501

MOST DEVASTATING DISASTERS

Dedicated to David Brown
1946–2009

Bon viveur, intrepid traveller, splendid raconteur, loyal friend and beloved husband, without whose efforts 'Team Brown' would not have written this volume and eight of its fellows in the *501* series. He is deeply missed.

501

MOST DEVASTATING DISASTERS

Bounty
Books

Publisher: Polly Manguel

Project Editor: Emma Hill

Designer: Ron Callow/Design 23

Production Manager: Neil Randles

Chapters Written By:
Natural Fid Backhouse/Roland Matthews/Kieran Fogarty/Joe Toussaint/Janet Zoro/
   Jackum Brown/Sal Oliver
Sports Joe Toussaint/Janet Zoro/Fid Backhouse
Transport Fid Backhouse/Roland Matthews/Jackum Brown/Janet Zoro/Joe Toussaint
Conflagrations Kieran Fogarty/Roland Matthews/Joe Toussaint/Fid Backhouse
Health Sal Oliver/Janet Zoro/Joe Toussaint/Roland Matthews
Political Roland Matthews/Fid Backhouse/Sal Oliver/Kieran Fogarty
Economic Fid Backhouse/Sal Oliver/Kieran Fogarty
Commercial Kieran Fogarty/Fid Backhouse
Military Roland Matthews/Fid Backhouse/Kieran Fogarty/Sal Oliver
Industrial Fid Backhouse
Engineering Roland Matthews/Jackum Brown/Janet Zoro/Kieran Fogarty/Fid Backhouse
Humanitarian Fid Backhouse/Kieran Fogarty/Roland Matthews/Sal Oliver/Joe Toussaint
Environmental & Ecological Fid Backhouse/Roland Matthews/Janet Zoro/Kieran Fogarty/Sal Oliver/
   Jackum Brown/Joe Toussaint
Terrorism Fid Backhouse/Roland Matthews/Kieran Fogarty/Sal Oliver/Joe Toussaint
Massacres Janet Zoro/Kieran Fogarty/Fid Backhouse
Consequences Fid Backhouse

First published in Great Britain in 2010 by Bounty Books,
a division of Octopus Publishing Group Limited,
Endeavour House, 189 Shaftesbury Avenue, London WC2H 8JY
www.octopusbooks.co.uk

An Hachette UK Company
www.hachette.co.uk

Copyright © 2010 Octopus Publishing Group Limited

A CIP catalogue record is available from the British Library

ISBN: 978-0-753719-58-9

Printed and bound in Hong Kong

Contents

Introduction

This unique collection featuring 501 of the world's worst disasters spans almost 2,500 years of history. It includes natural calamities such as the eruption of Vesuvius or the Indian Ocean tsunami, unstoppable diseases like the Black Death or AIDS and terrible accidents like the sinking of *Titanic*. Most shocking of all are those disasters that need never have happened, created by the sheer savagery and negligence of man – catastrophic devastation caused by war, genocide and massacre, or tragedies like Chernobyl or Bhopal. And then there are the all-too-frequent environmental, economic and political disasters brought about by the folly or greed of a few that ultimately wreak havoc on the lives of many.

It is intended that *501 Most Devastating Disasters* should serve as an intriguing but sobering reminder of how hazardous the world can be and of how little control individuals, communities or even countries may have over their own destinies – for anyone in any place can find themselves unexpectedly plunged into desperate circumstances by the fickle hand of fate. People understand only too well that life-or-death disaster can be just a heartbeat away. Drivers who slow to stare at a serious road smash or onlookers gathering to see if trapped occupants will be rescued as firefighters tackle a blazing house are being neither morbid nor ghoulish. Instead, they are reflecting on how fragile life can be and giving silent thanks that they and theirs were not involved . . . this time.

Much of what you read and see within these pages will seem grim. Yet within this catalogue of disaster may be found many stirring stories of fortitude, featuring those who have faced disaster with incredible courage. In a world increasingly characterized by the relentless quest for personal gratification, adversity often brings out the very best in people, serving as a reminder of the uplifting human capacity to help those in need without giving a passing thought to selfish considerations.

A related theme that runs throughout the book is that of human resilience, demonstrating mankind's ability to defy tragedy and face disaster time after time only to get back up and carry on, often against overwhelming odds. Since the ancestors of the modern human race migrated out of Africa 70,000 years ago, ultimately to colonize every continent, intelligence and drive have enabled *Homo sapiens* to thrive and become the world's dominant species. This indomitable spirit does not allow setbacks to become permanent, however serious, for instead they are regarded as challenges to be overcome.

But repeated triumphs for this indomitable spirit of endurance cannot hide the fact that Mother Nature still has the power to discipline her precocious children. Every so often she forcibly reminds us that our best efforts to tame her and exploit her bounteous natural resources may be impressive, but nonetheless remain pathetically puny in the face of a raging tornado, violent earthquake or lethal pyroclastic cloud that kills everything in its path as it bursts from an erupting volcano. There are many such disasters described in this book, including some that have taken tens or even hundreds of thousands of lives.

The death toll caused by such catastrophic occurrences can seem almost unbelievable to those in today's developed countries where the life of every single child is precious. Yet *501 Most Devastating Disasters* hints at fearful possibilities that might drastically affect not only those who live in impoverished Third World nations where mere existence often seems precarious, but also every single person on Planet Earth in generations to come. For the very success of the human race could ultimately prove to be its undoing, as an exploding world population consumes dwindling resources at an ever-increasing rate, while climate change accelerates to threaten the ecosystem that sustains us all.

Disaster can and does strike without warning at any time, in any place, as this fascinating book confirms . . . and *501 Most Devastating Disasters* sets out to offer thought-provoking insight into just about every sort of catastrophe the world has seen, or may yet witness in the future.

NATURAL DISASTERS

Vesuvius and the destruction of Pompeii

WHEN:
August 24–26 AD 79
WHERE:
Campania, southern Italy
DEATH TOLL:
Unknown, but estimates range from 10,000 to 25,000, based on the known populations of the affected communities. Evidence of over 1,500 bodies has been unearthed – including cavities created by corpses which had decayed in their casings of ash and pumice. The plaster casts made by archaeologists of bodies at the moment of death provide an extraordinarily potent and moving witness to the disaster.

Skeletons of victims killed in the eruption of Mount Vesuvius in the House of Neptune and Amphitrite at Herculaneum.

The ancient Romans were a superstitious people, forever looking for portents in natural events. They failed utterly, however, to predict the cataclysm which engulfed the fertile and heavily populated Campanian countryside south of Naples in AD 79. Had they possessed a modern scientist's understanding of the earth's behaviour they might have seen the link with the earthquake which had damaged many buildings in the region 17 years earlier. As it was, a comprehensive rebuilding programme was still underway in the busy provincial town of Pompeii when on a late summer's day its brooding neighbour Mount Vesuvius erupted without warning, casting day into night in a trice. At 1,280 m (4,200 ft) and only 17,000 years old, Vesuvius was a small and young volcano but the explosion nevertheless propelled a column of ash and gases some 25 km (15 mi) into the stratosphere.

Overwhelming though the initial eruption was, it was the subsequent pyroclastic flows which did the real damage. A pyroclastic flow is a relatively rare phenomenon in volcanic eruptions, caused by a temporary collapse of pressure in the

eruptive column which produces a dense cloud of incandescent ash, mud and volcanic debris. Nothing stands a chance in the face of this deadly cocktail as it roars over the ground at speeds up to 500 kph (310 mph) and temperatures as high as 500°C. In AD 79 there were no fewer than six such flows, at the end of which the entire communities of Pompeii and neighbouring Herculaneum lay buried beneath metres of volcanic ash and lava. In one of history's great ironies, this catastrophe became posterity's great gain, for the burial ensured the near-perfect preservation of complete townscapes which have yielded unparalleled insights into an ancient and vanished way of life.

YOU SHOULD KNOW:
Vesuvius has erupted more than 50 times since AD 79. The last occasion was in 1944, which means that another eruption is overdue.

Antioch earthquake

Lying on the Orontes River some 20 km (13 mi) inland from the Mediterranean coast in what is now the southeastern corner of modern Turkey, the ancient city of Antioch was an important centre of early Christianity. Founded in the late 4th century BC in Syria, as it then was, by Seleucus, one of Alexander the Great's generals, Antioch prospered as the capital of his new dominion and grew rapidly. In its heyday during the early Roman Empire the city had an estimated population of half a million; only Alexandria and Rome itself were more prestigious. Antioch was the destination for St Paul's first missionary journey following his conversion on the Damascus road, and the New Testament tells us that its gentile converts to the new religion were also the first to call themselves Christians.

Important though the city was, Antioch had the misfortune to be situated in one of the most unstable parts of the planet. In geological terms the Eastern Mediterranean is an area where four great tectonic plates meet. Antioch itself lay on the Anatolian plate and had a history of recurring earthquakes which damaged the buildings and fabric of the metropolis, including one in AD 115 while the Emperor Trajan himself was staying in the city before his ill-fated Parthian campaign. These were as nothing, however, to the massive quake of late May AD 526 which completely destroyed the city, including the great church built 200 hundred years previously by Emperor Constantius II, son of Constantine the Great. Few contemporary accounts of the disaster survive, but any buildings left standing after the initial tremor probably collapsed in a series of aftershocks; a huge fire which broke out the following day consumed what was left of Antioch 'the Golden'.

WHEN:
Late May AD 526
WHERE:
Antakya, Turkey
DEATH TOLL:
Although the population had declined since its heyday, it is estimated that the city's entire population of some 250,000 perished in the earthquake.
YOU SHOULD KNOW:
Its location made Antioch a key strategic bulwark of the Eastern Roman Empire against the Persian threat from the east. When Justinian assumed the Byzantine throne the year after the earthquake he spent lavishly on rebuilding the city. It was to little avail, however, as just a dozen years later it was sacked by the Persians.

Shaanxi earthquake

WHEN:
January 23 1556
WHERE:
Shaanxi Province, China
DEATH TOLL:
At least 830,000
YOU SHOULD KNOW:
Shaanxi forms part of the cradle of
Chinese civilization. It lay at the heart
of the state of Qin, the emperor who
first united the country in the 3rd
century BC and who gave his name
to the modern country.

The province of Shaanxi in northwestern China has the unenviable record of being the site of the world's most deadly recorded earthquake. It happened in the winter of 1555–1556 during the reign of the Jiajing Emperor of the Ming Dynasty, and is therefore often referred to as the Jiajing earthquake. Measuring an estimated 8.0 on the Richter scale, the quake destroyed an area of 830 sq km (520 sq mi); in some counties nearly two thirds of the population were killed. The epicentre was in the Wei River valley near Mount Hua and aftershocks were felt for a whole six months.

The main reason why this natural disaster caused such catastrophic loss of life – well over three quarters of a million people are thought to have died – was that a high proportion of the region's inhabitants were living in artificial caves called *yaodongs*. These had been dug out of porous and unstable loess deposits of which the cliffs and hillsides of the area were composed. Hundreds of thousands died when their primitive dwellings collapsed during the quake.

A scholar of the day, Qin Keda, was one of the lucky survivors and has left us a detailed account of the earthquake, describing vividly how rivers literally changed direction and new land masses and bodies of water were suddenly formed. He also left future generations in his debt through his observations on survival techniques. Noting how many people perished when, having abandoned their buildings, they were struck down by falling debris or else disappeared into huge cracks in the ground, Qin Keda opined that remaining indoors and crouching down in a safe place would undoubtedly have given them a better chance of survival.

Huaynaputina eruption

Huaynaputina is a strato-volcano situated in the Andes range in the south of Peru and is part of the infamous Pacific Ring of Fire. Its name translates as 'new volcano' and this huge, irregular crater, 2.5 km (1.5 mi) in diameter, has been formed over time from stratified layers of lava and other deposits. Its current shape was formed during the cataclysmic eruption which took place in 1600 – one of the largest volcanic explosions South America has ever witnessed. The previously dormant volcano spewed forth its deadly ballast of ash, rock and molten lava for two weeks, during which it is estimated that some 12 cu km (2.9 cu mi) of ash were released into the atmosphere.

The eruption was preceded and accompanied by a series of earth tremors and quakes, the most severe of which measured over 8.0 on the Richter scale. These were responsible for the obliteration of large parts of Arequipa, Peru's second city, whereas it was the *lahars* (volcanic mudflows) from the eruption which engulfed several entire villages as they made their lethal way down to the coast, 120 km (75 mi) away.

Survivors of the catastrophe started to rebuild their lives with their customary resilience, although the region's agriculture was a write-off for the next two years.

Perhaps the most distinctive feature of the Huaynaputina eruption, however, was its impact on global weather patterns. Recent studies by geophysicists in the USA have suggested that the unusually harsh winters experienced by many parts of the northern hemisphere in the years immediately following the eruption were caused by the large amounts of sulphur it released into the atmosphere; the resulting droplets of sulphuric acid acted as barriers to sunlight, with a consequent lowering of temperatures.

WHEN:
February 19 1600
WHERE:
Near Arequipa, southern Peru
DEATH TOLL:
Unknown, but its indirect consequences may make it one of the deadliest natural disasters of all. Scientists now believe that the extreme weather conditions in Russia which caused progressive harvests to fail at the start of the 16th century and led to the famines of 1601–1603, in which some two million people died, were due to the Huaynaputina eruption.
YOU SHOULD KNOW:
Arequipa is known as the 'white city' because of the distinctive white volcanic rock called *sillar* from which many of its buildings are constructed.

Genroku earthquake

WHEN:
December 31 1703
WHERE:
Edo (Tokyo), Japan
DEATH TOLL:
It may have been as high as 200,000.
YOU SHOULD KNOW:
The earthquake occurred during the historical Genroku Era and the name is used to distinguish it from subsequent major quakes which struck the city in 1855 and 1923.

Japan's spectacular economic success story over the second half of the 20th century is the more remarkable when you consider the shaky foundations on which it has been constructed – quite literally, since the country is one of the most geologically unstable parts of the entire planet. Japan comprises more than 4,000 islands, though the vast majority of the population lives on the four largest. The islands are actually a row of peaks in an underwater mountain range which includes hundreds of volcanoes – most notably iconic Mount Fuji, one of some 40 which are active. The explanation for all this activity is that Japan lies on a fault line between two of the earth's major tectonic plates.

It should not come as a surprise, then, that roughly one fifth of the world's earthquakes occur here. Even so, it is not easy for those of us who take living on *terra firma* for granted to comprehend that on an average day in Japan some half-dozen tremors are recorded somewhere in the Japanese archipelago. Few parts of the country have been spared over the centuries, but it is incidents affecting the most heavily populated areas that have attracted the greatest attention.

The capital, Tokyo, has had its fair share of earthquakes and as recently as May 2008 it suffered one which registered 6.7 on the Richter scale. At the start of the 18th century Edo (as Tokyo was then known) was the world's largest city, with a population of one million; on the last day of 1703, however, it was devastated by a massive earthquake. Most of the casualties were caused by the resulting fires which swept through the mainly wooden buildings, and by a tsunami which smashed into a wide coastal area around Sagami Bay and the Boso Peninsula.

Lisbon earthquake

One of Europe's most elegant capital cities was laid waste at a stroke when a ferocious earthquake – thought to have measured as high as 9.0 on the Richter scale – hit Lisbon in 1755. It was the morning of November 1, All Saints' Day, and thousands of citizens were attending Mass in the city's churches. Contemporary accounts described animals becoming unusually agitated in the hours preceding the disaster and water in the wells developing a strange taste. The epicentre of the earthquake was out in the Atlantic, some 200 km (125 mi) to the southwest of Portugal. When it struck Lisbon, the ground shook violently for ten terrifying minutes and vibrations were felt throughout the whole Iberian Peninsula.

Hundreds died when the quaysides on which they had gathered collapsed as they were trying to make their escape on the River Tagus. Worse was to follow, however. Fires broke out throughout the city; when they finally abated five days later, 85 per cent of Lisbon's buildings had been destroyed, including the cathedral, the royal palace and the new opera house. The earthquake also generated a huge tsunami which inundated the city and devastated the coastlines of Portugal, Spain and North Africa. Reaching a height of 15 m (49 ft), the giant wave had an effect which was noticed as far away as the West Indies.

The Lisbon earthquake sent shockwaves throughout Europe; literally, with waves noted on the surface of Loch Ness in Scotland, but also metaphorically in the worlds of thought and letters. Many intellectuals began to question the notion of divine providence and the view that such natural disasters were part of God's plan for the world. The most famous product of this new spirit of scepticism was Voltaire's satirical masterpiece *Candide*.

WHEN:
November 1 1755
WHERE:
Lisbon, Portugal
DEATH TOLL:
80,000–90,000 of Lisbon's inhabitants. One third of the city's population is thought to have perished and the overall death toll from the earthquake, fire and tsunami was probably well in excess of 100,000.
YOU SHOULD KNOW:
The Lisbon earthquake continues to puzzle seismologists and confound plate tectonics theory as the city lies nowhere near a plate boundary.

A dramatic engraving shows the destruction of Lisbon during the earthquake.

Great Atlantic hurricane

In October 1780 the Atlantic Ocean suffered its deadliest hurricane on record. This was before the era of modern data and tracking techniques so it is difficult to ascertain the precise course of the hurricane, but it probably originated at the start of the month somewhere near the Cape Verde Islands in the eastern Atlantic. It then moved westwards and on October 10 slammed into the island of Barbados in the West Indies. The island was buffeted relentlessly by winds of over 300 kph (200 mph) which stripped the bark off trees and tossed heavy cannons into the air. British Admiral Lord Rodney described the scene in a letter to his wife: 'The strongest buildings and the whole of the houses, most of which were stone, and remarkable for their solidity, gave way to the fury of the wind, and were torn up to their foundations.'

For the next seven days the hurricane continued to cut a swathe of destruction through many other islands in the eastern Caribbean, touching on Puerto Rico and Hispaniola also before eventually turning northeast and heading back out to the Atlantic. Thousands of islanders lost their lives and it was years before the local economies recovered. Caught up in the havoc and devastation were ships of the British, French and Dutch navies which had been vying for control of territorial waters while the American War of Independence raged. Lord Rodney, in fact, was in command of the British fleet which was anchored off St Lucia when the hurricane struck; eight of his ships were sunk and hundreds of sailors killed.

Laki eruption

The spectacular explosions of volcanoes such as Vesuvius and Krakatoa may dominate the popular imagination, but the eruptions which occur periodically in Iceland (itself a large and ancient volcanic island) are characterized, in contrast, by their extended duration and the high volume and comparatively low energy levels of their emissions. In 1783 the slopes around Mount Laki in the southeast of Iceland started to crack open, caused by the pulling apart of tectonic plates. A fissure on the mountain's southwestern flanks grew ever wider as it spewed out fountains of liquid basalt. In a matter of days a nearby river gorge was filled to the brim and a massive lava flow had spread out onto the coastal plain. Two months later the process repeated itself after a crack opened on the northeastern slopes. When activity finally stopped six months later, the fissures were 27 km (17 mi) long and had released 14.7 cu km (3.5 cu mi) of lava, covering an area of 600 sq km (230 sq mi).

While there were no reported human casualties, the eruption was still the worst disaster Iceland had ever suffered because of its impact on a predominantly agricultural economy. The loss of well over half the island's livestock and the decimation of fish catches led to a terrible famine which killed a quarter of the population.

The Laki eruption was one of the first natural disasters to have its global impact subjected to scientific scrutiny. Weather patterns throughout the world seem to have been affected: the winter of 1783–1784 in Europe and North America was the coldest in 250 years, water levels on the River Nile dropped to record lows and unseasonal frosts in Japan destroyed the rice harvest.

Tambora volcano

The largest volcanic eruption in recorded history took place in 1815 on the island of Sumbawa, which lies east of Bali in the Indonesian archipelago. After lying dormant for several thousand years Mount Tambora suffered a series of violent explosions over the course of a ten-day period which expelled a staggering 125 cu km (30 cu mi) of molten magma and volcanic debris. (To put this into some perspective, this is over 20 times the volume of material discharged in the Mount St Helens eruption of 1980.) In the process, the top 1,500 m (4,920 ft) of the volcano's cone was blown away and a giant hollow created, known technically as a caldera, 700 m (2,300 ft) deep and 6 km (3.75 mi) wide.

Tambora is an example of a Plinian eruption (so called after the Roman writer Pliny the Younger who first observed the phenomenon during the AD 79 eruption of Vesuvius). The distinguishing features are a towering column of ash and gases and deadly pyroclastic flows which obliterate everything in their path. In Tambora's case the eruptive column rose over 40 km (25 mi) into the atmosphere, while the flows laid waste much of the island and some 10,000 people suffered horrible deaths. A thick carpet of ash descended, killing animals and crops and destroying all vegetation on Sumbawa and neighbouring islands. It would be five years before new growth returned to the area.

The explosion, which was thought to have been caused by a massive build-up of pressure after ocean water had penetrated cracks in the earth's crust and reacted with magma deep inside the volcanic chamber, led to falls in temperatures worldwide in the following years; indeed, 1816 became known throughout Europe and North America as 'the year without a summer'.

WHEN:
April 5–15 1815
WHERE:
Sumbawa Island, Indonesia
DEATH TOLL:
92,000, the majority from the effects of starvation and disease following the disaster. This is the largest death toll from a volcanic eruption in recorded history.
YOU SHOULD KNOW:
The dust and acid aerosols which hung in the atmosphere for years afterwards produced strange and brilliant sunsets which were captured by many artists of the day, including the great British landscape painter J M W Turner.

Krakatoa eruption

Although considerably less powerful than the 1815 explosion of nearby Mount Tambora, the notorious Krakatoa disaster (Krakatau is its authentic Indonesian name but it was called Krakatoa by European colonists of the day) owes its reputation as the most famous volcanic eruption of all to timing. It was, in short, the first such disaster to occur in the modern communications age. The first undersea intercontinental telegraph cables had only recently been laid, which allowed news of the event to spread around the world in a matter of minutes.

Krakatoa is a small volcanic island in the Sunda Strait separating Java from Sumatra. Part of the Pacific Ring of Fire, its three volcanoes were observed spewing material in May 1883. Activity continued intermittently for the next three months but, because it was at a low level and the island was uninhabited, no significant threat was perceived by the local population.

All that changed on two terrible days at the end of August when a series of shattering explosions ejected a column of ash and gas 36 km (22 mi) high which turned the skies dark over Java and Sumatra. The final titanic blast on the morning of August 27 blew the mountain apart. It was reported as gunfire when heard

The volcanic eruption of Krakatoa in the Sunda Strait midway between Java and Sumatra

WHEN:
May to August 1883
WHERE:
Krakatau, Indonesia

5,000 km (3,000 mi) away and it remains the loudest single sound in recorded history.

Although the eruption generated pyroclastic flows, the enormous casualty figures and the massive environmental damage brought about by the disaster were actually caused mainly by the series of tsunamis which followed in the wake of the eruption. Reaching heights of over 30 m (100 ft), these giant sea waves laid waste entire coastal areas for hundreds of kilometres, leaving a gruesome tangle of shattered buildings, felled trees and corpses.

DEATH TOLL:
36,417
YOU SHOULD KNOW:
Although the new cone that has grown up inside the caldera or crater formed by the 1883 eruption (known as Anak Krakatau or 'son of Krakatoa') continues to be active, regularly lighting up the night skies over the Sunda Strait, this has not deterred thousands of small farmers from returning to the region, attracted by its rich and fertile volcanic soils.

'China's Sorrow'

Huang He (Yellow) River flood

The Huang He (Yellow River) is both 'the Cradle of Chinese Civilization' and 'China's Sorrow'. Only slightly shorter than the Yangtze, at 5,464 km (3,398 mi), it loops northwards from the Bayan Har mountains, then sweeps east, each year bringing 1.6 billion tons of fine-grained silt from the Loess plateau to the huge flat basin of the north China plains. That silt makes farming a joy – but at any time it can also be lethal. Silt replenishes the land. The Yellow River gets its name from its rich, fine-ground, golden mud. Unfortunately for the farmers, the only way the river can spread its bounty is by flooding the fertile fields; and the Huang He has flooded a recorded 1,593 times in four millennia, with catastrophic effects.

The worst of all was in 1887. The centuries of building and repairing the levees had pushed the river's main course higher and higher. It was banked up as much as 23 m (70 ft) higher than the surrounding land. After a long summer of non-stop heavy rain, millions of farmers squelched through their sodden fields, waiting for the inevitable. It came as a tidal roar. As the Huang He spilled over its banks, it tore down its levees, sweeping aside over 300 villages, 11 major cities, and millions of people. Already soaked, the land could absorb nothing. The floodwater created an instant lake the size of Lake Ontario, then seeped relentlessly forward over more than 50,000 square miles destroying everything in its path. A fierce wind completed the devastation. For several days it was impossible to effect rescue or repair – and by then diseases like typhus and dysentery had taken hold on survivors. Famine was inevitable.

It was the deadliest flood in history. 'China's Sorrow' had fulfilled its reputation.

WHEN:
September 28 1887
WHERE:
Huayenkou, near Zhengzhou, Henan Province, China
DEATH TOLL:
900,000 died in the first onrush and another estimated 1.3 million drowned. A further estimated three to four million died from flood-related, waterborne diseases. With a carpet of muddy silt 2.5 m (8 ft) deep, the most fertile fields in China were a desert which had to be cleared by bare hands and wheelbarrows. Yet with truly Confucian resilience, millions of Chinese farmers regained their land within two years. Their resignation seems to be hereditary – like their ancestors, they lived with the inevitable.
YOU SHOULD KNOW:
On occasion, the Chinese have sought to harness the Huang He as a natural defence. In 1938, Chiang Kai-shek, leader of the Kuomintang and the National Government, ordered the river levees to be blown up in order to halt the invading Japanese. The flood stopped the rapidly advancing troops in their tracks, but a military stalemate ensued. Disastrously, Chiang's order to flood the plain inadvertently killed more than 0.5 million Chinese farmers.

The great white hurricane

WHEN:
March 12–14 1888
WHERE:
Delaware to Maine,
on and offshore, USA
DEATH TOLL:
At least 400 people died during the blizzard, together with 100 sailors lost at sea. Although basic services were operating after a week, the snow took a long time to clear. One massive drift was still intact in July. Sadly, by the third day of the storm human nature had reasserted itself in New York City: coal barons doubled or trebled their prices, single ham sandwiches went from a nickel to a quarter, and cabbies demanded $50 a ride (that's about $600 now!).
YOU SHOULD KNOW:
It wasn't all bad: the editor of Wilmington's *Every Evening* noted the number of young men 'about to say adieu to the maidens of their choice' that evening, who discovered 'they needed no second invitation to come out of the storm and stay till morning by the side of the parlor stove, and ever anon, clasp a reassuring arm around the waist of their beloved'. The paper also reported a milkman, terrified his horse would freeze to death, who 'poured half a quart of whiskey down the animal's throat. It must have upped his horsepower, for he went to town in record time despite the drifts'.

Nobody was prepared for what happened. In New York City and along the eastern seaboard the temperature at midday was in the fifties and mild for early March. The next day's forecast from the US Weather Bureau was for more of the same: 'cloudy, followed by light rain and clearing'. Instead, that Sunday afternoon the temperature plunged as a huge mass of arctic air collided offshore in the Atlantic with a warm, moist system from the south. By midnight, a savage storm had developed over Chesapeake Bay. The energy of the collision generated hurricane-force winds as freezing temperatures turned driving rain into a thick blizzard. In the furious seas whipped up from Delaware to Maine, over 200 ships were driven aground, or overwhelmed by the icy, raging ocean. Even behind Wilmington's harbour breakwater, 21 of the 35 sheltering ships had their anchors ripped from the sea and were crushed into matchwood.

Inland, the blizzard was a complete surprise. By Monday morning New York City lay under 20 inches of snow, whipped up into mounting drifts of 12–15 m (40–50 ft) by recorded wind speeds of 75–100 mph. All forms of transportation stuttered to a halt. On the city's elevated trains 15,000 helpless passengers were stranded in unheated carriages. Overhead, the tangle of telegraph and telephone wires sagged under thick ice and snow, bowed and snapped. Delivery trucks and wagons slewed across the streets, spilling their loads into the maelstrom of broken glass, loose slates, branches and rubbish hurtling through the air. People who braved the arctic blast were simply blown off their feet; dozens were buried alive or 'drowned' in snow.

For nearly a week America's wrecked eastern seaboard had no transport and no communications. New Yorkers had had enough. As a direct result of the great white hurricane, the city got a subway system.

The great Galveston hurricane

WHEN:
September 8 1900
WHERE:
Galveston, Texas, USA
DEATH TOLL:
Over 6,000 died, and the horror stories are legion. Galveston suffered terribly, but the hurricane continued. It lacerated a 320 km (200 mi) wide corridor through five states, before hitting Chicago and tearing into Canada and roaring over New Brunswick and Nova Scotia, killing hundreds in its path and sinking 92 ships between Prince Edward Island and Newfoundland, and seriously damaging 100 others.

The port of Galveston is an island city. It sits at the east end of Galveston Island, an overgrown sandbar between 2–5 km (1.5–3 mi) wide and 50 km (30 mi) long that controls the entrance to Galveston Bay on the Gulf of Mexico. It was developed as a pirate's lair and slave market before it became an important commercial centre under the Texan and then US flags. By 1900 its 38,000 citizens were increasingly prosperous, but in September of that year they lost everything in one of America's greatest natural catastrophes.

The great Galveston hurricane slammed ashore as a storm surge of 5 m (16 ft) driven by winds of 208–224 kph (130–140 mph). The highest ground on the island was just 2–3 m (8–10 ft) above sea level. The wave splintered the smart wooden houses lining the beach, creating a battering

A damaged street in Galveston, Texas, after the deadly hurricane.

ram of debris that swept across the island. Nothing escaped. The land disappeared, leaving lines of skeletal timbers poking out of the water, supporting useless roofs at drunken angles. Galveston endured for four hours before the winds subsided to storm force; and as the sea fell back it became clear how the debris, piled up against what remained of stronger buildings, had in fact prevented utter destruction. Fifteen blocks were matchwood, the rest was shattered, but the shape of a community was still discernible – and that was enough for those who survived.

With nothing but optimism left, the people of Galveston decided not only to rebuild, but also to raise the height of the entire town. Behind a new sea wall the island doubled its height to 5 m (16 ft). All 2,100 buildings were raised on jacks while sand was pumped underneath them. It was stubborn (if not bloody-minded in the face of nature's power!), but it worked. Since the disaster, Galveston has withstood dozens of major hurricanes.

YOU SHOULD KNOW:
The hurricane eventually dissipated over Siberia on its fifth day. Its colossal destruction of life and property is immortalized in a folk song written a century later, called *Wasn't That a Mighty Storm?*.

The remains of the city following the devastating eruption of Mont Pelée.

Mont Pelée eruption

The vibrant port city of St Pierre, or 'Little Paris', in the lush tropical paradise of Martinique, was the commercial and cultural heart of the French West Indies. It lay in the shadow of Mont Pelée, a huge volcano at the northern end of the island. Pelée had been more or less dormant since an eruption of 1851; the only traces of activity were the delicate wisps of steam wafting from fumaroles in the summit craters – a source of wonder for visitors to the island.

As the 20th century dawned, Pelée began to wake up. The first sign was the smell of sulphur, but nobody was unduly alarmed by the volcanic rumblings until, in the spring of 1902, climbers noticed sulphurous boiling water filling the summit crater. Stuttering explosions and earth tremors signalled something serious. As the wealthy packed their bags, people poured into St Pierre from the surrounding countryside, seeking safety in numbers.

Pelée erupted at 07.52 on May 8: 'the whole side of the mountain . . . seemed to open and boil down on the screaming people' in a *nuée ardente* (glowing cloud) of incandescent lava. Vast quantities of gas, dust and ash darkened the sky for 80 km (50 mi) around as glowing tongues of lava descended on St Pierre in a pyroclastic flow so fast there was no escape. The boiling cloud was accompanied by a tsunami, causing havoc to ships at anchor, the city was smothered in lava and the harbour was awash with bodies.

Some months later a bizarre lava dome began to emerge from the crater floor, growing up to as much as 15 m (50 ft) a day. The 'Tower of Pelée' caused great excitement among vulcanologists. At night it glowed in the dark and it grew to 300 m (1,000 ft) before it suddenly collapsed in March 1903.

WHEN:
May 8 1902
WHERE:
Martinique, Windward Islands, Lesser Antilles
DEATH TOLL:
More than 30,000 people in and around the capital of St Pierre were burned or suffocated to death. There were only three survivors in the entire city – a shoemaker, a ten-year-old girl who took refuge in a cave on the seashore and a prisoner in the town's gaol.
YOU SHOULD KNOW:
Survivor Louis-Auguste Cyparis had been in a violent street brawl the day before the eruption and was thrown into the town's gaol. The thick stone walls of his dungeon protected him from the volcanic fallout. Four days later rescuers heard his cries for help and he was released, badly burned but very much alive. You can still see the cell today.

The 'Great Shake'

The San Francisco earthquake

Over a century later, seismology is still learning from San Francisco's 1906 'Great Shake'. The more we understand, the greater the disaster seems. In less than a minute the earth ruptured at a speed of 13,300 kph (8,300 mph) towards the north, and 10,080 kph (6,300 mph) towards the south, cracking open 477 km (296 mi) of the northern San Andreas fault from outside San Juan Bautista to the fault's triple junction at Cape Mendocino. The ninth biggest city in the USA collapsed. Its 400,000 residents woke at 05.12 buried in the rubble of their boom town, and with the flames of thousands of overturned cooking stoves already catching hold.

The water and gas mains had fractured and the fire chief had been killed. Lacking means and leadership, people already stunned and often badly injured could only watch the city burn. Many newer buildings were damaged but still standing when the fiercest tremors stopped; but nothing could resist the fire, especially since it was encouraged by unscrupulous people whose insurance covered fire but not earthquake. San Francisco burned for three days. The fire trebled the earthquake damage: 28,000 buildings were destroyed across some 500 city blocks, leaving 225,000 people homeless. In some places groups were isolated by fire against the shore.

Two days after the first shock, the USS *Chicago* evacuated 20,000 victims by sea. Back in the heart of the conflagration police and soldiers shot around 500 looters. Afterwards, the blackened skeletons of City Hall and other symbols of San Francisco's prosperity left little to the imagination.

Exhaustive analysis of the 1906 earthquake and fire has gradually revealed how the city fathers played down the casualties. With the opportunity to create a new San Francisco in their own, modern image, it's hard to blame them.

WHEN:
April 18 1906
WHERE:
San Francisco, California, USA
DEATH TOLL:
US Army relief operations in 1906 reported 498 deaths in San Francisco, 64 in Santa Rosa, and 102 around San Jose. More accurate, recent figures suggest at least 3,000 died and tens of thousands were injured or burned. The earthquake was the first large natural disaster to be recorded by photography, which greatly helped the research that led to Reid's 1910 formulation of the 'elastic-rebound' theory that remains the best model of why earthquakes happen. The discovery of plate tectonics 50 years later only confirmed in detail what he had hypothesized.
YOU SHOULD KNOW:
The 'Great Shake' was assessed in 1935 (when the scale was invented) as 8.3 on the Richter scale. On the more recent and accurate 'moment magnitude' scale it is measured as 7.8 or 7.9. The combined damage of the earthquake and fire was estimated at $400 million in 1906 dollars, which translates to about $9 billion today.

Survivors eat al fresco *after the earthquake.*

Messina

the deadliest earthquake in European history

WHEN:
December 28 1908
WHERE:
Messina, Sicily, and
Reggio di Calabria, Italy
DEATH TOLL:
Estimates of the dead go well beyond 200,000. In Messina, 75,000 (half the population) certainly died and 25,000 (nearly two thirds) died in Reggio. The quake's epicentre was just offshore from Messina, and buildings collapsed over 4,300 sq km (1,660 sq mi). Messina was rebuilt with wide streets and low buildings for future safety.
YOU SHOULD KNOW:
Sicily and Calabria have so many earth tremors they are known as *la terra ballerina* (the dancing land).

The ruins of a street in Messina, Italy, after the huge earthquake

Most people were sleeping when the tremors began at 05.21. The historic city of Messina shook violently for a full 30 seconds. Across the straits from Sicily, the Italian town of Reggio di Calabria imploded into rubble and dust in the same half minute. Buried in choking lumps of ragged stone and plaster, and tossed from their beds into a cold, wet and violent winter night, bewildered citizens had barely found their voices to scream in pain and for help when the tsunami followed. A series of three waves, rearing to a height of 6 m (20 ft), crashed simultaneously through Messina and Reggio, facing each other across the straits, and thundered along both coastlines wreaking havoc on villages and people. At Giampileri Marina the waves peaked at 11.8 m (39 ft). Ninety per cent of Messina was obliterated and 100,000 people died immediately. It is difficult to imagine the devastation.

The first shock measured 7.5 on the Richter scale. Hundreds of smaller aftershocks created a two-day nightmare. The dead stuck out from piles of rubble, smashed limbs easy prey for scavenging animals. With no communications and no civil structure left, help came slowly. The government in Rome took five days to organize lifting equipment, by which time the fleets of half a dozen Mediterranean navies were working as one to ferry the injured to hospitals in Naples, Rome and Malta. Their crews worked desperately, but rubble was 5m (16 ft) deep in Messina's centre. The last survivors, two starving children, were dug out after 18 days. It was the same in Reggio, and up and down the coastline. Sleep had concentrated the population in the most vulnerable circumstances. They died together – in full barracks, crowded hospitals and *en famille* in bursting tenements. Italian King Vittorio Emanuele came to look at them.

Wellington avalanche

the iron goat disaster

Avalanche and train wreck at Wellington, Washington

The Great Northern Railroad was one of those engineering triumphs that opened up America's Pacific northwest. From the Rockies, its final stage crossed Washington State from Spokane to Seattle, switchbacking through the steep defiles of the Cascade Mountains. The curves were dizzying. Trains crossed terrain too difficult for any living creature except goats – so in the US and Canada they were known as 'iron goats'.

In 1893 at Stevens Pass, locos laboured round 19 km (12 mi) of track to travel just 4 km (2.6 mi) forwards. Then, in 1900, the Cascades Tunnel was driven from Berne in the east to Wellington in the west, emerging on the lower slopes of 1,615 m (5,000 ft) Windy Mountain.

The blizzard had begun by the time the passenger express and the transcontinental mail trains left Spokane. It took them two days of delays to struggle as far as the tunnel and through it to Wellington. The line ahead was closed by heavy snow and the company's specialist snowploughs had run out of coal to power them. Usually trains would back up into the tunnel for shelter, but passengers were terrified of being blocked in as the storm raged for four more days. Fear proved fatal. On the fifth day, snow changed to rain as a massive thunderstorm hit Windy Ridge, towering above the trains. Lightning cracked and thunder boomed, shaking the earth until suddenly, in the darkness, a huge snow shelf 3 m (10 ft) deep, 400 m (1,250 ft) wide and 800 m (2,500 ft) long creaked once and broke off; and with a hissing roar swept both trains, like toys, crashing 50 m (150 ft) into the canyon torrent of the river Tye below.

In 1900, Americans believed in trains as representative of their civilizing mission to create technology capable of taming nature. The disaster stung the nation's pride.

WHEN:
March 1 1910
WHERE:
Wellington, Windy Mountain, Washington, USA
TOLL:
Officially, 96 people died and all 23 survivors were injured. In all probability many more died, because the Wellington depot – wiped out with the trains – was crammed with undocumented, immigrant work gangs drafted in to keep the line open, and the company didn't want the blue riband for 'deadliest train wreck'. It even changed the depot's name from 'Wellington' to 'Tye' to avoid the association.
YOU SHOULD KNOW:
In 1929, 'Tye' was abandoned after a new, longer Cascades Tunnel was built elsewhere. Recently, heritage organizations have developed the old railroad grade into one of the best interpretive hiking trails in America's West. Thousands of volunteers have created three trailheads – at Wellington, Martin Creek and Scenic. It's called the Iron Goat Trail.

Great Porcupine wildfire

WHEN:
July 11–19 1911
WHERE:
Timmins and South Porcupine,
Ontario, Canada
DEATH TOLL:
Officially there were 77 deaths.
Eyewitness estimates suggest at
least 200 died, with hundreds more
burned or injured trying to save
property. Around 2,000 sq km
(772 sq mi) of wilderness forest was
razed, and several townships were
fully or partly destroyed.
YOU SHOULD KNOW:
With the gold rush at its height, and
human nature so predictable, the
mines were working again within
two months. Even the injured
survivors stayed: whole communities
claimed the disaster had renewed
their sense of purpose. It was true –
eventually the Porcupine Gold Rush
produced 67 million troy ounces of
gold against the Klondike's total of
roughly 12 million.

The first train arrived on July 9 1911. Before that, most people reached Porcupine Lake by canoe, like the 18th century fur-trappers working for the Hudson Bay Company, or by wagon, like the thousands of raw hopefuls who followed the professional prospectors to Canada's gold fields. Porcupine's gold rush began in 1909. Northern Ontario was already full of miners and engineers attracted by the silver strikes at Cobalt further south. They flocked into Porcupine's wilderness of forest and lakes, 680 km (425 mi) north of Toronto, throwing up tent cities that became instant townships strung along 50 miles of sinuous gold seams. The early spring and long days of hot, dry weather in June and July of 1911 meant that progress was rapid; and the coming of the railroad meant quicker, easier rewards.

Two days after that first train, the wind changed to a southwesterly. Suddenly, local brush fires that were a regular part of the natural wilderness cycle blazed into a single, united front. Fanned by the growing gale, a consolidated wall of flame ripped through Timmins, South Porcupine and Porquis Junction. It enveloped Cochrane – 80 km (50 mi) from Porcupine – in a horseshoe-shaped inferno 36 km (22 mi) wide with flames 30 m (100 ft) high. It sucked the oxygen out of the atmosphere with such intensity that mature trees were ripped from the ground; and people sheltering like gophers in the mine shafts were asphyxiated as the wildfire stole their last breath. Others drowned when a boxcar of dynamite exploded by the shore of Porcupine Lake, lashing the surface of their refuge with waves 3 m (10 ft) high. One – the owner of one of the Big Three mines, and a gold millionaire in his first year – died saving his cat.

Only nature could end what it had begun. After eight days, heavy rain stopped the destruction.

The Florida Keys hurricane

The most powerful hurricane in its history hit Key West on September 10 1919. First sighted taking shape in the Lesser Antilles, it had been followed for a week as it travelled past the Dominican Republic into the Bahamas. The severe storm intensified as it turned west, heading for the Florida Straits as a Category Four 'large hurricane'. The US Weather Bureau noted the barometric pressure as a terrifying 27.37 inches (927 millibars) in the hurricane's centre – the fourth lowest ever recorded. Key West was well prepared, but with winds of over 60 kph (40 mph) sustained for 38 consecutive hours and lashed by 30 cm (13 in) of rain, damage was severe. Many houses were flattened, but at this point the casualties were mainly among shipping still at sea. Many ships just disappeared, like the Spanish passenger liner *Valbanera*, which was unable to enter Havana harbour because of the storm, and went down with only a deckchair as a trace of its 488 passengers and crew.

Having pounded the Keys, the hurricane kept its strength across the Gulf of Mexico. By now, there were no ships at sea to report its position and the Weather Bureau in Corpus Christi on the Texas coast downgraded their forecast in the belief that it had turned towards Louisiana. Too late, they saw their own barometer drop again. With renewed strength, the hurricane smashed into Corpus Christi with 5 m (16 ft) waves and sustained blasts of 200 kph (125 mph) winds. Residents had stood down their defences and in the catastrophic wreckage of their homes, factories and businesses hundreds died or disappeared, washed into the raging sea. Across Nueces Bay, 11 km (7 mi) away at White's Point, 121 bodies (and 87 survivors!) turned up. Downtown, Corpus Christi was a pile of dripping debris.

WHEN:
September 9–14 1919
WHERE:
The Atlantic, Florida Keys, Gulf of Mexico and southeast Texas coast
DEATH TOLL:
The official total is about 800 dead, of whom 500 were lost at sea, and 287 killed in Corpus Christi. But Corpus Christi was seeking official backing to develop a deep-water port, and determinedly underplayed the disaster. Its official '287' death toll conflicts with local authorities who put it at 'not less than 400, probably nearer 1,000'. Key West suffered fewer casualties only because it had battened down – and that couldn't save many of its buildings.
YOU SHOULD KNOW:
In Key West you can see a town shrine called 'the Grotto'. Built by nuns outside the Roman Catholic church in 1920, it carries the inscription: 'As long as the Grotto stands, Key West will never again experience the full brunt of a hurricane'. So far, so good(ish).

Extensive destruction in the main shopping district of Tokyo

The great Kanto earthquake

The epicentre lay deep beneath Oshima Island in Sagami Bay. The shock was estimated around 8.2 on the Richter scale, and tremors lasted between four and ten minutes. The earthquake's power devastated Tokyo, Yokohama and the entire Kanto Plain around them – the horseshoe of flat land hemmed in by hills and mountains that in 1923 was the heart of imperial Japan, and its economic centre. It was a uniquely Japanese catastrophe: the initial, natural disaster was magnified by exclusively Japanese circumstances and behavioural responses. The combination created a disaster of epic terror.

The quake struck at lunchtime, toppling over a million open charcoal or wood stoves, and spilling thousands of small fires into tightly packed houses made of wood, paper and bamboo. The first tremors snapped water pipelines as the soft terrain heaved. Before they even stopped, high winds associated with a typhoon off the Noto Peninsular to the north whipped the local fires into a series of firestorms across 50 miles. People died with their feet stuck in melting tarmac. Some 38,000 sought safety by cramming into the open space of the former army clothing depot in downtown Tokyo, and were incinerated together by a freak fireball. In the hilly coastal areas of Kanagawa and Shizuoka, landslides killed thousands. One pushed a train with 100 passengers, the station, the railway line and the local village down a cliff and out to sea. Meanwhile a succession of tsunamis smashed the coast with waves as high as 12 m (40 ft).

There was worse. In Tokyo and Yokohama, mobs accused Korean 'agitators' of 'poisoning wells'. Thousands of Koreans – and anybody with a foreign accent – were savagely beaten to death and, after offering their protection, police and army units massacred thousands more for sport, while looters stripped still-living, blistered, burning bodies unchallenged.

WHEN:
September 1 1923
WHERE:
The Kanto Plain (Tokyo, Yokohama, and the Prefectures of Chiba, Kanagawa and Shizuoka), Japan
DEATH TOLL:
Officially 142,000 died, including 40,000 who simply disappeared. Fire was the greatest killer but, with the violence and prolonged chaos, the death toll may well have been much higher. Burning oil slicks on the sea fried dozens of crews in their ships. On land hundreds of thousands were badly burned or injured. Some 575,000 buildings were levelled; 65 per cent of Tokyo and 90 per cent of Yokohama were destroyed or badly damaged. Reconstruction incorporated radical new building, safety and precautionary codes – but ethnic suspicions have lingered.
YOU SHOULD KNOW:
On the earthquake's first anniversary, the Tokyo municipal authorities published the *Taisho shinsai giseki* (Taisho-era Collection of Heartwarming Stories): 100 eyewitness records of acts of heroism, sacrifice and selflessness. Heartwarming indeed, until you see that the selection is a clever bit of self-serving official propaganda.

The tri-state tornado

Tornadoes form where warm, moist air is trapped below cold, dry air; when the cold air is punctured, the rapidly rising warm air begins to rotate as it cools. That creates clouds and thunderstorms – but it can also form a funnel that spins at speeds of up to 400 kph (250 mph). When the spinning funnel of cloud touches the ground, it becomes a tornado. They can happen anywhere, but the USA has more of them than anywhere else in the world. Americans understand that tornadoes are killers – and the tri-state tornado was the biggest killer of all.

The tri-state tornado of 1925 is the statistical Big Daddy of tornadoes. It spun faster, from 416–510 kph (261–318 mph); travelled faster, at an *average* 100 kph (62 mph), double the average speed of any other tornado; lasted longer, for three and a half hours instead of the usual 15 minutes; and went further, 350 km (219 mi), at least treble the average distance. It touched ground near Ellington in Missouri, on the edge of the Ozark Mountains, splintering trees as it took off on its rampage across Illinois into Indiana. It levelled whole villages and towns like Gorham, where it killed half the population. In Murphysboro it ripped apart three schools made of brick and stone, killing 25 of the 234 townsfolk who died there. It tore like shrieking Velcro across the countryside, tearing up farms and cattle, whirling cars, trucks, people and furniture into its vortex and spitting them out in broken shreds. It destroyed 15,000 homes across 164 square miles – roughly 50 times a greater area than other severe tornadoes.

The Tri-State Tornado was travelling so fast, across such a wide front (up to 1.4 km/1 mi), that people died because they couldn't believe it actually was a tornado.

WHEN:
March 18 1925
WHERE:
Ellington, Missouri, northeast across Illinois to just north of Princeton, Indiana
DEATH TOLL:
652 people died and more than 2,000 were injured (more than double the casualty list of the USA's next worse tornado). Because it was 'just' a freak of nature (i.e. there was nobody to blame) newspapers pursued the extraordinary human-interest stories that the tornado provoked – like the 800 miners near West Frankfort, Illinois, who were stranded 167 m (500 ft) down a shaft without any power or light, and survived the tornado only to find that 127 of their women and children had been killed, and 450 injured. The Tri-State Tornado really was a monster.
YOU SHOULD KNOW:
A *Tornado Watch* (as posted on the radio or in a newspaper, for example) means that conditions in the area are prone to severe weather. Be alert. A *Tornado Warning* means that a tornado has been sighted or tracked on radar in the vicinity. Go immediately to a safe shelter.

Devastating tornado damage

Great Mississippi flood

WHEN:
April to July 1927
WHERE:
The Mississippi from Illinois to
New Orleans, USA
DEATH TOLL:
Officially, about 500 died and 700,000
were displaced. Both figures are
grossly understated. When it became
clear that they would not be receiving
any of the money allotted as
compensation, hundreds of thousands
of African Americans migrated north.
The migration transformed the
cultural and political development of
the USA (and gave the world the
Chicago blues). The flood gave Herbert
Hoover (then Secretary of Commerce)
the national profile that carried him to
the presidency. The only significant
legislative action was Calvin
Coolidge's Flood Control Act, the
largest public expenditure in history
outside World War I. In the South, the
horrific exploitation shredded the
myth of a social contract between
rich whites and poor blacks.
YOU SHOULD KNOW:
In a brilliant analysis called *Rising Tide*,
John M Barry saw analogies with
Hurricane Katrina: 'Their struggle . . .
began as one of man against nature.
It became one of man against man.
Honor and money collided. White and
black collided. Regional and national
power structures collided. The
collisions shook America.'

*Tents were pitched on the levees
to house refugees.*

The Mississippi flood of 1927 was one of America's worst natural catastrophes. More significantly, it became the catalyst for one of the most profound changes in the country's social and political fabric. The flood began in Cairo, Illinois on April 16. After six months of record rainstorms had swollen the Mississippi's two main tributaries – the Ohio and the Missouri – to bursting point, and saturated the river basin further south with 40 cm (15 in) of rain in the preceding 24 hours, the first of 145 breaches in the levees released a wall of water that would eventually drown a total of 70,000 sq km (27,000 sq mi) across Illinois, Kentucky, Louisiana, Mississippi, Tennessee, Missouri, and worst of all Arkansas. By May you could look out from Memphis bluffs over a lake 100 km (60 mi) wide, stretching beyond the horizon down the delta.

Nobody was in charge – before, during or after the disaster. Levees were managed by a mixture of public and private resources, all of which used shoot-to-kill vigilantes to guard against sabotage (blow up one side of the riverbank, and the other side was guaranteed safety). Worse, the crisis revived barely latent racism across the former Confederacy. African Americans were rounded up at gunpoint to fight the floods. At Greenville, under 3 m (10 ft) of water, hundreds were swept away; and 10,000 were marooned on a tiny island of high ground while an entire rescue convoy was left empty rather than save them. Despite evidence that New Orleans was not threatened, the white elite went ahead and dynamited the levee protecting St Bernard Parish, consigning 12,000 of the poorest African Americans there to death or destitution. In several cases, living people were stacked like bricks, three rows high, to hold back water until sandbags arrived hours later. Held as prisoners and forced labourers for no wage and no future, it was August before 330,000 African Americans were moved to 154 relief camps, and forgotten.

The Thames Flood

Since Roman times, London has built its most important public buildings on or very near the banks of the Thames, and gradually embanked the river to protect them. By the 1920s London was the biggest city in the world, and the Thames was compressed into a sinuous coil that wound through its heart. On both banks, natural safeguards against flooding like mudflats and marshes were largely filled with buildings and concrete. London failed to notice: the river had ceased to be a primary benefit to its booming prosperity.

The river took its revenge in 1928. Heavy snow at Christmas in the Cotswold Hills, the Thames's source, swelled its entire length with meltwater and heavy rain. By the time it got to the tidal reach below Teddington, it coincided with both an exceptionally high, incoming tide and a storm surge from the North Sea. The water level at Southend, 50 km (30 mi) from central London was 1.5 m (4 ft) above normal. As it was funnelled into the sharply narrowing estuary and met the downstream flow it soared in a few hours to a peak of 5.5 m (18 ft), just where it could do most damage.

In parts of Greenwich and the Isle of Dogs, people struggled up to their waists, but it was worst in the heart of London. Where the river bends, at Charing Cross and Waterloo, water spilled over the embankments and flooded Southwark, the City, Lambeth, the Houses of Parliament, Westminster Hall, London Underground train stations, Hammersmith and all the way to Putney. At the Tate Gallery (now Tate Britain) nine galleries went under, threatening millions of pounds worth of irreplaceable fine art. Outside the gallery on Millbank, a section of the embankment actually collapsed, flooding the east side of Pimlico so quickly that 14 people drowned in their basements; and 4,000 people lost their homes.

A rowing boat was washed up from the Thames into Page Street, Westminster.

WHEN:
January 7 1928
WHERE:
London, UK
DEATH TOLL:
14 people drowned and a few were injured. The worst damage was to tunnels, underground electrical and other systems, and to the fabric of historic buildings and their often priceless contents along the flood's path. Cleaning and restoration took years in some cases. The embankments were raised, Millbank was entirely rebuilt, and the first discussions took place about creating some sort of 'barrier' to halt similar surges in the future (it took 50 years to happen). London has never been seriously flooded since.
YOU SHOULD KNOW:
HMS *President* is a former Royal Navy corvette once used by the Royal Naval Volunteer Reserve. It is still to be seen (now permanently) moored on the Thames at the Victoria Embankment, where it's been since 1922. On the day of the flood it floated majestically into the streets, and had to be tethered to Cleopatra's Needle.

Fallen coconut trees across the railroad tracks

Okeechobee

San Felipe's hurricane

The hurricane grounded first in Puerto Rico on September 13, feast day of San Felipe, killing 1,000 people. Along the Florida coast, everyone battened down as the storm gathered force. On September 16, it crashed into Palm Beach with winds driving solid sheets of water at 200 kph (125 mph), smashing buildings, boats and businesses, while most people had retreated to safe shelters. Unusually, hitting land did little to diminish the storm. Forty miles inland it actually gained strength for short periods, probing isolated farming communities for weak buildings it could tear apart. As it howled around the southern shore of Lake Okeechobee the hurricane reached a crescendo. For over five hours it beat the shallow waters into waves that pounded the 1.5 m (5 ft) defensive mud dykes. Suddenly, at Belle Glade, the dyke collapsed, and a wall of water surged through the breach, inundating every village from Clewiston to Canal Point.

An hour after the dyke broke the flood reached its peak of 3.8 m (12 ft). Swirling winds gusted up to 240 kph (150 mph), ripping up trees which became battering rams in the surging water. Death was a lottery, plucking six from a family of 18 clinging to the roof of their splintered farm as it surfed crazily, cannoning into chunks of tangled debris. Of 63 people huddled in another building, thought to be the strongest in the area, only seven survived after it, too, was wrenched from its foundations. One third of the 6,000 souls in the communities to the south of Lake Okeechobee were killed.

For survivors, the clear-up was a further disaster. You can't bury people in the Everglades. Coffins float on the ooze. In the heat and humidity 'bodies were stacked like cordwood' and burned, unidentified, in mass graves on firm ground miles away.

WHEN:
September 16 1928
WHERE:
Lake Okeechobee, the Everglades, Florida, USA
TOLL:
Officially 1,836 people died around Lake Okeechobee, but a separate mass burial of black farm workers numbered hundreds more. The true figure is probably around 2,500, not including further deaths in Puerto Rico and the Caribbean. The hurricane changed the Everglades permanently, because US Army Engineers rebuilt the Okeechobee dyke up to 15 m (45 ft) high – and it became the first in a series of flood control defences that has tamed the Everglades ever since.
YOU SHOULD KNOW:
Despite being one of the deadliest storms in US history, it has no official name (like 'Galveston' or 'Katrina'). It is difficult not to speculate that this is because the people – white or black – whose lives were devastated were exclusively poor. At the time, the big news story was 'how well' Palm Beach had come through the hurricane.

1931 central China floods

Most floods are known by a place name or geographic feature. In China, flooding is so endemic that only the date is relevant, and 1931 identifies the greatest natural disaster of the 20th century. Fifty million people were affected when all three of China's greatest rivers combined in a flood of biblical proportions between July and October 1931.

The plains of central China were recovering from a two-year drought when the winter of 1930 brought heavy snowstorms across the region and as far away as Tibet. The spring thaw arrived with heavy rains that culminated in no fewer than seven major cyclones during July alone (against an average of two per year). A final deluge on July 23 brought the month's rainfall to 0.61 m (2 ft), and central China began to submerge.

Hanyang, on a promontory where the Yangtze meets the Han river, was the first city to go under. Four dams protecting Wuchang collapsed and water undermined the city walls. Wuhan, known as 'China's Chicago', became 'China's Venice'; but since the flood peaked at neighbouring Hankou at 16 m (53 ft) above normal on August 19, it was no joke. The flood grew to an inland sea, spreading back upstream on the Yangtze to Chonqqing, isolating China's then capital Nanjing on a vast island downstream, filling the huge agricultural plain of Huguang, and finally uniting the Yangtze, the Huai and Huang He (Yellow) rivers across 107,000 sq km (41,000 sq mi).

The water moved with lethal speed. A torrent from the Huang He River in the north surged down the ancient imperial Grand Canal, smashing the dykes protecting Goayou Lake north of Suzhou and drowning 200,000 people as they slept. Even after the worst was over, the disaster grew as disease and famine took hold. The world clucked with horror long after the water receded in November. The Chinese ignored everyone and did what they had to do.

WHEN:
July to November 1931
WHERE:
Throughout the Yangtze, Huai and Huang He (Yellow) river basins, central China
DEATH TOLL:
Estimates vary widely because figures for individual rivers have been confused with totals for all three. The consensus is not less than three to four million dead, and 50 to 80 million left homeless. Millions more died from their injuries or diseases arising from the floods (or both). Accuracy in assessing the carnage is not helped by often careless official Chinese attitudes of the day. One report from a local bigwig dismissed local casualties as including '30,000 rickshaw coolie refugees and 100,000 wharf coolie refugees' and therefore beneath his dignity. Such officials did nothing to suppress infanticide, cannibalism or the selling of wives and daughters for food.
YOU SHOULD KNOW:
Plans for flood control systems on the Yangtze, Huai and Huang He (Yellow) rivers were abandoned as China went to war for some 15 years after 1931. The Three Gorges Dam scheme on the Yangtze, proposed in the 1930s and completed in 2009, is likely to protect one group of cities only at the expense of another.

A devastating torrent of water from the Grand Canal continues to pour through broken dykes near Goayou.

Dust bowl disaster

WHEN:
1931–1938
WHERE:
Great Plains, USA
DEATH TOLL:
It is impossible to estimate how many people died from dust-associated disease; 400,000 dispossessed souls left the dust bowl. In terms of human loss and suffering, America has known nothing on the scale of the 'Dirty Thirties', before or since.

This peaceful little ranch in Boise City, Oklahoma, is about to be engulfed in a gigantic dust cloud.

During America's Great Depression, the nation's economic collapse coincided with a drought in its heartlands, the semi-arid plains of the Midwest. As the rain failed, the 'black blizzards' or 'dusters' started, blinding black or red dirt that swept through 19 states: the panhandles of Texas and Oklahoma, Kansas, Colorado, Montana and New Mexico, and the High Plains of Dakota. The drought lasted for the best part of a decade and with each passing year the dusters increased in frequency and magnitude.

The 'Dirty Thirties' began in 1931 – great black clouds darkened the sky sending flying dust into every nook and cranny. In 1932 there were 14 dusters; the following year there were 38; by 1934, 40 million hectares (100 million acres) of arable land had lost its topsoil. With grim determination the farmers carried on ploughing their fields, sowing their wheat and waiting for rain, as an epidemic of 'dust pneumonia' raged and people and animals choked on the dust and died of suffocation.

The storms reached their height on April 14 1935 – Black Sunday. After weeks of storms, it was a clear day when suddenly a great cloud came rolling in from Oklahoma, enveloping everything in its path and blacking out all trace of daylight. Travelling at 100 kph (60mph) the cloud carried the dust northwards as far as Canada and east to the Atlantic seaboard.

Black Sunday was the tipping point for hundreds of thousands of smallholders: giving up the unequal struggle, they abandoned their land to roam the roads in search of work and food, joining the ranks of the millions of unemployed created by the Depression. But Black Sunday's dust storm finally made the government take action; it passed the Soil Conservation Act and implemented training programmes on sound farming practices. And finally, in 1938, it started to rain.

YOU SHOULD KNOW:
For years the grasslands of the Great Plains had been farmed too greedily. The usual methods of ensuring healthy soil – crop rotation and leaving exhausted land to lie fallow – had not been practised. And after years of over-grazing and deep ploughing, the natural prairie grasses that trapped moisture and kept the soil intact had been uprooted, leaving the abused topsoil vulnerable to erosion; as drought turned it to dust, the parched earth simply blew away leaving mile upon mile of barren land.

Great Labor Day hurricane

The hurricane built up gradually. In late August it was just a bit of local 'weather' near the Bahamas. Who was to know that it would evolve into one of the most powerful hurricanes ever to hit land in the USA? From landfall, it was to last for another ten days with winds reaching 296 kph (185 mph) accompanied by a 6 m (20 ft) storm surge.

From the afternoon of September 2 until 05.00 the next morning the hurricane ripped through Florida's Upper Keys with extraordinary ferocity, leaving a trail of destruction in its wake. Almost every building over a distance of some 50 km (30 mi) in the Upper Keys was torn up, while a 'wall of water' raced in from the south flooding everything in its path, sweeping away bridges and embankments and washing a train off the track on the Florida East Railway extension. The flimsy huts of three relief work camps (set up to provide jobs for World War I veterans under President Roosevelt's New Deal) were pulverized, with around 260 fatalities.

The storm curved northwards and then inland, crossing the Gulf Coast on September 4, damaging docks and fishing boats and causing tides to rise 1.5 m (5 ft) higher than usual. It then howled into Georgia and across the Carolinas on September 5, causing yet more damage, before losing intensity as it blew back into the Atlantic. Out at sea the wind picked up strength again. A week after hitting the Keys it was still a Category One force as it ploughed northwards, until eventually it was calmed down by the cooler temperature of the North Atlantic.

WHEN:
September 1–10 1935
WHERE:
Upper and Middle Florida Keys, USA
DEATH TOLL:
More than 400
YOU SHOULD KNOW:
The great Labor Day hurricane happened in what was already one of the grimmest years of the Great Depression. The unnecessary deaths of so many war veterans caused a political furore as to the competence of the federal authorities and rescue agencies.

The town of New London was one of the hardest hit by the West Indies hurricane which tore through Long Island and New England.

Great New England hurricane

Those who know no better might reasonably assume the Long Island Express speeds commuters into Manhattan from fashionable Nassau and Suffolk counties on the continental USA's longest island, which extends for 190 km (118 mi) up the Atlantic coast from New York City. But the phrase 'Long Island Express' has a darker meaning for Long Islanders – for that was the popular name given to the great New England hurricane that brought massive destruction in September 1938.

The Long Island Express began life off Africa, winding up to the maximum Category Five on the Saffir-Simpson hurricane scale before earning its nickname by making landfall on Long Island as a Category Three. With winds reaching 260 kph (160 mph), it was still powerful enough to become the deadliest hurricane in New England history – killing over 650 people, damaging or destroying nearly 60,000 buildings, felling forests and devastating infrastructure including railroads and the electricity grid.

The hurricane didn't touch New York City, but came close enough to cut the city's power supply and cause the East River to flood parts of Manhattan. High winds, combined with a violent storm surge, assaulted eastern Long Island, claiming around 70 lives – including the bizarre deaths of 20 cinema goers and the projectionist after a cinema in Westhampton was plucked into the stormy sky and deposited 3 km (2 mi) out to sea.

Rhode Island was hardest hit, with the storm surge engulfing Westerly and drowning 100 people. The state's entire coastline was seriously battered and several beach communities were obliterated. Eastern Connecticut, despite being sheltered by Long Island, saw extensive destruction. The hurricane then tracked up the Connecticut River and reached Massachusetts, where another 100 victims were claimed by floods, before weakening over New Hampshire and tracking into southern Ontario and petering out.

WHEN:
September 21 1938
WHERE:
New England, USA
DEATH TOLL:
There was no official casualty figure, but the number of fatalities was between 680 and 800.
YOU SHOULD KNOW:
The unfortunate victims of the great New England hurricane were entitled to feel both surprised and hard done by. No major Atlantic storm had struck the area since 1869, when the Saxby gale ravaged Maine before moving into Canada. The last 'biggie' to batter Long Island itself occurred over a century before, in 1821.

Chillán earthquake

Any time a seismograph gives a Richter scale reading of 8.3, lots of people somewhere suffer a terrible ordeal that many cannot survive. Late one night in January 1939 the 'somewhere' was central Chile, and the event with that awesome magnitude was the destructive 23-minute Chillán earthquake. The epicentre was near the city that gave this massive quake its name, located in the country's richest agricultural region, Ñuble Province.

The long, narrow country of Chile lies above a fault line and is prone to seismic activity. The normal pattern sees an imminent earthquake heralded by foreshocks, giving ample notice of what lies in store. But 1939 was different. With no advance warning and unfortunate timing that meant most citizens were abed, Chillán's inhabitants stood little chance. Few buildings were capable of withstanding such a powerful shock and 90 per cent duly collapsed. At least a quarter of the city's 40,000 population died in bed as their houses fell on top of them. Many public buildings were also destroyed, including the old cathedral that was subsequently replaced with a modernistic quakeproof structure. The nearby city of Concepción in the province of the same name was equally hard hit, with many buildings reduced to rubble and thousands killed. In all, an area of 45,000 sq km (17,375 sq mi) was seriously affected by the quake.

Chilean President Pedro Aguirre Cerda declared martial law and sent in the army to prevent looting and oversee initial rescue attempts. There were not many further casualties in the aftermath of disaster, thanks to a mild winter and effective relief efforts directed by the Red Cross. Both Chillán and Concepción were subsequently reconstructed to stringent safety codes designed to protect residents from earthquakes that are virtually guaranteed to strike again in the future.

WHEN:
January 24 1939
WHERE:
Bío Bío Region, Chile
DEATH TOLL:
It is estimated that around 30,000 people died as a direct result of the quake.
YOU SHOULD KNOW:
This wasn't the first time Chillán had suffered catastrophic damage. In 1835 the town was rebuilt to the north of its original location after being razed to the ground by a violent quake. Concepción was badly damaged at the same time but had already been moved to a new site after a great earthquake in 1751. Both were rebuilt on their existing sites after being flattened by the 1939 event.

This Concepción family rescued whatever personal belongings they could from the ruins of their home to start life again under the open sky.

Armistice Day blizzard

WHEN:
November 10–12 1940
WHERE:
Midwestern USA
DEATH TOLL:
154 deaths were directly attributed
to the storm.
YOU SHOULD KNOW:
In an echo of many a subsequent
weather disaster – including Britain's
great October storm of 1987 –
forecasters failed to predict the likely
severity of the Armistice Day
blizzard, thus contributing
significantly to the number of
casualties. As a result, a system to
improve local weather forecasts in
the Midwest was introduced.

The USA's Midwest is renowned for harsh winters. However, November 11 1940 brought welcome respite for Middle Americans. Temperatures soared past 18°C (60°F) and headed towards 21°C (70°F), bathing residents in unprecedented warmth for the time of year. But this extraordinary temperature rise did not bring lasting relief from winter's icy grip, instead heralding the imminent arrival of another freak of Nature – that rare but devastating storm system named the 'panhandle hook' after its genesis in the Oklahoma and Texas panhandles and subsequent curved course through the Midwest *en route* to the Great Lakes.

By late afternoon it became apparent that a major weather event was unfolding as an intense low-pressure front tracked northwards, simultaneously sucking in moisture from the Gulf of Mexico and arctic air from the north. Benign conditions deteriorated with frightening speed as temperatures plunged and high winds brought rain, sleet and snow in rapid succession. By late afternoon a severe blizzard was raging, hitting Nebraska, South Dakota, Iowa, Minnesota and Wisconsin before completing its home run by reaching Lake Michigan. The Armistice Day blizzard instantly gained notoriety as one of the Midwest's worst-ever winter storms.

With fierce winds, freezing temperatures and driving snow that precipitated to a depth of nearly 70 cm (28 in), communications and transport were paralyzed, while people literally started perishing. A large number of duck shooters died after being attracted to the Mississippi River by ideal hunting conditions and failing to appreciate how severe the weather would become. Two were killed in a train wreck, over 60 sailors perished as a number of boats sank on Lake Michigan and many individuals caught in the storm simply froze to death. Over 150 people died before the Armistice Day blizzard blew itself out on November 12.

San Juan earthquake

The central to western region of Argentina behind the Andes is prone to seismic activity, being one of the most active fold-and-thrust belt regions in the world. It was here the country's worst-ever natural disaster occurred. The San Juan earthquake struck one evening in January 1944, the first such occurrence in the area since 1894. It wasn't the most powerful of earthquakes, with an estimated magnitude of around 7.8 on the Richter scale and an epicentre at La Laja some 30 km (20 mi) north of the eponymous capital of San Juan province. But still the quake killed thousands and inflicted

terrible damage on the city and its environs.

Much of San Juan was destroyed, with barely one tenth of its buildings withstanding the event and almost all the adobe houses predominating in the city's residential quarters flattened. In fact, the devastation said more about the poor construction of San Juan's buildings than the earthquake's force. One notable casualty was a characteristic 18th-century Jesuit cathedral typical of the city's charming Spanish colonial architecture, but the destructive quake swept all that away forever. Medical teams and politicians rushed to San Juan – then relatively remote – only to be profoundly shocked by the scale of death and destruction.

In the aftermath, moving the city to a safer location was considered. But in the end San Juan rose like a phoenix from its own rubble to become Argentina's most modern city, with a current population of around 115,000 people. Reconstruction took place using a building code that required all new structures to be quake resistant and imaginative planners specified the wide concentric boulevards, tree-lined avenues, up-to-date housing and green spaces criss-crossed by running water that have given the city a lush Mediterranean atmosphere.

A car on the streets of San Juan is buried under fallen masonry.

WHEN:
January 15 1944
WHERE:
San Juan Province, Argentina
DEATH TOLL:
Estimated at 10,000, one tenth of the area's population
YOU SHOULD KNOW:
The region suffered further earthquakes – in 1952 and 1977 – but thanks to the robust nature of its reconstruction San Juan was not badly affected. Even so, it is estimated that another earthquake of similar magnitude to that of 1944 would still demolish more than a quarter of the city's buildings.

Mount Lamington eruption

WHEN:
January 18–21 1951
WHERE:
Oro Province, Papua New Guinea
DEATH TOLL:
The eruption is estimated to have caused between 3,000 and 4,000 deaths.
YOU SHOULD KNOW:
The complacency of the Australian administration was summed up by an official who – when criticism of official indifference reached fever pitch after the event – blandly stated: 'As Mount Lamington volcano was eight miles from Higaturu, I formed the opinion that there was no immediate danger to human life'. Unsurprisingly, vociferous demands for a public enquiry into the tragedy were turned down.

The world and almost everything in it was not nearly so well documented in the 1950s as it is today and back in January 1951 nobody even suspected that Papua New Guinea's Mount Lamington was a volcano, much less one that was about to erupt. But erupt it did, to fearful effect. The event began on January 18, with locals watching glowing volcanic bombs, minor landslips, ash emissions and lightning playing around the mountain. But nobody saw fit to inform Australian government vulcanologists about these unusual occurrences, much less consider what they might herald. Indeed, complacent officials discouraged apprehensive observers from leaving the area.

Three days later, at 10.40, a loud explosion was heard up to 320 km (200 mi) away. This blew out the side of the mountain and deadly pyroclastic flows killed everything within a 325 sq km (125 sq mi) area around Mount Lamington. The devastation did not have a uniform spread – going out as far as 12 km (8 mi) in some directions but only 6 km (4 mi) in others. The power of the exploding volcano may be judged by the fact that at Higaturu District Station, 10 km (6 mi) from the eruption, a Jeep was plucked up and hurled into a tree, where it lodged in the branches. Casualties were numbered in thousands, either killed by blast shock or instantly burned to death by the superheated pyroclastic cloud that burst from the shattered mountainside.

Rescue efforts were hampered by swirling fumes and suffocating dust, while the clean-up was repeatedly threatened by continuing volcanic activity. Lesser explosions and further tremors took place throughout January and February and on March 5 a secondary eruption caused a lava flow that travelled for 14 km (9 mi), igniting everything in its path.

North Sea storm tide

WHEN:
January 31 to February 1 1953
WHERE:
Netherlands, UK, Belgium, Denmark and France
DEATH TOLL:
It is estimated that around 2,500 people died in the great North Sea flood of 1953 (including 1,835 in the Netherlands, 307 in the UK and over 250 mariners lost at sea).

At the end of January 1953, a high spring tide in the North Sea was whipped up by a severe cyclonic European windstorm, creating a fearsome storm tide. This phenomenon is rare, requiring an unusual combination of natural forces, but also deadly. A storm tide can be up to 5 m (17 ft) higher than the tallest regular tide and have a disastrous impact on the coastal areas it assaults.

The one that struck on the night of January 31 sank numerous vessels and overwhelmed coastal defences in several countries, most notably the Netherlands and England. The low-lying Dutch province of Zeeland was hardest hit, although dykes collapsed and huge areas were flooded all along the coast, with over 1,800 casualties and 70,000 people evacuated from inundated or threatened areas. Some 30,000 farm animals were drowned, 10,000 buildings were destroyed and over 35,000 structures were badly damaged. Around 1,350 sq km (520 sq mi) of the Netherlands were flooded, including nine per cent of the country's agricultural land.

Across the North Sea, eastern England also suffered grievously as floods engulfed parts of Lincolnshire, Norfolk, Suffolk and Essex. The storm tide smashed into a 1,600 km (995 mi) stretch of coastline, overwhelming sea defences and putting 1,000 sq km (385 sq mi) of East Anglian countryside under water. At least 30,000 people had to be evacuated from their homes, around 25,000 residential and commercial properties were seriously damaged and the catastrophe claimed more than 300 lives.

In the aftermath of disaster, the Dutch government initiated a massive anti-flooding programme called Deltaworks that would finally be completed 45 years later. In England, sea defences along the East Coast were strengthened and the Thames Barrier was conceived to protect London from storm tides ripping up river. It was completed in 1982 and first used the following year.

YOU SHOULD KNOW:
In a dramatic variation on the famous Dutch legend of the boy Hans Brinker who saved his community of Haarlem by putting a finger into a leaking dyke, the river ship *Two Brothers* was navigated into a breached dyke on the Holland IJssel River to successfully plug the widening hole and thus prevent extensive flooding that would have affected 3,000,000 people in the South and North Holland coastal provinces.

Residents of flooded Canvey Island leave their homes in an unusual taxi.

Hurricane Hazel

WHEN:
October 5–18 1954
WHERE:
The main impact was on Haiti,
the USA and Canada
DEATH TOLL:
It is estimated that around 1,200
died, the vast majority in Haiti.
YOU SHOULD KNOW:
Because of the terrible damage and
extensive loss of life inflicted by
deadly Hurricane Hazel, the name
will never again be used for a
hurricane that occurs in the
North Atlantic.

Canada's most notorious female visitor was a certain Hazel, but she was not human. Hurricane Hazel was the largest Atlantic hurricane in the 1954 storm season and she discharged her sound and fury all the way from Haiti, across the eastern USA and into Canada. She was one of the 20th century's deadliest hurricanes and the fact that Hazel ranks as Canada's worst-ever storm pays eloquent testament to her awesome power – for by the time Hazel arrived in Canada she was technically no longer a hurricane, but merely a tropical storm.

The word 'merely' is relative, for Hazel retained unusual ferocity in travelling 1,100 km (680 mi) across land to reach Canada, a journey that should have dissipated her energy. There she stopped, after meeting a cold front, to batter Greater Toronto with high winds and intense rainfall. The impact was increased because the arrival of such a deadly tropical storm was unheard of in Canada. By the time Hazel moved through Ontario and Quebec before finally dissipating, over 80 people had been killed, most by drowning in flash floods.

But if Hazel was disastrous in Canada, she was catastrophic during her violent journey up from the Caribbean, pursuing an erratic course

*Damage at Myrtle Beach
caused by Hurricane Hazel.*

that repeatedly fooled weather forecasters. Grenada, Puerto Rico and the Bahamas were battered but Haiti took Hazel's full force, with more than 1,000 lives lost and massive property damage inflicted, along with ruination of coffee and cacao plantations. Moving on to the USA, Hazel built up steam from Category Two to Category Four and made landfall in North Carolina, causing extensive coastal chaos before rushing on through Virginia, West Virginia, Pennsylvania, New York State and Maryland *en route* to Canada. Again, property damage was extensive, there was serious flooding, power lines went down and 95 Americans perished.

Typhoon Vera

The Japanese prosaically identify Pacific storms by number rather than name unless they're very special – and the typhoon that brewed up in September 1959 most definitely earned a title. The Isewan Typhoon – known by the rest of the world as Typhoon Vera – was a massive storm by any name, becoming infamous as Japan's worst natural disaster after smashing into the southeastern coast of Honshu. Vera then tracked up the island, leaving widespread death and destruction in her wake.

It all began with a low-pressure area near Guam in the western Pacific, which slowly built into a tropical storm. Quickly intensifying and acquiring a name, Vera's 305 kph (190 mph) winds immediately qualified her as a super typhoon. These wind speeds had slowed to a still-ferocious 260 kph (160 mph) when Vera hit the Japanese coastline in the Kansai region on September 26. The next day the weakening typhoon crossed the northern tip of Honshu and sped off into the northern Pacific, losing momentum and strength before petering out. But by then Typhoon Vera's lofty status in the annals of natural destruction had been amply secured.

This violent storm brought high winds and heavy rainfall, along with a major storm surge that battered the coast and caused extensive flooding inland. Massive damage was done to sea defences in particular and infrastructure in general; vast areas of planted crops were ruined even as countless buildings were irreparably damaged or demolished, including 557,500 houses. Over 5,000 died, 39,000 reportable injuries were sustained and nearly 1,600,000 people lost their homes. The city of Nagoya was devastated and the Tokyo-Yokohama area also saw damaging carnage. A vicious sting in Typhoon Vera's tail was felt after the storm had passed, as various epidemics – including dysentery – raged among the legion of people left homeless.

WHEN:
September 21–28 1959
WHERE:
Honshu, Japan
DEATH TOLL:
The published figure was 4,697 dead with a further 401 missing.
YOU SHOULD KNOW:
The Japanese designation of 'Isewan Typhoon' was chosen because Isewan Bay at the main impact point suffered the most concentrated damage, experiencing and failing to repel a 4 m (13 ft) storm surge that overwhelmed sea walls and inundated an area up to 8 km (5 mi) inland.

Valdivia earthquake

The world's most powerful earthquake – impressively titled *Gran terremoto de Valdivia* in Spanish – rocked Chile in May 1960. It measured an unprecedented 9.5 on the moment magnitude scale (MMS), regarded by seismologists as the most accurate measure of energy released by a quake. The epicentre of the Valdivia earthquake was near Cañete, 900 km (435 mi) south of the capital, Santiago, but was named after the city that took the biggest hit.

There had already been a smaller earthquake that cut off communications to Southern Chile on May 21 and rescue efforts were underway when the big one struck on the following day, with terrible consequences. Two fifths of Valdivia's buildings were razed to the ground and many more were damaged, including much of the city's industrial capacity. Power and water supplies were knocked out, hundreds died and 20,000 people were made homeless. A landslide blocked the outflow of nearby Riñihue Lake, creating a dam that threatened to burst and unleash a devastating flash flood – a danger averted by feverish work to lower the dam and release water in a controlled manner. Beyond Valdivia, a vast tract of Chile was seriously affected as coastal settlements were wiped out by tsunamis, ships sank and extensive flooding was experienced.

Damage caused by this awesome natural phenomenon wasn't confined to Chile, as a tsunami raced across the Pacific Ocean with 10 m (35 ft) waves recorded 10,000 km (6,000 mi) from the epicentre, as far away as the Philippines and Japan. The impact was particularly severe in Hawaii, where the coastal town of Hilo was devastated and 61 people died. Valdivia itself never really recovered. Already subject to economic decline, in 1974 it lost regional capital status to Puerto Montt. Many sites in Valdivia where the quake destroyed buildings have never been redeveloped.

Typical earthquake damage

WHEN:
May 22 1960
WHERE:
Southern Chile
DEATH TOLL:
Estimates of the number of casualties directly attributable to the Valdivia earthquake (sometimes called the Great Chilean Earthquake) vary considerably, from around 2,000 to over 6,000.
YOU SHOULD KNOW:
Two members of the indigenous Mapuche community from Chile's Araucania region made a human sacrifice in an attempt to placate angry gods that had sent earthquake and flood. A five-year-old boy had his arms and legs cut off, with the severed limbs being stuck into the beach like talismanic posts to be carried away by the tide. Two men were convicted of the sacrifice but released when a judge ruled they had been compelled to act by the irresistible force of ancestral tradition.

North Sea flood

The city of Hamburg – Germany's second largest – stands on the River Elbe at the base of the Jutland Peninsula. The North Sea lies to the west and the Baltic to the east, but the city is 100 km (60 mi) from either coast. In February 1962 it therefore came as an unpleasant surprise when a severe storm in the North Sea led to extensive flooding in Hamburg.

The culprit was a European wind storm of the kind that initiated inundation of the Netherlands and eastern England a decade before, but this time the action was in the German Bight. Northwestern Germany took the full force of 200 kph (120 mph) winds that caused a powerful storm surge that rose to a height of 3 m (10 ft) above the highest tide. It was too much for sea defences. Late on the evening of February 16 the first dykes were overwhelmed and a domino effect swiftly allowed advancing waters to engulf large areas along the Rivers Elbe and Weser.

Because of the late hour and the fact that telephone and power lines were brought down by the sudden flood, Hamburg's population was not alerted to the onrushing threat. Before an effective civil defence response could be organized, a sixth of the city was flooded. Over 6,000 buildings were destroyed or damaged beyond repair and hundreds died. Hamburg was cut off as roads were impassable and the railway system became inoperable.

The local police commissioner took charge, calling in the German Army and requesting help from Germany's NATO allies. They responded by sending helicopters that made a significant contribution to rescue operations. The displaced and stranded people of Hamburg – especially in the hard-hit residential district of Wilhelmsburg - swiftly christened these saviours from the sky *Fliegende Engel* (Flying Angels).

WHEN:
February 16–17 1962
WHERE:
Hamburg, Germany
DEATH TOLL:
315 deaths were recorded in Hamburg as a direct result of the North Sea flood.
YOU SHOULD KNOW:
It was terrifying for those who experienced it, but the North Sea flood was nothing compared to the *Grote Mandrenke* (Great Drowner of Men) that happened in 1362, exactly 600 years before. This hit England, the Netherlands and northern Germany and resulted in at least 25,000 deaths, with some casualty estimates going as high as 100,000.

A flooded district of Hamburg where cars attempt to drive through axle-deep water while residents wade along the street.

Bou'in-Zahra earthquake

WHEN:
September 1 1962
WHERE:
Qazvin Province, Iran
DEATH TOLL:
12,225 confirmed fatalities resulted
from the quake, although the true
total was almost certainly higher.
YOU SHOULD KNOW:
Another earthquake hit Bou'in-Zahra
40 years on, in 2002. Although this
one registered a not-so-different 6.5
on the Richter scale, fewer than 300
people died with some 1,500 injured.
A mild casualty-free quake was also
experienced in 2005.

Northern Iran is a notorious earthquake zone and at the beginning of
September 1962 duly experienced a massive quake measuring 7.1 on
the Richter scale. The epicentre was near the town of Bou'in-Zahra
in rugged hill country between Qazvin and Hamadan. When
aftershocks finally subsided, a fissure 103 km (64 mi) long had
opened up. The tremor was felt over a wide area with minor damage
reported as far away as Tehran, 225 km (140 mi) to the east.

A truly terrible price was paid in Bou'in-Zahra; the town suffered
devastation and surrounding settlements fared no better. Around 100
villages were affected, at least 30 of them virtually flattened as their
mud-brick houses simply collapsed during the violent tremor, often
killing occupants or burying them alive. Numerous other dwellings
had already been swept away by landslides that occurred
immediately before the quake. In total, over 21,000 houses were
either destroyed or too badly damaged to be worth repairing. As a
further blow to embattled rural communities, around a third of the
domestic livestock that played such an important part in their
everyday lives perished during the quake.

In all, the Bou'in-Zahra earthquake killed over 12,000 Iranians
and injured thousands – with many of the more serious casualties
eventually being transferred to Tehran's hospitals after medical
facilities at the regional capital of Qazvin were overwhelmed. The
relief effort was patchy, with such emergency services as there were
extended far beyond their capabilities. Air searches were ineffective
and ground parties sometimes didn't even reach outlying villages for
a week or more. Private citizens organized relief convoys carrying
blankets and food, but for thousands of victims help came too late.

*The Iranian village of
Danesfahan after it was
destroyed by the earthquake.
In the centre is the mosque, the
only building left standing.*

Skopje earthquake

In the early 1960s Skopje was the capital of Macedonia, then an integral part of the Socialist Federal Republic of Yugoslavia, the disparate conglomeration of ethnic groupings put together towards the end of World War II and ruled with an iron hand by Stalinist dictator Marshal Josip Tito. Located on the Varda River in southern Yugoslavia, Skopje developed rapidly after the war ended – progress that was abruptly halted by an earthquake in July 1963.

This disastrous occurrence measured 6.9 on the Richter scale. It was particularly destructive because the epicentre was in the Varda River Valley close to the city, and the earthquake took place at the relatively shallow depth of 6 km (4 mi). The tremor lasted for only 20 seconds, but during that short period four fifths of Skopje's buildings were destroyed or badly damaged. Over 1,000 people died and up to 4,000 were injured, while around 200,000 were made homeless in and around the city.

The Skopje earthquake made headlines around the world and the story captured public attention, partly because it was one of the first disasters to attract massive TV coverage. Nearly 80 countries offered relief supplies and humanitarian considerations outweighed political differences as the USA was in the forefront of the relief effort, quickly flying in a mobile field hospital to care for the injured. Temporary housing was supplied by a dozen countries, allowing new settlements to spring up outside the devastated city.

In an early example of musical performers getting involved in disaster relief, the violinist Henryk Szeryng staged a charity concert in France – an example that would be followed two decades later by the spectacular Live Aid concerts for Ethiopian famine relief. Pablo Picasso was deeply moved by the plight of Skopje's people and donated his painting *Head of a Woman*.

Soldiers search through rubble after the earthquake wrecked the city.

WHEN:
July 26 1963
WHERE:
Skopje, Macedonia (then Yugoslavia)
DEATH TOLL:
1,100 deaths with around 4,000 injured (estimates)
YOU SHOULD KNOW:
Skopje's partially ruined old railway station serves as a haunting reminder of the disaster. Now the city museum, the large clock on the street elevation has not been touched since it stopped at 17.17, the precise moment when the earthquake struck.

Great Alaska earthquake

The Richter scale was developed to measure the magnitude of earthquakes and tops out at 10 – this being an epic event that has not yet happened. The more modern MMS (moment magnitude scale) has no upper limit, but by either system the great Alaska earthquake of 1964 registered over 9 and was then the second-largest megathrust quake then recorded (the biggest being Chile's Valdivia earthquake four years previously).

Had this violent four-minute event taken place within shaking distance of a major population centre, the consequences would have been unimaginable, with casualties up with the tens or even hundreds of thousands claimed by history's few super-quakes. As it was, the epicentre was off the mouth of College Fjord in the Prince William Sound region of thinly populated Alaska. But while the death toll was light for such a severe earthquake, it was felt over a vast area and damage was widespread across the state.

Wild water caused most of the casualties and much of the damage. An open-ocean tsunami assaulted British Columbia, Washington State, Oregon and California, with damage recorded as far away as Hawaii and Japan. Terrifying local waves reached the awesome height of 70 m (230 ft) at Valdez, which subsequently had to be relocated to higher ground. There were landslides and fissuring that significantly realigned the landscape, and all Alaska's major towns and cities were affected to some degree, though the fact that many buildings – especially houses – were constructed of wood ensured that property damage did not reach epic proportions. Anchorage, however, was hit hard. Many buildings and much of its infrastructure was destroyed and the village of Chenga in Prince William Sound vanished, along with the hamlets of Girdwood and Portage. Aftershocks were felt for 18 months.

Fourth Avenue and a row of cars some 20 feet below their former level, in Anchorage

WHEN:
March 27 1964
WHERE:
Alaska, USA
DEATH TOLL:
131 (115 in Alaska and 16 in Oregon and California)
YOU SHOULD KNOW:
The great Alaska earthquake had a long reach. A series of seismic waves travelled round the world, with water rising and falling as far away as South Africa. There was also considerable aquatic disturbance nearer home, right down to Texas and Florida on the other side of the continental USA, where the effects were so intense in enclosed areas like harbours and marinas as far south as Louisiana that a number of boats were sunk.

Romanian floods

In 1970 Romania suffered serious disruption when an unfortunate combination of circumstances combined to create a great flood in late spring. High winds and storms produced prolonged torrential rain, while unseasonable warmth caused massive snow melt in the Carpathian Mountains, further overloading Romania's river system. Resultant floods moved inexorably from the north down through the central regions to the low-lying Danube area. The mighty River Danube itself rose 2 m (6 ft) above its normal level, causing a destructive surge to travel downstream.

Floodwaters overwhelmed extensive dykes that carried irrigation water needed to improve the country's backward agriculture. The consequences were disastrous, with nearly 250 towns and villages inundated in the first few days and almost the entire country affected to greater or lesser extent. The waters did not recede for over a month and before doing so around 200 people died, more than 40,000 houses had been swept away or damaged beyond repair, tens of thousands of farm animals were drowned and crops on 400,000 hectares (1,000,000 acres) of land were ruined.

In addition, 250,000 people were rendered homeless and a similar number had to be evacuated ahead of the rising waters. Virtually all Romania's factories were brought to a standstill through power failure, flooding or inability to acquire raw materials as the country's infrastructure collapsed. Airports were closed, the railway network became paralyzed, roads were impassable as landslides blocked many that were not already under water. Problems were compounded as communications were further disrupted by widespread loss of telephone lines.

Many countries contributed to the relief effort, but Romania was the one country in the Eastern Bloc to operate an independent foreign policy, and China seized the chance to tweak the Soviet Union's nose by becoming the biggest short- and long-term donor.

WHEN:
May to June 1970
WHERE:
Romania
DEATH TOLL:
209 people died.
YOU SHOULD KNOW:
Times move on and warning systems have become more sophisticated, so the great European floods of 2006 took no Romanian lives. But in terms of damage done and people displaced, it actually hit the country harder than the 1970 flooding.

Rising floodwaters at the aeromechanical factory at Medias in Romania

Nevados Huascáran avalanche

WHEN:
May 31 1970
WHERE:
Mount Huascáran, Yungay Province,
Peru
DEATH TOLL:
Estimated at 20,000 (from a total of
up to 80,000 killed by the earthquake
as a whole)
YOU SHOULD KNOW:
The only foreign victims of the
avalanche were Czechoslovakian
climbers whose mountaineering
team was in the wrong place at
the wrong time. Their bodies were
never found.

*A massive avalanche scoured
this valley, burying the town of
Yungay and killing most of the
population.*

The great Peruvian earthquake in May 1970 took place off the north coast
of Peru. It measured an impressive 7.9 on the Richter scale and was the
deadliest seismic disaster in Latin American history. The quake had a
catastrophic impact on the Ancash and La Libertad regions with serious
damage caused over an area of some 35,000 sq km (13,500 sq mi). The
coastal city of Chimbote was hard hit, countless other towns and villages
were devastated and virtually everything in the Andean valley of Callejón
de Huaylas was obliterated. There was massive infrastructure damage
and 3,000,000 people were affected.

The most severe single consequence was the world's worst-ever
snow-and-rock slide – the Nevados Huascáran avalanche. The quake
destabilized a section of Mount Huascáran 1.5 km (1 mi) long by 900 m
(3,000 ft) wide and 900 m (3,000 ft) deep. This huge mass of rock and
glacial ice detached and thundered down the mountain, reaching a speed
of 160 kph (100 mph) and destroying everything as it gathered
momentum. The provincial capital of Yungay was in its path and didn't

stand a chance. Neither did the smaller town of Ranrahirca. Both were obliterated and buried 50 m (165 ft) beneath debris left by the avalanche. Just 400 of Yungay's population of 18,500 survived, while in Ranrahirca nearly 2,000 were killed.

It was two days before the scale of the disaster became apparent to outsiders, leaving survivors to claw at heaped rubble with bare hands. When rescuers finally arrived with heavy equipment and medical supplies, it was too late for those who had been buried alive and for many survivors, who had already succumbed to injuries. The Peruvian government has classified the site of Yungay as a mass grave where all excavation is forbidden.

Bhola cyclone

The most devastating tropical cyclone, ever, struck in November 1970 – the sixth cyclonic storm in that year's North Indian Ocean cyclone season, and the deadliest. The Bhola cyclone formed over the Bay of Bengal and travelled north, gusting to 205 kph (130 mph) before making landfall in East Pakistan on the evening of November 12, unfortunately coinciding with high tide.

The result of this deadly combination was a massive storm surge in the low-lying Ganges Delta region, already prone to serious flooding and quite incapable of withstanding an event with the destructive power of the Bhola cyclone, which generated a tide at least 4 m (13 ft) above average. The impact was shocking. West Bengal and Assam in India saw heavy rainfall and high winds that damaged housing and crops, as did the Andaman and Nicobar Islands, but the coast of East Pakistan suffered the most traumatic consequences.

Bhola Island and Hatia Island were completely devastated, along with neighbouring islands and the adjacent mainland coast. Some 3,500,000 people were seriously affected by flooding, with 85 per cent of homes destroyed along with crops and 300,000 valuable cattle. Around 9,000 fishing boats were destroyed and 45,000 on-shore fishermen were killed, subsequently creating a severe food shortage. Numerous larger vessels were sunk or damaged by the cyclone, but the major cost was measured in human lives, with hundreds of thousands killed.

The Bhola cyclone was then the world's worst modern natural disaster, and may remain so to this day. Either of two subsequent catastrophes – the 1976 Tangshan earthquake and the 2004 Indian Ocean tsunami – may have caused more deaths, but as casualty figures for each event were never officially established it is impossible to know which of the trio was the cruellest life-taker.

WHEN:
November 7–13 1970
WHERE:
East Pakistan (now Bangladesh) and West Bengal, India
DEATH TOLL:
Unknown, with estimates varying from 300,000 to 500,000 fatalities
YOU SHOULD KNOW:
The Pakistani authorities were widely criticized for a lacklustre response to the disaster – negligence that gave huge political impetus to East Pakistan's opposition Awami League and hastened the onset of the Bangladesh Liberation War, a struggle that would result in independence from Pakistan.

Iran blizzard

WHEN:
February 3–9 1972
WHERE:
Iran
DEATH TOLL:
Estimated at between 4,000
and 5,000
YOU SHOULD KNOW:
The USA's National Oceanic and
Atmospheric Administration (NOAA)
puts the Iran blizzard on its list of top
global weather, water and climate
events of the 20th century, along
with the great Iran flood of 1954 that
took 10,000 lives.

There had been a four-year drought in Iran, which came to a spectacular end in February 1972 not with long-awaited rainfall, but in the form of an intense blizzard that lasted for a week and blanketed the country. Virtually all Iran's 1,636,000 sq km (631,000 sq mi) landmass vanished beneath a covering of snow that was so deep in places it literally buried thousands of people, many of whom sat tight in houses that turned into freezing death-traps long before a slow thaw revealed the true horror of this extraordinary happening.

The tragic outcome is perhaps not surprising, for this was the worst blizzard ever recorded in world history. The snow was at least 3 m (10 ft) deep, though some places – mainly in southern Iran – saw coverage as deep as 8 m (26 ft). Furthermore, the extent of the blizzard was a surprise. Although a mountainous country, Iran's climate ranges from arid desert to subtropical and temperatures on the Caspian coastal plain in the north rarely fall below freezing. Inhabitants of the Zagros Mountains in the west were used to hard winters and heavy snowfall, but southerners living alongside the Gulf of Oman and Persian Gulf expected mild winters and hot summers.

Ironically, many of the casualties were recorded in and around the city of Ardakan in central Iran, the second city of Yazd Province, in a region containing several deserts and noted for being one of the most arid parts of the country. There were no survivors in Kakkan or Kumar and around 100 villagers were buried at Sheklab, by the Turkish border. At least 4,000 people died in this terrible blizzard, many because they simply weren't expecting or properly prepared to deal with such a totally unprecedented event.

Hurricane Fifi

WHEN:
September 14–24 1974
WHERE:
Western Caribbean and Honduras
DEATH TOLL:
Probably more than 8,000
YOU SHOULD KNOW:
Because of its devastating
consequences, the name Fifi was
retired from the list of Atlantic
hurricane names. The corresponding
name is the rather more serious
sounding Frances.

Fifi was designated a hurricane after it passed through Jamaica as a tropical storm and then reached maximum intensity when it raked the north coast and offshore islands of Honduras, before weakening after landfall in Belize. Renamed Hurricane Orlene, it later reached Mexico.

High winds and tides destroyed harbours, towns and crops along the coastal lowlands of Honduras, but it was the sustained torrential rain and subsequent flooding in the mountains that killed thousands, and left survivors destitute. In about 40 hours, 50 cm (20 in) of rain fell on the Sierra de Omaoa. Streams and rivers burst their banks, and walls of water deluged the fertile valleys, ruining the banana, coffee and bean crops. Flash floods and mudslides washed away villages and towns. The city of Choloma was engulfed during the night, and lost more than half its population

International aid – including US helicopters, British infantry and powerboats, and a Cuban medical team – arrived promptly, although continuous thunderstorms and thick fogs hampered work. Each day, hundreds of bodies were found, floating bloated in the rivers or buried in mud. They were hastily buried, but the stench of death was pervasive. The merciless sun and the snakes and tarantulas fleeing flooded banana groves added to the general misery. Relief agencies rushed aid to starving, isolated villagers whose access roads had been destroyed along with homes, stores and crops. They reported fierce fights among people desperate for food or for places on rescue helicopters – and the flagrant misappropriation and hoarding of supplies by the Honduran military.

Hurricane Fifi was the worst natural disaster in the history of Honduras, the poorest of the Central American republics. The country was left with countless dead and homeless, and damages in excess of its entire Gross National Product (GNP).

A row of houses surrounded by muddy water, some of which have their owners' possessions on the roofs, on a banana plantation near San Pedro.

Houses ripped apart by Cyclone Tracy, which hit Darwin early on Christmas morning.

Cyclone Tracy

For the people of Darwin, Christmas 1974 brought neither peace nor merrymaking. Just after midnight on Christmas Eve, Cyclone Tracy struck – leaving the city in ruins. The powerful and compact storm had travelled north of the city two days before, but swung round and headed straight back. Though warned of the cyclone's approach, most people chose to continue with Christmas preparations rather than evacuate. Cyclones were not uncommon and one predicted just ten days earlier had passed by harmlessly.

By the afternoon of Christmas Eve dark rainclouds covered the sky, and during the evening heavy downpours and gusts of wind caused some damage. Later, as Tracy swept over the northern suburbs and the airport, wind speeds of 217 kph (135 mph) were recorded. By dawn the town was absolutely devastated.

WHEN:
December 25 1974
WHERE:
Darwin, Northern Territory, Australia
DEATH TOLL:
70 died – 48 on land and 22 who were at sea when the cyclone struck.

In the stricken city, police, volunteers and hard-pressed hospital staff struggled to deal with wreckage and casualties. Darwin's remoteness, the damage to the communications systems and the fact that it was Christmas Day combined to delay news of the disaster. But relief medical teams arrived late the same day, and the seriously injured were airlifted to safety. The forces were called back from leave and deployed – the navy transported supplies, the airforce started evacuation and army teams worked tirelessly to search and clear collapsed buildings. Temporary water and power supplies were organized and an immunization programme was introduced to prevent epidemics. About three quarters of the population left in a government-supported evacuation and relocation programme; the men who stayed were involved in the rescue and reconstruction of the city.

A statement at the time declared that Darwin had 'ceased to exist as a city'. Later, the decision was made to bulldoze and rebuild; modern Darwin bears little resemblance to the town destroyed by Cyclone Tracy.

YOU SHOULD KNOW:
All over the country, funds were collected for the refugees. Small towns provided food and shelter as those travelling by road passed through. Large sums were collected at the Boxing Day Test Match in Melbourne.

Typhoon Nina and the Banqiao Dam disaster

Tropical storm Nina reached typhoon intensity on August 2 1975. It battered the central mountains of Taiwan, made landfall over southern China and moved northwest before turning south and dissipating. However, over the province of Henan, the collision of the typhoon's warm, humid air with a cold front produced a series of disastrous storms which, in three days, dropped more than a year's rain.

A 1950's project to control flooding and generate electricity had dammed rivers in the Huai Valley Basin. After the cracks which appeared in the structure of the largest dam, the Banqiao, had been repaired, it was known as the 'iron dam'. It had been designed to hold around 500 million cubic metres of water and to survive a 'one in 1,000 year flood' – 30 cm (12 in) rain per day. The rainfall Typhoon Nina delivered, however, was a 'one in 2,000 year flood' as a record amount – over 1 m (3 ft) – fell in 24 hours.

Flooding was inevitable and all forms of communication were wiped out by the appalling weather. The order to open the sluice gates was not received and only part of the area was evacuated. All the reservoirs were filled to capacity and at 00.30 on August 8, water topped the smaller Shimantan Dam and surged through. Half an hour later came the catastrophic failure of the Banqiao Dam, and a massive, fast-moving wall of water 13 km (8 mi) wide inundated towns, villages and farmland. In all, 62 dams failed or were breached to control flooding. Thousands of people drowned and even more died subsequently from famine and epidemics – nine days later, over a million survivors were still cut off by the floodwaters.

WHEN:
August 8 1975
WHERE:
Henan Province, China
DEATH TOLL:
25,000 from flooding, 135,000 subsequently (Henan Province Hydrology Department figures)
YOU SHOULD KNOW:
Eminent hydrologist Chen Xing recommended 12 sluice gates at the planning stage of the Banqiao Dam; it was built with only five, and other dams also had reduced safety features. Chen was 'removed' from the project for his outspoken criticism.

Damaged buildings in a popular shopping district in Beijing

The Tangshan earthquake

WHEN:
July 26 1975
WHERE:
Tangshan, Hopei, China
DEATH TOLL:
The official figure was 242,419, but it is thought to be much higher, possibly around 700,000
YOU SHOULD KNOW:
There is a traditional belief that the 'Year of the Dragon', which comes round once every 12 years, augurs ill. This one was later named the 'Curse of 1976'.

For China, 1976 was a year of political upheaval and power struggles. For Tangshan, an industrial city of over a million people in the Hailan coal basin of Hopei Province, it was a year of catastrophe. In July, a scientist at the State Seismological Bureau had predicted that the Tangshan region would suffer a significant earthquake around the end of the month. Although officials in Qinglong county risked their careers by organizing precautions, the city of Tangshan was considered to be in a low-risk area.

The earthquake, put by some sources as high as magnitude 8.3 and followed by a 7.1 aftershock, struck at 04.00 when most of the city's residents were sleeping. There had been no warning foreshock. In about 15 seconds, most of the city's houses and apartment blocks (very few of which were built to withstand earthquakes) collapsed, trapping survivors in the ruins. Bridges, stations and factories were also destroyed. Tremors were felt as far away as Beijing, whose residents were urged to stay in the city's open spaces.

In Tangshan, where casualties included coalminers buried alive and about 2,000 people in the city's largest hospital, survivors and rescue workers from the People's Liberation Army dug in the rubble, responding to the desperate cries of those beneath the wreckage. Tents were home for the survivors until they were moved to winter shelter.

The official line was that 'any grave natural disaster can be overcome with the guidance of Chairman Mao' and the Chinese government refused international aid, claiming there was ample food and medical supplies. Rebuilding began almost immediately. The new city is again home to more than a million and has been awarded the title 'Brave City of China'.

Vrancea earthquake

The Vrancea area lies in the southeastern 'corner' of the U-shaped Carpathian range which, with its beautiful Alpine pastures and high, wooded slopes, makes up about a third of Romania. Only 130 km (81 mi) north of the capital, Bucharest, Vrancea is a seismogenic zone where most of the seismic activity which affects a large swathe of the Balkans originates. Major earthquakes have taken place regularly here for centuries, but the 7.2 magnitude quake that struck in March 1977 was the most serious, with thousands of casualties and damage as far away as the Bulgarian town of Svishtov, south of the Danube.

Most badly hit was the city of Bucharest, which sustained about 90 per cent of the country's fatalities. In the countryside around Vrancea, hundreds of low, wood-framed village houses and farm buildings collapsed, but the worst architectural casualties were the city's prewar apartment blocks and public buildings. Bucharest still has a Parisian atmosphere, with wide boulevards lined by fine, tall residential buildings, and many of these fell in the quake, though they had survived a previous one in 1940. They were constructed of reinforced concrete with brick infill – most of the modern concrete buildings, such as hotels and offices, had been constructed to withstand quakes, and remained standing. Altogether, more than 30,000 apartments were damaged or destroyed, and many of the city's historic buildings were beyond repair.

In 1997 an international workshop on the earthquakes of Vrancea was held. Attended by more than 100 seismologists and engineers from 12 countries, it resulted in invaluable co-operative work and produced recommendations on hazard prevention and risk management.

WHEN:
March 4 1977
WHERE:
Vrancea and surrounding area, Romania, and parts of Bulgaria
DEATH TOLL:
Altogether, more than 1,500 died and more than 11,000 were injured.
YOU SHOULD KNOW:
In part of Bucharest's historic district conveniently 'cleared' after the earthquake, Ceausescu began his massive, Stalinist 'House of the People'. The second largest building in the world, it was unfinished at his death in 1989 and now houses Romania's parliament.

Mount St Helens eruption

WHEN:
May 18 1980
WHERE:
Washington State, USA
DEATH TOLL:
57
YOU SHOULD KNOW:
One of the fatalities was 84-year-old Harry Truman, who ran a motel on the shores of Spirit Lake. He refused to be evacuated and stayed, with his 18 racoons and 16 cats, to the end.

The Cascades Range, a remote region of the northern Rockies, is a place of mountains, rivers, forests and wildlife. Volcanic Mount St Helens, beautifully mirrored in Spirit Lake, had in 1980 been dormant for more than a century, when in March a series of eruptions began. The northern slopes developed a worrying bulge and a new crater opened, from which blue flames emerged. Geologists and seismologists monitored increasingly strong tremors and on April 3 a state of emergency was declared. While the suddenly active volcano attracted curious crowds, residents were evacuated. On May 17, after visible eruptions had ceased, home owners were allowed to retrieve their belongings.

At 08.32 the next morning, Mount St Helens exploded, with a 5.1 magnitude quake which triggered one of the biggest landslides in history. The whole north face collapsed and hurtled downwards at up to 241 kph (113 mph), displacing the water from the lake and burying a vast area under a deep layer of debris. In minutes, a cloud of ash rose 24 km (15 mi) while a massive lateral blast produced pyroclastic flows of hot ash, pumice and gas with temperatures up to 360°C (680°F). Volcanic mudflows wrecked roads and bridges, and restricted the flow of rivers for miles around. The scene was apocalyptic: air thick and black with burning ash, constant explosions, uprooted trees blazing in the intense heat, the entire mountain streaming with molten lava.

Afterwards, millions of tons of ash spread rapidly across the USA, falling thickly on towns hundreds of miles away, and then took just two weeks to spread all round the globe. The glorious mountain landscape had been mutated into a charred hell. Life is gradually returning but Mount St Helens is still scarred and shattered, and considerably lower than it once was.

An aerial view of Mount St Helens in full flow

The Armero tragedy

The remote town of Armero lay on the banks of the Langunilla River below Nevado del Ruiz, a volcanic peak in the Colombian Andes. This region is part of the 'Pacific Ring of Fire', an unstable area of the earth's crust circling the Pacific and including most of the world's active volcanoes. The Nevado del Ruiz was known locally as the 'Sleeping Lion', for there had been serious eruptions in the past, and Armero was within a hazard zone delineated by geologists (in fact, it was built on hardened mudflow deposits from the last eruption, in the 19th century).

In 1985, rumblings from the crater indicated new volcanic activity. The town's authorities were warned of potential danger but chose to reassure residents. On November 13, ash began to fall and evacuation started, but when the volcano went quiet again most people returned to their homes. Just after 21.00, the 'Lion' woke, and roared. In minutes Armero was obliterated.

The eruption melted the volcano's icecap and flung molten rock and ash into the river, which exploded into volcanic mudslides (*lahars*). These accelerated down the mountain, gathering momentum and sweeping up huge boulders before smashing into Armero. Most of the townspeople were indoors and the whole town was entombed in metres of mud and rubble. Like Pompeii, it was frozen in time.

International relief teams found a horrifying scene. People were trapped in the residue of the *lahars*, and there was no way to extricate them. The Colombian army, who could have provided equipment, numbers and muscle, had been mobilized to Bogota where there was political violence. Rescue workers could do little but offer comfort. A pilot, making a reconnaissance flight, reported that Armero had been 'erased from the map'. Later, the site was declared 'holy ground'.

Volcanic debris from the Nevado del Ruiz volcano swamps the town of Armero.

WHEN:
November 13 1985
WHERE:
Armero, Tolima Province, Colombia
DEATH TOLL:
2,300 (estimated)
YOU SHOULD KNOW:
Frank Fournier's photograph of the girl Omayra Sanchez, trapped in mud and gazing up at the camera as she waited to die, shocked the world and caused an outcry. It epitomized the tragic plight of the aid workers – without manpower and machinery, all they could do was watch.

The waters of Lake Nyos near Wum turned a murky brown following the deadly release of toxic gas.

Nyos Limnic eruption

In the autumn of 1986, a traveller made his way by bicycle from the remote Cameroon village of Wum towards the neighbouring village of Nyos. The dirt track was unusually quiet that day and when he found a newly dead antelope he strapped it to his bike. Soon he realized that there were dead animals wherever he looked. He surmised that they had possibly been killed by a lightning strike and journeyed on. When he came to a small hamlet he decided to call in to ask if anyone knew what had happened. On entering the first hut, to his horror he found that everyone was dead. It was the same story in each hut. He panicked, threw his bicycle to the ground and ran as fast as he could back to Wum.

By the time he reached Wum to tell his story, several other people from Nyos and neighbouring villages had arrived. Some spoke of hearing an explosion, others of smelling a foul odour. Some, still disoriented, had told of passing out for more than a day only to find the bodies of their friends and family strewn about lifeless all around them when they awoke. Such was the remoteness of Nyos that it took several days for news of the catastrophe to reach the outside world.

Soon a delegation of scientists from France and America arrived to try to shed some light on this terrible event. The bodies of the dead showed no signs of trauma or struggle; they had simply died where they were. As the research team approached Lake Nyos, they noted that the bodies became more numerous and on arriving at the lake they saw it was an unnatural dark-brown colour. That the lake was responsible for the deaths was clear, but the mechanism involved was not.

WHEN:
August 22 1986
WHERE:
Lake Nyos, Cameroon
DEATH TOLL:
Between 1,700 and 1,800 people and a huge amount of wildlife
YOU SHOULD KNOW:
Further scientific research found that carbon dioxide had built up under extremely high pressure in the volcanic lake. A landslip had probably caused the gas to be released into the air, poisoning those in its path and then dispersing. The usual level of carbon dioxide in the air is much less than a tenth of one per cent but near Lake Nyos levels may have reached ten per cent (more than a hundred times higher than normal). Attempts to rid the lake of the gas through controlled draining have been only partially successful and locals fear that what they call the 'bad lake' could strike again.

Yellowstone wildfires

Yellowstone is the oldest and perhaps most famous national park in the world. Established in 1872, it covers over two million acres of Wyoming and spreads into neighbouring Idaho and Montana. Over the years it has gradually become valued not simply as a vast outdoor play area but also as a national treasure – it eventually gained the status of United Nations World Heritage Site in 1978.

Management of the park has long been a source of controversy. In recent times, locals were outraged to find that emissions from snowmobiles there were higher than in the traffic of downtown Los Angeles. Also the culling of more than 1,000 bison, mistakenly thought to be carrying livestock-threatening disease, was misguided to say the least.

However, nothing has stirred more debate than the management of naturally occurring fires in Yellowstone. Until the 1970s it had been the procedure of the Park Service to tackle and extinguish these spontaneous blazes. This interventionist policy enabled older trees to survive and dead ones to lie where they fell, storing up problems for the future. So much dead wood made the entire park a giant tinder box just waiting for the right conditions.

In 1988, the ideal forest fire conditions duly arrived. Spring had been relatively warm and dry and these conditions stretched into the summer. Multiple lightning strikes hit the park and, combined with the parched conditions and a strengthening wind, the park authorities found themselves dealing with huge wildfires that they could do little to control. Despite the best efforts of around 10,000 firefighters who tackled the enormous conflagration from the air and on land, and the expenditure of nearly $120 million, the fires raged for months. On one August day alone, more than 600 sq km (232 sq mi) of Yellowstone were lost to fire, and cities downwind were covered in ash.

WHEN:
Summer of 1988
WHERE:
Yellowstone National Park, USA
DEATH TOLL:
There were two deaths outside the park attributed to the fires.
YOU SHOULD KNOW:
It is probable that the massive intervention by the authorities had little or no effect on the fires. In fact it may have harmed the area by introducing so much water which, combined with a subsequent wet spring, caused considerable soil erosion. While this level of wildfire occurs only about once in every 250 years, it is still part of the life cycle of the park. New vegetation has grown rapidly, seizing its chance to replace the old. In the decades following the fires the park has successfully regenerated.

The fire was fanned by tremendous winds as high as 95 kph (55 mph).

Great blizzard superstorm

WHEN:
March 12–15 1993
WHERE:
Cuba and the east coast of
North America
DEATH TOLL:
100
YOU SHOULD KNOW:
The storm was a triumph for weather
forecasters, who had predicted its
path and intensity several days in
advance. This information was vital
to at least 100 million people who
were in its path, allowing them to
hunker down in the warmth and
security of their homes

In mid March 1993 a powerful depression worked its way up the eastern seaboard of the USA. It sparked tornadoes in the Florida panhandle and record precipitation in many Atlantic states. Ferocious winds and bitingly low temperatures caused havoc, leading this freak weather occurrence to be dubbed the 'Storm of the Century'.

On March 12 a deep depression had formed in the Gulf of Mexico. As the storm moved northwards towards New Orleans the pressure dropped rapidly, producing hurricane-force winds in Florida and Cuba that spawned huge waves causing coastal flooding. The sheer scale of the storm was revealed when it hit Georgia. Laden with moisture, it dumped record-breaking rainfall to the south and east and as it moved inland over cold terrain this turned to snow. Transport was virtually shut down, interstate highways were closed, and at one point all the airports in the eastern United States lay idle.

By March 13 satellite imagery showed the full extent of the storm. Like a giant billowing tornado, it now stretched the whole way up the coast of North America as far as Nova Scotia. Blizzard warnings were issued for many locations, and upstate New York was particularly hard hit as snow turned to icy rain, making conditions even more treacherous. Parts of New Jersey experienced 90 cm (3 ft) of snow in a single day. Roofs collapsed under the weight of snow, economic activity slowed to a virtual halt, and the most vulnerable were cut off from help.

In all, 26 states of America were affected by the storm as well as Cuba and much of eastern Canada. By March 15 the storm had begun to abate, leaving many millions of people to mop up and count the cost.

Morning commuters negotiate their way over one of the many walls of ice that blocked street corners in Midtown Manhattan.

Great Hanshin (Kobe) earthquake

Located in the Kansai region of Japan, the trading city of Kobe was the scene of two great destructive episodes in the 20th century. During World War II it was virtually razed to the ground by American B-52 bombers in a series of incendiary attacks. The city was of such strategic importance to Japan that its rebuilding was essential and, like a phoenix from the flames, it emerged as a bustling port once more.

Just before dawn on a mid-January morning in 1995, the earth shifted near the Island of Awaji, located 20 km (12.5 mi) south of Kobe. This sent tremors along the Suma and Suwayama faultlines which run through the heart of the city. Such was the proximity and magnitude of the quake that the whole city juddered for 20 seconds and over 200,000 buildings were shaken to the ground. Many of the city's buildings had wooden frames and heavy roofs designed to withstand typhoons. As the ground was ripped open, gas mains ruptured and fierce fires broke out across the city. Rescue efforts were further hampered by the bursting of most of the water mains and the collapse of an elevated section of the Hanshin Expressway Route 43 – pictures of which remain the iconic image of the quake.

The quake shocked Japan in many ways. Although most of the city's buildings met with regulations at the time of their construction, these rules were clearly inadequate. The Japanese government also came in for criticism for initially refusing all outside help. Panic swept the floor of the Japanese stock exchange, and the day after the quake the Nikkei Index lost over 1,000 points. The tremor clearly prolonged the 1990's recession which became known as 'The Lost Decade'.

An elevated section of the Hanshin Expressway collapsed in the earthquake.

WHEN:
January 17 1995
WHERE:
Kobe, Japan
DEATH TOLL:
6,500
YOU SHOULD KNOW:
The damage caused by the quake amounted to one fortieth of Japan's annual economic production. The economic aftershocks were felt around the world, not least by Barings Bank, where the quake exposed large losses accrued by rogue trader Nick Leeson, leading to the bank's collapse.

Chicago heatwave

WHEN:
July 10–16 1995
WHERE:
Chicago and much of the
Midwest, USA
DEATH TOLL:
At least 739
YOU SHOULD KNOW:
The Mayor of Chicago called the
situation a unique, meteorological
catastrophe. But a public hearing
found that the city's support systems
had failed, and as a result warning
systems and procedures were
strengthened. In 1999, another
heatwave struck the city and this
time the death toll reached 110
people – still dreadful, but a
considerable improvement.

The American Midwest has suffered severe heatwaves throughout the years, but the one that struck in 1995 was extreme. From July 10–16, the heat was unbearable, exacerbated by super-high humidity. The city authorities were very slow to respond, only releasing an emergency warning on the final day.

In Chicago, a heat island aggravated the situation. These occur in urban settings, where buildings and roads absorb heat during the day without dissipating it at night, thus becoming and remaining hotter than normal. With no breeze, pollutants and humidity stayed at ground level. Indoors, at night, temperatures reached over 32°C (90°F), and people began to die. Those who could, left the city.

Air conditioning units worked overtime, and energy use reached record highs. Power failed and at one stage 49,000 households in the city were without electricity. Roads buckled, railway lines warped, and city employees watered the bridges to prevent expansion and locking. The Fire Department hosed down school children travelling in buses as hot as ovens, and by July 14 thousands of people had heat-related illnesses. Ambulances, supplemented by fire trucks, could not cope with the emergency calls, hospitals were overflowing and about 20 shut their emergency rooms to new patients. The city morgue, with 222 bays, needed a fleet of refrigerated trucks to contain the extra bodies.

The victims were mainly poor people living alone in the city centre. They either had no air conditioning or could not afford to use it, and fear of crime prevented many from opening their doors and windows, particularly at night. The worst hit were single, elderly, black men. Black women, Hispanics and whites fared a little better.

Afterwards, no official death toll was given, but figures show 739 extra deaths that week in comparison to all previous years on record.

Saguenay flood

WHEN:
July 19–20 1996
WHERE:
The Saguenay region of Quebec,
Canada
DEATH TOLL:
According to official records there
were seven fatalities; according to
other sources there were ten.

The Saguenay region of Quebec has suffered several natural disasters, including a landslide in 1971 and an earthquake in 1988. These events, however, cannot compare with the disastrous flooding that ripped the region apart in July 1996.

Between July 18–21 a vast storm system halted over the mouth of the St Lawrence River; more rain fell than is usual throughout the entire month. Around the Jonquiere, Chicoutimi and La Baie area of the Saguenay Valley over 20 cm (8 in) of rain fell between the morning of July 19 and the evening of the following day. The ground was already saturated with previous rainfall, and this triggered the catastrophe.

On July 19 the waters in Lake Kenogami began to rise. It was the height of the tourist season and the need to cater for holidaymakers had persuaded the Quebec government to keep the water level in the lake high.

By 03.30 on July 20 the crisis was recognized: engineers were forced to increase the evacuation of water from the dam to levels that they knew would flood houses downstream. Later that morning, Lake Ha!Ha! ruptured its earthen dyke and debris was washed through the forest to the Ha!Ha! River. This swamped a village with mud, rocks and uprooted trees, before hitting La Baie with the force of an explosion, annihilating an entire neighbourhood.

Altogether, more than 16,000 people were evacuated, 488 homes were destroyed and 1,230 were badly damaged. Several people were drowned, and others killed by mudslides. An entire shopping mall was swept away, and cars were buried under the layers of mud left behind. Much of the region's infrastructure just vanished, making rescue work infinitely more difficult. When all the losses were added up, they were estimated as being in excess of Can$1.5 million – the worst flood in Quebec's history.

YOU SHOULD KNOW:
The Nicolet Commission found that the 2,000 dams, dykes and embankments in the area – often privately owned – had mainly been built pre-1960, had not been upgraded and were poorly maintained. Many homes had been built on areas known to flood. The Commission made various recommendations, but geologists think that climate change will produce more such meteorological extremes, with catastrophic effects.

A dramatic aerial view of what used to be downtown Chicoutimi

The ice storm

WHEN:
January 4–10 1998
WHERE:
Ontario and Quebec, Canada; New England and New York State, USA
DEATH TOLL:
35 people died, 28 of whom were in Canada; 945 people were injured, and thousands of animals were killed.
YOU SHOULD KNOW:
The economic losses were enormous at about $4.4 billion US dollars, $3 billion of which were from Canada. Over one million maple trees were damaged; 22 per cent of Canada's maple syrup taps were affected, including 23 per cent of Quebec's 21 million taps and 285,000 of Ontario's. The industry estimates that it could take 40 years before production recovers from the ice storm.

In January 1998, North America fell victim to an absolute corker of an ice storm. Although not unknown in these regions, this storm was so extreme – affecting individuals, industry and infrastructure – that it has gone down in history as Canada's most expensive natural disaster.

Ice storms occur when warm and cold air collide. Warm air rises, cold air remains low and the snow in between melts, hitting the ground wet, and freezing instantly. Three storm fronts in quick succession left everything coated with ice that became thicker and thicker. Montreal and its rural environs received more than 10 cm (4 in) of freezing rain, twice the amount received in two previous record-breaking storms.

Power lines collapsed everywhere – Hydro-Quebec alone lost 3,000 km (1,850 mi). Steel pylons, said to be the strongest in the world, crumpled like tissue paper, wooden utility poles simply splintered under the weight of ice and phone lines collapsed. Trees fell on buildings and cars, and 100,000 people took refuge in hotels or emergency shelters. A state of emergency was declared.

By January 8 the military were involved. More than 4.7 million Canadians and 500,000 Americans were without power. Even after power was restored, large parts of Montreal were cordoned off as huge slabs of ice fell from buildings.

The rural areas were worst hit. Farmers could not feed, water or ventilate their livestock and almost a quarter of Canada's dairy cows died frozen, starving and trapped in barns collapsing upon them from the weight of the ice. Ten million litres (18 million pints) of milk were dumped, millions of trees were snapped, and both the orchard areas and maple syrup industries were devastated. Several hundred thousand people were still without power three weeks later.

National Guardsmen survey fallen power lines and ice-covered trees as they work to clear a road.

Texas floods

On October 17 1998, a catastrophic flood took place in southern and central Texas. The National Weather Service had predicted the coming storm, because a trough of low atmospheric pressure was approaching from the west. Thanks to Hurricane Madeline, which lay off the west coast of Mexico, the weather in Texas was very warm and moist. It was forecast that if the two fronts collided, thunderstorms would occur. And if the cold front, also moving across the western United States, were to coincide with the rain, a serious storm could take place, bringing floods in its wake.

Members of the Texas National Guard drive through the flooded streets of Wharton, looking for stranded residents.

Early on October 17 it began raining and peals of thunder rumbled around from time to time. By the evening the cold front had arrived and the heavens opened across the whole region. The deluge poured down continuously until the following evening, bursting the banks of every river, lake and creek in the area. In San Antonio and Austin, and their suburbs, the impact was enormous: 74 cm (29 in) of water fell upon a small area in Caldwell County, and between 50–76 cm (20–30 in) fell elsewhere, producing the highest levels of water in the many creeks and rivers ever recorded.

At first the conurbations suffered widespread flash floods, but by nightfall the deluge moved closer to the coast and became a major flood, affecting seven river basins. The Guadalupe River, normally 46 m (150 ft) wide, grew to a staggering 10 km (6 mi) in width. The National Guard came to the rescue and up to 10,000 people had to leave their homes. Houses were completely washed away and 15,000 cattle were thought to have drowned, although some managed to escape when their fencing was destroyed. Deaths occurred in nine Texan counties and, when the waters began to recede, everything was slicked with a thick coat of mud.

WHEN:
October 17–18 1998
WHERE:
Texas
DEATH TOLL:
31 deaths occurred in 24 incidents. The victims ranged in age between two months and 83 years.
YOU SHOULD KNOW:
The estimated cost of damage to property was estimated at about $750 million and total compensation for families, small businesses, unemployment assistance, public assistance and temporary housing was another $188 million. President Clinton declared it to be a major disaster and offered federal aid.

Austrian rescue workers and volunteers search for survivors after the avalanche partially buried the village of Galtur.

The Galtur avalanche

The pretty village of Galtur, situated in the Austrian Tyrol, has long been a popular tourist destination. Lying in a valley and lovely all year round, it comes into its own during winter, with 40 km (25 mi) of pristine pistes. There are lifts and mountain railways and, if you are experienced, professional skiers will take you onto seriously challenging slopes. With a permanent population of roughly 870, the numbers rise to about 4,000 at the peak of the season.

In January 1999 a series of storms occurred, bringing with them 4 m (13 ft) of fine snow and forming a huge snowpack on the mountains above Galtur. Later that month a melt-crust developed – the upper layers melting during the day and refreezing at night. As new snow fell, the melt-crust became unstable until finally, on February 23, it failed and caused an enormously powerful powder avalanche to crash down the mountainside, picking up more and more snow as it went.

The avalanche took less than one minute to hit Galtur. At 50 m (164 ft) high and travelling at 290 kph (186 mph), it hit with the force of a bomb, overturning cars, ruining buildings and burying 57 people. By the time rescue crews managed to arrive, 31 people – locals and tourists – had died.

As in most of the region, Galtur is risk-zoned for avalanches; but it was the safe, Green Zone that was worst hit. The Austrian government asked for assistance and thousands of people were airlifted out, using helicopters from both Europe and the USA. Since then, the risk zones have been extended, steel fences have been erected on the surrounding slopes to create smaller areas to reduce the extent of any similar disasters, and a 300 m (984 ft) 'avalanche dam' now protects the village itself.

WHEN:
February 23 1999
WHERE:
Galtur, Tyrol, Austria
DEATH TOLL:
31
YOU SHOULD KNOW:
Two dogs played a part in the Galtur avalanche. The first was Heiko, a rescue dog, which was responsible for finding many people buried under the snow. The second, a Labrador-Alsatian cross named Jack, was found alive after being buried under snow for 24 hours. His German owners had both died in the disaster, but a soldier in the search and rescue team adopted him.

Vargas mudslides

Vargas, in northern Venezuela, lies on the Caribbean Sea. Separated from the capital, Caracas, by the Avila Mountains, it was once densely populated. The mountains form a National Park, within which 23 rivers run down to the coast. Easy to reach from the city, Vargas had many residential communities and a thriving tourist economy.

The disaster that struck in December 1999 was of a magnitude never before experienced. Rain fell continuously for 37 days and the ground was at saturation point. Torrential storms that started on December 14 disgorged 9 m (36 ft) of water. Unable to absorb anything more, the soil finally gave way, bringing water, rocks, trees and mud crashing down the mountains to the sea. The mudslides completely devastated 100 km (60 mi) of coastline, consuming absolutely everything in their path.

Villages, shanty towns and mountainside shacks were buried beneath the mud or swept out to sea, and up to 30,000 people were killed. This figure could be considerably higher as there are no existing records. Over 100,000 people lost their homes and the entire infrastructure of the state – roads, bridges, dams, houses, hotels, apartment blocks, and all the services – vanished in minutes. For weeks there was no access to relief supplies, and hundreds of thousands were evacuated from the area.

President Chavez set up Corpovargas – a development authority to oversee the renewal – and in a speech to the nation promised that about $1.4 billion would be allocated to the clean-up, rebuilding the infrastructure, and the canalization of the rivers, funded by his administration and international contributions. Few of these projects ever came to fruition, and many questions exist as to what happened to the funds. Today, Vargas is a shadow of its former self.

WHEN:
December 14–16 1999
WHERE:
Vargas State, Venezuela
DEATH TOLL:
Unknown, but possibly more than 30,000, died. Only 1,000 bodies were found, the rest were buried under mud or swept out to sea.
YOU SHOULD KNOW:
The Venezuelan government asked the US to send engineers to help. The US responded by sending three ships, engineers, and an offer to donate the road needed to link Macuto to Caracas. Venezuela then changed its mind and the ships were obliged to turn back, thus delaying the building of a new road for years.

Survivors of the mudslides that killed up to 30,000 people in the village of Carmen de Uria.

Mozambique floods

WHEN:
February to March 2000
WHERE:
Mozambique
DEATH TOLL:
Approximately 800 people died and one million were displaced.
YOU SHOULD KNOW:
The iconic image of the flooding was of a woman giving birth in a treetop. Sofia Pedro and her newborn daughter were rescued by the South African Air Force and flown to safety.

Mozambique is situated on the southeastern coast of Africa. Between 1977 and 1992 it was in the grip of a violent and disastrous civil war that left the country in ruins. In 1994 the first multi-party elections were held and life began to look up for its inhabitants. War refugees were resettled and economic reforms led to a high growth rate, averaging over 10 per cent in the late 1990s. All these positive signs came to an abrupt halt in 2000, when catastrophic flooding during February and March devastated vast swathes of the country. This was the wet season and the whole of southern Africa was affected by heavy rainfall. But Mozambique was by far the worst hit.

On February 9 the capital city, Maputo, was flooded and the road to Beira, Mozambique's second city, quickly became impassable. Two days later, the huge amount of rain had totally saturated the ground and the Limpopo River burst its banks, flooding the valley, sweeping people and houses away, separating families and making thousands homeless. Little more than one week later, Cyclone Eline hit the country and five days after that, on February 27, flash floods devastated yet another region, producing 8 m (26 ft) of water that swept everything before it.

At first the rescue operation had very limited resources: a few Mozambican ships, and fewer than a dozen helicopters from neighbouring countries. It was three weeks before international help arrived. Meanwhile, 45,000 people were rescued from trees and rooftops, and 113,000 farming families were left with nothing: 1,400 sq km (540 sq mi) of agricultural land was ruined, 20,000 cattle vanished, 630 schools were closed and 42 health centres disappeared, including the second largest hospital in the country. Roads and bridges were swept away and dirty, contaminated water gave rise to outbreaks of dysentery and cholera.

Hundreds of Mozambicans wait for rescue on top of a building in the city of Xai-Xai, 200 km (125 mi) north of the capital Maputo.

European floods

In August 2002 central and eastern Europe were devastated by floods the like of which had not been seen for over 100 years. The torrential rainfall began in the Alps, where most of the winter snow had already melted, leaving bare ice behind. This meant that the earth could absorb nothing and rainfall poured straight off the mountains as though down a chute. The worst affected countries were Italy, Germany, Austria, the Czech Republic and Russia, while Spain, Slovakia, Romania, Bulgaria, Hungary and Ukraine also suffered.

In Germany much of the work that had been completed since unification in 1990 was wiped out. Bridges and roads as well as factories and homes were partially or wholly destroyed and thousands of people were evacuated. Dresden was badly hit when the River Elbe reached record heights, but despite damage to notable buildings such as the Semper Opera House, its world-famous treasures were saved.

Some regions of the Czech Republic received four times the amount of rainfall expected in August in only 36 hours. Many historic buildings in Prague were damaged, with much of the old town under water and the Metro system partially closed when 17 stations were flooded. Buildings old and new collapsed, and several chemical factories were inundated, raising fears of contamination of the River Elbe by dioxins, mercury and other toxic substances. Some rivers completely changed course, taking local residents by surprise.

Journalists in Austria and the Czech Republic began blaming 'greedy mayors' for the disaster, saying that they had levelled forests and built holiday homes on flood plains and river banks.

Russia's Black Sea coast, at the height of its tourist season, suffered terribly as villages, holiday apartments, tents, cars and people were swept away to sea.

Semper Opera House in Dresden, southern Germany, was hit by floods.

WHEN:
August 11–17 2002
WHERE:
Central and Eastern Europe, and Russia.
DEATH TOLL:
109 people were killed directly by the floods.
YOU SHOULD KNOW:
It seems likely that the rain was exacerbated by the El Niño effect and global warming, but possibly it was simply a natural phenomenon that only occurs once every 100–200 years.

Mud, rocks, and ice fill the Karmadon Gorge after an avalanche occurred when a section of a glacier in the Koban valley broke off and swept away everything in its path.

Kolka Glacier surge

The Republic of North Ossetia, in the northern Caucasus, is home to the Kolka Glacier, famous for its surges. The glacier lies at the head of the Genaldon River basin, in close proximity to Maili, another, larger glacier. Kolka is a cirque glacier, formed in a basin on the side of the mountains. Fed throughout the year by avalanches from above, it accumulates both ice and sub-glacial meltwater. These characteristics have, historically, led to instability and sudden surges. In the past villages were built only on the slopes but, more recently, settlements have unwisely been built on the valley floor.

During the evening of September 20 2002, a terrible disaster occurred when vast amounts of ice, water and rock broke free and plunged down into the Genaldon river valley. The avalanche devastated everything in its path, finally bursting into the Karmadon Depression – at the northern end of which a narrow entryway leads into a gorge. Here the avalanche should have been halted. Instead, the gap was blocked by huge chunks of rock and ice that still allowed mud and icy water to surge through and destroy everything for the next 17 km (11 mi). The ice within the debris quickly melted, flooding settlements and forming new lakes. Some 125 people were killed and the village of Nizhnii Karmadon, along with several rest houses beside the river below (the area was popular with trekkers), were totally obliterated.

This was the most powerful surge ever recorded here. The tongue of the glacier, which lies at about 3,000 m (9,842 ft), was ripped away, leaving the cirque completely empty. The vast amount of sub-glacial water that had accumulated produced so powerful a surge that the glacier was virtually thrown from its basin – the first time such a phenomenon has been observed.

WHEN:
September 20 2002
WHERE:
North Ossetia
DEATH TOLL:
125 people were killed and many others injured.
YOU SHOULD KNOW:
Among those who lost their lives in the Kolka Glacier surge were Russian actor and director Sergei Bodrov and a film crew of 27. The glacier itself was visible again a mere two years later and currently continues to grow.

The European heatwave

In August 2003, Europe struggled under the highest temperatures ever recorded in the northern hemisphere. The Earth Policy Institute (EPI) warned: 'Heatwaves are a silent killer, mostly affecting the elderly, the very young, or the chronically ill.' The European heatwave certainly proved that statement to be correct.

The worst hit country was France, where various additional factors contributed to the disaster. The nights are normally cool in France, even during the summer, and air conditioning is rare. During this period, however, temperatures remained high at night. Also, August is the main holiday period for the French; businesses shut and almost everyone goes away, including government ministers and doctors. Of the 14,802 people who died in France, most were elderly folk living alone, whose families had gone away and were unable to offer assistance.

The French government was quick to distance itself from responsibility, but the opposition blamed Health Minister Jean-Francois Mattei for failing to return from his holiday and for blocking hospitals from taking emergency measures – such as recalling medical staff. He lost his post in a reshuffle that took place in the following spring.

In Italy and Spain about 4,200 people died. In Switzerland, Germany, The Netherlands, Portugal and the UK, record temperatures were noted. Southern Europe suffered drought conditions which had a serious effect on agriculture. The total production of wheat in the EU was short by ten per cent and the grape harvest took place several weeks earlier than usual. It is thought that 2003 was a very good year for wine in terms of quality, although production was the lowest for ten years.

The EPI stated that more and more extreme weather events are likely to occur in future and that the world must cut its carbon emissions, which contribute to global warming and climate change.

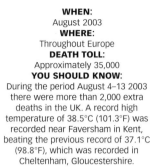

WHEN:
August 2003
WHERE:
Throughout Europe
DEATH TOLL:
Approximately 35,000
YOU SHOULD KNOW:
During the period August 4–13 2003 there were more than 2,000 extra deaths in the UK. A record high temperature of 38.5°C (101.3°F) was recorded near Faversham in Kent, beating the previous record of 37.1°C (98.8°F), which was recorded in Cheltenham, Gloucestershire.

Burnt out trees smoulder after a forest fire near Sant Llorenc Savall, in northeastern Spain.

Bam earthquake

WHEN:
December 26 2003
WHERE:
Bam, Kerman Province, Iran
DEATH TOLL:
The official casualty figure is 26,271.
YOU SHOULD KNOW:
In March 2007 Mother Nature delivered a reminder of her powers to survivors of the 2003 quake – a sandstorm whipped up by 130 kph (80 mph) winds that enveloped Bam, suffocating three children, causing fatal car accidents and injuring a dozen or more residents of the re-emerging city.

For countless centuries the world's largest adobe building was the Bam Citadel in the southeast of modern-day Iran, begun before 500 BC and still in use as late as 1850. This splendid complex on the famed 'silk road' connecting China to the Mediterranean was at the heart of a UNESCO World Heritage Site, and the modern town of Bam grew up around the citadel's impressive 7 m (23 ft) walls. Sadly, the word 'was' must be used because this magnificent ancient structure was virtually destroyed in 2003.

The Bam earthquake struck in the early hours of December 26. It measured 6.5 on the Richter scale but destruction was much greater than an occurrence of that magnitude might suggest because many buildings, including the citadel, were built of mud bricks. This construction technique had traditionally been used in surrounding villages and was continued as the city expanded. Iran introduced new building regulations designed to minimize earthquake damage in 1989, but by then it was too late for most of Bam's buildings – especially housing.

Because the city's population was asleep when the earthquake struck, more people were killed than would have been the case had everyone been out and about. Over 26,000 died on that terrible night, while about another 30,000 were injured in and around Bam – a fearful regional toll as the population of Bam itself was just 43,000.

A massive relief effort was mounted with the support of many countries and a meticulous reconstruction of the Bam Citadel was initiated by the Iranian government with help from the USA, France, Italy and Japan. A concurrent plan was devised to rebuild the devastated city. This did not meet with the general approval of survivors, but nonetheless proceeded along lines determined by central government.

The devastated Bam Citadel after the quake

Hurricane Ivan

If hurricanes had a motto, Ivan's would have been 'boom-bang-a-bang'. For Hurricane Ivan was in the top ten most intense Atlantic hurricanes, reaching the maximum Category Five on the Saffir-Simpson hurricane scale, growing to the size of Texas over the Gulf of Mexico, huffing and puffing at up to 275 kph (170 mph) and giving rise to around 120 individual tornadoes after arriving in the eastern USA.

The fourth major hurricane of the 2004 season was seriously scary. Ivan was born as a tropical depression near the Cape Verde Islands off the African coast. He raced across the Atlantic, became Tropical Storm Ivan along the way before maturing into Hurricane Ivan at ominously low latitude never before recorded for a full-blown hurricane. This was a harbinger of destructive intentions.

Ivan devastated Caribbean islands including Grenada (the hardest hit, with catastrophic damage that virtually wiped out the entire economy), Grand Cayman, Jamaica, Cuba, Barbados, St Lucia, Trinidad and Tobago. Venezuela and the Dominican Republic were also severely battered. Ivan's strength peaked over the Gulf of Mexico, where seven oil platforms were swept away. He reduced to a Category Three storm before reaching the USA at Gulf Shores, Alabama, along with a 4.3 m (14 ft) storm surge. Even in his weakened state, Ivan was still powerful enough to inflict widespread damage costing billions of dollars.

Prime targets were Florida, Alabama, Georgia and North Carolina. But heavy rain and high winds were experienced right up the eastern seaboard to Canada, while destructive tornadoes were recorded as far north as Maryland. High winds and extensive flooding did most of the damage to buildings and infrastructure, while thousands of boats were sunk or cast ashore. Awesome Ivan killed nearly 100 people, and claimed over 30 indirect victims.

WHEN:
September 2–24 2004
WHERE:
Atlantic Ocean, Caribbean Sea and USA
DEATH TOLL:
92 died, mainly in Grenada (39), the USA (25) and Jamaica (17).
YOU SHOULD KNOW:
North America's soybean (soya bean) crop had a narrow escape. Hurricane Ivan carried spores of soybean rust into the United States from South America. This virulent disease had never before broken out in the USA, despite regularly ruining soybean crops in South America. Luckily, most of the harvest had been gathered in so the soybean rust was contained with minimal economic damage to this important crop.

A massive wave, whipped up by Hurricane Ivan.

The third and largest wave of the tsunami invades the promenade on Ao Nang Beach.

Indian Ocean tsunami

When is an earthquake not an earthquake? Answer: when it's a tsunami. Of course that's just wordplay, because the Sumatra-Andaman earthquake is virtually unknown while the whole world has heard of the Indian Ocean tsunami of 2004. The latter was, of course, a consequence of the former – an undersea megathrust quake that occurred off the west coast of Sumatra. A moment magnitude of 9.3 made this the second most powerful earthquake ever recorded, and the consequences were catastrophic.

The resultant tsunami destroyed the nearby Indonesian town of Lhoknga before roaring off to inundate coastlines all round the Indian Ocean. In deep water the fast-moving tsunami barely rose above normal sea level, but as it approached land – and shallow water – it slowed and formed waves as tall as 30 m (100 ft). These developed unstoppable momentum capable of reaching inland for 2 km (1.24 mi) in places.

Although the tsunami hit Indonesia immediately, it took seven hours to arrive at the furthest point where it had significant impact: Somalia. Even so, there was no warning system and over 200,000 people, including thousands of tourists, were killed before this fearsome natural phenomenon was spent. Around a third of the casualties were children, who found it harder to survive the rushing waters than adults, while more women than men perished. This was because the menfolk of numerous fishing villages were at sea and rode out the wave while the women waited on shore for their return.

Deaths were recorded in 14 countries, and those who suffered the greatest number of fatalities were Indonesia, Sri Lanka, India and Thailand. A massive international response ensured that ample aid was offered, but as always delivery was patchy and it was predicted that many shattered communities would take a decade or more to rebuild.

WHEN:
December 26 2004
WHERE:
Indian Ocean
DEATH TOLL:
A precise figure was impossible to compute, but reliable estimates suggest around 230,000 people died, including 9,000 foreign tourists who had decided to travel to the welcoming Indian Ocean for a relaxing Christmas holiday.
YOU SHOULD KNOW:
The power of the Indian Ocean tsunami was calculated as being equivalent to five megatons of TNT – or to put it another way, more than twice the destructive force of all the munitions used in the whole of World War II, including the two atom bombs dropped on Japan.

Mumbai monsoon

Weather forecasters don't always get it right – or even agree with each other. So it was ahead of India's 2005 monsoon season, when battle was joined by the Centre for Mathematical Modelling and Computer Simulation in Bangalore ('monsoon rains in July will be 12 per cent below average') and the official India Meteorological Department in Delhi ('average rainfall expected'). Accusations flew back and forth, but in the event both sets of experts got it very badly wrong.

The monsoon season lasts from June to September and is vital to the Indian economy. A 'good' season with ample rain boosts agriculture while a 'bad' season has a negative impact that ripples out into the wider economy. But the monsoon is both a blessing and a curse, as it sometimes causes serious problems. Mumbai, on the northwestern coast, is a city with perhaps 17 million inhabitants. It originally consisted of seven developed islands, but has spread inland to become one of the world's largest urban conurbations. In late July 2005, Mumbai suffered an unprecedented deluge when a record-setting 94.4 cm (37.2 in) of rain fell in a single day.

The bustling Andheri, Borivili, Chembur, Kurla, Sion, Wandala and Worli areas were inundated, sometimes with shoulder-deep water, and there was general flooding all over. Electricity and telecommunications were knocked out, transport systems were paralyzed as roads and railways were flooded, and the airport was shut down. Intense rain also triggered devastating landslides that destroyed shanty towns. Tens of thousands were stranded in offices and people were killed by mudslides, falling walls, drowning in trapped vehicles or by electrocution; 15 children died in a stampede after hearing a false rumour that a dam had burst. The rains continued, albeit with lesser intensity, and the clean-up after Mumbai's disastrous day took many months.

WHEN:
July 26 2005
WHERE:
Mumbai (formerly Bombay),
Maharashtra State, India
DEATH TOLL:
Estimated at 1,000
YOU SHOULD KNOW:
In 2009 the combination of peaking monsoon rains and the year's highest tides caused another serious flood in Mumbai, though the consequences were nothing like as catastrophic as the terrible 2005 event.

People use a rope to cross a street after heavy rains in Mumbai.

Hurricane Katrina

WHEN:
August 23–30 2005
WHERE:
Southeastern USA
DEATH TOLL:
1,836 confirmed fatalities, with
another 705 missing
YOU SHOULD KNOW:
The official reaction to the Katrina
disaster was totally inadequate, with
confusion evident between local,
state and federal governments as to
who should do what across the
devastated areas. Relief efforts were
hampered by chronic
mismanagement and indecisive
leadership at all levels – a botched
response that was quickly labelled
'Katrinagate'.

The 2005 Atlantic hurricane season was a bad time to be living along the Gulf Coast in Florida, Mississippi, Louisiana or Texas – for that was the year when Hurricane Katrina came calling. She would inflict more damage than any hurricane before, cost the USA some $80 billion to put right, was the sixth-strongest ever recorded and the fifth-deadliest life-taker.

At her peak, Katrina's wind speed reached a frightening 280 kph (175 mph). The storm formed near the Bahamas on August 23 and crossed southern Florida as a relatively innocuous Category One hurricane, though causing flooding and a few deaths after a state of emergency was declared. Once over the Gulf of Mexico, the beast gathered strength and returned to make landfall in southeast Louisiana as a Category Three monster on August 29, creating a violent storm surge. After crossing the Breton Sound, Katrina made a third landfall in Mississippi before moving inland and finally being demoted to a tropical storm over Tennessee the following day. It was over, but not before a terrible price had been paid in devastation and lives lost.

Damage was widespread. The most severe devastation took place in New Orleans. This was a result of the failure of the levee (floodbank) system that protected the low-lying city. Levees were overwhelmed by rising water and many collapsed some hours after the hurricane had passed. Around 80 per cent of the city was flooded in consequence, but the catastrophe could have been much worse. Thanks to accurate advance warnings as to the storm's destructive potential, sensible precautions were taken in Katrina's projected path. These included a mandatory life-saving evacuation of New Orleans. Even so, many residents were unable to leave the city, and a large number perished in the subsequent terrible floods.

A plea for help is seen on the roof of a home flooded in the aftermath of Hurricane Katrina in New Orleans.

Cyclone Nargis

The worst natural disaster in the long history of Myanmar was caused by the ominously named Very Severe Tropical Cyclonic Storm Nargis – conveniently abbreviated to Cyclone Nargis – that struck in 2008. After forming over the Bay of Bengal in late April, Nargis was initially forecast to hit southeastern India or Bangladesh. Instead it wandered past causing relatively minor damage in Sri Lanka (4,500 people left homeless by floods), before gaining strength and approaching Burma with a well-defined 'eye' surrounded by winds gusting to 215 kph (135 mph).

When Nargis made landfall, the storm was at peak force. It struck the Ayeyarwady Division of Burma – formerly the Irrawaddy Division and consisting of that river's extensive low-lying delta. This is one of Myanmar's most populous areas where much of the country's vital rice crop is grown. Nargis then moved east across Burma as it quickly weakened, but the devastation left behind by this super-destructive cyclone was fearsome, with catastrophic impact on the lives of 1.5 million people.

The disaster was compounded by the initial reaction of the isolationist Burmese government, which failed to mount a significant relief effort and – worse still – categorically refused to admit outside aid agencies or take any support from countries that offered help. With many tens of thousands of people killed by the storm and the intense flooding that followed, this brutal rejection of its stricken citizens' needs undoubtedly caused a significant increase in the number of fatalities. When aid was eventually accepted, the junta still obstructed the process and refused to admit journalists and TV crews who could have confirmed the massive scale of death and destruction caused by Nargis. As it is, the number of dead will never be known, because the authorities feared negative publicity and deliberately failed to make an accurate count.

Myanmar residents walk past houses destroyed by Cyclone Nargis in Bogalay.

WHEN:
May 2 2008
WHERE:
Myanmar (known as Burma until the ruling military junta changed the name in 1989)
DEATH TOLL:
Unknown. Estimates range from 150,000 dead all the way up to the one million plus that would make Nargis the world's deadliest cyclone.
YOU SHOULD KNOW:
Nargis was the first named storm of the 2008 North Indian Ocean cyclone season and the chosen name belied this awesome storm's destructive nature. *Nargis* is the Urdu word for daffodil.

Sichuan Earthquake

One spring afternoon in May 2008 a terrible tragedy overtook the people of Sichuan Province in Central China, as one of the deadliest earthquakes of all time rocked an area that was home to 15,000,000 people. It had a moment magnitude of 7.9 and the epicentre was in Wenchuan County, 80 km (50 mi) from the provincial capital of Chengdu. The power of the Sichuan earthquake may be judged by the fact that buildings in Shanghai, 1,700 km (1,055 mi) away, rocked so alarmingly that many were evacuated.

Around the epicentre up to 80 per cent of all buildings collapsed in towns and villages, with many of the latter razed to the ground. No buildings fell in the province's five main cities, however, where much recent construction had been undertaken to quakeproof standards introduced after the Tangshan earthquake of 1976; but there was still damage.

Crops were also ruined and huge numbers of domestic livestock

Ruins of housing in Beichuan, with bodies in plastic bags lining the street after the great Sichuan earthquake.

were killed. Countless roads were destroyed and telecommunications were knocked out, hampering rescue efforts.

A huge relief campaign involving 50,000 soldiers did immediately get underway, but rugged terrain and total devastation in many areas hampered their efforts. The human toll was horrendous: around 90,000 killed – including 19,000 children.

Strong aftershocks – some exceeding a magnitude of 6.0 on the Richter scale – rocked Sichuan over a period of several months after the main event. These caused more damage and claimed additional lives, albeit on a much smaller scale. Sichuan was ranked number 21 on the list of life-taking earthquakes. The top spot is occupied by another Chinese quake – the Shaanxi event of 1556, thought to have caused at least 830,000 deaths.

WHEN:
May 12 2008
WHERE:
Sichuan Province, China
DEATH TOLL:
The official figures are precise, but probably not accurate: 68,712 dead and another 17,921 missing.
YOU SHOULD KNOW:
Although many tens of thousands of people were killed by the quake, huge media interested was generated by the fate of giant pandas at Wolong National Nature Reserve. Five keepers were killed but happily only two pandas died, although two more were injured.

Mont Blanc avalanche

The highest mountain in the Alps would be called White Mountain in English, but the French Mont Blanc or Italian Monte Bianco sound much better. This lofty 4,810-m (15,781-ft) peak has long presented an irresistible challenge to mountaineers, while skiing and snowboarding are hugely popular on the lower slopes. Climbing Mont Blanc is a dangerous business and every season sees this mighty massif claim lives from among the 20,000 who attempt the summit climb each year.

The occasional avalanche is typical of dangers faced on the slopes of Mont Blanc, and despite sophisticated rescue services these deadly snow slides can still surprise the most experienced climbers and claim victims when weather conditions are perfect. One such event occurred early one Sunday morning in August 2008. Climbers set off from the Refuge des Cosmiques in the early hours to scale the Mont-Blanc du Tacul. As they advanced up the mountain a serac broke loose above and, as it fell, this large ice block swiftly generated a lethal avalanche. Eight lead climbers were overwhelmed in the darkness, standing no chance of survival as a wall of snow and ice silently swept them 1,500 m (4,900 ft) down the mountainside, burying their bodies deep. Those following at a lower altitude survived after the avalanche split into two and lost momentum, though several were injured, some seriously.

This was the worst single accident the Mont Blanc range had seen in a decade, but a disaster described by a professional mountain guide who participated in the dramatic pre-dawn rescue as 'a scene from the apocalypse' could have been much worse. Only 45 climbers set out on the fatal route that morning, when a more usual number on a high-season Sunday would have been 100 or more.

WHEN:
September 21 2008
WHERE:
French Alps
DEATH TOLL:
Eight (five Austrians and three Swiss)
YOU SHOULD KNOW:
Avalanches regularly continue to take life on Mont Blanc. Two local men, both experienced climbers, were swept off a cliff to their deaths beneath the Tour des Courtes in June 2009.

Kenya drought

Is it global warming starting to impact negatively on millions of people in Africa, or is a normal weather cycle merely turning to bring prolonged drought? It's a question being asked with some urgency in Kenya. This East African republic was once the first choice of wealthy white settlers attracted by rich agricultural land and the pleasant climate of the interior highlands. After independence from Britain in 1963, Kenya's economy did fairly well but it was dependent on agriculture and the sector eventually went into steady decline.

Large areas in the north and east of Kenya are hot and dry. Inhabitants rely on wells to sustain a pastoral way of life, husbanding livestock or trying to scratch a subsistence living from poor soil. These remote, semi-arid lands make up 80 per cent of the country and when the rains were patchy in 2008, those occupying this inhospitable terrain were hard hit – not least because, for many, that year saw the third poor harvest in succession.

In 2009 the long rains failed again in many parts of Kenya, with disastrous consequences for the whole country. Large numbers of cattle died of thirst, crops never germinated and the price of Kenya's staple food – maize – rocketed, putting terrible strain on the urban poor who simply couldn't afford to eat. Nearly half the population already lived in poverty and before long as many as ten million Kenyans were in need of food aid. Despite the determined efforts of international agencies to help, malnutrition was rife along with associated diseases like cholera, malaria, Rift Valley fever and Kala Azar that stealthily invaded the nation. Children were, as always, particularly vulnerable. If climate change does indeed inhibit the regular rains that East Africans rely on for survival, Kenya's future looks bleak indeed.

Two Kenyan women make their way through a dust storm.

WHEN:
2008–2009
WHERE:
Kenya
DEATH TOLL:
Unknown, but acute malnutrition and disease has killed tens of thousands since the long drought began.
YOU SHOULD KNOW:
A hazard faced by rural populations already in dire straits is violence. In 2009 over 400 deaths were reported as cattle rustling and banditry became rife.

Black Saturday bushfires

Extreme weather conditions made it possible, but the evil hand of man made a fatal contribution to the series of bushfires that broke out in Victoria on February 7 2009, before raging for five weeks. Over 400 individual blazes were reported on that traumatic first day, which was quickly christened Black Saturday by the media.

The situation couldn't have been more conducive to conflagration. Prolonged drought conditions (linked by some to global warming) and a heatwave with temperatures reaching over 45°C (113°F) combined with wind speeds in excess of 100 kph (60 mph) to create optimum bushfire conditions. These duly broke out thanks to assorted causes including lightning strikes, electrical short-circuits, accidental ignition through human carelessness like discarded cigarette butts . . . and arson by persons unknown, described by Prime Minister Kevin Rudd as 'mass murderers'.

Although fires were reported in dozens of locations, an area to the northeast of state capital Melbourne was hardest hit, with firestorms accounting for the majority of casualties suffered on Black Saturday and during its aftermath. The largest and most destructive was the Kingslake-Maryville fire complex, but other major outbreaks included Beechworth, Bendigo, Bunyip State Park, Coleraine, Dandenong Ranges, Horsham, Maroondah/Yarra, Redesdale, Weerite, West Gippsland and Wilsons Promontory.

Cooler conditions and rain at the beginning of March assisted firefighters but by the time it was all over in the middle of the month 450,000 hectares (1.1 million acres) of forest, national parkland, agricultural land, rural communities and urban fringe areas had been laid waste. Over 170 victims had been killed, including one firefighter, and over 400 were seriously injured. More than 2,000 houses had been burned to the ground, along with 1,500 non-residential buildings, while thousands more had suffered damage. A total of 78 townships had been affected and 7,500 people were made homeless.

WHEN:
February 7 to March 14 2009
WHERE:
Victoria, Australia
DEATH TOLL:
173 people were killed by the bushfires.
YOU SHOULD KNOW:
On Black Saturday 3,500 firefighters were deployed in anticipation of trouble as the temperature soared to an all-time record 46.4°C (115.5°F) in Melbourne. At midday high winds felled power lines at Kilmore East, starting a bush fire that would rapidly generate a large pyrocumulus cloud and the most intense firestorm experienced in Australia's post-settler history. It was the beginning of the country's deadliest-ever bushfire event.

A wall of flames incinerates a clump of trees at the Bunyip Ridge bushfire, near Tonimbuk.

L'Aquila earthquake

WHEN:
April 6 2009
WHERE:
Abruzzo region, Italy
DEATH TOLL:
The quake killed 308 people.
YOU SHOULD KNOW:
Following the earthquake some spectacularly ill-judged remarks were made by Italian Prime Minister Silvio Berlusconi, reinforcing his reputation as the grand master of crass comments. A typical example was the billionaire politician's suggestion that displaced victims in their tented camps should look on the experience as a camping holiday where everything they needed was provided for free, adding that they might as well head for the beach and take a weekend break at the state's expense.

The lovely medieval city of L'Aquila and surrounding villages suffered horrendous damage in April 2009, after an earthquake measuring 5.8 on the Richter scale rocked the Abruzzo region in central Italy. The main event did not come as a complete surprise, as there had been significant foreshocks in the preceding months. Also, a month beforehand an expert predicted on television that a quake in the area was imminent, only for the authorities to rubbish his prediction and set the police on him for causing unnecessary fear among the local populace.

The quake was unusually severe by Italian standards. The country often suffers earthquakes, but only rarely do they result in extensive loss of life. But the L'Aquila event was the exception that proved the rule. Around 10,000 buildings were damaged, at least 3,000 of them seriously, and a number collapsed. A powerful aftershock occurred within an hour to exacerbate the situation and further aftershocks followed.

Much priceless heritage was destroyed, including a number of medieval churches that suffered severe damage. The top floor of a 16th-century castle housing the Abruzzo National Museum collapsed and the regional archive suffered when the cupola of St Augustine's Church fell. Nearby villages were badly hit; Onna was levelled and communities like San Pio delle Camere, Villa Sant'Angelo, San Gregorio and Poggio Picenze lost many houses. But the city's modern buildings suffered most, including a new wing of L'Aquila Hospital that was supposed to be quakeproof. As a result of corruption and inefficiency many structures had simply not been built to rigorous modern building standards.

In a few short moments, over 300 people died, 1,500 were injured and 65,000 people became homeless. Tented camps were set up for the displaced and a state funeral was held for more than 200 victims.

An aerial view of Santa Maria Paganica church in L'Aquila

Manila floods

Flooding is a regular problem in the Philippines, but the disaster that occurred in September 2009, when Typhoon Ketsana lashed the islands, was exceptional. Intense downpours created devastating flooding. The storm was known locally as Typhoon Onday and its impact was greatest on the island of Luzon – home of the capital city, Manila – and the nearby province of Rizal. Average rainfall for September is 39 cm (15.4 in), but a staggering 34 cm (13.4 in) of rain fell on Metro Manila's interlinked communities in just six hours – the heaviest precipitation for decades. The consequences were disastrous.

Filipinos wade through a flooded area in Cainta, east of Manila.

A large part of Manila was inundated, with raging floodwaters rising to chest height in places. The storm struck on a Sunday, when most people were at home, and tens of thousands of families had to take refuge on the roofs of their homes to await rescue by army helicopters. Roads were impassable, though many saw unusual traffic passing through – processions of cars floating atop muddy water. There were widespread power failures and sewerage systems were overwhelmed, along with the fresh water supply. Nino Aquino International Airport was shut down.

Rivers burst their banks in Rizal province, flooding numerous communities to a depth of 6 m (20 ft). The rains caused frequent landslips and building collapses, often resulting in fatalities. President Gloria Arroyo declared a 'state of calamity' and the Philippines government mounted a massive rescue operation. Boats toured Manila and rescued several thousand people. Aid centres were set up to cater for the vast number of people – up to 300,000 – displaced by the floods, offering temporary accommodation, food, clean water and adequate sanitation. Luzon's infrastructure sustained long-term damage, huge areas of standing crops were destroyed and hundreds died.

WHEN:
September 26 2009
WHERE:
Manila, Philippines
DEATH TOLL:
The official casualty figure for the Philippines was 464 deaths.
YOU SHOULD KNOW:
After hitting the Philippines, Typhoon Ketsana gathered strength and went on to make a second landfall, this time close to the port city of Da Nang in Vietnam. Despite an official evacuation of 170,000 people ahead of Ketsana's arrival, around 180 people died and hundreds were injured, while the storm itself and subsequent flooding did much damage, including shutting down much of the country's electricity grid.

Locals look on as heavy machines clear the rubble of a flattened market.

Padang earthquake

The infamous 'Pacific Ring of Fire' is the horseshoe-shaped area enclosing the Pacific Ocean renowned for seismic activity, where regular volcanic eruptions and earthquakes occur. One of its most recent – and deadly – quakes took place at the end of September 2009.

Although the epicentre was off the southern coast of Sumatra, this violent earthquake took its name from the nearby coastal city of Padang, capital of the Indonesian province of West Sumatra.

With an impressive moment magnitude of 7.6, this was a hugely destructive natural disaster in terms of physical damage and economic disruption. The epicentre was just 45 km (28 mi) from Padang, which suffered the most devastating consequences along with the neighbouring town of Pariaman. However, Pekanbaru on the other side of the island was also hard hit, along with many rural communities. More than 1,000 people were killed and another 3,000 were injured, 1,200 of them severely. Around 280,000 houses were damaged, half of them badly, along with public buildings like hospital and schools. Fires broke out in Padang and broken water mains caused temporary flooding.

Problems were exacerbated the following day, when a second earthquake rocked the province of Jambi in central Sumatra. It had a moment magnitude of 6.6 and was a separate event rather than an aftershock related to the first.

The world rallied round, with dozens of countries offering aid. The Indonesian military swung into action, initial efforts to recover trapped survivors quickly switching to the clearance of rubble and recovery of bodies. Helicopters were used to ferry relief supplies into remote areas cut off by the quake and carry injured victims to hospital on return trips. Rescue operations were helped by painful experience gained when the Indian Ocean tsunami claimed 130,000 lives in Aceh on the northern tip of Sumatra in 2004.

WHEN:
September 30 2009
WHERE:
West Sumatra, Indonesia
DEATH TOLL:
The Indonesian government announced an official figure of 1,115 confirmed dead, although the true figure is almost certainly higher.
YOU SHOULD KNOW:
The Padang earthquake was so powerful that the ground shook as far away as Singapore, with sufficient force to ensure that some high-rise buildings were evacuated as a precautionary measure.

Haiti earthquake

The island of Hispaniola is divided between Haiti and the Dominican Republic. With 10 million impoverished citizens, Haiti at the western end is one of the world's poorest countries – bearing the added burden of being in Mother Nature's bad books and regularly suffering hurricane damage. In 2008 four hurricanes ravaged the country inside 30 days, killing 800. But that paled into insignificance just before sundown on January 12 2010, when an earthquake measuring 7.0 on the Richter scale rocked the Port au Prince area, home to three million people.

The quake was followed by powerful aftershocks. Thousands of buildings were destroyed or seriously damaged, including the presidential palace, parliament building, UN peacekeeping headquarters and the city's cathedral. Houses were flattened or rendered uninhabitable. Shanty towns in the city's hills were razed and much infrastructure went, including services like electricity and running water. Many tens of thousands died instantly or succumbed to their injury or interment beneath rubble. Hundreds of thousands were made homeless.

As news of the disaster broke, governments worldwide swiftly pledged assistance. Unfortunately, in the quake's chaotic aftermath, good intentions proved completely inadequate. The harbour was blocked and Port au Prince airport couldn't handle the volume of incoming aid. Teams specializing in recovering trapped victims quickly arrived, but couldn't get in to start work until everyone beneath the rubble should have been dead. Even so, heart-warming rescues were made. Despite a terrible first week when the traumatized populace tried to comes to terms with their ordeal and stay alive in the absence of basic necessities like food and water, the willing but badly organized relief effort did slowly gather pace to alleviate suffering in the shattered city and its environs, with up to 1.5 million people eventually relocated to camps before the rainy season.

WHEN:
January 12 2010
WHERE:
Haiti
DEATH TOLL:
In the chaotic aftermath of this terrible quake countless bodies lay in the streets of Port au Prince and surrounding communities. Mass burials began at once, followed by many more as corpses were recovered from shattered buildings over time. But the absence of effective administration meant no definitive records were kept and therefore casualty figures were best estimates. These range from 150,000 to 250,000 dead.
YOU SHOULD KNOW:
Informed commentators suggested that Haiti – already an undeveloped nation by 21st-century standards – would be set back 50 years by the great earthquake of 2010. However, much short- and long-term aid flowed in.

Rescue teams work together to save victims from the collapsed cathedral in the centre of Port au Prince six days after the earthquake.

SPORTS
DISASTERS

Ibrox Stadium disaster

WHEN:
April 5 1902
WHERE:
Ibrox Stadium, Glasgow, Scotland, UK
DEATH TOLL:
25 dead 500 plus injured
YOU SHOULD KNOW:
In just over 100 years of its history Ibrox has witnessed almost 100 deaths. The words 'Ibrox' and 'disaster' have all too often been synonymous, most recently in 1971 when 66 died after a stairwell gave way.

Even though the football fixture between Scotland and the Auld Enemy England at Ibrox Park in 1902 was the 31st meeting between the two teams, stadium-based mass spectator sport was still in its infancy. Crowd control was little more than volunteer stewards holding up signs to indicate that parts of the ground were full, while the police were on hand to crack a few heads if things got rowdy, as they quite often did.

Fate played a hand in proceedings as the venue for the fixture, an unofficial world championship, was decided by the toss of a coin. Celtic lost out, so it was the home of Glasgow Rangers that would host this prestigious event. By the time of the 15.45 kick-off a partisan crowd of around 70,000 had assembled in the ground. Singing, clapping and stamping their feet, they roared as the players took to the field.

The match had barely kicked off when disaster struck the West End Stand. The wooden structure gave way under the stress of the heaving masses, creating a giant hole through which people began to fall. Panic ensued as thousands who were near the hole began to flee the terrifying pit. They rushed towards ground level, crushing those on the lower tiers whose attention was fixed firmly on the game. It soon became a scene of carnage as people lay injured and dying with little chance of medical assistance.

It is perhaps indicative of the times that the match was halted for a mere 15 minutes to allow the wounded and the dead to be stretchered away before play resumed. That people should attend a sporting fixture and not come home alive was, however, something that shook the whole of Britain, and benefit matches across Glasgow's sectarian divide were set up to support the bereaved families.

Injured spectators being carried away on makeshift stretchers after a section of wooden terracing collapsed.

The IV Olympiad:
Dorando Pietri's marathon run

An official assisting the Italian runner Dorando Pietri across the finishing line at the 1908 Olympic Games.

To become the defining symbol of an Olympiad, an athlete will normally have won one or more gold medals. That was the case with Mark Spitz, Jesse Owens and Nadia Comaneci, to name but a few. However, in the 1908 Olympic Games, an athlete who didn't even make the podium captured the hearts of a nation and became the face of the games.

The Games, held in London, were billed as a contest between New World and old – the brash parvenu Americans versus the stiff-upper-lipped British. In the event, a tragicomic character from Italy was to upstage them all.

Even Dorando Pietri's entrance into the sport of athletics is the stuff of legend. In September 1904 Pietri had been standing in the doorway of the delicatessen where he worked when the champion road runner sped past, during a 10 km (6 mi) race. The desire to race overcame him and, hitching up his apron, he matched strides with the champion all the way to the finishing line without breaking sweat. A star was born.

By the time of the 1908 Olympics, Dorando had already run a marathon in an astonishingly quick time of two hours 38 minutes. It was therefore no surprise that, coming into the stadium, he had gained himself a lead of over three minutes. From here on in, things began to go badly wrong for the Italian. Just feet from the line his legs turned to jelly and he collapsed. First aid was administered and when he came round the doctor and a steward helped him to his feet.

Unable to teeter more than a few steps, he dropped and was picked up again, before being helped across the line. The crowd of 100,000 roared their approval. But the Americans, whose athlete Johnny Haynes finished second, objected. Poor Pietri was subsequently disqualified.

WHEN:
July 24 1908
WHERE:
Between Windsor Castle and White City Stadium, London, UK
TOLL:
None
YOU SHOULD KNOW:
The 1908 Marathon was extended by 350 m (1,155 ft) so that it could start at Windsor Castle. It is quite possible that, had it been run over the previous traditional distance of 42 km (26 mi) Dorando would have made it across the line unaided. He did, however, become the darling of the games and a special medal was struck in his honour.

Happy Valley Racecourse

WHEN:
February 26 1918
WHERE:
Happy Valley Racecourse, Hong Kong
DEATH TOLL:
Around 600 people died. Injuries were relatively few because it was easy to jump clear unless you were directly in the path of the stands.
YOU SHOULD KNOW:
Though it remains one of Hong Kong's worst disasters, the Happy Valley fire did not attract the scandal it might have. Hong Kong habitually looked to its future – and disaster was bad for business. Today Happy Valley is still run by the Jockey Club elite.
The Hong Kong Jockey Club currently has around 20,000 members, for whom it provides 'dining, social and recreational facilities'.

In Queen Victoria's time, wherever Britons went a-colonizing they took with them the sporting institutions they were used to. In Hong Kong, thanks to a small patch of flat, marshy land on a ledge on the island, this included horse racing. Happy Valley Racecourse was laid out in 1845, and celebrated its first race at the end of 1846. Today, Happy Valley is a green oasis completely overshadowed by a skyline higher than Manhattan's. Then, the surrounding hills overlooking the busy bay were still gardens and cultivated fields. The oval circuit of the racecourse had tight corners. It was intended to resemble a Roman amphitheatre, with high stands close to the track.

Hong Kong's rapid growth saw British interests entrenched. At Happy Valley, that meant the Jockey Club became the sole arbiter of racing and racing etiquette. The racecourse became a fashionable place where ex-pats could practise being elegant, and the Chinese could satisfy their passion for betting. More and more stands were built to accommodate increasingly subtle social strata. Made chiefly of stout bamboo scaffolding and wood, their many tiers were steeply banked to give everyone the best view. The stands sheltered a small village of food stalls, bars and bookies, thronged with the *melée* from a great port attracted by the sizzling woks and appetizing smells.

One day, in the crush, a charcoal grill went flying and hot coals fired the lashed bamboo stand supports. The flames licked through the seating above, setting fire to people's clothes in an instant. Panic was as contagious as the fire and with the blazing stands now showering debris on those underneath, mere pandemonium became screaming agony. Most of the victims barely knew they were in danger before they were engulfed. No members of the Jockey Club were killed.

Burnden Park disaster

WHEN:
March 9 1946
WHERE:
Bolton, Lancashire, UK
DEATH TOLL:
33 spectators died of compressive asphyxia, with over 400 injured.
YOU SHOULD KNOW:
Incredibly by modern safety standards, the game began and continued for 12 minutes before the seriousness of the situation was realized and the two teams left the pitch. The danger area was swiftly cleared and after just 13 minutes play resumed. The match ended in a 0-0 draw that sent Wanderers to the FA Cup semi-final, where the club lost to Charlton Athletic.

The years immediately following World War II saw vast crowds flocking to football games in Britain, as entertainment-starved working men (yes, soccer was a male preserve back then) in flat caps flocked to see their sporting heroes in action. Professional clubs were deeply rooted in their communities in the era before blanket television coverage and stratospheric wage bills, enabling small-town clubs to compete on equal terms with big-city boys. Many professionals still played for their local team – often travelling home on the bus with fans after a home game.

As a founder member of England's Football League in 1888, Bolton Wanderers had an honourable history that included victory in the first-ever Football Association Challenge Cup Final at Wembley –

the famous 'White Horse Final' of 1923. 'The Trotters' played at Burnden Park, a stadium completed in 1895 adjacent to a railway embankment on Manchester Road, close to Bolton town centre.

The record attendance was 69,912, but a much greater number – estimates go as high as 85,000 – entered the ground in March 1946 for the second leg of an FA Cup Sixth Round tie against Stoke City. The official figure was 65,419, but turnstiles closed 20 minutes before kick-off with 15,000 fans locked out and more arriving. Frustrated would-be spectators simply climbed over turnstiles and walls, entered via the railway embankment or rushed a gate opened from the inside by a father who wanted to escape the crush with his small son.

When the teams emerged just before three o'clock the packed crowd in one corner of the ground surged forward. Two barriers collapsed and the sheer weight of numbers caused a deadly crush that killed and injured a large number of helpless victims.

The tragic scene at Burnden Park, where 33 fans were crushed to death.

Superga tragedy

They were sporting legends in their own lifetimes – which would be tragically cut short in 1949. Italy's Torino football club – popularly known as *Il Grande Torino* (The Great Turin) – had won the last wartime *Serie A* league championship in 1944, returning after hostilities ceased to win the next three titles (1946–1948).

In May 1949 Torino was just four games from clinching another *Serie A* triumph when this super-successful team flew to Lisbon to play a friendly match against Portuguese giants Benfica. It was a testimonial for the great Xico Ferreira, a Benfica legend, and Torino duly adhered to tradition by losing a high-scoring match.

On the return journey, Torino's three-engined Fiat G.212 – a nearly new aircraft chartered from Italian Airlines – encountered a thunderstorm and zero visibility approaching Turin, causing the pilot to descend in order to make a visual approach to the airport. Unfortunately, the combination of inadequate radio beacons, low cloud and a navigational error had a disastrous outcome. The plane crashed into Superga Hill, hitting the rear wall of the fabulous 18th century Basilica of Superga, resting place of kings and princes from the powerful House of Savoy. Everyone on board was killed instantly.

Italy was profoundly shocked by the tragedy. Torino lost all but one of its first-team players but carried on to win that fourth title, fielding its youth team. As a mark of respect, the remaining four opponents also fielded their youngsters, all of them losing to Torino. But that was the end of *Il Grande Torino*'s glory years. The club didn't win another *Serie A* title for nearly 30 years and the Italian national team was drastically weakened by the loss of Torino's ten international players.

WHEN:
May 4 1949
WHERE:
Basilica of Superga, near Turin, Piedmont, Italy
DEATH TOLL:
31 (18 members of the Torino first-team squad plus club officials, journalists and crew)
YOU SHOULD KNOW:
Torino's revered captain Valentino Mazzola left behind a great soccer legacy. His six-year-old son Sandro would grow up to become a top player in his own right, making 417 appearances for Inter Milan and representing Italy 70 times.

24 Hours of Le Mans

WHEN:
June 11 1955
WHERE:
Le Mans, France
DEATH TOLL:
80
YOU SHOULD KNOW:
The accident at Le Mans caused much soul-searching in the world of sports car racing. Mercedes-Benz withdrew from all motor racing and did not enter a car again until 1987. Switzerland banned all circuit motor racing – the ban was only lifted in 2007.

First held in 1923, the 24 Hours of Le Mans is a true test of speed, skill and, above all, endurance. Fans come from across the globe to witness one of the great spectacles of world sport. The 1955 event was billed as the greatest ever. All the best drivers of the day were there and over 250,000 fans had gathered to view the extravaganza.

In the first two hours of the race, drivers were breaking records on almost every lap of the circuit. However, just into the third hour, the British driver Mike Hawthorn was ushered into the pits for a fuel stop. He applied the brakes and, without realizing it, caused the car behind to swerve. This had a knock-on effect, ultimately causing a Mercedes driven by Pierre Levegh to hit a bank close to the grandstand.

The car exploded on impact sending the wreckage deep into the crowd. The driver and scores of spectators were killed instantly. Many more were injured and urgent medical attention was needed. This presented the race organizers with a dilemma and, though their decision not to stop the race may now seem harsh, it was probably the right one. Ambulances and fire crews were coming from the town and if such a vast crowd were to leave *en masse* they would have blocked their way. The circuit was so large that few had any inkling that something had gone terribly wrong.

Out of respect for their driver, Mercedes withdrew their cars from the race immediately, but all the other teams continued. The race was eventually won by the British Jaguar team of Mike Hawthorn and Ivor Bueb. At the official inquiry into the crash, it was ruled that Hawthorn had not been at fault – it was simply a tragic accident.

Police and bystanders frantically probe for survivors in the tangled heap of bodies and steel. In the background are the searing flames of the burning vehicle.

Manchester United and the Munich air tragedy

A view of the snow-covered front part of the crashed BEA-Elizabethan charter plane in Munich

Every so often in sport there arrives on the scene a team of such prodigious talent that future glory is all but assured. The Manchester United team of the late 1950s was just such a side. Dubbed 'the Busby Babes', they were both talented and cocksure. At last England had found a team to challenge the dominance of Real Madrid, who had won the first two European Cups with some ease. The Football Association had a stuffy attitude to European competition, but allowed English champions Man U to take part in the 1956–1957 tournament. They acquitted themselves well, but lost to Madrid in the semi-finals.

By 1958 'The Babes' were older and stronger and hopes of success were high.

Having secured their place in the semi-finals with a 3-3 draw against Red Star in Belgrade, the team boarded a plane to take them first to Munich and then back home for a fixture with Wolverhampton Wanderers at the weekend. Europe was in the grip of winter and, by the time they reached Germany, conditions were dreadful. After two aborted take-offs in near blizzard conditions, their plane finally took to the air . . . only to crash soon afterwards. Of the 44 passengers, 23 lost their lives, including eight players.

A singular act of heroism stands out: Harry Gregg, the United goalkeeper, scooped up both Bobby Charlton and Dennis Viollet (coincidentally the two goal scorers in Belgrade) and carried them to safety. Others were not so lucky and one name among the roll call of the dead stood out – that of Duncan Edwards, arguably the greatest footballer England has ever produced. He survived the crash but died two weeks later. Manager Matt Busby was so badly injured that the last rites were read for him – he eventually recovered after two months in hospital.

WHEN:
February 6 1958
WHERE:
Munich, Germany
DEATH TOLL:
23
YOU SHOULD KNOW:
Of the survivors, Bobby Charlton was to go on to the greatest success, winning medals at domestic, european and world levels. His survival of the crash gave him a steely determination to achieve success – as though to honour the memories of those who died. In his own words 'What happened still reaches down and touches me every day. It engulfs me with terrible sadness'.

Death of Kurt Jensen

WHEN:
August 26 1960
WHERE:
Rome, Italy
DEATH TOLL:
One
YOU SHOULD KNOW:
Kurt Jensen would not be the last competitive cyclist to die from performance-enhancing drug abuse. Notable future casualties include top British rider Tom Simpson, who died on Mont Ventoux during the 1967 Tour de France. An increasing number of current or former professional cyclists have suffered premature death from heart attacks thought to be associated with excessive drug-taking.

Doping in sport wasn't new when the 1960 Summer Olympics in Rome came around, and cycling had led the way with the first recorded death of modern times – that of a cyclist who ingested trimethyl in 1886. The Olympics itself had seen near-fatality in 1904 when marathon runner Thomas Hicks overdosed on brandy and strychnine. Amphetamines were used in the 1930s, and in the 1950s Soviet Olympic teams were giving athletes male hormones to increase strength and power, while Americans slyly countered with new-fangled steroids.

During the 1960 team time-trial 100 km road race, Danish cyclist Knud (known as Kurt) Enemark Jensen collapsed and fractured his skull, and was declared dead in hospital shortly afterwards. He was the first Olympian to die from a drug overdose and the first athlete to die in competition since marathon man Francisco Lázaro in 1912. Jensen had been taking a drug cocktail – supposedly prescribed by his doctor for medical reasons – that included amphetamine and the powerful stimulant Ronicol. Keen to avoid controversy, pathologists discreetly gave the cause of death as heat stroke. According to insiders, Kurt Jensen was the unlucky one, as most Olympic cyclists were doping themselves as a matter of routine.

If Jensen had a positive legacy, it was the International Olympic Committee's decision to ban doping, following the recommendation of a medical commission it had set up as a result of his untimely death. However, the real tragedy was that this decision merely served as a starting gun signalling commencement of a never-ending battle of wits between drug testers and athletes determined to cheat their way to victory, using ever more sophisticated chemicals and techniques to outwit the authorities. But doping was not made illegal in pro cycling until 1965, since when the sport has been dogged by seemingly endless doping scandals.

Loss of the US figure skating team

The US figure skating team of 1961 contained the golden girls and boys of their generation. That year's National Championships were the first to be screened nationwide on CBS's *Sunday Sports Spectacular*. Before the media exposure, the athletes were little known outside their sport, but by the end of the broadcast many were household names. Their grace and athleticism impressed a large TV audience and the sport's profile was high. With success in their sights, the team, along with a large entourage of coaches and family, headed to the World Championships in Prague.

Watching them as they posed for photographs on the steps of Sabena Flight 548 at New York's Idlewild Airport, nobody could have dreamed it was to be the last their admiring public would see of them. The plan was to fly to Brussels and then catch a connecting flight to Prague. On the approach into the Belgian capital the pilot overshot the runway and angled around to make a second attempt. Something had gone badly wrong with the flight controls and the plane came down in a nearby field, killing all on board as well as a farmer tending his cabbage field. The crash had a devastating effect on the tight-knit skating community, and the championships in Prague were called off. Among the dead was the nine-times US ladies champion Maribel Vinson-Owen together with her two daughters.

The disaster had a galvanizing effect on the sport of figure skating in America. With the loss of so many coaches and athletes, the US authorities decided to reach out far and wide to help the sport get going again. Overseas coaches were brought in and children across the nation were encouraged to take lessons. What had previously been regarded as a Boston-based sport now became a truly national pastime.

WHEN:
February 15 1961
WHERE:
Brussels, Belgium
DEATH TOLL:
73
YOU SHOULD KNOW:
The American authorities were so alarmed by the crash that they sent FBI officers to Belgium to help with the investigation. Though the final report into the crash was inconclusive, pilot error was ruled out.

Members of the US figure skating team pose before boarding their plane at Idlewild airport.

Lima National Stadium riot

WHEN:
May 24 1964
WHERE:
National Stadium, Lima, Peru
DEATH TOLL:
318 dead, more than 500 injured

As hosts of the South American qualifying section for the 1964 Olympics, Peru had high hopes of filling one of the top two spots that would ensure their place at the Tokyo Olympic Games. They had, after all, qualified for the previous Olympics in Rome. Their campaign kicked off with an inauspicious 1-1 draw with Ecuador, but by the time they confronted their perpetual nemesis, Argentina, they had dispatched Colombia and Uruguay. Argentina, on the other hand, brought with them a perfect record and Brazil lurked just beneath Peru in the table. Getting a result of some sort was crucial.

After a first half that brought stalemate, the game sprang into life when the Argentine Manfredi scored in the 60th minute. The home crowd then grew increasingly passionate as Peru strove for an equalizer. With minutes to go, their prayers seemed to have been answered as the ball crossed the Argentinian goal line. The stadium erupted, first with joy and then with fury, as the referee disallowed the goal. That fateful decision sparked what stands as the worst riot ever witnessed at a sports event.

Using tear gas police attempted to quell a riot sparked by a referee's decision that gave Argentina a 1-0 victory over Peru.

Two fans ran onto the pitch to attack the referee and many more surged forward. The police, who were greatly outnumbered, responded by firing tear gas. The scene rapidly descended into chaos. The crowd grew ever more enraged and were soon in a mood to fight. Fires were started in the stands and a mob began smashing up the stadium. The police responded by firing live rounds over the heads of the rioters. By now in a state of total panic, the majority of the spectators attempted to leave the stadium, only to find their way blocked by firmly closed iron gates. In the ensuing crush hundreds lost their lives and even more sustained serous injuries.

YOU SHOULD KNOW:
Once the fans finally escaped from the stadium, thousands of them marched on the Presidential Palace to call for the match to be declared a draw. Such was their crazy passion for football that they cared less for the dead and the dying than they did for the result. Rather than being kicked out of the tournament, the team was invited to play Brazil for the final berth at the Olympics. The game was held in Rio and Peru lost 4-0.

Atatürk Stadium disaster

There had always been keen competition for regional supremacy between the neighbouring Turkish cities of Kayseri and Sivas, but this had never spilled over into serious violence – until 1967. Provincial amateur football clubs were encouraged to merge in the mid 1960s to create single clubs capable of holding their own in the new Second Football League, a nationwide third tier for Turkish professional football.

Three clubs in each city amalgamated to form Kayseri Erciyesspor and Sivasspor respectively. They went toe-to-toe for the first time in September 1967, providing the perfect opportunity for rival fans to strut their stuff – a confrontation inflamed by the fact that both teams were sharing top spot in the league. Around 5,000 supporters of Sivasspor headed for Kayseri the day before the match, flooding bars and less salubrious houses of entertainment. Quarrels broke out, fans were stabbed and police made 50 arrests.

Suitably forewarned, security forces ringed the Atatürk Stadium on match day, searching spectators and removing assorted weaponry. When the match began at 16.00, tension among the 21,000 spectators was palpable, exploding into violence when Kayseri Erciyesspor scored after 20 minutes. Scuffles broke out among the players and the crowd responded. Rival fans exchanged a hail of unconfiscated rocks and missiles, before the outnumbered Sivasspor contingent tried to escape. In the ensuing stampede, 40 spectators died and over 300 were injured.

A general riot broke out, the referee abandoned the game and the two teams were locked into their dressing rooms to protect them from the angry mob. Sivasspor fans who got out of the stadium in one piece indulged in a little gentle window-smashing and vehicle-burning as they raced back to their coaches and headed for home, leaving a few of their compatriots behind to fight running battles with Kayseri fans.

WHEN:
September 17 1967
WHERE:
Kayseri, Central Anatolia, Turkey
DEATH TOLL:
40 (including 38 from Sivas), with Sivasspor supporters also featuring most prominently on the injury list.
YOU SHOULD KNOW:
Tragic events in Kayseri were just a starting point. Turkey's worst-ever sports-related violence really got into its stride in Sivas, where enraged inhabitants rioted for days, burning buildings, plundering shops and vandalizing pretty much everything they could lay hands on, with particular reference to the many properties owned by Kayseri folk. Two more people died in the week-long rampage.

Rescue workers searching the wreckage of a plane crash in Huntingdon, West Virginia. The plane carried the entire Marshall University football team and all passengers were killed.

Southern Airways Flight 932

Marshall University football team tragedy

College football is hugely important on the American sporting scene, attracting and showcasing the brightest and best future pro footballers, with success enhancing the reputation of institutions they represent. In 1970, West Virginia's Marshall University at Huntingdon ran the Thundering Herd football team. Most away games were easily reached by road from campus, and that year's game against East Carolina Pirates was the one-and-only time the footballers travelled by plane. The score at Greenville's Ficklen Stadium was 17-14 in favour of the home team, so the football squad's mood on the return flight was subdued.

The aircraft was a chartered twin-engined Southern Airways DC-9 capable of seating 95, though it was not full. Even so, quite a number of local supporters had joined the team for the rare airborne excursion, so Flight 932 was carrying 75 souls. The weather was not ideal, with controllers reporting rain, fog and ragged cloud in the area of Huntingdon's Tri-State Airport at Ceredo – conditions that would make a landing tricky but still perfectly feasible.

At 19.34 the crew reported passing Tri-State's outer runway marker and were given landing clearance. Seconds later, the DC-9 clipped treetops and ploughed into a hillside, bursting into flames and gouging out a charred impact zone 30 m (98 ft) wide by 85 m (280 ft) long. It was a crash described by investigators as 'unsurvivable', and instantly became the worst sports-related air disaster in American history.

The entire 37-man Marshall football squad perished, along with eight coaches, 25 prominent Huntingdon citizens (including a city councillor, state legislator and several doctors), four flight crew and one charter company representative. Many of the victims were interred at Spring Hill Cemetery after a mass funeral, some together; classes at Marshall University were cancelled and condolences were received from all over the USA.

WHEN:
November 14 1970
WHERE:
Ceredo, West Virginia, USA
DEATH TOLL:
75
YOU SHOULD KNOW:
The enduring effect of this tragic air crash on the local community may be judged by the fact that victims are still mourned at an annual ceremony on Marshall University's campus. In addition, the Huntingdon street where Spring Hill Cemetery with its commemorative cenotaph is located was renamed Marshall Memorial Boulevard and Marshall's Joan C Edwards football stadium has a large bronze memorial. There's also a memorial fountain and student centre on campus, while a plaque was dedicated at the crash site as recently as 2006.

The Munich Olympics

Whichever way you look at it, the Munich Olympiad of 1972 was tinged with a terrible irony. It was the first time Germany had hosted the event since the charade of the 1936 Nazi Games. The self-proclaimed 'Happy Games' had a logo of a sun spreading rays of hope for the future. It should have been an occasion remembered for the record-breaking seven gold medals won by swimmer Mark Spitz. However the Munich Games will go down in history for a brutal and audacious act of terrorism that had repercussions far beyond the Olympic Village.

On the morning of September 5, eight Black September Palestinian commandos dodged past lax security and took 11 Israeli athletes and officials hostage. Two of the hostages fought back and were killed immediately. The remainder were held in an increasingly tense stand-off that was to last throughout the day. Under the guise of a deal to take the captors and their hostages to a safe haven in the Middle East, a rescue attempt was launched. The German authorities had little experience of counter-terrorism at the time and things quickly went wrong. All of the remaining nine hostages were killed as well as a German policeman. Five of the attackers died and three were arrested.

Incredibly, the Olympic events were allowed to continue throughout the day. The president of the host's organizing committee lobbied for the remainder of the Games to be cancelled but, with the endorsement of the Israeli government, International Olympic Committee President Avery Brundage announced that 'the Games must go on'. A remembrance service was held the following day at a packed Olympic Stadium and the Games resumed. In retaliation, the Israelis launched 'Operation Wrath of God' to kill those involved in planning the assault, further polarizing Middle East opinion.

WHEN:
September 5 1972
WHERE:
Munich, Germany
DEATH TOLL:
17
YOU SHOULD KNOW:
The star athlete of the games, Mark Spitz, himself a Jew and therefore a possible target, was flown out of Germany before the closing ceremony. The three arrested Palestinians were released from custody in October to meet the demands of hijackers of a Lufthansa aeroplane.

A member of the International Olympic Committee speaks with a masked PLO (Palestine Liberation Organization) terrorist who invaded the Olympic Village.

Alive in the Andes

WHEN:
From Friday October 13 1972
WHERE:
Andes, South America
DEATH TOLL:
29

It is usual to describe the survivors of accidents as 'lucky', but in the case of the ill-fated Uruguayan college rugby team, stranded in the High Andes after a plane crash, luck had nothing to do with it – only the team's sporting spirit of co-operation and endurance ensured that any of them made it back alive.

On October 12 1972, a plane carrying Stella Maris College rugby team plus coaches and supporters took off from Montevideo. The team had an inter-college match fixture in Santiago, Chile. Bad weather forced an unscheduled landing in Mendoza, Argentina. After an overnight stop, the flight resumed but the terrible weather still hampered progress. The pilot plotted a new route across the mountains into Chile but he miscalculated the aircraft speed and sent an inaccurate location report.

Suddenly a blanket of cloud engulfed the plane and it crashed into the snow-covered mountainside; 17 passengers and crew were either killed instantly or died within minutes. The survivors were in the main extremely fit young men, but they were stranded on a barren

A body lying in snow outside the wreckage of the Uruguayan plane that crashed while flying members of the Stella Maris College rugby team from Montevideo to Santiago.

snow-covered rock face miles from anywhere in freezing conditions, with scarcely any food and no shelter apart from the plane's mangled fuselage. They huddled in the wreck of the plane and awaited rescue.

By the tenth day, two more had died of their injuries and the rest were starving. An avalanche killed another eight. The life-or-death situation demanded an extreme response. The remains of the team had to make an appalling decision: the only way to stay alive was to eat the flesh of their dead friends. After 60 days the two fittest youths, having regained some strength, set off on a 12-day trek through the mountains and finally found help. Of the 45 people on the flight, 16 survived their horrendous ordeal.

YOU SHOULD KNOW:
Robert Canessa, a medical student, is thought to have proposed cannibalism as a survival strategy. He was later to make an unsuccessful bid to become president of Uruguay. The ordeal of the plane crash and its aftermath was recounted by author Piers Paul Read in his best-selling book *Alive!*, later made into a film.

Karaiskakis Stadium disaster

Named after George Karaiskakis, a hero in the 19th century Greek War of Independence, the Karaiskakis Stadium was the velodrome at the inaugural 1896 Summer Olympics in Athens. This venerable venue became the home of soccer outfit Olympiacos FC, the most successful club in Greece.

However, two other great teams in the Greek capital – Panathinaikos and AEK Athens – are also constantly vying for supremacy. Derby matches between Olympiacos and its big-city rivals are eagerly anticipated by supporters, and so it was in February 1981 when two sets of passionate fans packed into the Karaiskakis Stadium for the big game between Olympiacos and AEK Athens.

In the event, the home side enjoyed a mighty triumph, beating arch rivals AEK 6-0. This was a cause for ecstatic celebration among the home contingent, but euphoria soon evaporated when disaster struck. After the final whistle, excited Olympiacos fans made a rush for the exits to continue their victory party outside the ground. At Gate 7 a partially closed exit was the cause of the biggest tragedy in Greek football history. Fans on the bottom steps hesitated and were pushed over by the solid mass pressing from behind. Dozens went down and were engulfed as the crowd continued to surge forward. When the *melée* was finally sorted out, 19 supporters had lost their lives and many more were injured. Most were young adults or teenagers.

The passion that Greek football fans bring to the game was matched by the intense sorrow with which they have mourned its victims since 1981. Every year on the anniversary of the catastrophic crush, thousands gather inside Karaiskakis Stadium for a memorial service, at which the massed fans sing the moving refrain 'Brothers, you still live and you are the ones who guide us'.

WHEN:
February 8 1981
WHERE:
Neo Faliro, Piraeus, Greece
DEATH TOLL:
21 (including two victims who subsequently died in hospital). Over 50 were seriously injured.
YOU SHOULD KNOW:
The Karaiskakis Stadium was rebuilt as a state-of-the-art venue to host the football competition at the 2004 Summer Olympics. But the Gate 7 tribute area has black seats among the standard red of Olympiacos, forming a giant figure 7, and there is a monument on the eastern side of the ground bearing the names of all 21 victims – gone but not forgotten.

Lenin Stadium disaster

WHEN:
October 20 1982
WHERE:
Lenin Stadium (re-named Luzhniki Stadium), Moscow (formerly USSR)
DEATH TOLL:
Official records put the death toll at 67 but the true figure may have run into hundreds.
YOU SHOULD KNOW:
Such was the secrecy in the former Soviet Union that, in spite of the presence of several journalists in the stadium, little was reported in the press. A local Moscow newspaper carried a small article stating merely that there had been an incident at the game and that some people had been injured. The Dutch team did not learn of the tragedy until many years later, and on the 25th anniversary of the disaster the original teams played a benefit match in aid of the victims' families.

The last 32 UEFA cup match between Spartak Moscow and Haarlem was hardly one to capture the imagination of the football-loving public. Though Haarlem had enjoyed their most successful season to date after finishing fourth in the Dutch league, they had been forced to sell their top player, Ruud Gullit. Spartak themselves could not boast any great talent either and only around 100 Dutch fans bothered to make the trip to Moscow.

The Moscow public was also decidedly lukewarm about the fixture and few bought tickets to brave the cold early winter air. Faced with such a meagre attendance, the authorities made the fateful decision to close off most of the ground and hem the 15,000-strong crowd into one stand. The match did little to warm the hands of the assembled audience, save for a Spartak goal in the 17th minute from their star striker Gess. It was a lead that they held onto until the game went into injury time. Satisfied with their team's work and keen to get back to the warmth of their homes, the crowd began to leave. Just seconds before the final whistle was due to be blown, Sergei Shvetsov doubled the home side's lead and put the game beyond doubt.

Hearing a roar, many in the departing crowd turned round and headed back to investigate its cause. The military police, who routinely managed sports events, were concerned only with blocking the returning fans, rather than opening more gates to ease a growing bottleneck. With underfoot conditions becoming ever icier, many began to slip and slide and this sparked a stampede. Hundreds of people lost their footing and hundreds more had no escape other than to clamber over the fallen. Scores were trampled to death and many more suffered severe injuries

Bradford Valley Parade stadium fire

By the spring of 1985 Bradford City looked like a football club that was finally going places. The 'Bantams', as they are affectionately known, had just secured promotion to the old second division when in early May the club hosted a match with Lincoln City. A bumper crowd of over 11,000 turned up to celebrate. The match failed to live up to the occasion and as half-time approached neither team appeared to be threatening to score. It was at this point that people in the antiquated wooden main stand began to notice a bright shimmering light coming from below. Others began to feel warmth under their feet. Within a few minutes flames were clearly visible

and police and stewards began evacuating the packed stand.

The combination of an old wooden structure and accumulated litter that had been allowed to collect beneath the stand acted like a tinder box. Within five minutes the fire had spread to the roof, sending ash, burning embers and choking smoke onto the spectators below. One side of the ground turned into a raging inferno and those who had not yet escaped were in serious danger. Although over 50 people lost their lives and many more were injured, the figure might have been much higher had it not been for the bravery of some spectators and the police on duty that day. Many risked life and limb to return to the heart of the fire and haul out the injured. Afterwards 22 spectators were given awards for bravery.

A subsequent investigation concluded that the fire was probably caused by a discarded cigarette end or a match. An inquiry chaired by High Court Judge Sir Oliver Popplewell reported a year later and recommended an overhaul of safety at all British sports grounds.

The stand burns while fans look on at Bradford's football ground.

WHEN:
May 11 1985
WHERE:
Valley Parade, Bradford, UK
DEATH TOLL:
56
YOU SHOULD KNOW:
A council report just a year before the disaster proved tragically prescient. It warned that the build-up of litter was a possible risk, even stating that it could be ignited by a dropped cigarette. The club had no legal obligation to heed the council's warning and the rubbish was not cleared away.

Heysel Stadium

WHEN:
May 29 1985
WHERE:
Brussels, Belgium
DEATH TOLL:
39 killed (38 Italians and one Belgian); 400 injured.
YOU SHOULD KNOW:
Heysel Stadium was built in the 1920s and was clearly not suitable for such an occasion. It had failed inspections and the threat of closure hung over it. Because of this, little was spent on maintenance. Local police had embarked on a policy of getting unruly fans into the stadium early rather than arresting them. All of these factors contributed to the tragedy.

It was the final that everyone wanted – the Champions of England and current European Cup holders versus the Champions of Italy and holders of the UEFA Cup Winners' Cup. Liverpool and Juventus were two teams at the height of their powers with international players in every position. A mouth-watering display of footballing talent was keenly anticipated by a TV audience of tens of millions across Europe. What they got instead was a slowly unfolding tragedy which formed a terrible backdrop to an increasingly irrelevant game of football. The name of the host stadium, Heysel, in Belgium, has since become a watchword for hooliganism, official incompetence and structural neglect.

The match was treated like any other big final. Tickets were allocated to the two sets of fans and they were to be separated by a neutral enclosure. Officials from both clubs had warned that many, mainly Belgians, in the neutral section were likely to sell their tickets, at a price, to partisan fans. There was a history of violence between English and Italian clubs and the previous year's final in Rome had ended in acrimony when Liverpool beat the local side Roma on penalties. Roma fans, the police and local hoteliers had all turned on Liverpool fans, who were forced to seek refuge in the British embassy.

Heysel was Liverpool supporters' chance for revenge. The neutral section quickly filled with mainly Italian fans and all that separated them from the Liverpool section was a flimsy fence. Taunts started and then missiles began to fly. The fence was quickly breached and the Liverpool fans advanced. Panic erupted as Juventus supporters tried to retreat, only to find their way blocked by a concrete wall. The pressure proved too much and the structure gave way, crushing the trapped Italian fans.

A clash between the Belgian police and Liverpool supporters.

Hillsborough

At the time of the FA Cup semi-final between Liverpool and Nottingham Forest, in the late spring of 1989, English football was a sport in turmoil. English clubs were banned from competing in Europe as a result of the Heysel disaster and hooliganism was endemic. It was still the custom to stand in large enclosures and fans were fenced in, often with the use of barbed wire, to prevent pitch invasions. Watching a soccer match was not a pleasant experience.

Hillsborough was one of the best grounds in the country and had a long history of hosting sell-out encounters. However, previous matches had not passed without incident and in 1981 around 40 fans were injured in a crush. This led to a redesign of the Leppings Lane End, dividing it into five pens – that decision was later to have dire consequences.

Fans had been instructed to arrive at the stadium in good time for the traditional 15.00 kick-off, but many found their journey to the ground delayed by roadworks on the M62 motorway. When the players took to the field some ten minutes prior to the scheduled kick-off, a large number of fans were still outside the ground. A fateful decision was made by the police to open the gates and allow the crowd in rather than risk disturbance outside the ground.

As more and more fans poured into the enclosure, those inside were pushed against the perimeter fencing. A catastrophic crush ensued but this remained unnoticed, except by those affected, as the game kicked off. BBC television cameras were at the ready to record the game, but instead a decision was made to go 'live' from the ground as the developing disaster unfolded. The game was halted after six minutes. Scores died, mainly through asphyxiation, and hundreds more were injured.

WHEN:
April 15 1989
WHERE:
Hillsborough Stadium, Sheffield, UK
DEATH TOLL:
94 people died that day and a further two died later in hospital. Over 700 were injured.
YOU SHOULD KNOW:
Sections of the press sought to blame hooliganism rather than poor crowd control by the police. In what must go down as one of the most shameful acts in tabloid journalism, *The Sun* newspaper, under a headline 'The Truth', published fabricated stories of fans attacking the police and even robbing the dead. Feelings still run high on Merseyside today and *The Sun* is seldom seen in newsagents there.

Fans trying to escape the crush of the crowd as more people pour into the ground.

Camp Randall Stadium crush

WHEN:
October 30 1993
WHERE:
Camp Randall Stadium, Madison, Wisconsin, USA
TOLL:
Six people were seriously injured.
YOU SHOULD KNOW:
The crush led to an overhaul in the design of Camp Randall and other similar stadiums. The security company in charge of the stadium was found liable for the poor crowd control and faced several hefty lawsuits.

It may be of little comfort to the handful of fans who were critically injured, but most of those involved in a 1993 crush at Wisconsin's Camp Randall Stadium got off relatively lightly. Serious flaws were uncovered in the stadium design and security, which provided a wake-up call for the whole of American mass spectator sport.

College football is no stranger to rowdy behaviour, and when home side Wisconsin Badgers scraped a win by three points against rivals Michigan, fans rushed to invade the pitch to celebrate. The news of a sell-out crowd had prompted the authorities to up the number of police on duty by ten to 65, but this was patently inadequate for a crowd of nearly 78,000 people.

A low mesh fence was all that separated the fans from the playing area; when they started leaping the barrier with ease, the police tried to push them back. This had the knock-on effect of causing some fans close to the fence to stumble and fall. They were now being crushed from behind while the police were still reacting by pushing the crowd back. In the commotion, appeals from police and club officials fell on deaf ears and fans at the back of the stands still rushed forward. Things were getting critical for those in the middle of the crush.

A horrified hush fell over the stadium as the crowd began to realize what was happening. Members of the young, athletic Wisconsin team acted heroically, diving into the melée to haul out the injured, many of whom were turning blue from asphyxiation. Six people suffered serious injuries, but it might have been very much worse had it not been for the actions of a few brave and level-headed individuals.

Ellis Park Stadium stampede

WHEN:
April 11 2001
WHERE:
Ellis Park Stadium, Johannesburg, South Africa
DEATH TOLL:
43 dead, over 250 injured.
YOU SHOULD KNOW:
The incident is the worst disaster at a sporting event in South Africa, but only just. A decade earlier 42 people were killed in a stampede when the two teams met in a pre-season friendly.

During the apartheid era, sport in South Africa played a central role both for those who wished to punish the regime through sanctions and others who wished to break those sanctions by setting up so-called 'rebel tours'. Rugby and cricket were in the forefront of these battles but the largely black sport of football was ignored. Because soccer requires little investment to play, it is the most egalitarian of sports and the black underclass took to it with great gusto. Post apartheid, soccer became the unofficial national sport and attendances grew.

In April 2001, Ellis Park Stadium in Johannesburg was to host the biggest club match in South Africa – the Soweto Derby between the Kaizer Chiefs and the Orlando Pirates. As kick-off approached, a capacity crowd of 60,000 was already in the ground but outside as many again were keen to gain entry. While many stadiums across the

country had fallen into disrepair, Ellis Park was one of the country's finest. However, poorly trained stewards could not cope with the sheer weight of numbers pressing to get in. The guards panicked and fired tear gas into the air. This led to a stampede, with people running everywhere, many of them into the already full-to-bursting stands. The pressure was at its most intense in the East Stand and, as the massed ranks of fans pushed against the perimeter fence, it gave way under the strain.

While some at the front escaped, many were unwittingly trampled by those coming up behind. The injured were laid out on the pitch alongside the dead and dying. Calls for medical assistance went largely unheeded as emergency planning was virtually non-existent. The walking wounded had to fend for themselves; the more seriously injured stood little chance of survival. The lack of crowd control had ended in tragedy.

Tragedy at the Ellis Park Stadium, Johannesburg, where 43 people were crushed to death during the Kaizer Chiefs v Orlando Pirates match.

Debris lying at the entrance of the Accra Sports Stadium after the deadly stampede.

Accra Sports Stadium stampede

The year 2001 was an *annus horribilis* for soccer in Africa. Within the space of one month the continent saw deaths at matches in Ivory Coast, South Africa and The Democratic Republic of Congo. Practically anywhere in Africa a mixture of rowdy behaviour and poor crowd control had made attending a match a risky business. In May of that year fierce rivals Asante Kotoko and Hearts of Oak met at the Accra Sports Stadium in Ghana's capital. The crowd was raucous and every adverse refereeing decision was booed, while the players themselves seemed to be letting the occasion go to their heads as several meaty challenges flew in.

For most of the game Kotoko fans were the happiest as their team led 1-0. Things started to turn ugly after a contentious equalizer and further fuel was added to the flames when Hearts took the lead. The Kotoko fans did not like what they saw and started ripping up the stands, using plastic seats as missiles against the police and rival supporters. The police in turn used tear gas, the most powerful weapon available to them short of live ammunition.

Tear gas is the bluntest of instruments when used against crowds. Designed to blind and disorientate, it is only really effective if the crowd has somewhere to run to. Many of the fans tried to flee the stadium only to find their path blocked by locked metal gates. In the ensuing crush more than 100 died through compressive asphyxiation and hundreds more were injured. To compound the unfolding tragedy, only a handful of medical staff were on duty that evening and even these had departed the scene before the trouble flared.

WHEN:
May 9 2001
WHERE:
Accra (Ohene Djan) Sports Stadium,
Accra, Ghana
DEATH TOLL:
Official figures put the death toll
at 127.
YOU SHOULD KNOW:
The coroner's inquiry was hindered
by the fact that many of the dead
were Muslims. It is the custom in
Islam that a burial should take
place within 24 hours of death
and this prevented detailed
forensic examination. Even the
official death toll may be a gross
underestimate as many families
took away their loved ones' bodies
to give them a decent burial in
accordance with their beliefs.

The Boys in Red

Across the territories and provinces of Canada, schoolchildren are considered a very precious cargo. The transport that is used to ferry them to and from school is deliberately robust. The iconic big yellow school bus is built like a tank and is driven by a highly trained driver. Flashing lights tell other drivers when not to pass and everybody obeys. However, these buses are expensive to run and it is often necessary to use other vehicles to transport children to extracurricular activities.

It was very late on Friday January 11 2008 when parents gathered to collect their sons who were returning from an away basketball fixture. This was a routine they had grown used to – the Bathurst High School 'Boys in Red' basketball team regularly travelled miles to play the game they loved. When midnight came and went and a mixture of freezing rain and snow began to fall, the assembled group grew increasingly anxious. Eventually a police car pulled up and an officer informed the parents that the 15-seat Ford Club Wagon carrying their children had been involved in an accident and they should go to the local hospital.

Only four of the 12 people on board had made it to the hospital – seven pupils and the wife of the 'Boys in Red' team coach (who was also the driver) had been pronounced dead at the scene. The tragedy shook the whole of Canada. A national day of mourning was declared and tributes and condolences poured in from far and wide. A Facebook page was set up to allow people to extend their sympathy. The boys' funeral, held at the Bathurst Civic Centre, was attended by more than 6,000 people and thousands more watched on a giant screen at the nearby ice rink.

WHEN:
January 12 2008
WHERE:
Bathurst, New Brunswick, Canada
DEATH TOLL:
Seven boys and their teacher
YOU SHOULD KNOW:
Laws were rushed through to ban vehicles like the one used to transport the boys. Some provinces began to require extra insurance, even for parents giving children's friends lifts to and from school-organized activities. While the laws are well meaning, there are fears that they may lead to children having fewer opportunities to engage in sports and social activities outside school.

Students from Bathurst High School placing flowers at a makeshift basketball court at the crash site where seven members of the school's basketball team were killed, along with the coach's wife.

Attack on the Sri Lankan cricket team

WHEN:
March 3 2009
WHERE:
Liberty Square Roundabout,
Lahore, Pakistan
DEATH TOLL:
Eight – six policemen, the minibus
driver and a civilian were killed.
YOU SHOULD KNOW:
Police involved in the attack were
later awarded medals for valour.
Coach driver Mahar Mohammad
Khalil was widely hailed as a hero,
and a grateful Sri Lankan cricketer
gave him his team shirt.

In the years leading up to Sri Lanka's ill-fated 2009 Test tour, Pakistan had experienced several incidents which led to international matches being abandoned or cancelled. Sri Lanka was playing as a replacement for the Indian team, which had pulled out after the Mumbai terrorist attacks; they had been promised 'presidential style' security.

On the morning of March 3, the vehicles transporting the team to Lahore's Qadhafi Stadium for day three of the second Test were attacked at Liberty Square roundabout. Masked gunmen opened fire on both the coach carrying the players and the minibus in which the referee and umpires were travelling. It was only fortunate that the grenades and rockets loosed by the assailants were ineffectual, else the carnage would have been far worse. Even so several players suffered shrapnel wounds and the driver of the minibus was killed, although none of his passengers was seriously injured. The coach driver courageously drove on through the hail of bullets to the safety of the stadium. A policeman who had boarded the minibus seeking cover had to be urged to take its wheel and follow the coach, which eventually he did. The match was abandoned as a draw and the team was airlifted from the stadium and flown home.

Those blamed for the outrage included al-Qaeda, Lashkar-e-Taiba ('Army of the Pure' – an outlawed militant group which had issued a *fatwa* against playing cricket) and the Tamil Tigers. The world was appalled by the attack, the first on a national sports team since the Munich massacre of Israeli athletes in 1972, and there was universal condemnation of the lax security. Footage from CCTV cameras had captured the whole scene: it not only showed the masked gunmen arriving, making their attack and escaping unchallenged but also recorded security forces running away.

A video grab shows damage to the windows of the Sri Lankan cricket team's bus.

Houphouët-Boigny Stadium stampede

West African soccer fans like to turn matches into carnivals and the 2010 World Cup qualifier between Cote d'Ivoire and Malawi was no exception. Tickets had sold out long beforehand and the newly refurbished Houphouët-Boigny Stadium in Abidjan was packed with an exuberant crowd, gloriously costumed and painted in the Ivorian team colours of orange, green and white, playing musical instruments, cheering and dancing. There were high hopes of success. Not for nothing are the Ivorian team known as 'The Elephants': robust athleticism combined with sound technical skills makes them a force to be reckoned with. Several of the national team play for European clubs and among the stars the fans had come to see were Hibernian defender Sol Bamba, Chelsea striker Salomon Kalou and Cote d'Ivoire team captain Didier Drogba.

Long before the match was due to start the crowd around the stadium was already heaving. Then, just before kick-off, a wall collapsed as fans jostled to get into the game. Pandemonium broke out and police fired tear gas into the surge of fans, making an already bad situation even worse; anyone who stumbled was crushed or trampled underfoot in the panic. Amazingly, the match went ahead as though nothing was happening; Cote d'Ivoire defeated Malawi 5-0.

Though officials blamed ticketless fans for the tragedy, a FIFA enquiry concluded that the Ivorian Football Federation (FIF) was responsible. The security staff had not been sufficiently trained or equipped to prevent a stampede. The FIF was fined and ordered to pay compensation to the victims' families. The Houphouët-Boigny tragedy was just the latest in a series of disastrous football stadium stampedes across the African continent, all due to lack of proper crowd control.

Men carrying out an injured spectator following the stadium stampede.

WHEN:
March 29 2009
WHERE:
Houphouët-Boigny Stadium, Abidjan, Cote d'Ivoire
DEATH TOLL:
At least 22 were killed and more than 130 injured
YOU SHOULD KNOW:
In high-scoring matches in 1992 and 2006, Cote d'Ivoire defeated Ghana 11-10 and Cameroon 12-11. Both matches were clinched by 24-shot penalty shoot-outs, the highest in international football.

TRANSPORT DISASTERS

Fort Washington great train wreck

WHEN:
July 17 1856
WHERE:
Camp Hill, Pennsylvania, USA
DEATH TOLL:
Between 59 and 67 people died in the crash, mostly children. Hundreds more were injured.
YOU SHOULD KNOW:
The Camp Hill disaster, as the crash is also known, remains one of the worst railway accidents in American history.

The children who attended the Sunday school at St Michael's Catholic Church in the Philadelphia suburb of Kensington were excited by the prospect of an outing to Fort Washington, outside the city, for a picnic in the park. They were up at dawn and were boarding the special excursion train by 05.00. Already the balmy mid July air gave promise of a warm day to come. There must have been plenty of lively chatter among the 1,500 children who clambered into the wooden box cars for the short journey. The year was 1856 and for many it will have been their first train ride as the North Pennsylvania Railroad on which they were travelling was just one year old.

The steam train was 20 minutes late leaving by the time everyone was safely boarded. The driver knew that a passenger train was scheduled to be approaching from the opposite direction on the same section of single-track line, but he reckoned that he could make up the time so that the two trains could pass each other at a siding along the route. The driver of the passenger train also knew about the excursion and he had slowed down to 16 kph (10 mph) and was blowing his whistle continuously as he approached a blind curve at Camp Hill. The excursion train, however, was on a downhill run and travelling much faster when it rounded the curve and smacked straight into the other. In the head-on collision the boiler of one of the locomotives exploded – it was said that the explosion could be heard 8 km (5 mi) away – and the Sunday school train came off the rails. The children stood no chance in the conflagration that followed as flames engulfed the tinder-dry box cars.

Sultana steamboat tragedy

WHEN:
April 27 1865
WHERE:
Mississippi River, north of Memphis, Tennessee, USA
DEATH TOLL:
Exact figures are unknown as there was no roll-call of the passengers, but estimates of deaths range between 1,500 and 1,900. Certainly there were only a few hundred survivors.

The bitter four-year civil war which had torn the American nation apart, pitting North against South, was finally over, and captured Union soldiers who had been held in Confederacy prisons in the South could at last look forward to a reunion with their families. Weakened and exhausted though they were by the harsh conditions of their incarceration, many hundreds of freed prisoners were in understandably high spirits as they boarded the paddle steamer *Sultana* at the Mississippi river port of Vicksburg on the evening of April 24 1865.

The *Sultana* was a typical Mississippi side-wheeler; built for the cotton trade, it had often plied the mighty river as a troop carrier during the war. It had left New Orleans three days previously on the long river journey north to Cincinnati, with a regular complement of cabin passengers and a cargo of sugar and livestock.

The problems started at Vicksburg when the crew were powerless to prevent the horde of ex-Union soldiers who pressed their way on board. When the steamer set sail again it was carrying some 2,300 passengers – six times its authorized capacity. The spring flood waters were at their height and the *Sultana*'s progress was slow against the strong current. When the boat docked two days later at Memphis its boilers were found to be leaking and had to be repaired. Shortly after resuming its passage the boilers gave out under the huge strain and a massive explosion lit up the night sky. The vessel was blown apart and soon ablaze. Those on board, many of whom were unable to swim as well as enfeebled by the ordeal of their captivity, were forced to make a ghastly choice between a watery grave in the ice-cold river or being burned alive.

YOU SHOULD KNOW:
The tragedy got very little press coverage at the time as everyone's attention was focused on the end of the war. The final surrender of the Confederacy forces had taken place only the day before.

The steamboat Sultana

Abergele rail crash

WHEN:
August 20 1868
WHERE:
Abergele, North Wales, UK
DEATH TOLL:
33 died. The bodies were so badly charred in the inferno from the exploding paraffin that only three could be positively identified; the remainder were buried in simple numbered coffins.
YOU SHOULD KNOW:
After the crash it became standard practice on the railways for steep gradients to be fitted with runaway catchpoints so that any vehicle which was out of control on the line could be derailed and stopped before there was a chance of it colliding with another.

Britain's first major train crash occurred in August 1868 in North Wales. The Irish Mail was a daily express service from London Euston to Holyhead in Anglesey, where many passengers embarked on the ferry to Ireland. The train, which was known for its speed and efficiency, frequently carried some of the country's wealthiest and most influential people on the way to their country estates in Ireland. On this particular day the Irish Mail arrived as usual in Chester, where four extra carriages were added to the front of the train, doubling it in size. Chester was an important junction and many more passengers joined the train at this point.

An hour or so later the express was approaching the small town of Abergele on the North Wales coast and preparing for the haul up towards Colwyn Bay. Some 5 km (3 mi) further up the main line at Llanddulas, a goods train was busy with a scheduled shunting operation which involved moving its wagons into sidings. Normally this would have been completed in good time before the express passed through. On this occasion, however, six goods trucks and a brake van which had been left secure on the main line during the operation somehow came free and started rolling down the incline towards the oncoming Irish Mail.

A sweeping curve in the track prevented the driver of the express from seeing the trucks before it was too late; nor could he have received any warning of the impending disaster as there was no telegraph connection between the local stations. Although he slammed his engine into reverse, a collision was inevitable, and made infinitely worse by the fact that two of the goods wagons were loaded with barrels of paraffin which exploded on impact.

Armagh rail disaster

A day out by the sea must have seemed an enticing prospect for the 940 passengers who packed into a special excursion train at Armagh station in Ireland one warm summer's morning. Such had been the demand for places that a further two coaches were added on the day to the 13 already assigned. This caused some concern to the driver, Thomas McGrath, who was by no means convinced his engine had the power to pull such a long train. Knowing in particular that the first stage of the journey down to Warrenpoint on Carlingford Lough involved the formidable climb to Dobbins Bridge Summit, McGrath, who was not an experienced driver, requested the assistance of a pilot locomotive for the 5 km (3 mi) ascent, but he was refused.

As McGrath had feared, the train lost significant speed on the climb until it finally stalled just short of the summit. The crew then decided they would split the train and take the first five coaches to the next station over the summit before returning to pick up the other ten. In those days coaches were not fitted with automatic brakes so as an extra precaution stones were wedged under the carriage wheels. Unfortunately, during the uncoupling of the front five coaches, the engine nudged them backwards, just enough to push the rear carriages over the retaining stones.

One can only imagine the sickening feeling in the stomachs of the passengers as the coaches started rolling back down the incline. On its way up was the regular service from Armagh which had left ten minutes behind the excursion. The runaway coaches crashed into the oncoming train and the first three were hurled down the embankment and completely destroyed.

Passengers and helpers scramble up the embankment.

WHEN:
June 12 1889
WHERE:
Armagh, Northern Ireland, UK
DEATH TOLL:
80 people died in the crash, including 22 children; 262 people were injured.
YOU SHOULD KNOW:
As a direct result of the disaster better braking systems were devised for trains. Within a year it had become mandatory for trains in the British Isles to be fitted with continuous automatic brakes.

119

General Slocum ferry disaster

Among the many immigrant populations who lived in the cramped and often squalid conditions of New York's Lower East Side the German community of *Kleindeutschland* (Little Germany) was one of the proudest and most distinctive. It was a tight-knit community, centred around important cultural markers such as St Mark's Lutheran Church. On June 15 1904, 1,358 members of the congregation – women and children in the main – set off on the church's annual picnic trip which this year was to be held on the North Shore of Long Island. They had chartered the SS *General Slocum* to take them there, a sidewheeler steam ferry which was a common sight in the waters of New York harbour. Having boarded at 3rd Street, the day-trippers were soon heading up the East River towards Long Island Sound.

As the *General Slocum* was passing through the narrow tidal strait known as Hell Gate (where the Triborough Bridge stands today), a fire broke out; spreading quickly, it caused panic on the crowded decks. Hoping to contain the fire, the captain maintained his course towards the sound but the stiff headwind simply fanned the flames further. He was able eventually to beach the ship on North Brother Island, the site of a hospital for infectious diseases. By this time there was complete pandemonium among the passengers, with hundreds leaping into the water to escape the flames. The ship's safety measures failed utterly; life-jackets were defective, the life-boats could not be accessed and the crew were inadequately trained.

Although there were many tales of remarkable escapes and of great courage and resourcefulness on the part of the rescuers, the tragedy of the *General Slocum* remained New York's worst civilian accident until the events of September 11 2001.

The excursion steamer General Slocum *burns in the Hell Gate passage of the East River. The* Slocum *sank, taking the lives of 1,021 people, many of whom were women and children.*

WHEN:
June 15 1904
WHERE:
East River, New York, USA
DEATH TOLL:
1,021
YOU SHOULD KNOW:
The disaster gets a mention in James Joyce's celebrated novel *Ulysses* which is set entirely on the following day, June 16 1904 (now known as Bloomsday after the main character).

Sinking of the *Titanic*

It must be the most famous shipwreck of all time, with the world still fascinated by a century-old event that is far from the worst maritime disaster on record. Perhaps it's the sheer glamour of the magnificent White Star liner RMS *Titanic*, built to opulent standards to service mega-rich passengers as well as less pampered below-decks travellers. Perhaps it's the pulsating drama of her final hours, or the fact that a great ship could be undone by a minor collision with an iceberg that could so easily have been avoided.

The fatal transatlantic maiden voyage began at Southampton on April 10 1912. Following stops at Cherbourg and Queenstown (now Cobh) she had 2,240 souls aboard, including 899 crew. Just before midnight on April 14 *Titanic* brushed an iceberg off Newfoundland, cutting a long gash in her starboard side. Five compartments filled with water, exceeding the number that let her stay afloat. It was not immediately apparent, but *Titanic* was doomed and would sink within three hours.

With lifeboats for only half those aboard and an icy ocean waiting to kill inside 15 minutes, it was always going to be a disaster. But inevitable tragedy was compounded by chaotic evacuation, where boats often left the ship without a full complement. Contrary to popular legend, *Titanic* was never billed as 'unsinkable' – but it *is* true that the ship's orchestra continued to play until the mortally wounded leviathan slipped beneath the waves.

The RMS *Carpathia* arrived on the scene after steaming for four hours at full speed. She picked up the last survivors at 08.30 and headed for New York. The SS *Californian* was much closer, but failed to act when distress rockets were seen shortly after midnight. However, her radio operator had earlier warned *Titanic* about pack ice and been brusquely rebuffed.

WHEN:
April 14–15 1912
WHERE:
North Atlantic Ocean
DEATH TOLL:
1,517 passengers and crew perished (including a disproportionate number of men as a result of the 'women and children first' principle). Only 706 survived.

The Titanic *leaving Southampton on its maiden voyage.*

YOU SHOULD KNOW:
After many attempts, the wreck of *Titanic* was located in 1985. She had split in half before sinking and was lying in water 4 km (2.5 mi) deep. There have since been tourist visits to the wreck using mini-submarines and thousands of artefacts have been recovered – only to become the subject of prolonged court battles in the USA.

SS *Mont-Blanc*

WHEN:
December 6 1917
WHERE:
Halifax, Nova Scotia, Canada
DEATH TOLL:
2,000 dead and 9,000 injured
(estimated).
YOU SHOULD KNOW:
Ironically, the crew of the offending
Mont-Blanc escaped largely unhurt
from the carnage caused by their
exploding ship – the only casualty
being one seaman killed by falling
debris. The French crew were unable
to make the clear and present
danger apparent to the
English-speaking locals, but
prudently retreated to a safe
distance themselves.

*A crowd amid debris from the
Halifax explosion.*

As World War I raged all sorts of unglamorous participants played a
part in sustaining global conflict. One such was an unremarkable
French tramp steamer, the SS *Mont-Blanc*. In November 1917 she
had collected a cargo of ammunition from New York before sailing to
Halifax in Nova Scotia to join a convoy bound for Europe. But as
Mont-Blanc entered Halifax Harbour, a relatively minor collision
took place with the outbound Norwegian ship SS *Imo* in the
infamous Narrows. It was the sort of maritime accident that
happened not infrequently without serious consequences, but this
time the result was truly awesome.

Sparks flew as the two ships collided head-on and fire broke out on
Mont-Blanc. Unable to reach firefighting equipment, her crew
abandoned ship. Some 20 minutes later, just after 09.00, *Mont-Blanc*'s
munitions cargo exploded in a massive fireball, obliterating the ship
and sending a vast mushroom cloud high into the sky.

A tsunami swept through the harbour and a pressure wave
flattened buildings and felled trees as though they were
matchsticks. Burning debris rained in all directions and the other
offender, *Imo*, was cast on shore. The force of the explosion may be

judged by the fact that a gun barrel from *Mont-Blanc* was later found 5.5 km (3.4 mi) away.

Large areas of Halifax and neighbouring Dartmouth were completely flattened by the blast, killing countless spectators who had been watching the blazing ship. Many more died in the tsunami and fires that subsequently broke out all over town, trapping and killing hundreds of people. Next day, adding to the misery, a blizzard precipitated a deep layer of snow on the devastated communities, hampering rescue efforts and adding to the huge death toll caused by history's largest accidental man-made explosion.

Iolaire sinking

It was the ultimate stroke of bad luck, or bad seamanship. Sailors who survived the dangers of life on the hostile ocean wave during World War I were about to be reunited with their loved ones, only to perish within a mile of home in one of Britain's worst peacetime maritime disasters of modern times. They were all from the Isle of Lewis, the northern part of the biggest Western Isle, Lewis and Harris. It wasn't a traditional Scottish Hogmanay celebration, but when the Admiralty yacht *Iolaire* ('Eagle' to the non Gaelic-speaking passengers) left Kyle of Lochalsh just before midnight on December 31 1918 all aboard were in high spirits at the prospect of being reunited with families and friends on Lewis.

The crossing wasn't long, and at 02.30 *Iolaire* was approaching the safe haven of Stornaway Harbour when she struck fearsome rocks known as the Beasts of Holm, close to shore and the notoriously tricky approach to port. Pandemonium reigned and most of the sailors – as was common at the time – couldn't swim. Even those who could were in uniform, complete with heavy boots, which made the short swim to shore in treacherous waters a dangerous proposition.

One brave islander did make the hazardous crossing. John F Macleod swam ashore with a line, along which many survivors made their way to safety. But over 200 would perish after *Iolaire* finally foundered. In best official tradition, the Admiralty held an inconclusive enquiry that failed to apportion blame, especially to itself. This angered islanders, who felt possible drunkenness and inept navigation were to blame for the catastrophic loss of life. Gaelic songs that recall the despair of island women who found the bodies of their menfolk washed ashore after the disaster are sung on Lewis to this day.

WHEN:
January 1 1919
WHERE:
North Minch Strait, off the Isle of Lewis, Outer Hebrides, Scotland
DEATH TOLL:
Officially 205, though it may have been higher as it is thought that some extra passengers who didn't appear on the manifest were on board.
YOU SHOULD KNOW:
The wreck site is marked by a granite pillar that rises from the water above the Beasts of Holm. It may be seen to the left as the ferry enters Stornaway Harbour, serving as a stark reminder of how close to safety *Iolaire* actually came.

One of the motors in the wreckage of the R101

R101 airship crash

During the early 20th century the first flying machines – hot air balloons used from the 1780s – were developed into mighty rigid-frame airships. Gas-filled German Zeppelins conducted air raids on Britain in World War I, but these lumbering giants were soon made obsolete as terror weapons by the invention of incendiary tracer bullets.

However, back when aircraft technology was primitive, airships had the potential to deliver the holy grail of international travel – long-distance air transport. The British government was keen to join the party and initiated the Imperial Airship Scheme in 1924, funding competition between an Air Ministry team's *R101* and the Vickers company's *R100*. The brief called for airships bigger than anything previously constructed, capable of lifting five fighter aircraft or 200 soldiers plus their equipment.

Construction of *R101* began in 1926, and this elegant craft was built to a superb standard. However, she suffered from serious design flaws caused by a meddling Air Ministry committee that kept changing the specifications; numerous problems had to be overcome before *R101* took to the air in October 1929. After further modifications she made an erratic appearance at Hendon Air Show in 1930 and was hastily readied for a maiden overseas voyage, carrying VIPs. *R101* was neither properly prepared nor fit for purpose, but Air Ministry prestige was at stake so go she must.

On the evening of October 4 1930, *R101* departed for India with one refuelling stop scheduled in Egypt. But she got no further than Northern France. After being observed flying at low altitude, the giant airship went into a slow dive and hit the ground – possibly attempting an emergency landing after a gasbag was punctured. The airship instantly exploded, and the intense fire that followed lasted for 24 hours. Just eight of the 54 passengers and crew survived *R101*'s catastrophic crash.

WHEN:
October 5 1930
WHERE:
Near Beauvais, Oise, France
DEATH TOLL:
48 (46 perished in the crash and two survivors died later in hospital)
YOU SHOULD KNOW:
Ironically, the rival *R100* was a much better airship, with a little help from 'bouncing bomb' designer Barnes Wallace and engineer Nevil Shute Norway (later famous as novelist Nevil Shute). It made a troublefree transatlantic return flight and although *R100* could have delivered what the Air Ministry wanted, the *R101* disaster caused the superior craft to be abandoned and with it British interest in airship development.

Loss of USS *Akron*

Great Britain's airship programme crashed and burned with the ill-fated *R101*, but others would be slow to learn the lesson. The US Navy was taken with the possibilities and commissioned a pair of helium-filled rigid airships, ZRS-4 and ZRS-5. These gaseous monsters, although slightly shorter than the hydrogen-lifted German Zeppelin *Hindenburg*, were, at 239 m (785 ft) long, the largest helium airships ever built. With eight engines, each driving a propeller that could swivel from horizontal to vertical, they carried enough fuel to make 16,900 km (10,500 mi) flights.

After being constructed at the Goodyear Airdock in Akron, Ohio, ZRS-4 was commissioned into the US Navy as USS *Akron* in 1931. After trials and exercises that included attempts to spot flotillas of warships, experiments to equip the ship with reconnaissance aircraft were conducted. After a visit to fly the flag on America's West Coast, *Akron* returned to home base in Lakehurst, New Jersey for intensive testing of her revolutionary 'flying trapeze' system that allowed for the in-flight launch and recovery of F9C-2 Sparrowhawk biplanes. She was also used to ferry military high-ups and inspection parties to sites as far apart as Cuba's Guantanamo Bay and Panama.

On a routine mission along the New England coast, *Akron* was helping to calibrate radio-direction-finder stations when she encountered severe weather. A series of violent gusts pounded the airframe and shortly after midnight on April 3 1933 she was hit by the worst possible combination – an updraught followed immediately by a powerful downdraught. As the crew struggled unsuccessfully to regain control, *Akron*'s tail hit the water and the mighty airship smashed into the sea, quickly breaking up. Despite the swift attendance of a rescue vessel, only four survivors were pulled from the stormy Atlantic, one of whom died. Over 70 passengers and crew didn't make it.

WHEN:
April 4 1933
WHERE:
The Atlantic Ocean off New Jersey, USA
DEATH TOLL:
73 of the 76 US Navy passengers and crew were lost.
YOU SHOULD KNOW:
One of those who died when USS *Akron* crashed was Rear Admiral William A Moffett, chief of the Bureau of Aeronautics and main promoter of the US Navy's rigid airships programme. Sistership ZRS-5 (USS *Macon*) was lost off the Californian coast in 1935, though this time only two of the 76-man crew perished. Thereafter the USA followed Britain's example and the disastrous flirtation with rigid airships abruptly ended.

The control cabin of Akron *being brought up from the depths.*

Hindenburg **Disaster**

WHEN:
May 6 1937
WHERE:
Lakehurst, New Jersey, USA
DEATH TOLL:
35 (22 crew and 13 passengers)
YOU SHOULD KNOW:
The art deco spire atop New York's iconic Empire State Building was originally designed as a mooring mast, thus creating a terminal where airships could dock. The 102nd floor was designated as a landing area, complete with gangplank, while an elevator carried outgoing passengers up from check-in on the 86th-floor observation deck. The idea was trialled but proved impractical as powerful air currents around the building made the whole operation too dangerous.

The airship Hindenburg *exploding into a huge ball of fire as she comes in to land at Lakehurst, New Jersey. Miraculously, many of the passengers and crew aboard managed to escape unharmed.*

Germany built the biggest and best airships, having honed the technology after constructing huge Zeppelins from the early years of the 20th century. The guiding light was Count Ferdinand von Zeppelin, who finalized his revolutionary design for a rigid-frame airship in the 1890s. Before World War I Zeppelins were being used for scheduled passenger flights by the world's first commercial airline, DELAG (short for German Airship Travel). These craft were modified for use as scouts and bombers after war broke out in 1914.

Count Zeppelin died in 1917 but, after the Armistice, colleague Dr Hugo Eckner resurrected the civilian air transport concept, finally making the breakthrough in 1924 when America ordered a dirigible and the Zeppelin company created LZ126, its finest airship yet. This served successfully as the USS *Los Angeles* until 1932 after an 8,000 km (5,000 mi) transatlantic delivery voyage lasting 81 hours. Thus energized, Eckner created the magnificent LZ127, christened *Graf Zeppelin* and launched in 1928. After this sturdy craft completed an impressive global circumnavigation in 21 days, commercial flights between Germany and Brazil began.

This service was very successful, but when the Nazis came to power they took over Zeppelin flights, including those by the most advanced airship of them all, LZ129. The *Hindenburg* was designed to be lifted by inert helium rather than flammable hydrogen and took to the skies in 1936, quickly being pressed into service on transatlantic crossings. Unfortunately, an embargo on strategic supplies meant insufficient helium could be obtained, so hydrogen was used. It was a fatal decision. In May 1937, at America's Lakehurst airship facility, *Hindenburg*'s swastika-decorated tail caught fire at the mooring mast. Within 34 seconds she was engulfed in flames as horrified spectators watched helplessly and a dramatic radio commentary was broadcast live. Of 97 on board, 62 survived.

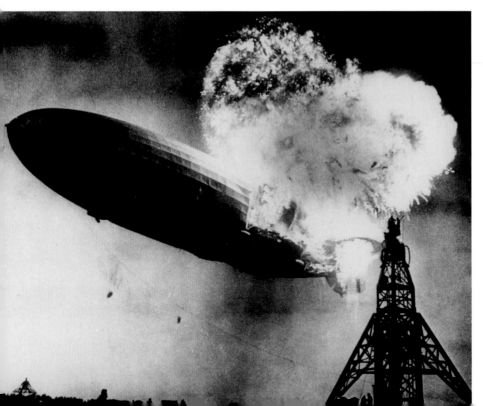

Lancastria sinking

Former Cunard liner
HMT Lancastria

The evacuation of 340,000 beleaguered British and French troops from Dunkirk by early June 1940 was a minor miracle for the Allies. But around 150,000 assorted British military personnel and civilians were left behind and word got around that those who could reach Saint-Nazaire, on the Loire Estuary, might yet escape the advancing *Wehrmacht*.

By June 17, assorted vessels were at the dockside or assembled off the port and HMT *Lancastria* was busy loading. This former Cunard liner carried 1,800 passengers in peacetime, but this was war. Around 9,000 were crammed aboard by the time she made ready to sail for England. Not far away HMT *Oronsay*, another requisitioned liner, was also embarking a seemingly endless stream of evacuees.

The *Wehrmacht* hadn't arrived, but the *Luftwaffe* ensured that this second mass evacuation would be subjected to maximum disruption. The *Oronsay* was hit but stayed afloat, though *Lancastria* was not so lucky. After waiting for a destroyer escort to protect her from submarine attack rather than leaving earlier, in mid afternoon she was hit three times by a Junkers JU-88 bomber and sank within 20 minutes. A large number of evacuees went down with the ship and many more died when German planes shot survivors in the water, igniting leaking fuel oil. Others simply drowned or choked on clinging oil. A total of 2,477 were rescued, thousands died.

The sinking saw the greatest loss of life in British maritime history and the worst casualty figure in a single engagement involving British troops in World War II. So great was the morale-sapping potential of the sinking that Winston Churchill suppressed the awful news and over time *Lancastria* became the forgotten disaster, though the number of casualties considerably exceeded the combined death toll of those famous earlier sinkings, *Titanic* and *Lusitania*.

WHEN:
June 17 1940
WHERE:
Off Saint-Nazaire, Loire-Atlantique, France
DEATH TOLL:
Unknown. However, best estimates suggest that over 5,000 evacuees perished during the attack and its tragic aftermath.
YOU SHOULD KNOW:
Despite being bombed, the *Oronsay* escaped from Saint-Nazaire with her full load of evacuees and returned to England, only to be subsequently sunk by an Italian submarine off the West African coast in 1942 with considerable loss of life.

Junyo Maru tragedy

WHEN:
September 18 1944
WHERE:
Off Java, Pacific Ocean
DEATH TOLL:
Around 1,500 POWs died, along with more than 4,000 Javanese and some Japanese guards and crew.
YOU SHOULD KNOW:
Survival didn't mean relief. The few remaining Javanese *romushas* (slave labourers) were worked to death, and barely 100 of 700 POWs saved from the sea survived the brutal conditions and intense heat of the Sumatra Railway construction camps.

In World War II the Japanese treated captives with extreme cruelty, and never was this more evident than when prisoners of war (POWs) were moved around the Pacific in rustbucket steamers from one forced-labour assignment to another. In defiance of the Geneva Convention, these hellish transports carried no red cross to identify them as prison ships, so many were sunk by Allied aircraft or submarines. This resulted in thousands of prisoners dying by 'friendly fire'.

No single disaster equalled that of *Junyo Maru*. The old single-stack steamer had been built before World War I and was just over 120 m (400 ft) long. In September 1944 she was sailing up the west coast of Java from Batavia (now Jakarta) to Padang, where her human cargo would work on the infamous Sumatra Railway, intended to transport coal from coast to coast. At least 6,500 unfortunate people had been packed aboard, comprising around 2,300 POWs – British, Dutch, Australian, Indonesian and American – together with 4,200 Javanese slave labourers. Conditions aboard were indescribably bad, with minimal latrine facilities and an acute shortage of water, compounded by sardine-like overcrowding.

The efforts of two escort ships were desultory. It was a serious omission. The British Triton-class submarine *Tradewind* was lurking and – with no idea what *Junyo Maru* was carrying – fired four torpedoes. Two struck home, causing pandemonium as packed prisoners fought to escape bamboo cages in the holds. Life rafts were tossed overboard but *Junyo Maru* settled quickly, the bow rose and she sank by the stern. As men in the water struggled to survive, the night filled with the desperate cries of dying men. When dawn broke and survivors were picked up, the extent of this terrible tragedy became apparent. More than 5,500 had gone down with the ship or died in the water.

MV *Wilhelm Gustloff* disaster

'Strength through joy' was the slogan of the state-controlled leisure organization in Nazi Germany. The *Kraft durch Freude* (KdF) was set up to persuade Germans of the benefits of National Socialism, becoming the world's largest tour operator in the 1930s. When taking cruises on the KdF's purpose-built flagship MV *Wilhelm Gustloff*, working-class Germans enjoyed the sort of holidays previously reserved for affluent vacationers.

Cruises abruptly ended as World War II loomed. In 1939 the ship brought the German Condor Legion back from Spain after the Spanish Civil War, before serving as a hospital ship. Thereafter, *Wilhelm Gustloff* became a floating barracks for naval personnel at Gdynia, a Baltic coast port. There the ship stayed until 1945, when it became part of Operation Hannibal, the German evacuation of over a million civilians and military personnel as the Red Army advanced on Prussia. In late January, the liner meant to transport fewer than 1,500 passengers was packed with over 10,000 people consisting of crew, various military personnel and nearly 9,000 civilians – all desperate to escape the rampaging Russians.

Ignoring the advice of an experienced submariner who suggested sailing close to shore, the senior captain headed for deep water. After nightfall, when informed of an approaching convoy of minesweepers, he obligingly put on *Wilhelm Gustloff*'s navigation lights. The Soviet submarine *S-13* needed no second invitation to join the turkey shoot, firing three torpedoes that all struck the nicely illuminated target. The carnage aboard the stricken ship was terrible. Torpedoes killed hundreds, many more died in the mad scramble to escape lower decks, and those who ended up in the water faced icy conditions. Rescue ships were quickly on the scene, saving around 1,200, but thousands died in the greatest loss of life ever recorded in a single maritime disaster.

WHEN:
January 30 1945
WHERE:
Baltic Sea
DEATH TOLL:
Unknown, as no civilian manifest existed. However, the latest research suggests that around 9,400 people perished in the disaster.
YOU SHOULD KNOW:
Not everyone knows this, but Switzerland had an active Nazi party and its leader was . . . Wilhelm Gustloff. Like the ship named in his honour, he came to a violent end – shot and killed in 1936 by a Jewish student incensed by Gustloff's rabid anti-Semitic activities.

A striking view of the gigantic Empire State Building with its upper stories enveloped in smoke and flame after it had been rammed by a US Army B-25 bomber.

WHEN:
July 28 1945
WHERE:
New York City, USA
DEATH TOLL:
14 people died (three crew and 11 office workers) and 26 were injured.

Empire State Building B-24 crash

If a pilot heading into the lofty urban jungle of New York City on a foggy morning rejects the chance to land at LaGuardia Airport and is told by the tower 'From where I'm sitting I can't see the top of the Empire State Building', the outcome would not be entirely unpredictable. That's precisely the situation that Lt Col William Smith found himself facing one Saturday morning in July 1945 as he piloted a USAAF B-25 Mitchell bomber towards Newark to pick up a senior officer. After showing up over LaGuardia, he requested a weather report and rashly carried on.

Diving low to get his bearings, Smith found himself among Manhattan's skyscrapers. After avoiding the New York Central Building he weaved between skyscrapers until he suddenly came face to face with the towering Empire State Building. Smith put the heavy bomber into a steep climb and tried to bank away, to no avail. The B-25 tore into the north side, smashing a hole 5.5 m (18 ft) wide and 6 m (20 ft) deep between the 79th and 80th floors, instantly killing the crew.

Aviation fuel ignited, immolating office workers and sending a cascade of fire down the outside of the building, also scorching stairwells and hallways within down to the 75th floor. Debris rained towards the street but, luckily, most landed on the structure's wider skirt. One engine was propelled right though the building, exploded through the opposite south-side windows and plummeted onto the roof of a building across 33rd Street, starting a fire that consumed the penthouse. Amazingly for such an explosive incident, the death toll was relatively light and there were not many serious injuries. The fire was put out inside 40 minutes and most of the Empire State Building was open for business the following Monday.

YOU SHOULD KNOW:
The B-25's second engine fell into a lift shaft and crashed down on an elevator car, which went into freefall until somewhat slowed by its automatic braking system. Miraculously, when rescuers reached the basement and untangled the wreckage, the two women in the mangled car were still alive. It remains the world's longest survived elevator fall.

Gillingham bus disaster

On a dark winter's evening in 1951 a 52-strong company of the Royal Marines Volunteer Cadet Corps set out to march from Gillingham's Melville Barracks to the Royal Naval Barracks in Chatham to watch a boxing tournament. Regular Marines officer Lt Clarence Carter was in charge, assisted by cadet non-commissioned officers. The youthful marchers formed a column 15 m (50 ft) long, arranged into three platoons.

In Dock Road, outside the gates of Chatham Royal Naval Dockyard, they had reached a dark section of road where a streetlight had failed when a Chatham & District Traction Company bus approached from behind. According to Lt Carter, who saw it coming and told the boys to edge as close as possible to the side of the road, the double-decker was travelling at 65 kph (40 mph). To his horror, the bus did not move out to pass, but ploughed straight through the marchers before eventually stopping.

At the wheel was 57-year-old John Samson, a driver with 40 years' experience. But he was using only sidelights, despite darkness and eddying fog, and most of the cadets wore dark-blue uniforms. Samson claimed he never saw the column and didn't realize he'd hit anyone, saying his speed was barely 30 kph (20 mph). After stopping, he found the street strewn with dead and dying youngsters. Lt Carter had been knocked down and seemed dazed, but was otherwise uninjured.

There had never been greater loss of life in a British road accident and there would later be a grand military funeral for victims in Rochester Cathedral, attended by many dignitaries, after which thousands of local people watched the cortege proceed to Gillingham Cemetery. One positive legacy of the disaster is that British military marchers on public roads always show a rear-facing red light at night.

WHEN:
December 4 1951
WHERE:
Gillingham, Kent, UK
DEATH TOLL:
17 died at the scene, some as young as ten years old, with a further seven dying in hospital, most on the same night. Another 18 were injured.
YOU SHOULD KNOW:
The inquest verdict was Accidental Death, but John Samson was still convicted of dangerous driving. He was fined just £20 and banned from driving for three years. The parents of dead boys shared £10,000 in compensation paid out by the Chatham & District Traction Company.

Harrow & Wealdstone rail crash

WHEN:
October 8 1952
WHERE:
Wealdstone, London, UK
DEATH TOLL:
112 died, 340 were injured.
YOU SHOULD KNOW:
Despite taking the full force of both collisions, the steam loco hauling the Perth express – Coronation class No 46242 *City of Glasgow* – was found to be reparable and returned to service. The other engines involved in this disastrous crash had to be scrapped.

October 8 1952 had been a foggy morning, but as the local passenger train from Tring stood at the up platform of Harrow & Wealdstone Station embarking passengers for London's Euston Station, the fog had cleared, the sun was breaking through and visibility was good. Even so, the driver of the overnight sleeper express from Perth in Scotland passed a distant signal set at yellow (caution) without slowing, possibly because it was momentarily obscured by the smoke from a passing goods train.

Driver Jones would not live to explain the lapse, for he also passed the outer home signal – a high-level semaphore arm set at 'stop', perhaps because he was still looking for the low-level distant signal. Only when he saw the inner home signal some 172 m (565 ft) from the station did he apply the brakes. It was far too late to avert England's worst-ever rail crash. At 08.19 the express ploughed into the back of the stationery Tring local at 97 kph (60 mph), the impact sounding like a massive explosion as wreckage was scattered across platforms and adjacent lines.

Immediately, a fast-moving express pulled by two engines, bound for Liverpool and Manchester, hit debris on the adjacent line and derailed violently, slewing across the down platform and bringing down part of the station's footbridge. In a few seconds of violent carnage, over 100 people died and nearly 350 were injured. A total of 16 carriages and vans were destroyed, 13 of which were compressed into a heap of wreckage just 41 m (135 ft) long, 16 m (52 ft) wide and 9 m (30 ft) tall. It took several days to remove bodies from the tangled mass of twisted metal. The accident enquiry found the cause of this major rail disaster to be inexplicable driver error.

Scenes of total devastation at the triple train crash at Harrow & Wealdstone Station.

Lewisham rail crash

St John's Station cannot be reached from the road, but is accessed by a pedestrian bridge from St John's Vale. It is located in the London Borough of Lewisham and was the scene of a terrible accident in December 1957. An early evening electric commuter train outbound from Charing Cross to Hayes was stopped by a red light just past the station, halting with the last carriage beneath a rail bridge carrying the Lewisham to Nunhead line.

Racing up from behind came a delayed Cannon Street to Ramsgate train, hauled by the steam loco *Spitfire*. There was fog in the cutting between New Cross and St John's, where signals were on the right. Steam engines were left-hand drive and exhaust smoke made visibility even worse on foggy nights, so it was customary for drivers to ask the fireman to lean out on the right to read the signals.

Driver W J Trew didn't do so, and failed to spot two yellow 'cautions' approaching St John's. He did see a red signal at the far end of the platform and braked, but *Spitfire* was still travelling at 55 kph (35 mph) when it hit the back of the stationary Hayes train at 18.20, telescoping rear coaches. The crashing steam train hit the Lewisham-Nunhead bridge, which collapsed onto the first three coaches, crushing them. Above, a quick-thinking driver managed to stop his train just in time to prevent it tumbling from the demolished bridge onto wreckage below. After a difficult and dangerous operation by emergency services, the last victims were extracted by midnight. There were 90 dead, with nearly 175 seriously injured.

Driver Trew was blamed for the crash and tried for manslaughter. The jury failed to agree a verdict and at retrial he was discharged owing to severe stress-induced mental illness.

WHEN:
December 4 1957
WHERE:
Lewisham, London, UK
DEATH TOLL:
90 were killed and 173 injured.
YOU SHOULD KNOW:
After Lewisham, British Rail was again criticized for not speeding up the installation of the Automatic Warning System (AWS) that would have prevented the crash. This had been called for after the catastrophic Harrow & Wealdstone crash five years earlier, but was still not mandatory when the Southwell rail crash happened 40 years later.

Firemen and rescue workers toil through the night to reach the trapped passengers at Lewisham.

USS *Thresher* sinking

WHEN:
April 10 1963
WHERE:
North Atlantic Ocean
DEATH TOLL:
139 US Navy personnel and civilian
technicians died.
YOU SHOULD KNOW:
The joint American-French
expedition aboard the RV *Knorr*
that located the wreck of *Titanic* in
September 1985 was secretly funded
by the US Navy, on condition that
the oceanographers first found
and photographed the sunken
USS *Thresher* and the US Navy's
other missing nuclear sub,
USS *Scorpion*, lost in 1967. This was
duly done before the dramatic
discovery of *Titanic*'s long-lost
remains was achieved.

In the early 1960s the pride of the US Navy's submarine fleet was SSN-593, the second sub to bear the proud name USS *Thresher* (the first served throughout World War II). The reborn *Thresher* was lead boat in a new class of nuclear-powered attack submarines.

Commissioned in 1961, she undertook extensive sea trials to test advanced technological systems. There were minor setbacks, as when her generator failed in port while the reactor was shut down, necessitating partial evacuation as temperature within the hull rose sharply. She was also hit by a tug in a separate incident, requiring repairs followed by a thorough overhaul.

In early April 1963, *Thresher* began more trials. First came deep-diving tests, some 350 km (220 mi) off Cape Cod, Massachusetts. Accompanied by the submarine support ship USS *Skylark*, she embarked on the first of a series of deep dives. As *Thresher* neared maximum test depth, a distorted message reached *Skylark* through the underwater telephone system suggesting that the crew was experiencing minor difficulties. It was the last communication ever received from the doomed submarine and gradually the awful realization that she had sunk with all hands dawned on those at the surface.

The subsequent enquiry concluded that a joint in the sub's salt-water piping system had failed, the leak creating a short-circuit that caused the reactor to shut down. With propulsion lost, *Thresher* was unable to 'drive' back to the surface or even blow her tanks successfully (the valves froze). She simply sank to the depth where she imploded under intense water pressure. The shocking loss of *Thresher* led the US Navy to accelerate SUBSAFE, a rigorous quality-control programme applied to the construction of nuclear submarines whereby hulls are built to maximum possible strength and systems within can function in the event of unexpected flooding.

Japanese air crashes

It's said that bad luck always comes in threes, and so it proved in 1966 when Japan experienced three catastrophic air crashes in quick succession. The first was a Boeing 727 that came down in Tokyo Bay in early February on final approach to Haneda Airport. Most passengers were returning from a winter carnival on the island of Hokkaido and all died, along with the crew – a total of 139 fatalities. The pilot was attempting a non-instrument night landing when the aircraft vanished from radar screens 10 km (6 mi) short of touchdown. It wasn't long before fishermen were pulling bodies from the sea and the shattered fuselage was found on the seabed and recovered – still full of corpses.

A month later, Canadian Pacific Airlines Flight 402 from Hong Kong to Vancouver had a stopover in Japan. Upon arrival above Tokyo International, poor visibility precluded a landing. After circling, the pilot decided to divert to Taiwan but the control tower told him visibility had improved and he attempted to put the McDonnell Douglas DC-8 down. He misjudged the approach and landing gear struck a lighting beacon. The plane went out of control and hit the sea wall bordering the airport, disintegrating into a trail of blazing wreckage. Amazingly, eight passengers survived. Ten crew and 54 passengers did not.

The next day, BOAC Speedbird 911 took off from Tokyo International bound for Hong Kong, from whence ill-fated Flight 402 had originated. Passing the still-smouldering remains of the DC-8, BOAC's Boeing 707 took off and soared away towards Mount Fuji. Above the iconic volcano the plane broke up in flight and crashed, killing all 124 souls aboard – 113 passengers and 11 crew. The cause was violent air turbulence, completing a tragic trio of disastrous air crashes in barely a month.

WHEN:
February 2, March 4 and March 5 1966
WHERE:
Tokyo Bay, Tokyo International Airport, Mount Fuji, Japan
DEATH TOLL:
The cumulative total for the three disasters was 327 casualties.
YOU SHOULD KNOW:
In fact, there were *five* air crashes in Japan during 1966. In August a Japan Air Lines Convair crashed and five died. Then All Nippon Airways lost Flight 533 in November when a Japanese-built turboprop airliner crashed after an aborted landing at Matsuyama Airport, killing 50. The combined effect of all these fatal crashes caused a sharp dip in demand for domestic flights within Japan.

Moorgate Tube crash

The London Underground system – not altogether affectionately known as 'The Tube' – had seen assorted accidents since the first section opened in 1863. None was as serious as a crash that happened at Moorgate Station in 1975.

The 08.39 train from Drayton Park on the Northern Line's Highbury Branch was due to terminate at platform nine, where passengers would transfer to alternative lines.

Instead of stopping, the six-car train accelerated past the platform on a spur that literally proved to be a dead end, entering a 20 m (66 ft) overrun tunnel. The train demolished a warning light, ploughed through a sand trap and hit hydraulic buffers – then a brick wall – at 65 kph (40 mph). It would have been catastrophic under any circumstances, but the run-off was a full-height railway tunnel allowing the first three cars to ride up over each other. The first was crushed into a V-shape, the second landed on top and was in turn telescoped by the third, which split in half.

Mangled wreckage filled the confined space, presenting emergency services with a daunting challenge. The final survivor was not freed for 12 hours and the body of driver Leslie Newson was recovered over four days later, the last of 43 confirmed fatalities. The cause of the disaster was obvious – Newson failed to brake – but the reason was never established. He definitely didn't release the 'Dead Man's Handle', a device that must be physically depressed to maintain power to Tube trains, and witnesses saw him sitting bolt upright and staring unnaturally ahead as the train gathered speed past the platform. The best explanations seem to be an inexplicable suicide or rare type of brain seizure where the victim is momentarily paralysed. The Coroner's Jury settled for a verdict of 'Accidental Death'.

Granville train disaster

It was a morning much like any Tuesday in New South Wales – until disaster struck a packed eight-car commuter train from Mount Victoria in the Blue Mountains as it approached the suburb of Granville, 22 km (14 mi) west of Sydney in January 1977. Just short of Granville Station, the train jumped the tracks at 08.10 and smashed into the overhead Bold Street road bridge supports. The carnage that ensued became Australia's worst-ever rail disaster, taking over 80 lives and injuring more than 200.

The derailed engine and two carriages emerged from beneath the bridge, whereupon the first carriage had its roof ripped off by an overhead gantry – with fatal consequences for several passengers. The remaining carriages ground to a halt, with the rear of the third carriage and front of the fourth under the bridge. Agonizingly, the bridge's heavy concrete and steel central section collapsed ten seconds later, bringing a number of cars down with it and pancaking half of each carriage below.

The aftermath was horrifying for those who struggled to deal with the shattered train. Emergency services were faced with the harrowing task of trying to extract survivors – plus horribly broken and mutilated corpses – from wreckage that been almost completely flattened in places. Many survivors were badly trapped and had serious crush injuries. Worse still, rescuers had to cope with many lucid victims who conversed bravely with them until finally freed, at which point they died almost immediately from crush syndrome – renal failure following the release of muscle myoglobins that build up in trapped limbs. The last survivor was not released for 48 hours but he, too, tragically died shortly afterwards.

The crash was caused by bad track maintenance, but it is now generally agreed that the full extent of official negligence was covered up at the time.

WHEN:
January 18 1977
WHERE:
Granville, New South Wales, Australia
DEATH TOLL:
83 died and over 213 were significantly injured.
YOU SHOULD KNOW:
The electric locomotive that derailed at Granville was an ill-starred engine. Built in 1957, the Co+Co 46 class No 4620 had previously featured in a dramatic accident in 1965, when the brakes failed as it hauled a goods train down from the Blue Mountains towards Sydney. The runaway train reached a speed of 160 kph (100 mph) before derailing. After Granville, 4620 was put into storage before being scrapped in 1979.

Tenerife aircraft collision

The holiday island of Tenerife was the scene of the world's worst aviation disaster in March 1977, as a result of pilot error, technical limitations at Los Rodeos Airport (now Tenerife North Airport), communications failures and appalling weather. The single-runway field was fogbound when KLM Flight 4805, a Boeing 747 jumbo jet, taxied out prior to take-off. After travelling to the far end of the runway, the Dutch aircraft did an about-turn and was ready to go.

Following behind was Pan-Am's Flight 1736, another jumbo. This was told to back-taxi – head up the runway against the direction of take-off – before turning onto a parallel taxiway at the third exit. Conditions were poor and the flight crew failed to spot their turn-off. Meanwhile, despite visibility being half the required 700 m (3,000 ft), 4805's captain commenced his take-off, assuming 1736 had cleared the runway and wrongly presuming he'd been given clearance by the tower. It was a catastrophic misunderstanding.

The KLM pilot saw the Pan-Am jumbo too late and – despite attempting desperate emergency lift-off – his aircraft's undercarriage and engines clipped the Pan-Am plane's spine above the wings, even as the American pilot took hopeless evasive action. KLM 4805 became airborne, but stalled before smashing into the runway – sliding for 300 m (985 ft) before coming to rest and, fully fuelled, exploding into a fireball that incinerated all 248 people aboard. Back down the runway Pan-Am 1736 was also ablaze, the deadly inferno trapping 335 passengers and crew who died. There were survivors – 56 passengers and five crew, including pilots.

Tragically, neither aircraft should have been at Los Rodeos. The destination for both had been Gran Canaria International on Las Palmas, but a terrorist bomb had exploded there, causing several aircraft to be diverted to the cramped regional airport on Tenerife.

Engines from the wrecked jumbos littered the area around the runway.

Los Alfaques disaster

The small Mediterranean resort of Sant Carles de la Ràpita in southern Catalonia has long been a popular tourist destination. July is prime holiday season in Spain and back in 1978 the nearby campsite of Los Alfaques (The Sandbars) was crowded with carefree vacationers, mostly foreign nationals. Little did they know or care that a tanker truck was loading flammable liquid propylene at a state-owned refinery north of Tarragona, further up the coast. The maximum permitted load was just over 19 tonnes, but the tanker took on 23 tonnes.

Furthermore, the driver had been instructed to take the old N-340 coast road, rather than pay a toll on the parallel A-7 motorway. The combination of illegal load and penny-pinching route would have fatal consequences. Accounts of what happened as the tanker reached Los Alfaques vary. Some say a tyre burst, causing the vehicle to swerve and hit a wall, rupturing the tank. Others claim the tanker sprung a pressure leak with an audible bang opposite the site, or was already leaking. In any event, it stopped outside the camp gates at around 02.35. A white cloud of gaseous propylene was carried into the camp on the breeze, drifting towards a disco as curious spectators gathered to observe the phenomenon.

When the deadly cloud got there, it found an ignition source. Flames flashed back to the tanker. It erupted instantly, a devastating BLEVE (Boiling Liquid Expanding Vapour Explosion) creating a huge fireball and large crater. Intense heat of over 1,000°F immolated everything within a 300 m (985 ft) radius, including tents, vehicles, caravans, people, the disco and all its occupants. Over 150 were killed instantly, including the tanker driver, and more than 200 were severely injured. Many burn victims would later die in hospital or be scarred for life.

The aftermath of the fuel tanker explosion at Los Alfaques campsite.

WHEN:
July 11 1978
WHERE:
Sant Carles de la Ràpita, near Alcanar, Catalonia, Spain
DEATH TOLL:
Around 220 died (on the day and subsequently).
YOU SHOULD KNOW:
Four employees of the ENPETROL refinery where the liquid propylene was loaded and two from the client company (Paular, now REPSOL, also state-owned) were convicted of criminal negligence and received short prison terms, later quashed or suspended. The two companies paid out massive compensation to survivors and victims' families.

The wrecked DC-10 resting on the runway.

Flight 191 crash

The worst airline disaster on American soil took place in May 1979 at Chicago's O'Hare International Airport. American Airlines Flight 191 was a three-engined McDonnell Douglas DC-10 jet bound for Los Angeles, taking off at around 15.05 with over 270 people aboard. The weather was clear and a brisk northeasterly breeze was blowing. As the airliner hurtled down the runway everything seemed normal – until a horrified air traffic controller saw the left-hand engine separate, flip back over the wing and crash to the runway.

The experienced pilots – Captain Walter Lux and First Officer James Dillard – knew it was too late to abort the take-off but immediately attempted the correct procedure for climbing on two engines. But the departing power plant had severed hydraulic lines that controlled leading-edge slats designed to lower a wing's stall speed, ripped a section from the front of the wing and disabled instruments that would have informed Lux of the precise situation. Hydraulic fluid drained away, wing slats retracted and the unbalanced DC-10 cartwheeled to the left and slammed into a hangar on the old Ravenswood Airport site after being aloft for just

WHEN:
May 25 1979
WHERE:
Chicago, Illinois, USA
DEATH TOLL:
There were 273 fatalities (258 passengers, 13 crew, two on the ground).
YOU SHOULD KNOW:
The crash was used to explain the sudden disappearance of one Diana Chorba. She was murdered around the time of Flight 191's crash and her daughter was told she had been aboard to avert suspicion. Her killer was finally convicted in 2001.

31 seconds. The impact and fire killed all aboard the plane and two workers on the ground, and showered a nearby trailer park with burning debris.

The engine separation that caused the crash was a result of poor maintenance by American Airlines, whose team had damaged the mounting pylon during an engine change two months earlier. But there had been an earlier fatal accident involving a Turkish Airlines DC-10 in Paris and two more DC-10 crashes followed swiftly – Western Airlines Flight 2605 in Mexico City and Air New Zealand Flight 901 in Antarctica. With over 650 lives lost, all DC-10s were grounded until minor design faults were rectified and maintenance procedures tightened up.

Sinking of the *Derbyshire*

The Liverpool-registered merchant ship MV *Derbyshire* was a state-of-the-art bulk carrier when she was launched in 1976. The length of three football pitches and as wide as a six-lane motorway, the *Derbyshire* had been built with the capability to convey both liquid and solid cargoes. When she set sail from the west coast of Canada on July 11 1980 she was carrying over 150,000 tonnes of iron ore and was bound for Japan.

Early September found her in the East China Sea making her way towards her final destination. It was the height of the storm season and the *Derbyshire* had the misfortune to run into typhoon Orchid. The last radio transmission from the ship was received on September 9; it reported a heavy tropical storm. Some time on that or the following day the giant ship sank without trace and with all hands on board. The area was searched for a week afterwards but nothing was found and the ship was declared lost.

There matters might have rested, and the loss of the *Derbyshire* would have been regarded as an unexplained and terrible maritime accident, had it not been for the tenacity of the families of the crewmen. It was seven years before the British government finally agreed to hold a formal inquiry into the incident, but the families rejected its conclusion as a whitewash. It was not until 1994 that an intensive search operation was finally mounted; remarkably, the wreck was located within 24 hours, even though it lay over 4 km (2.5 mi) down on the seabed. The formal inquiry was reopened in April 2000. The conclusion this time was that the vessel's buoyancy had been compromised and that the cargo hold covers had simply collapsed beneath the sheer weight of the mountainous seas.

WHEN:
September 9 or 10 1980
WHERE:
East China Sea, between Taiwan and Japan
DEATH TOLL:
All 44 people on board died: 42 crewmen and two wives.
YOU SHOULD KNOW:
The MV *Derbyshire* is the largest British merchant ship ever to have been lost at sea.

141

Bihar train accident

WHEN:
June 6 1981
WHERE:
Mansi, Bihar, India
DEATH TOLL:
The official death toll was given as 268, but over 300 passengers were never accounted for. Some estimates put the fatalities as high as 800.
YOU SHOULD KNOW:
Predominantly agricultural but with a growing service sector, Bihar remains one of the poorest and most heavily populated states in India.

One of the positive legacies bequeathed to India by the Raj (as the British rule there was known) was the network of railways which extended into every corner of the vast sub-continent. On June 6 1981 a typically crowded passenger train was travelling through the northeast Indian state of Bihar, some 400 km (250 mi) from Calcutta. Around 1,000 passengers had squeezed into the train's nine coaches. As the train was crossing the Baghmati River outside the town of Mansi, the rear seven coaches came off the rails and plunged into the water below.

It was the beginning of the monsoon season in India, so not only was the river swollen to well above its normal levels but the railway tracks were also wet and slippery. Hundreds of people were swept away and drowned in the swirling, muddy waters. It took the rescue services hours to arrive at the scene of the accident, and their work was hampered by the treacherous conditions of the monsoon rains. It is unlikely, however, that there were many people who could have been saved.

The reason for one of India's worst rail accidents is still disputed. Some sources maintain that it was caused by the atrocious weather conditions and that the train was struck either by a cyclone or a flash flood. However, a persistent story has it that the driver, a devout Hindu, braked hard on seeing a cow ahead about to cross the tracks. Cows are sacred animals in the Hindu religion and the driver would not have wanted to harm it. When the brakes were applied, the wheels failed to grip on the wet rails and so the carriages came off the tracks.

Crowds gaze in disbelief at an overturned railway carriage in the river.

Mount Osutaka air crash

A routine domestic flight from Tokyo to Osaka ended in the world's worst accident involving a single aircraft when a Japan Airlines Boeing 747 crashed into a ridge near Mount Osutaka in the Japanese Alps. Flight 123 took off from Tokyo's Haneda airport shortly after 18.00 on August 12 1985 for the 50-minute scheduled flight to Osaka. On board were 509 passengers, mostly holidaymakers, and 15 crew. Barely ten minutes into the flight the pilot reported a problem with the rear of the plane; he intended to turn back and make an emergency landing. Moments later, however, he radioed that he was no longer in control of the aircraft. The final message received at air traffic control said that the plane was lost. With the steering disabled, the aircraft veered off course and headed inland towards the mountains of central Japan.

Rescue workers struggling on the slopes of the mountain where the crash occurred.

When rescue and salvage teams got to the scene of the crash, they found debris scattered over a wide area of the remote mountainside. The desperate search for survivors was to little avail; only four people emerged from the tragedy alive. The accident happened just two months after another Boeing jet had crashed into the sea off southern Ireland with the loss of all hands, so there was intense pressure on the company to identify the cause of the Japanese crash and guarantee the safety of its fleet.

The cause was eventually found to have been a faulty repair seven years previously to the aircraft's rear pressure bulkhead, which had been damaged in a tailstrike incident during a landing. A single row of rivets had been used instead of the regulation double row; this caused the failure of the bulkhead, vital for maintaining cabin pressure. The resulting decompression ruptured the plane's hydraulics, thereby disabling its steering system.

WHEN:
August 12 1985
WHERE:
Near Mount Osutaka, Honshu, Japan
DEATH TOLL:
520
YOU SHOULD KNOW:
The well-known Japanese violin virtuoso Diana Yukawa lost her father in the crash. She never knew him as she was born three weeks after his death, but in 2009 on the 24th anniversary of the disaster she played her Guarneri violin at the accident scene.

Herald of Free Enterprise ferry disaster

WHEN:
March 6 1987
WHERE:
Outside the port of Zeebrugge,
Belgium
DEATH TOLL:
193
YOU SHOULD KNOW:
New safety measures and
regulations were introduced on all
British ships as a consequence of the
disaster; these included cameras
being fitted to a ship's bow so the
bridge can verify that doors have
been closed before sailing.

*The ferry rests on the sandbank
outside Zeebrugge.*

When the Townsend Thoresen car ferry *Herald of Free Enterprise*
left the Belgian port of Zeebrugge on the evening of March 6 1987
she was carrying some 650 passengers and their vehicles.
Conditions at sea were calm so they settled down to what should
have been a smooth passage across the English Channel to Dover.
The ferry was barely 100 m (330 ft) out, however, when observers
on shore watched in horror as the large vessel began to capsize;
within two minutes it had rolled over and come to rest on its port
side in the shallow water. Rescue services were quick to the scene
and took over 400 people off the ship; but the sheer speed of events
meant that many passengers had no chance of escape and perished
in the freezing waters. The *Herald* ended up on a sandbank; had
she gone over in deeper water, the death toll would undoubtedly
have been higher.

It seemed unlikely to most onlookers that a simple accident

could have caused the catastrophe. The *Herald of Free Enterprise* was a 'ro-ro' (roll-on roll-off) type ferry and it soon became clear that the bow doors had been left open when the ferry sailed; water had instantly flooded the car decks, destabilizing the ship and causing her to keel over. P&O, the company which now owned Townsend Thoresen, were heavily criticized in the public inquiry that followed; its report highlighted a 'disease of sloppiness' at all levels of the organization. The coroner's inquest held in Dover returned a verdict of unlawful killing, which led to P&O being charged with corporate manslaughter as well as seven employees facing individual manslaughter charges. Although the 1989 court case collapsed, it set an important precedent for corporate manslaughter being admissible in a British court of law.

Doña Paz ferry collision

Sea ferries are integral to the transport network linking the hundreds of islands which make up the Philippines. Millions of Filipinos use the ferries throughout the year; with air travel beyond the means of most it would be hard to imagine life there without them.

A few days before Christmas 1987 the MV *Doña Paz*, a Japanese-built ferry run by Sulpicio Lines, a Filipino ferry operator, set sail from the regional city of Tacloban on Leyte island, bound for the capital, Manila. It was an overnight journey and most of the passengers were asleep when late in the evening the *Doña Paz* collided with the oil tanker *Vector* as it was passing through the Tablas Strait, a busy shipping lane separating the two major islands of Mindoro and Panay.

A mid-sea collision in deep, shark-infested waters was bad enough, but what made this particular impact far worse was the cargo which the *Vector* was transporting: more than 8,000 barrels of gasoline. The deadly freight exploded and the resulting blaze spread rapidly through the passenger ship. The *Doña Paz* was grossly overcrowded, a far from uncommon occurrence in the region; many illegal tickets were sold on board at the last minute so precise passenger numbers will never be known, but there could well have been at least three times the vessel's authorized capacity of 1,500. Safety procedures were seriously deficient and would in any case have been of little use in such packed and chaotic conditions (it was claimed afterwards that the life-jacket cupboards had been locked). In an attempt to escape the inferno thousands leapt into the sea and drowned. Both vessels sank within hours.

WHEN:
December 20 1987
WHERE:
Tablas Strait, Sibuyan Sea, Philippines
DEATH TOLL:
The official death toll was given as 1,749. It is generally agreed, however, that over 4,300 people died in the tragedy, making it the world's worst peacetime maritime disaster.
YOU SHOULD KNOW:
It has never been established who was to blame for the collision. While there may have been only one junior crew member on the *Doña Paz*'s bridge at the time, it was also found that the *Vector* had been operating with a licence that had expired. As recently as July 2008 the oil company which had chartered the tanker was cleared by a Philippines court of any liability.

Iranians attending a 'Death to America' rally that was also a funeral for the victims.

Iran air flight 655

WHEN:
July 3 1988
WHERE:
Strait of Hormuz, Persian Gulf
DEATH TOLL:
290 passengers and crew, including 66 children.
YOU SHOULD KNOW:
Washington was eventually obliged to admit in the International Court of Justice that the USS *Vincennes* had been patrolling illegally in Iranian waters. Neither accepting responsibility nor apologizing for this disastrous action, Washington paid $131.8 million in compensation to Iran, further compensation going to the families of the 38 non-Iranians on board that day. In August 1988, George Bush Senior said 'I'll never apologize for the United States of America, ever. I don't care what the facts are'. Unsurprisingly, the incident has coloured relations between both countries ever since.

In 1980, shortly after Ayatollah Khomeini had seized power and declared Iran an Islamic Republic, Iraq invaded its neighbour (with the covert blessing of the USA). In the Persian Gulf there were attacks against oil tankers and merchant vessels, so the Americans sent warships and aircraft to provide protection for shipping. The USS *Vincennes*, carrying the state-of-the-art Aegis combat system, was deployed to the area, arriving in May 1988 under the command of Captain William C Rogers III.

On the morning of July 3 1988 a scheduled Iranian Airbus departed from Bandar Abbas, *en route* to Dubai – a mere 28-minute flight. Marginally delayed, it flew within its assigned Iranian commercial air corridor, transmitting the civilian aircraft code and speaking English to the civilian control tower. Seven minutes later, during its ascent, Flight 655 was shot down in flames by one or more missiles fired from USS *Vincennes*, taking with it 290 passengers and crew. There were no survivors.

USS *Vincennes* quickly reported that they had believed themselves to be under attack from an Iranian F-14 fighter plane, though it was immediately apparent that an appalling tragedy had occurred. The subsequent naval enquiry produced a startling whitewash, claiming Flight 655 was descending in attack mode outside its allotted airspace when it was destroyed. A month later the authorities admitted that it had in fact been at 3,658 m (12,000 ft) and was ascending well within its flight path. Later, the US Navy reported that the ship's crew were suffering from psychological stress due to first-time combat.

The crew of USS *Vincennes* all received medals and Captain Rogers, who was thought trigger-happy and arrogant by several high-ranking colleagues, retired in 1991 with the Legion of Merit. The 290 passengers who died were effectively forgotten.

Ufa train explosion

As Russian leader Mikhail Gorbachev struggled to push through his radical reform programme while at the same time holding together the Soviet Union and maintaining the Communist Party's commanding role, his nation was beset in the late 1980s by a series of disasters which brought home just how antiquated was the state of the country's infrastructure and ailing public services. Hungary had already started dismantling its border fences with Austria (the first step in a process which led to the collapse of the Soviet fiefdoms in Eastern Europe) when in early June 1989 Gorbachev's attention was suddenly drawn to events closer to home, albeit many hundreds of miles from Moscow.

As two busy trains were passing one another on a stretch of the Trans-Siberian railway east of the city of Ufa near the Ural Mountains, a huge explosion ripped both trains apart. Seven carriages were reduced to ash by the blast, while both locomotives and the remaining 37 carriages were destroyed. There were some 1,300 passengers on board the trains which were travelling between Novosibirsk and the Black Sea resort of Adler. Many of the passengers were children, either going on or returning from holidays at seaside Pioneer Camps.

Although rumours of sabotage started to circulate shortly afterwards, what looks on the surface to have been a freak accident turns out to have been caused in all probability by negligent maintenance. An undetected leak in a natural gas pipeline which ran alongside the tracks a few hundred yards away had created a highly flammable cloud in the air; this was ignited by sparks from the passing trains. Engineers on the pipeline had apparently noticed a drop in pressure a few hours before, but had restored it to normal levels without first checking for leaks.

WHEN:
June 4 1989
WHERE:
Near Ufa, Russia
DEATH TOLL:
The official death toll stands at 575, making it by far Russia's worst rail disaster. A memorial at the site, however, lists 675 names, and some sources state that as many as 780 may have died.
YOU SHOULD KNOW:
The force of the explosion was estimated to have been the equivalent of ten kilotons of TNT, not far short of the power of the atomic bomb dropped on Hiroshima in 1945.

The *Marchioness* disaster

WHEN:
August 20 1989
WHERE:
The River Thames, London, UK
DEATH TOLL:
51
YOU SHOULD KNOW:
In 1995, the jury returned verdicts of unlawful killing on those who drowned. For a decade, the action group founded by several survivors and their families pushed for an investigation. Bizarrely, Captain Henderson was allowed to retain his Master's Certificate despite the highly critical report that eventually appeared in 2001. As a result of the *Marchioness* tragedy many new safety measures were put into place on the Thames, including lifeboat rescue stations that have since proved their worth many times over.

Many people living in Great Britain still remember learning of the appalling disaster that befell a leisure cruiser on the River Thames in the early hours of the morning of August 20 1989.

Photographers' agent Jonathan Phang had put considerable effort into organizing the perfect 26th birthday party for his best friend, merchant banker Antonio de Vasconcellos. The evening began with dinner for eight, followed by champagne and birthday cake for 30. Jonathan had booked a River Thames pleasure cruiser for the party itself, collecting canapés, balloons and party poppers on the way. The *Marchioness*, packed with guests, finally set off after midnight.

Just 15 minutes later, near Cannon Street railway bridge, the *Marchioness* was holed through her side by the aggregate dredger *Bowbelle*. The *Marchioness* rolled, filling with water, the blow forcing her into the path of the *Bowbelle*, which ran straight over her. There were 131 people on board that night, including crew and party-goers. Most of those who survived the experience had been on the upper decks and were flung into the river by the collision. Like the birthday boy, many of the guests were only in their twenties – friends from student days, friends from the fashion industry and family. Of the eight who attended the dinner party, only Jonathan and Antonio's brother survived. Antonio himself did not.

The investigation found fault with both captains: no clear instructions were issued to the look-out of the *Bowbelle*, visibility from both wheelhouses was poor, and both vessels were in the centre of the river. Captain Henderson of the *Bowbelle*, who had downed six pints of beer during the course of that afternoon, was tried for failing to keep a proper look-out, but was acquitted by two separate juries.

The Marchioness *after the collision*

The sinking of the *Estonia*

On September 27 1994 the ferry *Estonia* set sail on a night voyage across the Baltic Sea from the port of Tallin in Estonia to Stockholm. She departed at 19.00 carrying 989 passengers and crew, as well as vehicles, and was due to dock at 09.30 the following morning, Tragically, the *Estonia* never arrived.

The weather was typically stormy for the time of year but, like all the other scheduled ferries on that day, the Estonia set off as usual. At roughly 01.00 a worrying sound of screeching metal was heard, but an immediate inspection of the bow visor showed nothing untoward. The ship suddenly listed 15 minutes later and soon alarms were sounding, including the lifeboat alarm. Shortly afterwards the *Estonia* rolled drastically to starboard. Those who had reached the decks had a chance of survival but those who had not were doomed as the angled corridors had become death traps. A Mayday signal was sent but power failure meant the ship's position was given imprecisely. The *Estonia* disappeared from the responding ships' radar screens at about 01.50.

The *Mariella* arrived at the scene at 02.12 and the first helicopter at 03.05. Of the 138 people rescued alive, one died later in hospital. Of the 310 people who had reached the decks, almost a third died of hypothermia. The final death toll was shockingly high – more than 850 people.

An official inquiry found that failure of the locks on the bow visor, which broke away under the punishing waves, caused water to flood the car deck and quickly capsize the ship. The report also noted a lack of action, delay in sounding the alarm, lack of guidance from the bridge and a failure to light distress flares.

The bow door of the Estonia *being lifted up from the seabed off Uto Island.*

WHEN:
September 28 1994
WHERE:
Near the Turku Archipelago, in the Baltic Sea
DEATH TOLL:
852 passengers and crew
YOU SHOULD KNOW:
The sinking of the *Estonia* was Europe's worst postwar maritime disaster.

The Mont Blanc tunnel fire

In 1954 a national charter was ratified by the French and Italian governments for the construction of a tunnel running beneath the Mont Blanc massif, between Chamonix in France and Courmayeur in Italy. It would be a two-lane stretch of road 11.6 km (7.25 mi) long and 8.6 m (28.2 ft) wide. The tunnel opened in July 1965 and quickly became a highly popular route for both passenger cars and freight lorries.

In March 1999 a Belgian freight vehicle, carrying margarine and flour, caught fire in the Italian section. At 10.53 driver Gilbert Degrave, realizing that smoke was appearing from beneath his lorry, halted immediately. He attempted to deal with the problem, but when his cab went up in flames he was forced back.

A couple of minutes later the tunnel fire alarm sounded, preventing further traffic from entering the tunnel. But almost 40 vehicles had already driven in from either side. Some tried to turn around and drive back, but larger vehicles couldn't manoeuvre in the narrow space. Most drivers closed their windows and waited for rescue, while a few escaped into the fire safety cubicles that were set at regular intervals along the tunnel walls. But the fire doors had been built to last for only two to four hours, not the 56 hours that the fire raged.

Thick smoke billowing out from the tunnel entrance.

WHEN:
March 24 1999
WHERE:
Mont Blanc Tunnel, Italy
DEATH TOLL:
39

150

The tunnel's ventilation system proved lethal, driving dense, black, toxic smoke and fumes back into the tunnel, which by now was without electricity. Fire trucks from both ends arrived fast, but their path was blocked by burning vehicles. Altogether 36 vehicles were involved in the fire, and 39 people died. Repairs and renovations took almost three years to complete. Today many new safety measures are in place and all HGVs are thoroughly checked before being allowed to travel.

YOU SHOULD KNOW:
In January 2005 16 companies and individuals were tried in Grenoble for manslaughter. On July 27 2005 13 of these were found guilty and received fines and suspended sentences. The head of security for the tunnel was given a six-month prison sentence.

Pile-up on Highway 401

The Macdonald-Cartier Freeway, or Highway 401, is the busiest freeway in North America. Starting just outside Windsor, Ontario, it ends 815 km (506 mi) later at the Quebec border. In September 1999 a terrible pile-up of 87 vehicles took place on the section running between Windsor and London, a stretch often referred to as 'Carnage Alley' due to the numerous accidents that have occurred there.

The 401, built during the 1950s, is narrow-laned, soft-shouldered and intersected by a strip of grass. It is mainly straight, which in itself has caused accidents with drivers occasionally falling asleep at the wheel. At 08.00 on September 3 1999 the sky was blue, with just a few puffs of fog left over from the previous night. No fog was forecast, but little did anyone know that there was a malfunction at the nearby Observation Station and that there was, in fact, a thick wall of fog on the road.

People were driving fast, many tailgating one another. Without warning, drivers in both directions were suddenly blanketed in dense fog. Braking hard, they found themselves slamming into the car in front while simultaneously being rammed by the vehicle behind, thus causing an unstoppable chain reaction. Car piled into car, vehicles slewed across the central strip into the opposite lanes, trucks piled into and over cars that had already crashed, and fire broke out.

When the fog lifted, broken glass lay everywhere and the horrific sounds of screaming victims could be heard. A total of 87 cars and trucks were scattered, wrecked and burning across 2 km (1.24 mi) of the freeway. Those who were able, ran for their lives but eight unfortunate people died and 40 were injured on that day in southern Ontario.

WHEN:
September 3 1999
WHERE:
Between London and Windsor, Ontario, Canada
DEATH TOLL:
Eight fatalities and 40 injured.
YOU SHOULD KNOW:
After the pile-up, paved shoulders, rumble strips and extra police patrols were added to the section, and improvements are ongoing. Extra lanes are being added and a central concrete barrier, known as an Ontario Tall-Wall, is being constructed in order to prevent accidents spilling across the lanes.

Ladbroke Grove rail crash

WHEN:
October 5 1999
WHERE:
Ladbroke Grove Junction, near
Paddington Station, London, UK
DEATH TOLL:
There were 31 deaths, including both
train drivers, and 523 were injured.
YOU SHOULD KNOW:
Two years earlier, this time at
Southall, there had been another
lethal crash on the Great Western
mainline in which seven people died
and 150 were injured. A joint inquiry
concerning both accidents made 39
safety recommendations. In 2004 a
£2 million fine was imposed on
Thames Trains for breaking health
and safety laws. In 2005 the Crown
Prosecution Service said it would not
prosecute any individuals. In 2007
Network Rail (formerly Railtrack),
who pleaded guilty to charges under
the Health and Safety at Work Act,
were fined £4 million, plus
£225,000 in costs.

The Ladbroke Grove rail crash, sometimes known as the Paddington train crash, occurred at 08.08 on October 5 1999. The accident involved a diesel train operated by Thames Trains, running from Paddington to Bedwyn, Wiltshire, and a First Great Western express train coming in from Cheltenham, Gloucestershire.

The trains crashed head-on at Ladbroke Grove Junction, just west of London's Paddington Station. A combined speed of 210 kph (130 mph) tossed and rolled carriages off the tracks. The first coach of the Thames train was wrecked and its load of fuel caused fire to spread throughout the train. The front coach of the express train was also totally burnt out. Altogether 31 people died and 523 others were injured, some extremely seriously. Ambulances and firefighters dashed to the site, and the vast plume of smoke that rose was visible for miles.

In December 2000 the Health and Safety Executive published their investigation on technical issues and the immediate handling of the aftermath of the crash. Lord Cullen conducted the Public Inquiry that followed in which it was established that Michael Hodder, driving the Thames train, had missed a red signal shortly before impact. Qualified for only 13 days, he appeared to have received no special instructions about his route.

A particularly shocking discovery was that, during the previous six years, eight other trains had also missed the same signal, fortunately without ill-effect; but drivers had already warned inspectors about the lack of visibility of both that and other signals. Lord Cullen criticized Railtrack, who were responsible for track maintenance and signalling, their staff in Slough for failing to send an 'emergency all stop' signal, and the Railway Inspectorate for their inspection procedures. Published in 2001, the report made 163 separate recommendations for improving safety.

Wreckage from the two rush-hour trains at Ladbroke Grove.

Concorde air crash

The iconic, supersonic aircraft Concorde was a remarkable engineering feat. Although no longer in service, no other passenger aircraft has yet surpassed it in speed or beauty. A joint venture between the English and French governments, Concorde was thus named because the French word translates as 'good understanding'.

On July 25 2000, Concorde (Air France flight 4590) took off from Charles de Gaulle airport near Paris, for John F Kennedy in New York – a three-and-a-half-hour trip – carrying 100 passengers and nine crew. The plane, chartered by a German tour company, was carrying passengers to New York to begin a 16-day cruise to South America. Their dream holiday was never to be because, within seconds of take-off, one of two engines on the left side burst into flames.

Two minutes later the plane crashed into a hotel in Gonesse, a town just north of Paris. Eyewitnesses saw a huge fireball and plumes of thick, black smoke when Concorde hit the ground. Parts of the hotel, as well as Concorde itself, were reduced to a horrific tangle of burnt and twisted debris. All passengers and crew were killed instantly, as were four others on the ground.

The French transport minister immediately halted all Air France Concorde flights pending investigation. The plane itself, which had been flying since 1980, was inspected just four days prior to the disaster and was passed as entirely fit to fly. Until the accident, Concorde had been the safest passenger aircraft in the world. The accident report of 2004 stated that, minutes earlier, a titanium strip had fallen from the previous plane's take-off, rupturing Concorde's tyres. The fuel tank fractured and ignited, rolling the aircraft into a rapid, unstoppable descent. Despite modifications, this heralded the end of Concorde. The final flight departed from Heathrow in November 2003.

The Air France Concorde taking off with flames trailing from the left engine.

WHEN:
July 25 2000
WHERE:
Gonesse, near Paris, France
DEATH TOLL:
113
YOU SHOULD KNOW:
British and French investigators had an alternative theory: that the plane was both unevenly and too heavily loaded, and that its landing gear was compromised.
In 2008 five individuals, including the former head of the Concorde Division in France, his chief engineer, and a former employee of the French airline regulator, were charged with manslaughter.
In early 2010 an official French inquiry claimed that the accident was the result of poor maintenance and that the Concorde in question had been 'unfit to fly'.

153

Fires burning at the scene of the Flight 587 crash in New York's Belle Harbor neighbourhood.

Flight 587 crash

On November 12 2001 most of the passengers flying to the Dominican Republic from JFK Airport were of Dominican descent; friends and relatives were waiting happily for their arrival at Las Americas International Airport. Then came the shocking news: shortly after take-off, the American Airlines Airbus A300 had crashed, killing all on board. Images of smoking wreckage and distraught families filled TV screens worldwide.

The crash came just two months after the attack on the World Trade Center and, inevitably, rumours circulated that this, too, was the work of terrorists. Though a member of al-Qaeda later claimed the plane had been blown up, the crash was in fact caused by structural failure. As the first officer tried to stabilize the plane when it entered turbulence caused by the take-off of another jet, first the tail-fin and rudder, then both engines separated, causing complete loss of control. Impact and fire destroyed the plane and many of the passengers' bodies.

Investigation ruled out terrorism, suggesting 'aggressive' use of the rudder as the reason for the disintegration. Airbus blamed pilot error, claiming training was at fault. American Airlines, who later modified training systems, held that the rudder controls were unusually sensitive. Subsequently, structural flaws, invisible to the naked eye, were found in similar fibre-reinforced composite plane bodies. Although Airbus stated that, even with such damage, their planes were safe to fly, some pilots felt inspection policies were inadequate.

Flights to the Dominican Republic are no longer numbered 587. A memorial near Belle Harbor, the scene of the crash, is angled to face the Atlantic, in the direction of the victims' homeland.

WHEN:
November 12 2001
WHERE:
New York, USA
DEATH TOLL:
251 passengers, nine crew members and five people on the ground were killed.
YOU SHOULD KNOW:
A woman who died in the crash *en route* to a holiday in her native land had, on September 11, escaped from the ground floor of the World Trade Center.

Al Ayyat train fire

The night train from Cairo to Luxor was packed with people, many of them families with children, travelling from the capital to their home towns for an important Muslim feast day. The third-class compartments were crammed with at least twice the official maximum load. As the train rattled southward and passengers slept, a cooking gas cylinder in the fifth carriage exploded and started a fire, which rapidly spread. Screaming people, their clothes alight, tried to get away from the conflagration, but the coaches were so crowded that no one could make their way to the front of the train to escape the flames, nor warn the driver of what was happening to his train.

The blazing train ran on as the fire inexorably engulfed rolling stock and occupants. Some passengers, desperate to escape the inferno, threw themselves onto the track, where many died of their injuries. Before the engineers discovered what was happening and uncoupled the burning section of the train, seven carriages crammed with third-class passengers had been completely consumed by the fire. The train eventually came to a halt in the small farming district of Al Ayyat, only about 48 km (30 mi) from Cairo. Farmers and villagers attempted to help the badly injured survivors. They could do nothing for the countless victims in the burnt-out carriages.

The official government figure for fatalities is woefully low. It chooses to ignore the overcrowding so common on Egyptian trains and the fact that so many travellers, together with their identities, had been reduced to ash.

WHEN:
February 20 2002
WHERE:
Al Ayyat, Egypt
DEATH TOLL:
The official figure is 383; many consider the real figure to be closer to 1,000.
YOU SHOULD KNOW:
Some time after the disastrous train fire, the people of Al Ayyat came to the rescue again when one passenger train ran into another that had stopped suddenly after hitting a water buffalo wandering on the line.

An Egyptian rescue worker walks beside the burnt-out train.

Igandu train disaster

WHEN:
June 24 2002
WHERE:
Igandu, near Dodoma, Tanzania
DEATH TOLL:
The official body count was 281 but it was probably far more; hundreds were injured, many critically.
YOU SHOULD KNOW:
Tanzania Railways Corporation was eventually bought by an Indian consortium.

In 2002 the government of Tanzania was looking for a private buyer to take over the run-down state railway system. The 22-car passenger train which left Dar es Salaam for the northwestern province of Dodoma was, like many trains at that time, dilapidated and overcrowded (there were probably more than 1,200 passengers aboard) and was maintained and manned by staff who, uncertain about the future of their jobs, may have been working less efficiently than usual.

After passing through the town of Msagali in the early hours of June 24, the train was slowly climbing the hill at Igandu when the driver realized there was something wrong with the brakes. Near the summit, he stopped the train and got down to re-adjust the braking system; then he got back up into the cab. As the train started moving again, the brakes failed completely and it began to roll backwards at ever increasing speed. In desperation, the driver abandoned the controls and raced along the train, shouting a warning that it was out of control. Many jumped out, terrified, onto the tracks.

At the bottom of the hill, a goods train was waiting to make the ascent. The runaway passenger train slammed into it at high speed and 21 of its carriages crashed off the tracks. In the ensuing nightmare of screaming, panic and injury, survivors and local people worked with ambulance teams but the vital heavy-lifting and cutting equipment did not arrive until the next day.

Victims' families received between $100 and $500 from the company. A government inquiry, ruling out sabotage by disaffected railway union members, blamed the 'slow reactions' of the driver.

Wreckage from the crash between the passenger and freight trains.

Le Joola ferry disaster

The south of Senegal is almost completely cut off from the north by the enclave of Gambia, and farmers of the poor but fertile Casamance region depend on coastal ferries to transport their agricultural produce to the rest of the country. The state-run *Le Joola* ferry provided the vital twice-weekly

The upturned ferry

service before it was withdrawn for maintenance and repairs. Without the ferry, traders had to use the long, dangerous and expensive alternative route – potholed, bandit-ridden roads and the ferry across the River Gambia, with its high fares.

After a year out of action, *Le Joola* resumed a once-weekly service in September 2002 to run in its new engine. On September 26 it left Ziguinchor for Dakar laden with cargo and more than three times its official capacity of 580 passengers. The weather was very hot and as night fell hundreds left the cramped, airless lower levels to sleep on deck.

At about 23.00 the ship hit an unexpected storm and it was so overloaded and unbalanced that it capsized, flinging hundreds into the rough sea. Many were killed instantly. Just one lifeboat was launched and fishermen in the area picked up some swimmers. But by morning, when the rescue teams arrived, most of those in the water had already drowned.

When the ferry went down hundreds more were trapped inside, and diving teams only retrieved some of the dead. Of a total of 551 bodies recovered, only 93 were identified. The actual number who died will never be known, for many passengers had no tickets. Families of the lost were offered about $22 per victim. Overcrowding, the weather and poor maintenance were blamed. Although several officers were fired, no one was prosecuted and the inquiry was closed after a year.

WHEN:
September 26 2002
WHERE:
Off the coast of Gambia
DEATH TOLL:
At least 1,860
YOU SHOULD KNOW:
Only one of the 64 survivors was a woman. About 600 women were on board, mostly travelling to sell palm oil and mangoes at the markets of Dakar.

157

Sinking of the ferry *Nasrin*

WHEN:
July 8 2003
WHERE:
Near Chandpur, Bangladesh
DEATH TOLL:
Probably over 400
YOU SHOULD KNOW:
Ferry accidents are all too common on the rivers of Bangladesh. A ferry which sank in the same stretch of river as the *Nasrin* in 1994 has never been found.

Southern Bangladesh and West Bengal occupy the world's largest delta, where a heavily indented coastline – the Mouths of the Ganges – is backed by the vast mangrove swamps of the Sunderbans and endless paddy fields threaded by waterways. Summer monsoon floods make roads impassable; ferries are then the only link between towns and villages.

The triple-decked ferry *Nasrin* embarked on its regular journey from Dhaka down the River Padma to the coastal towns of Lalmohan and Bhola. Near the ferry terminal at Chandpur, the River Meghna joins the main stream and the confluence of rain-swollen rivers produces an area of turbulence, always hazardous to shipping during the monsoon. On the night of July 8 2003, as the *Nasrin* entered this perilous stretch of water, one of her engines faltered. The fierce cross currents caught and spun the vessel, and it turned over.

Passengers, many of whom had settled down for the night, struggled to escape by climbing onto the roof and diving into the river. Suddenly, the ferry nose-dived and disappeared beneath the deep, wild waters. Local fishermen fought the currents to pick up swimmers; survivors and villagers on shore began a long, grim vigil. Navy and coastguard boats searched for survivors and for the sunken vessel as the monsoon rains pelted down. Some bodies were recovered downriver, but hundreds were never found.

Bangladeshi ferries rarely issue tickets and keep no record of passengers. On this journey, a whole boatload of travellers had swarmed onto the *Nasrin* when another ferry was cancelled, adding to the normal overcrowding. About 200 people survived, but many were trapped in the sunken ship and many more disappeared without trace. Staff at Dhaka's ferry terminal were 'relocated', with assurances that 'more efficient personnel' would be employed.

The 'Queen of the Sea' train disaster

Those who boarded the early train from Columbo on December 26 were heading south for an important Buddhist new-moon holiday. The railway line to Galle follows Sri Lanka's palm-fringed west coast, often within sight of the ocean, and this popular train was nicknamed the 'Queen of the Sea'. At Telwatta, a little north of Galle, it halted. As the driver waited for the signals to change, an enormous wave tore ashore and villagers rushed towards the higher ground of the railway line. The train seemed to offer protection from the waist-deep water, and some sheltered behind it while others clambered onto the roof. The wave surged around the coaches and retreated.

This is a telltale sign of a tsunami, which sucks up coastal waters into a vast, destructive wave, but those at Telwatta were unaware that an earthquake off the coast of Indonesia had set in motion a tsunami of cataclysmic power. The second wave flattened the village, snapped and uprooted trees and tossed the train off the tracks. Eight carriages crammed with terrified holidaymakers were tumbled over and over as seawater flooded in through open windows. Only a few managed to scramble out while windows remained, briefly, above the waterline. The rest drowned in the train or were buried in mud and debris.

The water ebbed, leaving the twisted, crumpled train in a wasteland of torn trees and razed buildings. Families and friends who searched and grieved alongside an army team in the waterlogged chaos did not know that this scene was being repeated all along Sri Lanka's ravaged coastline. At Telwatta, many bodies were never found, many more remained unidentified. Police displayed identification papers and unclaimed bodies were photographed and fingerprinted, and given a respectful burial by Buddhist monks.

WHEN:
December 26 2004
WHERE:
Telwatta, Sri Lanka
DEATH TOLL:
More than 1,700 – the world's worst-ever railway disaster.
YOU SHOULD KNOW:
A local woodcarver and his family saw the whole tragedy from the concrete roof of their latrine. In retrospect, they considered the tsunami nature's 'statement'. Like many other Sri Lankans, they tried to find meaning in the disaster.

A Buddhist monk looks at a wrecked carriage after an entire train was destroyed.

al-Salam Boccaccio 98

WHEN:
February 3 2006
WHERE:
In the Red Sea, between Egypt
and Saudi Arabia
DEATH TOLL:
Around 1,000 died.
YOU SHOULD KNOW:
An initial enquiry into the sinking was
a whitewash. The owner of the
shipping company, Mamdouh Ismail,
was also a member of Egypt's Upper
House and the report's findings
stank of corruption. Relatives of the
dead mounted a successful
campaign to have the case
re-opened and in 2009 the initial
enquiry was overturned, resulting in
a seven-year jail sentence for
Mamdouh Ismail and punishment for
other company officials.

Fire on board a ship throws up a unique set of problems. Water is usually the most convenient and effective way of tackling a blaze on dry land, but at sea the water must be removed from a ship almost as quickly as it is used to fight the fire. A fine balancing act is required. On the one hand the blaze must be stopped from reaching any fuel on board the vessel and on the other it must be ascertained that the boat doesn't shift its centre of gravity via a process known as the 'free surface effect'.

On an early February evening, the Italian built *al-Salam Boccaccio 98* set sail from Duba in Saudi Arabia. Its passengers were largely migrant workers and pilgrims returning home to Egypt. The *Boccaccio 98* was a boat that had seen much modification and the addition of extra passenger decks had made it top-heavy. Conditions in the Red Sea were rough and deteriorating rapidly, but this was nothing out of the ordinary for this vast body of water.

Just over half way into the nine-hour voyage, a fire started in or close to the engine room. Swift action was required to contain it, but the crew lacked adequate training in how to deal with the situation. As more and more water was used to tackle the blaze, the ship began to list to one side. Battered by waves, it sank in about seven minutes, putting the lives of all 1,400 on board in extreme danger. Rescue efforts were tardy to say the least and did not get under way until seven hours after the boat sank. Around 400 survivors were left to fend for themselves in lifeboats before help arrived.

The al-Salam Boccaccio

Flight Air France 447

Brazilian Navy divers recovering a huge part of the rudder of the Air France Airbus out of the Atlantic Ocean, some 1,200 km (745 miles) northeast of Recife.

On the evening of Sunday May 30 2009, Flight Air France 447 took off from Rio de Janeiro and skirted the Brazilian coastline before heading out over the Atlantic Ocean on its journey to Charles de Gaulle airport in Paris. Its usual flight path would have taken it over Senegalese air space and then on to France. When the plane took off it seemed that everything was normal, even though it was heading towards a band of thunderstorms that had bubbled up mid Atlantic. This in itself was nothing unusual and the highly trained Air France pilots and crew were used to flying through such turbulence.

Four hours into the flight the aeroplane sent an automatic signal indicating that there had been an 'electrical circuit malfunction'. The autopilot was disconnected, either as a result of the malfunction or manually by the pilot trying to regain control of the plane. No further messages were received and soon afterwards the plane plunged into the ocean, killing all 228 passengers and crew on board. It is highly unlikely that anyone would have survived for long after the plane hit the water. The Brazilian navy was dispatched to carry out a search, but it soon became clear that they were looking for wreckage and bodies rather than survivors.

Such was the scale of the task that faced them that in spite of having state-of-the-art equipment, it was not until June 6 that the first bodies were found. Two days later the tail section was recovered. The search for the dead was finally called off at the end of June, by which time 51 bodies had been recovered. Those who perished were mainly Brazilian, French and German, but nationals of 29 other countries were among the dead.

WHEN:
The early hours of June 1 2009
WHERE:
Midway across the Atlantic Ocean
DEATH TOLL:
228
YOU SHOULD KNOW:
The flight recorder has never been found and without it we will never know the full facts behind the loss of AF447. Air France reacted to the crash – the worst in its history – by replacing speed monitors in its Airbus fleet.

DISASTROUS CONFLAGRATIONS

Arson at the heart of the Roman Empire

WHEN:
July 18–27 AD 64
WHERE:
Rome, Italy
DEATH TOLL:
Fear and panic caused more death and injury than the fire. Not even the near-contemporary accounts speak of large numbers of casualties from the fire itself. The real death toll came later in the arena of the Coliseum, where Nero sent every Christian the Praetorian Guard could arrest. Christians – then a small but irritatingly vocal evangelistic sect – were convenient scapegoats for the conflagration. After the Great Fire of Rome, Nero derived amusement from holding torchlit dinner parties – using the flaming carcasses of Christians as human torches.
YOU SHOULD KNOW:
Rome wasn't rebuilt in a day – but Nero's new Palace, the 300-acre *Domus Aurea*, still survives in Rome's ancient centre, exactly where he 'dreamed' it would be.

In AD 64 Rome was the greatest city in the Western world – the capital of an Empire approaching the height of its power. With nearly a million citizens spread across its seven hills, Rome was accustomed to dealing with serious fires in the hot, dry summers. It had the means, the knowledge, the experience and the perpetual vigilance to cope without batting an imperial eyelid.

The fire that destroyed ancient Rome began by the Circus Maximus, sweeping through the wooden shops and tenements clustered in the warren of streets around the huge stone building. A strong southeast wind drove the flames simultaneously up the Aventine and Palatine hills, faster than anyone could contain them. The fire took on a life of its own, in six days reducing four of Rome's 14 districts to charred ash and leaving very little upright in seven more. When it looked like burning itself out, it re-ignited – according to the historian Tacitus, with help. Nothing important was spared, including Nero's favourite palace, the Senate House, the Forum, and the temple of the Vestal Virgins, one of Rome's oldest and most sacred sanctuaries. It swallowed up 1,700 private houses and 47,000 *insulae* (literally 'islands', meaning multiple-occupancy tenement blocks) and every slum in between.

If the Emperor Nero was directly or indirectly responsible, he got what he wanted – the space in the centre of Rome to build his cherished 'dream city'. But he also made a terrific show of helping to save the citizens, which diminishes the probable myth that he strummed the lyre while crooning a favourite verse-song called 'The Sack of Ilium'. However, the combination of malicious conspiracy and ostentatious generosity is entirely consistent with Nero's known instabilities – and frankly, it makes a much better story.

Nero fiddles while Rome burns.

The Great Fire of London

The Great Fire of London started in a pie shop on Pudding Lane, now commemorated by a 65 m (202 ft) Doric column surmounted with flames of gold. The Monument appears to celebrate the disaster, and there are good reasons why it should.

The fire consumed four fifths of the city within its Roman walls (then still standing, and enclosing roughly what is now known as The City). It swept away 430 acres of Saxon, Norman, Plantagenet, Tudor, Elizabethan and Jacobean development – 13,000 houses, 52 guild halls, 89 churches, and old St Paul's Cathedral – as well as the squalid accretions of a millennium of poverty, disease and crime, oozing filth from their interstices. Prohibition on building with wood and thatch and of workshops using open braziers or forges had been ignored for centuries, and the widespread practice of extending the upper floors of houses over the roadway meant that many already narrow lanes were virtual tunnels.

Medieval London had grown at random. Stone buildings were rare. Anyone who could afford to had long since moved westwards into what is now the West End and the City of Westminster. Burning slums held little interest, until the population as a whole realized that the mayor's indecision and inaction had allowed a firestorm to develop out of anyone's control. Worse, the City merchants had supported Cromwell in the recent Civil War; now they rejected King Charles II's offer of troops to create firebreaks. Only a firebreak on London Bridge – densely built over and one of the sights of Europe – stopped the fire from spreading to the markets and middens of Southwark; while beyond the walls to the west, the King's on-the-spot direction finally halted the flames at Fleet Street and Holborn.

The disaster had a silver lining. The inferno helped sterilize the bubonic plague that had decimated London only a year before. It was almost worth it.

WHEN:
September 2–6 1666
WHERE:
London, UK
DEATH TOLL:
The five known deaths take no account of the poor and homeless who simply disappeared. Contemporary estimates put property damage at £8 million, and £2 million more of merchant goods. But the Plague, which had killed 68,000 Londoners in the previous two years, scarcely troubled the city again.
YOU SHOULD KNOW:
King Charles II did a great job in organizing the recovery. He more or less kept London's medieval street plan, and encouraged the finest architects while restraining Christopher Wren's more grandiose schemes. By 1671 9,000 new buildings were complete; by 1700 London was Europe's biggest city. The influx of European craftsmen also initiated the effortless cosmopolitanism which has characterized London ever since.

The old St Paul's can be seen through the ruins of a wall near Ludgate Prison.

The burning of Atlanta

WHEN:
November 13–18 1864
WHERE:
Atlanta, Georgia, USA
DEATH TOLL:
Confederate and Union casualties
were both horrific, but there are no
figures more precise than 'tens of
thousands'.
YOU SHOULD KNOW:
Partly because its cold-blooded
ferocity was reinforced by the book
and film of *Gone With The Wind*, the
burning of Atlanta remains a vivid
and divisive landmark in American
culture. There is a truly remarkable
lateral insight to the burning of
Atlanta (and the march as a whole)
in the poems of John Allen Wyeth. He
fought Sherman as a Confederate
soldier at Chickamauga, and saw the
ruination of Georgia first hand. Then
he lived to serve as a US Army
translator on the Western Front in
France, in 1917. His war poems draw
together those two experiences.

It is taught at every military academy in the world, and engrained into the cultural memory of every American. General William T Sherman's 'march to the sea' from Chickamauga on the Tennessee state line through Georgia to Savannah is one of the most famous 'scorched earth' campaigns in history. Its lesson is how to break your enemy's will to fight. Its defining image is the burning of Atlanta.

After nearly four years, the Civil War was going badly for the Confederacy. Sherman entered Georgia with 100,000 men, but in their heartland the Confederates surrendered each mile dearly. It decided his tactics. He wrote to Union leaders: 'If the people raise a howl against my barbarity and cruelty, I will answer that war is war, and not popularity-seeking'. Atlanta's antebellum elegance equalled its strategic significance as a spur to Sherman's military vanity. It took him three months of bitter fighting to cross north Georgia, and two more of artillery bombardment to take the city. Civilians were ordered to leave while he regrouped. Then on November 15, Sherman marched 60,000 men in three columns towards Savannah. Behind him, the classical porticos of the wealthy, the vast warehouses that had housed two centuries of trading fortunes, the factories, railroad yards, plantations, and thousands of wood-framed houses and slave barracoons burned to ashes. Refugee columns looked back at biblical scenes of pillars of flame and choking smoke, helpless against Union irregulars drunk for loot. Even freed slaves ran from Sherman's troops.

It has become fashionable to rehabilitate Sherman from Georgia's still-current folk perception of the 'horned devil' and 'grand arsonist' of Atlanta; but when *Gone With The Wind* was written, there were still plenty of people alive who had seen his work for themselves. That sheet of crimson flame was for real.

Mobile magazine explosion

Mobile, Alabama had been a frontier town in French, British and Spanish hands before it became irrevocably American in 1813. During the cotton boom that followed, it grew in wealth and importance to become one of the United States' four busiest ports in the 1850s. The Civil War made it a strategic target, blockaded by the Union and heavily fortified by the Confederacy, who maintained a dribble of trade with a fleet of low-slung, sharp-prowed blockade-runners. Only after the Battle of Mobile Bay in August 1864, when Admiral Farragut of the Union defeated the ironclad CSS *Tennessee* (giving rise to the immortal quotation 'Damn the torpedoes, full speed ahead' used by every navy since), did Mobile surrender to the Union Army, to avoid bombardment and total destruction. After the end of the war, the city was invested by a Union garrison. With its superb port facilities, it was again used to stockpile necessaries to supply the army inland. One key installation was a warehouse on Beauregard Street, where Union troops guarded 200 tons of munitions.

In the afternoon of an early summer's day, preceded by a low rumble and a jet of black smoke, death and destruction erupted in Mobile. The shock wave levelled houses, blew bystanders to smithereens, and sent a rain of death in every direction as flying shells caused subsidiary explosions wherever they landed. Two ships in the Mobile River were sunk, but the worst damage was reserved for the northern part of the city, where incendiaries set simultaneous fires that joined together in an explosive fireball. Ironically, with the war over, warehouses had filled up, and cotton bales and other produce fed the inferno. For years afterwards the huge hole where the magazine had been served as a memorial to the dead and injured.

WHEN:
May 25 1865
WHERE:
Beauregard Street, Mobile, Alabama, USA
DEATH TOLL:
An estimated 300 died and thousands were injured. Bodies were burned beyond recognition: nothing at all was left of anyone in the immediate vicinity. For the wounded, it was almost worse – despite the war, few doctors could cope with the mangled limbs, horrific burns and mutilations.
YOU SHOULD KNOW:
Cynics blamed the blast on vengeful Confederate officers. More likely some hapless trooper accidentally dropped a percussion shell. Eight city blocks disappeared completely, and fire wrecked much more. Newspapers of the day estimated damage at anything between 'five and ten millions of dollars'.

Rubble and shells of buildings were all that remained after the Chicago fire.

The great Chicago fire

WHEN:
October 8–10 1871
WHERE:
Chicago, Illinois, USA
TOLL:
Chicago's characteristically energetic civic pride gave thanks for the relatively low death toll (estimated at 300) by rushing through tough revised building and fire codes that became a model for many other emergent US cities. Sadly, equally tough enforcement shattered the optimism of civic unity. Those who could afford to rebuild in stone blamed the fire on the poor who could not, as if poverty itself were feckless. City officials encouraged them, to distract attention from their own disorganization, and in the smart new Chicago the gap between 'have' and 'have not' widened to its present gulf.
YOU SHOULD KNOW:
The great Chicago fire remains the city's cultural landmark. Its Major League Soccer (MLS) team was founded on the fire's 126th anniversary, and is called 'The Chicago Fire'; and the athletics team at the University of Illinois at Chicago is known as 'The Flames'.

Chicago was born in a hurry to grow up, from a hamlet of 150 people in 1831 to a haphazard metropolis of 340,000 in 1871. Trains from the east decanted scores of immigrants while trains from the west decanted cattle and buffalo hides to market; and the end of the Civil War brought thousands displaced from the south. Chicago needed to build. Wood was quickest and cheapest so the city was built of wood, from its roofs and walls to its sidewalks, and even planked streets. It was a tinderbox and, at the end of an exceptionally hot, dry summer, the 'Queen of the West' burned.

A southwest wind fanned the flames from Mrs O'Leary's downtown milking barn up through the North Side along Lake Michigan. The fire surged in intensity as it leapt the Chicago River, filled with debris and oil from waterside factories, and swept through the blue-collar Irish district of Conley's Patch. Exhausted by dealing with a big local fire the previous day, the city's pitifully small fire service of 185 men could do nothing. Only the thin veil of rain on the third day stemmed the raging havoc, by which time 17,500 buildings lay in ashes along 70 miles of streets. Around 100,000 Chicagoans were homeless, and as many as 300 were dead.

But Chicago found common cause in its response to the calamity. The first wagonload of lumber for rebuilding arrived as the last flames were snuffed. Within a week some 6,000 new structures provided shelter for the bereft. Rich and poor worked side by side to put their city back on its feet. Improvement and expansion marched with renewal – and just 22 years later Chicago had re-invented itself to host 21 million visitors to the Chicago World's Fair. Its citizens turned disaster into a triumph of American 'can do'.

The great Boston fire

Even today visitors to Boston can feel the waft of the city's once evident superiority complex. In the 1870s it still had justification. The cradle of revolution and great trading centre of New England, Boston's tradition of Yankee thrift had created the habits of wealth and self-improvement. Every Bostonian knew God was on their side. Shipping crammed the harbour and warehouses overflowed with goods in and goods out.

By 1872, Boston had grown sloppy in guarding its assets. Building regulations were ignored and the practice of over-insurance was a better incentive to arson than to precaution. Only when the fire had started in the business district did everyone remember that fire alarm boxes were locked to prevent hoax calls, that hydrant fittings were not standardized, and that plans to increase the number of hydrants, and the water pressure available, had been shelved as 'extravagant'. Boston's fire chief had conscientiously visited Chicago to learn from its experience the year before – and been comfortably ignored on his return.

Few fires in history have been so well fuelled. Wool, textiles, paper and a thousand other flammables turned a warehouse accident into a firestorm that ripped through 65 acres in 15 hours, razing downtown and the financial district, and sending ships at anchor to a Viking funeral. Up to 100,000 people crowded to watch businessmen panicking, fighting off looters, and blocking fire teams – who had rushed to the city from all over Massachusetts – from saving anything at all. Exploding gas lines fed the heat until granite itself melted; the radiant glow was noted in ships' logs from far up the coast of Maine.

Boston's fire remains one of America's most expensive. It caused some $75 million of damage and hit Yankee pride where it hurts most – in the pocket.

WHEN:
November 9–10 1872
WHERE:
83–87 Summer Street, Boston, Massachusetts, USA
DEATH TOLL:
30 dead, including 12 firefighters. Despite his foresight and actual courage, the fire chief was made the scapegoat and lost his job.
YOU SHOULD KNOW:
Fire crews spotted two men stranded on a high ledge, waving. Understanding the men's fear of the nearby flames, they pointed their hoses up and drenched them; the two men appeared to shout encouragement, before sitting down calmly. When it was safe to rescue them, firemen discovered the men were dead. The water intended to save them had frozen them to death.

A large wall of fire sweeping up a hill as flames engulf Boston.

Matinee at the Iroquois Theater

WHEN:
December 30 1903
WHERE:
Randolph Street, Chicago,
Illinois, USA
DEATH TOLL:
602 dead, including 212 children.
Most of the survivors were injured
to some extent from being
trampled, gouged, choked,
suffocated or burned.
YOU SHOULD KNOW:
Chicago banned any celebration of
the New Year and went into official
mourning. An enquiry revealed a
catalogue of code violations
sanctioned by bribed inspectors.
The Iroquois' glamour masked
pitiless indifference to audience (or
staff) safety. Nobody was ever
convicted either for criminal
manslaughter, or for the cover-up.
The only person convicted of
anything to do with the disaster was
a businessman caught looting the
dead bodies for personal valuables.

*The ruins of the burnt-out
Iroquois Theater*

The Iroquois Theater was bang up-to-date. Designed like a Paris opera house with a 19m (60 ft) high marble-walled lobby and two sweeping staircases, its four storeys of polished wood and stained-glass windows seated 1,600 people in gilded galleries of velvet plush. Its rococo splendour incorporated every safety device yet invented, including an asbestos safety curtain between the stage and auditorium and 25 exits to guarantee a speedy evacuation if ever it should be needed. It was Chicago's newest showpiece.

The Iroquois was only five weeks old on December 30 1903 and the Wednesday matinee was sold out for the hit comedy *Mr Bluebeard*, starring the great vaudevillian Eddie Foy. This particular performance was for children on their school holidays, so management allowed 2,000 to cram into the seats and aisles. Backstage were another 400 actors, dancers and stagehands. Their irresistible cue came after the start of the second act. A coloured gel from an overhead light fluttered down in burning scraps. Without breaking rhythm, the onstage dancers tried to stamp them out but kicked them onto the red velvet curtains. The audience gasped as flash flames shot up to the proscenium arch – with delight, thinking it was part of the extravaganza. Nobody moved.

Then the stage set fell flaming round Eddy Foy's ears, the safety curtain jammed halfway down, and the theatre erupted in panic.

The ghastly inferno lasted 15 minutes. The 25 exits opened inwards, an impossibility against the surging crowd. Trampled bodies lay five deep. Terror-struck children hurled themselves from the balconies, crushing those below; and if they lived themselves, they later died burned and suffocated. Some got away – but when the crowd backstage opened an outside door, the surge of oxygen fanned the blaze to a tungsten-white fireball. The 'fireproof' theatre lay a shell, filled with human cinders.

Collinwood school

Fatal fires don't come more harrowing than the crackling inferno that took Collinwood's children in 20 awful minutes, and prompted the grief-stricken community literally to vote itself out of existence. It is the worst school tragedy in Ohio's history.

A crisp, sunny, midwest March morning is no time for a waking nightmare. In the two-storey, brick schoolhouse, teachers and children assumed it was a drill when they heard the booming gong sound three times for a fire alarm. Lake View School was well-practised, and in each class the little boys and girls quickly lined up to go to their designated exit. Down below, the school caretaker – who had arrived that morning at 06.30 for his usual routine of cleaning and stoking up the coal furnace, and been confronted around 09.30 by a girl shouting about 'fire in the basement' – had seen the smoke for himself. From the gong he rushed to open the front and back doors to help everyone get clear of the building more easily.

Air rushed in and, with an explosive roar, flames erupted out of the basement and filled the hall and front stairway, meeting the converging lines of children head-on. Singed and already choking, discipline went by the board. So many children rushed the back door that they jammed each other in a panicked tangle of arms and legs. Others behind them flung themselves on top, trying to scramble to safety. Pushed back by flames and blocked by the pile of screaming bodies, those still trying to come downstairs turned back, creating a new mayhem at the windows and fire escape.

Outside, the first adults to the scene pulled outstretched limbs as they burned, but the children were locked in fatal embrace, ten deep and screaming in agony. In 20 gruesome minutes, they died while their parents tried to beat the flames with naked fists. And it was Ash Wednesday.

WHEN:
March 4 1908
WHERE:
Lake View School, Collinwood, Ohio, USA
DEATH TOLL:
Of nearly 400 children, 172 died alongside two teachers and one of the rescuers; 19 could not be identified; many others were known only by some adjacent trinket, ring or watch. Nothing at all remained of the school except the blackened brick walls and a chimney stack.
YOU SHOULD KNOW:
The township of 20,000 was utterly devastated. Volunteers had to keep a suicide watch on parents driven mad with grief; but the town itself opted to disappear, by means of annexation to the city of Cleveland. The last act of residents was to vote for a memorial garden to cover the ground plan of the school. Among many heartbreaking mementoes was a piece of broken slateboard. Written on it in chalk was the beginning of the sentence 'I like to go to school . . .'. At least the disaster forced schools throughout America to revise safety regulations and codes of practice.

Firefighters at the Triangle Shirtwaist Factory

WHEN:
March 25 1911
WHERE:
Washington Place, New York, USA
DEATH TOLL:
146 women and men died, and 'many' were injured.
YOU SHOULD KNOW:
The owners of the factory were tried for manslaughter but acquitted. But thousands had witnessed the horror and seen the inhumanity of the women's working conditions. Public revulsion forced even the most recalcitrant to make improvements and led to the creation of the Factory Investigating Commission, whose recommendations initiated what has been called 'the golden era in remedial factory legislation'.

The Triangle Shirtwaist fire

If any single incident could provide a manifesto for the existence of labour unions, it is the horrific fire that incinerated 146 women and men at the Triangle Shirtwaist Factory in New York City in 1911. The conditions of their employment were brutal, and a direct cause of their deaths.

Their biggest handicap, of course, was that most of them were female. Underpaid, shamefully exploited, and prohibited on pain of the sack from doing anything about it, the women who worked at the Triangle Shirtwaist Company were mostly recent immigrants. There were roughly 500 of them, making women's blouses. Their speciality was the 'shirtwaist' – tight at the waist with puffy sleeves. They were crowded into the eighth, ninth and tenth floors of the Asch Building on the corner of Washington Place, working long hours six days a week. Some were as young as 13.

When fire started on the eighth floor, it took hold quickly. The fire hoses had no water supply. Everyone rushed for the elevators, but they burned out after only a few terrifyingly overcrowded trips. And in the *melée*, nobody told the women on the ninth floor about the fire. Most of the tenth floor crowded out onto the roof. On the ninth they found the fire escape had buckled, crashing down on their shrieking friends. Doors to other floors were locked as company policy. That left only the windows, or the flames. Outside the fire brigade's ladders could only reach the sixth floor. They watched as young girls in flames hurled themselves like meteors from the ninth floor. Nearly 100 of them lay dead or dying from injuries and burns. The rest were burned to cinders at their machines.

It was at least a form of martyrdom. Their deaths led inexorably to new legislation improving fire, safety and building codes.

Laurier Palace theatre

The Laurier Palace movie theatre in Montreal was nearly full for the Sunday matinee. The audience of 800 consisted mainly of children aged five to 17, excitedly relishing the comedy *Get 'Em Young*. An usher spotted a small fire – probably from a discarded cigarette – and, after giving the alarm, tried to deal with it using an extinguisher. He and other staff appealed for calm, but the thick smoke seeping into the auditorium panicked children in the balcony. It was contagious. As the first firefighters arrived, just two minutes after the alarm, it was clear that the ground floor was emptying fast. Upstairs, the terrified children had found one of the two exits securely locked, so they scrambled for the single stairway leading directly to the street. Hundreds threw themselves down the stairs. The immediate crush prevented those at the front from pulling open the doors; and moments later they were trampled under a kicking, scrabbling, screaming, human avalanche.

Ten minutes after it started, the fire was actually out. Nobody knew it. Oily, thick smoke and toxic fumes filled the theatre and rolled down the stairway, smothering the choking children. Quick-thinking fire fighters hacked through the outside walls to make exit holes and managed to pull several to safety. It was too late. Piled on the stairwell, a few feet from the safety of the sidewalk, the children were jammed and intertwined so densely that, later, 20 men pulling on a rope attached to a young body could not release it. Even then, the few children pulled out alive had scorched their lungs, and died when they breathed the cold fresh air.

Canada's 'saddest fire' should never have ended in tragedy. Nobody was killed by the flames and, had the doors opened outwards, the panic would not have been fatal.

WHEN:
January 9 1927
WHERE:
Laurier Palace, Moreau Street, Montreal, Canada
DEATH TOLL:
77 children died (12 crushed and 65 asphyxiated) and 24 were seriously injured. Most of the victims were French-Canadian. Montreal went wild with grief, as parents from every *quartier* rushed from hospital to hospital looking for their children. One fireman found all three of his children among the shrouded corpses on the sidewalk. French-speaking Canada mourned, but regarded the disaster as something like divine punishment. The fiercely Catholic culture of the region was intolerant of any Sabbath entertainment. The fire brought these issues into vociferous but futile public debate.
YOU SHOULD KNOW:
A commission reported on the fire. It ignored building safety codes completely and instead became a forum for the ultra-Catholic *Ligue du Dimanche* and other sabbatarians who wanted to ban working or having fun on Sundays. The commission got children under 15 banned from theatres, but for bizarre reasons. It concluded that 'immorality, free love, adultery, divorce, thefts, murders, suicides . . . and the depiction of people flouting legal and religious authority attract paying customers . . . [and] the portrayal of unpunished immorality promotes disrespect for authority'. That'd be the kids at fault, then?

Inspector J W Dagnall viewing what was left after the fire at Laurier Palace.

St Paul's Cathedral suffering a pounding during the Blitz.

The Blitz on London

The Blitz was not a single event. It was a World War II ordeal by fire and bombing that lasted from September 1940 until May 1941. It was a collective experience suffered by the whole of the United Kingdom – but London, the capital, bore the brunt. The Blitz – short for *Blitzkrieg*, Hitler's 'Lightning War' – began as the aerial Battle of Britain ended, taking with it the threat of imminent German invasion. Its first phase saw London bombed for 57 consecutive nights as Hitler sought to fragment civilian support for the government by destroying morale. The first raid alone, on London's docklands and East End, killed 430 and seriously injured another 1,600. Instead of crumbling, Londoners picked themselves up and united in outrage behind Prime Minister Winston Churchill. As the winter passed, other cities came to share their resolve to resist at all costs. The Blitz just grew worse.

Londoners accustomed themselves to extreme deprivation, cramming into underground stations and basements to escape the hellish conditions outside. Their slogan, to be seen freshly chalked each morning on still-flaming wreckage from the nightly raids, was 'Business as usual'. The Blitz just grew worse.

December 29 1940 was worst of all. In that single night, incendiary bombs started 1,400 separate fires, six of which were officially classed as 'conflagrations'. The City of London blazed. The 17th century Guildhall was reduced to blackened walls and many historic churches and buildings were damaged or destroyed along with five major railway stations, nine hospitals, 16 underground stations, the two principal telephone and telegraph exchanges and St Paul's Cathedral.

Still The Blitz grew worse. Raids by 500 and 700 German bombers were frequent. The death and destruction spiralled, but Britain's cities never flinched. The resilience of Londoners, especially, has passed into legend.

A firefighter in a bomb-damaged city street

WHEN:
September 7 1940 to May 10 1941
WHERE:
London and every major city and port in the UK
DEATH TOLL:
In London, over 20,000 people died in The Blitz. In each of the two fires of December 29 and May 10, roughly 1,500 were killed and 1,800 seriously hurt; 300,000 houses were destroyed in London, and fire-damaged public and historic buildings included the Houses of Parliament and Buckingham Palace.
YOU SHOULD KNOW:
The London Blitz may be the perfect demonstration of the adage 'what doesn't kill you makes you stronger'. It forged unbreakable loyalties between strangers and tempered an indomitable collective will to beat Hitler. Recordings of wartime broadcasts by Ed Murrow, an American newsman who stayed at his post voluntarily to report The Blitz for US radio, give an indication of what Londoners experienced. His calm, measured appraisal of raids belies the fact that he never took cover, preferring to see and hear exactly what was going on, and to record the courage of Londoners under fire.

Cocoanut Grove

The only entrance to the Cocoanut Grove was the revolving front door. Other exits had been bricked or welded shut during Prohibition when the club was one of Boston's hottest speakeasies. Now, a year into World War II, it was still one of Boston's swankiest nightspots – a version of Rick's Café Américain in *Casablanca*. It had edge, it had style and it had wide lapels. The owner was 'in with the mayor' – what he saved on taxes he added to by not bothering to rectify obvious safety violations; and city officials turned a blind eye.

Victims being hauled out of the Cocoanut Grove nightclub.

The legal capacity of Cocoanut Grove was 460 people. On Saturday November 28 1942 nearly 1,000 patrons, entertainers and staff were dining and dancing. Downstairs in the Melody Lounge a young couple looking for a moment's privacy unscrewed the light bulb over their booth. The barman told a busboy to replace it. The boy stood on a chair and lit a match to find the socket. As he leaned forward, the flame caught the silk ceiling hanging that covered the room. Fake palm trees turned the room into a fiery inferno which mushroomed up the stairwell and sent an explosive fireball through the dining room. The only exit from the Melody Lounge was bolted; piles of blackened corpses showed where terrified patrons had stormed the blazing stairwell. Upstairs the revolving door was jammed with people clawing for the freedom of the other side of the glass. The 26 fire engines and 187 firefighters could do nothing to prevent people dying.

There was talk of sabotage, because 50 sailors died and the club represented the America the boys were fighting for. But everyone also knew that its chic and gaiety were part of a rip-roaring, gangster mentality that sold escapism for profit – and fatally sold it short.

WHEN:
November 28 1942
WHERE:
Cocoanut Grove, Piedmont Street, Boston, Massachusetts, USA
DEATH TOLL:
492 dead, including a honeymoon couple, all four servicemen sons of a Wilmington family celebrating their leave, and Buck Jones, the Hollywood cowboy movie star.
YOU SHOULD KNOW:
The Grove's owner was jailed for involuntary manslaughter for three and a half years; the busboy was exonerated; and the Boston Licensing Board prohibited any club from ever again using the name 'Cocoanut Grove'. The disaster resulted directly in the creation and enforcement of safety laws in more or less the way we now recognize them. Witness statements referred to a 'flashover' and 50 years later this was confirmed by a former Boston firefighter whose research revealed the presence at Cocoanut Grove of methyl chloride – a highly flammable gas propellant used in refrigeration in place of freon, which in wartime was in short supply.

Hartford circus

WHEN:
July 6 1944
WHERE:
Ringling Brothers, Barnum and Bailey
Circus, Hartford, Connecticut, USA
DEATH TOLL:
169 dead and 487 burned, trampled,
asphyxiated and crushed, but living.
It transpired that the US Army had
vetoed the circus's request for their
fireproof compound, so the big top
was waterproofed with a mixture of
paraffin and gasoline. It acted like
napalm.
YOU SHOULD KNOW:
Ringlings behaved with total integrity,
accepting responsibility and offering
compensation. They wanted to do
the right thing and managed to stay
in business by promising their next
ten years' profit as compensation;
everyone got their money. The most
poignant story from the fire hit
headlines across America. 'Little Miss
1565' – named for the morgue
number assigned to her – was a
young girl whose sweet face was
(photogenically) unmarked. Though
her picture was briefly one of the
best known in the USA, she was
never claimed and never identified.

The disaster got its name from a front-page photograph of Emmett Kelly carried by the *Hartford Courant*. Kelly was the most famous clown in the most famous circus in an era when circus was big-time. The photograph showed him in full clown make-up, including the comedy big shoes, carrying a pail of water in a desperate effort to put out a fire.

It happened so fast. The Ringling Brothers, Barnum and Bailey Circus had reached Connecticut with their hugely anticipated wartime entertainment. The Great Wallendas high-wire act was in full swing at the matinee. From their vantage point, they signalled to the bandleader, who saw the lick of flame halfway up the side wall of the cavernous big top. Immediately he launched the band into 'Stars and Stripes Forever' – the signal to staff that a serious crisis was taking place. For a few seconds, the audience contemplated the diversion. Then, with a scarcely audible sigh, flame billowed across the whole roof of the tent above the main entrance and 8,000 women and children and the few men rose as one and scrambled down from their seats, intent on the exit. Grown men elbowed children out of the way and punched women to the ground. Wads of blazing canvas began to shower liquid flame from the disintegrating roof. Circus staff got the big cats out of the arena just in time; but the two caged-animal entrances blocked the only exits not on fire. Now the fire roared, and the six tent poles sagged one by one, and collapsed. Hundreds were still inside. From outside, the burning canvas heaved and rocked, and went still, a ghastly pyre of smoke and flames.

It took six minutes. Witnesses spoke of 'the awful sound of animals dying', but no animals were hurt. The agony was human.

Flames consumed the huge big top.

The Dresden firestorm

Symbolically, Dresden ended what began in Coventry. Early 1945 was getting towards the end of World War II. The Russians had broken the German army in the east; the British and Americans were at the Rhine and now the Allies wanted to end the war quickly. The Royal Air Force (RAF) had long followed a policy of area bombing, targeting entire cities to destroy civilian morale – just as Germany had done early in the war (one devastating raid obliterated Coventry and its medieval cathedral). Hoping for a knockout blow, the RAF chose to make an example of Dresden – the magnificent, baroque 'Florence-on-the-Elbe', Germany's pride and the only major German city still unscathed by bombing. Swollen with troops retreating from the eastern front and packed with refugees, Dresden contained nearly a million people instead of its usual 650,000.

The firestorm was planned; 773 Lancaster bombers alternated high explosive (to 'open' roofs, windows and walls) with thousands of small incendiaries and phosphorus bombs. The concentration of so many big fires among so many tall buildings super-heated the air above, drawing the flames together into an explosive fireball. On the scale of a city as big as Dresden the superheated fireball developed the uprushing power of a tornado with an air temperature so high people spontaneously combusted, or just melted. Thousands suffocated in cellars as oxygen was sucked from the atmosphere. Thousands more went insane as their skin bubbled and tore off in shreds. Wave after wave of aircraft left no respite, and the USAF fed the destruction for two more days with daylight raids by B-17 Flying Fortresses. Germany felt its soul had been seared and ripped out – as Britain had felt about Coventry. But the raid was not revenge. The destruction of Dresden was psychologically shrewd. However horrific, it shortened the war.

Dresden citizens in the Soviet sector of Germany attempting to board trams amid the ruins and chaos.

WHEN:
February 13–14 1945
WHERE:
Dresden, Germany
DEATH TOLL:
Estimates of the dead differ widely, from 40,000 to 100,000. Nobody had any idea how many people were in the city at the time, and thousands of bodies simply disappeared. Even more were terribly injured.
YOU SHOULD KNOW:
Arguments about the morality of mounting such a raid have reverberated ever since; but Dresden wasn't the only city of grace and culture to be annihilated, nor its people alone in the nature of their agonizing, unspeakable suffering. The moral horror of Dresden is perhaps the face of war itself. Happily, Dresden eventually became a symbol of reconciliation in 2004 when H M the Queen presented the city with a golden cross for the spire of its rebuilt baroque masterpiece, the Frauenkirche; and ministers from both Dresden and Coventry shared the consecration service.

Ballantyne's Department Store

WHEN:
November 18 1947
WHERE:
Cashel and Colombo Streets,
Christchurch, South Island,
New Zealand
DEATH TOLL:
41 members of Ballantyne's staff
were killed. There were few serious
injuries and burns – those who were
trapped, died.
YOU SHOULD KNOW:
The fire happened on Cup Day, so
Christchurch was full of extra visitors
who came to watch the disaster
unfold. Although some of the
obstruction was well-intentioned
(men seized firemen's hoses thinking
to help rather than hinder), the
crowds got so obstreperous with
anxiety that at one point firemen had
to turn the hoses on them to drive
them back.

The arcaded façade of Ballantyne's Department Store made a grand statement in the heart of Christchurch on South Island. Since opening in 1854 as the 'New Drapery Establishment', it had grown from one to seven buildings, mirroring New Zealand's booming prosperity. By 1947, Ballantyne's covered an acre. It was a maze of rooms and passages on two or three floors with 300 employees, and famous throughout the country. The store replicated New Zealand as a whole, including its subtle hierarchies and prevalent mores. And that proved fatal.

Midway through a November afternoon, a woman employee reported to her immediate superior, a floor salesman, that smoke was issuing from the cellar below the furnishings department. He passed the message up the staff chain, but called the fire brigade himself. They did not respond. In their offices the owners waited, then called again. The brigade arrived in two minutes, to find the ground floor already cleared of customers and staff, and flames licking through the floor of furnishings. Expecting a cellar fire, the firemen failed to bring a turntable ladder. That realization came as the whole centre of Ballantyne's exploded in flames, and it became obvious that no one had told the clerical staff and dressmaking department in their rambling, upstairs eyries.

It was grotesque. The firemen could not call for back-up because the telephone lines were overloaded. Department heads dithered for permission to evacuate their staff. The store's policy was not to allow staff to leave until all insured equipment had been signed off into a fireproof safe first – so the national culture of bureaucratic obedience made disaster inevitable. Worse, thousands of onlookers gathered to watch the spectacle, obstructing firemen, and exclaiming at tortured, flaming bodies being sucked back into the inferno. In every way, it was the worst fire in New Zealand's history.

Chongqing waterfront fire

Chongqing's importance is geographical: it sits on a hilly peninsula overlooking the confluence of the Yangzi and its principal tributary, the Jialing River. Today, people visit Chongqing to start cruises either to the nearby Three Gorges or downriver 2,400 km (1,500 mi) to Shanghai – but the city remains first and foremost a huge commercial port of vital strategic interest. It was China's capital from 1938–1945, ruled by Chiang Kai-shek for the Kuomintang National Government. Although the capital moved to Nanjing afterwards, Chongqing remained a Kuomintang stronghold with American assistance, until it was besieged and taken in 1949 by the People's Liberation Army of Mao Zedong. The waterfront fire that brought Chongqing such grisly fame took place during that siege.

Chaotianmen harbour runs along the Yangzi shore of the peninsula to its point, where the clear water of the Jialing runs parallel to the 'golden' (muddy) Yangzi. In 1949, although the port had been developed to handle massive civil and military traffic, this waterfront was still a district of narrow lanes with tall, ramshackle wooden buildings and warehouses. They had survived appalling Japanese bombing raids and represented a real link with the city's history.

Details of how a devastating fire started in September 1949 have been obscured by different propaganda interests. Chongqing waterfront still had lots of US installations and *matériel* given to support the Kuomintang, which they were reluctant to hand to the Communists. The Communists in turn like to refer only to the successful 'struggle' of the era. So was this catastrophic fire sabotage, military action, criminal arson, or just a simple accident in a highly sensitive area stuffed with explosives and flammable goods? The ghosts behind this veil of reluctance and secrecy make the fire seem more horrific. It was one of the worst fires the world has ever seen – but Chongqing's official guide makes no mention of it.

WHEN:
September 2 1949
WHERE:
Chongqing, China
DEATH TOLL:
At least 1,700 people died, trapped in a maze of old buildings whose usual entrances and exits were blocked by all manner of dead-ends, concrete walls, barbed wire and other defences that had accumulated in ten years of national and civil war.
YOU SHOULD KNOW:
The fire spread with the wind, helped by the presence of fuel oils, incendiaries and munitions. After the Japanese bombing (Chongqing holds the unhappy title of 'most severely bombed city') perhaps it didn't seem so awful; but each of the three parties involved – the USA, the Chinese Nationalists (Kuomintang) and the Communists – have, or had, good reasons to wish the fire to be remembered only as a 'local accident'.

Smoke pouring from Our Lady of the Angels Roman Catholic parochial school.

Our Lady of the Angels

The particular horror of school fires is that in addition to the personal tragedy of each child's death, the fire threatens the bond of trust whereby staff safeguard children *in loco parentis*. The fire that engulfed Our Lady of the Angels School in Chicago challenged even that basic assumption, not because the staff failed in their duty, but because they behaved impeccably according to the rules laid down by higher, external authorities, and their devotion to those rules caused the deaths of 95 children and nuns. The catalogue of pre-conditions, circumstances and mistaken responses is so comprehensive it hardly seems possible that such a disaster was not foreseen. In the light of its aftermath, it feels like a human sacrifice.

US school safety procedures were established in 1949, and incorporated huge technological improvements learned during World War II. They were not retrospective. Our Lady of the Angels was built in 1910 and extended in 1939, and despite appearances it was a firetrap. Up to 14 coats of highly flammable varnish covered the wood trim of open stairwells, and only the ground floor (US 'first floor') had fire doors. A small trashcan fire smouldered in the basement then swept up the stairwell, trapping 329 children and six nuns upstairs and causing a 'flashover' into the ceiling space above them, which then ignited. Only Mother Superior was allowed to activate the fire alarm, and she could not be found. When finally the fire brigade was alerted, it went to the wrong address. Two teachers tried independently to evacuate their classes; others obediently told the children to stay at their desks and pray for rescue. Nobody 'did' anything wrong. The catastrophe mushroomed out of goodwill and bad planning, and it's a miserable kind of satisfaction that at least it led to the most comprehensive review of national safety codes America had ever enforced.

WHEN:
December 1 1958
WHERE:
W Iowa Street, Chicago, Illinois, USA
DEATH TOLL:
92 children and three nuns died, and at least 120 others were severely injured with burns and broken bones sustained when jumping to safety. Although the school was officially blamed, forensic analysis concluded that, given the U-shaped building and the cumulative mistakes made (in good faith), it was a miracle that the death toll had not been higher.
YOU SHOULD KNOW:
There were many acts of courage and ingenuity. One Sister saved most of her class by blocking smoke and flames with books beneath the classroom door; and a parish priest was badly burned as he swung students from one blazing classroom window to another. Incredibly, it took 1 h 25 min to control the fire after it was first noticed. The Catholic Archdiocese of Chicago swiftly doled out individual compensation packages to avoid lawsuits.

Summerland holiday centre fire

If ever there was a contrast between the high hopes of a project's designers and that project's eventual outcome, the Summerland entertainment complex on the Isle of Man surely affords an all too sobering example. When this indoor holiday centre on the seafront at Douglas opened in 1971 it was the last word in design and innovation in the leisure industry. Summerland was going to do nothing less than confront head-on the challenge of cheap package holidays in the Mediterranean. Why bother to go to the Costa Brava when all your holiday needs could be met at home – and under one roof? You could spend the whole day at Summerland if you wanted – swimming in one of the two indoor pools, 'sunning' yourself in the Sundome, even pretending you were on a cruise ship with a game of deck quoits, or just enjoying the rides, amusement arcades and other traditional attractions of the British seaside.

The Summerland centre had been open only two years when on a cool, drizzly evening in early August 1973 the unimaginable happened: it caught fire. The fire started outside but spread rapidly through the interior of the building, where 3,000 people were thought to have been at the time. The fire alarm failed, there was no sprinkler system and little in the predominantly open-plan design to impede the flames. Survivors spoke afterwards of locked fire exits and inadequate evacuation routes. The building was completely destroyed in the blaze.

The police investigation established that the fire had been started accidentally by three lads who had been smoking outside the centre. The inquest into the deaths was highly critical of elements of the building's design and many of the construction materials but eventually returned a verdict of death by misadventure.

The skeleton of Summerland still ablaze.

WHEN:
August 2 1973
WHERE:
Douglas, Isle of Man, UK
DEATH TOLL:
50 people, mostly holidaymakers from northern England, died in the fire; a further 100 needed hospital treatment for their injuries.
YOU SHOULD KNOW:
The tragedy traumatized the tight-knit island community. In its report the Fire Commission said that it 'would leave a permanent scar in the minds of Manxmen.'

Firemen shovelling rubble from the shell of the club.

Beverley Hills Supper Club blaze

It was a typically busy Saturday night at the Beverley Hills Supper Club, a North Kentucky nightclub which was a magnet for people from the region looking for a good night out. There was an extra buzz in the air at the sprawling entertainment complex because this was the Memorial Day holiday weekend and some 1,200 customers had crowded into the Club's main Cabaret Room for the floor show featuring popular American singer John Davidson. As many people again were elsewhere in the building, dining and enjoying other facilities, when in the middle of the evening a fire burst out, spreading rapidly through the complex. The investigation afterwards showed that it had started in a small function room at the back of the building and had probably been caused by an electrical fault. Because the room was not in use at the time, the fire had burned for a while before being discovered.

When firefighters arrived they were met with a blazing inferno. There had been a stampede to evacuate the Cabaret Room and it was here that most of the deaths occurred. Many who managed to escape the flames succumbed to the deadly smoke from the cocktail of chemicals released by burning plastics. There was no hope of saving the building itself, which burned throughout the night. When daylight came, the grim task of salvaging corpses from the smouldering ruins could finally begin.

The subsequent inquiry into the disaster revealed various breaches of fire and safety codes, including a lack of alarms and sprinklers. Some of the construction materials also turned out to have been highly combustible. Worst of all, on that fateful night the club was thought to have had double the number of patrons it could safely accommodate.

WHEN:
May 28 1977
WHERE:
Southgate, North Kentucky, USA
DEATH TOLL:
165
YOU SHOULD KNOW:
This was one of the first public disasters in American history in which the victims' families pursued a class action suit for negligence against various manufacturers and equipment suppliers. Litigation lasted for years but settlements were finally obtained totalling some $50 million.

Stardust disco fire

Friday the 13th turned out to be a tragically unlucky day for 48 young people who died in a 1981 fire that consumed a Dublin disco. It was St Valentine's Eve and a crowd of youngsters had gathered at the Stardust Club in the Artane area of North Dublin for an evening of dancing and romance. When the fire was first discovered some time after midnight staff attempted to bring the blaze under control by sealing off the area, but this simply fanned the flames and drove them into the main ballroom where the disco was being held. With lights failing and walls and ceiling tiles emitting thick plumes of black smoke, panic erupted among the dancers. In the stampede for the exits some were trampled underfoot while others collapsed in the noxious atmosphere.

While the patrons at another function in the club were alerted in time and successfully evacuated, the young dancers were less fortunate. The building which had promised a good night out turned with horrifying speed into a prison from which many of them never escaped; fire exits had been locked with chains and windows barred by iron grilles. Rescue workers afterwards described their helpless horror as they watched people inside claw vainly at the bars.

Although a tribunal of inquiry concluded that arson was the probable cause, no criminal charges have ever been laid in respect of the Stardust fire. The victims' families have never accepted this finding and in the years since have resolutely campaigned for the government to re-open the inquiry. They believe that the club's owners, a local business family with connections to prominent Irish politicians, should be held criminally liable for the disaster.

WHEN:
February 13 1981
WHERE:
North Dublin, Ireland
DEATH TOLL:
The 48 young people who died had an average age of just 19. Over 200 more were injured.
YOU SHOULD KNOW:
As recently as January 2009 a new and independent examination of the case concluded that the finding of arson by the original tribunal of inquiry was wrong. Evidence has emerged in the years since of certain flammable materials having been dangerously and inappropriately stored in the club's premises.

Salang Tunnel fire

The difficult and dangerous Salang Pass crosses the Hindu Kush mountain range that bisects Afghanistan, traditionally making travel between southern and northern regions a laborious process, particularly in winter. But one useful legacy of the Soviet Union's aggressive interest in Afghanistan was the Salang Tunnel, providing all-weather vehicular passage beneath the forbidding pass. This engineering marvel is 2.6 km (1.5 mi) long at the lofty altitude of 3,400 m (11,150 ft) and upon completion in 1964 greatly facilitated north-south travel, cutting the journey time to ten hours from three days. It also greatly improved communications between the Soviet Union and the Afghan capital, Kabul.

But this was a legacy that turned to ashes – literally. The tunnel became a vital strategic facility during the Soviet-Afghan War that erupted in 1979, allowing Soviet military traffic to move freely both ways. In November 1982, a Soviet army convoy travelling south was engulfed by fire, in a catastrophe that may well be one of the most disastrous conflagrations the world has ever seen. But the world didn't see and will never know for sure, as the Red Army wasn't about to announce details of such a terrible reverse to comfort its enemies during a hard-fought war.

The fire may have resulted from a *mujaheddin* operation, as these fearsome guerrilla fighters frequently mounted ambushes on tunnel traffic. However, the general consensus suggests a fuel tanker exploded after a collision within the tunnel, with the resulting flash fire made infinitely more serious by the tunnel's narrow confines – its tube being just 7 m (22 ft) wide and tall. There were a considerable number of Afghan casualties – certainly over 100 – although the Russian death toll remains a closely guarded secret to this day. But the true figure may well have run into the thousands.

WHEN:
November 3 1982
WHERE:
Hindu Kush mountains, Afghanistan
DEATH TOLL:
Unknown. The top estimate is 2,750 dead, mainly Red Army soldiers, but this is pure speculation. However, it is generally accepted that the casualty figure does put this tragic event right at the top of any list of all-time fire-related disasters.
YOU SHOULD KNOW:
The Soviet cover-up was comprehensive. In a fit of apparent candour, it was officially announced that there had been a collision in the Salang Tunnel between two military convoys numbered 2211 and 2212, causing a serious traffic blockage. This led to the deaths of 64 soldiers and 112 Afghanis through a build-up of carbon monoxide, but of course there was definitely no fire or explosion.

King's Cross fire

WHEN:
November 18 1987
WHERE:
London, UK
DEATH TOLL:
31 died and over 60 were injured
(suffering various degrees of burns
and smoke inhalation).
YOU SHOULD KNOW:
One male victim of the fire was not
identified and became known as
'Body 115' after his mortuary tag.
The mystery was finally solved with
the help of DNA analysis nearly
20 years later, when it was
confirmed that he was Alexander
Fallon, a 73-year-old from Scotland.

A major interchange on the London Underground system is King's Cross St Pancras, a station complex that serves both overground lines and the Tube. There are in effect two Tube stations, the shallow one for the Circle, Metropolitan and Hammersmith & City Lines plus a deep-level station for the Northern, Piccadilly and Victoria Lines. One Wednesday in November 1987 the escalator shaft serving the Piccadilly line was busy with early evening travellers when a small fire broke out at about 19.30.

The 50-year-old elevators were partially constructed from wood, and a carelessly dropped lit match fell down the side of the moving staircase, igniting the oily running mechanism below. Minor escalator fires were not uncommon, and the potential severity of this one was not initially appreciated. Emergency services were in attendance and an orderly evacuation was under way when a combination of circumstances turned an unfortunate incident into a major tragedy.

Down below, a westbound Tube train departed just as an eastbound train arrived. This created a powerful up-draught through the escalator shaft and this piston effect caused a flashover – the phenomenon where hot gases given off by over-heated combustible materials ignite, consuming everything flammable in a deadly burst of flame and intense heat. A jet of flame roared into the ticket hall,

The top of the fire-damaged escalators

which quickly filled with toxic smoke so that even many of those who escaped the flames were overcome – including fireman Colin Townsley, who died from smoke inhalation after trying to rescue a woman in difficulties. He was one of over 30 victims of the fire, which burned until the early hours of the following morning. As a result of the King's Cross fire, the partial ban on smoking first introduced in 1984 was rigorously enforced throughout the Tube network and almost all London Underground's ageing wooden escalators were replaced by new all-steel versions.

Kader Doll Factory

In 1993, Thailand's worst-ever industrial disaster killed more than 180 workers in a catastrophic conflagration. Indeed, although it received little publicity outside Thailand, the Kader Doll Factory fire is the worst industrial factory fire ever recorded, claiming a greater number of victims than the infamous and well-publicized Triangle Shirtwaist Factory fire that took place in New York back in 1911.

The Kader Doll Factory manufactured plastic dolls and stuffed toys, mostly branded items for big American corporations like Mattel and Disney. The workforce mainly consisted of young women from rural families who toiled in a badly designed E-shaped multi-storey production facility, built to poor standards. Despite fire exits being shown on original construction plans, these were not actually included in the finished building. Furthermore, it was usual practice to keep the exit doors that were there locked during working hours.

It was a recipe for disaster, which duly unfolded on a May afternoon after a small fire started in a first-floor area of Building One, used to store finished goods. This was thought to be so insignificant by management that the fire alarm wasn't sounded and workers were instructed to remain at their posts. But the fire spread with frightening speed, not only within their section but also to flammable raw materials elsewhere in the factory.

As workers in Building One scrambled to escape, they found ground-floor exit doors locked. The building's skeleton consisted of unprotected steel girders that soon buckled and twisted in the intense heat, making the staircase unusable. As terrified workers jumped from upper floors the building collapsed, just as firefighting teams arrived on site.

Nearly 190 workers died in the blaze, or subsequently from burns and smoke inhalation, while 500 were injured. The other buildings were evacuated without loss of life.

WHEN:
May 10 1993
WHERE:
Sam Phran, Nakhon Pathom Province, Thailand
DEATH TOLL:
188
YOU SHOULD KNOW:
Despite agonized public utterances by Thai politicians after this horrifying disaster, and solemn promises of a review of industrial safety standards and proper enforcement of those that did exist, little changed. As is so often the case, the imperative to sustain economic growth at any price ensured that bold promises to shut down every Thai factory without adequate fire safety systems were quietly forgotten once the Kader Doll Factory fire faded from the headlines.

Gothenburg Discotheque fire

WHEN:
October 29 1998
WHERE:
Hisingen Island, Gothenburg, Sweden
DEATH TOLL:
63 dead and more than 200 injured.
YOU SHOULD KNOW:
In the days after the arson attack, leaflets began to appear calling for revenge against the perceived Swedish perpetrators. One particularly unsavoury handout called for 60 Swedes to be killed to avenge the loss. Physical and emotional scars have taken time to heal. A beautifully crafted granite and gold memorial was unveiled ten years after the tragedy.

The disco held in a Macedonian community centre in Gothenburg was intended to provide some Hallowe'en fun for the youth of the city's immigrant communities. However, this innocent evening of music and dancing turned into a nightmare as fire engulfed the premises, leaving over half the attendees dead or injured.

The centre's upstairs dance hall was licensed to hold 150 people, but there was little chance of stopping the revellers piling in and as many as 400 were present by 23.00. Shortly after 23.30 the smell of smoke began to drift over the dance floor, but most of the partygoers thought this was coming from a smoke machine. Then a DJ noticed flames and issued a warning to the crowd, but this too was dismissed by many as a prank. The large group of young adults were there to party and little could distract them. By the time the fire took hold on one of only two stairwells that could facilitate their escape, it was too late. The noise was so great that, when a call was finally made to the emergency services, the operator had difficulty in hearing the address. That said, once called, the fire brigade arrived on the scene quickly and were well prepared. The firefighters were greeted by a panic-stricken scene – people were hurling themselves out of windows and rushing to escape out of one narrow doorway.

For some time the authorities refused to disclose what many had suspected – that the fire was the result of arson. Rumour was rife and some in the immigrant community pointed the finger of blame at Swedish Neo-Nazis. Tensions ran high, until four young Iranians were found to have started the blaze in an idiotic and deadly game of dare.

The interior of the hall after the fire where teenagers died while they were celebrating Halloween.

Enschede fireworks warehouse

One moment the neighbourhood of Roombeek in the eastern Dutch city of Enschede was there, the next it was gone. Some 400 houses were destroyed and 15 streets obliterated within a 40 hectare (100 acre) area, with damage caused by a massive explosion rippling outwards to engulf a further 1,500 houses. Nearly 1,000 people were injured, many seriously, and 22 had been killed. Around 10,000 residents were subsequently evacuated and the final damage bill exceeded 450 million euros.

A huge smoke cloud hangs over the fireworks warehouse.

The culprit was a disastrous conflagration at the SE Fireworks facility. The company imported large quantities of fireworks from China for pyrotechnic displays at major events and boasted a good safety record. The premises had been inspected just one week before the accident, confirming the fact that relevant official regulations were being complied with. This made the subsequent catastrophe all the more puzzling, and the precise cause has never been determined.

What is known is that the chain of events leading to this huge detonation began with a fire in the central building, where a considerable quantity of fireworks was kept – either set by an arsonist or sparked by an electrical short-circuit. This ignited the stored fireworks and initiated a chain reaction. Next, two container-loads of fireworks – illegally stored outside the building – went up. Finally, the main bunker containing 177 tonnes of fireworks exploded in a massive fireball, sending a dense cloud of black smoke skywards.

This was an outcome that shouldn't have been possible, as the warehouse had been carefully designed to isolate firework stores from any possible source of accidental ignition. It was suspected – but never proved – that internal safety doors had been left open by careless staff. After the event, two SE Fireworks managers were convicted of criminal negligence and received short prison sentences. The Roombeek area was rebuilt.

WHEN:
May 13 2000
WHERE:
Enschede, Netherlands
DEATH TOLL:
22 dead and 947 injured
YOU SHOULD KNOW:
The Eurovision Song Contest 2000 was taking place on May 13 and telephone voting in the Netherlands was suspended in the aftermath of the explosion, both as a mark of respect for presumed victims and to free up the communications networks for urgent use by emergency services.

Workers try to contain the fire at the rubber factory.

Lagos armoury explosion

Nigeria is a country split by religion and factionalism. It is home to Christians and Muslims in equal number and even within these groupings there are innumerable tribal subdivisions. Fighting in the north continues and the riches gained from large oil reserves do not trickle down to the majority of the population. Above all it is a country held together by a powerful military, who can more often than not do as they please. It is also a place that seems cursed by bad luck – if something can go wrong it invariably will.

When, in 2001, the government asked the army to decommission a large munitions warehouse located in the densely populated northern district of the capital, Lagos, the generals ignored the request. They wanted their armaments to be easily accessible and hang the risk. On a January evening in 2002, a fire broke out in a market adjacent to the warehouse. This sparked a cataclysmic sequence of events.

At around 18.00 the fire spread to the armoury and despite frantic attempts to control it, little could be done. A series of small blasts preceded several huge explosions as the whole store spewed out its ordnance like an erupting volcano. Buildings for several miles around were shaken to their foundations, with many collapsing and crushing the people inside. Many fled in panic as shells, grenades and bullets rained down on them. Hundreds died in the crush. In the confusion, many sought refuge in a neighbouring banana plantation, little knowing that their path was blocked by an overgrown, but deep, canal. As darkness fell, more and more people plunged through the vegetation to their deaths, pushed by a confused crowd fleeing the mayhem.

WHEN:
January 27 2002
WHERE:
Lagos, Nigeria
DEATH TOLL:
Around 1,500 killed, thousands more injured and tens of thousands left homeless.
YOU SHOULD KNOW:
The explosions caused such widespread damage to the area's infrastructure that it took years to recover. Many people who lost loved ones suffered the double tragedy of homelessness and extreme poverty.

The Station nightclub fire

When it was announced that the 1980s rock act Great White would be headlining an evening of retro rock music at The Station nightclub in West Warwick, Rhode Island, their small but loyal following turned out in force. The warm-up acts went down well and, by the time Great White took the stage, shortly after 23.00, spirits were high. The band started with their traditional opening song 'Desert Moon', accompanied by a pyrotechnic display laid on by the group's manager.

The band had scarcely got going when the fireworks sent a spray of sparks up into the sound-proofing foam above the stage. The foam quickly ignited, surrounding the band with flames. Most of the audience thought this was all part of the act and just carried on enjoying the show. The fire quickly engulfed the whole ceiling, sending billows of black smoke across the arena, at which point the lead singer shouted 'this ain't good' and the band headed for an exit behind the stage. Soon all anyone could hear was the penetrating squeal of the club's fire alarm system. Despite the fact that the club had four functioning exits, in their haste to get out most of the audience chose to leave through the narrow hallway through which they had arrived. The passage soon filled up and became impassable, leading those in the club to push even harder as the fire sucked the oxygen from the room. One hundred lost their lives in the stampede, either through being trampled or as a result of smoke inhalation and severe burns. Only around one quarter of the 470 present escaped unharmed.

The fire had a huge impact on the local community. Scores of children lost their parents, the band lost their lead guitarist, Ty Longley, and lawsuits totalling $180 million were initiated.

WHEN:
February 20 2003
WHERE:
West Warwick, Rhode Island, USA
DEATH TOLL:
100
YOU SHOULD KNOW:
The fire was caught on film by cameraman Brian Butler, who was on the scene to do a piece for a local television station about safety in nightclubs. Two main lessons can be learnt from this and numerous other similar tragedies: indoor pyrotechnics are a bad idea and you should always check out the fire escapes when attending a crowded venue.

Investigators with plaintiffs' law firms were allowed by authorities to inspect the remains.

República Cromañón nightclub fire

WHEN:
December 30 2004
WHERE:
República Cromañón nightclub,
Buenos Aires, Argentina
DEATH TOLL:
194 dead and more than 700 injured
YOU SHOULD KNOW:
A subsequent inquiry revealed that
the inspection system was severely
flawed. In 2006, the mayor of Buenos
Aires was impeached and removed
from office and, in a trial some four
years after the fire, the club's owner,
its manager and a local official
received lengthy prison sentences.

There is a growing body of opinion in developed countries that people's freedom is becoming stifled by health and safety legislation and that somehow society has become too risk averse. However, it might be worth imagining a culture where such legislation is thin on the ground and where even this can be circumvented by greasing the palms of dishonest officials with relatively small amounts of money.

Although by 2004 Argentina had shaken off the shackles of a brutal military junta, its civilian infrastructure was riddled with corruption. The events on New Year's Eve of that year at República Cromañón nightclub came to embody much that was wrong with the new Argentina. More than 3,000 revellers crammed into the venue to see Los Callejeros, a popular local rock band. The arena was lavishly decorated with, at its centrepiece, a *Media Sombra* ('half shade') in the form of a giant net. Literally everything that was used to adorn the venue was highly flammable.

Fireworks are a central part of seasonal celebrations in South America and, despite warnings from the band, a flare was set off in the crowd. The overhead netting immediately caught fire and showered the crowd with fragments of molten plastic. Overcome with fright, everyone made a dash for the exits only to find most of them firmly locked. Within a few minutes the whole place became a raging inferno as the foam decorations began to burn, spewing noxious fumes into the nightclub. The air turned more and more poisonous and scores of people died from asphyxiation while hundreds more suffered lung damage from the toxic smoke.

A fireman inspects the damage following the fire at República Cromañón nightclub.

Momart fire

When in 2004 fire ripped through an East London warehouse housing a large selection of British contemporary art, certain sections of the print media could scarcely contain their glee. Purporting to speak for their readership, they had always seen the Britart movement as a scam foisted on the British public by talentless artists and funded by a rich patron – Charles Saatchi. For them art should be nothing more challenging than a rural idyll in a gilt-edged frame. One artist in particular got their goat and when Tracey Emin burst on the scene with 'that unmade bed' they took great delight in mocking it. But, by putting it on the front page of newspapers that sold in their millions, they ensured that the work of the Turner Prize-winning artist reached a truly mass audience. Any publicity was good publicity and, fuelled by their notoriety, artists such as Emin, Damien Hirst and the Chapman Brothers flourished and prospered.

When not being displayed, many of their works were housed in the Momart warehouse – a storage facility leased from a removals company. A fire started when burglars sought to cover their tracks in an adjacent building by torching it. The fire quickly spread throughout the whole complex, destroying such notable works as Emin's 'Everyone I Have Ever Slept With 1963–1995' and the Chapman Brothers 'Hell'. The fire was not fully extinguished for a full two days and it was feared that all the artworks stored were lost. Miraculously some works did survive the blaze, including 'Charity' –a bronze by Hirst.

While the art world mourned its loss, Tracey Emin put things into perspective stating that, when set against the suffering in places such as Iraq and the Dominican Republic, the destruction of her work was of only minor importance.

Firefighters walk from the blaze.

WHEN:
May 24 2004
WHERE:
Leyton, East London, UK
TOLL:
The artworks lost were valued at between £30 and £50 million.
YOU SHOULD KNOW:
Many artists, patrons and curators questioned the wisdom of housing such important works in what was a multiple-occupancy building. Even after the fire those who lost their collections were treated to the further indignity of seeing Uri Geller sifting through the wreckage. He told the media that he wished to create a single piece from the fragments he found – thankfully the threat of legal action put a halt to his ill-conceived plans.

Investigators walk around the back of the day-care centre.

Hermosillo day-care centre fire

When in June 2009 fire spread from a warehouse to a centre minding the children of local workers, it set in motion a chain of events that shocked the whole of Mexico and left the residents of the northern city of Hermosillo inconsolable with grief. The fire started at around 15.00 in a heating unit and soon breached the thin walls of the centre, filling it with noxious fumes. Around 150 staff and children were present at the centre when the blaze began.

There were several notable acts of individual bravery as fire crews, parents and passers-by strove to rescue children from the inferno. One desperate father drove his vehicle through the walls of the centre. His actions led to the rescue of many children, though sadly not his own. With anguish etched on their faces, the families could do little more than wait behind a yellow police line to see if their children had been spared. Thirty children died at the scene, mainly through smoke inhalation and the collapse of a ceiling, while 40 needed urgent hospital attention. A further 17 children died later as a result of their injuries.

Although government funded, the centre was privately run. A lax system of inspection allowed it to function even though it had no working emergency exits, no sprinkler system and a partially obscured fire alarm. Proper safety measures were made all the more important by the fact that the authorities had allowed the setting up of a childcare centre on an industrial estate containing a large amount of highly combustible material. The bereaved parents' grief soon turned to anger and they demanded greater transparency in the childcare system and, above all, that someone should be held to account for their heartbreaking loss.

WHEN:
June 5 2009
WHERE:
Hermosillo, Sonora State, Mexico
DEATH TOLL:
47
YOU SHOULD KNOW:
Even though the centre was licensed to cater only for children over two years, such was the demand for their services that some as young as six months were being looked after.

Perm nightclub fire

The city of Perm, lying on the European edge of the Ural Mountains 1,400 km (780 mi) east of Moscow, rarely appears in the international headlines, even though it is Russia's sixth largest city with a population of over one million. On a weekend in early December 2009, however, it found itself facing the full glare of the world's media, but not for a reason it would ever have chosen. A private party was in full swing at the Lazy Horse, a city-centre nightclub that was celebrating its eighth anniversary. Between 250 and 300 guests were enjoying a floor show which apparently included fireworks. When one of these set light to wickerwork decorations on the ceiling, the flames spread through the building in seconds. In the pandemonium that followed many people were overcome by the heat and thick smoke, while others were crushed in the stampede to flee the building. Most had little chance of getting out unscathed as there was only one narrow exit from the club and fire regulations had been patently ignored.

There was a national outcry following the tragedy, by far Russia's worst fire disaster since the fall of communism. The government in Moscow lambasted local and regional officials for having ridden slipshod over basic fire and safety procedures. In the immediate aftermath four people, including the club's owner and the supplier of the fireworks, were arrested and charged with manslaughter. They had apparently ignored repeated demands from the authorities to modify the interior to make it comply with safety standards. The city's mayor and entire regional administration also resigned *en masse*, amid accusations of endemic corruption among fire inspectors who were alleged to turn a routine blind eye to fire code violations in return for bribes.

WHEN:
December 5 2009
WHERE:
Perm, Russia
DEATH TOLL:
149 people died, including many later in hospital from the severe burns and other injuries sustained.
YOU SHOULD KNOW:
Lax enforcement of fire and safety regulations is sadly not untypical in Russia which, with some 18,000 fire-related deaths a year, has the worst such record of any developed country.

Russian men light candles in front of the Lazy Horse nightclub.

HEALTH
DISASTERS

The plague of Justinian

WHEN:
AD 541–542
WHERE:
Constantinople (Istanbul) in
present-day Turkey
DEATH TOLL:
Without any accurate historical
record, it is impossible to be certain
of the mortality rate: estimates vary
between 25 million and 100 million
deaths – a vast number. At the height
of the plague 10,000 people a day
were dying in Constantinople.
YOU SHOULD KNOW:
Bubonic plague is a a virulent
flea-borne bacterial infection that
primarily affects rodents. The plague
spreads to other mammals, including
humans, when infected fleas looking
for a new host settle on them. The
flea-bite injects the plague bacteria
into the victim, causing 'buboes',
excruciatingly painful swellings that
quickly turn gangrenous. Today
bubonic plague is easily treatable
with antibiotics but there are still
about 2,000 deaths a year across
the world.

Although there is plenty of evidence that bubonic plague has been around for as long as mankind, the plague of Justinian is the first properly documented bubonic plague pandemic. The Greek historian Procopius wrote a history of the Byzantine Roman Empire during the reign of Justinian, in which he recounts the devastation wreaked by the plague on Constantinople (later renamed Istanbul), at that time the most important political and cultural centre of the Western world and the hub of Christian civilization.

The plague appears to have started in Lower Egypt in AD 540 and gradually spread across the Mediterranean in the ships that transported grain to the centre of the Empire. The first few cases appeared in Constantinople in the spring of 542. The disease soon took hold and started to spread like wildfire, raging for four months. People died faster than they could be buried. The Emperor ordered vast pits to be dug to dispose of the rotting corpses; when these overflowed, bodies were stuffed into the towers of the city walls with quicklime poured over them to speed up decomposition, or were loaded onto ships that were pushed out into the Sea of Marmora and set alight. Constantinople came to a standstill, food started to run out and law and order broke down. By the time the plague had run its course nearly half the city's population was dead.

The plague spread throughout western Europe where it became endemic with localized outbreaks occurring for the next two centuries. However, the worst was over by AD 590, by which time about a third of Europe's population had been wiped out. Not for another 1,000 years, when the Black Death ravaged Europe, would a pandemic on the scale of the plague of Justinian be experienced again.

The Black Death

WHEN:
Peaked 1348–1350
WHERE:
Europe
DEATH TOLL:
An estimated 25 million

Mid 14th century Europe was debilitated by years of war, the cruel winters of the 'Little Ice Age', poor harvests, and diseases which struck man and beast. In 1347 the Black Death arrived in Sicily via trade routes with the East and by 1348 had spread to England.

The 'Great Pestilence' or 'Great Mortality', as it was called at the time, was incredibly virulent, taking hold within hours and killing within days. It has recently been suggested that the Black Death may have been some sort of contagious human-to-human infection, but it is more usually thought to have been one or more sorts of plague, spread by black rats carrying infected fleas.

To the people of medieval Europe the plague was an inexplicable and unstoppable nightmare. When doctors, priests and prayers all

proved equally ineffectual, terrified people tried everything from imbibing herbal remedies to ringing church bells. The plague was thought to be a punishment from God and bands of flagellants took to roaming from town to town whipping themselves in penance. People fled from their homes, abandoning their dying families, and whole villages were evacuated leaving starving animals to stray through the untended fields. In some parts of Europe, Jews bore the brunt of people's terror – in many places they were tortured and burned, leaving their communities shattered.

Around half the population of Europe died within four years and for the next two centuries outbreaks of plague continued to wreak havoc on society. People started to question the infallibility of the pope while the drastic decrease in the peasant population meant there was a shortage of manual workers, increasing the worth of both labourer and artisan. The Black Death completely disrupted the social and economic order and was a major factor in bringing about the end of the feudal system.

Dancing mania swept through Europe during the medieval plague. Penitents prayed for mitigation of the plague.

YOU SHOULD KNOW:
Plague is caused by the bacterium *Yersinia pestis*. The disease manifests itself in one of three ways: bubonic – infecting the lymph nodes with gangrenous swellings (buboes) in the groin, armpits and neck; septicemic – infecting the bloodstream, causing blood poisoning; pneumonic – infecting the lungs. Only the pneumonic variety could be passed from one person to the next – in the droplets that went into the air when a victim coughed; otherwise it was transmitted by flea bites.

197

The Indians believed in curing smallpox and pneumonia by building a sweat hut on the bank of a creek, they then placed heated rocks inside the hut and covered the hut with a blanket. The sick would disrobe and enter the hut and stay inside until thoroughly drenched in perspiration. They then plunged into the cold water of the creek.

Smallpox among the American Indians

The New World that Columbus discovered in 1492 was rich in wonders but devoid of immunity to old-world diseases. Smallpox, a feared killer in Europe and Asia for centuries, was unknown in the Americas before the 'white man' arrived. The disease stripped North and South America of its indigenous inhabitants far more effectively than any amount of war with the colonizers.

In 1520 when Cortez and his men retreated from the Central American Aztec capital Tenochtitlan they left smallpox in their wake. When the *conquistadores* finally captured the city in 1521 they found it strewn with smallpox victims. Around 40 per cent of the Aztec population died of the disease. Altogether, more than two thirds of Mexico's population was lost. Similarly, the Incas of Peru were weakened by European diseases and eventually between 60 and 90 per cent had been killed by smallpox, while some of the Caribbean peoples were almost entirely wiped out.

Smallpox did its destructive job far more slowly among the scattered tribes of the North American Plains. European settlers suffered epidemics throughout the 17th and 18th centuries which inevitably spread to the 'biologically naive' Amerindian population, carried by the fur trade to the remotest regions. The first major epidemic of 1617–1619 decimated tribes throughout the Great Plains. The Native Americans tried traditional remedies to no avail. At first they thought they were being punished for violation of tribal laws but, as soon as they realized that smallpox came from the European colonists, they thought they were being deliberately infected. By 1800 the population of the Plains Indians was reduced by two thirds.

Vaccination programmes were established in the 19th century and smallpox was gradually eradicated from the Americas. But by then it was too late. Whole civilizations had been destroyed and unique cultures lost for ever.

WHEN:
1492–1900
WHERE:
North and South America
DEATH TOLL:
The population of the Americas before 1492 is unknown. It is possible that smallpox wiped out as much as 80 per cent of the Amerindians; some groups became extinct.
YOU SHOULD KNOW:
The sweat lodge (a sort of sauna) was traditionally used by North American Indians as a remedy for disease. Tragically, it was inappropriate for smallpox victims – the steaming herbs used as analgesics and decongestants were often emetic, the heat worsened the sores and the cold plunge afterwards weakened resistance and caused shock.

198

The Great Plague of London

Since the Black Death, London had suffered several outbreaks of plague and had established a quarantine system to restrict infection – houses shut and guarded, doors marked with a cross, disposal carts for dumping the dead in mass graves. But this epidemic was different: the population of London had tripled between 1650 and 1665, when the plague arrived; rats scurried everywhere through the squalid streets of the city and invaded the over-crowded slum dwellings of the poor – and rats carried infected fleas.

The first case in April was followed by one of the hottest summers in memory. Deaths escalated as the plague spread through London. The King's Court and the nobility hastily departed, followed by the middle classes – lawyers, merchants, clergy and doctors. The 'plague doctors' who remained were unqualified opportunists and the sick and the dying were abandoned. Normal daily life came to a halt: inns were closed, markets banned, shops shut, and dogs and cats were destroyed for fear they carried contagion – giving the rats free reign. Parishes employed local residents to carry out the Plague Orders – reporting sickness, nursing, moving bodies. Thousands of families were confined to their homes, waiting to die.

In August the plague spread around the country. It reached Eyam in Derbyshire where the villagers heroically quarantined themselves to prevent the disease spreading further – three quarters of the village died. In London thousands died in the first week of September, and thousands more camped on boats in the Thames to escape infection. Fires burned in the streets; church bells tolled continually.

As the weather began to cool, the rate of infection slowed and Londoners started to come home. The King returned in February 1666. But new plague cases were still appearing in September, when the Great Fire destroyed much of the city and finally purged London of the infection.

WHEN:
1665–1666
WHERE:
London, UK
DEATH TOLL:
Contemporary Bills of Mortality list 68,576 deaths. Records were not always kept for the poor, and some deaths went unreported to avoid quarantine, so the true figure was probably nearer 100,000.
YOU SHOULD KNOW:
The famous diarist Samuel Pepys stayed in London throughout the plague. Much of our knowledge of events comes from the detailed and moving eye-witness record he left for posterity.

Illustration depicting the effects of London's 17th-century plague.

Caragea's plague

WHEN:
1813–1814
WHERE:
Bucharest, Romania
DEATH TOLL:
An estimated 60,000–70,000 deaths in two years, of which 20,000–30,000 were in Bucharest itself and the remainder in the surrounding countryside.
YOU SHOULD KNOW:
Plague is fatal in approximately 50 per cent of cases unless treated with antibiotics.

In the centuries following the Black Death, bubonic plague reappeared spasmodically in Europe, gradually receding eastwards where it continued to ravage the Ottoman Empire. The last major European outbreak was in 1813 in Bucharest, capital of the Ottoman principality of Wallachia, in what is now Romania.

In 1812 Ioan Caragea was appointed governor of Bucharest. He travelled from Constantinople to take up his post and on the way one of his retainers died of plague. Whether this single case was responsible for introducing the disease to Bucharest is uncertain; but, together with persistent reports of cases in Constantinople and the surrounding provinces during the following months, it alerted Caragea to prepare for the worst. He established two quarantine hospitals in January 1813, and the city waited . . .

On June 11 the first case was officially notified and Caragea immediately implemented emergency measures, putting Bucharest into lock-down: the city gates were guarded to prevent unauthorized people roaming to and fro; all markets, schools, bars and cafes were closed; and coins were soaked in vinegar to disinfect them. But of course none of these precautions was in the least use against the fleas that spread the disease; the quarantine hospitals were soon filled to overflowing and effectively became charnel houses.

The stench of death hung in the city air as public morgue officials wheeled their carts from house to house collecting corpses for disposal, indiscriminately piling up the sick together with the dead. If the former tried to resist they were simply cudgelled to death, though occasionally the odd sturdy specimen managed to fight back and escape. By autumn there were far too many corpses to bury, so bodies were simply slung into open pits and left to rot. Before the epidemic was over, Caragea's plague had wiped out half the population of Bucharest.

Cholera pandemics

The first documented account of cholera appears in an Indian medical report of 1563, but the disease seems to have been restricted to Bengal until the 19th century, when unprecedented population growth and increased mobility facilitated its transmission across the world. The expansion of global trade, rapid urbanization and extensive military campaigns all contributed to a series of six devastating pandemics that killed millions of people.

An outbreak in Calcutta in 1816 led to the first pandemic. Carried by pilgrims and troops across the subcontinent, by 1820 it was being transmitted along trade routes: eastwards into China, Japan and the Philippines, westwards to the Persian Gulf, and northwards through central Asia to the borders of Russia. Europe was spared – just.

Almost as soon as the first pandemic had receded, a second one started in 1829. This time it took hold in Russia, from where it rapidly spread through Europe. Paris and London were stricken in 1832, with thousands dying in both cities. Emigrants carried the infection across the Atlantic to New York, and by 1834 it had spread to the west coast, southwards into Latin America and north to Canada.

London was again badly affected by the third pandemic of 1852–1863, 'the most terrible outbreak of cholera which ever occurred in the kingdom'. In Soho people were dropping like flies when Dr John Snow tracked the source of infection to a public water pump that was being contaminated by a nearby cesspit. Through his use of statistics and spot maps, Dr Snow single-handedly founded the science of epidemiology.

The pandemics of 1863–1875 and 1881–1896 again hit Europe hard, but by the time of the sixth pandemic of 1899–1923, when mortalities ran to 800,000 in India and 500,000 in Russia, most of Europe escaped relatively unscathed because of improved sanitation.

WHEN:
1816–1852
WHERE:
Across the world, spreading from Bengal, India
DEATH TOLL:
Millions. Between 1817 and 1860 there were 15 million deaths in India alone. In Britain, 55,000 deaths were recorded in the outbreak of 1832 while an 1848 epidemic killed 52,000. Between 1847 and 1861 more than two-and-a-half million Russians contracted the disease and over a million died.
YOU SHOULD KNOW:
Cholera is spread through contaminated food and water. Prevention is straightforward – strict public health measures and decent sanitation. The *Vibria cholerae* bacterium, of which there are at least 16 different strains, causes extremely painful muscular spasms in the intestines with diarrhoea and vomiting of such severity that the victim often dies of dehydration within 24 hours. At present the world is suffering from a seventh pandemic. It started in Indonesia in 1961 and shows no signs of receding. In many parts of the world cholera is now endemic.

The plague and cholera costume suggested to frantic citizens of Vienna during the 19th-century epidemic. At that time scores of recipes and sanitary measures were devised. The woman pictured has a cholera band around her body and her skirt is weighted down by bags of aromatic herbs. Her shoes are of double width and size to prevent infections from the street. The small windmill on her hat was to chase away evil winds. All the fantastic superstitions that cholera created are here adorning the lady's dress.

Fiji: a tragic epidemic

WHEN:
January to June 1875
WHERE:
Fiji
DEATH TOLL:
Around 40,000 – a third of the
population
YOU SHOULD KNOW:
Measles is a highly contagious viral
disease of the respiratory system
with accompanying symptoms of
high fever and rash. An otherwise
healthy person is unlikely to be
seriously ill but it can be very
serious indeed for anyone whose
immune system is already
compromised by malnourishment,
leading to secondary complications
such as pneumonia or encephalitis
and, all too often, death or
permanent disability.

Fate played a cruel trick on the natives of Fiji. The islands emerged from appalling inter-tribal wars in 1874, hopeful of a peaceful and prosperous future under British colonial governance, only to immediately suffer the loss of entire tribes – wiped out not by war, but measles.

In October 1874, Fijian chief Ratu Cakobau was persuaded to voyage to Australia on HMS *Dido* for an official state visit to the governor of New South Wales. Cases of measles had just started in the city of Sydney and Cakobau and his entourage caught the disease. With attentive nursing care, they had all more or less recovered by the time they landed back home in January 1875 and the newly posted British authorities did not deem it necessary to impose any quarantine restrictions.

A week later, the islanders began to be struck down with what was for them a mysterious new disease. Despite the protestations of British administrators, the suspicions of the hill tribes that they were the victims of sorcery and that the British had taken Cakobau to Sydney with the specific intention of poisoning him could not be allayed. The increasingly hostile islanders refused all conventional measles treatment and attempted to allay their fever by bathing in icy rivers, laying themselves open to the all-too-common secondary complications of a disease against which they had in any case no natural immunity. The outbreak coincided with a spell of appalling weather: howling gales did nothing to help weakened immune systems stave off serious illness.

The epidemic was the worst disaster in Fiji's history. In the end the British government blamed the tragedy on the ship's doctor and the captain of HMS *Dido* for failing to put their passengers into quarantine. But, whoever was to blame, it was too late for the Fiji islanders.

Spanish flu pandemic

Despite its name, the flu pandemic of 1918 did not start in Spain. In fact it spread there rather late in the day; but the uncensored Spanish press was the first to report the outbreak. The countries engaged in fighting World War I had a news blackout on anything that might cause panic, so . . . 'Spanish flu' it became. The first cases were probably in Kansas, USA, where the virus started as 'ordinary' flu in March 1918. It soon mutated into a virulent strain which, unusually, proved most deadly in the young and healthy.

The war enabled the flu to spread rapidly. It was almost certainly brought by US servicemen to the Front, where the appalling conditions in the trenches ensured that it got a grip on already weakened soldiers. When the sick were shipped home, the infection was transmitted to the

A policeman wears a face mask in an attempt to avoid the flu

civilian population. Soon flu victims were dying worldwide. Eventually about a third of the world's population was affected.

Symptoms were so severe that at first the flu was often misdiagnosed as cholera, typhoid or dengue. The disease worked rapidly – victims might start to feel ill in the morning and be dead by nightfall. Recent research suggests it may have been a strain of H1N1 virus which killed by triggering an allergic overreaction of the body's immune system – thus explaining the high mortality rate in young adults with strong immune systems.

As the Armistice was celebrated, the pandemic took hold. Hospitals were already overflowing with war-wounded and because many doctors and nurses were still at the Front, care of flu victims was hopelessly lacking. The virus galloped round the world until late 1919 when new cases dropped sharply, although deaths continued into 1920 as the virus mutated again.

WHEN:
1918–1919
WHERE:
Worldwide
DEATH TOLL:
50–100 million
(16 million in India alone)
YOU SHOULD KNOW:
Altogether some 675,000 Americans died in the flu pandemic, 43,000 of whom were servicemen. In the USA restrictions were placed on travel and gauze face masks distributed in an attempt to control the pandemic.

Sleeping sickness epidemic

WHEN:
1915–1928
WHERE:
Worldwide
DEATH TOLL:
Possibly up to a million, with
countless others condemned to
living death
YOU SHOULD KNOW:
One theory links 'sleeping sickness'
with the Salem witch trials in New
England in the 1600s. Many of the
symptoms described in the
'bewitched' are strikingly consistent
with those of the victims of
Encephalitis lethargica.

The 'sleeping' or 'sleepy' sickness that swept the world in the 1920s had nothing in common with the tropical disease. It was a strange form of encephalitis which attacked the brain, leaving victims speechless and unable to move. It was named *Encephalitis lethargica* – 'inflammation of the brain that makes you tired'. Its cause remains a mystery, though research continues and isolated cases still occur. One theory is that it is triggered by an excessive immune response to bacteria. At the time it was thought to be connected with the Spanish flu pandemic, and some current research points to a viral infection.

The epidemic began as early as 1915, though most cases were reported in the 1920s. It could affect anyone, but was most common in young people, particularly women. Early symptoms of fever, sore throat and headache were quickly followed by double vision, tremors, delayed response, then drowsiness and lethargy; many patients became comatose and completely unresponsive. And many of those who survived remained in a coma for months or years.

Those who appeared to make a recovery often went on to develop a form of Parkinson's disease, with unpleasant and permanent symptoms. In 1969, a newly developed anti-Parkinson's drug, Levodopa (L-Dopa) was used to treat some of the comatose patients. A number made dramatic recoveries, regaining movement and speech after 30 years of unconscious immobility. Most slipped back into coma within days or weeks, and could not be roused again. Dr Oliver Sacks was working in the USA at the time and his 1973 book *Awakenings* (later a film) examines the case histories of these tragic living statues.

The mystery epidemic came to an end in 1928. But by that time hundreds of thousands were permanently institutionalized, trapped inside useless bodies.

Jamaica Ginger (Ginger Jake)

It goes by the name of 'potcheen' in Ireland, 'hooch' or 'moonshine' in North America and *batti sarai* in India. History is littered with those who wish to make a fast buck by producing illicit liquor and those who are ready to take a chance by drinking it to get high. This normally takes the form of a cottage industry but, during the crazy Prohibition era in America, the distilling of illegal alcohol became a multi-million dollar business.

The iconic image of the era is the speakeasy, a joint where people drank and danced, listening to jazz while trying to keep one step ahead of the law. On the street things weren't quite so glamorous and a brew called Ginger Jake was much in demand. Although the laws of Prohibition had the intention of banning all alcoholic beverages, there were several medicines which had to be diluted in alcohol to make them palatable. This was to prove a very big loophole and ultimately drove a horse and cart through the legislation.

An extract of Jamaican ginger had been sold as an aid to digestion in America since the 1860s and to dissolve the powdered root of the plant, a high concentration of alcohol was required. Demand for the tincture mushroomed, outstripping supply, and the price skyrocketed. In January 1930, hoping to make easy money, chemist Harry Gross of Boston decided to add a component of varnish to the hooch. The ingredient, triorthocresylphosphate, was cheap, plentiful and, most importantly, legal. Gross mixed the brew himself and shipped it across the USA. But what he was shipping was slow poison, as the brew attacked cells in the spinal column. Blues songs of the day picked up on this, describing sufferers as having 'Jake leg' some years before the medical profession noticed that anything was amiss.

WHEN:
Late 1920s onwards
WHERE:
USA
TOLL:
Sufferers probably numbered in the hundreds of thousands but, because they were largely street people with all sorts of other problems, no one really counted.
YOU SHOULD KNOW:
'Jake leg' wasn't fatal, it just meant that sufferers had to walk with a cane and their speech was slurred. In the words of one of the songs of the day 'I can't eat, I can't talk – Been drinkin' mean jake, Lord, now can't walk – Ain't got nothin'.

Poster advertising the delights and benefits of Jamaica Ginger.

Minamata disease

WHEN:
1932–1968
WHERE:
Minamata Bay, Kumamoto, Japan
DEATH TOLL:
Over the years 2,265 people have
been officially certified as
permanently disabled, of whom
1,784 have died; but compensation
payments of more than $610 million
to another 10,000 people have been
wrung out of the Chisso Corporation
and the Japanese government, and
at least another 20,000 victims are
thought to have been affected.
YOU SHOULD KNOW:
After the event, which was itself a
tragic mishap, neither the Chisso
Corporation nor the Japanese
government behaved well. Every
possible attempt was made to
cover up the true extent of the
poisoning. Although it paid 'sympathy
money' to some of the most affected
victims and their families, for years
Chisso refused to accept liability and
used strong-arm tactics to stop
people speaking out.

Doctors first noticed something strange in the Japanese coastal town of Minimata towards the end of April 1956. Patients were presenting with unusual symptoms – loss of balance, shambolic gait, impaired speech, tingling in fingers and toes and, in more serious cases, convulsions, coma and even death. In his official report of May 1, Dr Hajime Hosokawa concluded that Minamata had been hit by an 'epidemic of an unknown disease of the central nervous system'.

As the weird new disease spread, an atmosphere of panic and suspicion pervaded the whole town. Anyone walking oddly was ostracized for fear of contagion, houses were disinfected, people reported seeing 'dancing cats', dogs running in frenzied circles, birds dropping out of the sky, and dead fish floating in the waters of Minamata Bay. At first Dr Hosokawa and his fellow researchers were baffled, but eventually it dawned on them that the illness must be caused by some sort of poisoning: all the symptoms pointed to ingestion of heavy metal.

For centuries the inhabitants of Minimata had scraped a livelihood from fishing. Then in 1908 the Chisso chemical plant was established, providing much-needed employment. For years the factory had been pumping out waste water into Minimata Bay without ill-effect. But investigations revealed that in recent years the waste had been tainted with mercury that had got into the food chain: it was being ingested by fish which were in turn eaten by humans and animals.

The tragedy of Minimata was that Chisso had been a major benefactor to the community – everyone had wanted the factory built, benefited from the employment opportunities and enjoyed the rise in living standards that accompanied the industry. Nobody could possibly have foreseen that the town's enduring legacy would be incurable illness and congenital birth defects.

*A woman holds a girl with a
malformed hand who is
suffering from Minamata
disease, or mercury poisoning.
Many victims of the disease
suffer from physical
deformities, among other
symptoms.*

The Cutter incident

Poliomyelitis is a peculiarly nasty, highly contagious disease of the central nervous system that all too often leaves its victims permanently disabled with withered limbs. Polio epidemics swept through postwar America with alarming frequency, growing more virulent every year. An epidemic of 1952 killed over 3,000 people and left more than 21,000 with varying degrees of paralysis. So when medical researcher Jonas Salk developed a viable vaccine, he was hailed as a saviour.

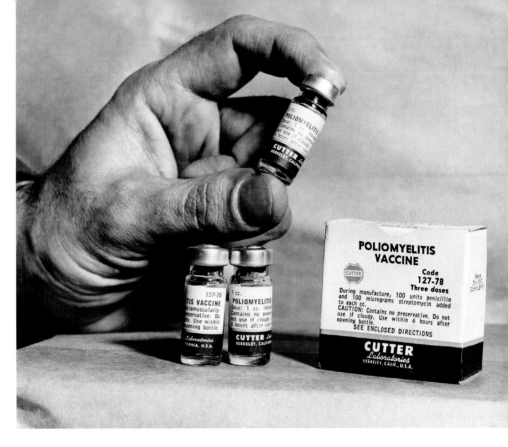

Dr Jonas Salk's polio vaccine as shown in April 1955.

There followed the largest medical experiment in history, involving 1,800,000 children in a rigorous double-blind trial. On April 12 1955 the vaccine was hailed a success: it was deemed safe and effective. The public health authorities immediately licensed several pharmaceutical companies to produce the vaccine in bulk so they could carry out a mass immunization programme to rid America of this latter-day plague. Among the chosen companies was Cutter Laboratories of Berkeley, California. A terrible mishap in their laboratory led to what is known as the Cutter incident.

Cutter manufactured 120,000 doses of vaccine in which the polio virus had not been deactivated properly. In two out of eight batches produced at the laboratory, some of the polio virus had survived the formaldehyde treatment designed to kill it. It was one of the worst disasters in the history of the US pharmaceutical industry. Cutter was sued and, when the case came to court in 1958, although the firm was cleared of negligence it was ordered to pay damages for breach of warranty – having claimed that the vaccine was safe when it manifestly wasn't. The company never again produced polio vaccine and in the 1970s was taken over by German pharmaceutical giant Bayer, the third largest pharmaceutical company in the world.

WHEN:
1955
WHERE:
California, Idaho, New Mexico and Arizona, USA
DEATH TOLL:
Of 164 people who developed paralysis in response to the vaccine, ten died; 40,000 suffered a milder polio that, fortunately, did not affect their central nervous systems
YOU SHOULD KNOW:
Famous people who were crippled by polio include US President F D Roosevelt and Ian Dury of the Blockheads – a 1970s British punk rock band. Today polio is virtually non-existent in the developed world and is only endemic in four countries: India, Pakistan, Afghanistan and Nigeria. Worldwide, there were 350,000 cases in 1998, but by 2007 the number had been reduced to 1,310.

Children crippled by Thalidomide writing with the aid of pencil-holding devices.

Thalidomide

Images of the effects of Thalidomide are firmly etched into the public consciousness. What was originally seen as a safe treatment for morning sickness quickly became one of the worst tragedies in medical history, as thousands of children were born without limbs and with damaged vital organs.

Thalidomide was discovered by chance in 1954, by the small yet ambitious German firm Chemie Grünenthal while trying to create new antibiotics. The firm had a history of releasing new drugs onto the market without proper testing and when no antibiotic qualities were found they tried it on people with epilepsy. Again no curative effects were found, but patient reports of particularly sound sleep led to the identification of the drug's sedative properties. Thalidomide had finally found its lucrative market. If they had truly found a safe alternative to the highly toxic barbiturates available at the time, then scientific prizes as well as great remuneration awaited them.

Heralded by a huge marketing campaign, Thalidomide was launched in Germany, under the name of Contergan, as a safe sedative. It was so benign, argued the manufacturers, that accidental overdoses by small children had resulted in no harm. Distillers, a UK whisky maker with only marginal experience in pharmaceuticals, became interested. They launched the drug in

WHEN:
Most cases date from 1959–1961.
WHERE:
Practically worldwide. Germany and the UK had a high number of cases due to the drug's early release. Japan was badly affected as the drug was made available over the counter. Thalidomide was never given full approval in the USA, resulting in comparatively few cases there.
TOLL:
More than 10,000 people were affected.
YOU SHOULD KNOW:
Many victims of Thalidomide have gone on to lead long and fulfilling lives. Most notably Nicaraguan guitarist Tony Meléndez and Mat Fraser, a British rock musician-turned-actor.

Britain under the name of Distaval in April 1958. In the summer of 1958 the German company announced that Thalidomide was safe for use by expectant mothers to combat morning sickness. Distillers simply accepted this as true and it was prescribed accordingly. Even when evidence of nerve damage began to surface, the drug was still marketed as safe.

Work by scientists in Australia and Germany proved the link between Thalidomide and birth defects and the drug was withdrawn in December 1961 – but not before more than 10,000 children had been born with deformities.

Iraqi seed grain poisoning

After a series of disastrous harvests in the late 1960s, Saddam Hussein applied for an aid shipment of 90,000 tons of American barley and Mexican wheat seed. The seed grain was for planting not eating. It had been coated in methylmercury fungicide and had been dyed bright pink, with 'Do Not Eat' warnings on the bags printed in English and Spanish.

When the consignment arrived at the port of Basra some of it was immediately stolen and unscrupulous dealers sold it as fit for consumption. By the time the rest of the shipment had been distributed to the illiterate and semi-starving peasant farmers in outlying rural areas it was long past the planting season. Unable to read the labels on the bags but wary of the pink dye, people washed the seed and started cautiously feeding it to chickens and livestock. There were no immediate ill effects, so they started using it to make bread.

A few months later there was a sudden influx of patients to hospital suffering from mysterious symptoms. Doctors soon realized they were dealing with an outbreak of poisoning; moreover, the symptoms were identical to Minimata disease, or mercury poisoning. Once the source had been traced to the pink grain, the government ordered all remaining supplies to be handed in on pain of death. Panicked, everyone dumped their grain anywhere – scattered at roadsides, in rivers and irrigation channels – to be eaten by fish, birds and wildlife and absorbed into the food chain with who knows what long-term consequences.

To this day nobody knows the long-term effects on the population of Iraq. And of course, since then, so much worse has happened that the toxic seed grain has faded to become just one more tragic incident in the tale of that nation's appalling suffering.

WHEN:
December 1971 to March 1972
WHERE:
Iraq
DEATH TOLL:
There were 6,530 hospital cases officially recorded and the authorities admitted to 459 deaths, so the likelihood is that the actual number, including those who died at home, is far more, with thousands left permanently brain-damaged.
YOU SHOULD KNOW:
The seed grain was distributed all over Iraq but a disproportionate amount found its way to farmers in the northern provinces that were most at odds with Saddam Hussein's dictatorship. When the toxic nature of the seed came to light, many people thought it was a deliberate conspiracy on the part of the government to kill them.

Tainted blood on the NHS

WHEN:
1973 onwards
WHERE:
UK
DEATH TOLL:
Out of 4,670 haemophiliac patients infected with Hepatitis C (a chronic, potentially fatal liver disease) 1,243 were also infected with HIV and 1,756 have since died.
YOU SHOULD KNOW:
Haemophiliacs suffer from a disorder of the blood that prevents it from clotting properly, thus risking bleeding to death. Their condition can be controlled by regular injections of a blood-clotting factor. Health authorities in England and Wales continued to use clotting factor from human blood plasma long after most developed countries had started to use much safer synthetic alternatives. Heat treatment to decontaminate human blood product was not introduced until the 1980s and routine testing of donated blood only began in 1991. Government procrastination has potentially put at risk another 4,000 lives from vCJD-contaminated blood between 1980 and 2001.

Described as 'the worst treatment disaster in the history of the NHS', the tainted 'Hemofil' blood product that was used to treat haemophiliacs from the end of 1973 was imported from the USA, despite an earlier recommendation that the UK should become self-sufficient in blood product as soon as possible. In 1974 an outbreak of hepatitis among haemophiliac patients was the first sign that something was seriously amiss. It gradually emerged that nearly 5,000 NHS patients had been infected with potentially life-threatening Hepatitis C, often in combination with HIV.

Successive governments have consistently refused to hold a public enquiry, maintaining that the NHS could not be held responsible because it could not have known the blood was tainted. But, unlike UK blood which is always freely donated from carefully screened donors, much of the US donated blood had come from a single source – the Arkansas prison system. Inmates at high risk of disease – mainly drug addicts and 'skid row' down-and-outs – had been selling their blood to pharmaceutical companies to get extra money while they were in gaol. The pharmaceutical companies' commercial interests had taken precedence over concern for patient safety. And the NHS had used this blood product in the full knowledge that it had not been properly screened.

It has been an uphill battle for the past two decades to get the British government to accept liability. Eventually, affected patients organized a privately funded investigation, chaired by Lord Archer of Sandwell, former Solicitor General. The Department of Health not only refused to give evidence to the enquiry but also 'lost' incriminating documents, while the government withheld more than 30 documents on grounds of confidentiality. When Lord Archer published his report in 2009 he called for a government apology, describing the affair as a 'horrific human tragedy'.

MPs and haemophiliacs outside 10 Downing Street in London, calling on the prime minister to intervene personally to ensure that compensation is paid to haemophiliacs who contracted AIDS after treatment with infected blood. From left: Danny Morgan from Sydenham; Liberal Democrat Sir Russell Johnston; Conservative MP Patrick Cormack; Labour's Jack Ashley and Nicholas Medley from Oxford.

Spanish toxic oil syndrome

Confiscated drums of colza oil

It started with the death of eight-year-old Jaime Garcia in his mother's arms on the way to hospital. When doctors learned that his five siblings were also ill, the whole family was rushed to hospital to be treated for 'atypical pneumonia'. But, as more people in the satellite towns around Madrid started suffering from high fevers, fluid on the lungs, skin lesions and excruciating muscle pain, doctors became increasingly baffled.

On May 12, a newspaper report indicated that the illness might be organo-phosphate poisoning, but no further mention was ever made of this link. In June another theory was propounded: the symptoms were caused by aniline poisoning from cheap cooking oil doctored with industrial rapeseed oil by unscrupulous dealers. This explanation fitted the facts sufficiently to suit the health authorities and on June 10 the Toxic Oil Syndrome (TOS) disaster was officially announced.

Six years later, in March 1987, 40 back-street traders appeared in court. They didn't dispute the fact that they had mis-sold industrial rapeseed oil, but denied that their oil had caused TOS. Dr Manuel Posada of the National Health Research Centre gave evidence that 'the correlation between the illness and the oil is so impressive, it is the only viable theory' and was backed up by expert British epidemiologist Sir Richard Doll and the World Health Authority. Several defendants were given hefty prison sentences.

But it didn't add up – people who had ingested quantities of cheap oil had often not displayed any TOS symptoms, while many who had not touched it had been severely stricken. Conspiracy theorists delight in the idea that scientists have colluded with the Spanish authorities in covering up the truth behind the disaster. But it is equally probable that nobody really knows what caused TOS, nor ever will.

WHEN:
May 1981
WHERE:
Provinces of Madrid, Segovia and Palencia, Spain
DEATH TOLL:
Over 300 people died and more than 20,000 were affected; many were left permanently disabled.
YOU SHOULD KNOW:
Some think TOS was an outbreak of organo-phosphate poisoning from fruit or vegetables, mass-produced in the plastic polytunnels of southeast Spain with the aid of massive amounts of fertilizer and pesticides. An alternative theory blames an accident involving biological weapons at the US air base at Torrejon, just outside Madrid. It has been suggested that the doctored rapeseed oil was a convenient myth to protect Spain's burgeoning agro-industry or military interests. However, TOS has been extensively studied and it would take a cover-up of truly monumental proportions to perpetuate such a falsehood if there was any clear evidence to the contrary.

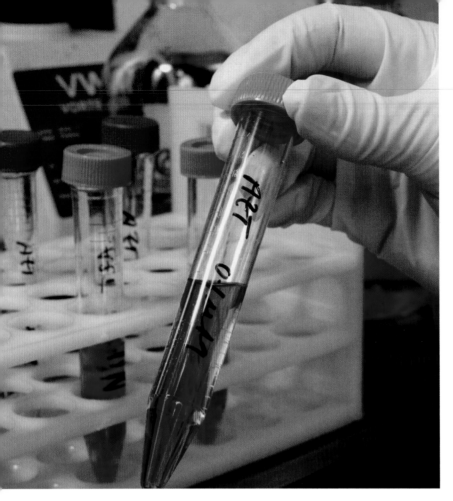

AZT to fight AIDS

AIDS pandemic

It is difficult to pinpoint exactly when the AIDS epidemic began. The first death assumed to be caused by Acquired Immuno-Deficiency Syndrome probably occurred in the late 1950s. No one can be sure because no one from the medical or scientific community was joining up the dots. What is clear is that by the 1980s the dots were getting ever more numerous and people from specific communities were dying from rare diseases alarmingly early in life.

In the early days AIDS was seen as a disease of the gay community, particularly in North America, Germany and the UK. At that time it was even defined by those who were perceived to be most at risk, earning the name GRID (gay-related immune deficiency). In France it affected those who had contact with Central Africa – the picture was getting more confusing. One thing that was certain was that the disease was having a devastating impact on the communities it affected. By the end of 1985, of the 23,000 people diagnosed with AIDS more than half had died. Panic spread and ignorance was rife. Those affected were discriminated against in the workplace while newspaper headlines proclaiming a 'gay plague' served no one well.

Research in France had discovered that the blood-borne (HIV) virus was responsible, but this was little publicized until the baton was taken up by scientists in the USA. Once identified, it was clear that it was a condition that could affect us all. Politicians and the media were still in denial and only gradually were barriers broken down. The death from AIDS of the American icon Rock Hudson in 1985 proved a watershed in public awareness and coincided with the Federal Drug Administration's approval of an antibody test. In 1987 AZT, a drug that combats the AIDS virus, was approved by the FDA. Today people can live with AIDS rather than die from it.

WHEN:
1980s to present
WHERE:
Worldwide
DEATH TOLL:
More than 25 million people have died of AIDS since 1981.
YOU SHOULD KNOW:
Today AIDS is more a disease of poverty than of lifestyle. In the rich industrialized world drug treatment has greatly prolonged life expectancy. Two thirds of sufferers live in sub-Saharan Africa and, because of poor public health, political posturing and the unreliable availability of life-prolonging drugs, the disease is having a devastating effect on many communities and economies. In November 2009 the World Health Authority announced that the pandemic is officially in decline.

Goiânia accident

Nothing goes to waste where people are living on the breadline, and few opportunities to make a little extra money get overlooked. And so it was in the Brazilian town of Goiânia in September 1987. Scavengers were combing through an abandoned clinic when they found a radiation therapy source that had been carelessly left.

The lead and steel canister looked innocent enough, but its deadly heart was a tiny capsule with an iridium window, full of highly radioactive caesium chloride. Two men found the container and trundled their trophy home in a wheelbarrow. It was the start of a process subsequently described as one of the world's worst nuclear accidents.

They would survive – though both soon felt nauseous and later developed radiation burns, while one eventually had an arm amputated. Before the danger became apparent they broke open the iridium window and found the radiation source, which emitted a strong blue light. After five days, the finders sold the partially dismantled unit to a local scrapyard, where the glowing source became an object of curiosity that attracted dozens of spectators.

A brother of the scrapyard owner took some caesium home, where his six-year-old daughter played with the lethal powder. She would die a month later and be buried in a lead coffin encased in concrete. Her aunt would also be a victim. Gabriela Maria Ferreira – wife of scrapyard owner Devair Ferreira – was the first to appreciate that something was desperately wrong and took the deadly capsule to a hospital where it was identified as dangerous. Her action undoubtedly saved lives, though not her own. The other two immediate fatalities were young men employed at the scrapyard. In all, around 250 people were irradiated, some seriously, and the authorities were forced to mount a major clean-up of contaminated locations.

WHEN:
From September 13 1987
WHERE:
Goiânia, Goiás State, Brazil
DEATH TOLL:
Four directly attributable deaths and severe contamination of another 250 people.
YOU SHOULD KNOW:
Three doctors from the abandoned clinic were charged with criminal negligence for leaving such a dangerous piece of equipment behind when the facility was closed down.

The discovery of a radioactive lead and steel canister at Goiânia caused the death of four people and the severe contamination of another 250.

BSE and vCJD

WHEN:
BSE: 1985 to present;
vCJD: 1996 to present

WHERE:
Britain has been worst affected, but there have been cases of both diseases across Europe, North America and Japan. In countries where cattle were fed hay and soya the diseases are non-existent.

DEATH TOLL:
180,000 cattle died from BSE in the UK. The annual death toll from vCJD has stabilized at around 20, but it is highly likely that this figure is an underestimate.

YOU SHOULD KNOW:
In Papua New Guinea in the mid 20th century there was an outbreak of laughing disease, known locally as *Kuru*. It is believed that the disease was spread via cannibalistic practices where it was traditional to eat the brains of the dead to preserve their spirit. The practice is now taboo and the fatal disease has been eradicated. Studies of its pathology have given us vital clues in the understanding of all Transmissible Spongiform Encephalopathies.

Cows on a farm in the Scottish Borders

In scientific terms Bovine Spongiform Encephalopathy (BSE) and variant Creutzfeldt-Jakob Disease (vCJD) are Transmissible Spongiform Encephalopathies (TSEs). Put simply this means that the diseases can be passed on to animals or humans through eating contaminated tissue. Once it takes hold, the disease produces innumerable microscopic holes in the brain by the production of an abnormal protein (misfolded prions). This gives it a spongy appearance when analyzed at autopsy.

In 1985 vets and farmers across Britain began to notice that a large number of cows were displaying erratic behaviour – losing coordination, rolling around as if drunk and eventually dying. Autopsies on the dead animals showed alarming similarity in brain damage to the sheep disease scrapie. A disease, it seemed, had crossed species. This discovery had a devastating effect on the British beef industry. The public were treated to the spectacle of the Agriculture Secretary, John Selwyn Gummer, feeding a beefburger to his daughter and declaring British beef safe to eat. The rest of the world was not so sure and most countries banned imports, costing the UK economy billions of pounds. All herds where the disease was present were slaughtered.

Just over a decade later, the worst fears were realized when it was found that BSE could affect humans in the form of vCJD and that the disease had once again jumped a species barrier. In that time more than five million cattle had been destroyed across Europe

and cattle over 30 months old had been removed from the food chain. Though these measures will probably prevent future cases of vCJD, its long incubation period may mean we are looking at the tip of an iceberg. Diagnosis can only be made after death, and research from America shows that many deaths that were previously thought to be from Alzheimer's may in fact have been caused by vCJD.

Zaragoza radiotherapy accident

When the Zaragoza Clinic's electron accelerator malfunctioned and was repaired in early December 1990, it was fortunate that the machine's annual inspection was due. When the Spanish Nuclear Safety Board carried out tests just before Christmas, it was discovered that the electron beam accelerator control was still malfunctioning, meaning that patients treated for tumours since the equipment was returned to service had received dangerous levels of radioactive overexposure, averaging six times more than the correct dosage. As soon as the error was discovered, the machine was taken out of service, a fortuitous intervention that almost certainly ensured that many lives were saved. But for patients already exposed the damage was done.

Those who had been irradiated suffered skin burns and inflamed internal organs. The first mistreated patient died after just two months and by the time the last unfortunate victim passed away a year later, on Christmas Day, the number of casualties was approaching 20. Nine of those who received a radiation overdose did survive, but all of them suffered from incurable long-term disabilities.

The blame game soon began. Operators using the faulty machine had noticed that when they selected the correct energy level a gauge on the control panel showed the electron beam was at full strength. It was assumed that the gauge had stuck, but in fact a faulty transistor meant the machine could generate a beam only when the maximum amount of electron energy was used. In the end a Spanish court ruled that responsibility rested not with the hospital or its radiological unit, but with the technician who carried out the faulty repair and the American General Electric Company (GE), who supplied the equipment and were responsible for maintenance. It therefore fell to GE to compensate survivors and families of those who died.

WHEN:
December 10–20 1990
WHERE:
Zaragoza, Spain
DEATH TOLL:
18 (though perhaps up to seven might have died of cancer anyway).
YOU SHOULD KNOW:
The machine at the centre of this medical scandal was recalibrated and continued in use until 1996, when it was taken out of service and scrapped – very discreetly, to ensure that no adverse publicity was generated to remind the Spanish public of the disaster.

African meningitis outbreak

WHEN:
1996–1997
WHERE:
Africa
DEATH TOLL:
Around 25,000
YOU SHOULD KNOW:
In 2008, health ministers from across the region signed an accord (The Yaoundé Declaration) resolving to make such outbreaks a thing of the past through the availability of an effective and affordable vaccine. However, the disease continues to be one of the world's biggest killers.

Meningococcal meningitis is a bacterial infection of the slender lining that envelops the spinal cord and the brain. Even if treated with antibiotics, it has a high mortality rate and a large number of those who do survive it suffer long-term health problems. These include loss of limbs, deafness and epileptic seizures. It is a truly terrible disease and is particularly prevalent in a belt across Africa from the Horn in the east all the way to Senegal in the west.

Although *Neisseria meningitides*, the bacterium responsible for the African outbreaks, was identified in 1887, it has proved fiendishly difficult to treat or even to predict when epidemics may occur. It is believed that up to a quarter of the population may carry it and since it affects only humans, testing potential treatments has been complicated. What is known is that the disease goes in cycles, with epidemics occurring every ten years or so. The dry season, with its dusty days and cold nights, provides a fertile breeding ground, when widespread coughs allow the bacterium to be passed from one person to the next. Those living at close quarters, such as schoolchildren and those on pilgrimages, are particularly vulnerable.

In 1996 Africa suffered its largest outbreak in history. A quarter of a million cases were reported, but the actual number was probably higher. Of those, 25,000 people died and tens of thousands more were left disabled. After this most devastating outbreak, the World Health Organisation (WHO) launched a twin approach of preparedness and response. Health centres were set up to monitor outbreaks closely, while a distribution network to provide vaccines swiftly was formed. It is estimated that, if this proper response is made, over two thirds of cases can be avoided.

SARS virus

WHEN:
November 2002 to July 2003
WHERE:
Worldwide, but predominantly in the Far East (China, Taiwan, Vietnam and Singapore)
DEATH TOLL:
According to the WHO, over 8,000 people are known to have been infected with the SARS virus during the outbreak, of which some 750 died. Although this represents less than 10 per cent of infected cases, the mortality rate was much higher among older people.

Towards the end of 2002 reports began to emerge from China of a virulent and potentially fatal respiratory disease that was proving highly resistant to treatment. The Chinese authorities were slow to alert the world to what quickly became a major health crisis. The World Health Organisation (WHO), by contrast, fearing a global pandemic, acted swiftly in drawing up and implementing a plan to combat the spread of what became known as SARS (Severe Acute Respiratory Syndrome).

The SARS virus had originated in the Guangdong Province in southern China, where a large rural population of peasants lived in close contact with animals. Scientists believe that the animals had been carrying the virus and that at some stage it must have leapt the species barrier to infect humans. Reported symptoms were similar to flu and included a high fever, breathing difficulties, dry cough, muscular aches and loss of appetite. In a remarkable example of international cooperation the WHO organized a worldwide coalition of scientists who worked resolutely to identify the cause of the disease and devise treatment programmes. SARS was found to be caused by a previously unknown type of coronavirus, a form of animal virus which infects the upper respiratory tract. Although the virus was spread like the common cold, it was not as contagious as initially feared, and rigorous infection control and preventative measures meant that the vast majority of cases were restricted to the Far East. Nevertheless, international air travel led to smaller outbreaks also occurring in other parts of the world, such as Canada, before the WHO was able to declare in July 2003 that the epidemic had been contained.

YOU SHOULD KNOW:
Although in the end no specific treatment was found to be particularly effective against SARS, scientists were helped in their investigations by the fact that the virus barely mutated from the moment when it emerged.

Chinese security guards wearing masks to ward off SARS as they monitor the quarantined dormitory buildings of Beijing's Northern Jiaotong University.

Northwick Park drug trial

WHEN:
March 2006
WHERE:
Northwick Park Hospital, London, UK
DEATH TOLL:
None. However, but for the prompt
and effective response of hospital
staff all six volunteers would almost
certainly have died.
YOU SHOULD KNOW:
The long-term effects of the trial on
the volunteers remain unknown.
One man has since had a cancer
diagnosis (which may or may not be
connected) while another believes
that his auto-immune system has
been permanently damaged.
Ironically, the drug has probably left
the six at greater risk of contracting
the very diseases it was designed to
help cure.

In March 2006 six healthy men, all under the age of 40, signed up as volunteers in a drug trial that was being conducted at a research unit based at Northwick Park Hospital in northwest London. The drug being tested was TGN1412, an anti-inflammatory drug designed to treat conditions such as leukaemia, rheumatoid arthritis and multiple sclerosis. Manufactured by TeGenero, a German pharmaceutical company, the experimental drug was supposed to work by subtly 're-tuning' the body's immune system. Following extensive testing in laboratories and on animals, the trial marked the first phase of the three-stage human testing process – the purpose of which was to check for side-effects rather than to see if the drug worked.

Within hours of the drug being administered all six volunteers suffered catastrophic organ failure, accompanied by sharp falls in blood pressure, swellings and excruciating pain. Seriously ill, they were admitted to the hospital's intensive care unit. Here they made a gradual recovery and most were discharged after a few weeks, although one man remained in hospital for four months and had to have fingers and toes amputated after contracting septicaemia. The victims' puffy and bloated appearance, caused by the steroids with which they were treated, led to them being dubbed 'elephant men', a phrase that promptly resonated around the world's media.

Parexel, the US-based clinical research organization that was administering the trial, has never admitted any liability or apologized to the victims, who have launched a multi-million pound damages claim against the company. The MHRA, the UK regulatory authority responsible, found no initial evidence of errors or irregularities, but was itself criticized for having approved the trial in the first place and did subsequently conclude that Parexel had given insufficient information to the volunteers and had not followed proper procedures.

Ivory Coast waste dumping

The multinational company Trafigura did a nifty deal in 2006, buying a large amount of coker gasoline from Mexican oil giant Pemex. This waste by-product of oil refining contains concentrated silica and sulphur, but Trafigura intended to process the waste to extract saleable naphtha. Better still, the company cleverly came up with a scheme to extract the valuable chemical *in situ* aboard the Panamanian-registered tanker *Probo Koala*, a vessel chartered to carry the coker gasoline. This involved 'washing' it with caustic soda, which separated the naphtha but greatly increased the toxicity of remaining waste.

An Ivorian man wears a mask at Akuedo.

As soon as a Dutch company contracted to dispose of the waste realized how dangerous it had become, the price quoted for the job went up twentyfold. Trafigura wouldn't pay and *Probo Koala* set out in search of a contractor who *would* handle the foul-smelling toxic liquid, conveniently finding a newly formed outfit called Compagnie Tommy in the port city of Abidjan in the Côte d'Ivoire (Ivory Coast) who agreed to process the waste for a tiny fraction of the price demanded in Holland.

Unfortunately, Compagnie Tommy's idea of 'processing' was to dump 500 tonnes of waste in a dozen landfill sites in and around Abidjan. After a few weeks, people started complaining of problems ranging from headaches, nosebleeds and vomiting to severe skin burns and seared lungs. Nearly 100,000 Ivorians sought medical attention, over 30,000 sustained recordable injuries and 17 deaths were directly attributable to acute poisoning caused by the dumped toxic waste. The cumulative effect was a catastrophic medical emergency that brought down the Ivory Coast's government, though Trafigura denied that there had even been any toxic waste aboard *Probo Koala* – and was quick to threaten (or take) legal action against anyone who suggested that the company was complicit in the illegal dumping.

WHEN:
August 2006
WHERE:
Ivory Coast
DEATH TOLL:
17 known fatalities (though the real figure may be much greater).
YOU SHOULD KNOW:
Trafigura may have emphatically denied responsibility for, or knowledge of, the illegal dumping of toxic waste in Côte d'Ivoire – but still came up with £100 million to pay for a clean-up operation. The Ivorian boss of Compagnie Tommy was sentenced to 20 years' imprisonment for his contribution to this large-scale medical disaster.

Parents being offered ultrasonography check application forms at Hebei People's Hospital in Shijiazhuang, capital of north China's Hebei Province. China's Health Ministry pledged free health care for all babies sickened after drinking the Sanlu brand contaminated formula milk powder.

China baby milk scandal

A parent's worst nightmare came true for thousands of families in China in 2008 when they found out they had been innocently feeding their babies with contaminated milk powder. Reports of infants falling ill with urinary problems and kidney failure began to emerge in March, but it was six months – and after the Beijing Olympics – before China acknowledged it had a major health crisis and before Sanlu, the country's biggest producer of powdered milk goods, halted production and recalled stock from retailers' shelves. By then four babies had died and tens of thousands had been taken ill.

The contamination had been deliberate; some 60 people were arrested in connection with the scandal, including the head and three senior executives of Sanlu. Both infant milk formula and liquid milk were found to have been tainted with melamine, a toxic industrial chemical used in the manufacture of plastics and banned from use in food products. At the root of the problem lay the desperately harsh and competitive conditions prevailing in China's food production industry; at the start of the chain stood small dairy farmers and the temptation, in the face of margins endlessly squeezed, to water down the milk they produced, in some cases by as much as 30 per cent. The diluted product had then been disguised by the addition of melamine which raised the product's all-important protein levels.

Although the Chinese government was quick to offer free medical treatment and some compensation to families affected, it was publicly excoriated for its perceived delay in tackling the crisis. In particular, its food inspection and regulation apparatus was exposed as chaotic and massively deficient. To date 21 people involved in the scandal have been convicted, including two middlemen who were sentenced to death and executed in November 2009.

WHEN:
2008
WHERE:
China
DEATH TOLL:
At least six babies died from drinking contaminated milk, with an estimated 300,000 thought to have been infected and taken ill.
YOU SHOULD KNOW:
The scandal further undermined public confidence in food safety in China, already at a low ebb after a series of earlier incidents involving other consumer products.

Zimbabwe cholera epidemic

In 2008, Zimbabwe's suffering people had a glimmer of hope to lighten the dark decades during which Robert Mugabe and his ruthless ZANU-PF henchmen had bankrupted their once-prosperous country. The Movement for Democratic Change won parliamentary and presidential elections and – though Mugabe rigged the latter and refused to go – opposition leader Morgan Tsvangirai agreed a power-sharing deal that offered some prospect of better times to come.

But an insidious legacy of Mugabe's ruinous regime was about to add a new burden to the impoverished population – cholera. This deadly gastroenteritis is highly infectious, killing around five per cent of Africans who catch the disease, though the death rate is lower elsewhere. In Zimbabwe, the year of hope also saw the start of a major cholera outbreak that August which would become Africa's worst for 15 years. The cause? Services like a clean water supply, sanitation and garbage collection had collapsed as a result of the Mugabe regime's chronic mismanagement. Zimbabwe's urban population had little choice but to drink any water they could find, though this was almost invariably contaminated by human waste containing cholera bacteria, which thrives in an aqueous environment. As city and town dwellers became widely infected, they spread the disease to rural areas by visiting relatives and repatriating cholera victims to their home villages for burial.

The epidemic spread like wildfire in the dying months of 2008, reaching a peak in December when the government belatedly declared a national emergency and appealed for international help. It even spilled over into neighbouring countries. For the suffering Zimbabweans, weakened by prolonged under-nourishment and wide incidence of HIV and AIDS, the death rate was terrifying, averaging ten per cent and reaching double that in some areas of the country. The epidemic started a slow decline in 2009, but not before killing thousands.

WHEN:
2008–2009
WHERE:
Zimbabwe (also affecting parts of Botswana, Zambia, Mozambique and South Africa)
DEATH TOLL:
Over 4,200 deaths were reported by mid 2009, probably representing a considerable underestimate of the actual figure.
YOU SHOULD KNOW:
The vituperative anti-British rhetoric that Mugabe's government used to justify every setback in his beleaguered nation soon came in to play when cholera took hold. Information Minister Sikhanyiso Ndlovu claimed that the epidemic had been caused by a bio-chemical weapon attack that was designed to create a diversion ahead of an imminent British invasion.

Men fill up a container from a borehole in the high-density suburb of Mabvuku in Harare.

221

POLITICAL
DISASTERS

The Dreyfus affair

The front cover of Le Petit Journal *showing prisoner Alfred Dreyfus, imprisoned on Devil's Island, in 1899.*

WHEN:
1894–1906
WHERE:
France
TOLL:
The Dreyfus Affair permanently altered political consciousness in France, where left and right remain polarized at extremes. It directly motivated the 1905 legislation separating Church and State and established the political philosophies of both radical republicanism and right-wing nationalism that were subsequently transplanted to Spain, where they clashed in unholy civil war.
YOU SHOULD KNOW:
Both the Tour de France cycle race and *L'Auto* (*L'Equipe*) daily sports newspaper owe their existence directly to the Dreyfus affair. Anti-Dreyfusards started *L'Auto* in 1900 to challenge the Dreyfusards' paper *Le Velo*; then when *L'Auto's* readership fell, created the Tour de France in 1903 to boost circulation.

For over a decade the Dreyfus affair dominated French political and cultural life. It began with the rigged court martial for treason of Captain Alfred Dreyfus. The only Jewish officer on the French General Staff, Dreyfus was purposely picked as the scapegoat for a major spying scandal. Evidence against him was either spurious or forged. He was publicly stripped of his insignia and sentenced to life imprisonment on the pestilential hellhole of Devil's Island.

The blatantly corrupt conviction magnified the existing anti-semitism that stained France's deepest sentiments. It opened a fault line of implacable hostility between the far right and left-leaning liberals: strident bigotry faced a growing coalition of those from every stratum of French society who were unwilling to allow the most fundamental principles of truth, justice and humanity to be trampled into dust.

Protest became fury in 1896 when the real culprit, Major Ferdinand Walsin Esterhazy, was exonerated at a court martial. The evidence against him was suppressed, and new forgeries used to reconvict Dreyfus. It was too much. The intermittent salvos of virulent propaganda exploded into a war for the moral soul of France. The affair was already consuming careers, reputations and whole governments when the 'Dreyfusards' found their champion in France's greatest writer, Emile Zola.

Zola's inimitable denunciation '*J'Accuse!*', an open letter to the president of the Republic, managed simultaneously to summarize Dreyfus's innocent plight, savage the military and political racist skulduggery, and demand of all Frenchmen what kind of country they wanted to live in. Zola was convicted of libel, but he had shifted the weight of public opinion. After five more years, two more trials, and a public rehabilitation including the *Legion d'Honneur*, Dreyfus was freed – blameless but broken. France tore itself apart in his name; and the repercussions were still discernible in the line that separated Vichy from Free France during World War II.

Prohibition

By the time the Eighteenth Amendment to the US Constitution was ratified more than half the states of America were already dry. A complete ban on alcohol seemed the logical next step. In the rough and tumble of frantic expansion, the authorities had been rushing through state laws covering a whole range of socially progressive reforms; women had identified the role of liquor in domestic and child abuse, the police knew alcohol's contribution to social crime, and industrialists like Henry Ford blamed drink for low productivity and safety issues. World War I had made sobriety look patriotic because so many breweries had German origins, and by the end of the war the various interest groups had forged such an influential popular temperance movement that no politician could ignore it even if he wanted to.

At midnight on January 16 1920 Prohibition politely welcomed the impending criminalization of the majority of American adults, and instigated the biggest and most violent crime wave in the country's history. The vice that Americans condemned in principle was condoned as part of their social culture. As always, they enshrined morality in legislation but couldn't reconcile it to individual behaviour.

So drinking went openly underground into the 'speakeasies', supplied by increasingly well-organized gangs of bootleggers, rum-runners and beer barons who stopped at nothing to fuel the colossal demand for a drink – manufactured or home-made, certified champagne or blindness-inducing 'mountain dew'. Rich and poor shared in the euphoric glamour of illicit thrills . . . and the rampant violence of the armed gangs' ruthless, black economy. Every shot of whiskey embedded corruption deeper, at city, county, state and federal level, rotting the fabric of American society.

WHEN:
Midnight January 16 1920 to
15.32 December 5 1933
WHERE:
USA
TOLL:
Prohibition created the economic model of modern America: if you want it, take it – if necessary, by force. More than 90 years after its introduction, Prohibition mores, style and language remain fundamental to American (and therefore global) culture, even among those who try to resist all three. Each decade adds a new twist, but fashion, literature and films (like *The Terminator* or *Star Wars*) still draw on Prohibition as the Great American behavioural archetype.
YOU SHOULD KNOW:
Cleveland, Ohio, was fairly typical. In 1919, before Prohibition, it had 1,200 legal bars. In 1923 it had 3,000 illegal speakeasies and 10,000 stills. Around 30,000 of its citizens sold alcohol in the course of Prohibition and 100,000 made some kind of 'bathtub gin' for themselves and friends. The quality was often dangerous (adulterated liquor killed 50,000 Americans in seven years), and it is said that when one potential customer sent a sample of moonshine for laboratory analysis, the chemist's report read: 'Your horse has diabetes'.

Children watch as a prohibitionist destroys a barrel of beer with an axe.

The League of Nations

WHEN:
1920–1946
WHERE:
International organization with headquarters in Geneva, Switzerland
TOLL:
The failure of the League of Nations meant Europe was plunged into World War II with all its concomitant horrors.
YOU SHOULD KNOW:
For all its failures the League bequeathed a significant legacy to the United Nations, including its principal instruments of a General Assembly and smaller Council made up of permanent and elected member states.

Best known today for being the precursor body to the United Nations, the ill-fated League of Nations emerged from the devastation wrought by World War I. As conceived by its founders at the 1919 Versailles peace conference, the League was a permanent international body that would provide a forum for resolving disputes between nation states by diplomatic, non-military means, and would thus act as the principal guarantor of peace in the world. The League's ethos was underpinned by the twin principles of self-determination for a nation state and of collective security (countries acting together rather than individually).

The high-minded idealism which accompanied the League of Nations' establishment proved sadly and all too soon to be just that. By the end of 1920 48 states had signed the League's Covenant, pledging to work together to eliminate aggression between nations; but in spite of minor early successes (for example, resolving a 1925 border dispute between Greece and Bulgaria), the limitations of the League's powers quickly became apparent through a series of ever more brazen challenges to its authority. The writing was already on the wall when in 1923 France, one of the key founder states, disregarded its international obligations and occupied the Ruhr. The League looked on helplessly from its headquarters in Geneva, powerless to intervene because it lacked a military force of its own.

The other crucial factor which undermined the League's effectiveness from the outset was that the USA, the world's most powerful nation, never signed up as a member, in spite of the League having been the brainchild of President Woodrow Wilson himself. The weakness of the League was ever more cruelly exposed as the Axis powers flexed their territorial muscles during the 1930s, culminating in the flagrant, unchallenged expansionism of Adolf Hitler's Germany.

The first meeting of the Council of the League of Nations in 1920

Teapot Dome

Near Casper in Wyoming, a strangely shaped butte soars out of the prairie. It is known by its shape as Teapot Dome, and it towers over an unseen oilfield.

The scandal of Teapot Dome is synonymous with the presidency of Warren Harding. It owes its notoriety to its unequivocal moral; compared to the jumble of corruption and sleaze discovered in its wake, the rights and wrongs of Teapot Dome are crystal clear.

In the early 20th century various US presidents set aside vast tracts in Wyoming and California to be held as unexploited oil reserves for the US Navy. In 1921 incoming President Harding appointed Albert Fall as Secretary of the Interior. Fall lost no time in persuading the Secretary of the US Navy to pass him responsibility for two of the oil reserves; and indecently soon he leased them to two personal friends who each headed a major oil company. It was common gossip in Washington that the oil corporations had made huge, unsecured 'loans' to Fall by way of thanks. But Harding defended his man by citing earlier presidential approval for the deals. The truth might have stayed suppressed despite an investigation mounted by the outraged Senate, but Harding died suddenly in 1923 and Vice President Calvin Coolidge stepped up. He was having none of it. Fall was convicted of receiving at least one bribe of $100,000.

The Jazz Age was in full swing, fuelled by the Charleston and the ubiquitous hip flasks of Prohibition. Perhaps Teapot Dome should not have disgusted people already so contemptuous of the law – but apart from its demonstration of naked greed and abuse of power, it was just the tip of an iceberg of corruption to which it gave a collective name. It still does, though in scale it has long been outmatched. People remember the first time, and their worst-ever president.

A Teapot Dome hanger from the 1924 US presidential election, featuring Charles W Bryan and John W Davis.

WHEN:
March 1921 to January 1924
WHERE:
Teapot Dome, Wyoming; Elk Hills, California; Washington DC, USA
TOLL:
Worst hit was the credibility of government itself. Teapot Dome lodged in popular consciousness like no previous wrongdoing and gave movies like *Mr Smith Goes to Washington* their meaning years afterwards, because trust between government and governed simply evaporated.
YOU SHOULD KNOW:
Albert Fall was the first cabinet member to be jailed for a crime committed while in office. Ever since, American journalists (and conspiracy theorists) have kept a weather eye on 'sticky' oil money, its provenance, and its influence on every level of elective office. With the Enron debacle recalling Teapot Dome so forcefully, observers have been quick to record the painful details of the uneasy relationship between George W Bush, Enron's $1.76 million campaign contribution, former oil executive Vice President Dick Cheney and the protection of so many corporate oil interests. They've gone – but the story has yet to be revealed.

Crowds celebrating the proclamation of the Second Spanish Republic.

Seed of disaster: the Spanish Constitution of 1931

WHEN:
April 1931
WHERE:
Madrid, Spain
DEATH TOLL:
Five years of growing civil unrest culminated in the revolt of the garrisons of Ceuta, Melilla and Tetuan on July 17 1936, and the start of a bloody civil war between General Franco's Nationalists and the Republic in which some 100,000 lost their lives. After the civil war ended in the winter of 1938–1939, Franco abolished the 1931 Constitution and sought revenge. Between 1939 and 1943 an estimated 200,000 people died in his prisons.
YOU SHOULD KNOW:
The 1931 Constitution of Spain's Second Republic survived just eight years in all its variations. It is sometimes compared to Guernica's 'shattered tree', the symbol of the town's disaster immortalized by Picasso. Today, residents point at the tree on the same spot in the same square and tell you 'It's not the actual tree, but it's like the one that was here'. They should know.

Over the centuries, the Spanish monarchy learned very well how to use religion as an instrument of social control. Catholicism had been enshrined as the official religion of the State since AD 859. These twin strands of Spanish political DNA were broken for the first time by the new Constitution of 1931.

King Alfonso XIII abdicated, swept away by broad popular support for the liberal reforms of the newly elected Republicans; and Church was separated from State. The Catholic hierarchy was horrified to find its traditional privileges threatened by the new constitution's integral anti-clericalism, and openly supported the coalition of right-wing opposition to a government seeking reforms through negotiation rather than the traditional Spanish route of repression and violence.

Without the intransigence of the Catholic Church, the moderate government might have survived; but in the see-saw of right- and left-wing power coups that followed, the essentially bourgeois government was forced to use the same tools of repression created by the Church during its centuries of dominance. Public order disintegrated as left- and right-wing extremists weakened the moderate centre by inciting violent response to each other's violent provocations.

The 1931 Constitution was characterized by decency and nobility of purpose. It established universal suffrage, women's fundamental rights, regional autonomy and freedom of speech and worship. It was a disaster because it was far too radical for the *exaltados* (bigwigs) of the political right (monarchists, falangists, the army and the Church) and not nearly radical enough for the socialists and anarchists of the left. Its offer of human rights for all polarized Spanish society by invoking centuries of prejudice: in fact nobody knew how to implement such a manifesto of social magnanimity. The subsequent tragedy of the civil war was inevitable – but the 1931 Constitution also planted the seeds of Spain's transforming success after Franco's death, during the late 20th century.

The German Reichstag election of 1933

The Weimar Republic that followed German defeat in World War I proved a switchback of political fortunes. In the 14 years after the Treaty of Versailles 20 separate government coalitions revealed the weaknesses of democracy as a system. The economic chaos of the Wall Street Crash and the death in 1929 of Gustav Stresemann (peacemaker among the democratic splinter groups of the centre, stabilizer of German currency, and the only man to face down Hitler), created conditions in which the anti-democratic Nazis and Communists thrived.

By the November 1932 elections the Nazis held more seats but steady Communist gains were sufficient to alarm Germany's right-wing industrialists. The useless outgoing Chancellor Franz von Papen was able to persuade his fellow-aristocrat President Hindenburg (who loathed the 'foreign corporal') that with a government weighted by reliable Prussians, it was safe to replace Chancellor von Schliecher with Hitler, who would 'safeguard corporate interests' against the Communists. Hindsight makes you want to scream 'Behind you!'

Hitler now had the position, but not the numbers. Two months later, the Reichstag burnt down. Rumour blamed the blameless Communists, and a week after that another election gave the Nazis a much-increased 44.5 per cent of the seats. It still wasn't enough. Hitler ran circles round the old buffer Hindenburg to make rapid alliances with the conservative DNVP and the Catholic Centre Party. With stardust in their eyes, they gave Hitler the two-thirds majority he needed to ram through the Enabling Act of March 23 1933 – a law which permitted him to pass any legislation without even consulting the Reichstag. It gave Hitler real teeth, and he bit immediately.

The communist KPD and Social Democratic Party (SPD) were outlawed. There was no other opposition. Hitler had his legally sanctioned dictatorship. The ninth German federal election of the Weimar Republic was the last election before World War II.

WHEN:
March 5 1933
WHERE:
Germany
TOLL:
The fragile codes of civilization melted before an onslaught of barbarity worthy of the Four Horsemen of the Apocalypse. Hitler had set out his political stall in *Mein Kampf* years earlier. Germany – admittedly bone-weary from unemployment, hunger, despair and continuous exploitation by an obsolete Prussian hierarchy – voted for what they thought Hitler offered, and turned their backs in fear once they realized what the pact actually entailed. Could a single event have a worse outcome?
YOU SHOULD KNOW:
An immediate consequence of the 1933 election was the start of the diaspora of German artists, architects, scientists, film makers, philosophers, writers, circus performers and many others who had contributed to making the Weimar republic such a vibrant, creative powerhouse in spite of the daily contest to stay alive. Their individual disasters under Hitler's persecution transformed and enriched the rest of the world, wherever they were transplanted.

German Chancellor and Nazi leader Adolf Hitler casting his vote in a polling station in Königsberg, East Prussia.

'Peace for our time' – the Munich agreement

WHEN:
September 1938
WHERE:
UK and Germany
TOLL:
Czechoslovakia very soon paid a heavy price – the surrender of all its territory – for the sake of Chamberlain's policy; and who knows how Hitler would have reacted if Chamberlain had not conceded?
YOU SHOULD KNOW:
Britain's view of Nazi Germany in the 1930s was crucially coloured by its fears of the threat posed by the Soviet Union – Germany being seen as an essential bulwark against the westward spread of communism.

When British Prime Minister Neville Chamberlain arrived home from Munich at the end of September 1938 flourishing the text of his agreement with Adolf Hitler, an agreement that he memorably described as delivering 'peace for our time', he was greeted as a popular hero who had saved the nation from the dire threat of another all-encompassing war. With the horrors of pan-European conflict barely a generation earlier seared indelibly on the national consciousness, there was no appetite in Britain for any resumption of hostilities, still less for standing up to the calculated provocations of Hitler's warmongering.

Chamberlain was sure he was reflecting the public mood, as well as his own convictions, when he flew to Munich to negotiate with Hitler over the fate of the three million ethnic Germans in the Sudetenland region of northern Czechoslovakia. Hitler cleverly used the notion of self-determination to support his claim that this group be reunited with Germany. Anxious to preserve peace at any cost, Chamberlain acceded to Hitler's demands, giving an assurance that Britain would not intervene if Germany occupied the Sudetenland, as it duly did. The Munich agreement effectively pledged Britain and Germany to leave each other's territorial ambitions alone.

Just six months later Germany seized the rest of Czechoslovakia, making a nonsense of an agreement dubbed by a Labour politician of the time as that 'scrap of paper torn from *Mein Kampf*' and by the historian Simon Schama as 'the holy scrip of appeasement'. Britain's subsequent guarantees to protect Poland were too little and too late. When in September 1939 Britain declared war on Germany following its invasion of Poland, Winston Churchill's assertion, in a parliamentary debate a week after the Munich settlement, that 'there can never be peace between the British democracy and the Nazi Power' was proved chillingly true.

British Prime Minister Neville Chamberlain waving to the crowd at Heston Airport and declaiming, 'Peace for our Time', after returning from signing the Munich agreement.

Vichy government

Any head of state convicted of treason and sentenced to death by firing squad is entitled to feel overwhelmed by political disaster – and that's precisely what happened to French elder statesman Marshal Philippe Pétain after World War II. In 1940, as German troops stormed into France and abject defeat loomed, the old soldier emerged from the maelstrom of French politics to become the Third Republic's last prime minister. Endowed with extraordinary powers by the National Assembly, he signed a peace treaty with Hitler.

This allowed the conquered nation to retain a semblance of self-government, with Marshal Pétain's administration retaining nominal authority over France. In fact, the Germans divided the country into two zones and occupied the larger northern zone, leaving 84-year-old Pétain to govern the unoccupied southern zone and France's overseas colonies from the spa town of Vichy.

The authoritarian Pétain was genuinely concerned about the degenerate state (as he saw it) of *La Belle France*, for he announced a *Révolution Nationale* designed to regenerate the nation. Whatever his motivation, the result was a collaborationist regime that did everything the Germans asked of it, and more, including the rounding up of Jews and 'undesirables' for deportation and concerted efforts to destroy the increasingly active French Resistance.

Any notion of French autonomy was quickly exposed as a sham. German occupiers trampled on the Vichy government's sensibilities whenever it suited them and their laws always took precedence. And in November 1942, after Allied forces landed in North Africa, Marshal Pétain's humiliation was complete. The *Wehrmacht* swiftly occupied the southern zone and – while the Vichy regime continued to enjoy nominal authority – any real power Pétain once enjoyed was nullified. He became a sad political figurehead whose government would forever be disastrously tainted for collaborating so enthusiastically with Hitler and the Nazis.

German Chancellor Adolf Hitler, right, shaking hands with Marshal Philippe Pétain.

WHEN:
1940–1944
WHERE:
France
TOLL:
Pétain's damaging political legacy was international perception that France had collaborated with the Germans rather than suffer the sort of harsh oppression experienced by most occupied countries. Subsequent claims that the *Vichy* government was an illegal administration run by traitors was an attempt to neutralize that view by blaming Pétain and his cronies rather than the nation that voted him in. It didn't work. When French support for the USA's Second Gulf War in 2003 was lukewarm, hawkish American commentators were quick to call the French 'cheese-eating surrender monkeys'.
YOU SHOULD KNOW:
General Charles de Gaulle, France's first postwar president, commuted Pétain's death sentence to life imprisonment on the grounds of his advanced age and outstanding service to France in World War I. He was imprisoned on an island off the French coast, became completely senile and died in 1951, aged 95.

Muslim refugees sitting on the roof of an overcrowded train in their attempt to flee India.

Partition of India

The vast subcontinent of India was the prized jewel in Britain's imperial crown, but controlling British India was never straightforward. After World War II, the exhausted colonial power faced the inevitability of granting India the independence for which momentum had long been building, led by charismatic leaders like the Hindu Mohandas Gandhi and Muslim Allama Mashriqi. Both wanted to replace the British Raj with a united India where Hinduism and Islam could co-exist peacefully, but influential leaders on both sides disagreed and whipped up tension.

The Hindu-majority Indian National Congress led the independence movement. It had many Muslim members despite formation of the breakaway All India Muslim League in 1906, which felt the Muslim minority was unfairly treated within Congress. By the late 1930s there were calls for a separate Muslim state. By 1946, when independence was imminent, friction between the two religious groups reached boiling point. Fearful of a post-independence bloodbath, Britain decided to create Hindu India and Muslim Pakistan (consisting of the geographically separate West and East Pakistan). It was a fateful political decision, with dire consequences for hundreds of millions of human lives.

Partition was overseen by the last British Viceroy, Lord Louis Mountbatten, and took place in August 1947. There is still argument as to the long-term merit of a one-state federal solution following independence, but it is generally agreed that Britain was so eager to be rid of its troublesome colonial dominion that it rushed Partition. Final boundaries of the new nations were not even agreed, leading to tension between India and Pakistan that lasts to this day. Around 14 million people were displaced, moving to their respective religious homelands and creating an intractable refugee problem. Racial violence during this mass migration was endemic, costing countless lives. It was not Imperial Britain's finest hour.

WHEN:
August 14–15 1947
WHERE:
India, Pakistan and Bangladesh
DEATH TOLL:
It is estimated that Partition cost between 300,000 and 1,000,000 lives, while the tense aftermath would include four wars between the uneasy neighbours over disputed territory. To this day Kashmir is still a running sore between India and Pakistan.
YOU SHOULD KNOW:
M K 'Mahatma' Gandhi was murdered shortly after Partition by an assassin who reflected the widely held Hindu view that the Congress Party had treated Muslims *too* fairly – allowing Pakistan to be exclusively created for Muslims with their rights enshrined in law, while India itself remained a country where Hindus and the remaining Muslim minority enjoyed equal rights.

McCarthyism

If ever there was a blot on the USA's political escutcheon, it was paranoid anti-communist activity as the Cold War heated up after World War II. Senator Joseph McCarthy never belonged to the congressional House Committee on Un-American Activities with its famous question 'Are you now or have you ever been a member of the Communist Party of America?' but would give his name to the sort of witch-hunts it mounted.

After becoming Wisconsin's youngest circuit judge in 1939, McCarthy volunteered for the US Marines and flew combat missions, subsequently embroidering his war record to gain political advantage. He became the Junior Republican Senator for Wisconsin in 1946 but only found his vocation in 1950, making endless demagogic speeches after being pleasantly surprised by avid media attention after he claimed to have a list of 205 communists working in the US State Department. The term 'McCarthyism' was soon coined by a *Washington Post* cartoonist and passed into the language.

McCarthy became chairman of the Senate Committee of Government Operations and used its Permanent Subcommittee on Investigations to mount virulent attempts to expose imaginary subversion and espionage. It came to a head when McCarthy took on the US Army, inventing rumours of dangerous spy rings to justify this unpopular action. His extended confrontation with the military, much of it televised, revealed him as a bombastic bully and led to a collapse in his popularity. In 1954 the Senate censured McCarthy for his intemperate behaviour, a rare dishonour that effectively destroyed his political influence.

The Senator from Wisconsin died of hepatitis and alcoholism at Bethesda Naval Hospital in 1957, but his name lives on as the description of any political activity that involves reckless accusations made without proof, or frenzied public criticism of the character and patriotism of political rivals.

WHEN:
1940s and 1950s
WHERE:
USA
TOLL:
Although the patent excesses of Senator McCarthy's reckless and unjustified attacks eventually led to a reaction against the sort of 'reds under the bed' hysteria that had been gripping the nation, his rabid anti-communist crusade was a reflection of the USA's genuine abhorrence of the rival political ideology and McCarthyism helped to reinforce the attitudes that led America into its disastrous Vietnam misadventure.
YOU SHOULD KNOW:
As an indication of the intellectual rigour with which America's pursuit of closet communists was pursued, at one pre-war session of the House Committee on Un-American Activities a reluctant witness – who headed the Federal Theatre Project, an organization allegedly riddled with communists – was asked if the Elizabethan playwright Christopher Marlowe (1564–1593) was (or ever had been?) a member of the Communist Party.

Senator Joseph McCarthy shaking a finger during his second appearance before the Senate Foreign Relations Subcommittee.

Arab-Israeli conflict

Civilians walking through the debris-laden Ben Yehuda street in Jerusalem after an Arab bomb attack.

One of the world's most enduring and disastrous conflicts is that between Israel (consistently supported by the USA) and Palestinians displaced after the state of Israel was established, or subsequently placed under Israeli control by force of arms. Palestinians are seen as oppressed victims by Middle Eastern nations and extreme regimes still promote the destruction of Israel.

To support their cause in World War I, Britain promised Palestinian territory to both Arabs and – in the Balfour Declaration of 1917 – Jews. The postwar British mandate over Palestine saw a sharp rise in Jewish immigration and serious friction between Arab and Jew. The argument was eventually settled when the United Nations voted for the partition of Palestine and establishment of a Jewish state in 1948.

This led to war, with neighbouring Arab states immediately attacking when Israeli independence was declared. The new Jewish state survived, was boosted by mass immigration and became a prosperous modern democracy. But along the way it fought further wars, in the process seizing the West Bank, East Jerusalem, Gaza Strip and Golan Heights. The indigenous Palestinian population of occupied territories was horrified as Jewish colonization threatened to overwhelm their ancestral lands, while Israel actively encouraged invasive settlement.

The United Nations declared Israel's land-grab illegal, but UN Security Council Resolution 242 suggests a 'land for peace' deal might be negotiated to create a Palestinian state in the occupied territories that would also provide a homeland for displaced Palestinians, allowing normalization of Arab-Israeli relations. But the long history of passionate competition for this small patch of land on the eastern Mediterranean ensures that enduring bitterness and mutual mistrust make a settlement almost impossible. Sadly, though it is in the interest of neither Arabs nor Jews, the intractable conflict seems likely to run and run.

Iran coup

The full story of the 1953 *coup d'état* in Iran has yet to be told but it is generally agreed today that it was this event that sowed the seeds for the Islamic Revolution of 1979 and the era of religious and political fundamentalism it ushered in. With its strategic location and vast oil reserves Iran was always going to be of special interest to the major powers; this particular debacle had its roots in World War II when Britain established a presence in the country to protect a vital supply route to its ally the Soviet Union and to prevent the oil from falling into German hands. After the war Britain effectively retained control over Iran's oil through the establishment of the Anglo-Iranian Oil Company.

This cosy arrangement changed abruptly in 1951 when the Iranian parliament, led by the nationalistic but democratic government of Mohammed Mossadeq, voted to nationalize the country's oil industry. Seeing its interests thus threatened, Britain embarked on a secret campaign to weaken and de-stabilize the Mossadeq government. When this evolved into the idea of a full-scale coup to overthrow the government, Britain, reluctant to shoulder the responsibility alone, persuaded the USA to join forces by playing on Cold War fears and raising the spectre of the communist bogeyman to the east.

The USA now took on the leading role in a covert operation where CIA-funded agents were used to foment unrest inside Iran with the harassment of religious and political leaders and a campaign of media disinformation. These efforts came to a head in the coup of August 1953 when the democratically elected government was deposed and the despotic authority of Shah Reza Pahlavi and his pro-Western monarchy was re-asserted.

Shah Reza Pahlavi being saluted upon his arrival at Tehran airport.

WHEN:
August 1953
WHERE:
Iran
DEATH TOLL:
Total unknown, but some 300 people were killed in the final fighting in the streets of Tehran.
YOU SHOULD KNOW:
The coup nearly failed because the Shah, fearful for his throne, vacillated over signing the royal decrees the CIA had prepared to sanction the change of government.

Soldiers waiting to land and Westland Whirlwind helicopters of No.845 Naval Air Service share the flight deck of HMS Theseus outside a blazing Port Said.

Suez crisis

The sun was already setting on Britain's empire and its status as a major player on the world stage when in 1955 a weary and disillusioned Churchill stepped down as prime minister, handing the reins to his foreign secretary, Anthony Eden. The following year the final nail in the coffin of Britain's imperialist aspirations was driven home when catastrophic political misjudgement combined with old-fashioned muscle-flexing in one of the most humiliating fiascos in the country's history, one whose repercussions would echo through British political life for generations to follow.

The Anglo-Egyptian Treaty of 1936 proclaiming Egypt a sovereign independent state also allowed Britain to maintain a garrison to protect the Suez Canal, a vital trading route then jointly owned by Britain and France. A phased withdrawal saw the last troops leave in 1956, not a moment too soon for Egypt's ambitious new leader, Gamel Abdul Nasser, who had recently announced the construction of a great dam on the Nile at Aswan which he hoped would transform his country's economy. When the USA and Britain reneged on promises of vital finance for the massive project (in part because of American misgivings over an increasing Soviet influence in Egyptian affairs) Nasser nationalized the Suez Canal to secure an alternative source of funds. In retaliation, Britain and France held secret discussions with Egypt's sworn enemy, Israel, coming up with a strategy, duly executed, whereby Israel attacked Egypt across the Sinai peninsula and thereby gave the European powers a pretext to invade under the guise of a peace-keeping force. On the brink of military success Britain and France were forced into an ignominious withdrawal following United Nations' condemnation of the action – led by a furious USA which had always preferred a diplomatic solution – and the threat of a Soviet counter-attack.

WHEN:
July to November 1956
WHERE:
Suez Canal region, Egypt
DEATH TOLL:
There were an estimated 650 Egyptian deaths, including civilians. Israeli losses were 189 and Anglo-French forces lost 26.
YOU SHOULD KNOW:
Anthony Eden's decision to call off the British action in Suez was also influenced by considerable popular opposition at home together with the threat of economic meltdown following a run on Sterling (and no prospect of a bail-out from the USA).

The Profumo affair

Harold Macmillan, the Conservative prime minister of the day, may have declared that Britain had 'never had it so good' but, beneath the more relaxed atmosphere ushered in by the 1960s after years of postwar austerity, lay hidden undercurrents. Against a background of a nation still smarting from the humiliation of Suez and alive with Cold War jitters following the Cuban missile crisis, the early 1960s saw a number of high-profile spy trials, including the conviction of double agent George Blake. Then, on March 22 1963, John Profumo, the Minister for War and a rising star in Parliament, made a statement to the House of Commons in which he categorically refuted accusations levelled by fellow MPs of an affair with a young model, Christine Keeler.

The charge against a married minister of the Crown was serious enough given the prevailing mores, but what gave it far greater substance were the revelations that Miss Keeler was in fact a high-class call girl among whose clients was a military attaché at the Russian Embassy. Rumours circulated that Profumo's liaison with Keeler might have led to classified information on Britain's nuclear capability being passed to the Russians. Profumo explained that he and his wife had met Keeler in 1961 at a party on Lord Astor's Cliveden estate where they had been guests of Stephen Ward, a well-connected London osteopath. Profumo had met her several times subsequently but strenuously denied there had been any 'impropriety'.

Less than three months later on June 5, Profumo tendered his resignation from government, admitting he had lied to Parliament. Although a subsequent inquiry found no evidence of security breaches, the scandal proved a fatal blow to the government, leading to Macmillan's own resignation that autumn and victory at the following year's polls for Harold Wilson's Labour Party.

WHEN:
1963
WHERE:
UK
DEATH TOLL:
Stephen Ward died in August 1963 after taking a fatal overdose towards the end of his trial on a charge of living off immoral earnings.
YOU SHOULD KNOW:
John Profumo, who died in March 2006 at the age of 91, devoted the rest of his long life to charitable work in the East End of London, winning huge respect and admiration in this role and resolutely shunning the public spotlight.

Christine Keeler, right, and Marilyn (Mandy) Rice-Davies, were two of the principal witnesses in the vice charges case against osteopath Dr Stephen Ward.

Prague Spring

WHEN:
1968
WHERE:
Czechoslovakia
DEATH TOLL:
Unknown, but at least 100 people died in street skirmishes in Prague. In January 1969 student Jan Palach burned himself to death in Prague's Wenceslas Square in protest against the invasion.
YOU SHOULD KNOW:
After his dismissal Alexander Dubcek spent 18 years in a humble clerical post in his native Slovakia but returned in triumph after the Velvet Revolution of 1989 to become the first Speaker of the new Federal Assembly.

Prague residents carrying a Czechoslovakian flag and throwing burning torches, attempt to stop a Soviet tank in Prague.

The central European country of Czechoslovakia had fallen under the Soviet sphere of influence after World War II; from 1948 it was ruled by the Communists as a one-party state. In the mid 1960s poor living conditions and the weak economy gave rise to increasing rumblings of dissent in the populace, not least in Slovakia (then still part of one Czech nation), where Alexander Dubcek was party leader. In January 1968, responding to the popular mood, Dubcek replaced the discredited Novotny as leader of Czechoslovakia. The progressive Dubcek bided his time but in April he announced a wide-ranging reform programme, designed, as he famously put it, to present 'socialism with a human face'. While insisting that the Communist Party preserved its 'leading role' in the state, Dubcek attempted to liberalize the regime through a series of key measures including freedom of speech and assembly, an end to censorship, a strengthening of trades unions and relaxations on travel abroad.

Although Dubcek had been careful all along to pledge the country's continuing allegiance to the Soviet Union and the Warsaw Pact alliance, the bosses in Moscow took a rather different view of the new freedoms being enjoyed by the Czech people during what

became known as the 'Prague Spring'. The whole world was stunned when on August 21 1968 Soviet troops invaded Czechoslovakia and tanks rolled through the streets of Prague. Officially this was a Warsaw Pact operation, Moscow cannily justifying its naked aggression as the legitimate provision by fellow Pact states of fraternal assistance against 'counter-revolutionary forces'.

Despite valiant popular resistance on the streets, the brave experiment of the Prague Spring was summarily snuffed out and a defeated Dubcek duly dismissed from his post the following April. The Czech people would have to wait another generation before enjoying such freedoms again.

The Chappaquiddick incident

Senator Ted Kennedy's car being pulled from the water at Edgartown.

The death of Senator Edward Kennedy in August 2009 marked the end of an era in which the Kennedy family dominated American political life. The youngest of nine children of ambitious parents, Edward's long and distinguished life of public service was marred by personal difficulties and private tragedy, most notably the assassinations of his two older brothers, Jack (JFK) and Robert. Edward had been particularly close to Robert; when the latter was gunned down in June 1968 during his campaign to secure the Democratic nomination for the presidency, his grief was compounded by the enormous weight of expectation that then fell on his shoulders.

One year later, on the night of July 18 1969, Edward, who shared the family taste for living it up, attended a party on Chappaquiddick Island, just off the exclusive Massachusetts retreat of Martha's Vineyard. At midnight Edward left the party to drive a fellow guest, 28-year-old Mary Jo Kopechne, to catch the ferry. Driving at speed, Kennedy missed the road and ran off a bridge into a tidal creek. Kennedy escaped from the capsized car but Kopechne drowned in the accident. Although he claimed to have tried to rescue her, Kennedy's failure to report the incident for over ten hours and the subsequent inquest held in private led to accusations of a cover-up and public outrage that Kennedy had seemed prepared to put his political career ahead of a young woman's life.

That career never recovered from Chappaquiddick. Although he remained a member of the US Senate until his death, becoming a conscientious and hugely effective legislator, Edward Kennedy had to abandon any serious aspirations to follow his brothers into high office, a move only underlined by an ill-judged campaign in 1980 for the party's nomination in which he ran against President Jimmy Carter.

WHEN:
July 18–19 1969
WHERE:
Chappaquiddick Island, Massachusetts, USA
DEATH TOLL:
A single person died, Mary Jo Kopechne, but the incident had far-reaching repercussions.
YOU SHOULD KNOW:
Edward Kennedy was the third longest-serving member of the US Senate in American history.

The Pentagon Papers

WHEN:
June 1971
WHERE:
USA
TOLL:
The publication of the Pentagon Papers weakened President Nixon's ability to wage the Vietnam War, as the revelations of official misconduct at the highest level further hardened already disenchanted public opinion against the conflict. Humiliating military defeat duly followed in 1975 when the last US helicopter fled Saigon on April 30.
YOU SHOULD KNOW:
Ellsberg and Russo were tried on treason and theft charges in 1973, fully expecting to be sent to prison for life. However, Judge William Byrne declared a mistrial after the government tried to influence him with an offer of the FBI directorship and evidence emerged of massive illegal activity against the accused pair, including unauthorized wiretapping and a failed break-in at the office of Ellsberg's psychiatrist by White House 'plumbers' Liddy and Hunt who hoped to discredit Ellsberg by making him appear mentally unstable. It was their unsuccessful rehearsal for the subsequent Watergate affair.

If there's one thing Americans like nearly as much as a good conspiracy theory, it's a juicy political leak. One of the best poured out in 1971 when *The New York Times* started publishing excerpts from the so-called Pentagon Papers. This top-secret 7,000-page review of US conduct in Vietnam after World War II was dryly entitled *United States-Vietnam Relations, 1945–1967: A Study Prepared by the Department of Defense*. Completed in 1968, it was political dynamite.

In 1971 one of the joint authors, disillusioned military analyst Daniel Ellsberg, enlisted the help of Anthony Russo and they copied the Pentagon Papers – before handing most of them to *The New York Times*. As soon as serialization began, political controversy and street demonstrations erupted, closely followed by the inevitable lawsuits.

What was the fuss about? Quite a lot – for the Pentagon Papers revealed that four US Presidents, from Harry Truman to L B Johnson, had persistently lied about their intentions and conduct in Vietnam. Notable revelations included the fact that the war had been deliberately escalated with the carpet-bombing of Laos and Cambodia and that various raids and offensives had taken place without being publicized. The damning cumulative message to the American people was that their government had distrusted and misled them.

President Richard Nixon accused Ellsberg and Russo of treason and obtained an injunction that plugged the leak in *The New York Times* . . . though not for long. On June 18 *The Washington Post* waded in and was immediately silenced by injunction. On June 29, Alaska's Senator Mike Gravel entered over 4,000 pages of the Pentagon Papers onto the Congressional Record, ensuring that nobody could be prosecuted for publishing or discussing no-longer-secret contents. The message was underlined the following day when the US Supreme Court vacated gagging injunctions in a pro-free-speech First Amendment judgement.

Members of The New York Times *composing room looking at a page proof containing the secret Pentagon report on Vietnam.*

Watergate

The events which led to the resignation, on August 9 1974, of President Richard Nixon began in a relatively low-key way with the red-handed arrest in the early hours of a June 1972 night of five burglars. The building they were apprehended in, however, was no ordinary one but the headquarters of the Democratic Party in Washington DC, housed at the time in the Watergate apartment complex. As it emerged in the subsequent trials and investigations, the burglars had been part of a covert operation, known as the 'plumbers unit', which had already engineered one break-in of the Watergate offices to install bugging equipment.

In the background was Republican President Nixon's campaign to secure a second elected term and the eerily well-named CREEP, the Committee to Re-elect the President. In the November poll Nixon gained a landslide victory, winning over 60 per cent of the popular vote. But any sense of triumph was short-lived as the Watergate clouds darkened and *Washington Post* reporters Carl Bernstein and Bob Woodward kept the public supplied with fresh revelations of murky dealings in the administration. Although Nixon initially denied any prior knowledge of the break-in or involvement in a subsequent cover-up, the string of trials and resignations that followed ensured no let-up for the White House.

In June 1973 John Dean, the former presidential counsel, formally implicated President Nixon in testimony to a Senate committee; the killer blow came, however, with the revelation that tape recordings existed of White House conversations covering this period. When the president refused to testify or to hand over the tapes, Congress began an impeachment process against him. As a vote for impeachment drew ever closer, Nixon bowed to the inevitable and, three days after finally releasing the tapes, announced his resignation in a televised address to the nation.

Bob Woodward (left) and Carl Bernstein, staff writers on The Washington Post, *who investigated the Watergate case.*

WHEN:
June 1972 to August 1974
WHERE:
Washington DC, USA
TOLL:
Three of Nixon's co-conspirators were jailed. Watergate cast doubt on the probity of politicians in general and severely dented the reputation of the legal profession because so many of those involved were lawyers. The affair made such an impression on the public consciousness all over the world that since then almost any public scandal is suffixed with '-gate'.
YOU SHOULD KNOW:
One month after Nixon's resignation, the new president, Gerald Ford, who had been Nixon's Vice President, granted him a 'full free and absolute' pardon for 'all offenses against the United States'. Richard Nixon is the only US president to have resigned from office.

The downfall of Jeremy Thorpe

In 1967, when MP for North Devon Jeremy Thorpe became leader, the Liberal Party was long past its heyday. But he galvanized the Party back into action to place it firmly at centre stage of British politics. At just 37 years old with saturnine good looks, rapier wit and a foppish taste in clothing, Thorpe radiated an extraordinary charisma that won the hearts of the electorate.

There was only one problem – despite the fact that he was married, he was rumoured to have had a passionate affair with male model Norman Scott back in 1961 when homosexuality was still a criminal offence. The whispers were so persistent that eventually, in 1971, the Liberal Party was forced to hold a 'whitewashing' inquiry to squash the story.

At the general election of 1974 Thorpe was at the top of his game. The Liberals won 14 seats, holding the balance of power in a hung parliament. This was Thorpe's moment . . . until the homosexuality smears resurfaced, to devastating effect. A man named Andrew Newton had been charged with the attempted murder of Norman Scott and, as a trial witness, Scott ensured that Thorpe's name was dragged through the mud. The embarrassment was too much and Thorpe was forced to quit as Liberal leader in May 1976.

Scott continued stirring and the story refused to die. In August 1978 Thorpe was charged with conspiracy to murder. With incredible bravado he stood in the general election of May 1979. But the allegation was too much for North Devon to swallow – he lost his seat, and a few days later appeared in court. The jury ultimately found Thorpe not guilty but the damage had been done – he had provided the nation with a sensational political scandal, his reputation was in tatters and the Liberal Party was permanently tainted.

Jeremy Thorpe leaving the National Liberal Club in London's Whitehall.

WHEN:
1975–1979
WHERE:
London and Devon, UK
TOLL:
Politics was the poorer – parliament and the nation lost a major talent. Jeremy Thorpe's career was in ruins and tragically he was diagnosed with Parkinson's disease shortly after. It was a terrible waste of a brilliant politician, and the Liberal Party was a spent force thereafter, ultimately merging with the Social Democratic Party to form the Lib-Dems.
YOU SHOULD KNOW:
Norman Scott sold love letters written by Thorpe, one of which contained the line 'bunnies can and will go to France' – 'bunny' supposedly being Thorpe's pet name for his lover. At Thorpe's trial the judge summed up Scott as '. . . a fraud; he is a sponger; he is a whiner; he is a parasite'.

Lancaster House Agreement

The 1960s was a decade in which Britain was busy divesting itself of its colonies in Africa. In most cases this process was smooth and free from conflict; Southern Rhodesia, however, proved an exception and by 1968 it was the sole remaining British colony on the continent. In discussions some years earlier about the transition to independence, the country's white settlers – a minority group which exercised political and economic control – refused to countenance any move to majority rule, fearing that Rhodesia's black population would be incapable of effective self-government.

In 1965 the white Rhodesian government of Ian Smith defied Britain and declared UDI (Unilateral Declaration of Independence). Britain did not of course accept this and won UN backing for a programme of economic sanctions which lasted for the next 15 years. External pressures were exacerbated internally by a debilitating civil war against the guerrilla forces of Robert Mugabe and his black Patriotic Front. As the 1970s wore on, popular support for the Patriotic Front grew until Smith was forced in 1979 to agree to multi-racial parliamentary elections. When these proved inconclusive Britain, in one of the first major acts of Margaret Thatcher's new Conservative government, persuaded the principal parties to participate in talks held at Lancaster House, London.

Under the chairmanship of the Foreign Secretary, Lord Carrington, the Constitutional Conference met for three months in autumn 1979. The resulting Agreement, signed on December 21, gave Rhodesia (soon to be renamed Zimbabwe) a new constitution and guaranteed a peaceful transition to full independence. Although hailed as a success at the time, the Lancaster House Agreement's failure to resolve underlying problems, such as the key issue of land ownership, has left a country which today is in a state of near-total collapse with tensions between blacks and whites as high as ever.

WHEN:
September to December 1979
WHERE:
Lancaster House, London, UK
DEATH TOLL:
The Agreement brought an end to the extended guerrilla war in Rhodesia which caused thousands of military and civilian deaths.
YOU SHOULD KNOW:
The Agreement gave white Rhodesians certain 'protective rights', including a guaranteed 20 per cent of the seats in parliament. This quota was abolished by Mugabe in 1987.

The scene at Lancaster House, London, after the signing of the Rhodesia ceasefire agreement.

The winter of discontent

WHEN:
Winter of 1978–1979
WHERE:
UK
TOLL:
The Labour Party lost the confidence of the working classes.
YOU SHOULD KNOW:
A popular and widely respected parliamentarian, Jim Callaghan was nevertheless criticized for a certain complacency in his handling of the winter of discontent. 'Crisis? What crisis?', trumpeted a famous headline in *The Sun* newspaper at the time.

The so-called 'winter of discontent' of 1978–1979 which brought down Jim Callaghan's Labour government marked a low point in Britain's postwar industrial relations. When Callaghan took over as prime minister from Harold Wilson in 1976 he inherited an unenviable catalogue of national woes. Chief among these was Britain's poor economic health. The country was already struggling to adapt to the new realities of international trade and accept the terminal decline of its traditional manufacturing base, so it was ill-equipped to withstand the huge inflationary pressures generated by the OPEC countries' dramatic hike in oil prices after 1973.

In the same year that Callaghan took office, the Labour government, in order to stem a potentially catastrophic fall in the value of the pound, had to go cap in hand to the International Monetary Fund for a £4 billion loan. There were of course conditions to the loan, the chief one being that Britain must make savage cuts in public expenditure. The Callaghan government managed to reduce its public spending by £1 billion, but such draconian measures were achieved at the cost of a massive increase in unemployment (1.6 million in 1978) and, most significantly, of the alienation of its traditional allies in the trades union movement.

As 1978 drew to a close, the public service unions, whose members bore the brunt of the cuts, rejected the government's attempts to impose a cap on wage rises and organized a series of strikes and walk-outs, causing serious disruption around the country. While the tales of uncollected refuse, understaffed hospitals and even unburied bodies at cemeteries were fuelled by media exaggerations, the 'winter of discontent' nevertheless demonstrated to the electorate that the government was no longer up to the job, and the resulting general election in May 1979 saw a decisive victory for Margaret Thatcher's Conservatives.

An unpleasant official rubbish dump in Leicester Square, London

Iran-Contra affair

The background to what became known as the Iran-Contra affair of the mid 1980s lay in US President Ronald Reagan's pre-occupation with the spread of communism internationally, in particular in the United States' own backyard of Central America. In 1979 the Sandinista liberation movement in Nicaragua had finally overthrown the brutal dictatorship of General Somoza and Reagan became increasingly convinced that the presence of an actively left-wing regime would spark revolution throughout the region and threaten the security of the USA itself. In the early 1980s his administration ploughed massive amounts of military aid into a number of governments in Central America that were beset by civil war and guerrilla fighting.

In the case of Nicaragua, the focus was on destabilizing the government and engineering the overthrow of the Sandinista regime. Military aid was channelled to right-wing militia groups – the so-called 'contras' – fighting to achieve this. The American public, however, grew increasingly opposed to such funding and when Congress passed a law banning it, the White House resorted to covert means to continue its support. The scandal broke in November 1986 when the Reagan administration was forced to admit that it had been continuing secretly to fund the Nicaraguan 'contras' by means of arms sales to Iran which were themselves illegal and in breach of a trade embargo against that country.

In testimony to the subsequent congressional hearings on the affair Lieutenant-Colonel Oliver North, who had been in charge of the covert operation, declared that Reagan and his Vice President, George Bush, had been aware of it, though both denied any knowledge of the details and no evidence was ever brought linking them to any wrongdoing. The affair nevertheless raised serious questions about the power of the executive and the extent and effectiveness of Congress's oversight of foreign affairs.

Oliver North being sworn in on his first day of testimony at the Iran-Contra hearings.

WHEN:
1985–1987
WHERE:
USA, Nicaragua, Iran
DEATH TOLL:
The 'Contra' war against the Sandinista government caused tens of thousands of civilian deaths in Nicaragua.
YOU SHOULD KNOW:
An immunity agreement with the Senate regarding his testimony in the affair meant that Oliver North's criminal conviction was subsequently quashed. He is now a radio talk show host and columnist. Daniel Ortega, leader of the Sandinistas and Reagan's chief bogeyman, is currently the democratically elected President of Nicaragua.

Labour Party rally in Sheffield

As the 1992 general election approached, Britain was sliding into recession. The electorate were more than ready for change after 13 years of Tory rule, but not entirely convinced by Neil Kinnock's Labour Party. In the weeks leading up to the election the polls were neck and neck – it looked as though the result could be a hung parliament.

On the morning of April 1 the latest opinion poll showed Labour ahead. Labour supporters were over the moon. With only eight days until the election, the scent of victory was in the air. The auspices couldn't be better for that evening's Sheffield Arena rally, a gathering of 10,000 Labour Party members that was costing £100,000 to stage.

The rally had all the razzmatazz of an American campaign convention with live music and celebrity backing. Kinnock flew in by helicopter, his entrance timed to coincide with the nine o'clock news. The nation watched as an ecstatic-looking Kinnock, followed by his beaming shadow cabinet, paraded through the audience to delirious applause and bounced onto the podium flushed with triumph.

Whether he bellowed 'Well, all right! Well, all right!' or 'We're alright! We're alright!' is disputed but, whichever it was, it wasn't so much the words as the tone that was the mistake. Kinnock sounded like a tinpot preacher. And with national flags fluttering overhead and party apparatchiks fanatically chanting 'We will win. We will win', the scene had altogether too many echoes of Nuremberg for the liking of the British electorate.

Voters went to the polls a week later with the image of a rabid Welsh evangelist fixed firmly in their heads. It was not a pretty picture. Kinnock's triumphalism stuck in the craw of the electorate. The Sheffield rally had turned into a public relations debacle and the Tories won the election.

Labour leader Neil Kinnock at a Labour Party election rally in Sheffield, April 1 1992.

WHEN:
April 1 1992
WHERE:
Sheffield Arena, UK
TOLL:
A disappointed Neil Kinnock resigned as Labour leader and the country had to suffer another five years of a government it detested.
YOU SHOULD KNOW:
The Sun newspaper has always asserted that 'it wos *The Sun* wot won' the 1992 election. The paper ran a virulent anti-Kinnock campaign with an election day headline: 'If Neil Kinnock wins today, will the last person to leave Britain please turn out the lights'. But the Conservatives certainly credited their unexpected victory to the misconceived Sheffield rally.

Guantánamo Bay detention camp

Guantánamo Bay on the southern tip of Cuba has been an American naval base ever since 1898, used from the 1970s as a detention camp for Cubans and Haitians caught attempting to slip into America by sea. After the invasion of Afghanistan in October 2001, President Bush found a chilling new purpose for it: Guantánamo was converted into a high-security detention centre and declared to be beyond the jurisdiction of US law and the articles of the Geneva Convention.

Governments on both sides of the Atlantic deemed it a perfectly reasonable ethical response to an extreme situation and hid behind euphemistic catchphrases: apparently the 'war on terror' demanded the 'extraordinary rendition' of 'enemy combatants' to undergo 'coercive interrogation' for the sake of our very survival.

Since its inception, at least 775 captives have been detained in Guantánamo, around 420 of whom were eventually released without charge. Many of these had been rounded up randomly by Afghan tribesmen in exchange for bounty money; among them were children as young as 13. It was US policy to keep the prisoners' identity secret and information as to what was going on in Guantánamo dripped out slowly: detainees were routinely subjected to 'unorthodox interrogation techniques' including beatings, sexual and cultural humiliation, sleep-deprivation, prolonged stress positions and exposure to heat, cold and unbearable noise, and the infamous 'water-boarding' torture of semi-drowning.

The world was aghast at the depravity of the US administration. But it was not until 2006 that the British government, after much blustering, tentatively declared that Guantánamo was 'an anomaly'. Its very existence demonstrates just how easily the democratically elected government of a 'civilized' country can trample on fundamental human rights. America's reputation as the world's guardian of liberty, justice and truth was in tatters.

WHEN:
From January 2002
WHERE:
Guantánamo Bay, Cuba
DEATH TOLL:
Unknown
There were many attempted suicides, at least four of which were successful, and three deaths have been attributed to suicide by the Pentagon. The detainees have all been left with permanent physical and psychological scars. At least 60 of the detainees were boys under the age of 18, some as young as 13.
YOU SHOULD KNOW:
In January 2009 some 245 detainees were still incarcerated; by November this had been reduced to 215. Of these it is anticipated that between 60 and 80 will eventually stand trial, though it is not known when nor what they are to be charged with. The remainder will be freed – eventually. No more than 24 prisoners were closely linked to the terrorist organization al-Qaeda and only one is an important international terrorist – Mohamed al-Kahtani, who is thought to have helped plan 9/11. On January 22 2009 President Barack Obama ordered that Guantánamo detention camp be closed within a year. This is turning out to be easier said than done. No country is willing to accept the remaining detainees, so the US government doesn't know what to do with them.

Detainees in orange jumpsuits sitting in a holding area under the watchful eyes of military police.

Scandal of the September dossier

WHEN:
September 24 2002 to July 18 2003
WHERE:
House of Commons, London, UK
DEATH TOLL:
The death of Dr David Kelly was directly attributable to his exposure as Gilligan's informant. During the actual invasion of Iraq 33 British soldiers died. Another 146 died in its immediate aftermath and 790 were seriously wounded. The invasion cost over 7,000 Iraqi civilian lives and there have been at least another 110,000 (possibly as many as 600,000) violent deaths in the subsequent years of insurgency.
YOU SHOULD KNOW:
The September dossier scandal may not be over yet. On December 5 2009 six doctors started a legal action demanding an inquest into Dr Kelly's death on the grounds that there was not enough evidence to prove that he killed himself.

When British Prime Minister Tony Blair agreed to support America's invasion of Iraq he was on shaky ground – under international law there was no *casus belli*. But in September 2002 the government published a dossier based on British intelligence reports. It claimed that Saddam Hussein was armed to the teeth with biological and chemical weapons of mass destruction (WMD) which could be deployed within 45 minutes. Blair argued that 'the stability of the world' was at stake and 'unless we face up to the threat . . . we place at risk the lives and prosperity of our own people'. The next day *The Sun* newspaper's headline trumpeted: 'Brits 45 Mins from Doom'.

In May 2003, a few weeks into the Iraq war, Radio 4's *Today* programme broadcast an interview with journalist Andrew Gilligan in which he declared he had it on good authority that the September dossier had been 'sexed-up' by government spin doctors and, more specifically, the 45-minute claim (the government's main grounds for declaring war) was fictitious.

A massive row broke out between Downing Street press secretary Alastair Campbell and the BBC which led to the first of many parliamentary inquiries. Gilligan's information source was 'outed' as Dr David Kelly, a Ministry of Defence weapons expert. Kelly was hauled before the inquiry and, a few days later on July 18, was found dead in the woods near his home. Instead of an inquest, the investigation into Kelly's death came within the remit of the postwar Hutton Inquiry where, without further ado, it was declared an open-and-shut suicide case.

The 'sexed-up' dossier led to a complete breakdown of trust between the New Labour government and the British people. It became clear that the government was tailoring facts to suit its policy and that Blair had misled parliament and the nation.

A journalist holds a copy of a dossier setting out British Prime Minister Tony Blair's case for military action against Iraq.

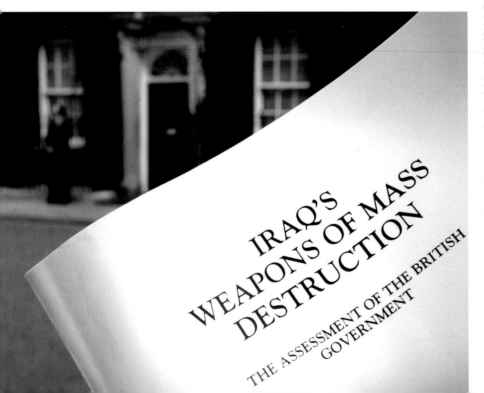

IRAQ'S WEAPONS OF MASS DESTRUCTION

THE ASSESSMENT OF THE BRITISH GOVERNMENT

Afghan election

The fiasco of the Afghan presidential election of 2009 is an object lesson in the consequences of blithely marching into alien territory and attempting to impose by force Western notions of liberal democracy on an ancient and complex kinship culture in which clan loyalties invariably take precedence over national identity.

An Afghan woman casting her ballot at a polling station in a mosque in Kabul, Afghanistan.

After the UN (United Nations) forces ousted the Taliban in 2002, pro-western Hamid Karzai was installed as a 'safe' transitional leader. At the first presidential election in 2004 Karzai, backed by America, unsurprisingly obtained the necessary 50 per cent of the vote to grant him a five-year term. But by 2009 he was no longer the golden boy. The Americans were rooting for his main opponent, Dr Abdullah.

In southern Afghanistan, where the Taliban still hold sway, the election was boycotted – the polling stations simply did not open. Karzai's campaign team went to the other extreme – they indulged in bare-faced corruption by inventing ghost polling stations, registering literally millions of fake voters and stuffing the ballot to achieve a 54.6 per cent majority. America tried to pressurize Karzai into a power-sharing deal. When that failed they demanded a second round of the election; at which point Dr Abdullah had the grace (or was persuaded – who knows how a kinship culture works?) to bow out and Karzai was reinstated as president.

The UN was left with egg on its face. The election had to be seen to be a success in order to justify the eight-year military occupation. By the standards of Western democracy the entire electoral process was a nonsense – but then in Afghan cultural terms the very concept of individual political enfranchisement is a nonsense. The farcical level of corruption merely demonstrated the impotence of the occupying forces in the face of the complex problems of the region.

WHEN:
August 20 2009
WHERE:
Afghanistan
TOLL:
According to Amnesty International 'the highest level of civilian casualties since the fall of the Taliban in 2002 has been registered in Afghanistan in the period around the elections'. The security situation grew worse than ever and any Afghanis relying on the UN to create political stability have seen their hopes completely dashed.
YOU SHOULD KNOW:
America had decided to invade Afghanistan and overthrow the Taliban long before 9/11. The terrorist attack on the Twin Towers merely provided a pretext and ensured UN backing.

ECONOMIC DISASTERS

Tulip bulb mania

WHEN:
1634–1637
WHERE:
The Netherlands
TOLL:
Although the Dutch economy was strong enough to absorb the collapse of the tulip market, confidence was badly shaken, which slowed down economic growth. The poorer members of society bore the brunt: people who had scraped together everything they owned in exchange for a tulip contract were left penniless.
YOU SHOULD KNOW:
The amazing multi-coloured flowers of the most highly valued 17th-century tulips were in fact caused by a plant disease known as 'mosaic' or 'tulip break', a virus that breaks up the colour of the petals making them appear attractively streaked. A similar but less dramatic effect is achieved in modern tulips by cross-cultivation.

In his authoritative work on the subject of human folly *Extraordinary Popular Delusions and the Madness of Crowds*, Victorian journalist Charles Mackay cited the Dutch mania for tulip bulbs as a perfect illustration of a speculative 'bubble'. During the 1630s The Netherlands was gripped by a sort of national insanity. In retrospect, it was an outbreak of delusional frenzy that almost defies belief.

The 17th century was the Dutch Golden Age: Holland was a great global trading power, the arts and sciences were flourishing and the aspirational middle classes were prospering, until . . . a craze for tulip bulbs swept through the nation.

Originally introduced to Europe from Turkey in the late 16th century, the tulip was having its heyday. Growers produced eye-catching new cultivars with exotic names, and rare specimens were sought after as fashionable garden plants. As the seasonal tulip trade became increasingly profitable, speculators devised a system of 'futures' contracts so that tulips could be bought and sold even when the bulbs were planted in the ground. The tulip contracts market became known as the 'wind trade' because there were no visible goods.

Tulipmania reached its peak towards the end of 1636. Everyone, from all walks of life, wanted to invest and contract prices rose to dizzying heights. A single bulb of the rare *Semper Augustus* variety, admired for its flamboyant blue-and-crimson-streaked flower, cost the equivalent of the entire annual income of a well-to-do merchant.

Suddenly, in February 1637 at the Haarlem bulb-contract auction, asking prices weren't met. The news spread like wildfire, panicking investors into offloading their contracts, sending prices plummeting. Many ordinary people were faced with ruin, having invested in tulip contracts that were now only worth a tenth of what they had paid for them, and only government intervention prevented the disastrous 'wind trade' from destabilizing the entire Dutch economy.

The Mississippi bubble

Early 18th-century France was in the economic doldrums. The government was drowning in debt and the Regent, the Duke d'Orleans, enlisted the aid of Scots adventurer John Law (1671–1729). Law was a financial wizard, a gambling man with grandiose ambitions. He had fled from Scotland after killing a duelling opponent and now sought to make a name for himself by putting his economic theories into practice in France. Having persuaded the Duke that he could get the government back into the black, he was made Controller General of Finance and given *carte blanche* to turn round the French economy.

Law's first move was to set up the Banque Générale, which

accepted deposits in coin and issued credit notes in return. Law believed that by replacing coin with credit he could control money supply and kick-start the economy. He was right. His bank notes were a huge success. Then, in 1717, he established a trading venture, the Mississippi Company, to exploit the rumoured gold and silver deposits of the French-owned colony of Louisiana. Investors were gradually seduced into this scheme and throughout 1719 the share price rose rapidly as speculators fuelled demand. Shares bought for 500 livres soared to 10,000 livres, creating instant paper millionaires.

The fatal flaw in Law's economic theory was that the Mississippi Company had no assets. Law was simply increasing money supply by issuing bank credit notes to fund share purchases. Eventually the bubble had to burst. In 1720 the Mississippi Company began to unravel. Law attempted to control the falling market but his desperate measures only panicked investors even more. By September 1721 shares were back where they started, at 500 livres. His disastrous experiment in monetary control unstuck, Law was forced to flee a country for the second time in his life. He died in Venice, a poor man.

WHEN:
1717–1721
WHERE:
France
TOLL:
Thousands of small investors were bankrupted and the French economy spiralled into hyperinflation. It was another 80 years before the French dared to re-introduce paper money.
YOU SHOULD KNOW:
Despite his disastrous mishandling of the French economy, John Law had monetarist ideas that were way ahead of his time and many of his theories are standard practice today. He was in large part responsible for the introduction of paper money.

Street speculators during the Mississippi bubble

An engraving by William Hogarth satirizes investors in the South Sea Company.

The South Sea Bubble

At the beginning of the 18th century Europe was in political chaos and by 1710, after a decade of war, the British government was millions of pounds in debt. Robert Harley, the Lord Treasurer, dreamed up a brilliant (if dishonest) financing scheme not unlike the French Mississippi Company.

The South Sea Company was set up in 1711 specifically to underwrite the national debt. The company would make money from a monopoly on all trade with South America (then known as the 'South Sea') and lend money to the government at a guaranteed return of six per cent interest. Harley put the company in the hands of financiers who, if nothing else, understood the value of marketing: they set themselves up in plush London offices and issued free shares to several leading politicians so that influential names would be listed as shareholders, giving the South Sea Company a reputable air.

The value of the shares kept rising as rumours of the South Sea Company's trade potential spread through the drawing rooms of the chattering classes. Before long it was an apparently well-established, rock-solid investment opportunity. Little did anyone realize that trade was more or less non-existent and the company was being kept afloat solely by the continual issuing of shares. As the share price rose, it only confirmed what everyone had been led to believe – that the company was a sound investment – which lured yet more people into investing.

Eventually, in 1720, the supposed success of the company led to a buying frenzy and the share price rocketed from around £100 to nearly £1,000 in six months before crashing spectacularly and bankrupting thousands of investors. Among them was Sir Isaac Newton who, on hearing the news, said 'I can calculate the movement of the stars, but not the madness of men'.

WHEN:
August to September 1720
WHERE:
UK
DEATH TOLL:
Thousands of small investors were financially ruined. But far worse, the only profitable trade the South Sea Company undertook was the transportation of 34,000 West Africans to the colonies, of whom 4,000 (over ten per cent) died in transit; the remainder were sold into slavery.
YOU SHOULD KNOW:
The company's collapse nearly brought down the entire UK financial system and the government had to rush through a series of panic measures to restore stability. Amazingly, the South Sea Company remained in existence: after its directors had been arrested for fraud, the company was restructured and carried on servicing government debt until the 1850s when it was finally wound up.

Overend, Gurney and Company

Mid-Victorian global economics evolved under the ever-increasing arch of the British Empire. The City of London was the Empire's engine-room, fuelled by expanding colonial trade; but by the 1860s entrepreneurial confidence was replaced by opportunistic greed. Tennyson, Trollope and Dickens were among the great literary figures who fulminated against what Thomas Carlyle denounced as 'Cheap and Nasty' – a phenomenon of commercial immorality as much as of shoddy manufacture.

Corruption flourished in a speculative boom, effectively financed by a discount banking house whose indirect importance to retail banking made it second only to the Bank of England itself: Overend, Gurney and Company was the most powerful privately owned financial institution in Britain. Supreme wealth wasn't enough. The company wanted more – but its willingness to waive collateral on increasingly risky speculations backfired in a catastrophic spate of scandal, fraud and multiple bankruptcies among its clients.

The collapse of Overend, Gurney and Company in 1866 signalled the most notorious bank run in British history. On May 10, the company suspended cash payments and the Bank of England declined its support, sparking a run on all the banks until by midday 'tumult became a rout' with 'throngs heaving and tumbling about Lombard Street'.

Though Gladstone (then Chancellor of the Exchequer) suspended the Bank Charter Act to stop the rot, the consequences steamrollered on. Ten banks and over 180 major companies failed; and the damage to colonial economies and Britain's trade could barely be imagined, let alone calculated. Whole sectors, like the Lancashire cotton industry, never fully recovered.

Overend, Gurney's failure (to the tune of £11 million) instilled a conservatism in banking that enabled Britain's economy – alone in Europe – to survive the hammering of the interwar years. It's taken 140 years for those lessons to be forgotten . . . and for history to repeat itself.

WHEN:
May 1866
WHERE:
London, UK
TOLL:
Whole communities that depended on a single industry for at least partial employment suffered prolonged hardship.
YOU SHOULD KNOW:
Overend, Gurney and Company was once nicknamed 'the bankers' banker' because of its probity. Only when it began lending direct to 'finance companies' involved in unsecured mortgages did its troubles begin. Curiously, in 2007 Northern Rock collapsed for the same reason – and the run on Northern Rock was the first on a British bank since Overend, Gurney and Company in 1866.

Black Friday

WHEN:
September 24 1869
WHERE:
New York, USA
TOLL:
The public's faith in the presidency and trust in politicians was rocked to the core. The stock market dropped by 20 per cent and thousands of investors lost their savings. Public confidence remained so shaken that when, a few years later in 1873, the banking firm J Cooke & Co became insolvent, it triggered the historic Long Depression that lasted until 1879.
YOU SHOULD KNOW:
During the American Civil War (1861–1865) the government raised money by issuing 'greenbacks' – paper dollars backed only by a government promise that they would be swapped for gold at the end of the war. But 'greenbacks' stayed in circulation and it was the difference in value between this paper money and 'double eagles' (gold coins) that profiteers like Fisk and Gould attempted to exploit, hoping to make a fortune by price-rigging.

Panic on Black Friday in the New York Gold Room.

On Friday September 24 1869 Wall Street was paying close attention to the price of gold. In the previous three weeks it had been rising rapidly and brokers were getting jittery, though that hadn't stopped them from investing. Suddenly the price started to fall . . . and didn't stop. In under 15 minutes, the price per ounce dropped from $162 to $133. Pandemonium broke out as Wall Street lost its nerve and sent the market crashing.

The cause of 'Black Friday' was a complex money-making scheme cooked up by a notorious pair of racketeers – financier James 'Barnum of Wall Street' Fisk, who was renowned for his entertaining persona, and Jay Gould, a shrewd railway magnate. Using every means at their disposal including charm, nepotism, government-nobbling and insider trading, they set about cornering the gold market. To ensure their success, they enlisted the aid of the President's brother-in-law and the Assistant Secretary to the Treasury. They even had the gall to approach President Ulysses S Grant himself (although he had the good sense to blank them).

Throughout September, Gould and Fisk were bulk-buying gold and hoarding their stock to create an artificial shortage, thus forcing the price up. In an attempt to calm the market, the government ordered the sale of $4 million worth of its gold reserves. But it miscalculated badly – the sudden flood of government gold for sale sent the price nose-diving, triggering a stock market crash, which turned into a bank run when panicked depositors tried to access their savings.

Despite the failure of their outrageous scheme, Gould and Fisk still managed to walk away with a cool $11 million between them. Within five years Gould had become boss of the Union Pacific Railway. Fisk was less fortunate – he was shot dead in an argument over a Broadway starlet.

Crash of the Paris Bourse

From the mid 19th century the French stock exchange was based in the Palais de la Bourse, in the heart of Paris. Some 60 *agents de change* – official stockbrokers – operated here in a syndicate. There was a common fund which any of them could dip into to cover temporary trading losses, thus providing individual brokers with a safety net; the prospect of a systemic breakdown had never even been considered. But that's what happened in 1882: the common fund was insufficient to prop up Bourse trading, causing the most serious French economic crisis of the 19th century. Only government intervention prevented the stock exchange from closing and the entire financial system from unravelling.

The crash was triggered by the collapse of l'Union Générale, a bank established by Catholic grandees in 1876 to compete with the famous German-Jewish Rothschild bankers. L'Union Générale produced excellent company reports and its shares appeared a safe investment in a turbulent market. Demand pushed up the share price, encouraging ever more investors to believe it was a safe bet. By January 1882 the price had risen from an initial 500 francs to 3,000 francs.

Suddenly it all seemed too good to be true. Nervous investors started to sell and the price plummeted accordingly, causing mass panic. The Lyons branch of l'Union Générale was besieged by depositors demanding their money. But the bank didn't have it. Instead it had to close its doors. At the same time all share prices started to fall and the Bourse didn't have the means to continue trading.

It was rumoured that the crisis had been engineered by enemies of the Catholic Church, either Freemasons or Jews. In fact the directors of l'Union Générale had over extended themselves and falsified the accounts. It was nothing but brazen dishonesty that broke the Bourse.

WHEN:
January 1882
WHERE:
Paris, France
TOLL:
Around a third of stockbroking firms' *agents de change* were either brought to the edge of ruin or completely bankrupted and many people, the artist Paul Gauguin among them, lost their jobs. France slid into a deep recession that lasted for most of the decade.
YOU SHOULD KNOW:
The French recession was part of a much wider economic depression that affected the whole of Europe and the USA.

People and horse-drawn carriages in the street in front of the Paris stock exchange, in the 1880s.

The Knickerbocker Trust Company and the New York bank panic

WHEN:
Tuesday October 22 to
Monday October 28 1907
WHERE:
New York, USA
TOLL:
Charles Barney, President of the
Knickerbocker Trust Company shot
himself. The New York Stock
Exchange lost 50 per cent of its
value and many ordinary small-time
investors lost their savings.
YOU SHOULD KNOW:
The 1907 New York bank panic led to
the creation of a central banking
system – the Federal Reserve.

The bank panic of 1907 demonstrates that crises in the banking system are nothing new. Once confidence is lost, panic spreads like a contagious disease. The Knickerbocker Trust Company was the third largest of the New York trust companies. The failure of such a prestigious financial institution inevitably caused the jitters to spread throughout the banking system.

It started with an attempt by shady copper magnate Augustus Heinze and his equally dishonest brother Otto to corner the copper market – dodgy dealing to gain control of enough shares to manipulate the price. Their cornering bid failed dismally. Instead of getting control of their target – the United Copper Company – their shenanigans caused the sudden collapse of its share price.

There were whispers that the Knickerbocker Trust Company's President, Charles Barney, was one the Heinze brothers' cronies. Depositors panicked and on October 22, a week after the United Copper Company collapse, they started a run on the Knickerbocker Trust. In under three hours $8 million was withdrawn, completely wiping out the company's funds. Barney begged financier J P Morgan for help but Morgan refused; Barney had no choice but to order the company to cease trading.

By Thursday October 24 banks and trust companies across the USA were affected. At the same time the stock market was collapsing. J P Morgan realized that if the Stock Exchange were forced to close, the entire US financial system would crash. He persuaded New York's most influential financiers, John Rockefeller (the wealthiest man in America) amongst them, to contribute enough funds to temporarily restore liquidity. On Friday he made a press announcement outlining a financial rescue package and instructed the clergy to calm their congregations during that Sunday's sermon. The weekend break calmed nerves and on Monday the Stock Exchange opened for business as usual. Complete meltdown had been prevented . . . for the moment.

Hyperinflation in the Weimar Republic

During World War I prices in Germany had doubled, but the real trouble started afterwards. The new German Weimar government was bound by the Treaty of Versailles – designed to ensure that the grandees of the now defunct German Empire could never wage war on their neighbours again. The Treaty's terms put the Weimar government under intolerable financial pressure; it would have been a miracle if the ailing German economy had recovered. The stupendous amount the Germans had to pay the Allies in reparation for the war meant they couldn't afford to buy imported goods, and the loss of their colonies meant they couldn't rely on cheap raw materials. At the same time billions of marks hoarded during the war suddenly came back into circulation.

The rising cost of goods combined with a dramatic increase in the money supply created perfect conditions for inflation. Before World War I the exchange rate was just over four marks to the dollar. By 1920 the value of the mark was 16 times less. Here it stabilized at 69 marks to the dollar for some months. The government was still in a position to get a grip on the economy; instead it chose to print yet more money in order to pay the reparation debt. By July 1922 prices had risen by some 700 per cent and hyperinflation had arrived.

The government had to print million-mark notes, then billion-mark notes. By November 1923 $1 was equivalent to 1,000 billion (a trillion!) marks. A wheelbarrow full of money couldn't buy a newspaper. Shopkeepers couldn't replenish their stock fast enough to keep up with prices, farmers refused to sell their produce for worthless money, food riots broke out and townspeople marched into the countryside to loot the farms. Law and order broke down. The German attempt at democracy had been completely undermined.

WHEN:
1922–1923
WHERE:
Germany
TOLL:
Millions of Germans were bankrupted – an entire life savings sometimes wasn't enough to buy a loaf of bread. Conspiracy theories sprouted and extremist political views became acceptable. Ultimately, hyperinflation enabled Hitler to gain power.
YOU SHOULD KNOW:
A new currency, the Rentenmark was introduced in August 1924, backed by the US gold reserve, and realistic reparation payments were agreed. Although economic mismanagement on the part of the Weimar government is usually blamed for causing hyperinflation, evidence suggests that speculators were in large part responsible: they started 'short selling', effectively betting on the value of the mark dropping.

A housewife uses millions of Deutsche marks to light a stove during a period of hyperinflation in Germany.

The Wall Street Crash and the Great Depression

WHEN:
1929–1939
WHERE:
USA
DEATH TOLL:
At least 110 people died directly of starvation and countless more died from secondary illnesses caused by malnutrition.The suicide rate rose by more than 20 per cent.
YOU SHOULD KNOW:
The Great Depression was exacerbated by severe drought and dust storms in the Mid West, which forced thousands of rural families to abandon their land and travel westwards in search of food and work.

The high life of the Roaring Twenties came to a juddering halt on Black Tuesday October 29 1929 with the Wall Street Crash. Politicians who had welcomed in the 'New Era' of a continually rising stock market in an ever-expanding economy were shown up for the frauds they were. The New Era turned out to have been a con trick – a bubble fuelled by speculators and easy credit – and the boom years of the 1920s had enriched only a privileged few on the backs of the many. Banks had over extended themselves, lending funds that they didn't have, and panic-stricken depositors caused a bank run that resulted in more than 1,500 finance companies going to the wall.

Whether the Wall Street Crash was merely a symptom or the main cause of the Great Depression, it was certainly the single largest factor in triggering it. The catastrophic effects of the crash rippled across America: thousands of small-time investors suddenly found themselves bankrupt, more than 100,000 businesses collapsed, and unemployment soared to more than 12 million.

By the winter of 1932, America was in the ferocious grip of the worst depression in its history. Poverty became the norm and thousands of people were forced to take to the road in search of work. Industrial output and international trade dropped by half and a deflationary cycle set in for the rest of the decade, spreading from America across the globe. The US economy didn't fully recover until America entered World War II in 1941.

The suffering of the Great Depression years is deeply etched into the American consciousness and has found lasting romantic expression through the arts: John Steinbeck's prize-winning novel *The Grapes of Wrath*, the hobo folk songs of Woody Guthrie, and Dorothea Lange's iconic documentary photographs of the dispossessed.

Migrant Mother *by Dorothea Lange. A poverty-stricken migrant mother (Florence Owens Thompson, 32) with three young children gazes off into the distance. This photograph, commissioned by the FSA, came to symbolize the Great Depression for many Americans.*

UK stock market crash and stagflation

Cars queueing to buy petrol on Sunday December 23 1973 at a gas station in New York City. The gas station remained open despite President Nixon's plea for stations to close on Sundays.

'When America sneezes, the rest of the world catches a cold' so it's not really surprising that when America got the collywobbles at the beginning of the 1970s, the result was pneumonia on the London Stock Exchange – more than 70 per cent was wiped off share values in the worst bear market (market downturn) of the 20th century.

By the end of the 1960s, after a decade of consistent growth on both sides of the Atlantic, America's economic advisers reckoned they had solved the problem of 'boom and bust'. They congratulated themselves on having successfully applied the theories of 'the new economics', boasting that the idea of a business cycle was old hat and that consumer capitalist economies could enjoy continuous uninterrupted growth.

In the context of President Nixon's politically troubled world of the Vietnam War, the Watergate scandal and a partisan involvement in the Arab-Israeli Yom Kippur War that was to lead to the Arab nations imposing an oil embargo, it was inevitable that the good times would come to an end. The experts hadn't realized that the prosperity of the 1960s was nothing to do with their clever theories but had simply been caused by a long-lasting economic bubble.

The crash precipitated a lengthy period of 'stagflation' – an economic Catch-22 that was particularly keenly felt in the UK. The economy was trapped in a wage-price spiral: when the government took measures to stimulate growth, inflation rocketed; but attempts to control inflation made the economy shrink. Fuel shortages caused by the oil crisis and the government's battle with the National Union of Mineworkers resulted in the misery of the 'three-day week'. Not surprisingly, at the general election in February 1974 the Conservatives lost their overall majority and Britain limped on with a hung parliament.

WHEN:
November 1 1973 to June 12 1974
WHERE:
USA and UK. It also affected the whole of Europe.
TOLL:
Recovery was extraordinarily slow. The UK stock market did not return to its pre-crash real level until 1987.
YOU SHOULD KNOW:
The economic boom of the 1960s was brought to a sudden end by Richard Nixon's decision to remove the dollar from the gold standard. The international money market was thrown into turmoil and the loss of confidence spread to the stock market, sending the whole house of cards tumbling down.

Latin America's lost decade

WHEN:
1982–1991
WHERE:
Latin America, notably Mexico,
Costa Rica, Brazil, Argentina,
Venezuela and Peru
TOLL:
The poor and the weak, women,
children and Amerindians suffered
disproportionately. Income per head
plummeted, the gap between rich
and poor, which had been
narrowing, grew even wider and
any improvements in social welfare
that had occurred in the 1970s
were eroded.
YOU SHOULD KNOW:
The IMF (International Monetary
Fund) and World Bank are the twin
pillars that prop up the global
financial system. The difference
between them is obscure and their
roles overlap but the World Bank is
primarily responsible for financing
economic development while the
purpose of the IMF is to maintain
monetary order and fair currency
exchange between nations.

It is generally agreed that Latin America's 'lost decade' can be traced back to 'petrodollar recycling' in the 1970s. The Middle East had suddenly grown phenomenally wealthy as oil prices rocketed and the Arab states needed somewhere safe to stash their billions. The big international banks were only too happy to help. They used the dollars deposited by the oil sheikhs to invest in Latin America, a part of the world that looked an excellent bet.

Latin American countries had all been doing pretty well but in order to further their development they either had to restructure their economies, which would have been politically unpopular, or take up the international bank loans that were practically being forced on them at temptingly low interest rates. Naturally, they went for the loans.

Initially the repayments were perfectly manageable, but then interest rates started to soar and Latin America got caught in a trap – the only way of maintaining interest payments was by borrowing more. By 1982 the interest payments alone were so crippling that Mexico decided to default. The international bankers were stunned. Then Argentina, Brazil, Venezuela and Chile followed suit and the situation was out of hand. It emerged that major US and European banks had over extended themselves and couldn't absorb the loss if the debts weren't repaid.

Rather than let big-name banks go under, the International Monetary Fund (IMF) restored order by restructuring repayments. In exchange for financial help via the World Bank, the IMF required the debtor countries to slash public health and education budgets, make public-sector job cuts, devalue their currencies to stimulate exports and freeze vital infrastructure projects like roads and buildings. The IMF had chosen to bail out investors and international bankers at the cost of a 'lost decade' for the deprived underclasses of Latin America.

Crash of the Souk al-Manakh camel market

WHEN:
August 1982
WHERE:
Kuwait
TOLL:
The collapse of the Souk al-Manakh
cost a staggering $92 billion, cast a
terrible shadow over business in the
Gulf and, combined with disruption in
oil revenues due to the Iran-Iraq war,
tipped the whole region into
recession.

The 'camel market' or Souk al-Manakh was a semi-illicit Kuwaiti stock market that operated from unlikely premises – an air-conditioned underground garage in Kuwait City. The rise in oil revenues in the 1970s had created a surge of wealth in the Arab Gulf countries and investing in shares seemed sensible. But the *nouveaux riches* couldn't get a look in at the official Kuwait Stock Exchange, which was dominated by a few elderly sheikhs. Besides, it was so dull, so tightly regulated, there was no fun in it. The Souk al-Manakh operated on credit, using a system of postdated cheques, and bored young men with money to burn were drawn there like moths to a flame, attracted by the thrills of high-stakes gambling on the stock of unregulated non-Kuwaiti companies.

Since the Souk al-Manakh wasn't subject to government controls, the deals were highly speculative in nature. The promise of rich pickings started to attract all the biggest players in the Kuwaiti shares business. Almost unbelievably, the 'camel market' grew to be the third most highly capitalized market in the world – even bigger than the London Stock Exchange and only outdone by New York and Tokyo.

One day the garage was closed. No rumours. No panic. No spectacular crash. Overnight the Souk al-Manakh had simply ceased to exist. But for a Kuwaiti government investigation, the disappearance of the Souk al-Manakh might still be a complete mystery. It emerged that the market had been quietly closed by the police after a spectacularly large cheque bounced. Further investigation revealed that many of the investors were flash young men from influential families who had used their connections to obtain such massive amounts of credit from the banks and the only one still solvent was the National Bank of Kuwait!

YOU SHOULD KNOW:
Souk al-Manakh literally means camel market and it has been mistakenly assumed that the unofficial stock exchange acquired its name because the underground garage premises had once been used to trade camels. Camels in a garage? Hardly likely. The name almost certainly derived from the febrile, crowded atmosphere which was comparable to the ambience of a camel market.

Black Monday

There have been several Black Mondays in history, but the daddy of them all arrived in 1987. October 19 was the day when global stock markets went into collective meltdown, destroying nearly half the world's paper wealth in a series of dramatic hits that went through the time zones like falling financial dominoes.

Rapid growth in the USA had started to slow and the Dow Jones Industrial Index reflected declining optimism, falling steadily from its August peak. Where America leads in these matters, the world tends to follow. Stock markets around the world were already jittery when Hong Kong's Hang Seng Index crashed. The ripple effect reached Europe and after US warships shelled an Iranian oil platform in response to a missile attack on an American ship, alarms went off all over Wall Street. The Dow Jones Industrial Index fell 508 points on Black Monday, wiping out $500 billion in the biggest-ever one-day stock-market loss.

Even the benefit of hindsight and studious application of the finest economic and financial brains failed to come up with an explanation for this extraordinary event, thus introducing another 'black' to the equation – the Black Swan. This is a major happening with massive impact that is hard to predict and beyond the scope of established expectations or – to explain it in another colourful phrase – a bolt from the blue.

Some say Black Monday was simply a case of fear eclipsing greed, others claim the likely cause was newly computerized trading programs that sold stocks automatically as the markets fell, exacerbating the slide. Whatever the cause, the effect on worldwide financial markets was disastrous and it took quite a while for the global patient to get over the shock and start recovering.

WHEN:
October 19 1987
WHERE:
International
TOLL:
Was it really that bad? Despite the ravages of Black Monday, the Dow Jones actually managed to end 1987 with a small increase. On January 2 it stood at 1,897 points and rose to 1,939 by December 31. In between, however, it had reached a dizzying 2,722-point peak in late August – a figure not attained again until 1989.
YOU SHOULD KNOW:
In Australia and New Zealand the dreadful day is known as Black Tuesday, because that's what it was by the time the crash had crossed all the time zones to arrive in the Southern Hemisphere. The Antipodean neighbours didn't escape financial carnage – Australia's stock market fell by over 40 per cent and New Zealand's was decimated by a dramatic drop of nearly two-thirds from its 1987 peak.

A frenzied trader on Black Monday

Nikkei bubble

WHEN:
1990
WHERE:
Japan
TOLL:
With the puncturing of the Nikkei bubble, the Japanese economic miracle came to an abrupt end.
YOU SHOULD KNOW:
Despite a brief recovery after 2003, the Nikkei share index reached a 26-year low of 6,994 points during the global financial crisis of 2008. Way back in December 1989, at the height of the Nikkei bubble, it stood at a heady 38,915 points.

In 1945 Japan was a feudal monarchy that had suffered catastrophic defeat in World War II, but in fewer than 50 years this ruined nation would transform itself into a prosperous industrial democracy. Peasants became factory workers and the middle classes became white-collar workers – salarymen – who were promised jobs for life in the mighty *zaibatsu* (banking and industrial conglomerates) that grew from the determined efforts of the hard-working Japanese people. As the economy boomed, *zaibatsu* morphed into even more powerful entities called *keiretsu*, alliances where big business and government worked together for the common good.

But the frugal Japanese saved rather than spent, ensuring that financial institutions were awash with investment capital – a fact leading inevitably to speculation. The *keiretsu* invested in each other's shares, inflating values, and there was a massive real-estate boom. Banks also made increasingly risky loans as they put surplus capital to work, creating an overheating economy and an asset-price bubble that just couldn't last.

Japan's Nikkei share index hit an all-time high on December 29 1989, but that was as big as the bubble got. It didn't exactly burst, but deflated rapidly through 1990 and into 1991.

The stock market dropped to half its peak level by August 1990 and continued to fall until hitting rock bottom in 2003. Land and property prices started a similar downward journey in 1991.

The long-term effect of the deflating Nikkei bubble on the Japanese economy was disastrous. Capital was redirected abroad. Manufacturers lost their competitive edge. Thrifty consumers further depressed the ailing economy as exports declined and – despite the fact that interest rates were reduced to zero – there was a vicious deflationary spiral. Economic stagnation and recession followed, unemployment rose and those valued 'jobs for life' inevitably started disappearing as the government ran enormous budget deficits.

An overhead indicator shows 160.03 yen at the Tokyo Stock Exchange on April 18 1990.

Soviet economic collapse

A woman rests her bag on symbols of the Communist state in Moscow.

The big winners to emerge from World War II were two superpowers that – like mighty stags that feel compelled to do battle – locked horns for 40 years. The resulting Cold War was a fierce struggle to secure global dominance, with the USA and Soviet Union representing diametrically opposed political systems. One was the torchbearer for democracy, individual freedoms and *laissez-faire* capitalism. The other espoused autocracy, tight social control and a centrally managed economy.

Intense rivalry led to an arms race based on the appropriately named doctrine of MAD (Mutually Assured Destruction), requiring each side to possess nuclear weapons capable of destroying the world. There were other expensive contests, like the space race and aid to Third World client states. Desire to reign supreme even led the participants into disastrous foreign wars. The USA notably failed to roll back the tide of communism in Vietnam, while the Soviet army was humiliated by ragged mujahideen resistance fighters in Afghanistan.

It was the latter that determined the outcome of this titanic struggle. The cost of fighting the Afghan war – from 1979 until 1985 – bankrupted the Soviet Union's command economy, already stagnating as a result of intrinsic inefficiency and widespread corruption. But cometh the moment, cometh the man – in this case reforming leader Mikhail Gorbachev. The Soviet economy had long been guided by five-year plans that delivered infrastructure, heavy machinery and military hardware, but couldn't satisfy the complex demands of a modern consumer economy.

Gorbachev's new policy of *Perestroika* (economic reform) saw brief improvement, but it wasn't enough. By 1991 the economy was in such dire straits that the Soviet Union simply disintegrated, with autonomous republics declaring independence and subjugated Eastern Bloc states regaining their freedom. In the end it was not a rival superpower that destroyed the once-mighty Soviet Union, but economic incompetence.

WHEN:
1979–1991
WHERE:
Soviet Union
TOLL:
Russia and the 15 former Soviet republics that rose from the ashes of economic disaster found it hard to come to terms with the realities of global commercial life in the post-Soviet era.
YOU SHOULD KNOW:
The Soviet Union passed a law in 1988 that effectively marked the end of central economic control. The Law on Cooperatives allowed the private ownership of businesses, but merely hastened the process of economic collapse. By 1990 the government had lost control of the economy as the weakening of central control led to the economic and financial anarchy that would prove terminal for the toppling superpower.

Black Wednesday

If there was one thing the Conservative Party cherished – and the British electorate admired – it was a reputation for economic competence. In the early 1990s, the opposition Labour Party was struggling to reinvent itself as an alternative government that could be trusted with the national piggy-bank, but that wasn't easy . . . until Black Wednesday arrived in 1992 like a spectre at the Tory feast.

The European Union's Exchange Rate Mechanism (ERM) was set up in 1979 as a prelude to a single Euro-currency, but Britain refused to join. Subsequently, Chancellor Nigel Lawson decided to 'shadow' the Deutschmark, unofficially linking Sterling to Germany's stable currency. But squabbling broke out within government, his approach was criticized by Alan Walters – Prime Minister Margaret Thatcher's economic advisor – and Lawson resigned.

But the pro-ERM faction prevailed and the UK joined in 1990. ERM membership required economic and monetary policies that would maintain exchange rates within narrow bands, but Britain was in the grip of high inflation and high interest rates. As a result, Sterling fell to its lowest permitted level by 1992 and was coming under pressure from international speculators led by American George Soros, who were betting the pound would be forced to leave the ERM and devalue.

How right they were. Their inexorable short selling (entering future sale contracts at today's price in anticipation of buying the necessary currency more cheaply when it has to be delivered) finally broke the pound on September 16, when the Treasury's increasingly frantic efforts to prop up Sterling had cost £27 billion. Chancellor Norman Lamont was forced into the humiliating admission that Britain would leave the ERM with immediate effect and let the pound find its own level. Black Wednesday is estimated to have cost Britain £3.5 billion, and earned George Soros $1 billion.

WHEN:
September 16 1992
WHERE:
UK
TOLL:
The Conservative reputation for economic competence was shattered, paving the way for the crushing election victory of Tony Blair's New Labour in 1997. Ultimately, however, the devaluation of the pound proved to be beneficial for the British economy, which would soon come out of recession and then enter an era of unprecedented annual growth.
YOU SHOULD KNOW:
To rub salt in the wounds, had the Treasury and its political masters been more astute, Black Wednesday could have become a nice little earner for the British taxpayer. If the country's large foreign currency reserves had not been squandered in that doomed attempt to prop up Sterling, it is estimated that the nation could have made a £2.5 billion profit on the subsequent unavoidable devaluation.

A foreign exchange dealer in London shouts orders following a two per cent rise in British interest rates to 12 per cent.

Dot-com bubble

Every so often, something happens to change the world, from invention of the wheel through the first smelting of iron to gunpowder and the development of the steam engine. But none of the many discoveries that transformed the way people lived could hold a candle to the biggest innovation of them all – the internet, aka the worldwide web.

The personal computers that became increasingly available from the early 1980s made it all possible. In 1988, the internet arrived – and within a decade this interconnected global system of computer networks using a common protocol was reaching billions of individuals and growing fast. Possibilities were infinite and a Wild West mentality took hold – this was a new frontier and plenty were willing and able to join the technological gold rush.

All sorts of clever ideas for exploiting this exciting newcomer were devised and – just as a gold rush rewards the fortunate few who come up with nuggets that make them rich – prescient backers of some internet start-up companies saw relatively modest investments increase in value beyond their wildest dreams. Massive returns soon led to feeding frenzy and there were plenty of young entrepreneurs happy to put forward imaginative proposals for dot-com enterprises (named after the 'com' suffix that completed universal website addresses).

Normal commercial caution went out of the window as a combination of ignorance of the new medium and greed saw the rapid inflation of a financial bubble as dot-com stocks boomed for two heady years from 1998. But confidence in the potential of technological advance rather than more traditional methods of assessing investment potential proved to be unsustainable, and after reaching a high point in March 2000 the dot-com bubble burst. In the next 12 months dozens of dot-com companies failed and their investors lost billions.

WHEN:
2000–2001
WHERE:
International
TOLL:
Numerous over-hyped internet start-ups where hard-headed analysis would have shown that they could never make a fraction of the profits dazzled investors were prepared to bet on.
YOU SHOULD KNOW:
The business model that fuelled the dot-com bubble (and so singularly failed) is summarized by the phrase 'get big fast'. The idea was to spend vast sums establishing public awareness of a new dot-com enterprise, on the assumption that once a large number of regular users had been hooked they could subsequently be profitably exploited.

Former employees of Pseudo Programs Inc move their possessions out of the company's Broadway offices in New York City as the once-mighty Internet content provider closed down after running out of funding.

Zimbabwe hyperinflation

WHEN:
2000–2009
WHERE:
Zimbabwe
DEATH TOLL:
The number of deaths specifically caused by malnutrition and related diseases since Zimbabwe's economy collapsed and hyperinflation took hold can only be guessed at, but best estimates start in the high tens of thousands and don't stop there. Average life expectancy in Zimbabwe declined to 37 years of age for men and 34 for women, the world's lowest figures.
YOU SHOULD KNOW:
The inflation nightmare eased somewhat – for some – in January 2009 when Zimbabwe citizens were officially permitted to use hard currency to purchase the few goods and services that were available. But this was little consolation for those unfortunate sufferers without relatives abroad who could send back life-saving remittances or helpful contacts in the regime.

Southern Rhodesia was created by acquisitive British colonial entrepreneur Cecil Rhodes, after whom landlocked territory south of the Zambesi River was named. The country became a self-governing British colony in 1923, but when majority governments started replacing colonial administrations all over Africa, Rhodesia's white rulers made a Unilateral Declaration of Independence (UDI) in 1965, joining neighbouring South Africa in trying to roll back the advancing tide of black nationalism.

Stakes were high, for the fertile land was ideal for growing maize and tobacco, with white-owned farms producing excellent yields. But the breakaway was doomed. Prolonged armed struggle between Ian Smith's government and two groups of freedom fighters – Robert Mugabe's ZANU and Joshua Nkomo's ZAPU – ended in defeat for the beleaguered regime, though the war lasted for 15 years.

Robert Mugabe's ZANU won a landslide victory in free elections held in 1980, then ruthlessly crushed rival ZANU in its Matabeleland power base. Although the newly named Zimbabwe was nominally a parliamentary democracy, and it took some time to erode established institutions like an independent judiciary, Mugabe set about becoming an autocratic dictator.

White farms were seized from 2000 – the best by government high-ups, most of the rest by roaming bands of war veterans. Agricultural production imploded, exports dried up, economic activity stagnated and the country ran out of hard currency. The result was disastrous for Zimbabwe's population, leading to hyperinflation that ravaged the country. Between 1998 and 2007 the annual inflation rate rose from 32 per cent to 2.31 million per cent in 2008, going off the scale in 2009 with prices doubling every 1.3 days and banknotes reaching dizzying denominations of Z$100 billion and more. It had taken fewer than 30 years for Mugabe's corrupt regime to destroy Zimbabwe's economy and turn the prosperous 'bread basket of Africa' into a basket case.

A Zimbabwean woman holds a handful of bundles of the new 10 trillion (10,000,000,000,000) Zimbabwe dollar note in Harare, Zimbabwe.

Global financial crisis

The causes of catastrophic financial events that started unfolding in 2007 were many and varied, but one inescapable fact is that consumers in America and Europe (especially the UK) had been living in a fools' paradise. For years inflation had been low – mainly as a result of cheap imports from the Far East – while interest rates were depressed by vast inflows of capital from those self-same Asian economies as well as the oil-producing countries.

A manic spending spree saw house prices rocket and complacent politicians announcing that the era of 'boom and bust' was over. They were so wrong. Over-optimistic consumers had kept a dangerous economic model afloat, eagerly indulging their every whim with easily borrowed, cheap money. They were assisted by creative bankers, who earned massive bonuses by creating financial instruments that turned out to consist of no more than smoke and mirrors – many involving vast loan packages sold to fellow banks that purported to be sound, though actually were based on debts incurred by companies and individuals who couldn't afford repayments.

It couldn't last. The first ominous cracks appeared in 2007, when housing bubbles burst. This was followed by a run on the highly leveraged (over-borrowed) Northern Rock Bank in the UK that presaged the demise of numerous mortgage lenders. It came to a head in September 2008 with the collapse of New York's once-mighty investment bank, Lehman Brothers. International financial markets panicked, vital inter-bank lending dried up and governments had to step in with massive bailout packages to prevent the world sliding into another Great Depression.

It would be two years before signs of recovery appeared in developed Western economies – with the vast sums borrowed by governments to combat the crisis sure to be a heavy financial burden on their citizens for a generation or more.

A broker gestures under the German stock index DAX at Frankfurt Stock Exchange.

WHEN:
2007–2009
WHERE:
International
TOLL:
No Wall-Street-Crash-style suicides were recorded at the height of the crisis, but numerous banks and businesses failed with severe consequences for countless individuals and the shocked world economy.
YOU SHOULD KNOW:
Even as tentative recovery got under way in the recently humbled economies of the USA, Europe and Japan – with the hesitant return to annual growth sometimes measured in a fraction of one percentage point – countries such as China were already powering ahead with growth rates that in some cases approached ten per cent. This serves as a potent reminder that the balance of global economic power is sure to tilt in favour of the Far East's emerging tiger economies as the 21st century unfolds.

The headquarters of Lehman Brothers investment bank on Sixth Avenue in New York City.

Collapse of Lehman Brothers

Lehman Brothers was founded in 1850 by three brothers who emigrated to the USA from Germany, initially running a store in Alabama. But they soon turned to cotton trading and shifted operations to New York. Lehman remained a commodities house until the early 20th century, when the focus switched to public offerings, laying foundations for a financial services institution that would become one of the world's great investment banks.

By 2008, after a short-lived merger with American Express, Lehman had reinvented itself as an independent asset-management company, with over 28,000 employees and turnover up from $2.7 billion in 1994 to more than $19 billion. But there had been difficulties along the way – disruption when its World Trade Centre offices were destroyed in the 9/11 attacks and an expensive run-in with regulators over the way the bank's investment division influenced the findings of its research analysts.

These setbacks paled into insignificance during 2008. Lehman was heavily involved in the subprime loans business, an activity that was driving unsustainable economic growth. But these were by definition the riskiest of loans, to consumers without security whose ability to repay was recklessly taken on trust. Despite suffering a $50 million hit by closing its own subprime mortgage lender in 2007, Lehman was still badly exposed. When securitizing vast mortgage packages for onward sale, the company sold the best mortgages and kept the worst, a decision that proved catastrophic.

Huge losses were reported, Lehman Brothers stock lost three-quarters of its value, then plunged again when rumours of a takeover came to nothing. A mass exodus of clients took place, the firm's assets were drastically downgraded by credit agencies and the firm was forced to file for bankruptcy in September 2008. Unbelievably, this great financial behemoth had been slain by its own misjudgements.

WHEN:
September 15 2008
WHERE:
New York City, USA
TOLL:
Disastrous – the collapse of Lehman Brothers was the shove that finally pushed the tottering global financial system off a cliff, precipitating a crisis that threatened to become another worldwide Great Depression.
YOU SHOULD KNOW:
The world financial meltdown might have been avoided (or at least mitigated) if the demise of such an important investment bank had been averted. But the US government failed to appreciate the potential gravity of the situation and refused to mount a bail-out that would have cost but a tiny fraction of its subsequent mega-investment in economic stimulus measures and rescue packages for broken financial institutions.

Iceland goes bust

Even the largest of corporations can go bankrupt, and the Third World has many countries that constantly teeter on the verge of insolvency. But the financial cataclysm that brought the proud little nation of Iceland to its knees in 2008 shocked the world.

This volcanic island in the North Atlantic with a population of just 320,000 people became an independent republic in 1944 after severing formal constitutional ties with Denmark. Following World War II, Iceland was almost entirely dependent on fishing, a resource fiercely defended during the 'cod wars' with Britain from the 1950s to the 1970s, before the country started to evolve a more broadly based free-market economy. Pre-eminent among the new commercial activities were financial services, with a low-tax regime and light-touch regulation encouraging spectacular growth. By 2007 Iceland not only had an enviable welfare system, but was also an extremely prosperous country. There would be a vicious sting in the tail.

The global economic crisis of 2008 revealed severe structural weakness in the Icelandic economic powerhouse. The country's banks had liabilities of over 80 billion euros – an awesome sum compared with Iceland's annual GDP (gross domestic product) of around 15 billion euros. When the world's financial markets went south, this imbalance was bound to end in tears – floods of them.

Emergency legislation enabled the government to take control over the operation of Iceland's three largest banks – Glitnir, Kaupthing and Landsbanki – and renege on international debts. This caused huge losses to resentful overseas investors, but wasn't sufficient to rescue the economy. A bailout loan was received from the IMF (International Monetary Fund), interest rates reached 18 per cent and Iceland appealed to its fellow Nordic countries for additional aid. The Icelandic króna was devalued by two-thirds and by late October the country was bankrupt.

WHEN:
October 2008
WHERE:
Iceland
TOLL:
Apart from unfortunate international depositors who lost billions when the banks went bust, the most immediate casualty of financial mismanagement was the Icelandic government, which was forced out of office and replaced by a new left-wing administration. Its first act was to request the resignation of the Central Bank of Iceland's governors.
YOU SHOULD KNOW:
Riches to rags? In 2007, just one year before financial Armageddon, the United Nations ranked Iceland the wealthiest country on earth, with the highest per capita income – and also put it high on the list of the world's most productive nations.

Thousands of demonstrators taking part in a rally in Reykjavik on November 15 2008, calling on the government to resign over the national financial crisis.

COMMERCIAL DISASTERS

Charles Ponzi's Securities Exchange Company

WHEN:
July 1920
WHERE:
Boston, USA
TOLL:
17,000 investors got taken for a ride.
YOU SHOULD KNOW:
One of the most brazen Ponzi schemes operated in China between 1999 and 2007. Its perpetrator, Wang Fengyou, persuaded thousands of dirt-poor farmers to invest 10,000 yuan ($1,500) in boxes of 'special ants', which had to be kept and fed for 74 days according to very strict rules (the most important being never, ever, to open the box!) and were then collected to be ground and sold as aphrodisiacs in pharmacies across China. Wang's company achieved a turnover of 15 billion yuan ($2 billion) before it was exposed as a pyramid racket.

More affable scoundrel than kingpin of crime, Charles Ponzi sits astride criminal history as the man who gave his name to Ponzi schemes. A Ponzi scheme is a swindle based on a financial pyramid unsecured by any actual assets. The incremental maths is remorseless: by the 20th round of investment, a Ponzi scheme that starts with 1,000 participants will need more new investors than the entire population of the USA. Such pyramid schemes have always existed, but it wasn't until 1920 that they became a genre with a name.

Charles Ponzi's humdrum career as a petty criminal changed gear in 1919 when he realized that, thanks to the discrepancy in currency exchange rates, an International Reply Coupon (IRC) from Spain, worth five cents, could be exchanged for its US equivalent, worth ten cents. Multiply by hundreds of thousands, and serious money could be made. Ponzi invited 'friends and neighbours' to invest in IRCs via his new Securities Exchange Company (several years before the US government used a similar name!) with a guarantee of 50 per cent profit in 45 days. It was too easy. Money poured in after the first investors were paid in full. Ponzi stopped bothering with IRCs, because he made so much money just holding the money in the bank.

By July 1920, after just seven months, he was making $250,000 per day. Sudden wealth turned his head and attracted notice: the US Postal Service realized that for Ponzi's company to be solvent, 160 million IRCs should be circulating against the 27,000 registered. Arrested in August and tried for fraud in October, Ponzi almost sweet-talked his way out of trouble – and even his victims (perhaps ashamed to admit their own gullibility) defended him, convinced that if he were left alone, his Midas touch would somehow restore their bilked millions. Ponzi was a very plausible crook.

Charles Ponzi – an affable scoundrel?

The Edsel

A Ford Edsel Citation Convertible in a showroom

Even though nobody knows better how to put a positive spin on failure, not even auto manufacturers can blag their way around self-inflicted hubris. The Edsel wasn't just a car. It was a whole new division within the Ford Motor Company, created to compete with General Motors' Oldsmobile. Planned in the mid 1950s' flash flood of optimistic consumerism, it was developed behind a screen of blinkered hype. Its details were so secret not even official Edsel dealers were allowed to see it in advance; but the pre-launch marketing blitz promised something revolutionary that Ford just could not deliver.

Bad timing (the USA was entering recession and had no need at all for another set of expensive gas-guzzlers), bad marketing, bad design and bad workmanship invited what business academics call 'consumer blowback'. The public had been teased into expecting nothing less than a 'plutonium-powered, pancake-making supercar'. What they got looked like an overpriced, regular Ford Mercury with a front, 'horsecollar' grille described by *Time* magazine as looking 'like a midwife's view of labor and delivery' – and by the motoring press with far greater ribaldry and vulgarity.

Disappointment mushroomed in direct proportion to public anticipation. Post-launch incompetence compounded the fiasco. In the rush to meet launch deadlines, cars were shipped incompletely or wrongly assembled – and with no customer loyalty to fall back on, the brand was born into its own death spiral of recrimination and closed dealerships. Edsel survived just 26 months, and cost the Ford Motor Company $350 million.

More than half a century later, retro-chic appeal has muted the original knee-jerk response to the Edsel name. In 1958, Vice President Richard Nixon rode a convertible Edsel through Lima, Peru: when his motorcade was pelted with eggs, the unlovely man could smirk 'they were throwing eggs at the car, not me'. Yes, that bad.

WHEN:
1958
WHERE:
USA
TOLL:
Edsel Ford's blameless good name
YOU SHOULD KNOW:
The Edsel was intended to honour Henry Ford's second son. Edsel Ford had been the much loved and appreciated Ford company president up to his death, aged 49, in 1943. He shared his name with thousands of other American boys and men – but following the Edsel disaster, the name has all but vanished from US culture. It's still considered a laughable synonym for failure.

275

Strand cigarettes

WHEN:
1959
WHERE:
UK
TOLL:
Existentialism suffered. Coffee-houses lost their 'edginess' as centres of philosophical discussion, even though black polo-necks flourished for another five years as the uniform of jazz clubs and the modern art scene.

YOU SHOULD KNOW:
Existentialism was the mainspring of films made by Hitchcock, Orson Welles, Wajda, Polanski, Truffaut and Renoir. The Strand man's success as an icon of alienation froze further discussion – except as a satirical butt for the likes of *Monty Python's Flying Circus* and Douglas Adams (*The Hitchhiker's Guide to the Galaxy*). The Strand disaster may have been worth it just for the quality of satire it provoked.

The new brand was launched with the reassuring reminder that 'You're Never Alone with a Strand – the Cigarette of the Moment'. A series of ads showed a Frank Sinatra lookalike (from his *Pal Joey* period) in a trilby hat and trench coat, apparently satisfied that a good smoke was proper antidote to the night-time emptiness of the rain-slicked streets. They were beautiful photographs, taken by Bert Hardy, one of the stars of *Picture Post* and famous for the gritty realism of his photo-journalism. They exactly captured the fashionable mood of the era, as expressed in film noir and in the novels of Camus and Sartre. They implied that with a Strand cigarette to draw on, existential angst was bearable; and the suggestion was reinforced (in an accompanying TV commercial) by the haunting, jazz-tinged 'Lonely Man' theme (written by the prodigious Cliff Adams) that reached the charts. Strand's 'man in a mackintosh' became an immediate and enduring icon of cool, with a cultural significance ranking alongside *The Third Man* and Mickey Spillane heroes.

But the advertising image also touched a raw nerve in the public psyche. At the time, smoking was considered a social, and sociable, activity. Nobody wanted to be seen as a Billy No-Mates loser, 'alone with a Strand'. Sales evaporated, and the cigarette brand was quietly withdrawn. It wasn't just a commercial disaster, either. When the ad campaign for Strand hijacked existentialism, it turned a branch of authentic philosophy into a joke which offered alienation merely as an urban lifestyle statement. The highly memorable imagery associated that choice forever with failure – and even now, though most people no longer know or care that it was cigarettes that failed to sell, the powerful existential imagery of the Strand ad campaign remains a staple target of comedy writing and performance.

Decca rejects The Beatles

WHEN:
January 1 1962
WHERE:
Decca Studios, Maida Vale, London, UK
TOLL:
Decca's blooper made life much easier for new bands in the next decade. Big record companies were terrified of making a similar mistake, and for the only time in popular music history, were prepared at least to listen to anyone with something remotely new in sound or song.

On New Year's Day 1962, the fledgling Beatles performed 15 songs in one hour at the Decca Records studio in north London. They hoped for a recording contract. Instead, they were advised by Decca's A&R bigwigs that 'guitar groups were on the way out' and were rejected in favour of a local band whose travel expenses would be lower. Just 18 months later, the decision was already being cited as one of the biggest mistakes in musical history – and by any financial yardstick it's been getting bigger ever since.

And yet . . . even if you're besotted by The Beatles, the Decca audition tape isn't very good. Only hindsight enables you to identify what would develop into signature musical features. Beatles' manager Brian Epstein's selection of songs reveals his own, muddled, musical taste; and though they are played with the fluency acquired doing three, finger-splintering sets a night in Hamburg's Reeperbahn, the songs cover too broad a stylistic range to establish a strong identity. Even so, Decca's lack of enthusiasm was typical of Londoners' attitudes to 'north of Watford'. If they'd been listening, they'd have picked up the new buzz from the Liverpool area.

From Epstein's and The Beatles' point of view, the Decca rejection turned out to be a blessing. It meant the unwanted tape could be played to an EMI subsidiary producer, who spotted the originality of the feisty personalities behind it. And the whole world knows about the symbiotic relationship of The Beatles and their producer George Martin.

It was a disaster for Decca – but even they derived ultimate triumph from The Beatles success. By 1963, already stratospheric, George Harrison felt sorry for Dick Rowe, head of Decca's A&R. So George gave Dick a hot tip to go and see a new band – and Decca signed the Rolling Stones.

YOU SHOULD KNOW:
Decca was not the only label to reject The Beatles. Brian Epstein approached numerous companies in his mission to get a recording contract, among them Philips, Pye and Columbia.

The Beatles, from left to right, Paul McCartney, John Lennon, Ringo Starr and George Harrison

Lionel Bart's *Twang!!*

WHEN:
1965
WHERE:
London, UK
TOLL:
Millions of unhappy fans who loved Lionel Bart's music, and mourn the wasted years as much as he did.
YOU SHOULD KNOW:
The failure of *Twang!!* left the field clear for the new kinds of musicals like *Hair* and the many hits of Rice/Lloyd Webber and Mackintosh. In fact it was Cameron Mackintosh who acknowledged the debt due to Lionel Bart by reviving *Oliver!* in 1994, and restoring a percentage of the profits to him.

Lionel Bart was the man who wrote some of Britain's earliest pop chart hits, including 'Living Doll', 'Rock With The Cavemen' and 'Little White Bull'. The list of his successes is endless and includes musicals like *Lock Up Your Daughters*, *Blitz!* and *Fings Ain't Wot They Used To Be*, but it was the smash hit musical *Oliver!* that assured his immortality.

First produced in London in 1960, *Oliver!* arrived on Broadway in 1963. It brought Bart every kind of theatrical award, international fame and the more or less constant flood of royalties that proved to be his undoing. Generous to a fault, sociable and rich, he was welcome at the most glamorous tables of showbiz, rock 'n' roll and high society. In that glittering milieu, there was little stigma attached to hard partying, and unfortunately for Lionel, who was still flashing out new triumphs like the 1964 Bond theme 'From Russia With Love', he didn't know when to stop. By 1965 his creativity had wandered into a different dimension – and there he wrote *Twang!!*

Twang!! was a musical about Robin Hood. The most amusing bit is the title, which anticipated the semi-satirical comedy then coming into vogue, but which had no place in a family musical show that in any case lacked Bart's hallmark freshness and originality. Everything about it might be safely forgotten except for the fact that Bart believed in it. When it flopped, comprehensively, he tried to keep it alive with his own money. He sold the rights to his existing and future material, including *Oliver!*, until he was hamstrung by bankruptcy in 1972 and retreated into the bottle.

Happily, Lionel Bart eventually recovered his health; but until his death in 1999, he referred to *Twang!!* as 'my famous flop' – the personal disaster that swallowed his dreams as well as his money.

Pages from the court of Prince John in a dress rehearsal of Lionel Bart's Robin Hood musical Twang!!, *at the Shaftesbury Theatre.*

Silver Thursday

Apart from a handful of reigning monarchs and despots, in 1961 Nelson Bunker Hunt was the richest man in the world. Like his father, the legendary oilman H L Hunt, Bunker gambled big and got lucky. By 1970, although his wealth was accumulating faster than he could spend it, he foresaw a volatile economic future. Prevented by F D Roosevelt's 1933 prohibition on US citizens owning gold, Bunker and his brother Herbert chose silver, then standing at $1.50 per ounce, as their speculative hedge.

Billionaire Nelson Bunker Hunt appears before a House subcommittee investigating the crash of the silver market.

Their initial caution vanished after Colonel Gaddafi nationalized Bunker's Libyan oil fields in 1973. Furious, and paranoid that paper money would soon be worthless, in 1974 the Hunt brothers bought futures contracts on 55 million ounces of silver – but instead of selling the contracts like normal commodity traders, they took delivery of the bullion and chartered three Boeing 707s to airfreight it to Switzerland.

By 1979 they had engineered a genuine shortage. The Hunts owned $4.5 billion-worth of shiny, glittering silver, safely stashed in Swiss vaults. Still the price climbed, until on January 17 1980 an ounce cost $49.45. Then the goal posts were moved.

Almost simultaneously, trading in silver was suspended and the Federal Reserve raised interest rates. Without these props, the silver boom was suddenly over – but Bunker still had to honour contracts to buy at prices over $50. The day after he decided to get out – 'Silver Thursday', March 27 1980 – silver fell from $21.62 to $10.80, the metal's biggest single collapse. The Hunts became the (then) greatest debtors in financial history; and though the New York banks allowed them $1.1 billion credit towards clearing their obligations, Bunker was personally bankrupted and later convicted of illegally trying to corner the market. He had gambled that silver was undervalued: he failed because he made the price of silver too attractive for its own good.

WHEN:
March 27 1980
WHERE:
USA
TOLL:
Nelson Bunker Hunt and William Herbert Hunt were bankrupted.
YOU SHOULD KNOW:
J R Ewing in *Dallas* and the Duke Brothers in *Trading Places* all drew inspiration from Bunker's story, and his larger-than-life, characteristically 'Texan', persona.

Actors Kris Kristofferson, left, and Isabelle Huppert star in director Michael Cimino's, right, 1980 film Heaven's Gate.

Heaven's Gate – the movie

Hollywood's film studios felt expansive during the 1970s. Relatively young directors like Spielberg, Lucas and Coppola could hope for big-budget projects after just one or two successes, and even expect the studio suits and bean-counters to give them a free, unsupervised hand. So in 1978 when Michael Cimino approached United Artists, proposing to revitalize the classic American genre of the western, the studio rolled out the red carpet for him.

Cimino had just released *The Deerhunter* to universal critical and public acclaim. He was officially a 'genius', entitled to big money and big stars for his next big story. He disappeared with all three to Montana to film a fictional account of the 1890s Johnson County War between the Wyoming land barons and the immigrant wave of European farmers. The studio confidently expected Cimino to weave his magic in 'them thar hills'.

Heavens Gate proved to be epic in every sense. Months overdue, and nearly four times over an already colossal budget, Cimino presented a coma-inducing five-and-a-half-hour edit of a total 220 hours of film. After a recut to make it shorter, *Heaven's Gate* was still so dreary and plain awful that it was withdrawn after its premiere. *The New York Times* damned it as 'an unqualified disaster . . . a forced four-hour walking tour of your own living room'.

Released on circuit six months later, slashed by another 70 minutes, the film's total box-office was just $3.5 million – making it proportionately one of the biggest flops in movie history. *Heaven's Gate* ruined Cimino's reputation, earning him the 1982 Golden Raspberry ('Razzie') for Worst Director; and it pushed United Artists into bankruptcy. Most disastrously of all, *Heaven's Gate* killed off a golden opportunity to create a new impetus for the whole western genre.

WHEN:
1980
WHERE:
USA
TOLL:
Countless stillborn ideas for westerns; and the artistic licence to be quirky in any genre. For years afterwards, quirky in Hollywood equalled expensive and dangerous.
YOU SHOULD KNOW:
Over the years, no amount of editing, even into a mini-series, has made anything successful out of the wreckage of *Heaven's Gate*. However, inevitable critical revisionism means that the film now has a coterie of new champions, whose claims for the film range from 'artistic integrity of the epic form' to 'postmodern parable'. Mainly they want the original edit of the final battle scene released as a whole movie – at roughly two hours, it would still be longer than most films.

DeLorean DMC-12

Oh what a lovely car . . . or was it? In fact, the DeLorean DMC-12 was an innovative sports car with gull-wing doors and stainless-steel body panels. The problems were all commercial. Savvy entrepreneur John Zachary DeLorean had honed his engineering and management skills in the cut-throat world of American auto manufacture, notably when developing the iconic Pontiac Firebird muscle car. Keen to repeat the trick on his own behalf, he founded the DeLorean Motor Company (DMC) in 1975 and developed the futuristic DMC-12 for the US market.

In an early move towards the manufacturing outsourcing that would later become commonplace, DeLorean shopped around for the best start-up deal. He was about to sign with Puerto Rico when a better offer landed on DMC's table – from a British government desperate to stimulate the stagnating economy of Northern Ireland to help reduce rising sectarian tension. A huge manufacturing plant was built near Lisburn and the first DMC-12 rolled off the line early in 1981.

But the workforce was inexperienced, resulting in quality-control issues. The car looked good but was underpowered and overpriced compared with its competition. The DMC-12's revolutionary stainless-steel exterior showed every mark from a fingerprint upwards and was hard to paint successfully. So every car leaving the factory looked identical, displeasing image-conscious American consumers whose sporty purchase was supposed to underline their individuality.

Sales faltered and financial problems ensued as surely as night follows day. The British government refused to mount a rescue unless matching funds were forthcoming. John DeLorean failed to attract other investors and – despite proclaiming that it was a viable business with money in the bank and a healthy order book – his company went bust in 1982. And the DMC-12 itself? Over two thirds of the 9,000 produced survived to become popular cult classics in the USA.

WHEN:
1976–1982
WHERE:
Dunmurry, Lisburn, Northern Ireland, UK
TOLL:
When DMC folded 2,500 jobs were lost together with over $100 million of investments . . . and so was John DeLorean's reputation. After his acquittal on charges of illegal drug dealing, DeLorean joked 'Would you buy a used car from me?'.
YOU SHOULD KNOW:
It should have been the commercial coup of the century, leading to massive worldwide sales of the DMC-12 – for this was the car chosen to star in the blockbusting *Back to the Future* trilogy. Unfortunately, DMC had already gone bust and production of the car ended before the first movie was released.

John DeLorean and his famous DeLorean DMC-12

The Hitler diaries

WHEN:
April 25 1983
WHERE:
Germany, UK and USA
TOLL:
Aside from the reputations of great men, journalistic ethics took the biggest beating.
YOU SHOULD KNOW:
Resignations over the Hitler diaries included *Stern*'s editor and senior colleagues; but Murdoch's *Times* organization cynically demanded its money back from the German magazine. The actual forgers served prison sentences, becoming so famous that their own artworks began to be forged for profit. The Hitler diaries twisted normal morality into a Gordian Knot that disabled the careers and reputations of everyone involved with them.

Conspiracy theorists quickly piled in with suggestions of East discrediting West and vice-versa, but Cold War skulduggery had no part in the 20th century's most brazen hoax.

Like it or not, Adolf Hitler cast – and casts – a monstrous shadow over the era. Curiously, though, he left astonishingly few relics or personal papers. The possibility of finding anything as intimate as his diary was a postwar grail of journalism. Apart from the fame, it was worth circulation-busting millions to its publisher.

On April 25 1983, with its cover screaming 'Hitler's Diaries Discovered', German news magazine *Stern* anticipated demand with an extra two million copies. Simultaneously in London, Rupert Murdoch's *The Sunday Times* rushed into print. Both journals were determined to get the most from their sensational investment.

They should have waited. Even as the diaries hit the streets, their veracity was being questioned by the very historians who had authenticated them. None of the experts suffered more than Hugh Trevor-Roper (Lord Dacre), whose authorship of *The Last Days of Hitler* had brought him fame, fortune, and immense academic prestige. Trevor-Roper, like so many others, very badly wanted the diaries to be real – so reality was what he saw. As he shook free of the spell of his desire, it became clear that the diaries were a crude forgery: the paper and ink were wrong, the entries were like a catalogue of Hitler's known stylistic clichés, and referred to 'facts' which simply were not available to the dictator. The 'banality of evil' was one thing; the banality of the diaries merely laughable.

Only the German word *schadenfreude* (literally 'joy in another's discomfit') describes the crowing editorials of the world's press when they realized. Their response was as ugly as *Stern* and Murdoch's greed, in the cause of which they had put expediency over the need for history to be accurate.

One of the 60 diaries of Adolf Hitler discovered by the West German magazine Stern, *Hamburg, is marked with a note saying it is the personal property of the Führer, signed by Reichsleiter Martin Bormann.* Stern *magazine made public, during a press conference on April 25 1983, that reporter Gerd Heidemann had discovered the diaries. Bonn Interior Minister Friedrich Zimmermann said on May 6 1983 that the purported diaries are falsifications after the Federal Criminal Office and the Federal Bureau of Standards jointly examined three of the volumes.*

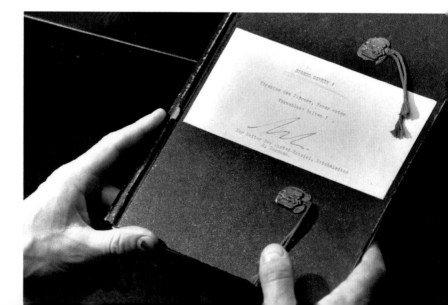

Sinclair C5

Talented inventor and not-so-lucky entrepreneur Clive Sinclair could have ended up as a billionaire, but didn't. Always fascinated by miniaturization, he invented the electronic pocket calculator in 1972 and followed that success story with a series of affordable home computers in the early 1980s – the ZX80, ZX81 and ZX Spectrum. These futuristic devices should have been hugely successful, but suffered from the chronic British disease of brilliant inventiveness coupled with poor commercial exploitation.

Sir Clive Sinclair demonstrating his C5 electric vehicle at Alexandra Palace.

But Sinclair's Cambridge-based company was briefly profitable, and Sir Clive (he would be knighted in 1985) again demonstrated technical foresight by forming Sinclair Vehicles to develop electric propulsion, two decades before this became a priority of car manufacturers reacting to global warming. He had long been interested in this revolutionary technology and invested heavily – too heavily – in making his dream of an electric car come true.

The resultant open-top Sinclair C5 was a pedal tricycle with plastic single-seater body and electric motor that allowed the driver to sit back and enjoy the ride. It was steered by means of handles and could reach the reckless speed of 24 kph (15 mph), though in fairness the advertising featured racing driver Stirling Moss and a modified model reached 240 kph (150 mph), seizing the land-speed record for electric vehicles.

Its quirky design was inspired by new regulations that allowed the C5 to be driven on British roads without a licence. But press and public alike ridiculed Sinclair's baby, claiming it was unsuitable for inclement British weather and sure to prove hazardous in traffic. Extras like weathershields and a reflector on a pole singularly failed to dampen criticism. Just 12,000 units were built in ten months before production ceased, making the C5 a catastrophic failure that swallowed most of its creator's fortune and effectively ended his business career.

WHEN:
January to October 1985
WHERE:
UK
TOLL:
None (despite fears that the low-slung C5 would be dangerously vulnerable on busy roads).
YOU SHOULD KNOW:
It was perhaps not the best of omens that Clive Sinclair chose a certain Barrie Wills as the managing director of Sinclair Vehicles. The new boss had been a senior manager at Belfast's ill-fated DeLorean Motor Company, which went bankrupt in 1982 after a short but turbulent commercial life – a fate all too soon shared by TPD (the successor to Sinclair Vehicles).

Coca-Cola billboard for the short-lived New Coke

Introduction of New Coke

After decades of losing market share to the 'Pepsi Challenge', Coca-Cola found a new formula for their 99-year-old product which consistently came top in nationwide blind tastings. On April 23 1985 at New York's Lincoln Center, the company proclaimed the birth of 'New Coke'. Henceforth, production of original Coca-Cola would cease, and 'New Coke' would be the standard bearer of the Red and White in what the marketing division called 'the beverage landscape'. The announcement sparked a furore, and within a few days the decision to discontinue original Coke was denounced as 'the biggest marketing blunder of all time'.

In their ivory towers at Atlanta, Coke's blinkered executives had forgotten what Coke meant to American culture. In the 1930s a Pulitzer Prize-winning Kansas newspaperman had described the carbonated fizz as the 'sublimated essence of all America stands for – a decent thing, honestly made . . .' and nobody blinked when the Coke company hung out a sign for the Apollo astronauts reading 'Welcome back to earth, home of Coca-Cola'. More insensitively, after telling the world for years that Coke was 'the real thing', the company was now saying it wasn't. On the street it was considered a national disaster: Coke ads on screen at the Houston Astrodome were booed; original Coke was hoarded, or sold at Prohibition-style prices; Coca-Cola delivery men were literally assaulted by irate housewives; and in Seattle New Coke was dumped publicly in the sewers.

After 77 days, original Coke was brought back as 'Classic Coke'. The Coca-Cola company lost millions in research and advertising costs, but gained three times as much in free advertising of the highest quality. Indirectly, New Coke eventually restored the company to its present unassailable position at the top of the 'beverage tree' – which conspiracy theorists say is what 'they' planned all along . . .

WHEN:
April 23 1985
WHERE:
Lincoln Center, New York City, USA
TOLL:
None (apart from a few bruised delivery men)
YOU SHOULD KNOW:
The best verdict on the New Coke affair came from Pepsi-Cola's CEO Roger Enrico, who wrote '. . . by the end of their nightmare, they figured out who they really are. Caretakers. They can't change the taste of their flagship brand. They can't change its imagery. All they can do is defend the heritage they nearly abandoned in 1985.'

Ishtar

Movie director Mike Nichols described *Ishtar* as 'the prime example that I know of in Hollywood of studio suicide'. The comment highlights the distinction between *Ishtar* and most other box-office turkeys: *Ishtar* went way over budget, but it wasn't a bad film. It failed because of bad blood between Columbia's new CEO, David Puttnam, and its Oscar-winning stars, Warren Beatty and Dustin Hoffman.

Ishtar was conceived as an intelligent comedy about a pair of talentless songwriters trying to make it as a ritzy lounge act. Too dumb to work out why their songs inspire hilarity instead of romantic wonder (even with titles like 'That a Lawnmower Can Do All That') they get a last-ditch gig entertaining US troops in the North African Emirate of 'Ishtar'. *En route*, the boys and their blind camel get involved with a mysterious *houri* (Isabelle Adjani) and a CIA agent trying to depose the Emir. You can see the obvious parallels with Bing, Bob and Dorothy Lamour's 'road' movies and, with 'comedy legend' Elaine May as director, why Hollywood foresaw a guaranteed success.

Instead, the delays mounted under Elaine May's perfectionist direction (she even had the Moroccan sand dunes bulldozed a few metres to improve a desert shot). Every delay was scornfully evaluated by the media, burying the film in negative publicity. Rumours of revenge were rife. Did David Puttnam bear a grudge against Warren Beatty? Was the media punishing Warren for treating them like low life? It was enough to convince audiences that the film couldn't be fun, and that its $55 million cost represented megastar arrogance towards the paying public.

Ishtar was nominated for three 'Razzies' (1987 Golden Raspberry Awards), but the negative reviews were all about the money. People who actually saw the film found it entertaining. In fact, during the 20-odd years *Ishtar* has been synonymous with 'box-office flop', the more of a cult it has become.

Actor Dustin Hoffman and his wife Lisa are joined by co-star Warren Beatty, right, as they arrive for the world premiere of the motion picture Ishtar *at the Century Plaza Theatre in Los Angeles on May 14 1987.*

WHEN:
1987
WHERE:
USA
TOLL:
Despite the growing number of fans, the business end of Hollywood still regards *Ishtar* as a bitter betrayal and over 20 years later the film has never been issued on DVD in North America. Hollywood minded the financial disaster less than the fact that *Ishtar* made stars and suits alike aware of their changing power relationship – and wary of attracting knives in their backs.
YOU SHOULD KNOW:
The negative PR campaign against *Ishtar* brainwashed even the brightest and most perceptive audiences. Gary Larson, the cartoonist, drew a 'Far Side' comic strip showing 'Hell's Video Store' stocked solely with piles of *Ishtar* tapes. Much later, after seeing it as an inflight movie, he praised it, admitting 'there are so many cartoons for which I should probably write an apology, but this is the only one that compels me to do so'.

Carrie The Musical

WHEN:
May 12 1988
WHERE:
Virginia Theater, New York City, USA
TOLL:
Recriminations in 'luvvie land' caused deeply hurt feelings on both sides of the Atlantic. In addition, *Carrie*'s composer baulked at college and small independent theatre attempts to adapt the musical. Twenty years later, its iconic status as the flop musical has revived interest in new adaptations.
YOU SHOULD KNOW:
In 2008, the composer of *Carrie The Musical* hit a small community theatre with a 'cease and desist' order on their homespun, technically illegal production. The theatre promptly reworked the show, adapting songs from the charts and other musicals. It was a huge success under the new title of *Telekinesis!*

Most people know the story of Carrie, the awkward teenager with a fanatically religious momma. Bullied at school and bewildered by her own, inarticulate isolation, she wreaks telekinetic havoc on the world that has humiliated her. A smash hit movie elevated Stephen King's original novel into a cult; and after seeing Alban Berg's opera *Lulu* at the Metropolitan, the film's screenwriter thought he saw *Carrie*'s potential as a musical. It was com*plex* (provided you emphasized the second syllable) with intellectual credibility plus lurid effects. The project took off, gathering major choreographers, librettists, directors and stars. In the end, production money proved as hard to find as a finalized script, until England's Royal Shakespeare Company (where whole teams of Broadway-accoladed theatrical professionals were in collective residence) premiered it early in 1988.

The transatlantic cast included Darlene Love (original singer of immortal songs like 'Da Doo Ron Ron' and 'He's a Rebel') as 'the teacher', but the RSC's show was a nightmare of script and technical problems. On opening night, Carrie was almost decapitated by falling scenery and, in the key scene, she couldn't be drenched in pig's blood without her body-microphone shorting out. The audience hooted at what they thought was a comedy musical – so the laughs were ruthlessly chopped to secure a transfer to Broadway.

Two months later, still with no settled script or staging, *Carrie The Musical* opened on May 12 1988 in New York. After 15 catastrophic previews, the critics were ready with an official mauling. The audience may have (allegedly) 'buzzed', but the official First Night reviews were brutal. After five performances, *Carrie The Musical* closed without making a cast soundtrack for later record sales. It lost $8 million, and you can't even hum it: quite apart from the money, that makes *Carrie* 'Broadway's biggest flop'.

Actresses Betty Buckley and Linzi Hateley are engulfed in fog.

The case of the contaminated Perrier

Panic engulfed the French Perrier company when a North Carolina chemist found traces of benzene in bottled Perrier water. Perrier was the gold standard by which the US state judged the purity of its own water. Fear became its corporate spur. Desperate to protect the reputation of the 'naturally sparkling' mineral water that gushed so obligingly from its limestone aquifer near Nimes, Perrier launched what is now regarded as a textbook demonstration of self-destructive damage limitation.

Perrier's initial reaction seemed exemplary: only 12 bottles were contaminated; it was an isolated incident – probably caused by a worker's dirty rag at the US regional bottling plant. The company issued an immediate (voluntary) product recall. But things started to look more sinister when benzene-tainted bottles were also found in Denmark and the Netherlands. The explanation rapidly changed: benzene was naturally present in the spring water, but was filtered out before bottling – so the contamination was caused by dirty filters. The recall became global and 260 million bottles were destroyed.

Meanwhile, rumour and suspicion created beneficiaries from Perrier's misfortune – LaCroix and San Pellegrino became the preferred taste in US restaurants and hotels. Perrier lost 50 per cent of its sales and the decades of prestige that went with being the 'choice of presidents' at the White House.

Perrier's mishandling of the whole affair led to serious, long-term repercussions. Detailed analysis of the production process caused US and Canadian authorities to reclassify it as an artificially carbonated 'beverage' (with a sales tax, payable retrospectively as a huge fine) instead of tax-free 'water'. Once the Rolls-Royce of spring waters, Perrier's label could no longer even claim to be 'naturally sparkling'. The irony was that the trace benzene was indeed caused by a natural chemical process within Perrier's French spring. The fuss could have been avoided.

Perrier being removed from store shelves due to a threat of benzene contamination.

WHEN:
February 1990
WHERE:
France, the USA and across the world
TOLL:
Perrier's shareholders suffered and the company had to bear the commercial humiliation of losing a huge proportion of US market share to brands like Aquafina and Dasani, which used municipal water supplies.
YOU SHOULD KNOW:
Perrier was a favourite of British royalty during the early 20th century. Its worldwide status was so exalted that Salvador Dali and Andy Warhol designed poster ads for the company, and Orson Welles was its spokesman.

Polly Peck tycoon Asil Nadir at his London home, after being released on bail from Wormwood Scrubs prison.

Polly Peck

In 1940, a new fashion house was formed in London, which traded in a modest way for four decades under the name Polly Peck. What followed was spectacular. Turkish Cypriot Asil Nadir bought a majority stake in 1980, then used Polly Peck as a vehicle for overseas investments. Rights issues raised the capital necessary to create or purchase enterprises of extraordinary diversity in fields such as packaging, food, fruit, resort hotels, textiles, mineral water, housewares and electronics – the latter category including the first recorded foreign takeover of a major Japanese player.

The stock-market rise from zero to hero was astonishing. In ten years Polly Peck went from a market capitalization of $300,000 to $1.7 billion, becoming a member of the elite *Financial Times* 100 Share Index in 1989. It then had around 17,000 employees and was making an annual profit of over $160 million. Financial institutions and wealthy individuals whose investments supported this soar-away success story congratulated themselves on their acumen and collected handsome dividends.

And then Polly Peck hit a brick wall – at speed. Asil Nadir tried to take the operation private, but when the attempt failed it quickly became apparent that the company was in deep financial trouble. The Nadir holding company was raided by police and Polly Peck shares went into free fall. The business collapsed in 1990 as Nadir faced 70 charges of theft and false accounting.

Though strenuously denying the charges – which were sufficiently grave to justify bail set at $3.5 million – Asil Nadir didn't stay around to argue the point. Bail was allowed to lapse (as a result of official negligence rather than the conspiracy in high places that some alleged) and the disgraced entrepreneur slipped out of Britain in a private plane, to find refuge in his native Northern Cyprus – which conveniently lacks an extradition treaty with Britain.

WHEN:
1990
WHERE:
UK
TOLL:
Numerous investors lost megabucks and thousands of workers lost their jobs.
YOU SHOULD KNOW:
Asil Nadir was able to flee from the short arm of British justice because police detectives who were supposed to be watching his every move were not on duty, having been stood down during a public holiday to save the cost of their overtime pay.

Ratner's gaffe

Honesty is not always the best policy. Gerald Ratner inherited a small jewellery business from his father and expanded it into the UK's biggest chain of high street jewellers. He persuaded millions of customers that in addition to providing the enduring symbols of birth, marriage and death, a jeweller's could be part of high-street fashion – a place you might drop into every so often for some casual bling to match a new dress or liven up a shirt cuff. He was a natural salesman, but his commercial success was equally due to his ready bonhomie, sense of humour and generosity of spirit.

Inevitably, such a man was a popular after-dinner speaker, and Ratner became accustomed to delivering speeches at sporting, charity, and business functions. He learned the ropes by trial and error, until he knew which jokes would work for almost any occasion. And he learned – from experience and from advertising – that people respect candour: tell the truth about your product and they buy more of it.

Ratner was at the top of his game on April 23 1991, though a little wary of his after-dinner audience at the Institute of Directors in London. He decided to include two of his regular jokes to loosen them up. One was enough. Describing a sherry decanter set that sold for £4.95, he joked 'People say "How can you sell this for such a low price?" I say "Because it's total crap!".' . . . The room rocked with laughter.

Next morning, Ratner was assailed for 'insulting his customers' and 'sneering at the recession-hit poor'. The tabloids crucified him. *The Sunday Times* called him 'Gerald Crapner'. He lost his job and his company, and finally his name (when Ratner's was renamed Signet in 1994) – only because, short of news, the papers decided to twist his joke into a headline declaration of class war.

WHEN:
April 23 1991
WHERE:
Institute of Directors' dinner, London, UK
TOLL:
Gerald Ratner personally lost £500 million. Though his self-belief was severely dented, he bounced back ten years later with an online jewellery business called 'Geraldline'. For years, banks and former business associates refused to help him, so his subsequent success represents an even greater personal triumph over his very personal commercial disaster.
YOU SHOULD KNOW:
The 'law of candour' is the 15th law of *The 22 Immutable Laws of Marketing*, one of the 'bibles' of marketing experts. Yes, everyone admires you for admitting a problem – but doing so goes against corporate and human nature unless you instantly qualify the negative with a positive solution. 'Ratner's gaffe' is now shorthand for the consequences of ignoring that principle.

The Ratners Jewellery store in Regent Street, London, part of the chain owned by Gerald Ratner

Hudson Hawk

WHEN:
1991
WHERE:
USA
TOLL:
One blessing was that after winning the 1992 Worst Screenplay 'Razzie' (Golden Raspberry Award), Bruce Willis shelved his ambition to write. The film lost some $50 million and was Tri-Star's final failure. Soon afterwards, it merged with Columbia (still suffering from *Ishtar*) and both studios were financially subsumed into Sony Studios.
YOU SHOULD KNOW:
Hudson Hawk was neither postmodern nor surreal. Furthermore, if Willis's constant gurning was comic, 'the joke', according to *Entertainment Weekly*, 'is on the audience. *Hudson Hawk* is a Hollywood first, all right – a fiasco sealed with a smirk.'. Not pretty, and not at all comprehensible.

In 1990, Bruce Willis was a newcomer to Hollywood's high table, riding high on the success of *Die Hard*. The role of Hudson Hawk, a wisecracking action-man burglar, was made for him. He leads a screwball cast in a comedy heist caper which (somehow) involves Leonardo da Vinci's accidental recipe for making gold out of lead. Willis wrote the script himself. It was an amalgam of every fantasy he'd ever had, playing for gags and one-liners whether they fitted or not.

Hudson Hawk is crammed with coy and often laboured homages to people Willis admires, from Buster Keaton, Abbott and Costello and Bing and Bob, to James Bond, the cartoon Katzenjammer Kids and Leonardo himself. The exhausting, non-stop patter has its action equivalent, straining even the dash of credulity necessary for comedy; but the running gag of the burglars choreographing pop songs (like 'Swinging on a Star' – '. . . one moonbeam, two moonbeam . . .') to monitor the split-second timing of their evil deeds eventually makes you scream.

The Washington Post referred to 'crafty satire with a swashbuckling soul', the combination of 'suavity with punkish comedy', the patter and stunts with 'a Dadaist twist', and the 'connections between surrealism and slapstick'. Every other reviewer placed it firmly among 'the most legendary turkeys', 'so disconnected from itself that it's like watching someone flip cable TV channels with a remote'; and dismissed 'the banality of the screenplay . . . that crash lands in a sea of wretched excess and silliness'.

Just like the rest, *Entertainment Weekly* was appalled by Willis constantly pulling faces at the camera, but cleverly hedged its criticisms by suggesting that 'in a peculiarly self-conscious, show-offy way, *Hudson Hawk* may be the first would-be blockbuster that's a sprawling, dissociated mess on purpose, making it a perverse landmark: the original postmodern Hollywood disaster'.

BBC TV's *Eldorado*

WHEN:
July 1993
WHERE:
Coin, Costa del Sol, Spain, and London, UK
TOLL:
The BBC effectively abandoned *Eldorado* long before it was finally cancelled; and the nature of its demise explains why, ever since, the BBC has avoided launching any new soaps in favour of financing drama

A legendary lemon, *Eldorado* was BBC TV's new soap opera for the 1990s. Conceived as Spain became second home to many Britons, it was supposed to replace the gritty realism of no-frills urban drama like *EastEnders* and *Coronation Street* with the sun-kissed bounty of sea, golden beach and sizzling paella.

The set was purpose-built at Coin on the Costa del Sol. With a fountain at its heart, and multi-level nooks and crannies to provide an infinity of camera angles, it was an *urbanizacion* of arches, steps and white stucco so typical of Spanish developments of the era. Its

The set of BBC TV's Eldorado

drawback was the ex-pats who 'lived' there: how could they be constantly complaining when they had already achieved the nirvana of living it up in lotus land? Even in Australian soaps like *Neighbours* and *Home and Away*, the beach and the glorious weather were mere extras. The action should have been head-to-head in the kitchen or garage. The psychology of an intimate, daily, domestic drama didn't work in what looked like an open-air holiday haven.

Mismatch apart, the early scripts were nearly as awful as the amateur acting – but those were faults that could be and were (nearly) set right. Far away at Television Centre, the greater threat to *Eldorado* was a new Controller, temperamentally committed to restoring the BBC's high moral purpose. Populism was fine, as long as it wasn't just a rehash of something already covered by independent TV. Big-budget populism that swallowed funds which could have paid for more edifying drama drew scowls and pursed lips. Despite a regular audience of five to six million towards the end of its run, *Eldorado* closed. At a cost of £10 million, it was a disaster for the BBC's managers – but quite good value for a national joke.

series like *Casualty*, allowing them to be developed in a soap-like fashion once their 'brand' has been established. As for the series itself, memory plays strange tricks, and in retrospect it has never been more popular – as it showed every sign of becoming had the BBC not had John Birt as Director General, whose unfavourable opinion nobody dared disagree with.

YOU SHOULD KNOW:
One of the best-ever 'episodes' of *Eldorado* was the satirical sketch on *The Ruby Wax Show*, starring Ruby as an 'extra' in mantilla and castanets. She exactly captured the so-bad-it's-really-good response that kept millions watching the soap while it slowly improved.

Nick Leeson and the collapse of Barings Bank

Baring Brothers was Britain's oldest merchant bank, founded in 1762. It collapsed when a single employee committed the bank to losses of roughly $830 million, which it could not cover. Embarrassingly, Barings had only itself to blame. Its culture had evolved from the collision between its own illustrious history and the contemporary, ruthless avarice typified by its rival, Morgan Stanley (whose president, on discovering that big names were haemorrhaging losses from trading derivatives, told his team 'There's blood in the water. Let's go kill someone.').

Snobbery flourished: as long as the profits rolled in, Barings' old-money merchant bankers tolerated the new breed of securities traders . . . but not enough to actually talk to them or try to understand what they did. Barings' culture meant that 28-year-old Nick Leeson in the Singapore office could trade securities without direct supervision. Staggeringly, he was in charge of both buying and selling ('trading' and 'settlement'). The temptation was biblical. Leeson was uniquely placed to commandeer huge sums of cash from London; to gamble them; and to report the results to his best advantage.

In 1993 (the year known by Barings' staff as 'The Turbulence'), what was effectively an internal takeover created the unworkable situation of investment bankers supposedly overseeing investment traders. Leeson began trading between Singapore's Simex and Japan's Nikkei, feeding a steady stream of profits to London, and hiding losses in what became the notorious account 88888. By December 1994 the file hid losses of S$373.9 million. Leeson kept doubling his bets on the Nikkei staying above 19,000 points during January 1995 – but on January 17, the Kobe earthquake sent the Nikkei crashing. Desperate, Leeson doubled and redoubled until on February 23 he fled Singapore leaving losses of S$2.2 billion to be revealed by the auditors in his wake. Three days later Barings went into administration.

Ex-Barings trader Nick Leeson escorted by police in Singapore.

WHEN:
February 27 1995
WHERE:
London, UK; Singapore; and Osaka, Japan – then globally
TOLL:
Nick Leeson surrendered voluntarily. In December 1995 he was sentenced to six-and-a-half years in prison, and was released on July 3 1999. Barings was sold to the Dutch company ING for a token £1. Immediate steps were taken to toughen both internal and international company law – but as history shows, fraud was already endemic at every level of the financial services industries. More than a decade after Leeson's release, fresh reforms continue to be framed at national and international levels.
YOU SHOULD KNOW:
In The Army, if one soldier steals from another man's locker, it used to be not the thief, but the victim who was punished – for leaving temptation in the other man's path. Barings may have saved Britain by financing the Napoleonic Wars, and much else, but they also brought disaster on themselves in 1995. It's all in Leeson's book, now filmed, called *Rogue Trader*.

Kevin Costner's *The Postman*

Let's be clear: this movie is not to be confused with the Oscar-nominated *Il Postino* (released in the US as *The Postman*) one of the most profound and beautiful films ever to come out of Italy. By complete contrast, Kevin Costner's *The Postman* heads several 'Top Ten Career-Killing Movies' lists, which is a surprise only because most people have never heard of it, having lost interest after *Waterworld*.

The Postman is another post-apocalyptic wham-bam, spliced with an extra 45 minutes of dithering morality. James Berardinelli's Reelviews website kindly suggested that 'with all its rampant jingoism, clichéd melodrama and shameless attempts at emotional manipulation, [it] could easily be viewed as a clever satire of epic adventures', but admitted that although its 'cloying dose of patriotism' enabled the rest of the world to enjoy its comedy, it wasn't meant to be a joke. It was, said *The New York Times*, 'a bald-faced exercise in cinematic self-deification'.

Costner plays another loner, a wandering minstrel doing one-man Shakespeare shows for bread and alms. Fleeing conscription into the racist, psychopathic army of thugs that runs America (the year is 2013), he finds a dead postman in the Utah Salt Flats and takes both uniform and full mailbag off the skeleton. Siddartha in a US Postal Service jacket, he sets out to deliver mail, wisdom and nobility of purpose. Will he? Won't he? Can he? Can't he? inspire the shattered outposts of decency to a common weal, aided by the usual 'crazy', called Ford Lincoln Mercury, and the usual girl, Abby, whose big line is 'you give out hope like it was candy in your pocket'.

Heaven only knows what Costner was thinking. Apart from losing $63 million, *The Postman* stripped him of any credibility remaining from the excellence of *Dancing With Wolves*. It was a disaster for the actor, the director, and intelligence itself.

WHEN:
1997
WHERE:
USA
TOLL:
It's all been downhill for Kevin Costner. The steady stream of work confirms Hollywood's belief in his core talent, but his choices have done little or nothing to redeem his reputation. Even the political comedy *Swing Vote* (2008) lost millions on a meagre budget of $21 million. Happily, however flawed, there's still something very likeable about the man.
YOU SHOULD KNOW:
Since 2007, Costner has been touring extensively with his country music band 'Kevin Costner and the Modern West'. Though it's usual to dump on middle-aged men fulfilling boyhood dreams of rock stardom, and plenty have – one review called the band 'so unbelievably cornball it becomes laugh-out-loud funny' – he's actually pretty good. In any case, all his films are about fulfilling impossible dreams, so why should his band be any different?

US actor Kevin Costner waves to fans during the celebration for the German premier of his new movie The Postman *in Hamburg.*

Dorling Kindersley

WHEN:
January 2000
WHERE:
London, UK
TOLL:
DK could not have survived the *Star Wars* fiasco without Pearson – and Peter Kindersley valued his independence above everything. The affair caused what one well-known media analyst called a 'sea change' in subsequent film merchandising deals.
YOU SHOULD KNOW:
Christopher Davis, a Dorling Kindersley board member for 25 years, wrote: 'It would be intriguing to hear Peter Kindersley . . . give an insight into those conflicts that arise from Founder's Syndrome . . . Is there ever a satisfactory exit point for the founder and chief architect of a creative business forged largely in his own image? How does he resolve the Faustian pact which decrees that the price for personal wealth is to lose control of your creation? I can only guess . . .'

From the outset in 1974 (Christopher) Dorling and (Peter) Kindersley were successful book packagers (they created finished books for other companies to publish). They specialized in large-format, heavily illustrated books on almost any subject. By 1982 they themselves had become publishers, internationally famous for 'visual guides' which made complex non-fiction subjects readily accessible. Typical of their many successes are titles like *Universe, Earth, History, Animal,* and *Human*; the Eyewitness series and a host of others usually created by their own teams of writers and editors. Margins are wafer thin, but Dorling Kindersley bulldozed its way to the top of its field by sticking to its unmistakable formula. Peter Kindersley – nothing if not passionate about his product – made sure of that.

In 1999 Dorling Kindersley won the right to publish the lavishly illustrated book to accompany the first 'prequel' to George Lucas's *Star Wars*. Called *Star Wars: Episode I The Phantom Menace*, it was the most-hyped film in history. As part of the collateral merchandising, Dorling Kindersley printed 13 million books, expecting a Christmas sales surge. 'Only' three million were sold (enough to put it on *The New York Times* bestseller list) but Dorling Kindersley was forced to announce a £25 million pre-tax loss, of which some £18 million related to *Star Wars*. Peter Kindersley, the executive chairman, revealed the immediate departure of the chief executive. By giving no details, he appeared to blame him for the loss; but Peter Kindersley was famous for his hands-on approach to major projects, and nobody can name one in which he has not been intimately involved. He stayed, proudly proprietorial.

It was no use. Dorling Kindersley had to go and the Pearson Group (owners of Penguin) bought it. The packager was ultimately clobbered by the ambition that had deterred his earlier partners.

Boo.com goes bankrupt

The dotcom frenzy reached its zenith around the millennium. At every stage of its explosive development and violent decline, its standard-bearer was Boo.com, the European online sports and high-fashion 'e-tailer'. From its conception in 1998, Boo had value-added glamour in the form of its founders, a Swedish poetry critic and a former *Vogue* model. They parlayed their youth, their previous experience of running an online bookshop, and their innate style into $80 million of backing from the most prestigious sources in the USA and Europe.

To the envy of potential rivals, their investors included J P Morgan, Goldman Sachs, Benetton and Bernard Arnault of LVMH (Louis Vuitton Moet Hennessy); but instead of funding a staff of 30 and a suitably corporate mindset, the money evaporated in demonstrations of the cachet and chic they were supposed to be selling. They used Concorde like a bus (though by their own later account 'after the pampered luxury of a Learjet 35, Concorde was a bit cramped') and redefined 'partying' as a fundraising mechanism. They opened for business a year late, with 400 staff in eight offices round the globe, waiting. Before they sold a single thing, *Fortune* magazine described Boo.com as Europe's coolest company. Its reputation turned out to be its epitaph.

Within six months, the dotcom boom was over as venture capitalists realized technology had outstripped consumers' awareness of, and familiarity with it. Buying online was too new, and too slow. The banks were closed, even for high fliers like Lastminute.com. Boo's 'passion' built a brilliant internet edifice which very few customers understood how to use properly. The company did too much too soon – and did it with such champagne-fuelled gusto that nobody noticed the achievement behind the hangover. If go you must, then what a way to go.

WHEN:
May 18 2000
WHERE:
London, UK
TOLL:
Boo.com's high-profile bankruptcy attracted unfair censure during the tech-stock crash of 2000. The other dotcom ventures would have failed anyway. However, it did real damage to perceptions of European internet start-ups, and US internet giants colonized the resulting vacuum – just in time to take full advantage of the huge increase in domestic broadband availability that would have given wings to Boo.com's original plans.
YOU SHOULD KNOW:
When the BBC referred to Boo.com's 'all-singing, all-dancing website', it surely included one of its most delightful features. The site had an online hostess and personal shopper called 'Miss Boo', a compelling character who very much resembled a pixellated version of Boo's co-founder, the former *Vogue* model Kajsa Leander. It is said that 'Miss Boo' was responsible for much of the euphoria with which users responded to the internet site.

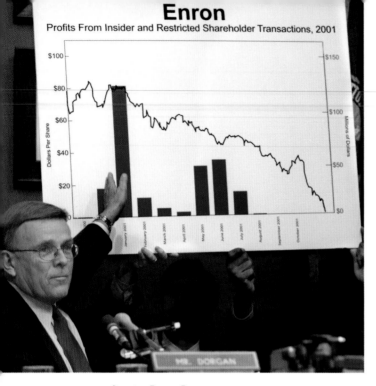

Enron

Profits From Insider and Restricted Shareholder Transactions, 2001

Senator Byron Dorgan with a graph showing profits from Enron insider and restricted shareholder transactions for 2001 during a hearing investigating the company's collapse.

WHEN:
2001

WHERE:
Houston, Texas, USA

TOLL:
Arthur Andersen, one of the world's 'big five' accounting firms, shrivelled in size and reputation, the first of over 700 companies required 'to restate their earnings' in the light of their creative accounting. The scandals, rip-offs and prosecutions brought legislation, passed by the US Congress in 2002, intended to reform corporate ethics and protect 'the little guy'. Enron links to Dick Cheney and the Bush administration have allegedly slowed the reform process.

YOU SHOULD KNOW:
Ken Lay, CEO and then Chairman of Enron, was George W Bush's biggest private contributor, giving $2 million. He took home $67 million in 2000. CEO Jeffrey Skilling took $42 million and was so adept at selling that 13 of the 16 analysts who covered Enron were still advising investors to buy, a month before its bankruptcy.

Enron and the SPEs

For five years straight, *Fortune* magazine named it 'most innovative company of the year'. By then Enron was a colossus, one of the world's top seven financial services groups, and the accolade was a stunned acknowledgement of Enron's peak – $100 billion revenues and soaraway $90 share price. Enron's winning formula baffled the shrewdest financial minds, who in any case preferred to get in on the action instead of digging too deep.

Protected by its success, wealth, and stockholders representing every level of political clout up to the White House itself, Enron's only Achilles' heel was its imitators. Many companies had tried to follow Enron without understanding what it actually did – and their mistakes provoked Federal agencies to speculate more closely on Enron's slick operations. Like Al Capone, Enron was taken down by tax accountants.

Enron's 'innovations' were twofold. Firstly, it refined old-style creative accounting to a new art form. Secondly, it used a perfectly ordinary financing technique that would attract no attention, in a novel way and on a scale without precedent. 'Special Purpose Entities' (SPEs) enable a company to lessen risk by placing assets in a smaller partnership that can be sold independently. Enron placed only assets that were already losing money in such partnerships; and instead of isolating the SPE from the parent company as the law required, continued to run them with its own managers, and back them with its own stock.

When federal auditors insisted that Enron treat over 4000 SPEs as part of Enron, the resulting $1.1 billion 'charge against earnings' caused the whole financial house of cards to collapse. Ten years later, charges of wire fraud, securities fraud, mail fraud, money-laundering and conspiracy are still hitting senior executives – including the same 140 people who took home $680 million in the year before Enron's bankruptcy, knowing at the time that, apart from everything else, the 21,000 lesser employees' retirement fund had been wiped out.

Equitable Life

Founded in 1762, the same year as Barings Bank, Equitable Life used to share the same reputation for probity. That reputation evaporated in 1999 when the insurance company went to court in an effort to renege on its promises to policyholders. It won a shameful judgement, but lost in the Appeal Court. By December 2000, unable to fulfil its £1.5 billion obligations, or find a buyer who would, it closed to new business.

That was just the tip of an iceberg of scandal revealed during the following decade, and marked by a series of stitch-ups involving the government, the courts and every regulatory body supposed to safeguard innocent consumers. The affair is still unresolved, and though all parties continue to use the euphemistic language of diplomacy and the law, it's a saga of unremitting greed, vicious disregard for responsibility and evasion of the most straightforward truth. Claim has followed counterclaim in the cause of delay. Blame for 'regulatory failure' passes back and forth while newly sensitized financial services authorities alternately support and excoriate schemes to buy out arbitrarily selected groups of policyholders.

A 2008 enquiry found that a million people had lost half their life savings because the government painted 'a wholly misleading picture' of their investment risk. Or someone else did. Meanwhile some 30,000 policyholders have died, waiting. More poignantly, the other few hundred thousand need their money to live in the manner they saved so assiduously to achieve. Currently, Equitable Life presents itself as one of the hapless victims, and is visibly delighted that after so many years and 13 reports, it looks as though the company will not only survive, but won't have to pay a red cent where it is due. Roll on the bonuses!

The 'collapse' of Equitable Life is proving to be as much a humanitarian disaster as a commercial one. It's not as though it presents any moral dilemma.

WHEN:
2001
WHERE:
London, UK
TOLL:
Many thousands of Equitable Life's policyholders have suffered greatly following its collapse and prevarication. Collaterally, the disaster has caused intense scrutiny of aspects of the insurance industry and other financial services; and further legislation is being drawn up to replace the interim, provenly toothless, reforms. Unfortunately, so far they don't include a bill to outlaw the corporate and political abuse of legal nitpicking.
YOU SHOULD KNOW:
In 2008 one of the many reports proposed an independent body to decide how much of the policyholders' losses was caused by maladministration (as distinct from the company's later market collapse). According to *The Independent* 'the Equitable Members Action Group (EMAG) suggests this amounts to £4.65 billion'.

Chairman of Equitable Life Assurance Society Vanni Treves, left, and Chief Executive Charles Thomson during a photo call in London.

Coca-Cola's Dasani water

WHEN:
February to March 2004
WHERE:
UK
TOLL:
Apart from its embarrassment and financial loss in the UK, Coca-Cola faced reviews of its water bottling procedures in many places, including the USA.
YOU SHOULD KNOW:
In the US, Dasani is promoted as 'better than natural' water. Among a series of ads using actors dressed in 'what look like off-off Broadway animal costumes' is one showing a 'camel' to suggest 'natural' means tasting like 'sandy' water; and a 'bear' to suggest 'natural' can mean 'tastes fishy'. What's not clear any more is whether it is the manufacturer or the consumer who is losing the plot.

Five years after its 1999 launch in the USA, Coca-Cola had achieved a marketing miracle with its Dasani bottled water. It was time to 'grow' the brand in Europe. Early in 2004, the company spent £7 million introducing Dasani to the UK as 'pure' bottled water, meaning (as *The Grocer* trade magazine pointed out) water taken from municipal sources, purified according to Coca-Cola's own process, and revived 'for taste purposes' with added mineral salts. It was tap water.

Worse, the 'highly sophisticated purification process' proved to be identical to that used in household-sized domestic water purifiers. Half a litre from the tap cost 0.03p; half a litre of Dasani cost 95p. Underlying economic outrage gave an edge to cackling headlines like 'Eau Dear!', 'Coke's in Hot Water' and 'The Real Sting!'. But Dasani performed well in much of the world, and the company sniffily observed that the UK market for bottled water is 'relatively immature'. If their intention was to 'diss' Britain for failing to subscribe fully to the 'lifestyle choice' of Coke's superior branding, they provoked only more gales of laughter.

Mirth turned to irritation when UK trading standards monitors looked closely at Dasani. Analysis challenged its use of the word 'pure'. It also dropped the bombshell that among Dasani's additives there were illegal levels of bromate, a dangerous carcinogen. There was no bromate at all in the source water. Britain's Food Standards Agency (FSA) announced that 'Any increased cancer risk is likely to be small [but] presents an unnecessary risk'.

Five weeks after its glitzy launch, Coca-Cola withdrew all half a million bottles from circulation, and Dasani abandoned the UK. Coke had suckered itself with a PR disaster.

Bottles of Dasani water on sale at a central London supermarket, March 19 2004

Société Générale trading loss

The world now knows to its cost that the great investment banks lost all sense of disciplined prudence as they greedily grabbed glittering profits in deregulated markets. By developing ever-more sophisticated and complex financial instruments, sharp traders were able to make massive gains for their employers and earn huge cash bonuses themselves. But these flawed practices were a recipe for disaster, leading to the near-collapse of the international banking system in September 2008. For those with eyes to see, events at one of France's most respected banks earlier that year provided a dramatic pointer to the trouble in store.

The Société Générale trading loss is a tangled web that has never been unravelled, but there's no dispute about the bottom line. Over three January days, at a cost of 4.9 billion euros, the bank closed out positions built up over time by a single trader named Jérôme Kervie, in the process losing a staggering sum that would represent a respectable annual budget for many a small country.

According to the bank, Kervie engaged in unauthorized trades totalling around 50 billion euros – thus personally exceeding Société Générale's total market capitalization. Kervie countered by claiming that the bank was aware of his complex wheeling and dealing but turned a blind eye because it was so profitable. He added that others were doing similar business with management's tacit approval. Kervie's story was given credence by the fact that – while he expected a 300,000 euro bonus – he earned it by making a two billion euro profit for the bank and didn't fraudulently divert any funds into his own pocket. In the end, despite the mayhem caused by his actions, Kervie admitted to no more than exceeding his credit limits and faced only minor charges of illegal access to computers and abuse of confidence.

WHEN:
January 21 to January 23 2008
WHERE:
Paris, France
TOLL:
None (though Société Générale's reputation was hardly enhanced).
YOU SHOULD KNOW:
There were international repercussions when Société Générale started the forced sale of Jérôme Kervie's complex positions. The bank's action contributed to a sharp fall in European stock markets, which in turn led to an emergency cut in the US Federal Reserve's inter-bank lending rate. It was the start of a steep and slippery slope leading to the global banking crisis.

Former French trader Jérôme Kervie arriving for a hearing at the financial investigation unit of the Paris courthouse on October 13 2008.

*Bernard Madoff at Manhattan
Federal Court in New York*

Bernie Madoff's
$billion Ponzi scam

It was inevitable that the fallout from the collapse of international banking and the global government bailouts would add the scum of fraud to the froth of scandal, bubbling to the top of the cauldron of financial disaster. Bernie Madoff is the Big One, but there is absolutely nothing heroic about his Slim Shady wheeling and dealing. Madoff was an unsophisticated, low-rent criminal. Running a Ponzi scheme – paying non-existent profits from an ever-widening circle of new investors, and creaming a bit of 'personal' off the top while it's in your hands – is tacky stuff.

Madoff differs from your local flim-flam man only because of the colossal scale on which he eventually operated. The hugely sophisticated methods of concealing both his actions and the money were devised by paid accomplices, as motivated by greed as he was. It's the scale that makes him interesting, and the celebrity world he moved in as a consequence. The combination made a story worthy of Aesop, if the wise old Greek had run a red-top gossip column.

Bernie Madoff's personal take was $65 billion. After decades of deceit, his 150-year prison sentence probably feels like a holiday from it all. Still cushioned by his wealth (via his wife) he can literally relax while officials wrangle over the authorities' failure to stop him. Theirs is a separate catalogue of cowardice prompted by personal and departmental ambition or greed. Many among his victims have remained quiet, too well aware of temptations and misgivings pushed to the back of their well-heeled minds. Across a great divide are the other victims, whose trust was sought and given and betrayed; and others still, employees of crashed businesses and their families, who won't even get their wages, never mind million dollar repayments of all-too-willing investments.

There ought to be something funny about Bernie Madoff. But there isn't.

WHEN:
December 11 2008
WHERE:
New York City, New York, USA
TOLL:
The SEC (Securities & Exchange Commission) is planning far-reaching reforms which will have to pass Congressional and Senate hearings to take effect – but first the squabbling over the spoils and blame has to be resolved. The Madoff scandal will run and run.
YOU SHOULD KNOW:
Zsa Zsa Gabor (Princess and national treasure!) has instructed her lawyers to argue an impertinent IRS (Internal Revenue Service) tax claim for $118,000 on grounds of Bernie Madoff's failure to pay her. If Madoff had ever had that kind of chutzpah, he might never have turned criminal.

Honda F1 withdrawal

From the early 1990s Honda pursued high-profile success in the premier international motor-racing series, supplying engines to established teams in The Formula One World Championship with some success. But the mighty Japanese car maker eventually decided to ditch partnership deals and go solo, forming the British-based Honda team that performed well in 2006, though two disappointing seasons followed.

No matter, for 2009 promised to be a good year. Honda lured a giant of the sport in 2008, appointing Ross Brawn as team principal. The canny Englishman had enjoyed spectacular success with Benetton and Ferrari, and abandoned the lacklustre 2008 Honda car to its lowly fate and threw the team's efforts into developing a competitive car for 2009. But disaster struck.

Despite Brawn's forceful assertion that the new car was a winner, Honda panicked and abandoned Formula One as global recession bit, writing off a billion-pound-plus investment that never quite delivered the glory, headlines and valuable exposure the company so desperately craved. To avoid losing face, Honda offered a trifling parting gift of £100 million that enabled Ross Brawn to effect a management buyout, secure an engine deal with Mercedes-Benz and enter the 2009 F1 World Championship with the renamed Brawn GP team.

The rest is history. Brawn driver Jenson Button won the inaugural Grand Prix in Australia and went on to win five more, hotly pursued by team-mate Rubens Barichello. The Constructors Championship was finally clinched in Brazil, along with Button's Drivers Championship. The reaction in Honda's Tokyo HQ can only be imagined. The ultimate prize pursued at vast expense for a decade and more should have been Honda's for the taking, but the company simply tossed it away – along with international publicity worth hundreds of millions. It was surely one of the worst business blunders of all time.

WHEN:
2008–2009
WHERE:
International
TOLL:
None. Fortunately, *hara kiri* is no longer mandatory in Japan in the event of humiliating failure, so the knives didn't actually come out at Honda.
YOU SHOULD KNOW:
Honda's marketing people may have missed the biggest showboat in history, but shrewd entrepreneur Sir Richard Branson swiftly boarded with a cut-price sponsorship deal that put the Virgin name on fledgling Brawn cars, thus reaping the most handsome of dividends – securing brand exposure worth an estimated £40 million for a fraction of that sum.

Jenson Button testing his successful Brawn GP car in Barcelona, Spain.

MILITARY
DISASTERS

A painting depicting the Battle of Salamis.

Battle of Salamis

When the ancient Persian Empire was at its height the Athenians were constantly fomenting trouble in the eastern Mediterranean. The Emperor Xerxes mustered a massive force of several hundred thousand men and marched into the Balkans, while his fleet of 1,200 ships sailed across the Ionian Sea to the shores of Greece. He looked unstoppable. Meanwhile the Athenians under the brilliant leadership of Themistocles organized an alliance of Greek city-states, nominally led by Sparta but in which Athens played a starring role. Xerxes, having thrashed the Greeks at Thermopylae, confidently marched on Athens. But he found the city deserted.

Themistocles had evacuated the entire city to Salamis, an island 2km (1 mi) off the mainland. Here the Athenian fleet was joined by the rest of the alliance ships, 378 in total. They holed-up in the harbour awaiting the Persian onslaught. The Greek forces were woefully inadequate and many of the allies, dubious about Themistocles's strategy, considered beating a hasty retreat and abandoning the Athenian fleet to its fate. But it was too late – they were hemmed in by the Persians.

What followed was an incredible sea-battle – some 1,500 battleships engaged in mortal combat in the narrow strait between Salamis and the mainland. The confined space worked to the Greek advantage, just as Themistocles had predicted. The Persians, relying on strength of numbers, had rushed into battle without any plan whereas the Greeks, in a last-ditch bid to defend their homeland, kept in formation and were able to pick off Persian ships as their fleet, too tightly packed to manoeuvre freely, descended into chaos. Despite the vast superiority of the Persian forces, the battle ended in a rout. Salamis was the turning point in the Greco-Persian Wars. The mighty Xerxes was humbled and Athens won dominance of the Ionian Sea.

WHEN:
September 480 BC
WHERE:
Mediterranean
DEATH TOLL:
Probably at least 50,000. Many of the Persian forces had been recruited from landlocked regions and couldn't swim: vast numbers died from drowning rather than enemy blows.
YOU SHOULD KNOW:
The battleships used by the Greeks and Persians were all of the same basic design: about 40 m (150 ft) long with three banks of oars rowed by about 150 men and packed with infantry. The boats had a battering ram at their bows and could reach speeds of about 10 knots. A boat could be sunk by ramming a hole in it or captured by hand-to-hand combat. At the Battle of Salamis the Greeks sank or captured some 200 Persian ships and chased the rest of Xerxes's fleet back across the Ionian Sea.

Battle of Lepanto

In the 16th century the expansionist ambition of the Turkish Ottoman Empire was a major threat to the interests of other Mediterranean countries. When the Turks invaded Cyprus, Pope Pius V decided it was a step too far – Catholic Europe was in danger of being overrun by the infidel! He formed the Holy League in alliance with Spain, Venice, Genoa and the Knights of Malta. Overall command was given to Don John of Austria, the King of Spain's half brother. He was an adept commander and he had soon assembled an awesome fleet of 212 ships which included six Venetian galleasses equipped with side-mounted cannons. They set off from Messina in Sicily to confront the Turks in the Gulf of Patras off Lepanto. The Ottoman fleet under Ali Pasha was even larger than that of the Holy League with 286 galleys and galiots (small galleys that used both sails and oars).

Straight away, the Turks made a fatal error of judgment: mistaking two galleasses in the vanguard of the Holy League fleet for supply ships, they immediately attacked. The galleasses responded by blowing eight Turkish galleys out of the water before the battle had even begun. Then, within hours of the opposing fleets engaging, the Turkish flagship was boarded by Spanish forces and, after a desperate hand-to-hand struggle, Ali Pasha was captured and executed on the spot. Seeing their commander's bloodied head staring down at them from the end of a pike on Don John's flagship, the Turks completely lost heart and the battle turned into a rout.

The cost in terms of human life was utterly appalling, especially considering how little effect the Battle of Lepanto had on the balance of power in the region. Any political significance was largely symbolic: the myth of Ottoman invincibility had been destroyed.

WHEN:
October 7 1571
WHERE:
Gulf of Patras, near Lepanto, Greece
DEATH TOLL:
In a battle lasting less than five hours the Turks lost 210 ships with 25,000 dead. Many more thousands were wounded and 3,500 were taken prisoner. The Holy League lost only 15 ships with 7,500 men killed and 16,000 wounded (but at the same time some 10,000 Christian galley slaves were rescued from the Turkish boats).
YOU SHOULD KNOW:
The Turks were still a force to be reckoned with. Even though Lepanto prevented any further western expansionism, the Ottoman Empire had rebuilt its fleet within a year and not only held onto Cyprus but also continued to exert its influence in the Mediterranean.

The Turkish fleet under Ali Pasha was almost completely destroyed by the Holy League under Don John of Austria.

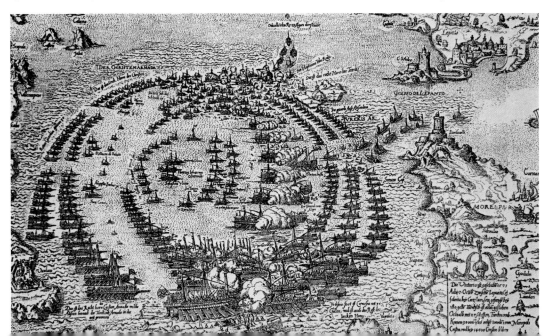

Spanish Armada

WHEN:
July to September 1588
WHERE:
The seas around the British Isles
DEATH TOLL:
An estimated 20,000 Spaniards perished in the Armada. It was said that there was no noble family in Spain that had not lost a son.
YOU SHOULD KNOW:
There is no reliable evidence to support the famous story of Drake's insouciance when told the Armada had been sighted in the English Channel. Playing bowls on Plymouth Hoe, he is supposed to have reacted by insisting on finishing his game.

King Philip II of Spain regarded himself as the principal defender of the Catholic faith in 16th-century Europe. Provoked by England's support, under Protestant Queen Elizabeth, for the Dutch independence struggle against their Spanish overlords, and also by English looting raids on his treasure galleons arriving from the New World, Philip began in 1586 to make plans for an invasion – the so-called 'Enterprise of England' – as much to protect his own dominions as to restore Catholic rule to England. Persisting against the advice of his senior commanders, who always doubted that such an invasion could succeed, the Spanish monarch's resolve was only strengthened the following year when Elizabeth executed her Catholic cousin Mary, Queen of Scots, and Francis Drake brazenly attacked the Spanish fleet at Cadiz.

After numerous delays, the enormous Armada fleet, comprising 122 ships and some 30,000 men, set sail from Lisbon in July 1588. It made its stately way up the English Channel, largely unaffected by the harrying sorties of the smaller English fleet. At the heart of the Spanish plan was a rendezvous off the coast north of Calais with the Duke of Parma's invasion army from Flanders; the ships were to ferry the army across the Channel. It was always an ambitious undertaking and it failed thanks to unfavourable winds and the havoc wrought when Drake sent fireships into the moored Spanish fleet.

Even now the Armada remained a formidable force, but following an inconclusive naval engagement and with supplies running low, the Spanish commander decided to escape into the North Sea and return home by sailing around the British Isles. The weather sealed the Armada's fate. Buffeted by savage storms off the Scottish and Irish coasts, one-third of the Spanish ships foundered on the return voyage and at least 21 were destroyed altogether.

Unmanned British ships with flammables explode among Spanish ships.

Sinking of the *Vasa*

While the Thirty Years War was raging in Europe, King Gustavus Adolphus of Sweden realized he needed a stronger naval presence if he were to retain his dominance in the Baltic. He ordered five heavy-duty warships to be built.

The *Vasa* was to be a mighty vessel – with two gundecks, her broadside would be capable of hurling 267 kg (588 lb) of shot, making her arguably the most powerful warship of the time. But the project became fraught with problems: the King was pressing for quick delivery yet he kept interfering with the plans, endlessly fiddling with measurements and demanding constant modifications; a shortage of money mid project led to more delays; and to cap it all the head shipwright suddenly dropped dead.

At long last the *Vasa* was ready for her maiden voyage. It was a calm day with a light breeze – perfect sailing weather. The gun ports were opened ready to fire a salute. After sailing only 1,130 m (3,700 ft) the sail suddenly billowed and the *Vasa* heeled violently to port. She immediately righted herself, but at the next gust she leant even further and disaster struck – water poured into the open gun ports. The inrush made her heel so far that she collapsed on her side. The pride of the Swedish fleet met her ignominious end a mere 120 m (390 ft) from land in full view of a crowd of thousands.

Gustavus Adolphus was incandescent with rage. The ship's captain was immediately arrested while the shipbuilders and the crew blamed each other. It soon became clear that it was the actual construction at fault. There was nobody to blame: the original contractor was dead and the King himself had personally overseen every single measurement. Everyone else had just obeyed orders.

The salvaged Vasa *in Stockholm*

WHEN:
August 10 1628
WHERE:
Baltic Sea
DEATH TOLL:
Between 30 and 50 crew drowned despite the fact that the *Vasa* was so near the shore.
YOU SHOULD KNOW:
The *Vasa* was eventually salvaged on April 24 1961. When it was measured, calculations proved that it was so unstable it would have heeled over even in a light breeze of four knots. It was top-heavy, weighed down by the second gun-deck and the massive sculptures on the prow with which warships of the period were customarily decorated.

An engraving depicting the Battle of Zenta between the Habsburgs and the Turks.

Battle of Zenta

Just over 300 years ago the Turkish Ottoman Empire was within striking distance of assimilating Europe. But, in one of the defining moments of European history, Ottoman dominance evaporated in a mortifying military defeat. At Zenta in northern Serbia, the 80,000-strong Turkish army was annihilated by the Habsburg forces under the leadership of a brilliant military tactician, Prince Eugene of Savoy.

After Sultan Mustafa II had captured Belgrade, he headed northwards along the River Tisza towards the strategically important Hungarian city of Szeged. It was too late in the year for further campaigning so he decided to cross the Tisza at Zenta to ensconce his troops in Ottoman-held territory for the winter. Meanwhile Prince Eugene, one of Europe's ablest commanders, had hastily mustered an opposing army.

The Sultan, unaware that he was being pursued by Eugene, entrenched his troops and prepared to cross the Tisza. Eugene sneaked up behind him, positioning his heavy artillery in the high ground overlooking the river. He chose his moment carefully: just as the Sultan's own artillery was fording the river, and therefore out of action, he gave the order to start raining shot down from above. At the same time he mounted an assault on the rear flanks of the Turkish army. The Turks found themselves hemmed in between the river and Eugene's army. Mayhem broke out as thousands plunged into the water to escape being slaughtered.

Zenta was arguably the most ignominious defeat ever inflicted on the Turkish Empire. Not only were all the Sultan's arms and treasure captured but he even lost his Imperial state seal and personal harem. The threat of Ottoman hegemony was ended for good; it was Austria's turn for dominance over Europe.

WHEN:
September 11 1697
WHERE:
Zenta (Senta), Hungary (now Serbia)
DEATH TOLL:
The Turks lost some 20,000 men killed in action, while more than 10,000 drowned in the River Tisza. The Habsburg forces suffered only a few hundred casualties.
YOU SHOULD KNOW:
The Battle of Zenta signalled the end of the Austro-Ottoman Great Turkish War of 1683–1699, forcing the Turks into signing the Treaty of Carlowitz, which ceded a large chunk of Hungary, the whole of Croatia and Slovenia, and most of Transylvania – all the territory that the Ottoman Empire had gained in central Europe since 1526 – to Austria.

Battle of the Wabash

In the long and troubled history of the United States' relations with its indigenous population, the Battle of the Wabash in 1791 stands out as the worst defeat ever inflicted on US forces by Native Americans. That it continues to occupy an important place in the nation's psyche is indicated by the alternative name by which the action is still popularly known: St Clair's Defeat. General Arthur St Clair was governor of the Northwest Territory, a volatile region in the years following the formal recognition of American independence in 1783, whose Indian tribes disputed the fledgling nation's territorial claims. In 1791, following an abortive campaign the previous year, President Washington ordered St Clair to mount another expeditionary force to secure the lands northwest of the Ohio River and quell any resistance encountered.

The 2,000-strong force which St Clair led out from Fort Washington (near modern-day Cincinnati) in mid September was undisciplined and poorly equipped; the troops were ill prepared for the cold temperatures of the advancing winter. After establishing two new forts, St Clair made camp on a slight rise above the Wabash River in Ohio. By this time the effects of sickness and low morale (there were many deserters) had reduced his force by over one third. Nevertheless, it still outnumbered the 1,000 or so Native American warriors who launched a dawn raid on St Clair's encampment on November 4. Led by Little Turtle of the Miami tribe and Blue Jacket of the Shawnee, the attack took the troops completely unawares. After two hours' fighting, in which he sustained heavy losses, St Clair ordered a retreat which quickly turned into a rout. News of the defeat shocked the country and the President demanded St Clair's immediate resignation.

WHEN:
November 4 1791
WHERE:
Wabash River, Ohio, USA
DEATH TOLL:
Over 800 US troops and ancillaries were killed, and some 250 wounded. Native American losses numbered fewer than 100.
YOU SHOULD KNOW:
It was another 100 years before American Indian resistance on the continent was effectively brought to an end, by which time the indigenous population had been largely confined to designated reservations.

Lithograph of the defeat of Arthur St Clair's army, depicting uniformed soldiers on horseback in battle with Native American Indians near Fort Wayne, Ohio.

ST. CLAIR'S DEFEAT.

WHEN:
October to December 1812
WHERE:
Russia and Belarus
DEATH TOLL:
Over 400,000 soldiers in Napoleon's
Grande Armée died, the vast majority
from cold and starvation.
YOU SHOULD KNOW:
Kutuzov was an eccentric but wily
old general who had many enemies
at the Russian court. Immortalized by
Tolstoy in *War and Peace*, he was the
same age (67) when appointed
commander-in-chief as Churchill was
when he became British prime
minister in 1940.

Napoleon's retreat from Moscow

In spite of his naval defeat at Trafalgar in 1805, Napoleon Bonaparte remained supreme on land; a series of decisive victories over other European powers, including Russia, gave France unchallenged authority in the succeeding years. The treaty Napoleon signed with Alexander I, Tsar of Russia, at Tilsit in 1807 was thus negotiated very much on the French Emperor's terms, even though ostensibly it committed the two nations to an alliance. Recognizing Russia's weakness, Alexander bought himself time by playing a shrewd diplomatic game over the next few years.

By 1812, Napoleon could no longer overlook Russia's disregard of its treaty obligations. Napoleon's *Grande Armée*, numbering nearly half a million, invaded Russia in June. The Russian army was not only half the strength of the French but did not know at first whether Bonaparte's objective was Moscow or St Petersburg. It adopted a policy of strategic retreat, harrying the invaders and stretching the French supply lines, but refusing to engage in pitched battle. When Marshal Kutuzov took over command, he accepted reluctantly that Russian morale required a

Napoleon Bonaparte at the head of the French army in the retreat from Moscow, 1812.

confrontation; the battle at Borodino resulted in predictably huge Russian losses.

One week later Napoleon entered Moscow and waited there for the peace embassy which he assumed would come from the Tsar. A month passed; with fires breaking out all over the city and his French troops growing hungry and unruly, Napoleon ordered a retreat. Kutuzov shadowed the French on their return west, refusing to engage them in spite of his generals' urgings. He saw no need to fight another battle since Napoleon was leaving anyway; he was content to let Cossack raids deplete the French lines and, as temperatures plummeted, to leave the rest to his greatest ally, 'General Winter'. Less than one-tenth of the once-mighty Grand Army made it back into Poland.

Elphinstone's retreat from Kabul

Throughout the 19th century Russia and Britain were embroiled in their 'great game', vying for supremacy in Central Asia. In 1838 the British initiated the ill-advised First Afghan War and in 1839 installed a puppet regime under Shuja Shah, a Pashtun tribal leader. The British settled confidently into Kabul with a contingent of some 4,500 troops and around 12,000 civilians. Major General William Elphinstone was put in command of the garrison.

But Afghanistan then was as Afghanistan now – 'the graveyard of empires'. The British were harried by constant insurgency, fomented by Pashtun warlord Akbar Khan. In November 1841, after they had murdered a British political officer, tribesmen attacked the British army camp. Belatedly, Elphinstone saw he could not hold Kabul. He agreed to hand over most of his arms to Akbar Khan in return for safe passage so that the garrison could withdraw to Jalalabad 140 km (90 mi) away.

The British column that set off from Kabul on January 6 was ill-prepared for the journey ahead. The way led through snowbound mountains yet Elphinstone made no provision for food or shelter, nor did he think to send out any advance guard. For the next five days, soldiers and civilians alike stumbled through the hostile terrain at the mercy of the elements and marauding tribesmen, dropping down dead from cold or being picked off by bullets. In desperation, Elphinstone handed himself over to Akbar Khan so that the column would be left alone. But on January 12 it was attacked yet again; the following day fewer than 40 men were left to make their last stand at Gandamak, still 56 km (35 mi) from Jalalabad. Medical officer William Brydon reached Jalalabad on January 13, seriously injured. When asked where the army was, he replied 'I am the army'.

WHEN:
January 6–13 1842
WHERE:
On the road between Kabul and Jalalabad, Afghanistan
DEATH TOLL:
The entire British force of 690 British soldiers, 2,840 Indian soldiers and 12,000 camp followers were virtually wiped out, with the exception of a few prisoners. It is not known how many Afghan tribesmen died.
YOU SHOULD KNOW:
The retreat from Kabul was the most humiliating defeat in the history of the British Empire. The prestige of the British in the East was permanently undermined by Elphinstone's incompetent command. The First Afghan War provided a clear lesson that it is easy to invade Afghanistan, but the country cannot be held for long without the full co-operation of the inhabitants.

An illustration of the Charge of the Light Brigade when 600 horsemen were ordered to charge by Lord Raglan during the Crimean War in 1854.

Charge of the Light Brigade

In one of warfare's great ironies the Crimean War of 1854–1856 is remembered chiefly for one act of pointless heroism which was of marginal relevance to the military outcomes. Thanks to the verses penned by Victorian England's favourite poet, Alfred Lord Tennyson, the ill-fated charge of the Light Brigade at the battle of Balaclava has come to represent the very essence of British valour and derring-do.

British forces under the overall command of Lord Raglan had taken up positions on the heights above the small harbour of Balaclava in southern Russia. On October 25 the Russians launched a surprise assault but were repulsed first by the British infantry and then by the cavalry squadrons of the Heavy Brigade, in spite of the Russians' markedly superior numbers.

At this point the now legendary incompetence of the generals took over, resulting in one of the great botched orders in military history. Observing the Russian retreat from a somewhat removed position, Raglan sent his adjutant with written orders to the cavalry commander, Lord Lucan, 'to advance rapidly to the front' and 'to prevent the enemy carrying away the guns'. The guns in question were Turkish outposts on the heights flanking the valley on the east, which the Russians had just captured; from his lower vantage point, however, Lucan was unable to see these and assumed the order must refer to enemy artillery further down the valley.

Although he understood the futility of such an assault, Lucan reluctantly ordered his brother-in-law, Lord Cardigan, to lead his Light Brigade forward. In the ensuing charge into 'the valley of Death' they were sitting targets in the cross-fire from the surrounding hills and from the Russian guns ahead.

WHEN:
October 25 1854
WHERE:
Balaclava, Crimean peninsula, Russia
DEATH TOLL:
113 cavalrymen of the 673-strong Light Brigade were killed, and 134 wounded. Most of the horses died or had to be destroyed.
YOU SHOULD KNOW:
When Raglan's adjutant saw the disastrous course on which the Light Brigade was set, he tried to divert the charge by galloping across the front of the advancing horses and gesturing frantically with his sword; to no avail because he was shot down before anyone could take heed of his warning.

American Civil War

The young nation that was the United States of America grew vigorously in the decades following independence; but beneath the confidence and optimism a canker festered in the body politic. The affirmations of the founding fathers that everyone had a right to 'life, liberty and the pursuit of happiness' rang hollow for the underclass of black slaves on which much of American society was constructed. Whereas the more affluent, enlightened farmers and industrialists of the North forswore slavery and advocated its abolition, the conservative states of the South, where slave-owning had become a key element of the cotton-growing economy, were fiercely resistant to any challenges to the *status quo*. Conflict was almost inevitable, especially after Abraham Lincoln was elected president in 1860 from the newly formed (and anti-slavery) Republican Party.

In 1861 11 Southern states, led by South Carolina, seceded from the Union and formed a breakaway government known as the Confederacy. The four-year civil war that followed saw the bitterest and most bloody fighting ever to take place on American soil. That the war lasted as long as it did, given the overwhelming superiority of the Union in both manpower and resources, was due to the more skilful leadership displayed by the Confederate generals in its early years. The turning point came in July 1863 when the North struck two decisive blows: taking control of the Mississippi River, they effectively split the Southern forces in two; and, in the defining battle of the war, at Gettysburg, Pennsylvania, the Union army halted the Confederacy's advance north, though not without heavy casualties on both sides. When the Confederacy capital, Richmond, Virginia, fell to the North in early April 1865 the final surrender soon followed, bringing to an end a devastating conflict which has left deep and lasting incisions in the American psyche.

WHEN:
1861–1865
WHERE:
USA, especially the Deep South
DEATH TOLL:
Some 620,000 Americans died in the Civil War, of which 200,000, or one third, were killed in action; the remainder died from various diseases.
YOU SHOULD KNOW:
The trauma of the Civil War may live on, but so do the many legends it gave birth to, with the names of generals such as Ulysses Grant (later US president) and William Sherman (Union), and Robert E Lee and Thomas 'Stonewall' Jackson (Confederacy), preserved for ever in the nation's memory.

Colour lithograph showing the Battle of Gettysburg

Battle of the Little Big Horn

WHEN:
June 25 1876
WHERE:
Little Big Horn River, Montana, USA
DEATH TOLL:
It is generally agreed that Custer and his entire detachment of 264 soldiers were killed at the Little Big Horn. Native American casualties are unknown, with estimates varying between 45 and 200.
YOU SHOULD KNOW:
The alternative name by which the battle is known, Custer's Last Stand, says it all about the place it has come to occupy in American mythology. A more truthful and authoritative assessment was given by President Grant, himself a famous Civil War general: 'I regard Custer's massacre as a sacrifice of troops, brought on by Custer himself, that was wholly unnecessary.'

After Custer's Last Charge
by Feodor Fuchs

The protracted conflict known to US history as the Indian wars was due to the vigorous resistance of Native American tribes of the Great Plains to the remorseless expansion westwards of white settlers. The Sioux were one of the largest such tribes, with vast homelands that included the sacred Black Hills of Dakota. When an 1874 expedition into the Hills led by George Custer himself gave rise to tales of gold strikes, the resulting influx of prospectors and settlements inflamed the Sioux who refused a government offer to buy their lands.

When the Commissioner of Indian Affairs ordered all Sioux bands to enter designated reservations early in 1876, Sitting Bull and Crazy Horse, Chiefs of the Lakota Sioux, refused to leave their traditional hunting grounds. During a ritual sun dance Sitting Bull had a vision of white soldiers falling out of the sky. Seeing this as a presage of victory, a force of 1,000 Sioux and Cheyenne warriors fought a fierce but inconclusive battle against US troops.

Shortly afterwards General Custer, now at the head of the Seventh Cavalry, was sent to locate the villages of the tribes involved. On June 25 he came across a large encampment by the banks of the Little Big Horn River in eastern Montana. Fatally underestimating the Native American numbers, Custer, who had developed a reputation for both flamboyant bravery and a decidedly cavalier attitude to the lives of the men under his command, resolved to attack the camp immediately, without waiting for the main army. Custer divided his cavalry forces in order to launch attacks from three different directions. Soon realizing they were outnumbered, two groups retreated over the river; Custer, however, remained on the east bank where his small force was surrounded and ruthlessly cut down by some 4,000 warriors.

Battle of Isandlwana

In 1874 Sir Henry Bartle Frere was appointed High Commissioner of South Africa and sent to unify the country as a British dominion. There were two stumbling blocks – the Boer-controlled South African Republic and the Kingdom of Zululand. In 1879 Frere tackled the latter. He issued an impossible ultimatum to the Zulu King Cetshwayo, before sending troops under Lord Chelmsford to invade Zululand. Cetshwayo understood that fighting back would harden British public opinion and make ultimate defeat inevitable, but was left with no choice and assembled 24,000 warriors.

Victorian Britain's army was a steely fighting force that bestrode the globe and policed the mighty British Empire. Conventional wisdom suggested a relatively small number of trained troops with modern weapons could outmatch any native army, whatever the numerical imbalance. Chelmsford split his main column without a second thought and sallied forth with 2,500 men to find the Zulu *impi* (fighting force). Around 1,300 – a mixture of European and African troops – were left behind. Secure in the knowledge that they had artillery and were armed with breech-loading Martini-Henry rifles, the remaining Brits took no special defensive measures – a disastrous decision.

A reconnaissance party from the reserve encampment near Isandlwana discovered the main Zulu force who, armed with cowhide shields, spears and elderly muskets, fell on the disorganized British troops on the morning of January 22. The defenders fought hard, but by mid afternoon were overwhelmed. Everyone wearing a red coat was slaughtered in final hand-to-hand combat, and the vaunted British army had suffered its worst-ever defeat at the hands of indigenous fighters. But King Cetshwayo's worst fears were soon realized. Having learned the hard way never to underestimate Zulu tactical awareness and fighting prowess, Chelmsford summoned reinforcements and his second campaign resulted in defeat for the Zulus, though not before a further series of bloody engagements was fought.

WHEN:
January 22 1879
WHERE:
Isandlwana Hill, now in KwaZulu-Natal Province, South Africa
DEATH TOLL:
Around 2,300 combatants (1,300 British and African troops, 1,000 Zulu warriors). The Zulus spared black-coated civilians.
YOU SHOULD KNOW:
Immediately following the battle over 4,000 Zulu warriors attacked the fortified mission station at nearby Rorke's Drift on the Buffalo River, defended by just 139 British soldiers. In a determined defence, the tiny garrison repulsed the Zulu assault and inflicted hundreds of casualties, thus salving wounded British army pride and earning 11 Victoria Crosses.

Lieutenants Melvill and Coghill (24th Regiment) dying to save the Queen's colours on January 22 1879.

Khartoum and the death of General Gordon

One of the iconic images of the glory days of British Empire shows a tall, stiff-backed soldier standing defiant at the top of stairs against an advancing horde of turbaned natives brandishing spears. Joy's painting of *General Gordon's Last Stand*, which now hangs in Leeds City Art Gallery, immortalizes the death of one of 19th-century Britain's greatest soldiers and administrators. Impressive as George Gordon's resistance undoubtedly was, the image is, however, a piece of Victorian myth-making designed to reflect the public mood. The reality, as so often, was grimmer and altogether more brutal.

The Sudan region of northeast Africa had been under the joint control of Britain and Egypt for most of the 19th century. When a Muslim radical named Muhammad Ahmad led a savage uprising in 1881 against colonial rule, he soon prevailed and established an independent Islamic state over a large area of the Upper Nile. Although Khartoum, the capital, remained under colonial control, Gladstone, the British prime minister, had no appetite for further imperial expansion, so in February 1884 he sent General George Gordon, a career soldier who had distinguished himself in the Crimea and in China, to the Sudan to oversee the evacuation of Khartoum and the withdrawal of Anglo-Egyptian forces down the Nile to Cairo. Within weeks of arrival Gordon found himself under siege by the forces of the 'Mahdi', as the rebel leader came to be known.

Gladstone initially resisted the strong public calls for action, including from the Queen herself. When a relief force did finally leave Cairo in September 1884 to go to Gordon's assistance, it was hampered by complacent and incompetent leadership. An advance detachment eventually reached Khartoum on January 28 1885, two days after the town had fallen to the Mahdi and Gordon and his entire garrison had been slaughtered.

General Gordon's Last Stand *by George William Joy*

WHEN:
January 26 1885
WHERE:
Khartoum, Sudan
DEATH TOLL:
General Gordon and his entire garrison of 7,000 troops were killed, as well as an estimated 4,000 civilian inhabitants. Losses on the Mahdist side are unknown.
YOU SHOULD KNOW:
The exact circumstances of Gordon's death may never be known. It is possible that he was not killed along with his troops, but captured and then executed in the Mahdi's camp. What is certain is that his head was afterwards paraded through the streets on the end of a pike.

HMS *Victoria* collision

In the late 19th century Britannia did indeed rule the waves, having enjoyed supremacy since the Battle of Trafalgar. The British navy was well equipped with new ironclads, including HMS *Camperdown*, a battleship commissioned in 1889 and posted to warmer climes as the flagship of Britain's powerful Mediterranean Fleet.

Once there, she swapped crews with HMS *Victoria*, which became the flagship of fleet commander Vice-Admiral Sir George Tryon. He was a martinet who believed constant exercises were the key to efficiency, priding himself on an ability to direct complex ship movements. In June 1893 he decided to try a new manoeuvre. Two parallel columns of ships would perform inward U-turns that reversed the direction of travel before anchoring. Tryon miscalculated the distance between columns required to execute his plan but brusquely rebuffed queries.

Tryon's deputy – Rear-Admiral Markham, aboard *Camperdown* – commanded the second column and appreciated that the manoeuvre was dangerous. He failed to acknowledge Tryon's 'turn' signal but when his superior publicly humiliated him by sending a follow-up 'what are you waiting for?' gave the order anyway. As *Victoria* and *Camperdown* inexorably converged, both ships' captains expected Tryon to give one of his last-minute-change-of-plan orders designed to keep everyone on their toes. He didn't.

Moments before impact Tryon shouted across to Markham on *Camperdown*'s bridge 'go astern, go astern'. It was too late. *Camperdown*'s ram smashed through *Victoria*'s starboard side. Even then, the accident could have been prevented from turning into disaster had it not been for Tryon's last order to Markham. With screws reversed *Camperdown* backed off, allowing water to flood through *Victoria*'s gaping wound before watertight doors could be closed. Just 13 minutes later *Victoria* capsized, precipitating her crew into a vicious whirlpool of deadly debris where half would die. Perhaps wisely, Tryon elected to go down with his ship.

WHEN:
June 22 1893
WHERE:
Mediterranean Sea off Tripoli
(then Syria, now Lebanon),
DEATH TOLL:
358 of *Victoria*'s crew died, 357 survived. There were no casualties aboard *Camperdown* though she, too, nearly sank.
YOU SHOULD KNOW:
Second in command of *Victoria* was Commander John Jellicoe, who survived the disaster and went on to command the British Grand Fleet at the Battle of Jutland in 1916, the largest naval battle of World War I and the only one to feature a major clash of battleships.

British naval ship HMS Victoria *colliding with HMS* Camperdown.

Sinking of the *Lusitania*

WHEN:
May 7 1915
WHERE:
Off the coast at Kinsale,
County Cork, Ireland
DEATH TOLL:
1,198 people died when the *Lusitania*
sank, including 291 women and 94
children. There were 761 survivors.
YOU SHOULD KNOW:
Although the Germans claimed that
the liner had been a legitimate target
because it had been covertly carrying
munitions for the war effort, this was
denied by the Allies and there was
widespread condemnation of the
German action on both sides of the
Atlantic. The tragedy undoubtedly
contributed to the USA's decision to
enter World War I in April 1917.

The Lusitania *leaving on
her last voyage.*

When the Cunard company launched its latest passenger liner at
Clydebank in Scotland on June 7 1906, RMS *Lusitania* was the last
word in luxury maritime travel. The first British civilian ship to be built
with four funnels, the *Lucy*, as she was affectionately known, had also
been designed with the power and speed to win back for Britain the
Blue Riband for the fastest trans-Atlantic crossing. The ship duly did so
on only its second voyage, in October 1907, sharing the record with its
sister ship the *Mauretania* for the next 22 years.

When war broke out between Britain and Germany in August 1914
the Admiralty did not requisition the *Lusitania* for military use and
the liner continued to ply the Atlantic in monthly crossings to North
America. It left New York on its fateful final journey on May 1 1915,
with a full complement of almost 2,000, the paying passengers on board
undeterred by German warnings issued in the American press shortly
beforehand that anyone travelling on Allied ships in the European war
zone did so at their own risk.

The voyage passed without incident until, on May 7, the ship was in
sight of the southern Irish coast. The threat of German submarines had
made the coastal waters around the British Isles especially perilous, so
the captain doubled the look-outs and maintained high steam pressure
as the *Lusitania* approached Queenstown (modern-day Cobh in
County Cork). Unfortunately, they had been sighted by a German
U-boat; the torpedo it fired struck the *Lusitania* on the starboard
side. A second explosion followed, generally thought now to have
been one of the ship's boilers exploding, and the great vessel sank in
just 20 minutes.

Gallipoli landings

Even in a conflict characterized by poor strategic leadership, the Gallipoli Campaign of 1915 was one of the more shamefully chaotic episodes of World War I. Turkey had entered the war as Germany's ally, prompting Winston Churchill, then First Lord of the Admiralty, to formulate a plan to attack the Dardanelles, the narrow straits in Turkey controlling maritime access to Constantinople (Istanbul) and the Black Sea. Churchill hoped that opening another theatre of war would relieve the stalemate on Europe's Western Front.

When an Allied naval operation in the area proved inconclusive, plans were hastily drawn up for a supporting military campaign involving landings on the Gallipoli Peninsula. The campaign depended for any chance of success on the element of surprise, but in the event the Turks had long since been tipped off and knew about an imminent assault. Moreover, the determined resistance they put up was a factor consistently underestimated by the Allied commanders.

The landings began on April 25 1915. Of the three separate beachheads attempted, one comprised a force of 16,000 soldiers from Australia and New Zealand – the Anzacs: volunteers, mostly, who had signed up with patriotic fervour at the outbreak of war to help defend the mother country but whose long sea passage to Europe had been diverted by Churchill. Their dawn landing in a small bay flanked by steep cliffs was met with ferocious shelling from the Turkish gun emplacements above; by nightfall over 2,000 Anzacs lay dead.

The initial landings having been repulsed, the Allied forces had no choice but to dig in for a sustained campaign. They failed, however, to establish any effective foothold on the peninsula, and after a second seaborne assault in August failed, the order was sent from London for a wholesale evacuation of Gallipoli in December 1915 and January 1916.

Troops landing at Anzac Cove in the Dardanelles during the battle between Allied forces and Turkish forces at the Gallipoli Peninsula.

WHEN:
April 1915 to January 1916
WHERE:
Gallipoli Peninsula, Turkey
DEATH TOLL:
More than 60,000 Allied troops died in Gallipoli, with an estimated 120,000 wounded. Of these deaths, over 11,000 were Anzacs – over half the contingent that had sailed from Australia. The Turks lost 66,000 men and 140,000 were wounded.
YOU SHOULD KNOW:
The battle for Gallipoli has been elevated in Australian history to the status of a national legend and a decisive factor in shaping Australian identity. Anzac Day on April 25 is a public holiday in Australia and New Zealand, marked each year with parades and commemorations.

Battle of the Somme

Can there ever have been a greater military disaster than the Battle of the Somme? It seems unlikely. One side's disaster is often the other side's triumph, but this fearful encounter on the Western Front was a catastrophe for Allied and German troops alike. It was World War I's most infamous battle – a prolonged engagement lasting for nearly five months that claimed over 1,100,000 lives with over 60,000 falling on the first day, July 1 1916.

British troops going over the top during the Battle of the Somme.

WHEN:
July to November 1916
WHERE:
On both banks of the River Somme, northern France
DEATH TOLL:
Around 1,120,000 casualties were recorded during the battle (500,000 German, 420,000 British and 200,000 French). In addition, countless combatants were seriously wounded.
YOU SHOULD KNOW:
As an indication of how outmoded British military thinking was in 1916, a key element of the General Staff's plan for the Battle of the Somme involved unleashing a regiment of cavalry to charge through the hole that was supposed to be punched in the German lines by advancing infantry. It never happened. The tactic had worked well in the English Civil War over 250 years before but was ludicrously inappropriate for 20th-century trench warfare.

The battle ostensibly took place to relieve German pressure on Verdun, where French defenders had been taking heavy casualties. But in reality both British and French governments were under intense pressure to deliver military achievements. Despite serious reservations expressed by the head of the French army, General Foch – backed by senior British commanders – political pressure ensured that the view of Britain's commander-in-chief prevailed. Field Marshal Douglas Haig believed grinding attrition – whatever the cost – was the way to weaken and beat the Germans.

He also wrongly believed that artillery would destroy enemy defences. Over 1,700,000 shells were fired on the eve of battle, but the Germans retreated to deep dugouts and popped up when the barrage stopped, ready and able to repel the Allied advance. This came on a 40 km (25 mi) front and marked the start of a bloody stalemate. When the Battle of the Somme finally ended in November, the Allies were able to claim pyrrhic victory. They had gained a strip of ground 48 km (30mi) wide and 11 km (7 mi) across at its deepest point.

If ever a single event epitomized the tragic futility of the trench warfare for which the Western Front became notorious, it was the Battle of the Somme. This one inconclusive encounter made a major contribution to the war's overall casualty figure of 15,000,000 dead.

Sinking of HMS *Royal Oak*

The Royal Navy's HMS *Royal Oak* was a Revenge-class battleship that saw action in World War I. But by 1939 *Royal Oak* was too cumbersome to engage in the new sort of flexible naval warfare that would no longer involve mighty battleships pounding each other in set-piece battles. Six weeks into World War II she lay in Scapa Flow, Britain's great naval base in the Orkneys. It wasn't a safe harbour. German submarine commander Karl Dönitz was planning a daring raid that would exact revenge for the humiliating scuttling of the German fleet in Scapa Flow in 1918, and also weaken Britain's ability to protect Atlantic convoys.

His chosen weapon was U-47, commanded by Günther Prien. On the moonless night of October 13 the submarine brazenly entered Scapa Flow on the surface, only to find the anchorage almost empty. Prudently, much of the fleet had been dispersed, though *Royal Oak* and a few others remained. At 00.58 U-47 fired a salvo of torpedoes at the unsuspecting battleship. One struck her bow six minutes later, causing the startled crew to think there had been an on-board explosion. Prien fired again, using his stern tube, and missed. But a second salvo from the bow tubes struck home, wreaking havoc. A fireball engulfed *Royal Oak*'s interior and she rolled onto her side before sinking at 01.29, just 13 minutes after the second attack. Over 800 crew members perished on the stricken ship and in Scapa Flow's icy waters.

The loss of *Royal Oak* had a seriously negative effect on morale, but at least the ease with which U-47 slipped in and out of Britain's main naval base and sank a capital ship ensured that home sea defences were immediately tightened, making any repeat of the disaster much less likely.

WHEN:
October 14 1939
WHERE:
Scapa Flow, Orkney Islands, Scotland, UK
DEATH TOLL:
833 from the ship's complement of 1,234 perished
YOU SHOULD KNOW:
Today, *Royal Oak*'s upturned hull lies just 5 m (16 ft) below the surface of Scapa Flow. The wreck is a designated war grave that may not be visited by divers, save those from the Royal Navy who go down each year on the anniversary of the sinking to place a White Ensign at her stern.

HMS Royal Oak *off Southend, Essex, in 1919*

Battle of France

WHEN:
May 10 to June 25 1940
WHERE:
Northern France
DEATH TOLL:
Approximate casualty figures in the Battle of France were 170,000 Allied and 49,000 German dead.
YOU SHOULD KNOW:
Hitler later suggested that he allowed the BEF to escape from Dunkirk as a gesture of goodwill, in the hope that Britain would appreciate his merciful gesture and be encouraged to enter into a negotiated peace settlement. But the facts don't support this claim – the German army's *Directive 13* issued on May 24 called for the total annihilation of all forces within the Dunkirk pocket.

The so-called phoney war ended in May 1940 when the Battle of France began. It would end in disastrous defeat for the Allies. In phase one of the battle, *Fall Gelb* (Operation Yellow), the *Wehrmacht*'s rapid advance outwitted Allied Forces defending Belgium in anticipation of Germany repeating its World War I attack plan. This time Germans poured through the Ardennes Forest (a feat thought impossible by Allied strategists) and outflanked the defences.

After fierce fighting, the British Expeditionary Force (BEF) – along with many French soldiers – was driven back to the sea and mounted a defiant last stand. This – and Hitler's decision to hold back his generals for three days and leave the task of preventing the BEF's escape to the *Luftwaffe* – allowed Britain to organize Operation Dynamo. The dramatic evacuation of 338,000 mainly British troops from the beaches of Dunkirk by the Royal Navy and the famously gallant flotilla of small boats took place between May 27 and June 4.

Having mopped up resistance in the northwest, the Germans began phase two of the battle on June 5. *Fall Rot* (Operation Red) involved outflanking France's vaunted (but ultimately useless) defensive Maginot Line, smashing through demoralized defenders and heading through the French heartland towards Paris. The government fled to Bordeaux and Paris fell on June 14. Newly elected French leader Marshal Pétain sued for peace and an armistice was signed on June 25. The Battle of France was over, barely six weeks after it began.

If there was a glint of silver in the Allies' dark cloud, it was Dunkirk, where the soundly trounced BEF turned the tables by slipping away before the *Wehrmacht*'s steel jaws snapped shut, living to fight another day . . . a great escape that probably prevented Germany from winning World War II in 1940.

British prisoners of war captured at Dunkirk, France, in June 1940

Operation Barbarossa

If there was one thing at which Germany's well-trained and disciplined *Wehrmacht* excelled, it was *Blitzkrieg* (lightning war). This was modern warfare at its most shock-and-awesome, involving air supremacy and the rapid advance of powerful tank columns supported by mechanized infantry. And it was *Blitzkrieg* that Hitler relied on when he ripped up his pact with Stalin. It had suited the two dictators to carve up Eastern Europe between them in 1939, but uneasy peace between two diametrically opposed ideologies was never going to last.

German forces invaded Soviet territory in June 1941 in a pre-emptive strike codenamed Operation Barbarossa. The prolonged conflict that followed would become the largest military offensive and most lethal battle in world history. Despite occupying huge swathes of the Soviet Union, including key economic areas like oil-producing Ukraine, Operation Barbarossa would prove disastrous. German troops got to within just 16 km (10 mi) of Moscow in December 1941 before revitalized defenders – aided by the onset of harsh winter – held them off in the desperate Battle of Moscow. It was the turning point.

As with Napoleon before him, Hitler's ambition to slay the Russian Bear had been thwarted by the iron hand of winter. From the Christmas of 1941, the *Wehrmacht* would be driven back inexorably in a long and bloody fight that included terrible episodes like failure of the prolonged siege of Leningrad and catastrophic defeat in the battle of Stalingrad. Along the way, millions of lives would be lost on both sides. The final drama was eventually played out when rampaging Russian troops entered Berlin in April 1945. If the self-delusional Adolf Hitler still refused to accept that his decision to mount Operation Barbarossa had led directly to Germany's defeat in World War II, he must surely have known it then.

WHEN:
From June 22 1941
WHERE:
Western Soviet Union
DEATH TOLL:
Uncountable. War on the Eastern Front is estimated to have cost Soviet forces 7,000,000 casualties, while Axis powers lost 4,200,000 troops. Civilian deaths are thought to have reached 20,000,000.
YOU SHOULD KNOW:
Stalin can have been under no illusion about Adolf Hitler's intentions. Hitler's views on the Soviet Union were made clear in *Mein Kampf* (*My Struggle*), published in 1925, wherein the future Führer promised to invade vast lands to the east to provide the Aryan German master race with *Lebensraum* (living space), simultaneously subjugating 'lesser' Slav peoples.

German Wehrmacht *infantrymen of Army Group North crossing a pontoon bridge over the Niemen near Vilkija, northwest of Kowno.*

Pearl Harbor

World War II had been taking its grim course for two years without the involvement of the world's richest and most powerful nation, the United States of America. All that changed on the morning of December 7 1941 when Japanese aircraft launched a surprise attack on the US naval base at Pearl Harbor, Hawaii. The attack was as devastating as it was unexpected; in two separate strikes over 350 Japanese fighters and bombers unleashed their deadly cargo on the pride of America's Pacific fleet, sinking five battleships and damaging 15 others. During the two-hour attack 188 US aircraft were destroyed; Japan lost just 29 planes. Never imagining such a brazen act of aggression, the Americans had moored their ships in lines, making them even easier targets for the bombers.

Although the standard American portrayal of Pearl Harbor is that of an unprovoked attack that came quite literally out of the blue, Japanese resentment over US economic power in the Pacific and its own dependence on imported natural resources had been festering for some time. In pursuing its expansionist policies in Southeast Asia, Japan may have achieved its short-term objective of disabling the US fleet and thus buying vital time to conquer prized targets in the region such as the Philippines, Malaya and Burma; but the assault on Pearl Harbor failed spectacularly in the long term, for, far from forcing the USA to abandon its presence in the Pacific or indeed to sue for peace, it served to galvanize the previously reluctant nation.

The very next day President Roosevelt declared war on Japan, prompting Germany in its turn to declare war on the USA, achieving finally what Churchill had been praying for since 1939: America's entry into the European conflict on Britain's side.

Sailors scrambling to escape the sinking battleship USS California *after the surprise attack by the Japanese.*

WHEN:
December 7 1941
WHERE:
Pearl Harbor, Oahu,
Hawaiian Islands (USA)
DEATH TOLL:
2,402 Americans were killed in the attack, including 1,177 on the USS *Arizona* alone when it was blown up and sunk. Japanese losses were 64.
YOU SHOULD KNOW:
There has been much debate over the failure of US intelligence to gain advance warning of the Japanese plan. It seems particularly strange that no one detected a 30-strong fleet which spent 11 days travelling 6,500 km (4,000 mi) across the Pacific.

Fall of Singapore

It's said that pride comes before a fall, and the efficiency with which Japanese forces overwhelmed 'impregnable' Singapore in February 1942 certainly dealt a crushing blow to British military pride. The island fortress off Malaya's tip was nicknamed 'Gibraltar of the East' and served as a vital power base from which British tentacles uncoiled into Southeast Asia.

Japanese forces invaded Malaya in December 1941 – a move co-ordinated with the attack on the US Navy at Pearl Harbor. Numerically superior British and Indian army battalions hurried north, even as a sustained campaign of air raids on Singapore began. But their opponents were battle-hardened veterans and, when the Japanese gained air superiority, disastrous defeat was assured.

The catastrophe began unfolding when – two days after the invasion – the British capital ships HMS *Prince of Wales* and HMS *Repulse* were sunk by torpedo bombers while attempting to shell Japanese landing sites. Light tanks and bicycle infantry allowed invading troops to make a swift advance, arriving at the gates of Singapore on January 31 1942. British sappers blew up the causeway linking Singapore to the mainland, but merely postponed the inevitable.

An intense air and artillery bombardment began and on February 8 a Japanese assault hit Sarimbun beach in the northwest. Once the last of Singapore's Hawker Hurricane fighter aircraft were neutralized, further tank landings soon outflanked defenders who were driven back into a small pocket in the southeast. Despite Winston Churchill's rousing 'fight to the last man' instruction, surrender seemed the only option. On January 15 the Japanese Rising Sun flag was hoisted atop the Cathay Building, Singapore's tallest, and what Churchill bitterly called 'the largest capitulation in British history' was complete. His anger was righteous. The Japanese commander later admitted that he would have lost the battle had the British fought on.

WHEN:
February 15 1942
WHERE:
Singapore
DEATH TOLL:
During the Malayan campaign Allied forces suffered 50,000 casualties (with 130,000 taken prisoner). The Japanese lost 9,600 men.
YOU SHOULD KNOW:
The supremely complacent British attitude before the crushing defeat at Singapore could be judged by gung-ho talk among young army officers who repeatedly expressed disappointment that potential attackers would be frightened off by Singapore's impressive defences, thereby denying the Brits a sure-fire opportunity to inflict a huge defeat on 'inferior' Japanese forces.

Triumphant Japanese troops, hoisting their flag over Singapore after the British surrender.

Dieppe raid

WHEN:
August 19 1942
WHERE:
Dieppe, Seine-Maritime, France
DEATH TOLL:
Precise figures are not known, but around 1,000 Allied soldiers were killed (mainly Canadians), plus some 550 Royal Navy personnel. German losses were in the low hundreds.
YOU SHOULD KNOW:
The only Allied success during the Dieppe raid was the copybook attack by the British army's No. 4 Commando under Simon Fraser, 15th Lord Lovat. The well-trained commandos stormed ashore on Orange Beach and destroyed their target – a German coastal battery on the right flank of the main landing – before returning safely to England having suffered only minor casualties.

Soon after the evacuation from Dunkirk in 1940, Combined Operations Headquarters was set up to harass the all-conquering Germans by any means possible. Combined Ops was taken over by Lord Louis Mountbatten in 1941 and a major success was achieved in March 1942 when a British seaborne assault on St Nazaire put the strategically important dry dock out of action. Thus emboldened, a further attack on the French coast was planned. Operation Rutter would evaluate the possibility of capturing and briefly holding a port, also testing invasion techniques, destroying valuable equipment and gaining useful intelligence from captured Germans. This time the target would be the port of Dieppe.

Unfortunately, on the very day of departure – July 5 1942 – German bombers attacked the assembled fleet and Operation Rutter was aborted. Undeterred, Mountbatten revived and modified the plan as Operation Jubilee. It was an ill-starred initiative, as the Dieppe raid would turn out to be a major military reverse. On August 19 around 6,000 Canadian infantrymen went ashore from landing craft on the town beach, supported by new Churchill tanks, even as flanking British commandos and US army rangers attacked gun batteries on the headlands. Overhead, Allied fighter aircraft waited to pounce when the *Luftwaffe* was drawn into the fray.

The attack went in at 05.00 and was dogged by bad luck, poor planning and lack of communication. By 09.00 it was all over and Allied forces retreated, confirming the painful World War I adage that it's easier (and safer) to defend than attack. The Royal Navy's bombardment had been ineffectual, 119 Allied aircraft were shot down (against 46 *Luftwaffe* planes), the 58 Churchill tanks couldn't get off the beach and half were lost. Casualties were heavy and the Dieppe raid went down in history as a disastrous debacle.

With a burning LST in the background and a disabled tank next to them, two wounded Canadian soldiers await medical assistance, during failed Allied landing operations.

Battle of Arnhem

In the months following D-Day in June 1944 the success of the Allies in driving Germany out of France and Belgium made them increasingly confident the war could be brought to a swift conclusion, perhaps by the end of the year even. With Allied forces now close to the Dutch border the British commander, General Montgomery, came up with an audacious plan. Montgomery believed that a powerful, narrow thrust deep into the German lines would be more effective than an advance on a broad front.

The plan, code-named Operation Market Garden, would involve the largest airborne offensive in the history of warfare, with around 35,000 men being parachuted behind enemy lines. The key objective was to capture a number of strategic bridges spanning the waterways on the Dutch/German border, thus opening the way for a rapid assault on the Ruhr, Germany's industrial heartland.

On September 17 in clear blue skies some 1,500 aircraft and 500 gliders dropped the first wave of 10,300 paratroopers of the British 1st Airborne Division close to the town of Arnhem in occupied Holland. Hopes were high, but the operation had already been compromised by a lack of planes which meant three separate lifts would be needed to transport the entire force. Once the paratroopers had captured the bridges they would be relieved by more heavily armed ground forces advancing north from Belgium.

Some bridgeheads were indeed established, but German resistance was stiffer and better organized than expected. Only one parachute battalion reached the ultimate objective, the bridge over the Rhine at Arnhem. Vastly outnumbered and outgunned, the 700 British soldiers held the bridge's northern end for four heroic days waiting for the relief force to arrive before being overrun. The Germans recaptured the bridge and Operation Market Garden had failed.

WHEN:
September 17–26 1944
WHERE:
Arnhem, Netherlands
DEATH TOLL:
1,300 men of the 1st Airborne Division were killed at Arnhem and over 6,400 captured. Only 2,400 British and Polish paratroopers – less than a quarter of the original landing force – were rescued when the area was evacuated by the Allies and the operation abandoned. German losses are estimated to have been at least 1,500.
YOU SHOULD KNOW:
The 1st Airborne Division was so badly hit by casualties at Arnhem that it ceased to exist as a fighting unit and was never reconstituted. It would be another four months before the Allies crossed the Rhine again for the final offensive against Germany.

Paratroopers and gliders taking part in Operation Market Garden, during which the Allies dropped 10,300 paratroopers behind German lines. Only 2,400 survived.

Citizens of Leningrad scoop up water from a broken main, during the 900-day siege.

The siege of Leningrad

Leningrad was a primary objective of Operation Barbarossa, Hitler's invasion of the Soviet Union. Its importance as Russia's second city (even as St Petersburg, and Russia's Tsarist capital, it never displaced Moscow) was secondary to its strategic value at Russia's northwest corner. Take Leningrad – and with the Finns as allies in the north and west, and the *Wehrmacht* rolling up Belarus and Ukraine to the south, Moscow could be encircled and the USSR either defeated or pushed over the Urals out of Europe.

By September 8 1941 Leningrad was cut off, an enclave backed onto the shore of Lake Ladoga. The lake made it possible (just) to cut and run. Leningrad snorted its contempt for Hitler, stayed and fought. Knowing they faced winter with no food, fuel or public utilities, some three million people sacrificed themselves to keep going the city's factories, schools, businesses and shops, and supporting whatever Soviet army units survived in their midst with hurriedly organized militia. In 1942, in January and February alone, 200,000 died of cold and starvation. The city shrank as Leningraders contested each building and street in hand-to-hand fighting with the Nazis. If you couldn't fight you did what you could: surviving was an act of war. Old man Shostakovich composed a symphony to inspire the besieged; others braved incessant shelling on the *Doroga Zhizni* (Road of Life) across Lake Ladoga – a road of ice or open water which was Leningrad's only lifeline for food, ammunition, or evacuation of the wounded. The dead were left unburied. The dying hurled one last grenade.

Leningrad survived carnage and starvation for 872 days, creating a propaganda triumph from the city's disaster. It took Stalin to turn it back again: terrified that Leningrad's exhausted leaders might acquire a popular following, he had them executed.

WHEN:
September 8 1941 to January 27 1944

WHERE:
Leningrad (now St Petersburg), USSR (now Russia)

DEATH TOLL:
At least 641,000 people died. Many survivors believe the figure is closer to 1.1 million. For Russia, Leningrad's disaster was also a moral victory. For Hitler, Leningrad's resolute will was an early harbinger of the disaster of ultimate defeat.

YOU SHOULD KNOW:
The brutal conditions of the siege left survivors unwilling even to describe it. When the only 'food' came from boiling leather boots or extracting the glue from wallpaper, cannibalism was inevitable.

Dien Bien Phu

As Fat Man and Little Boy brought World War II to its nuclear end, former colonial powers elbowed their way through coalitions of tribal, sectarian and nationalist interests to fill the power vacuum left by the defeated Japanese throughout the Far East. In Vietnam, France found itself violently opposed by the Viet Minh, a nationalist force that had resisted the Japanese with the hope of simultaneously kicking out their colonialist overlords. Led by Ho Chi Minh, an inspirational leader trained in both Paris and Moscow, the Viet Minh were old-school communists, and thoroughly accustomed to the self-sacrifice demanded by a common weal. With the legendary Vo Nguyen Giap as their military commander, and a stubborn reluctance to be bullied, the Viet Minh evolved into a field army capable of bringing their enemy to battle almost where and whenever they chose. Dien Bien Phu was the climax of their seven-year war.

Dien Bien Phu was 'the key to Laos', a crossroads in the mountainous northwest of Vietnam. As soon as the French began to fortify it, Giap saw his chance. The battle – essentially between outmoded Staff College tactics and what we now recognize as 'modern', combined operations based on information and close support – included ambush, hit-and-run, artillery siege, extended trench warfare, and brilliantly extemporized opportunism.

It lasted 55 days. Giap's military genius won a decisive victory that Ho Chi Minh, in the Geneva Accords of 1954, was able to translate into France's permanent withdrawal from Vietnam, Laos and Cambodia. France's military and political disaster was eventually equalled by Vietnam's. The Accords also partitioned the country at the 17th parallel, handing South Vietnam to one of history's most corrupt figures, US-backed President Diem. By 1959, Giap and Ho Chi Minh had it all to do again. And they did.

WHEN:
March 13 to May 7 1954
WHERE:
Dien Bien Phu, northwestern Vietnam
DEATH TOLL:
Only 70 French soldiers escaped Dien Bien Phu to Laos, leaving 2,293 killed, 5,195 wounded, and 10,998 captured (of whom only 3,290 were ever repatriated). Viet Minh casualties were (estimated) at 23,000.
YOU SHOULD KNOW:
For all their public protestations, the US was covertly and intimately involved with French military and political strategy at Dien Bien Phu. There is French evidence to suggest the US discussed 'lending atomic bombs' in their support; and in 2004–2005 it became known that at least 37 US pilots flew 682 missions, and two were killed in action during the battle. On February 25 2005 the seven US pilots still living were invested as members of the *Legion d'Honneur* by the French Ambassador to the USA.

ARVN paratroops during heavy street fighting along the Boulevard Gallieni.

Bay of Pigs invasion

*Cuban leader Fidel Castro,
lower right, sitting inside a
tank near Playa Giron,
Cuba, during the Bay of
Pigs invasion.*

Lying only 300 km (200 mi) from the US mainland, the Caribbean island of Cuba had become an increasingly irritable thorn in America's side since Fidel Castro had led a popular revolution in 1959 to overthrow the dictatorship of General Batista. Castro helped to finance the socialist policies he introduced, including universal health care and free education, by nationalizing US-owned businesses in Cuba. America's response was to impose a crippling trade embargo and to cut all diplomatic ties.

The loss of influence and commercial opportunities in Cuba continued to rankle, and the embers of resentment were fanned by the large population of Cuban exiles in Florida: supporters and beneficiaries of the old regime who had fled the island. In 1960 the CIA devised a covert plan to use these exiles to oust Castro and restore a pro-American government. This became one of the first issues confronting the new president, John F Kennedy, when he took office in January 1961. Kennedy initially was unconvinced but was persuaded to sanction the operation when a smokescreen of 'plausible deniability' was put in place to protect his reputation. Following a successful US bombing raid on Cuba's airfields, on April 17 1961 five US merchant ships landed 1,500 armed Cuban exiles in the Bay of Pigs, an inlet on Cuba's south coast 145 km (90 mi) southeast of Havana.

The operation was bungled from the outset: two transports were sunk, jeeps were landed without fuel, the troops had inadequate maps of the island and ended up firing on each other. Worst of all, the CIA's assumption that the invasion would spark a popular uprising against Castro proved a disastrous misjudgement. The invaders were soon surrounded and pinned down on the beach by Castro's militia; within 72 hours they had all surrendered.

Vietnam war

The protracted and brutal war that laid waste one of Asia's most ravishingly beautiful countries was a classic example of a Cold War conflict. In the early 1960s US foreign policy was in thrall to the 'domino theory', which held that if one country were to fall under the communist spell, neighbouring states were bound to follow suit. After the 1954 division of Vietnam into North and South at the 17th parallel, the communist North, under charismatic leader Ho Chi Minh, continued to pursue its goal of national unity by infiltrating South Vietnam with troops and arms; thus began a bitter civil war that was to last 16 years.

Although fearful of the spread of communism, the USA restricted its initial involvement to supplying the South Vietnamese army with military advisers, but when Lyndon Johnson assumed the presidency following Kennedy's assassination he quickly raised the stakes by ordering bombing raids against North Vietnam. In March 1965 the first American ground troops landed in South Vietnam; numbers steadily increased until by the end of 1968 they had reached over half a million. In January of that year Ho Chi Minh launched the Tet offensive, a massive combined assault by the North Vietnamese army and the Viet Cong (as the guerrillas fighting in the South were known) which took the Americans completely by surprise. Although they ultimately beat back the assault, the offensive marked the turning point of the war.

Peace talks started in Paris soon afterwards and eventually, in 1973, a ceasefire was agreed, involving the complete withdrawal of US troops. Just two years later the North invaded the South; now without US support, its government capitulated rapidly. Vietnam was once again united, but under a communist flag, and the myth of an invincible America had been shattered.

Children fleeing from their homes after South Vietnamese planes accidently dropped a napalm bomb on their village.

WHEN:
1959–1975
WHERE:
Vietnam
DEATH TOLL:
58,193 US troops were killed or listed as missing in action. It is thought as many as 250,000 South Vietnamese soldiers died. Combined North Vietnamese and Viet Cong losses are estimated at over 1,000,000. In addition to the horrendous military loss of life, around 4,000,000 Vietnamese civilians (10 per cent of the population) were killed or injured during the war. The country's economy and infrastructure were destroyed and its ecology suffered devastating and irreversible damage.
YOU SHOULD KNOW:
Key factors in the North's ultimate victory were its use of guerrilla tactics and the Viet Cong's success in winning the 'hearts and minds' of the rural peasantry in the South who disliked the regime in Saigon.

Afghan Mujahideen *standing on a destroyed Russian helicopter.*

The Soviet invasion of Afghanistan

Since time immemorial Afghanistan has been riven by tribal, ethnic and religious conflict. In its harsh geography, authority expands and contracts beneath a patina of centuries of shifting loyalties. The process of forming reliable alliances has been too subtle for foreign invaders – including Alexander the Great, the Moghuls, the British (repeatedly), and in 1979, the Russians. The USSR had promoted its own interests for years with a massive aid programme, until in the 1970s Afghanistan 'voted' a communist government to power. Urban communism, backed only by the military, was a direct challenge to deeply entrenched Muslim culture and belief. Countryside protest became nationwide revolt, and the USSR invaded Afghanistan in defence of the 'Brezhnev doctrine' of surrounding the mother country with kowtowing, client communist states.

On Christmas Eve in 1979 Russia flooded the country with 100,000 troops, tanks, artillery and aircraft. They thought they were fighting the usual, unruly dissidents, but their enemy was Islam itself: common religious cause over-rode internecine tribal antagonism. From Russia's point of view this redefined the *mujahideen* to include every town, village or farm that sheltered them (voluntarily or not). During the next ten years Russia razed the heart and soul out of Afghanistan's rural culture, ably assisted by the actual *mujahideen* guerrillas, who gratefully accepted the CIA's $2.1 billion investment in their resistance, and grew too excited by weaponry to care who got damaged in the cross-fire. Russia, confined to heavily fortified enclaves, haemorrhaging young lives to no conceivable benefit, threatened by its own allies with trade sanctions, and pressurized by international moral censure, gave up. Using the pretext of the botched, 1988 Geneva Accords, its armies fled with indecent haste. Afghanistan was a wasteland, robbed of its culture, its civil structures and democratic potential. And thanks to Russia, worse was yet to come.

WHEN:
December 24 1979 to February 15 1989

WHERE:
Afghanistan

DEATH TOLL:
Of the 620,000 Russians who served in Afghanistan, 15,000 were killed and 54,000 wounded. The country is still carpeted with land mines. Hundreds of thousands of Afghanis died, and millions fled as refugees to Pakistan. With traditional tribal structures irrevocably fractured by the war, new alliances have been forged linking the refugee communities with both Taliban fundamentalists and Afghani 'tribal nationalists'. The USA must share the blame with the USSR for playing an almost genocidal game of one-upmanship in this period.

YOU SHOULD KNOW:
Zbigniew Brezhinski of the US State Department confessed years later that the US had planned to support Russia's Afghani opponents five months *before* the USSR invaded: 'On July 3 1979 President Carter signed the first directive for secret aid to the opponents of the Pro-Soviet regime in Kabul . . . The day the Soviets officially crossed the border, I wrote to President Carter: We now have the opportunity of giving to the USSR its Vietnam war . . .'

Operation Eagle Claw

Now it seems either breathtakingly arrogant or plain mad, but in 1979 global diplomacy had no public voice for, nor knowledge of, Muslim fundamentalism. When President Jimmy Carter, as Commander-in-Chief, sent in his newly formed Delta Force to rescue 53 American hostages seized with the US Embassy in Tehran, he was behaving as the heads of superpowers had behaved since Roman times. An embassy has always physically represented the 'national soil' of a country. An invasion of it is an act of war.

Carter's may have been a knee-jerk reaction, but it seemed reasonable: Britain felt the same way when Argentina invaded the Falkland Islands. The difference was the circumstances that forced Carter to hedge his entire bet. The Shah of Iran – a long time 'client' of NATO – had only recently been forced out, and might conceivably return to nominal or real power. The antagonism between Iran's new, civilian politicians and its religious leaders under Ayatollah Khomeini was neither understood nor resolved. Eagle Claw had to look like a 'punishment' raid, not war. Nobody must be offended.

Eagle Claw was inspired by the Israeli success at Entebbe in 1976, but it was much more complicated. Several huge C-130 transports had to land 'in the Iranian desert', wait while nine helicopters deposited Delta Force 'specialists' in Tehran itself, and after roughly 24 hours to cover the 'extraction', pick up the hostage group from Tehran airport (secured, improbably, from any opposition!) and fly them somewhere with decent hamburgers. A sandstorm reduced the airworthy helicopters to five and exhausted the pilots beyond the endurable. Eagle Claw was aborted – leaving eight dead in a desert fireball after a C-130 transport collided with a helicopter, the hostages in captivity, the global influence of Iran's student fundamentalist group massively enhanced, and Carter's presidency in ashes. The hostages were released to mark incoming President Reagan's inauguration.

WHEN:
April 24 1980
WHERE:
The Iranian 'desert'
DEATH TOLL:
Eight US servicemen died and America suffered a disastrous humiliation, enabling Khomeini to consolidate his grip on power. From being an embarrassment to the new regime, unskilled at the propaganda game, the 52 remaining hostages became a major bargaining chip. Eagle Claw cost Carter a second term, and shocked America's allies (who had been neither informed nor consulted about it) into forming premature policies preferring sanctions to any show of force. The mission's failure created the political suspicion that led, eventually but unerringly, to George W Bush's 2002 inclusion of Iran in his 'Axis of Evil'.
YOU SHOULD KNOW:
President Carter said (April 25 1980): 'I ordered this mission . . . *to reduce the tensions* in the world that have been caused among many nations as this crisis has continued.'

The scorched wreckage of an American C-130 cargo aircraft lying in the Iranian desert.

Palomares incident

WHEN:
January 17 1966
WHERE:
Palomares, Andalucia, Spain
DEATH TOLL:
Seven US crewmen were killed in the accident. Whilst there were no direct civilian casualties on the ground, the local population are still given annual medical checks to this day.
YOU SHOULD KNOW:
As recently as October 2006 the USA and Spain agreed to undertake a further clean-up of radioactive land in the Palomares area.

Although some progress towards *détente* had been made with the signing in 1963 of the Test Ban Treaty between the USA and the Soviet Union, there were still plenty of itchy fingers around nuclear buttons when, on January 17 1966, during a routine mid-air refuelling operation off the Mediterranean coast of southern Spain, a US B-52 bomber collided with a KC-135 tanker aircraft. The B-52 was patrolling the European skies on a typical Cold War sortie when the accident occurred at 9,000 m (30,000 ft). Both planes crashed to the ground outside the fishing village of Palomares in Andalusia, killing the entire tanker crew and three members of the bomber crew; the remaining four crewmen managed to parachute to safety.

What made this mid-air collision no ordinary accident was the fact that the B-52 bomber was carrying a nuclear payload comprising four H-bombs. Three bombs crashed with the plane; although the hydrogen cores remained intact, the non-nuclear explosives in two of them detonated upon impact, contaminating a wide area of agricultural land with plutonium dust. Although the American authorities played down the significance of the incident, the massive clear-up operation that followed gave ample evidence of how worried they were. Two thousand US servicemen were involved and blanket embargoes were placed on the local tomato crop and fishing industry.

The fourth bomb, which had been jettisoned over the water, was eventually found on the sea-bed after an intensive 80-day search by more than 30 ships. The Palomares incident remains the worst accident ever to have occurred involving American nuclear weapons; the clean-up and subsequent compensation claims are said to have cost the USA over $180 million.

Crewmen on board the submarine USS Petrol *lashing down the US hydrogen bomb, still partially wrapped in its parachute, after its recovery from the sea.*

Iraq invasion of Kuwait

In the late 1980s, after the failure of his long and costly war against Iran, which had lasted for most of that decade, Iraq's President Saddam Hussein started to cast around for a new target for his warmongering aspirations. His sights alighted on another neighbour, the small but oil-rich Gulf state of Kuwait. On August 2 1990, under the pretext of a border dispute over oil exports and distribution arrangements, Saddam launched a large-scale invasion of Kuwait with more than 100,000 troops backed up by 700 tanks. Kuwait was quickly overrun and in no time Saddam was declaring its annexation by Iraq. With customary bellicose rhetoric he threatened to turn the capital, Kuwait City, into a 'graveyard' if any other country dared to challenge the 'take-over by force'.

The response of the United Nations was immediate and decisive. Meeting in emergency session, the Security Council called on Iraq to withdraw its forces from Kuwait and imposed sanctions until it had done so. Saddam, however, gave no indication that he would bow to UN demands. Over the following months a US-led Coalition force involving troops from 30 countries was assembled. It was widely assumed that Saddam would back down in the face of intense international pressure, but when he failed to respond to a UN ultimatum for withdrawal, the Coalition forces launched Operation Desert Storm on January 17 1991, a major offensive to expel Iraq and liberate Kuwait. For more than a month a sustained and devastating aerial bombardment of key military targets, including the Iraqi capital Baghdad, brought the country to its knees. When the ground forces finally moved in at the end of February the conflict was effectively over; within days the Iraqi army had fled, Kuwait was free, and a ceasefire had been declared.

An American soldier standing on top of a destroyed Iraqi tank. Kuwaiti oil wells, ignited by Saddam's retreating forces, burn in the distance.

WHEN:
August 2 1990 to February 28 1991
WHERE:
Kuwait and Iraq
DEATH TOLL:
Iraqi casualties are unknown, but estimates of military deaths range as high as 100,000. Some 3,500 civilians are thought to have died in the bombing raids, tens of thousands more from diseases and other effects of war. Coalition troops lost 381 lives, including a number from so-called 'friendly fire' incidents.
YOU SHOULD KNOW:
What has become known as the First Gulf War must rate as one of the most unequal engagements in the history of warfare. The Coalition forces' equipment, resources and firepower were vastly superior to that of their Iraqi opponents.

The *Kursk* disaster

Some time over the weekend of August 12–13 2000, while on a naval exercise inside the Arctic Circle, the Russian nuclear submarine *Kursk* sank to the bottom of the Barents Sea with all hands on board. The entire 118-strong crew perished on the Oscar II class submarine, built in 1994. According to the Russian navy, it had not been carrying nuclear warheads so there was never a danger of radiation leaks. A desperate Russian rescue operation over the following days, in which other countries including Britain offered their

The Russian nuclear submarine Kursk *in the Barents Sea near Severomorsk, Russia*

assistance, failed to establish radio communication with the stricken vessel, still less gain access to save the crew. Rescuers' efforts were hampered by the icy waters, stormy weather and poor underwater visibility.

No one will ever know for sure what caused the disaster. The explanation generally held today, and one borne out by the findings of the official Russian inquiry, is that it was due to a faulty torpedo exploding as it was being prepared for use. The Russians admitted afterwards that the liquid fuel they had been using in their missiles was known to be unstable in certain conditions. As the captain struggled to bring the submarine to the surface there was a second and much bigger explosion – most likely another warhead – which tore a hole in the bow and probably killed most of the crew instantly. This explanation is supported by reports of two underwater explosions picked up by Western agencies monitoring the area at the time, as well as by the physical evidence of the wreck when it was finally brought up from the seabed by a Dutch salvage team more than a year after the accident. Public reaction in Russia to the authorities' handling of the disaster was hostile, with victims' families branding the official inquiry a whitewash.

WHEN:
August 12 or 13 2000
WHERE:
Barents Sea, off the Arctic coast of Russia
DEATH TOLL:
118 Russian sailors died.
YOU SHOULD KNOW:
Vladimir Putin, who had taken over as president of Russia from Boris Yeltsin at the start of the year, was on holiday at the time and did not return immediately to Moscow. His handling of his first major crisis in office was widely criticized for its inadequacy and lack of sensitivity.

Operation Iraqi Freedom

Operation Iraqi Freedom is the name given to the invasion of Iraq on March 19 2003. Its objective was 'regime change' – a euphemism for the removal of Saddam Hussein from his post as leader of Iraq, and his replacement by a 'democratically elected' Iraqi government with whom the USA could 'do business'. The *casus belli* was, according to US President George W Bush and UK Prime Minister Tony Blair, the 'clear and material threat' posed to their countries by Iraq's 'proven' possession of 'weapons of mass destruction' (WMD).

Having failed to win support from either the United Nations (UN) or the UN Security Council for UN Resolution 1441 ('to disarm Iraq'), Britain and America cited Iraq's 'breach of 17 prior UN resolutions' and went to war anyway. Operation Iraqi Freedom ended as a conventional war on April 10 2003, though Saddam was not captured until December. That same month, a US battalion commander in the town of Abu Hishma summarized Iraqi Freedom's success: 'With a heavy dose of fear and violence, and a lot of money for projects, I think we can persuade these people that we are here to help them.'

Now – long after Saddam Hussein's execution, the ruination of Iraq's economy and the effective sequestration of its valuable oil assets – Iraqi Freedom's legacy of civil strife between Sunni and Shi'ite and Kurd merely multiplies the bitter ashes of the entire episode. As the UN's Inspector said before it began, there never were any WMD. Bush and Blair lied about them, having planned to go to war with Iraq a whole year earlier. Iraqi Freedom is an ongoing disaster for Western democracies, for Iraq, and for truth itself. It shames us all.

WHEN:
March 19–20 to April 10 2003
WHERE:
Iraq
DEATH TOLL:
By 2009 the total number of deaths as a direct result of the invasion and its aftermath had been estimated at 1,366,350. Nobody has ever counted the injured and displaced in Iraq.
YOU SHOULD KNOW:
As early as July 23 2003, a US game company issued a PC game called 'F/A-18 Operation Iraqi Freedom', offering players the chance 'to fly the Marine and Navy's workhorse fighting machine, the F/A-18 Hornet, as navigated above Iraq, Iran, Kuwait and the Gulf during Iraqi Freedom'.

The statue of Saddam Hussein being toppled in Firdaus Square, Baghdad.

INDUSTRIAL DISASTERS

Monongah mining disaster

WHEN:
December 6 1907
WHERE:
Monongah, West Virginia, USA
DEATH TOLL:
No definitive total has been established. The official death toll was 361, but unofficial estimates are considerably higher.
YOU SHOULD KNOW:
The sole survivor of the Monongah blast was a man called Peter Urban, who managed to find a hole through which to escape before toxic gases killed him, though his twin brother did perish. It was only a reprieve – he was subsequently killed in a mine cave-in.

West Virginia and mining go together like coal and dust, which means the impoverished state has seen more than its fair share of serious industrial accidents – including the worst mining disaster in American history. The scene of this tragedy was the Consolidated Coal Company's mine at Monongah, consisting of an elaborate labyrinth of tunnels with entrance shafts connected by a steel bridge above the West Fork River.

On the morning of December 6 a full complement of men and boys were working their shift. Many – over half – were immigrants from southern Italy who lived in houses built on the hillside above the mine. Mid morning a massive underground explosion shook the ground. As a result of a carelessly opened lamp or botched dynamite blast, firedamp (methane gas) had exploded, starting a chain reaction with suspended bituminous dust that ripped through shafts six and eight of the mine.

The result was disastrous for the unfortunates below ground. Many survived the explosion, but the ventilation system had been destroyed and poisonous fumes swiftly permeated the mine. Wreckage blocked escape routes and rescuers could only work for short periods before they, too, suffered from gas inhalation. A large crowd of distraught family members and spectators gathered at the ruined main entrance awaiting news, which was all bad. As bodies were carried out – many mangled or burned beyond recognition – it became apparent that there were few if any survivors. By the end of the day 250 widows and 1,000 fatherless children were in mourning, along with their community.

The Monongah disaster provided impetus to the growing movement towards greater mine safety. America's mine owners subsequently fought hard against government regulation – with considerable success – but the fact that accidents reduced productivity caused them to start improving safety measures for themselves.

A black granite monument in Mount Calvary Cemetery in Monongah commemorates the mine disaster.

Boston molasses disaster

The Purity Distilling Company was an alcohol manufacturer based in the North End area of Boston, Massachusetts. A key ingredient of their industrial process was molasses, the syrupy by-product of sugar processing that served as a domestic sweetener and could be fermented to produce rum or (in Purity's case) industrial ethyl alcohol.

January 15 1919 was an unusually warm day. Purity's vast crude molasses storage tank at 529 Commercial Street was brimming with some 8.7 million litres (2.3 million US gallons) of molasses. The precise cause of what happened next was never established. It was probably a combination of factors – the hot day encouraging internal fermentation, a poorly maintained cast-iron tank and a stress crack near its base that had been overpainted rather than repaired.

Whatever the cause, there is no argument about the event itself. At 12.40 the 15 m (50 ft) tall tank fractured with a rumble, accompanied by the machine-gun popping of exploding rivets. The ground shook and a wave of molasses up to 4.5 m (15 ft) high engulfed the surrounding area, moving at an awe-inspiring 55 kph (35 mph) – a sticky tsunami that flattened buildings, invaded a fire station, tossed a train off the tracks and demolished bridges. When its energy was finally spent, several city blocks were flooded to a depth of 1 m (3 ft).

Rescue efforts were a nightmare, as clinging molasses hampered attempts to pull out the injured and recover the dead. A makeshift hospital was set up to treat the wounded as they emerged and it took four days – working day and night – to comb through the disaster scene. The last two bodies were so solidly glazed with molasses that they were never identified. The subsequent clean up required over 3,600 arduous man-days. Purity's owners eventually paid out $600,000 in compensation.

This aerial view shows the site of the molasses storage tank explosion. In the background is the Navy Yard in Charlestown.

WHEN:
January 15 1919
WHERE:
Boston, Massachusetts, USA
DEATH TOLL:
21 dead (plus around 150 seriously injured).
YOU SHOULD KNOW:
It may be folklore coupled with autosuggestion, but locals living around the site of the great molasses flood (now a community baseball field) insist that it's still possible to smell the unmistakable sweet odour of molasses on hot days.

Oppau explosion

Ignorance can be bliss – until disaster strikes. Before World War I the BASF (Badische Anilin- und Soda Fabrik) dye works in Oppau made – among various other chemicals – ammonium sulphate, an inorganic salt with assorted applications including widespread use as fertilizer. From 1914, ammonium nitrate was added to the factory's repertoire as it was a vital component of explosives needed to sustain the German war effort. After the Armistice BASC continued to produce both ammonium sulphate and ammonium nitrate, mixing them to produce rich fertilizer.

Unfortunately, the combination produced a putty-like substance that sometimes set hard inside the factory's giant storage silo. This build-up couldn't be removed manually, so was dislodged by using small dynamite charges. Though the properties of ammonium nitrate as an oxidizing agent in manufactured explosives were well known, it was not appreciated at the time that the compound was potentially volatile in its own right. If anyone had suspicions, they were nullified by the fact that the dynamite method had been thoroughly tested and thousands of firings had taken place without incident.

That changed in a microsecond on the morning of September 21 1921. Nobody was left alive to explain what went wrong, but it is assumed that a routine blasting session set off a mixture that had a higher-than-usual concentration of ammonium nitrate. Up to 4,500 tonnes of ammonium mixture went up. The massive blast killed over 500 people instantly, injured thousands and flattened the factory. Most of Oppau's buildings were destroyed, leaving 6,500 residents homeless. A pressure wave ripped roofs off over a 25 km (15 mi) radius and shattered windows over a wider area. The explosion was heard in Munich, 300 km (185 mi) away, ensuring that the world would no longer be in ignorance of the awesome destructive power of ammonium nitrate.

The enormous crater in the foreground, about 91.4 m (300 ft) wide by 12 m (40 ft) deep, was filled with water from burst pipes and subterranean infiltration.

WHEN:
September 21 1921
WHERE:
Oppau, Ludwigshafen, Rhineland-Palatinate, Germany
DEATH TOLL:
Never officially confirmed, but many sources claim the figure to be 565. Despite early press reports that the Oppau death toll was over 1,000, it is now generally accepted that the figure was between 500 and 600, with around 2,500 injured.
YOU SHOULD KNOW:
Terrorists and freedom fighters everywhere use widely available ammonium nitrate fertilizer as the main component in the IEDs (improvised explosive devices) that range from relatively small roadside devices targeting passing vehicles to massive truck bombs used to devastate urban areas and cause extensive loss of life.

Hawk's Nest Tunnel tragedy

It seems bizarre that one of the USA's worst-ever industrial disasters happened without a single casualty being recorded, but that's exactly how it was . . . until the true scale of an unfolding tragedy became apparent. The Depression Era was hard for working-class Americans, so when an ambitious engineering project in West Virginia was announced men hurried from all over the South to join locals from the pretty riverside town of Gauley Bridge as a workforce of 3,000 assembled.

The Hawk's Nest Tunnel would be a 5 km (3 mi) shaft beneath Gauley Mountain, designed to divert most of the dammed New River's flow to power huge turbines that would generate electricity for Union Carbide's industrial plant downstream at Alloy. The dam was to be built by US Army Engineers, but tunnelling was subcontracted to a private firm and work began in the late 1920s.

The rock to be penetrated turned out to be sandstone, consisting of almost pure silica – a mineral that is valuable after being pulverized and melted. The diameter of the tunnel – originally set at 5 m (16 ft) – was increased to 11 m (35 ft) and it became a mining operation that also happily delivered the planned tunnel. This awesome engineering achievement generated its first electricity in 1936 and has been doing so continuously ever since.

But silica is deadly, creating fine airborne powder when mined that can cause immediate breathing difficulties and often leads to silicosis, a fatal lung disease. As times were hard, two men clamoured to replace every tunneller who was unable to carry on. Managers wore masks, workers did not. The first silicosis deaths occurred before work was completed, and hundreds more would die in the years ahead. The impressive Hawk's Nest Tunnel would indeed prove to be a major industrial tragedy.

WHEN:
1930s
WHERE:
Gauley Bridge, Fayette County, West Virginia, USA
DEATH TOLL:
Uncertain, since many workers dispersed to their homes when the project was complete and were never monitored. But a subsequent congressional hearing placed the figure at 476 and more realistic estimates put the true total at around 1,000, a third of the workforce.
YOU SHOULD KNOW:
The Hawk's Nest Tunnel was a great feat of engineering, but the price paid may be gauged by the fact that the picturesque river settlement of Gauley Bridge became known as 'the town of the living dead'.

Some of the men doomed to die from the tunnel dust disease

Benxihu (Honkeiko) Colliery

WHEN:
April 26 1942
WHERE:
Benxi, Liaoning, China
DEATH TOLL:
1,549 miners killed
YOU SHOULD KNOW:
There was no respite for lucky survivors. The Japanese reopened the mine as soon as the clear-up was complete and it continued to operate until the Japanese surrender in 1945, when it was taken over by the exploited workers.

Being a coal miner in China has never been the easiest or safest of careers, but today's Chinese miners operate in conditions infinitely superior to those endured by their forebears. Mining was particularly demanding under Japanese rule, when the conquerors used forced labour. Miners wore tattered clothing and frequently went barefoot, food was in short supply and disease was rife in the labour camps.

One such mine was the Benxihu (Honkeiko) Colliery in Manchuria. It was a joint Chinese-Japanese commercial venture ('Honkeiko' being the Japanese name), but during the Sino-Japanese War of 1937–1945 it was under Japanese control. Overseers were brutal but there was no escape. The mine was surrounded by a barbed-wire perimeter and weakened miners who refused to work were brutally beaten.

The miner's worst enemy is firedamp – explosive gases (usually methane) that can build up, especially where coal is bituminous. The other serious danger is a coal-dust explosion, where fine suspended particles of flammable material combust instantly in a confined space with stunning force. On April 26 one, the other or both exploded within a shaft.

The earth shook and flame burst from the entrance. In the immediate aftermath of the blast, miners' families rushed to the scene of the disaster, only to be prevented from approaching by Japanese guards, who erected an electric fence to prevent anxious spectators from getting too close. The clean-up operation lasted for ten days, with a succession of charred bodies being carried out of the shaft on carts, many too badly burned to be identified. They were interred in a mass grave with scant ceremony, and when the final death toll was known over 1,500 souls – a third of the miners working that day – had perished in the world's worst mining disaster.

Cleveland East Ohio Gas explosions

At first, nobody noticed a cloud of vapour pouring from an Ohio Gas Company storage tank on Cleveland's East 61st Street. Even if they had, no alarm bells would have rung on that October Friday in 1944 – liquefied natural gas was a new product and its explosive capabilities had not yet been appreciated. They soon would be. Wind off nearby Lake Erie pushed the heavy gas cloud inland, where it flowed into the sewer network via street drains. Once there, it was only a matter of time before the dangerous mixture of air, sewerage gases and natural gas ignited.

The flashpoint came in the early afternoon, when a violent underground detonation hurled manhole covers high into the air (one was found several miles away) as plumes of fire erupted from the depths. The number of casualties caused by this dramatic occurrence is not recorded, for the worst was yet to come. As residents got over their initial shock and the fire department appeared to gain control, crowds of spectators gathered . . . to their cost.

Some 20 minutes after the initial blast, one of the Ohio Gas Company's tanks exploded, flattening the tank farm and unleashing a second conflagration. Survivors claimed that their clothes caught fire instantly – and they were the lucky ones. Many died, some being burned beyond recognition. A second wave of fire roared through the sewers and erupted from drains, engulfing homes and those who had sought safety within. When the flames finally died down over 70 houses, two factories, countless vehicles and the sewerage system had been destroyed. Around 600 people were homeless, having lost everything, and more than 100 had died. If the disastrous event had occurred after school was out and adults returned from work, the casualty list could have quadrupled.

Birds fell flaming from the sky when the tank exploded, leaving this scene of devastation near the centre of Cleveland.

WHEN:
October 20 1944
WHERE:
Cleveland, Ohio, USA
DEATH TOLL:
131 dead, plus 225 with serious burn injuries
YOU SHOULD KNOW:
As a result of explosive events in Cleveland, utility companies that were using liquefied natural gas started phasing out above-ground storage tanks in favour of less vulnerable underground facilities.

View of the wreckage that resulted along the Port Chicago waterfront after the two ammunition ships blew up.

Port Chicago munitions explosion

WHEN:
July 17 1944
WHERE:
Port Chicago, California, USA
DEATH TOLL:
320 dead, 390 injured
YOU SHOULD KNOW:
Safety conditions for loading munitions were not improved and the Port Chicago disaster had a significant sequel. African-American sailors who subsequently refused to load munitions were court martialled for mutiny, dubiously convicted and sentenced to long prison terms. It became a *cause célèbre* that highlighted racial inequality in the US Navy and led to the first serious efforts to lessen discrimination. The convicted mutineers were released after serving barely a year.

America prides itself on defending national shores and protecting its people against hostile incursion in times of war, but that's not to say there have never been US war casualties on American soil. One of the greatest losses of life occurred in World War II at Port Chicago, California (not to be confused with Port of Chicago, Illinois).

At the Port Chicago Naval Magazine, munitions to support America's Pacific Theatre of Operations were delivered by train prior to loading onto cargo ships. In July 1944 the naval base was a hive of activity, working around the clock as crews – mainly enlisted African-Americans – competed to see who could load munitions fastest, though these US Navy stevedores were poorly trained and badly supervised.

One night, the Liberty ship SS *E A Bryan* was being loaded with bombs and depth charges at Port Chicago's single pier, opposite the SS *Quinault Victory*. At 22.18 an explosion occurred and fire broke out. A few seconds later there was a massive detonation as all the munitions in and around *E A Bryan* went up in a huge fireball, killing everyone on the pier and injuring hundreds more in the nearby barracks and town.

The *E A Bryan* was completely destroyed, *Quinault Victory* was blown out of the water and disintegrated, a fireboat was hurled 180 m (600 ft) before sinking and the pier and its environs were completely flattened. It was later calculated that the explosion was equivalent to the detonation of 2,000 tons of TNT (or a small nuclear bomb) and the shock wave measured 3.4 on the Richter earthquake scale. When the dust settled, over 300 navy personnel were dead (most so badly burned that they were never identified) and nearly 400 sailors and civilians had been injured, many seriously.

Texas City disaster

Sometimes painful history lessons aren't learned. Sometimes they are simply ignored. Either way, the disastrous explosion that devastated Texas City in April 1947 could still have been avoided. The deadly properties of ammonium nitrate were well known, but Federal regulations were lax in regard to almost every aspect of dealing with the potentially volatile compound.

Some did learn – Houston did not permit loading of ammonium nitrate, though nearby Port Texas was not so scrupulous. There, the French-registered SS *Grandcamp* was packed with ammonium nitrate fertilizer when fire broke out in the engine room, quickly spreading to the cargo hold. A crowd gathered on shore to watch the drama at what was presumed to be a safe distance. It wasn't. The crew attempted to put out the fire by using live steam, a method more likely to preserve the cargo than the use of water. But the consequent heat only succeeded in causing the ammonium nitrate to reach its explosive threshold.

A massive blast ripped through the port and sent a tsunami surging along the Texas coastline. Most ships in harbour were sunk, while the SS *High Flyer* with its own cargo of ammonium nitrate was set ablaze (it would explode 15 hours later, adding to the initial disaster). The entire volunteer Texas City Fire Department was wiped out, over 1,000 buildings were flattened and a couple of low-flying aircraft were incinerated. A chain reaction set waterfront refineries ablaze and ignited various chemical plants and explosives facilities, while blazing debris rained down over a wide area.

It took a week to put out fires and a month to recover all the bodies. America's worst-ever industrial disaster claimed nearly 600 lives and caused devastating property damage, later estimated at $100 million – an awesome sum in 1947.

WHEN:
April 16 1947
WHERE:
Texas City, Galveston County, Texas, USA
DEATH TOLL:
Officially 581 (405 identified, 63 unidentified, 113 missing) – but the force of the explosion and fierceness of subsequent fires probably killed and incinerated many more who were not missed. Of more than 5,000 reported injured, nearly 1,800 required serious hospital treatment.
YOU SHOULD KNOW:
They love them in America – but the class-action lawsuit only appeared on the legal map in 1948 following an Act of Congress, thus enabling victims of the Texas City disaster to participate in the very first collective action against the US government. It eventually failed after a contentious Supreme Court decision.

Heavy black smoke rises from the fires raging in the refinery and oil storage tank area.

Kyshtym nuclear disaster

WHEN:
September 29 1957
WHERE:
South Ural Mountains, Russia
DEATH TOLL:
At least 200 people died of radiation
sickness and it is estimated that
several hundred more died from
radiation-related cancers. Over a
period of 45 years more than
500,000 people were exposed to
radiation, many of them at levels 20
times greater than the victims of
Chernobyl.
YOU SHOULD KNOW:
Although rumours of a nuclear
accident in Russia circulated in the
West for years, the Soviet cover-up
was so effective that the Kyshtym
disaster was only officially
admitted in 1990. America's Central
Intelligence Agency knew all about
it almost as soon as the accident
happened, but kept the information
quiet to avoid raising public
concern about the USA's own
nuclear industry.

Nuclear fission was a sensitive subject in the Soviet Union during
the Cold War years – to the point where Russia's Mayak nuclear
fuel reprocessing plant and the closed town of Ozyorsk that was
built around it in the Ural Mountains didn't even feature on maps.
But they existed all right, even though the nuclear catastrophe that
occurred there in 1957 had to be named after the nearest 'official'
town, Kyshtym.

After World War II, the Soviet Union lagged behind the USA in
the vital arena of nuclear technology and scrambled to catch up
with a little help from information gathered by its spies in the West.
But the need for weapons-grade uranium and plutonium led to bad
decision-making when it came to building and operating nuclear
plants. Nowhere was this more evident than at Mayak, where
ignorance about proper safety procedures was coupled with gross
environmental negligence – highly toxic radioactive waste initially
being dumped straight into the nearby river.

In 1953, in an effort to curb the radioactive pollution, 40
underground storage tanks for liquid waste were constructed. The
self-generated heat from this radioactive waste rose to a
dangerously high temperature, so cooling units were added. But
neither these nor the tanks themselves were adequately monitored.

When one of the cooling systems failed in September 1957, the
temperature in one bank of tanks rose rapidly and the waste within
exploded. There were no immediate casualties, but a radioactive
cloud swiftly spread to the northeast, severely contaminating an
area of 800 sq km (310 sq mi). The authorities belatedly reacted a
week later, evacuating some 10,000 people from the affected zone –
but without telling them why. Many became hysterical when
symptoms such as radiation burns and peeling skin occurred. The
truth only came out when the USSR collapsed in 1990.

Windscale fire

Generating electricity by means of nuclear energy was a young
industry in 1957. The Windscale plant on the Irish Sea was not
about providing electricity for the people, but weapons-grade
plutonium for the military. The on-site Calder Hall nuclear
power station did generate power, but the two air-cooled
reactors at Windscale commissioned back in 1950 (Piles 1
and 2) had only one purpose – producing plutonium-239 for
Britain's H-bombs.

In October, the graphite core of Pile 1 caught fire, initially

without its operators realizing there was a problem. But when radiation gauges on the cooling-tower filters redlined, two men suited up and went to inspect the reactor. They removed an inspection plug and to their horror saw fuel within the core was red-hot. It was more than possible that the fire would reach temperatures at which the reactor's reinforced concrete containment would collapse, releasing a disastrous cloud of radioactive contaminants.

Initial firefighting attempts failed miserably. The ejection of undamaged fuel cartridges merely stopped the raging inferno from becoming even more intense. An attempt to blow out the fire by using the reactor's powerful fans merely exacerbated the situation, and the injection of carbon dioxide to starve the fire also proved unsuccessful. As the soaring temperature became critical, there was only one highly risky option left – water.

This was incredibly dangerous. The molten metal core would oxidize in water, creating hydrogen that could mix with air and cause a massive explosion, which would undoubtedly demolish the reactor and scatter lethal radioactivity far and wide. Mercifully, the forced gamble paid off and 24 hours later the fire was out and Pile 1 was cold, with a relatively minor radiation spill in comparison with what might have been. A mass tragedy had been averted. But it was the nearest of misses.

Aerial view of Calder Hall and Windscale power stations

WHEN:
October 10 1957
WHERE:
Near Seascale, Cumbria, UK
DEATH TOLL:
There were no casualties at the time. Whether or not the later cancer cluster in the area is attributable to Windscale is a matter of controversy. It is estimated that some 240 cancer deaths probably resulted from the radiation released into the atmosphere.
YOU SHOULD KNOW:
Late in the construction of Windscale Piles 1 and 2, Sir John Cockcroft – director of Britain's Atomic Energy Research Establishment and an eminent nuclear physicist – asked that bulky and expensive high-performance filters should be fitted to the cooling towers. He was roundly criticized for this demand, but insisted. In the event his foresight would prevent a serious industrial accident becoming a major nuclear catastrophe.

Springhill Mines bump

WHEN:
October 23 1958
WHERE:
Springhill, Cumberland County,
Nova Scotia, Canada
DEATH TOLL:
74 miners died, 100 were rescued.
YOU SHOULD KNOW:
The Springhill operation was closed
down after the 1958 disaster,
devastating the community and
leaving some of the world's deepest
coal workings to fill with water. But
the flooded mines would later be
used to provide a useful source of
geothermal energy for local
industries.

*A second miner is brought to
the surface after nearly ten
days in the dark.*

Canada's Springhill coalfield in Nova Scotia opened in the 19th century, and was the scene of more than one serious accident. Way back in 1891 a coal-dust fire broke out in Number 1 and 2 collieries, which were connected by a tunnel. With 125 miners killed and scores more injured, it was a disaster that horrified the nation. In 1956, Number 4 colliery suffered an explosion when runaway train cars carrying coal dust hit a power line. A huge blast destroyed surface buildings and killed or trapped over 100 miners (39 dead, 88 pulled out alive after a superhuman effort by rescue crews).

Just two years later, Number 2 colliery was rocked by the worst 'bump' in North American mining history. A bump is an underground quake caused when bedrock weakened by mining activity gives way, creating a shockwave with a domino effect that causes further collapses. The bump that occurred on October 23 was so severe that it was felt as a small earthquake on the surface. The mining community of Springhill immediately appreciated that this presaged disaster and hurried to the mine to begin a long vigil as a frantic rescue effort was mounted.

Rescue teams found survivors at the 4,200 m (13,800 ft) level, but tunnels were blocked by rock falls and shafts were filled with debris. It looked bad but, after seven days of frantic digging, 12 lucky miners were pulled out. Two days later a final group of survivors was found, but after that only bodies were recovered. It wasn't the world's worst mining disaster but the Springhill bump attracted widespread attention because the Canadian Broadcasting Corporation beamed out pictures of the unfolding drama, making it the first major accident ever to get international coverage on live TV.

Knox mine disaster

Just one year after Nova Scotia's Springhill community went into mourning for miners lost in its infamous 'bump', another bizarre mining disaster occurred in North America. This time the location was Jenkins Township in Pennsylvania. There was nothing sylvan about the River Slope Mine, an anthracite pit operated by the Knox Coal Company near the grimy coal-mining city of Pittston.

The eponymous river of the mine's name was the mighty Susquehanna, the longest on America's East Coast. In January 1959, management ordered miners to tunnel upwards towards the Susquehanna from existing workings below the river, reducing the thickness of rock separating the riverbed and mine to a recklessly dangerous 1.8 m (6 ft) – when 10.5 m (35 ft) was considered to be the minimum safety margin in such situations. The consequence of this folly was predictable, and catastrophic.

River water broke through into the workings and gushed down into the mine. Amazingly, although there were casualties among the 81 mining crew, the vast majority somehow managed to escape – 32 of them being led to safety by a resourceful miner called Amadeo Pancetti who was consequently awarded a Carnegie Medal, reserved for civilians who perform extraordinary acts of heroism.

Some 10 billion gallons of water cascaded into the mine, a process that created a large whirlpool in the Susquehanna River. Desperate attempts to plug the hole by depositing rail cars into this maelstrom were unsuccessful and the river eventually had to be diverted before the breach could be sealed. The tragedy led to the abandonment of deep coal mining in northeastern Pennsylvania's Wyoming Valley. Ten people – including the mine superintendent and a senior official of the United Mine Workers Union – faced assorted charges, but only three went to prison for their negligent contribution to the Knox Mine Disaster.

WHEN:
January 22 1959
WHERE:
Jenkins Township, Greater Pittston, Luzerne County, Pennsylvania, USA
DEATH TOLL:
12 died (though no bodies were recovered) and 69 escaped.
YOU SHOULD KNOW:
The Knox mine disaster may have been the Pittston area's most unusual mining disaster, but it wasn't the worst by quite some way. In 1896 a massive explosion had caused a cave-in that killed 58 miners at the Newton Coal Company's Twin Shaft Colliery.

Aberfan

Coal was the life-blood of industry in South Wales, with whole communities dependent on the top-quality steam coal found beneath the valleys and hills. One such was Aberfan, a village close to Merthyr Tydfil in the historic county of Glamorgan. Opened in 1875, Aberfan's Merthyr Vale Colliery became the biggest pit in the South Wales Coalfield, generating huge quantities of waste.

For half a century this was dumped in spoil tips on the flanks of Merthyr Mountain, directly above Aberfan, with little thought given to the underlying geology. Unfortunately, this consisted of porous sandstone riddled with underground springs. One Friday morning in October 1966, subsidence occurred in Tip Number Seven after heavy rain, precipitating a slide of liquefied debris that flowed swiftly down the sunny mountainside towards the mist-shrouded village below, reaching a depth of 12 m (40 ft). It hit Aberfan and smashed into the Pantglas Junior School minutes after the pupils had assembled.

Everyone heard the ominous rumble, but the mist meant nothing could be seen. Before evasive action could be taken, the school was engulfed. Frantic villagers raced to the scene and started digging with their bare hands, soon joined by trained rescue personnel, but few children were pulled alive from the slurry. When the final death toll was known, 116 youngsters had perished, along with five teachers. There were further casualties in the village.

The aftermath was scandalous. Coal Board Chairman Lord Robens suggested that the disaster could not have been predicted – despite the fact that safety concerns had frequently been raised – and it took a lengthy public enquiry to apportion blame to the Coal Board. Worse still, the Board appropriated money from the disaster fund – generously subscribed by the public for victims and their families – to help pay for clearance of remaining tips.

WHEN:
October 21 1966
WHERE:
Aberfan, Wales, UK
DEATH TOLL:
144 deaths
YOU SHOULD KNOW:
The Merthyr Vale Colliery was renovated and modernized at great expense in the 1960s, thus surviving the subsequent wave of mine closures in South Wales, but it never recovered from the miners' strike in 1984–1985 and was closed in 1989.

Buffalo Creek flood

Don't always trust a US Federal Mine Inspector – that was the painful lesson learned by unsuspecting residents of Buffalo Creek Hollow in West Virginia. On February 22 1972 the Pittston Coal Company's Slurry Dam Number Three had been declared 'satisfactory' after inspection, despite having been built on accumulated coal waste created by large-scale strip mining rather than bedrock.

Four days later, after prolonged seasonal heavy rain, the 'safe' dam burst, overwhelming Dams Number One and Two downstream and unleashing 500 million litres of liquid coal waste on the unfortunate residents of Buffalo Creek Hollow. A number of coal-mining hamlets were engulfed by a 10 m (33 ft) wave of black water and there was further damage in communities like Lundale, Saunders, Latrobe and Laredo.

Some 4,000 people were left homeless and over 500 houses were destroyed, along with business premises, mobile homes and 1,000 trucks or cars at a total cost of around $50 million. The local population was devastated by the loss of 125 lives (including seven bodies never found) and over 1,100 people were injured. The Pittston Coal Company and its Buffalo Creek Mining subsidiary described the event as that old blame-dodging favourite, 'an act of God'. The official enquiry hardly demurred, vaguely calling for legislation and a further investigation. An unofficial Citizen's Commission was less forgiving, returning a 'murder' verdict against Pittston Coal.

Equally surprising was the financial outcome in the litigious USA. Pittston Coal's act-of-God defence didn't stand up but the company managed to settle with survivors for $18.5 million (against $290 million claimed) while the state's demand for $100 million for disaster relief costs was miraculously settled for just $1 million in 1977, days before the outgoing Governor left office. It all went to show that Big Coal was indeed king in West Virginia.

WHEN:
February 26 1972
WHERE:
Logan County, West Virginia, USA
DEATH TOLL:
125 dead, 1,121 injured
YOU SHOULD KNOW:
Although coal impoundment dams like those at Buffalo Creek were banned by Federal statute in 1969, the regulations simply hadn't been enforced. West Virginia passed a Dam Control Act in 1973 but failed to attach funds for its implementation – and in the 1990s it was estimated that there were still over 400 hazardous dams in the state.

Debris from houses in Buffalo Creek Valley.

Flixborough chemical disaster

WHEN:
June 1 1974
WHERE:
Flixborough, North Lincolnshire
(formerly Humberside), UK
DEATH TOLL:
28 (including a driver who died of a
heart attack), with 36 seriously
injured
YOU SHOULD KNOW:
Despite the tragic loss of life at
Flixborough, it could have been so
much worse – had the plant
explosion not occurred at the
weekend, the entire workforce
of over 500 people would have
been killed.

People characterized as NIMBYs ('Not In My Back Yarders') are the curse of would-be developers everywhere. They are often dismissed as selfish by said developers, who counter with the argument 'but it has to go somewhere'. Yet NIMBYs often have genuine cause for concern, and so it proved when the residents of Flixborough near Scunthorpe in North Lincolnshire fought and lost the battle to prevent a major chemical plant from being sited close to the village in the 1960s.

The chemical factory produced caprolactam, used in the manufacture of nylon. This process involved the oxidation of cyclohexane, by combining benzene with hydrogen in six linked reactors. When a crack was discovered in one reactor, a large bypass pipe was installed so repairs could be effected. At 16.53 on June 1 1974, a Saturday, this temporary pipe ruptured. A volatile vapour cloud formed as 40 tonnes of cyclohexane leaked out in seconds. Almost instantly, this found an ignition source and a massive explosion demolished the plant and killed 27 employees.

Nearly 2,000 buildings in the surrounding area were destroyed or damaged and the wrecked chemical plant blazed for ten days before the fires were finally extinguished. Those apprehensive NIMBYs were proved tragically right when Flixborough village suffered severe structural damage, as did the neighbouring communities of Amcotts and Burton-upon-Stather. There was even significant damage reported in Scunthorpe, 13 km (8 mi) away.

Despite their case being validated in such dramatic fashion, Flixborough's NIMBYs were again ignored – the ruin was rebuilt and resumed production. But market forces achieved what locals had failed to do. Demand for nylon declined and the plant became commercially unviable. It was demolished in 1981 and the site is now occupied by an industrial estate.

Emergency services attend to the fire at the chemical plant at Flixborough.

Seveso

The small chemical plant owned by Hoffmann-La Roche subsidiary ICMESA near Meda, 15 km (10 mi) north of Milan, was not considered by the locals to pose any threat, perhaps because it had been operating for many years without serious incident. But that changed in July 1976. Building B housed a complex chemical reaction producing 2,4,5-trichlorophenol, used as an intermediate for hexachlorophene and a herbicide. On July 10 operations were being shut down ahead of the weekend, when Italian law prohibited production. Unfortunately, a runaway reaction forced a relief valve to open, releasing six tonnes of wind-borne material that swiftly spread over an area of 18 sq km (7 sq mi).

A policeman pins up warning signs around the town of Seveso.

Contained within this toxic emission was just 1 kg (2.2 lb) of – wait for it – 2,3,7,8-tetrachlorodibenzodioxin (shortened for obvious reasons of convenience to TCDD or simply 'dioxin'). This potent compound gained notoriety as a constituent of Agent Orange, a lethal herbicide used by the Americans in the Vietnam War, and even such a relatively small quantity exposed local people to an amount that was fully 100 times more concentrated than the acceptable trace amount of one part per million.

Animals died, soil was contaminated and some 37,000 people suffered varying degrees of exposure to TCDD. Many – especially children – developed skin lesions and several pregnant women chose to have abortions, only permitted in Italy under such extraordinary circumstances. The event became known as the Seveso Disaster after the town that suffered most. Two senior executives of ICMESA – technical director Herwig von Zwehl and production director Paolo Paoletti – were arrested and the Italian government mounted a massive long-term clean-up operation. As a result of this disastrous dioxin leak, the set of regulations drafted to govern industrial safety in the entire European Community is known as the Seveso II Directive.

WHEN:
July 10 1976
WHERE:
Meda, near Seveso, Lombardy, Italy
DEATH TOLL:
Around 3,300 domestic animals (including poultry) perished within days and another 80,000 were slaughtered to prevent them entering the food chain. As no people died as an immediate result of the spill, a human total is harder to estimate but there is no doubt that adverse long-term health effects contributed to a large number of early deaths – notably from respiratory and heart diseases.
YOU SHOULD KNOW:
In February 1980 ICMESA's production boss Paolo Paoletti was assassinated by a member of the radical Marxist-Leninist Italian terrorist group *Prima Linea* (Front Line) as part of a violent campaign against uncaring capitalism.

Aerial view of cooling towers at a nuclear power plant on Three Mile Island

Three Mile Island

For an event that fascinated the world and sent a frisson of fear scorching through the USA, the nuclear accident at Three Mile Island was in fact the disaster that never (but nearly) was. The accident could have developed into a 'China Syndrome', that hypothetical catastrophe where the core of a nuclear reactor melts down and spews out lethal radioactivity. But it didn't actually happen. So what did?

The Metropolitan Edison Company operated two pressurized water reactors on an island in Pennsylvania's Susquehanna River. Unit One (TMI-1) came on line in 1974 and Unit Two (TMI-2) in 1978. The following year, in the early hours of the morning of March 29, a minor cooling system failure in TMI-2 initiated an unfortunate series of events.

Reactor temperature rose, causing automatic shut down. A relief valve failed to close, draining coolant from the reactor core. Inadequate instrumentation meant that control-room staff assumed the valve had closed, so they mistakenly reduced the flow of replacement cooling water. The reactor's core then overheated and started to melt,

WHEN:
March 28 1979
WHERE:
Londonderry Township, Dauphin County, Pennsylvania, USA
TOLL:
None – or at least no proven consequences
YOU SHOULD KNOW:
In a rare example of life imitating art, a near-disaster movie entitled *The China Syndrome* (starring Jane Fonda, Jack Lemmon and Michael Douglas) was released just 12 days before Three Mile Island hit the headlines, featuring safety cover-ups at a nuclear plant. Events at Three Mile Island ensured that the film became an instant international blockbuster.

contaminating the remaining coolant. This subsequently released radioactive gases into the atmosphere on March 30 and 31.

Once the operators realized what was happening, they plugged the leak and initiated cool-down. After an anxious month, reactor shutdown was finally achieved on April 27. The containment building did its job and – despite acute public apprehension resulting from poor communication – there were no further radioactive leaks.

In 1996, a class action lawsuit claiming damages for ill-health effects was dismissed for lack of hard evidence. Some studies suggested that leukaemia and lung cancer rates increased significantly in the population exposed to radioactive krypton gas and iodine-131, but the official line remains that there were no adverse medical consequences of Three Mile Island. Meanwhile, TMI-1 remains one of the most productive nuclear energy plants in the USA.

Church Rock uranium spill

Quizmasters of the world sit up and take note. Here's the question: 'Name the worst radioactive accident in US history – clue, it took place in 1979'. Sit back with an evil smile as all those pencils instantly scribble 'Three Mile Island', and later enjoy the shocked expressions when the answer is given: 'Church Rock uranium spill'.

Radioactive spills aren't confined to nuclear facilities or faulty manufactured items. The raw material is uranium. Uranium is mined. Mining creates waste. Waste has to be stored. The plan at the United Nuclear Corporation's Church Rock Uranium Mill in New Mexico was depressingly familiar in mining history – store the effluent in a large pond behind an earth dam built on poor foundations. In this case, the plot had a nasty twist – when cracks start appearing in the dam don't tell anyone and don't do anything. That's just what happened in 1977, and the weakened dam duly collapsed in July 1979.

Over 1,000 tonnes of radioactive mill waste in 352 million litres (93 million gallons) of contaminated water spilled into the Rio Puerco, producing a level of radioactivity 7,000 times greater than that permitted in drinking water. Nobody bothered to notify residents, who used the river extensively. Those suffering radiation burns were diagnosed with heat stroke and there was a half-hearted clean-up effort. End of story.

Why did this disastrous spill slip under the world's radar? The area was remote and those most affected were Navaho Indians – many of whom worked as uranium miners and were already exposed to associated risks. The USA does not have the best of records when it comes to Native Americans. Trucked-in water was provided until 1981 but then farmers had to return to the use of irrigation water from the river, allowing residual radioactivity to pass into the local food chain.

WHEN:
July 16 1979
WHERE:
Church Rock, New Mexico, USA
TOLL:
Unknown. Unlike many other serious pollution incidents no serious epidemiological studies were ever done to assess the health effects – nor have there been studies of the low-income labour force in uranium mines – despite the fact that some types of cancer have a significantly higher incidence than the national average among the Navaho people.
YOU SHOULD KNOW:
In 1994 the US Environmental Protection Agency belatedly mounted an investigation and clean-up at the Church Rock mine site.

San Juanico

WHEN:
November 19 1984
WHERE:
San Juan Ixhuatepec, Mexico
DEATH TOLL:
Estimates put the death toll at 500 to
600, with perhaps 6,000 to 7,000
severely injured.
YOU SHOULD KNOW:
Mexico's state-run petroleum
company, the giant PEMEX energy
combine, owned the San Juanico
facility. In true 'not our responsibility'
style, the company initially tried to
suggest that the disaster was
initiated not by its own negligence
but an explosion in a nearby factory.

If you've got a storage and distribution terminal containing a third of Mexico City's liquid petroleum gas (LPG) supply stored in 54 tanks, it pays to buy the best gas-detection system money can buy. Unfortunately, the San Juanico facility had the tanks – filled with a mixture of butane and propane – but lacked a sophisticated gas-detection capability.

Early one November morning in 1984, as the surrounding town of San Juan Ixhuatepec slept, a pipeline ruptured during a transfer procedure. An insidious cloud of heavier-than-air LPG accumulated and slowly travelled towards the western end of the site, where a flare pit burned off waste gas. Naked flame and a huge pool of flammable gas are a lethal combination.

The startled residents of San Juan Ixhuatepec were awoken by a massive explosion, which was followed by an intense fire fed by gas escaping from blast-damaged tanks. A few moments later, the next detonation in a percussive hour-long series took place as individual tanks went up. These were BLEVE explosions, the bland acronym standing for Boiling Liquid/Expanding Vapour Explosion. Each blast contributed more burning gas to the conflagration and when two of the largest spherical tanks blew, seismic instruments registered 5.0 in the Richter scale – equivalent to a moderate earthquake. The terminal would burn for over 24 hours.

It soon became apparent that this catastrophic event was not only the worst LPG accident ever recorded, but also one of the world's worst industrial disasters. San Juan Ixhuatepec – mainly consisting of simple one-storey concrete houses with tin roofing – was devastated by blast waves, flying debris and a deadly firestorm. Hundreds of the 40,000 inhabitants died and many thousands were badly injured. Casualty figures were vague because the vast majority of the dead were reduced to ashes as the inferno raged.

Bhopal

In 1969 the American Union Carbide Company established a factory at the Indian city of Bhopal. It would produce the pesticide carbaryl, marketed as Sevin – a process made more efficient in 1979 when a methyl isocyanate (MIC) plant was built on site. Union Carbide knew this chemical was hazardous, but it was cheaper than alternative ingredients of Sevin and managers wrongly believed that a first-class handling strategy was in place. On the night of December 2 1984 water flooded Tank 610, which contained 42 tonnes of methyl isocyanate, and initiated a complex chemical reaction that rapidly heated the contents.

By midnight a temperature of 200°C (392°F) had blown a safety valve, releasing a toxic mixture of poisonous gases into the atmosphere. Residents of Bhopal started waking with symptoms that included burning lungs, violent coughing, severe eye irritation and vomiting. Many died almost immediately and others were killed in the panic-stricken melée that followed. Even as Union Carbide denied that there had been a leak, police started evacuating residents and hospitals filled to overflowing with victims, many of whom had been blinded. Fatalities were measured in thousands, with terrifying implications for those who survived but would face chronic medical problems and premature death in the years ahead.

Union Carbide scientists had identified the danger of a runaway reaction of the kind that occurred in Bhopal, but their report never reached senior management. Before 1984 there had been numerous minor industrial accidents at the plant, some involving MIC, but these ominous signs were ignored, along with dire warnings from visiting American experts and the Indian authorities. Leaving all that aside, the tragedy would have been averted if Tank 610's refrigeration system hadn't been switched off to save money. This was an industrial massacre that should never have happened.

WHEN:
December 3 1984
WHERE:
Bhopal, Madhya Pradesh, India
DEATH TOLL:
Officially, it stands at 3,787. Unofficially, it is thought that a more realistic total is around 35,000 (10,000 within days and another 25,000 who died later from diseases related to the gas poisoning).
YOU SHOULD KNOW:
The Union Carbide factory site became a permanent dumping ground for some 400 tonnes of toxic waste that polluted ground water and thus continued to damage the health of the local population.

Bhopal victims wearing eye patches.

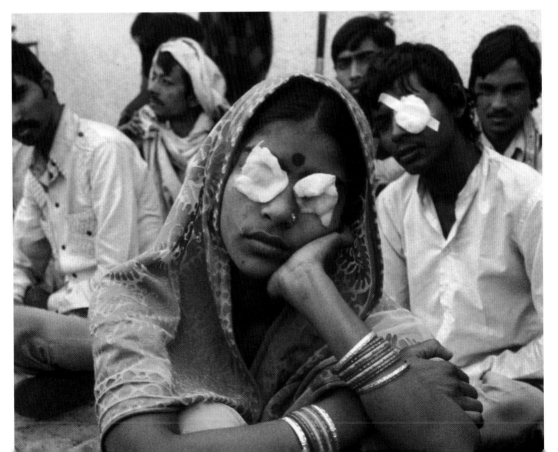

Chernobyl

WHEN:
April 26 1986
WHERE:
Prypiat, near Chernobyl, Ukraine
DEATH TOLL:
Over 200 people suffered acute radiation sickness in the immediate aftermath of the explosion, of whom 31 died within three months. The total number of deaths directly attributable to the accident was 56, mostly irradiated rescue workers but including some children who died of thyroid cancer. The number of premature deaths to be expected from related diseases was estimated at 5,000.
YOU SHOULD KNOW:
The radioactive fallout from the disaster at Chernobyl was 400 times greater than the amount released by the atom bomb dropped on Hiroshima at the end of World War II.

The catastrophic nuclear disaster the world had long feared finally happened in 1986 at the Chernobyl plant in Ukraine. Reactor number four exploded early one morning in April, sending a vast plume of radioactive fallout into the atmosphere. This would contaminate large areas of the western Soviet Union and Europe, with nuclear rain being recorded as far away as Ireland.

The initial power excursion (nuclear chain reaction) was followed by further chemical and gas explosions, then fire. Unlike those in most Western plants, the reactor building was not a reinforced containment vessel designed to limit the effects of just such an accident. It was therefore destroyed, allowing disastrous quantities of radioactive material to escape. Yet this was an accident that could have been avoided.

Ironically, the catalyst was an experiment carried out to test reactor safety. Operators were worried that a power failure might result in the reactor core overheating, as vast quantities of cooling water were required and standby generators didn't get the pumps back up to speed for over a minute. They therefore decided to test whether an emergency core-cooling procedure would work should such a situation arise. Had regulations been followed there would have been no problem, but safety features were disabled in order to complete the test. This decision proved fatal. After complex set-up procedures were completed, the test commenced but within seconds the core went critical and a powerful explosion rocked the plant.

The aftermath was horrific, though Soviet authorities initially tried to conceal the scale of the disaster. The town of Prypiat was evacuated the following day and remains a deserted time capsule. The accident site was contained within a vast concrete sarcophagus at the centre of the 30 km (19 mi) exclusion zone around Chernobyl that is in force to this day.

An aerial view of the Chernobyl nuclear power plant, the site of the world's worst nuclear accident, two to three days after the explosion. In front of the chimney is the destroyed fourth reactor.

Piper Alpha

WHEN:
July 6 1988
WHERE:
North Sea
DEATH TOLL:
167 died (including two crew
members from a rescue boat); 59
survived.
YOU SHOULD KNOW:
The initial fire on Piper Alpha would
have burnt out and the death toll been
greatly reduced had the platform not
been a staging point for pipelines from
the Tartan and Claymore platforms.
The cost of shutting these down was
so great that both continued pumping
into the heart of Piper Alpha's fire,
creating an unstoppable conflagration
that destroyed the rig and cost the
lives of so many crew members.

The discovery of North Sea oil and gas was a boon to Britain. Piper Alpha made a productive contribution. Originally an oil platform, it was later modified for gas production and consisted of four safety modules separated by firewalls. In July 1988 Piper Alpha was producing ten per cent of the North Sea's annual production. The revenue amounted to millions of daily dollars, but events soon proved that harvesting black gold from beneath the sea could exact a terrible price.

Two pumps on Piper Alpha compressed gas for onward transmission, but on July 6 Pump A's safety valve was removed for maintenance and the open pipe sealed with a metal plug. At 21.45, Pump B failed. Supply had to be maintained at all costs and control room staff tragically failed to find the written notification that Pump A was out of commission. They started it at 21.55, immediately initiating a major leak through the temporary plug.

The gas ignited, causing an explosion that demolished safety walls built to withstand fire only. The control room was abandoned and events ran out of control. A second explosion rocked the platform at 22.20, intensifying the blaze. The *Tharos* rescue and firefighting vessel drew alongside at 20.30, only to be driven off as the second gas line went, creating a massive fireball.

The crew were either sheltering in the fireproofed accommodation block or leaping desperately into the sea, but the end was nigh. At 23.50 most of the platform collapsed into the sea, the rest soon following. As dawn broke, all that could be seen above the sullen swell was the skeletal remains of one module, its top still burning. Of 226 people on the platform that fatal night, fewer than a third survived the world's worst offshore oil disaster.

Texan expert firefighter Red Adair on the still-burning Piper Alpha offshore platform, before he was forced to retreat by a combination of a surge of flames from one of the wells and worsening weather.

Camelford water pollution

Anyone who wants to damage the largest possible number of people in the shortest possible time could find few better methods than slipping a large amount of poison into the public water supply system. That's not actually what happened at South West Water's unmanned Lowermoor Water Treatment Works in North Cornwall, but the incident that occurred in July 1988 is still regarded as Britain's worst-ever breach of water-quality guidelines.

There was no malicious intent, and the compound that went into the drinking water – far from being poisonous – was actually aluminium sulphate, a chemical that helps to purify water by solidifying particulate matter. But it is applied in minute quantities compared to the amount of water being treated, and a delivery driver accidentally dumped 20 tonnes of the stuff into the wrong tank.

This resulted in a massive overdose of aluminium sulphate entering Camelford's water supply – over 3,000 times the maximum permitted amount, a concentration that stripped all sorts of other chemicals from lead and copper piping as it went. Though residents quickly started complaining about acidic water quality, it was two days before the problem was identified and action taken to prevent 20,000 users suffering additional exposure. Public anger erupted, along with claims of mismanagement and even cover-up.

People immediately started suffering from all sorts of symptoms, from hair turning blue though acute skin irritation to sore throats and short-term memory loss. As time went on, many developed severe joint complaints and even brain damage. As always in these cases, where official enquiries tend to rule that there's no proven link between cause and effect, the Lowermoor Incident Health Advisory Group concluded that there had been real suffering in the community, but decided it had been caused by anxiety rather than genuine physical ill-effects.

WHEN:
July 6 1988
WHERE:
Camelford, Cornwall, UK
TOLL:
Studies continue into the long-term health implications of the Lowermoor pollution, as public perception (and considerable scientific opinion) suggests that the metallic chemical cocktail ingested in 1988 may eventually lead to the premature development of assorted but serious medical conditions.
YOU SHOULD KNOW:
South West Water was prosecuted and fined £10,000, plus £25,000 in costs. But they didn't get off that cheaply. In 1994, 140 victims were awarded compensation totalling £400,000 for documented injuries caused by the incident.

Vaal Reefs elevator disaster

WHEN:
May 10 1995
WHERE:
Orkney, Klerksdorp, South Africa
DEATH TOLL:
105 dead
YOU SHOULD KNOW:
The one person who did actually survive the catastrophic accident was the driver of the runaway train, who managed to jump clear before it toppled into Shaft Number Two and fell towards the rapidly ascending elevator cage.

Becoming a miner in South Africa during the 20th century was a dirty and dangerous case of needs must. With a chronic lack of alternative employment, a workforce of black miners came from all over the country to live in dormitories and earn modest wages that nonetheless meant survival for families left behind. Sadly, many never returned to their loved ones, as around 70,000 were killed in mining accidents between 1910 and 2000.

In May 1995 over 100 of that total perished at the Anglo-American Corporation's Vaal Reefs Mine near Orkney, southwest of Johannesburg. Even a nation hardened to mining tragedy was horrified by the gruesome disaster at one of South Africa's largest and most profitable gold mines. Miners had finished their shift in the sweltering depths of the 2.3 km (1.4 mi) Shaft Number Two and were returning to the surface in an elevator cage. High above, their fate was sealed when an underground train entered a tunnel that was supposed to be closed, went out of control and careered into the shaft.

The falling train hit elevator cables, sending the cage plunging downwards in free fall. A second after it hit bottom, the heavy locomotive smashed into the already compressed cage and further reduced the substantial two-tier structure to what the President of South Africa's National Union of Mineworkers (NUM) later described as 'a one-floor tin box'. The occupants were pulverized, body parts were scattered everywhere and identifying individuals proved to be a long and distressing process. Two days after the accident a representative of Anglo-American grimly told a press conference: 'The bodies are badly mutilated, it's hot and they're beginning to decompose'. The NUM established a trust fund for dependents of victims, who were located as far apart as the rural areas of Lesotho, Transkei, Swaziland and Botswana.

Los Frailes Mine pollution

WHEN:
April 25 1998
WHERE:
Andalucia, Spain
TOLL:
Long-term environmental damage
YOU SHOULD KNOW:
In 2000, without giving any advance warning, Boliden abruptly abandoned its mining activities in Spain, before filing for bankruptcy later that same year to avoid paying a hefty fine imposed by the out-of-pocket Spanish government.

A vast area in the marshy lowlands of Las Marismas, around southwestern Spain's Guadalquivir River, was designated as a wildlife refuge and national park in 1963. Doñana National Park became a UNESCO World Heritage Site in 1994, but not before suffering persistent threats to its unique ecosystem caused by water extraction for agricultural irrigation and burgeoning coastal tourist facilities.

Four years on, this unique area faced an even more severe threat – a massive spill of mining waste from a storage lagoon at the Los Frailes lead-zinc mine operated by the Swedish-Canadian Boliden company at nearby Aznalcóllar. A dam wall collapsed, sending millions of cubic metres of concentrated zinc, lead and cadmium sludge into the River

Guadiamar, a tributary of the Guadalquivir that flowed through Doñana National Park. This toxic cocktail polluted a 60 km (37 mi) stretch of the river, killing all aquatic life, depositing lethal heavy-metal waste in wetlands, polluting wells, permeating ground water, ruining farmland and destroying standing crops.

Boliden inevitably claimed that the disaster could not have been foreseen, though it probably happened because pollution fines were so low in Spain that it was cheaper to let things happen than take expensive remedial action. This theory is supported by the fact that a report commissioned by the company two years earlier identified the failed dam's weakness. After the event, contributory factors such as unsuitable subsoil and blasting at the opencast mine were identified. But whatever the cause, its effects were disastrous and despite a 250 million euro clean-up it will take four decades for the polluted area to recover fully.

However, there was a silver lining. The rapid construction of an emergency dam across the River Guadiamar prevented any toxic waste contaminating Doñana National Park's fragile ecology, which therefore remained undamaged by this avoidable disaster.

A massive spill of toxic mining waste into the River Guadiamar wipes out all aquatic life.

Petrobras 36 Oil Platform

WHEN:
March 20 2001
WHERE:
Campos Basin, Atlantic Ocean
DEATH TOLL:
11 of the rig's crew of 175 were killed – ten in the explosion and one who died of severe burn injuries after being evacuated.
YOU SHOULD KNOW:
The accident enquiry showed that P-36's emergency response teams were not properly trained – or equipped – to deal with any eventuality. They didn't have the portable gas detectors that would have enabled them to monitor the threat . . . and perhaps prevent any loss of life.

In March 2001 the Petrobras 36 Oil Platform (P-36) was the world's largest floating oil production platform, operating 130 km (80 mi) off the Brazilian coast in the Roncador Field. Tragically, by the end of the month it was floating no more.

The platform had started life as the drilling rig *Spirit of Columbus*, before being refitted as a production platform. It was a semi-submersible with two pontoons that supported four large columns. They in turn carried the main deck with its production facility. Although capable of processing 180,000 barrels of oil per day, P-36 was operating at less than half capacity.

Just after midnight on March 15, less than a year after production had begun, an emergency drain tank in the starboard aft column ruptured due to excessive pressure. Water, oil and gas flooded in. The emergency firefighting team rushed to the scene but 17 minutes later dispersed gas caught fire, causing a major explosion that killed ten crew members.

P-36 had become a dangerous place to be and a full-scale evacuation began almost immediately. By 06.00 all 165 surviving crew members had been lifted off, two hours before the stricken rig suddenly tilted by more than 15 degrees. But the owners weren't about to abandon their valuable baby without a fight, and attempts were made to stabilize the damaged platform. Salvage teams pumped nitrogen and compressed air into the submerged pontoon, but bad weather hampered their operations.

On March 20 one final effort was made, but it was all in vain. At 05.30 that morning the inclination reached 31 degrees and P-36 continued to topple. By 09.00 the angle was 45 degrees and at 10.45 34,600 tonnes of metal worth $350 million – plus 1,500 tonnes of crude oil – started the 1,375 m (4,500 ft) journey to the bottom of the Atlantic Ocean.

A rescue boat near Petrobras platform P-36.

Jilin chemical plant explosions

Anywhere in or around the Number 101 Petrochemical Plant in Jilin was definitely not the place to be on November 13 2005. For that was the day when explosions ripped through the state-owned China National Petroleum Corporation's facility when a nitration unit malfunctioned. The sequence of powerful detonations lasted for an hour, shattering windows over a wide radius and starting fierce fires that would not be extinguished until the following morning. Six workers were killed with around 75 injured, many seriously.

The very real fear that there could be further blasts and possible chemical contamination caused the evacuation of 10,000 from the area around the plant. Suspicion that the disaster had caused severe pollution was eventually confirmed when it became apparent that a large quantity of carcinogenic benzene and nitrobenzene had leaked into the Songhua River. An 80 km (50 mi) toxic slick drifted down river, causing widespread disruption to drinking-water supplies as it went. Efforts were made to mitigate the disastrous leak – hydroelectric dams upriver opened their sluices in an attempt to dilute the dangerous level of benzene – but it was still more than 100 times greater than the national safety level.

China's tenth-largest city was particularly hard hit. Harbin in adjacent Heilongjiang Province is located on the banks of the Songhua River downstream of Jilin, and public water supplies had to be cut off for more than three days as the pollution slick approached, causing great inconvenience to nearly four million inhabitants. With impressive efficiency, 100 new artesian wells were drilled to provide Harbin with uncontaminated ground water and ease the supply shortage, but the benzene continued to cause problems as it went on to enter the Amur River and passed through the Russian Far East *en route* for the Strait of Tartary and the Pacific Ocean.

Smoke rises into the sky after the explosion in Jilin.

WHEN:
November 13 2005
WHERE:
Jilin City, Jilin Province, China
DEATH TOLL:
Six
YOU SHOULD KNOW:
In typical knee-jerk fashion, the initial reaction of Jilin Petrochemicals' management was to deny that pollutants had entered the Songhua River. Only when it became obvious that a serious benzene slick was heading for Harbin did they own up. The Chinese press was critical of the official response to the accident, forcing a senior government environmental minister to resign.

Halemba mine accident

WHEN:
November 21 2006
WHERE:
Ruda Slaska, Silesia, Poland
DEATH TOLL:
23 dead
YOU SHOULD KNOW:
Despite the Polish prime minister's suggestion that the fatal explosion might be seen as an act of God, state prosecutors did not agree. After an exhaustive investigation, 27 individuals faced criminal charges in 2008, ranging from endangering the lives of miners resulting in death down to negligence and falsifying documents.

Silesia is Poland's industrial heartland and the region's coal mines – employing more people than any other sector and fuelling 90 per cent of the country's electricity generation – are vital to the national economy. But it's a dangerous business, with miners operating in difficult conditions, often exacerbated by lack of investment following the collapse of the Communist regime in 1989. With its poor accident record, the Halemba mine was no exception, though there had been nothing to compare with the tragedy that occurred on November 21 2006.

On that day, a kilometre below the surface, equipment was being recovered from Halemba's 1,030 m (3,380 ft) level – closed the previous March after a dangerous concentration of methane gas was detected by a specialist, who was trapped there for five days after a minor explosion. But the equipment left behind was valuable and – despite the continuing presence of methane – management eventually sent in a recovery crew

that consisted of 23 miners ranging in age from 20 to 60, including inexperienced young hands supplied by private contractors.

It would prove to be a fatal assignment. A violent gas explosion ripped through the mine, almost certainly killing the unfortunate victims instantly. Six bodies were quickly recovered, but the remaining 17 were not found for two days, after rescue teams braved persistent methane to dig through collapsed tunnels.

Polish Prime Minister Jaroslaw Kaczynski declared a state of national mourning and arrived at the mine to commiserate with victims' families in particular and the shocked mining community in general. In the manner of politicians everywhere after such happenings, he promised a thorough official enquiry but offered little hope that it would get to the root cause of the problem – poor safety standards in Poland's mines – by suggesting that the likely culprit was that old scapegoat 'natural forces'.

Miners from a rescue team in Halemba coal mine in Ruda Slaska, southern Poland. After a 38-hour-long rescue operation all 23 remaining missing miners were found dead.

A man rinses soot from his face at the scene of a gas pipeline explosion near Nigeria's commercial capital, Lagos.

Abule Egba pipeline explosion

WHEN:
December 26 2006
WHERE:
Abule Egba, Lagos, Nigeria
DEATH TOLL:
The number of casualties has never been officially established. After the event, an experienced Reuter's news photographer did an approximate body count and came up with a figure of 500.
YOU SHOULD KNOW:
Abule Egba wasn't the first pipeline disaster in Nigeria during 2006. Back in May a pressurized pipe at Atlas Creek Island was drilled by petrol thieves, the resultant explosion incinerating everyone within a 25 m (85 ft) radius and killing at least 150 people, many of whom were interred in a mass grave.

Black gold has proved both a boon and a curse to the West African republic of Nigeria. The world's eighth most populous country is a major oil producer, has membership of OPEC (Organization of the Petroleum Exporting Countries) and possesses huge proven reserves. However, constant agitation by the population of the oil-producing Niger Delta – concerned by pollution and central indifference to their needs – has meant that the government's main source of income is constantly being disrupted by protest action.

Nor has this lucrative revenue stream transformed the lives of the country's people, with many living in grinding poverty and shanty towns. To the inhabitants of Abule Egba in Lagos State, the overhead pipeline that carried petroleum products was a constant reminder of the valuable national resource that had somehow failed to transform their lives. Some resented it, and some decided to do something about it.

In 2006, around midnight on Christmas Day, thieves set out to give themselves a late present. They punctured the pipe and proceeded to help themselves to a large quantity of fuel before going on their way, possibly driving a full tanker, leaving behind a leaking pipeline. It may have been the small hours, but word spread quickly and soon hundreds of residents with assorted containers were trying to collect their share, amid pools of spilled fuel that formed beneath the breach.

At dawn, these were ignited and the pipeline exploded, causing a catastrophic fire. Numerous houses were destroyed, along with a church and mosque, and hundreds of people died. When the Nigerian Red Cross arrived to help, they were confronted with a scene of carnage. Charred corpses were scattered everywhere, though the team was able to find and help 65 seriously burned residents who survived the inferno.

Qinghe Special Steel Corporation disaster

Once a Chinese state enterprise, the Qinghe Special Steel Corporation had been transferred to the private sector before its plant in Tieling became the scene of a terrible accident in April 2007 – the worst to befall the modern Chinese steel industry. A large overhead ladle, that carried molten steel from a blast furnace, separated from its overhead track and fell. Instead of remaining upright, it hit a flatbed truck and tilted, spilling its deadly contents.

Some 25 tonnes of liquid steel at a temperature of 1,500°C (2,730°F) flowed out of the 2 m (6 ft) ladle, burst through the door of a meeting room where workers had assembled during an early-morning shift change and killed over 30 occupants. By some miracle, six workers who were out on the factory floor survived – they were able to turn and run, though all were badly burned and required prolonged hospitalization. Rescue services couldn't gain access to the area until the intense heat cooled. The bodies they eventually recovered were too badly burned to be recognized and had to be identified through DNA testing.

There was public outrage when news of the tragedy broke. The authorities immediately sealed off the plant and launched a full investigation. The findings were not reassuring. It seemed that safety measures were poor, management was ineffective and the hoist that fell was not suitable for the job it was being asked to do. More significantly, the report concluded that this was not an isolated case of inefficiency, but indicative of a malaise that had spread throughout the Chinese steel industry. In a situation where steel making had to expand rapidly – perhaps too rapidly – to support the rapacious demands of a booming national economy, corners were being cut and a lax safety culture had become endemic.

WHEN:
April 18 2007
WHERE:
Tieling, Liaoning Province, China
DEATH TOLL:
32 died
YOU SHOULD KNOW:
In the immediate aftermath of the Qinghe Special Steel Corporation disaster, the plant's owner and three senior employees were arrested and charged with safety violations, while officials quickly offered generous compensation to bereaved families to ensure that public anger did not get out of hand.

ENGINEERING DISASTERS

Dee Bridge collapse

WHEN:
May 24 1847
WHERE:
River Dee, Chester, UK
DEATH TOLL:
Of the 20 or so passengers on the train, five were killed and many others injured.
YOU SHOULD KNOW:
Following the accident Robert Stephenson used only the tougher material of wrought iron in his future railway bridges, such as those at Conway and across the Menai Straits.

Chester in Northwest England had been an important settlement since Roman times but its status as a regional centre received a major boost when a new long-distance railway line opened in the 1840s, running between London and Holyhead on the island of Anglesey. The line passed through Chester and had to cross the River Dee just outside the city at a point where the river is still tidal.

One of the principal engineers for the line, Robert Stephenson, designed a bridge for the crossing. He was the son of George, of Rocket fame, who was often called the 'father' of the railways. Although a span of some 80 m (250 ft) was called for, Stephenson's bridge had just two stone piers because of concerns about the foundations; these were linked by a construction of cast-iron girders on which oak joists were laid that supported the twin tracks.

The bridge opened with great ceremony in November 1846, but just six months later, in May 1847, a local passenger train was passing over the bridge when it suddenly collapsed. The driver had nearly completed the crossing when he felt the final span start to give way beneath the steam engine. He managed to get the locomotive onto firm ground on the far bank, but the tender and train behind him fell 10 m (30 ft) into the river below. The subsequent investigation revealed that a cast-iron beam on the bridge had fractured at its centre. Although it was not understood as such in those days, it is now generally accepted that metal fatigue was the cause. After the accident the widespread use of cast iron in bridge construction ceased on account of its brittle nature.

An early engraving of the bridge collapse

Pemberton Mill disaster

Lawrence was an important mill town situated on the Merrimack River in northeastern Massachusetts. Appropriately enough, one of its grandest buildings was Pemberton Mill, a mighty five-storey brick edifice with an overall length of 85 m (280 ft). Built in 1853, this busy cotton mill produced woven textiles and clothing on some 700 looms. The mill was at full capacity on January 10 1860 when, late in the afternoon and without warning, the whole construction suddenly came crashing down. A large proportion of the 900 workers in the mill at the time were women and Irish immigrants. Most of them were buried in the ruins. The site of the collapse resembled a battlefield with piles of shattered beams, mangled iron and crushed brickwork littered with human bodies.

A frantic rescue operation was mounted and many victims were dug out and pulled to safety. But this tragedy had yet to deliver its final and cruellest act. A lantern being used by one of the rescuers was knocked over and started a fire which quickly consumed the entire ruins. Contemporary accounts describe the terrible screams of people trapped in the rubble who had sensed that rescue was close at hand but then suffered an even more horrifying fate in the flames. The investigation into the disaster found that the collapse had been caused by defects in the cast-iron pillars supporting the factory floors and by weak mortar used in the brick walls. As so often with accidents during the industrial age, a subsequent inquest did not find anyone accountable, even though managers had almost certainly known that the loading of the upper floors with heavy machinery had exceeded normal safety limits.

WHEN:
January 10 1860
WHERE:
Lawrence, Massachusetts, USA
DEATH TOLL:
More than 120 people were killed and at least 160 injured.
YOU SHOULD KNOW:
A local magazine reported many remarkable tales of survival, including the feat of a young woman who with great presence of mind managed to escape by climbing down a chain hoist from the upper floors as the building collapsed about her.

The ruins of Pemberton Mill in Lawrence, Massachusetts

The bridge collapsed in a storm, killing the entire crew and all the passengers on a train that was crossing at the time.

Tay Bridge disaster

WHEN:
December 28 1879
WHERE:
Firth of Tay, Scotland, UK
DEATH TOLL:
75
YOU SHOULD KNOW:
William McGonagall, the 19th century poet dubbed the worst in the English language, was a native of Dundee. His most famous – or infamous – poem is devoted to the disaster and begins with the line 'Beautiful Railway Bridge of the Silv'ry Tay!'

It took engineer Thomas Bouch 20 years to persuade the operators of the east coast London-to-Scotland railway line to commit the funds for a great bridge to cross the Firth of Tay in Scotland. When the bridge was completed in 1877 it was, at over 3 km (2 mi), the world's longest by far. Bouch was only able to use brick piers at the southern end of the bridge where the foundations were in solid rock; for most of the bridge's 85 piers he had to resort to the lighter alternative of piers composed of cast-iron columns. The bridge also had a central raised section of 13 piers over the estuary's deep channel so that shipping could pass beneath; the clearance was further enhanced by the expedient of placing the bridge's trusses for that section on top of the track, creating in effect a latticework tunnel.

On December 28 1879, little more than 18 months after the Tay Rail Bridge had opened for passenger traffic, the mail train from

Edinburgh was heading for the city of Dundee on the north bank. Approaching the south end of the bridge the driver slowed down; a storm was raging and there were vicious cross-winds in the estuary. As he eased his engine gently over the high section the piers gave way, spilling the entire train into the turbulent waters below. There were no survivors.

The official inquiry cited the extreme weather conditions as a major factor in the disaster but also castigated aspects of the construction method and the materials deployed, in particular the use of cast iron. Although this had also been at the root of the Dee bridge collapse 30 years before, it was still another dozen years before the British government banned the use of cast iron in bridge construction.

Detroit Wonderland Theatre

Detroit was on the cusp of its re-birth as Motor City and Henry Ford was cutting his teeth as a young automobile engineer when Messrs Wiggins and Moore, two developers and impresarios, secured a prestigious city-centre plot to be the new home for their popular and much-loved Wonderland Theatre. The plan was for a new building that would rise to an impressive five storeys and be a significant addition to Detroit's entertainment scene.

The shell and the steel skeleton of the new theatre had been completed when, early one Saturday afternoon in the late autumn of 1898, the roof suddenly collapsed, dragging down the structures beneath it. Both of the galleries in the auditorium were crushed underneath the weight of falling debris, much of which ended up in the theatre pit. Within minutes the building had been transformed into a huge mound of dusty rubble, littered with twisted beams, broken timbers and great chunks of brickwork and cement. One newspaper of the day described it as a 'fatal hillside'.

When the accident happened 35 labourers were at work in the building and they were all swept down in the deluge of debris. The lower balcony at least held up, which probably saved the lives of a number of the builders, though they suffered injuries. The walls survived the initial collapse but one side-wall had clearly been damaged very badly; a few hours later it, too, collapsed.

It appears that the roof was simply too heavy for the structure, having been topped with a 20 cm (8 in) thick layer of cement. There were also questions about the toughness and durability of the steel girders used for the framework.

WHEN:
November 10 1898
WHERE:
Detroit, Michigan, USA
DEATH TOLL:
15
YOU SHOULD KNOW:
Undeterred by the tragedy, Wiggins and Moore continued to prosper as major promoters of vaudeville entertainments in Detroit.

Quebec Bridge

WHEN:
August 29 1907 and
September 11 1916
WHERE:
St Lawrence River, Quebec, Canada
DEATH TOLL:
74 (1907) and 11 (1916)
YOU SHOULD KNOW:
Quebec Bridge finally opened in
December 1917 and has stood
without incident since. It is still the
world's longest single-span
cantilever bridge.

Looking today at the imposing bulk of Quebec Bridge as it straddles the St Lawrence River, you would be hard pushed to imagine its inauspicious origins. The crossing of the mighty St Lawrence was always going to be a major engineering challenge, but by the beginning of the 20th century a solution to the efficient transport of goods to the city on the north bank had become imperative. The design of the prestigious project was entrusted to one of America's most eminent bridge builders, Theodore Cooper. The site, to the west of the city, would not only mark the easternmost crossing of the river but would also have to allow the passage of large ocean-going vessels.

Cooper produced a design for a steel cantilever bridge with a single central span 46 m (150 ft) above the water. In order to reduce costs the original dimensions were altered, producing a central span with an unparalleled width of 549 m (1,800 ft). This modification fatally compromised the integrity of the design. When work on the bridge began in 1904 Cooper was old and infirm; he relied on reports from his engineers, sent to his New York office. In August 1907 the south cantilever was already projecting 230 m (750 ft) from the pier when buckling was noticed on some steel plates. Cooper's instructions to suspend construction pending investigation failed to reach the builders and on August 29 the whole structure collapsed, taking with it 85 men. Even though the replacement structure used two-and-a-half times as much steel, it too ran into difficulty. Nine years later the new central section was being raised carefully into position between the cantilevered arms when a rupture caused it to crash into the water.

Quebec Bridge collapsed twice during construction, with fatal consequences.

St Francis Dam catastrophe

One of the key issues affecting the development of Los Angeles was the provision of an adequate and dependable water supply. The city's Bureau of Water Works and its chief engineer, William Mulholland, attracted national attention in the early 1900s with the bold construction of the Owens River Aqueduct which brought water a staggering 380 km (237 mi) from the mountains. By the 1920s, however, the rapidly expanding city was experiencing regular water shortages. Mulholland's solution was to create a network of new water storage facilities closer to the city.

One of these, the St Francis Dam, was built between 1925 and 1926 across the St Francisquito Canyon, 56 km (35 mi) northeast of Los Angeles. The dam was an imposing curved structure 56 m (185 ft) high built of concrete on the gravity principle. The artificial lake behind it was 4.5 km (2.8 mi) long and took two years to fill. Just five days after the reservoir had reached full capacity the dam suffered a catastrophic breach. The concrete wall shattered, sending a terrifying wall of water raging down the valley. The torrent swept up everything in its path, abating only when it reached the Pacific Ocean near Ventura, 86 km (54 mi) away. In just 70 minutes the St Francis reservoir had been emptied of 12.4 billion gallons of water.

At the official inquest afterwards the blame for the disaster was placed on the dam's foundations and the unpredictable nature of the rock on which it had been built. Although the existence of a minor fault line was known, the understanding of geological movements was not very advanced at the time. More recent research suggests that the real culprit was an ancient and unknown landslide that had been re-activated.

Remains of the St Francis Dam after it collapsed and released 12 billion gallons of water.

WHEN:
March 12 1928
WHERE:
Santa Clarita, near Los Angeles, California, USA
DEATH TOLL:
More than 450 people were killed in the flood waters; the bodies of many who had been swept out to sea were never recovered.
YOU SHOULD KNOW:
The City of Los Angeles paid out more than $7 million dollars in compensation to the victims' families and those who had lost homes and livelihoods.

The concrete roadway falling into the water after the bridge started to sway.

Tacoma Narrows Bridge

The first half of the last century witnessed a burgeoning enthusiasm for the suspension bridge, especially for the clean lines and simple elegance of the so-called suspended deck design. The world's most famous example, the Golden Gate Bridge straddling San Francisco Bay, opened in 1937. Three years later the quest for ever more slender and graceful structures culminated in the Tacoma Narrows Bridge across Puget Sound in Washington State. Connecting the under-developed Olympic peninsula with the Washington mainland, the bridge was not designed for heavy traffic volumes so, even though it had a central span of 853 m (2,800 ft), it had a width of just 11.9 m (39 ft) – enough for a single carriageway and walkway in each direction.

The Tacoma Narrows Bridge opened with much fanfare in July 1940. For all the high expectations its life proved spectacularly short. Just four months later the deck of the bridge began to twist in the lateral forces of a stiff cross-wind blowing up the Narrows one autumn morning.

WHEN:
November 7 1940
WHERE:
Puget Sound, Washington, USA
DEATH TOLL:
The bridge's protracted death-throes gave good notice of the collapse so there were fortunately no human casualties on this occasion. The only fatality was a dog too frightened to leave a car that had been abandoned on the bridge.
YOU SHOULD KNOW:
Because of World War II it was ten years before a new bridge was built across the Narrows, this time with a wider deck and open trusses used as stiffeners instead of the previous solid-plate girders.

A certain amount of vibration along the length of the deck had in fact been observed in lighter winds as soon as the bridge was finished, and this had gained it the nickname of 'Galloping Gertie'. On this occasion the carriageways were not only rippling lengthwise but the torsional oscillations were also pushing one side of the deck as much as 8.5 m (28 ft) above the other. This extraordinary sight continued for over an hour until the bridge could take the strain no longer and its central span broke and fell into the water. This has become a particularly famous engineering disaster because the whole episode was captured on film and many a school physics lesson has been enlivened by this remarkable footage.

Malpasset Dam collapse

When the French government decided to build a dam to improve the water supply and irrigation for the notoriously dry agricultural region around Fréjus on the country's Mediterranean coast, it chose the site of a narrow gorge on the Reyran River a few kilometres inland. Geological tests indicated that the surrounding rock was suitably solid, although some concerns were expressed when construction started. The dam was of the double-curvature arch type, built of concrete. At the time of its completion in 1954 it was the thinnest of its kind in the world.

The prevailing climate meant that it took several years before the reservoir was filled to its full capacity of some 50 million tons of water. This was only achieved late in 1959 when unusually heavy rainfall had raised it to unprecedented levels.

On December 2 officials released excess water through the dam in an attempt to control the level, but with limited success. Shortly after nine in the evening the dam came away from its foundations on the left bank and burst, releasing a wall of flood water over 40 m (130 ft) high which raced down the valley at speeds approaching 70 kph (44 mph). After passing through the outskirts of Fréjus, the deluge of mud and water finally discharged into the sea. In just half an hour the entire landscape had been devastated.

In spite of its thinness, the design of the dam was not at fault. The cause of the collapse seems to have been a combination of exceptional water pressure induced by the torrential rains; the composition of the rock on the left bank; and a fault line a little distance downstream.

WHEN:
December 2 1959
WHERE:
Near Fréjus, Côte d'Azur, France
DEATH TOLL:
Estimates vary, but it is generally accepted that more than 420 people were killed.
YOU SHOULD KNOW:
The name of the site – Malpasset – derives from the French *c'est mal passé* ('bad passage') since in former times the road through the narrow gorge had been a notorious spot for ambushes by highwaymen.

Baikonur launch-pad explosion

WHEN:
October 24 1960
WHERE:
Baikonur Cosmodrome, Kazakhstan
DEATH TOLL:
At least 120 people were killed in the explosion, including Marshal Nedelin himself. Some sources put the death toll as high as 200.
YOU SHOULD KNOW:
In an effort to conceal its true location from the West, the Soviet Union deliberately named the launch site after a mining town that was in fact 320 km (200 mi) away.

The rocket launching site of Baikonur in Central Asia was at the heart of the Soviet Union's space programme. Located on the steppes of what is now Kazakhstan the vast facility covered at its peak an area of over 10,000 sq km (4,130 sq mi). Baikonur was also an important test site for missiles during the Cold War and has witnessed well over 400 launches. Many of the landmark events in the space race began there, including the launch of the Sputnik satellite in 1957 and the first manned space flight by Yuri Gagarin in April 1961.

The achievement of getting the first person into space represented a huge propaganda coup for the Soviet Union. What the Russians kept quiet about, however, was the terrible explosion that occurred at Baikonur just six months previously. Only since the fall of the Soviet Union has anything like a full picture emerged of an incident which remains the worst single accident in the history of rocket science.

The R-16 was a new type of intercontinental ballistic missile the Russians had been developing. In October 1960 a prototype was being prepared for a test launch at Baikonur under the personal supervision of Marshal Nedelin, head of Soviet Rocket Forces. Wishing to impress the Soviet top brass, Nedelin put huge pressure on the scientists and engineers to have the launch ready for the anniversary of the Russian Revolution. Inevitably this meant overlooking safety procedures, so that when the rocket was being fuelled some 150 personnel remained on site instead of evacuating the area. As electrical repairs were being carried out, the second stage engine accidentally ignited; its exhaust ripped through the fuel tank on the first stage, producing a massive explosion which was reportedly seen 50 km (30 mi) away.

Vajont Dam landslide

WHEN:
October 9 1963
WHERE:
Dolomites, Friuli, Italy
DEATH TOLL:
At least 2,000 people died; the toll may have been as high as 2,600.
YOU SHOULD KNOW:
Remarkably, the dam itself survived the disaster intact and can still be seen today – though it is of course no longer in use.

The postwar recovery of the Italian economy was driven by the great industrial cities of the north and the Vajont Dam was one of a number of major hydroelectric schemes designed to service their increasing power needs. Sited in a deep valley in the Dolomites 100 km (62 mi) northeast of Venice, the double-curved arch dam was 265 m (870 ft) high and the artificial lake it created could hold 150 million cu m (33 billion gallons) of water. Although there was evidence of past landslides in the area and some concern over the stability of the slopes of Monte Toc which formed the south side of the reservoir basin, none of this impeded construction and the dam was duly finished in 1960.

A minor landslide occurred in November that year but this did not prevent the filling of the basin, which proceeded on a controlled schedule over the next three years. The reservoir was full nearly to capacity when on October 9 1963 a massive landslide dumped 260 million cu m (9 billion cu ft) of earth and rock into the water from the feared south bank. Not only did this push water up the opposite slope, engulfing a village hundreds of feet above, but it also created a giant wall of water which overwhelmed the dam. It is estimated that the landslide expelled nearly half the water in the reservoir. The sight of the *seiche* wave, which probably exceeded the crest of the dam by as much as 250 m (820 ft), must have been truly terrifying. The wave crashed down the valley, consuming everything in its path. By the time the flood waters finally settled, several more entire villages in the neighbouring Piave valley had been utterly destroyed.

View of Longarone, the village that was wiped out after the landslide.

Ronan Point

WHEN:
May 16 1968
WHERE:
Newham, London
DEATH TOLL:
Four people died and 17 were
injured.
YOU SHOULD KNOW:
The Larsen-Nielsen construction
method was intended for buildings
of up to six storeys – in the UK it
was used for tower blocks. The
Ronan Point disaster forced the
demolition of other similarly
constructed tower blocks and was
responsible for the tightening of
building regulations everywhere.

*Rooms exposed after the
collapse of the flats.*

Much of London's East End was flattened by German bombs in World War II and in 1961 a programme of slum clearance and tower-block construction was started. Many of these towers were built according to the Larsen-Nielsen method: reinforced, pre-cast concrete sections assembled on site. The construction of 22-storey Ronan Point in Newham began in 1966 and the tower was completed two years later. Newham Council tenants moved in during March 1968.

Just two months later Ivy Hodge, a cake decorator living in a corner flat on the 18th floor, woke early. She went sleepily into her kitchen and lit the cooker to boil a kettle: a massive explosion hurled her across the room and ripped out the load-bearing outer wall. With nothing left to support the flats above, they began to collapse, their weight soon bringing down the entire southeast corner of the tower.

Fortunately three of the four flats above Ivy were unoccupied and, amazingly, she herself survived. The living rooms of the flats beneath her broke away from the rest of the building, but the bedrooms remained intact and luckily most people were still asleep when the explosion occurred. Whole families, in their nightclothes, rushed downstairs – the lifts had failed – and out into the street, as a great chunk of Ronan Point collapsed like a house of cards.

The ensuing investigation found that a gas leak had caused the explosion but that high winds or fire would probably have caused a similar collapse. The tower was repaired but in 1984 a survey revealed structural cracks suggesting that, despite the re-building and strengthening that had taken place, Ronan Point was disintegrating. During the tower's demolition in 1986 it was found that the section joints had been poorly fitted and that the original building work was sub-standard.

West Gate Bridge

Melbourne's West Gate Bridge across the Yarra River links the city to the suburbs and leads out to an industrial zone and the port of Geelong. Construction began in 1968 and appeared to progress well for the next two years. But in October 1970, while two half girders on the west side were being connected, a camber difference between them was noticed. Ten eight-tonne concrete cubes were placed on the northern span, to level them out. It was noted that a buckle had developed around one of the joints as a result, but work still continued. On October 14 written instructions were given to straighten the buckle forthwith; at 08.30 the following morning this was started.

At 11.50 a 112 m (367 ft) section suddenly collapsed, bringing 2,000 tonnes of concrete and steel crashing down onto the riverbank and into the water below. Some workers were taking a break beneath the bridge while others were working on the girder itself. The collapse killed 35 men and the force of the impact caused an explosion that shook all the surrounding buildings and splattered them with flying mud. The noise could be heard for miles. To add to the havoc, some spilt diesel oil caught fire, hampering rescue attempts

A Royal Commission set up to investigate the disaster heard evidence from 52 witnesses. Its report of August 1971 left none of the parties involved in the project entirely free of blame. Error had been piled upon error and 'the events which led to the disaster moved with the inevitability of a Greek tragedy'. What became abundantly clear was that not only was the construction site unsafe, but the bridge also would have been unsafe upon completion. The West Gate Bridge collapse was 'the most tragic industrial accident in the history of Victoria'.

A section of the West Gate Bridge lies in twisted ruins in the mud of the Yarra while rescue squads work in the debris.

WHEN:
October 15 1970
WHERE:
Yarra River, Melbourne, Victoria, Australia
DEATH TOLL:
35 construction workers were killed and there were numerous injuries.
YOU SHOULD KNOW:
In June 1970 part of the Milford Haven Bridge in Wales collapsed during construction, resulting in the strengthening of the steel spans in the new West Gate Bridge build. Work resumed in 1972, and was completed in 1978. In 2007, following the collapse of a bridge in Minneapolis, a project was proposed to identify structural weaknesses in West Gate Bridge, as it was carrying far heavier loads than it was designed to bear. The strengthening project should be completed in 2011.

Water pouring through the collapsed dam.

Teton Dam flood

The Teton Dam in the northwestern US state of Idaho enjoys a dubious reputation as one of the most short-lived constructions in the history of dam building. The earthfill dam had just been completed – workmen and machinery were still on site – when in June 1976 it burst, sending an estimated 80 billion gallons of water down the valley to inundate a huge area of farmland. A project of the US Bureau of Reclamation, the dam had been sited in the canyon of the Teton River, part of the Snake River system and 71 km (44 mi) northeast of Idaho Falls. Standing to a height of 93 m (305 ft) and with a crest width of 975 m (3,200 ft), it was built for a variety of purposes, including, ironically, flood protection.

WHEN:
June 5 1976
WHERE:
Teton River, near Idaho Falls, Idaho, USA
DEATH TOLL:
11
YOU SHOULD KNOW:
There was considerable disagreement over the cause of the dam's failure, but it is now widely assumed to have been due to the permeable nature of the loess soil used in the core of the dam.

The 27 km (17 mi) long reservoir was almost full with spring melt water when the breach occurred. Some seepage had been noticed several hours beforehand but was considered to be within normal operating limits. When a hole appeared near the right bank, however, bulldozers attempted to plug it. When they failed and the hole got steadily larger, workers watched helplessly as the whole western side of the dam collapsed and an angry cascade of water surged forth. Collecting rocks and debris from the valley floor as it moved down the canyon, the flood water had turned a muddy brown by the time it swamped the towns of Wilford and Rexburg. Because there had been a few critical hours' notice of impending disaster, warnings had been issued and local residents had evacuated their homes. As a result, although damage to land and property ran into the tens of millions of dollars, loss of life was mercifully low.

Alexander Kielland oil rig

Having to deal with potentially hazardous substances in some of the fiercest weather the planet has to offer has made workers in the offshore oil and gas industries an exceptionally tough breed. High rates of pay and generous shore leave have helped to ensure that there has never been a shortage of willing labour prepared to brave the elements. Although a generally good safety record has also helped, 123 North Sea workers tragically paid the ultimate price when in March 1980 their accommodation rig capsized in gale-force winds.

The Alexander Kielland was a semi-submersible rig situated in the Ekofisk oil field in the North Sea, midway between the Scottish and Norwegian mainlands. It was being used as a so-called 'flotel': an accommodation rig for the 300 or so workers drilling on the Edda rig. The two rigs were linked by a bridge, although this was not connected at the time of the accident. In the early evening, as winds of almost 100 kph (60 mph) buffeted the rig, one of the rig's leg braces snapped, causing the others to fail in turn and then the leg itself to break. The whole enormous 10,000 tonne structure toppled over; for some 15 minutes it balanced precariously at a 35 degree angle before capsizing and turning over completely. Many of the survivors owed their escape to those crucial minutes, during which two lifeboats were successfully launched.

The rig now lay upside down in the storm-tossed seas with only its legs visible above the surface. A huge international rescue mission was immediately organized, involving ships, helicopters and diving vessels from Norway and the UK. The terrible weather made rescue efforts very difficult and some survivors had to endure an ordeal lasting many freezing hours before being picked up.

WHEN:
March 27 1980
WHERE:
North Sea (between Scotland and Norway)
DEATH TOLL:
123 people died out of the 212 crewmen on board the rig at the time of the tragedy.
YOU SHOULD KNOW:
Although rumours of sabotage have continued to surround the incident, the official explanation for the disaster was metal fatigue in the leg brace.

The sinking remains of the rig

Kansas City hotel disaster

WHEN:
July 17 1981
WHERE:
Kansas City, Missouri, USA
DEATH TOLL:
114
YOU SHOULD KNOW:
The Hyatt Regency Hotel re-opened in due course. Sadly, but perhaps not surprisingly, the new building contains no memorial or other reference to the accident.

The wreckage of two catwalks is scattered through the lobby of the hotel.

When the Hyatt Regency Hotel opened its doors for business in downtown Kansas City local leaders were understandably proud of this sumptuous addition to their city's facilities. It was July 1980, and many features of the building were at the cutting edge of design, in particular the impressive atrium which connected the hotel's tower block to an adjoining function complex. One year later, on a Friday evening, some 2,000 guests had filled the atrium for a dance party when two suspended walkways running the length of the atrium suddenly gave way and fell onto the crowded lobby below. Many party-goers had been standing on the walkways when the disaster occurred.

The collapse was caused by the failure of connections supporting the fourth-floor walkway ceiling rods. This walkway crashed onto the second-floor walkway directly beneath, which in its turn fell onto the lobby. Most of the deaths were of people either in the lobby or on the second-floor walkway, crushed by falling masonry and other objects. The subsequent investigation brought several disquieting facts to light, not least that the design of the rod connections had been changed at a late stage by the manufacturer to simplify the assembly. This was probably the critical error, but analysis of the surviving offset walkway on the third floor revealed that it had been barely capable of supporting the expected load. There had also been an indication of possible trouble ahead when, during construction in October 1979, a large section of the atrium roof had caved in following the failure of another connecting device. Although the hotel's design engineers were cleared of criminal negligence, they were all subsequently stripped of their licences to practise their trade.

The Ocean Ranger capsize

As the name suggests, Ocean Ranger could indeed range. But in February 1982 this mobile semi-submersible offshore drilling platform was firmly anchored 267 km (166 mi) off Newfoundland in the Grand Banks area of the North Atlantic. Granted the location, it was as well that Ocean Ranger was built to withstand the worst weather and sea conditions nature could conjure up.

This rugged capability would be tested to the limit. Along with two other platforms drilling Hibernia Field, Ocean Ranger received reports of a fast-approaching storm whipped up by a major Atlantic cyclone. There wasn't time to go through the full procedure to isolate the drilling system, but the crew managed to disconnect from the sub-sea blowout preventer. During the evening, wind speeds reached 100 knots (190 kph, 118 mph) and waves towered to 20 m (65 ft). Messages from Ocean Ranger reported minor problems but nothing to hint at the disaster that was about to occur.

At 00.52 the following morning, a Mayday signal went out, reporting that Ocean Ranger had suddenly developed a severe list and requesting help. Even as the rig's *Seaforth Highlander* support vessel stood by and those from the two neighbouring rigs raced to provide assistance, a final communication was received at 01.30 – Ocean Ranger was doomed and the crew was taking to the lifeboats. It was a badly botched evacuation, made even more difficult by darkness and atrocious sea conditions. Observers on *Seaforth Highlander* watched helplessly as many crew members struggled in the water, unable to do anything because their ship was neither equipped to rescue casualties from the water nor capable of even attempting the feat. By the time rescue helicopters arrived at 02.30, Ocean Ranger's entire crew had perished in the icy sea by drowning, hypothermia or a combination of both.

WHEN:
February 15 1982
WHERE:
Grand Banks, North Atlantic
DEATH TOLL:
84
YOU SHOULD KNOW:
The disaster was triggered by a freak wave that broke a portlight window, allowing water into the ballast control room. Consequent short-circuits caused ballast valves to open in the forward tanks (or be opened by the controller in error when the instrument panel malfunctioned), creating a list too severe to be corrected by the pumps and leading inevitably to capsize. The crew's chances were lessened by the fact that evacuation training was inadequate and there were no survival suits on board.

Hatchie River Bridge

WHEN:
April 1 1989
WHERE:
Tennessee, USA
DEATH TOLL:
Eight motorists died.
YOU SHOULD KNOW:
The Hatchie Bridge collapse pointed
to the dangers inherent in many
bridges built before World War II that
were reaching their sell-by date with
a little help from intense modern
traffic volumes. To underline the
point, another Tennessee bridge
failed two weeks later. The wooden
structure crossing the Southern
Railway at Oliver Springs collapsed
under the weight of a truck, killing
one and injuring two.

The 1930s was a good time for infrastructure works in the USA, as that vast country rapidly developed its national road system with a little help from President Roosevelt's New Deal. Route 51 was a major north-south artery created in 1926 to connect Wisconsin and New Orleans. Ten years later, the Tennessee section was improved by the construction of a two-lane highway bridge across the Hatchie River north of Memphis. This impressive 1,220 m (4,000 ft) structure not only crossed the river, but also spanned its flood plain. In 1974 a parallel bridge was built to provide two southbound lanes, leaving the old bridge to handle northbound traffic. Unlike the original, the new bridge did not sit on piles for its full width, instead being built with a restricted opening of around 300 m (985 ft) in the centre for the main river channel.

This feature would have unexpected consequences, as it concentrated the Hatchie River's powerful flow in wet winters. That of 1988–1989 saw particularly heavy and prolonged rainfall, causing the river to remain in flood from November 1988 to the following April. On the first day of that month, three sections of the old bridge collapsed without warning. Four cars and an articulated truck plunged over 6 m (20 ft) into the fast-moving torrent below, as a 26 m (85 ft) gap was left in the carriageway. All eight occupants of the five submerged vehicles perished.

Blame fell squarely on the Tennessee Board of Transportation, which had regularly inspected the old bridge and noted ten years earlier that the main channel of the Hatchie River had shifted, with the result that piles – the very ones that eventually failed – were permanently submerged, though they were never designed to stand in water. No remedial action was taken, and disaster ensued.

Highland Towers collapse

The township of Taman Hillview in Malaysia's Klang Valley is conveniently close to Kuala Lumpur and became popular with expatriates from the 1970s, despite being in landslip country. That didn't deter developers from erecting three 12-storey apartment blocks collectively known as Highland Towers in this verdant setting, starting in 1975 and completing the project in 1978. The buildings were erected on a flat section of elevated ground at the base of a steep hill terraced with randomly constructed retaining walls. A stream was diverted into a pipe culvert and a further web of drains was created to serve an extensive bungalow development. It was an ambitious scheme that would end in tears.

After a prolonged period of heavy rain towards the end of 1993 a huge mudslide overwhelmed a retaining wall in the three-tier Highland Towers car park. The sheer force of the slide, combined with ground weakened by the diverted stream and foundation pilings that were simply not deep enough, caused Building One to topple on its side – a terrible event captured in a dramatic series of photographs shot by a visiting American. Rescuers had to halt their efforts after a further slide occurred and when they finally finished combing through the rubble 48 bodies had been recovered.

Although the Malaysian government placed an immediate ban on hillside development after Highland Towers, this risky form of construction continued apace and 15 years later another catastrophe occurred close to the site of the original tragedy, when four people died, many were injured and 5,000 had to be evacuated after a large development area in nearby Bukit Antarabangsa was declared a disaster zone following . . . a massive mudslide. The Malaysian government's reaction to the latest disaster was predictable. It placed an immediate ban on hillside development.

WHEN:
December 11 1993
WHERE:
Taman Hillview, Selangor, Malaysia
DEATH TOLL:
48 residents were killed in the collapse.
YOU SHOULD KNOW:
Abandoned after the destruction of Building One for safety reasons, the vandalized Buildings Two and Three of Highland Towers still stand today above the Kuala Lumpur ring road, rising incongruously above encroaching jungle greenery that is fast reclaiming the site.

The collapsed Sampoong store

WHEN:
June 29 1995
WHERE:
Seoul, South Korea
DEATH TOLL:
501 were killed and 937 injured.
YOU SHOULD KNOW:
The massive concrete floors of the
fifth floor restaurants were fitted
with pipes for hot-water heating. In
traditional Korean restaurants diners
sit on the floor and underfloor
heating is essential in cold weather.

Sampoong Department Store

South Korea's construction boom in the 1980s and 1990s often meant corners were cut, rules bent and palms greased; the Sampoong Department Store was no exception. When work started in 1987, planning permission had been granted for a four-storey office block. But property developer Lee Joon redesigned it as a department store, with modifications which compromised its safety. His building contractors objected but they were simply sacked and replaced. The bright-pink store opened in 1989 and was a huge success, with around 4,000 shoppers a day 'thinking pink'.

Lee Joon decided to add another floor. Further retail development was prohibited, so he opted for restaurants and a pool. Again his contractors protested, saying that the combined weight of additional concrete and air-conditioning equipment would be dangerous. Like their predecessors, they were fired.

On June 29 1995, when cracks appeared in the ceiling of the fifth floor, it was simply closed off. The shop was particularly busy that day and management were unwilling to evacuate the entire building. By lunchtime the cracks had widened and the fourth-floor ceiling was sagging, so the upper floors were shut. The staff finally sounded the alarm at 17.50 and a few minutes later the roof caved in, the support columns gave way and, in less than 20 seconds, a huge section of the five-storey building collapsed into the basement, trapping shoppers and staff.

Thanks to the efficiency of the rescue team, hundreds were pulled out from the wreckage, the last survivor being freed after 17 days. Initially the disasters was blamed on a gas leak or terrorism, but investigations showed that the building had been seriously overloaded and constructed with inferior concrete. Loo Joon was imprisoned, as were several city officials. The corruption came as no surprise to the people of South Korea.

The Hintze Ribeiro Bridge

Entre-os-Rios is an attractive, prosperous town in lovely countryside north of the River Douro. By contrast, Castelo de Paive, just to the south, is a poor rural municipality isolated by mountainous terrain and narrow, twisting roads. The Hintze Ribeiro Bridge, completed in 1886, was an impressive steel and concrete structure which for the people of Castelo de Paive was an invaluable link to jobs, schools and hospitals.

March 4 2001 was a dark and stormy night. The flow of water around the bridge, just below the confluence of the River Douro and the Tamega, was unusually fast. Both rivers have dams upstream, but these were open, and the bridge was pummelled by swirling currents. One of the pillars suddenly gave way and the central section of the bridge plunged into the turbulent river, taking a bus and three cars with it. The exceptionally powerful currents and thick sediment in the water made immediate rescue impossible and all the occupants of the sunken vehicles drowned. The tidal current swept away the bodies and some were washed up as far away as the north coast of Spain.

The whole country was horrified. The transport minister was forced to resign and bridges throughout Portugal were immediately closed for remedial work. However, the Hintze Ribeiro Bridge's age and the force of the swollen river were not the only causes of its collapse. Years of theoretically illegal sand extraction in the vicinity had weakened its foundations and compromised its safety. Warnings from divers and engineers had been repeatedly ignored by the authorities. Now a new bridge spans the Douro and a winged figure commemorates those who died.

WHEN:
March 4 2001
WHERE:
River Douro, near Porto, Portugal
DEATH TOLL:
53
YOU SHOULD KNOW:
River conditions ruled out the use of divers and sonar could give only a rough location of the submerged vehicles. This led to the invention of a flexible 'diving bubble', weighted and fitted with camera, lights and rudder, which sends images of anything it bumps into and is capable of operating in water made opaque by mud or pollution.

A Portuguese navy diver checks the collapsed bridge on the Douro river.

Chicago balcony collapse

WHEN:
June 29 2003
WHERE:
Lincoln Park, Chicago, Illinois, USA
DEATH TOLL:
11 people died at the scene and two more in hospital. There were 57 serious injuries.
YOU SHOULD KNOW:
The wooden balconies on Chicago's older buildings are often rotten after years of snow and rain, and used as spaces to keep air conditioning units, garden furniture and even paddling pools. Unsurprisingly, disintegration is still not uncommon.

Chicago, the windy city, is bitingly cold in winter but breezes from Lake Michigan are very welcome in the heat of summer. Much of the city was built in the 19th century, before the days of air-conditioning, and apartment blocks were usually built with balconies. Unlike New York's famous metal fire escapes, the Chicago versions were generally built of wood.

In the summer of 2003 a group of young people were holding a large party, using two floors of a block in the Lincoln Park neighbourhood of Chicago's North Side. Most of the guests were in their early twenties and had been friends at High School. As the party got livelier, more and more revellers squeezed their way out onto the balconies to cool off. Just after midnight the overloaded floor of the upper balcony gave way and crashed down, taking the first- and ground-floor balconies with it into the basement area.

When the fire department rescue team arrived they found the distraught survivors desperately trying to dig their friends out from beneath the mound of debris. Partygoers and residents alike stood by in shock as the firemen used chainsaws to cut the injured and dead free from the wreckage.

Subsequent enquiries blamed a combination of overcrowding and structural weakness. When the owner had modernized the block he had renovated the balconies without obtaining specific planning permission. In fact, the old-fashioned balconies were larger than modern regulations allowed and constructed of materials which would nowadays be considered sub-standard. He was fined for his part in the tragedy and ordered to bring balconies on all his properties up to the required standard. Since the Lincoln Park incident, stringent inspections city-wide have gone a long way to reducing the incidence of collapsing balconies.

Demolition crews remove the balcony from the building.

Bad Reichenhall ice rink

Bad Reichenhall is a small town in the lovely Bavarian Alps, a popular winter sports area close to the Austrian border. New Year 2006 began with normal, seasonal weather – heavy snow. On the afternoon of Monday January 2, as families on their Christmas holidays were skating on the town's indoor rink, the snow-covered roof collapsed, burying more than 50 people.

Several hundred firefighters were joined by specialist rescue teams from Austria and Germany and dogs trained to locate earthquake victims. Hopes faded as night fell and temperatures plummeted for, although a little girl had been rescued after five hours, hypothermia threatened those still trapped. Using heavy lifting gear, the rescuers worked on despite continuing snow, while firemen, their weight taken by supporting cranes, shovelled snow off the roof. In a two-day operation all the missing were rescued or retrieved.

The shocked community was assured that the usual checks of snow depth on the roof had been made and the accumulation was well within safety limits. The cancellation of ice hockey practice, scheduled for later that day, was queried. Spokesmen for the rink answered that this precautionary measure had been taken because further heavy snow was forecast, and the roof was not due to be cleared until the next day. The grief of the townspeople was mixed with anger. Many claimed that the whole building, which dated from 1971, was in urgent need of a thorough overhaul. Although the official explanation was that the renovations discussed the previous summer were of a cosmetic rather than structural nature, families and friends still blamed the loss of their loved ones on those involved in the construction and management of the ice rink.

Rescuers in front of the collapsed ice rink

WHEN:
January 2 2006
WHERE:
Bad Reichenhall, Bavaria, Germany
DEATH TOLL:
15 died, including eight children; 32 were injured.
YOU SHOULD KNOW:
The former head of the local building office, together with an engineer and an architect who had both been involved in the building of the rink, were brought to trial in 2008 on various charges of negligence. The engineer was given a suspended prison sentence after he admitted his failure to calculate how much weight the roof could bear and the use of an unsuitable kind of beam in the construction. His co-defendants were acquitted.

The snow-covered roof of the collapsed exhibition hall

Katowice trade hall roof collapse

It was Poland's worst building disaster of recent times. On January 28 2006 at 17.15 the huge, flat roof of the Katowice International Fair (MTK) building crumpled like aluminium foil, and collapsed onto more than 700 exhibitors, delegates, visitors and children. The avalanche of snow concealed glass shards and spears of jagged steel that crashed down. Despite regular sweeping, it seemed that heavy snowfall had pushed the MTK roof structure beyond its limits.

Katowice, in southwestern Poland, was justifiably proud of the MTK, built in the late 1990s with every facility to host events – such as Pigeon 2006, the 56th National Exhibition of Carrier Pigeons. Pigeon-fancying may be a minority sport, but breeders and exhibitors are consumed by a passion for their hobby and the fair had attracted an international crowd with more than 1,000 birds on display. Many survived, protected by their cages. Humans weren't so lucky. The collapse plunged everyone into sub-zero temperatures, threatening death by exposure as much as from injury. Around 1,000 firefighters, 230 police with sniffer rescue dogs and several army units battled temperatures as low as -15°C with hot-air jets, until melting snow caused the wreckage to settle, crushing trapped victims. For 24 hours rescuers tore at the rubble with bare hands. After that they used heavy lifting equipment – because they knew no one could have survived the cold any longer.

It was a total calamity; the nation had been proudly investing in 'modernity' so, when MTK's steel frame buckled, the Polish people felt it as a direct blow to their new-found self-esteem. But first the victims had to be remembered; the president of Poland declared three days of national mourning. Then Poland had to make sure it could never happen again.

WHEN:
January 28 2006
WHERE:
Katowice, Poland
DEATH TOLL:
65 dead and 170 seriously injured.
YOU SHOULD KNOW:
It took workers 22 days to reach the last major pile of collapsed rubble. They found two carrier pigeons, still alive.

Can Tho bridge

Can Tho, 170 km (105 mi) southwest of Ho Chi Minh City, is both a province and the biggest city and hub of the Mekong delta. The region is Vietnam's breadbasket, but the country has always found it difficult to make the most of its prime agricultural resource. Transport has never been straightforward in the huge network of waterways that lie between each of the Mekong's principal tributaries. The River Hau separates Can Tho from Vinh Long province, and the Can Tho road bridge across the Hau was to be the clearest demonstration of Vietnam's commitment to providing the infrastructure proper to a modern, rural economy. Its 16 km (10 mi) of ramped approach roads would lead to a 2.75 km (1.7 mi) central span – a beautiful cable suspension bridge arcing across the flat, green waterscape. Construction began in 2004 and three years in the project was going well.

It might have been the heavy rain that softened the ground, or just one shortcut too many, or the still-drying concrete poured just the day before. Whichever it was, the scaffolding along the 87 m (270 ft) length of the double span buckled in slow motion and crashed more than 30 m (100 ft) to the ground taking the massive, four-lane, concrete deck with it. The wreckage stood higher than a five-storey building. None of the 250 workers stood a chance as 2,000 tons of concrete and twisted steel just collapsed. Fewer than a dozen workmen and engineers survived totally unscathed.

The bitter irony is that the disaster was not caused by corporate greed. If anything, it was caused by goodwill – the genuine desire of the Japanese building consortium and the Vietnamese government to help the delta farmers get their produce to market quickly.

WHEN:
September 26 2007
WHERE:
Hau River bank, Can Tho, Vietnam
DEATH TOLL:
65 dead and 180 injured (most of them severely) out of 250 on site.
YOU SHOULD KNOW:
The bridge's opening was delayed from 2008 to 2010, upsetting collateral regional improvement including Tra Noc airport, which re-opened in 2009 as 'Can Tho International' but could only offer onward transit by ferry. The Japanese consortium showed immense dignity by apologizing even before the independent enquiry was announced. Safety procedures were immediately reviewed and work was started again as quickly as possible.

Workers search through the remains of the bridge that was under construction.

I-35W: the Minneapolis bridge disaster

WHEN:
August 1 2007
WHERE:
Minneapolis, Minnesota, USA
DEATH TOLL:
13 dead and 145 injured.
YOU SHOULD KNOW:
Surprisingly few people were hurt.
It seems a pity that with providence
on the survivors' side for once,
teams of lawyers are still pursuing
class actions in the hope of
squeezing someone – anyone – for a
few bucks. Even though I-35W was a
disastrous accident, lawyers are bent
on finding someone to blame.

Gusset plates are not glamorous, but like the two-dollar O-ring seals on the space shuttle *Challenger*, you take them for granted at your peril. When NASA was still a gleam in John Kennedy's eye, Eisenhower's Interstate Defence Highway system was pushing its concrete capillaries across America. In 1967 Minnesota completed its contribution to Interstate 35 West (I-35W) with an eight-lane bridge across the river Mississippi in the heart of Minneapolis. For 40 years it eased the city's spectacular growth, and it was bumper-to-bumper with rush hour traffic at 18.05 on a hot summer's evening when stalled drivers heard a screeching cacophony of groans and explosive snapping sounds.

The roadway reared up beneath them, twisting in mid air – catapulting the helpless concertina of cars like smashed dominoes into the pillar of dust and debris roiling up from the gaping hole in front. Ribbons of highway hung by a single steel thread, tilted down and sideways into the fast-flowing Mississippi. Chunks of road dropped 35 m (110 ft) perfectly flat to the river banks, like concrete salvers still bearing cars and trucks with their stunned and shaken occupants. But where the three central spans – 330 m (988 ft) of I-35W's 615 m (1,907 ft) total – crumpled in a mockery of their former geometric confidence, the ugly detritus of steel tresses was woven with human rag dolls, and trickled blood.

The collapse was Minnesota's worst-ever man-made disaster. It inspired heroism and provoked a blizzard of lawsuits. A 15-month enquiry found that at the very bottom of the well of minor mishaps that had accumulated coincidentally into a disaster were 24 (out of many) gusset plates of the wrong size. They had not been spotted in the original review process, and had therefore been incorporated into I-35W's design and original construction.

Vehicles scattered along the broken remains of the I-35W bridge.

Sayano-Shushenskaya power station

WHEN:
August 17 2009
WHERE:
Yenisei River, Cheryomushki, Khakassia, Russia
DEATH TOLL:
74 dead and one missing
YOU SHOULD KNOW:
Local feeling about the incident's probable cause is best expressed by the ban imposed in Cheryomushki on strong alcoholic drinks.

The Yenisei River runs 5,494 km (3,534 mi) northwards from Mongolia to the Arctic Ocean, dividing west from east Siberia. Rushing off the Hangayn Mountains, it is already a mighty force of nature by the time it enters the Russian region of Khakassia; and since 1978 it has driven Russia's biggest hydroelectric power station. At Sayano-Shushenskaya, a 245 m (800 ft) high dam across the 1 km (0.6 mi) wide Yenisei dwarfs the massive RusHydro turbine hall at its downstream foot. The ten colossal turbines spun remorselessly to supply 25 per cent of Russia's hydroelectricity and it was a model renewable energy resource. Then it exploded.

Three turbines simply ceased to exist. The explosion ripped the concrete roof off the hall as water from the Yenisei swamped what was left, drowning anyone left standing in a toxic flood of 40 tonnes of spilled transformer oil that later found its way into the river. It took several days even to be sure how many had died. By then, the outcry of the bereaved was magnified by local, regional, national and international alarm about the sequence of the disaster, some of it for shared reasons. The Sayano-Shushenskaya dam supplied 70 per cent of the power for the world's biggest aluminium producer, RUSAL.

The loss of half a million tons of aluminium was only one of the associated economic disasters. Another was the huge oil slick on the Yenisei, heading towards the Arctic and decimating fish farms on which huge numbers of people depend. PCBs in the specialist oil threatened drinking water. On a different level, Russian utilities and hydro-reliant heavy industries took a hammering on stock exchanges round the world. And it still isn't clear which came first – an explosion causing the flood, a flood causing the explosion, or a human error known only to one of the victims.

The explosion highlighted the need to modernize the ageing Russian infrastructure.

Korba chimney collapse scandal

Bharat Aluminium Co (Balco) is one of India's major companies, a subsidiary of Vedanta Plc, the conglomerate listed on the London Stock Exchange. Balco is building a new power plant at Korba, in the northeast of Chhattisgarh state, using the firm Sepco as its chief sub-contractor. Sepco in turn hired Gannon Dunkerley (GDCL) as project managers for a 275 m (852 ft) specialist chimney. The half-built chimney collapsed and, six weeks later, Balco tried to distance itself from the whole affair when one of its own vice-presidents and two of its engineers were caught on the run. Balco's spokesman would only comment 'The arrest has come as a surprise to us.'

There were over 3,000 workers on the site on the day in question. The weather was foul, with heavy rain shot through with lightning. Those not assigned to a specific task huddled anywhere they could in search of shelter. A large number found it in and around the shell of the nascent chimney, already 106 m (330 ft) high. It was the worst place to be. Without warning the labourers were showered with tons of ragged concrete blocks as the chimney crashed to the ground, burying them in mud, steel and rubble.

By the next day only nine survivors could be found; another two were pulled out six days later. After two weeks rescue workers with 30 earth-moving machines had found some 40 bodies – but a witness estimated there must be at least another 60 still buried. There was no reliable list of employees to guide rescuers; and site security had no real idea how many people were even working there. The charges against Balco's men include 'culpable homicide' and 'conspiracy'.

Site of the Korba chimney collapse

WHEN:
September 23 2009
WHERE:
Korba, Chhattisgarh, India
DEATH TOLL:
An estimated 100 dead and 11 injured, although it could be many more.
YOU SHOULD KNOW:
According to the United Nations International Labour Organisation nearly 50,000 Indians die from work-related accidents or illness each year. A senior official confirmed that the Indian government was looking into trades union leaders' accusations that Balco had been using 'low-quality materials' for the building of the Korba chimney.

401

HUMANITARIAN DISASTERS

The transatlantic slave trade

The seal of the Society for the Abolition of Slavery in England shows an
African on bended knee proffering his manacles, above the impassioned
plea: 'Am I not a man and a brother?' It is the *cri de coeur* of moral
repugnance: nothing so belittles Europe and the Americas as their
willing involvement, for economic gain, in the enslavement of millions
of Africans over three centuries, and in the continuing exploitation of
their descendants.

The Portuguese and Spanish may have started the transatlantic
slave traffic, but as soon as they could find the ships and a market,
everyone else joined in. Slavery was not new. It is as old as mankind,
and was prevalent in African tribal cultures of the 17th century. The
novelty consisted in Europeans reviving that as a justification, centuries
after abandoning it as morally worthless. They all had colonies to
develop. Slavery was expedient, and created a triangular trade between
Europe, Brazil and the Caribbean islands, and – in the hands of the
French and British especially – the United States. Soon hundreds of
specially built slavers, called 'blackbirders', were crating Africans in
worse conditions than sardines direct to market in America.

More than 11 million human beings were wrenched from family
and culture, and worked to death. Their inhuman treatment further
brutalized their abusers, infecting American culture itself. Conscience
died. Everyone (of every nationality) condoning slavery had to persuade
themselves that Africans were savages beyond understanding 'civilized'
processes: it became a subconscious credo that survived the US Civil
War and legal emancipation (as late as 1888 in Brazil). Ever since, the
institutionalized belief in racial superiority or inferiority has remained a

*Slaves in chains on the island
of Zanzibar in the 19th century*

Slave family in a cotton field near Savannah, USA

powerful driving force in international relations, and a fundamental ingredient current in both military and economic wars. Even in its mildest social forms, it's a sickening legacy of a sickening trade.

Famine in Bengal

At the time of the 1770 Bengal famine, the British East India Company was governing the region and the Company has to bear some of the blame for the indescribable suffering in one of the worst famines in the history of Bengal. When a partial crop failure in 1768 led to food shortages in 1769, the Company had little sympathy for the peasants' plight. It rigorously enforced land taxes, even raising the levy by ten per cent. Bengalis are a resourceful, uncomplaining people; they made no protest, and the Company blithely assumed all was well when in fact most of the population had started to suffer from lack of proper nutrition.

The autumn rains of 1769 didn't come, and the rice crop that was expected to reverse everyone's ill-fortune failed. By early 1770 malnutrition had become starvation proper, and by the middle of that year people were dying like flies. Whole villages starved to death, having first sold their livestock and then their children. People were reduced to eating leaves and grass, and finally the bodies of their dead. Cultivated land soon reverted to jungle as people downed tools and poured into the towns in search of sustenance. The streets were strewn with corpses that couldn't be buried quickly enough; and where starvation had been, disease epidemics soon followed.

The autumn monsoon came with a vengeance that year. It did nothing to alleviate suffering: torrential rain flattened the crops, overflowed the rivers and flooded the fields. Middlemen made exorbitant profits out of what little produce there was, while any remaining struggling farmers were still financially crippled by impossibly high taxes. For the next three years, the harvests were unusually abundant, but it was too late. In a few short months the entire economy of Bengal had collapsed and millions had died.

WHEN:
1770
WHERE:
Bengal, India
(now Bangladesh and West Bengal)
DEATH TOLL:
Around ten million, or one in three people. A disproportionate number of these were children, which led to de-population of the countryside for the next 15 years. Roving gangs of thugs and *dacoits* terrorized the villages, and were joined by many a hitherto honest villager with nothing left to lose.
YOU SHOULD KNOW:
It is generally agreed that the severity of the Bengal famine was caused not only by lack of rain but also by the bungling ignorance of the British administration. Instead of making provision for the foreseeable consequences of the poor rainfall, they forbade hoarding and increased the land tax that farmers had to pay, thus adding an extra burden to farmers already on the edge of extremity.

The arrest of a peasant royalist

The Vendée

Genocide in the name of revolution

Afterwards, French General Joseph Westermann wrote to Robespierre's Committee of Public Safety: 'There is no more Vendée . . . according to the orders you gave me, I crushed the children under the feet of horses, massacred the women . . . I have exterminated everyone . . . Mercy is not a revolutionary sentiment.' More than 200 years later the Vendée 'war' and its aftermath remain the dirty secrets of the French Revolution, still officially ignored – and still capable of arousing furious passions.

The Vendée is in western France south of the Loire, a coastal quilt of slow rivers and deep forests, haphazard fields and scrubby pine enclaves. In 1793 it was deeply royalist and deeply Catholic. Enraged by the Convention's suppression of their religion and conscription of their men, the peasant farmers of the Vendée and their immediate neighbours revolted. Early success was crushed within the year at Savernay. The remnants of the 'armies of the Chouans' split into guerrilla bands across the Vendée and Brittany – and 'Butcher' Westermann's brutal rape of the country, culture and people was taken up early in 1794 by General Turreau's *Douze Colonnes Infernales* (Twelve Columns of Hell).

Their scorched-earth policy was a tame beginning to annihilation. These troops had a malevolent genius for new forms of torture and mass execution; and they killed even proven loyalists without discrimination. Long before the Nazis and Auschwitz, they burned their victims in huge ovens; tanned human skins for officers' saddlery; tied men, women and children naked together for mass drownings (*les noyades*) they jokingly called 'republican marriages'; tossed babies on bayonet points; and dozens of far more disgusting atrocities.

They slaughtered a third of the Vendée's population – and though the army records of this genocide still exist at Vincennes, the world and most Frenchmen have never heard this terrible scream from history. Conscience demands we all listen now.

WHEN:
December 1793 to February 1795
WHERE:
France. The Vendée Militaire included the Vendée itself and parts of Anjou and Poitou. The Convention's barbarity later extended to include Brittany.
DEATH TOLL:
An estimated 300,000 died (of the Vendée's 800,000) in gruesome circumstances. Some historians reject the term 'genocide' because the Chouans fought back; but what else can you call planned, systematic extermination of an entire population?
YOU SHOULD KNOW:
Napoleon sought to reconcile the Vendée in 1801 by signing a Concordat with the Vatican that restored Catholicism in France, but the scars have never healed because post-Jacobin French Republics have always wanted to retain pride in a Revolution founded on the *Declaration of the Rights of Man* and have never acknowledged its ugliest manifestation. The Vendée genocide remains a corrosive canker in French politics.

The great Irish famine

During the Napoleonic Wars, Irish landlords enjoyed a successful period as the price of food was high. Once peace was restored, prices fell and more profit could be gained by turning the land from small tenant farms into pasture. In brutal acts typical of the times, farmers were evicted from the land and their dwellings were razed to the ground. The result was mass homelessness and great privation. Any dissent was harshly dealt with and even minor offences were punished by transportation.

As the century progressed the Irish poor grew dependent on the potato as almost the sole means of subsistence, while grains, meat and poultry were all exported to Europe. Various voices in England had warned of the dire consequences of the failure of the potato crop, but the government in Westminster feared that any assistance given to Ireland would be used against them to fund rebellion.

In 1845 people's worst fears were realized when the potato crop failed. Accustomed as they were to hardship, the population harvested a meagre bounty and prayed that the next year would be better. Not only was the following year far worse, but the country also saw the harshest of winters. Cruelly, it was only this foodstuff of the poor that was affected and, during the period of the famine, food exports actually rose. By now many of the Irish who had survived the great starvation had had enough and sought any possible way out of their homeland. The first group of migrants went to Canada on board returning lumber ships which offered low fares to the New World. By the end of the famine in the early 1850s, Ireland's population had fallen by more than one quarter. Half of those gone had left the island and the other half had died from disease and starvation.

WHEN:
1845–1852
WHERE:
Ireland
DEATH TOLL:
Estimated at between 750,000 and 1.5 million
YOU SHOULD KNOW:
In 1849, a royal visit was arranged for Ireland. As if to highlight the disparity in wealth, no expense was spared and one banquet alone cost £5,000 – a vast sum in those days. One William Kindles became something of a local hero when he severed the ropes supporting a giant Union Flag and brought it crashing down on a marching band performing for Queen Victoria. He then promptly boarded a ship bound for America to join many of his fellow countrymen and women.

A poor Irish family desperately searches for potatoes during the famine.

407

Manifest Destiny and Indian Removal

WHEN:
19th century
WHERE:
USA
DEATH TOLL:
The true figure is hotly debated. Some argue that the effect of European settlement on the native peoples was genocide without parallel in history. The best estimates are that between ten million and 100 million deaths can be linked to colonization.
YOU SHOULD KNOW:
Wars, disease and forced migration took a heavy toll on the native people throughout the 19th century. While some small bands are now successful, the vast majority of First Nations have not fared so well. For some bands unemployment is over 80 per cent and life expectancy is under 50 years.

First Nation women and children massacred in Idaho by white scouts and native allies.

'Manifest Destiny' has at its core the assertion that not only were the European people of America right in their beliefs, but that they also had the divine right to force these beliefs on other, usually unwilling, peoples. Although the term did not appear in print until the late 1830s, it had long been a guiding principle for post-revolutionary America. Taking its lead from the Enlightenment in Europe, it sought to evangelize the basic belief systems that had so successfully thrown off the yoke of British rule. It was used as the rationale for furthering the expansion of the United States northwards into Canada and southwards into Mexico, but its main impact was the drive westwards into the lands of the First Nation 'Indian' Peoples

It was argued that if the hunter First Nation bands could be encouraged to settle and farm like the Europeans, there would be enough land for everyone. This in reality was a smoke screen for a land-grab on a massive scale. In 1814 Andrew Jackson led a force which defeated the Creek Nation and seized great swathes of what is now Georgia. In 1818 an invasion of Spanish Florida was ordered under the pretext of recapturing fleeing slaves. Faced with overwhelming military might, several native bands saw no alternative but to sign peace deals that would at least give them some land. Liberal thinkers among the European Americans thought that indigenous people would do better if they lived apart; hardliners saw them as little more than savages and an obstacle to progress.

In 1823 the Supreme Court ruled that the European's 'right of discovery' was paramount over the native peoples' 'right of occupancy' – in effect their country now no longer belonged to them. In 1830, the Indian Removal Act was passed, imposing internal exile on the native people.

The fate of Australian Aboriginals

The once widely used catch-all phrase 'Australian Aboriginals' is being replaced by 'Indigenous Australians'. In fact, both descriptions are misleading, entirely failing to reflect the diversity of Australia's first inhabitants. There were many distinctive 'nations' when English settlers arrived in the late 18th century, speaking 300 languages and spread throughout the continent and Torres Straits Islands.

Aboriginals had been around for upwards of 50,000 years, developing a unique culture and advanced hunter-gatherers' survival skills. But they shared a catastrophic experience with native South Americans when a pandemic of diseases – notably smallpox – brought by the incomers proved devastating, killing half the indigenous population in the first decades of European settlement.

This was a major humanitarian disaster but insult was added to injury by the harsh treatment meted out to Aboriginals, showing that the new European colony cared little for its original inhabitants. Ancestral lands were expropriated throughout the 19th century and children were forcibly removed from families in large numbers between 1870 and 1970. The disrespect with which Aboriginals were treated is typified by the fate of Tasmania's tribes. They were systematically hunted down or lured into camps from the 1820s and had effectively been wiped out by the 1850s. The last surviving Tasmanian Aborigine was Truganini, who died in 1876 – the Tasmanian language dying with her. As a final insult, her skeleton was put on public display.

The movement to grant proper recognition to Aboriginals began in the 1930s and gathered pace from the 1960s, but despite 'official' acknowledgment of past wrongdoings and relatively isolated examples of individual achievement, the vast majority of the downtrodden Aboriginal population still lives in Third World conditions, reflecting the inhumanity with which native peoples were always treated when Europeans arrived to create new colonies at the expense of long-established indigenous civilizations.

Aboriginals getting together to discuss tribal matters.

WHEN:
1850 onwards
WHERE:
Australia
DEATH TOLL:
Impossible to calculate. Latest estimates suggest the current population of Indigenous Australians to be in excess of 450,000, against a high estimate of 750,000 when Europeans first arrived and low point of some 100,000 in 1900.
YOU SHOULD KNOW:
Ironically, Australia's jealously guarded reputation as a top sporting nation was initiated by an Aboriginal cricket team. It visited England in 1868 on one of the first-ever international sporting tours and performed creditably before large crowds, winning 14, drawing 19 and losing 14 matches. Delighted spectators were treated to boomerang- and spear-throwing displays after matches.

Southern India famine

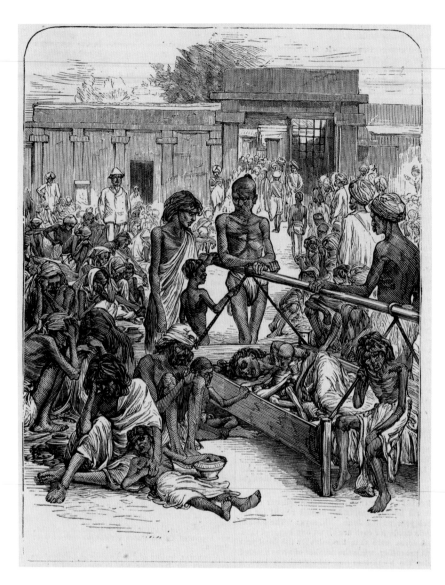

Starving citizens of India died in the streets.

For two years in the 1870s over 58 million people in the Bombay, Madras, Mysore and Hyderabad areas of southern India endured famine that eventually blighted an area of 670,000 sq km (257,000 sq mi). The specific cause was crop failure, but the decision of British authorities to deny a serious relief effort was the reason that huge numbers actually died.

Earlier in the decade a potentially disastrous famine in Bengal had been ameliorated by a massive programme of food imports, mainly rice from Burma (now Myanmar), supported by a public works programme to build roads. There was little loss of life but this successful humanitarian effort was roundly criticized on cost grounds. It had been organized by Bengal's Lieutenant Governor, Sir Richard Temple, who by 1876 had become famine commissioner for the British-run government of India. Keen to avoid further recrimination on cost grounds as famine again reared its ugly head, he introduced rigorous criteria for granting relief. The programme included public works for the able bodied – effectively hard labour for a minimal wage – and very limited charitable handouts for the old, infirm and young. Worse, these dubious benefits were only offered after the famine had taken serious hold and offered in patchy fashion across affected areas.

WHEN:
1876–1878
WHERE:
Southern India
DEATH TOLL:
In areas directly administered by Britain over five million died, while additional fatalities from starvation or disease in the princely states were never estimated.

After two years of severe malnutrition – and millions of deaths – a malaria epidemic swept through the population, killing many more people who were too weak to resist the greedy disease. In the aftermath of famine, it was ironic that a spirited debate broke out – this time focused on awareness that the relief effort had been totally inadequate, with less than one fifth of the amount per head spent compared with the successful Bengali effort. The no-win Sir Richard Temple learned that both generosity and parsimony attracted severe criticism in equal measure.

YOU SHOULD KNOW:
One lasting legacy of the Southern India famine was the foundation less than a decade later of the Indian National Congress, the political party that would eventually steer India to independence. Among the founder members were senior British civil servants who were largely motivated by the colonial administration's disastrously inadequate efforts to counter the terrible famine.

Ethiopian great famine

Africa's traditional subsistence economies have been subject to the whims of nature since time immemorial – as evidenced by events as diverse as decades-long drought and famine in Upper Egypt that destroyed the sophisticated Old Kingdom four millennia ago, or half remote Timbuktu's population dying of starvation in the 1730s. But nowhere has been more prone to humanitarian disaster than landlocked Ethiopia in the Horn of Africa, one of the world's most ancient countries.

A disastrous episode began in 1888 and lasted four years. The Ethiopian great famine started with an outbreak of a deadly epidemic affecting cattle – the rinderpest epizootic – that arrived from India via Eritrea, to the north. This spread southwards and would eventually reach South Africa, causing havoc within many cultures that relied on cattle as a vital part of everyday life. In Ethiopia, all but 10 per cent of the national herd perished, bringing destitution to both rich owners of many beasts and humble herders of few.

Subsistence farming was the mainstay of Ethiopia's economy, but this inefficient activity produced no surpluses so the vast majority of the population relied on one year's harvest to tide them over to the next. In 1888, the shock of mass cattle death was compounded by lack of rainfall that swiftly led to drought, crop failure and famine. It is thought today that the main culprit was the usual suspect – an irregular El Niño weather pattern – but whatever the cause, the effect on Ethiopia was tragic. As so often in times of drought, malnourished people proved incapable of withstanding illness. Smallpox, cholera and typhus epidemics ravaged those resisting starvation, while plagues of caterpillars and locusts destroyed such crops as survived prolonged drought conditions. By the time the Ethiopian great famine started to ease, one third of the country's population had perished.

WHEN:
1888–1892
WHERE:
Ethiopia
DEATH TOLL:
The great famine is estimated to have caused 3.5 million deaths.
YOU SHOULD KNOW:
Ethiopia's climate is of the tropical monsoon type, with average annual rainfall of 120 cm (47 in) that largely falls in summer (June to September). But when the monsoon rains fail, the consequences are invariably serious for the majority of the population, which relies on subsistence farming to this day.

Herero and Nama genocide

WHEN:
1904–1907
WHERE:
Namibia (known as South West Africa until 1990).
DEATH TOLL:
Between 25,000 and 100,000 Herero and 10,000 Nama were exterminated; the survivors of the concentration camps were sold to German farmers as slaves.
YOU SHOULD KNOW:
Responding to international criticism, Germany argued that its actions against the Herero were not in breach of the 1864 Geneva Convention of human rights because the tribesmen were not 'human' but 'animal'. A thriving trade developed in native skulls and body parts; these were regularly shipped back to German museums and universities for anthropological research purposes, and geneticist Eugen Fischer even went to the Herero concentration camps to research his 'race science' – a eugenics theory that would later be invoked by Hitler to justify his attempted extermination of the Jewish race. In 1985, the UN declared Germany's attempt to wipe out the Herero and Nama peoples as the first genocide of the 20th century.

During the late 19th century, when territorial expansionism was at its height, the nations of Europe vied with each other in the 'scramble for Africa'. Germany achieved a formidable presence in the 'dark continent' with ambitions founded on a garbled paternalistic philosophy of eugenics and racism, including notions of 'survival of the fittest'.

In 1884 Germany occupied Damaraland in southwestern Africa, establishing the protectorate of Deutsch-Sudwestafrika. Great tracts of land and herds of cattle were expropriated from the nomadic Herero and Nama tribes of the region. With an ingrained sense of their own cultural and racial superiority, the Germans reduced these proud indigenous peoples to the status of labourers, imposing Christian beliefs and European dress with missionary zeal.

In January 1904, under the leadership of Samuel Maharero, the Herero finally erupted in a full-blown rebellion in which 120 German settlers were killed. Germany responded by sending in a 15,000-strong contingent of Schutztruppe colonial forces commanded by Lothar von Trotha. In August, at the Battle of Waterberg, he hemmed in the Herero rebels on three sides and pushed them back into the Omaheke desert, where thousands of them died of thirst. Trotha was utterly ruthless in his determination to finish the job; he had the Herero watering holes poisoned, positioned guardposts along 240 km (150 mi) of territory and gave an order that: 'All Herero must leave the land . . . Any Herero found within the German borders with or without a gun, with or without cattle, will be shot'. He then rounded up any remaining Herero, included the Nama for good measure, and imprisoned them all in forced-labour camps. By 1908 up to 80 per cent of the Herero and 50 per cent of the Nama had been killed by a combination of overwork, starvation and disease.

The 'Great Calamity' Armenian genocide

The Armenians have inhabited the Caucusus, between Russia and eastern Turkey, since time immemorial. They were among the earliest Christian converts and clung zealously to their faith after the rise of Islam in the 7th century.

War between Turkey and Russia resulted in the division of Armenia, with the eastern part under Russian control and the west governed by Turkey. When a surge of Armenian nationalism began to threaten this rather shaky *status quo*, Russia responded by clamping down on the intelligentsia, and confiscating Armenian church property. The Turks were more overt in their repression – they carried out several massacres between 1894 and 1896. At the outbreak of World War I, mindful of its eastern border, Turkey decided it was time to settle the problem of Armenia once and for all, by the simple expedient of extermination under the guise of relocating all 1.75 million inhabitants.

The plan was carried out systematically through a series of official emergency measures, under cover of the war. Armenian community leaders and intellectuals were arrested on April 24 1915, then all males aged 20 to 45 were conscripted to the front line while older men aged up to 60 were put to work on military transport. Finally, the rest of the population were evacuated for 'security reasons'. In practice, through a system of concentration camps and forced marches, old men, women and children were forcibly driven southwards to the Mesopotamian desert – a journey of one or two months – where, if they had not already died from exhaustion, rape or massacre *en route*, they were abandoned to die from thirst, starvation and exposure.

In the postwar political repositioning, eastern Armenia was absorbed into the Soviet Union (until the collapse of the USSR in 1990). Turks settled in the western part, and the disappearance of an entire population was simply ignored.

WHEN:
April 24 1915–1918
WHERE:
Armenia, Caucasus
DEATH TOLL:
At least a million
YOU SHOULD KNOW:
The Armenians are one of the world's most dispersed peoples. Among the Armenian diaspora, the genocide is known as the Great Calamity. More than 20 countries have now formally recognized the mass killings as genocide; the UK and USA are not among them. To this day Turkey denies that a planned ethnic cleansing programme ever took place. Instead it continues to claim that around 300,000 Armenians and thousands of Turks were killed in the general turmoil of war, with atrocities and massacres on both sides.

Armenian girls and women who escaped death.

Holodomor: murder by hunger

WHEN:
1932–1933
WHERE:
Ukraine
DEATH TOLL:
Around eight million. Those who did not die of starvation were killed in the gulags.
YOU SHOULD KNOW:
It later emerged that the thousands of tonnes of grain seized by the state had not been redistributed around the Soviet Empire. Whether through sheer bungling incompetence or by design, the authorities had simply put it into storage; while entire villages starved to death the local granaries, locked and guarded, were piled high with grain supplies.

Ukraine has always been invaluable to Russia as a ready source of grain. For centuries, the fertile black earth of the eastern European plains was cultivated by *kulaks* (prosperous peasant farmers) who led a traditional way of life attached to their patches of land. When Stalin came to power in 1924, he instigated a reign of terror in the Ukraine that ranks among the foremost of his crimes against humanity. Over the next few years, he imposed a ruthless policy of collectivization. The *kulaks'* land was seized for state farms and they were forced to work their own land as state employees. Many rebelled and were shot. In 1928, Stalin piled on the pressure by increasing the *kulaks'* taxes at the same time as requisitioning ever-larger quotas of grain.

By 1932 the demands of the state had become insatiable. At the end of that year the *kulaks* were forced to surrender their seed grain, without which they could not plant the following year's harvest. From February to August 1933 they were ordered to hand over all foodstuffs; at the same time travel restrictions were imposed and the secret police brutally sniffed out any hoarders. The effect was to create a famine of such horrendous proportions that, having devoured first their livestock then cats and dogs and rodents, the starving finally resorted to infanticide and cannibalism.

The quota demands were lifted in 1933, by which time whole villages lay deserted. Survivors were transported to the Siberian *gulags* (forced labour camps) and Russian settlers were sent into the Ukraine to replace the dead. For years, successive governments of the USSR denied the famine had ever happened. To this day, although Russia accepts that incompetent agricultural policies contributed to mass starvation, it still denies there was any deliberate policy of genocide – officially, Holodomor never happened.

The Holocaust

WHEN:
1940–1945
WHERE:
Europe
DEATH TOLL:
It is generally accepted that the Holocaust claimed six million Jewish lives, while 200,000 Roma people (Gypsies) and a similar number of mentally or physically disabled Germans were also murdered.

There cannot be a word in the English language that conjures up more haunting – and terrifying – images. The literal meaning of 'holocaust' is 'sacrifice by fire', but with a capital letter it represents the most devastating humanitarian disaster in world history, starting when Germany's Nazi regime embarked upon its 'Final Solution' in 1940. This ruthless programme aimed to eliminate the entire Jewish population of Europe, which stood at nine million before the Holocaust began.

State-sponsored racism designed to isolate Germany's Jews, appropriate their assets and drive as many as possible from the country began after the Nazi Party was elected in 1933, reaching a

savage climax on *Kristallnacht* (the Night of Broken Glass) in 1938, when a wave of systematic anti-Jewish attacks took place across Germany, Austria and Czechoslovakia's occupied Sudetenland. With the outbreak of World War II, virulent Nazi anti-Semitism was exported to conquered territories in the east.

The Germans first established ghettos where entire Jewish populations were penned in terrible conditions. Following the invasion of the Soviet Union in 1941, large numbers of Jews were executed by shooting or gassing in mobile vans. But this process wasn't speedy enough for the Nazis, who swiftly established camps like Sobibor and Treblinka in Poland as 'death factories' that could murder thousands of Jews every day. The deadliest such establishment was the Auschwitz complex – three camps (Auschwitz 1, Auschwitz-Birkenau and Auschwitz-Monowitz) specifically designed to work Jewish prisoners to death, or despatch them immediately in the notorious gas chambers and dispose of bodies in crematoria that operated around the clock.

In the short space of five years, the Holocaust would claim millions of victims and reduce the Jewish population of Europe by two thirds, creating the ugliest of testaments to mankind's unspeakable ability to impose the most brutal inhumanity on fellow human beings.

Frightened Jewish families surrender to Nazi soldiers in the Warsaw ghetto in 1943.

YOU SHOULD KNOW:
The Holocaust did not mark the limit of Nazi atrocities. Millions more were 'eliminated' – including Soviet prisoners of war, forced-labour-camp victims from most of the occupied countries plus specific target groups such as homosexuals, religious dissidents and political opponents from Germany itself or conquered territories.

Locals suffering from the famine queue for supplies in Calcutta. Often, people died before they could reach the food.

Bengal famine

Way back in the 19th century the Bihar and Bengal famines of 1873–1874 were dealt with by the import of rice from Burma, ensuring that there was no loss of life through malnutrition. But 70 years later things couldn't have been more different. Britain was at war and suffered a huge reverse when Burma and Singapore fell to the Japanese in 1942. This halted rice exports to India, but losing a Burmese food supply was not the reason why there was a savage famine in Bengal the following year.

The loss of rice imports was indeed significant, but insufficient to create famine. A reduced rice harvest caused by a cyclone in October 1942 that damaged the autumn rice crop was not the cause, either. It put pressure on the following year's crop, because to survive many subsistence farmers and their families were forced to eat rice reserved for planting. But in fact the 1943 crop would still have been perfectly adequate to feed everyone, but for special wartime factors that turned a difficult situation into disaster.

Fearing Japanese invasion, British authorities stockpiled food to feed defending troops, and also exported considerable quantities to British forces in the Middle East. They also confiscated boats, carts and elephants in Chittagong, where the invasion was expected. This deprived fishermen and their many customers of the ability to operate and generally inhibited the sort of low-level commerce upon which many peasants relied for survival.

But the real killer was fear – fear of an imaginary shortage that caused hoarding, speculation and consequent price inflation – that put even a basic subsistence diet beyond the means of Bengal's legion of poorly paid labourers. An incompetent and complacent government failed to halt rice exports or seek relief supplies from elsewhere in India, precipitating a humanitarian disaster of epic proportions.

WHEN:
1943
WHERE:
Bengal, India
DEATH TOLL:
Around three million Bengalis died of malnutrition or disease.
YOU SHOULD KNOW:
During 1943 the Bengal government – with a lot of help from the British Army – did manage to distribute over 110 million free meals, and it is an indication of the intensity and scale of the famine that this effort barely scratched the surface of the starving populace's need.

Hiroshima and Nagasaki

In August 1945 a B-29 bomber named *Enola Gay* after the pilot's mother took off from Tinian Island in the western Pacific, heading for Japan. Intensive American bombing of Japanese cities had failed to end the Pacific War, though Hiroshima had been spared aerial bombardment. Little did the inhabitants know they were merely enjoying a stay of execution.

For *Enola Gay* was carrying the 4,000 kg (8,900 lb) *Little Boy*, the first nuclear bomb to be used in anger – and the Americans wanted to assess how effectively this untested weapon would destroy an undamaged city. This bomb derived its explosive power from the inefficient but still deadly method of blasting two pieces of uranium together to create critical mass. The awesome detonation at 600 m (2,000 ft) above Hiroshima flattened a large area of the city and set the rest ablaze. Around 12 sq km (4.7 sq mi) vanished into a wasteland of destruction, with 70,000 inhabitants killed and as many again irradiated.

Still Japan didn't surrender, and three days later President Harry Truman authorized the use of *Fat Man* on Nagasaki. The second (and final) atom bomb ever dropped was a more sophisticated plutonium weapon. This rotund device weighed 4,630 kg (10,200 lb) and was more powerful than *Little Boy*, but did less damage owing to Nagasaki's hilly geography. Even so, 40,000 died and the final casualty figure would double within months. It was punishment enough. Within a week Emperor Hirohito announced Japan's surrender and World War II was over.

Abruptly ending a war that could have taken many thousands of American lives as US forces battled across the Pacific Ocean towards Japan was President Truman's rationale, but the wisdom of a decision that inflicted death and terminal suffering on more than 200,000 Japanese civilians is still debated today.

ABOVE: A mushroom cloud towers above Nagasaki after the second nuclear bomb.

BELOW LEFT: The wrecked framework of the Museum of Science and Industry after the blast.

WHEN:
August 6 and 9 1945
WHERE:
Hiroshima and Nagasaki, Japan
DEATH TOLL:
The two blasts and their immediate aftermath killed 220,000 Japanese, mainly civilians (140,000 in Hiroshima and 80,000 in Nagasaki), with many hundreds more dying of radiation-related illnesses as time passed.
YOU SHOULD KNOW:
Japan was warned of the devastating consequences of fighting on when the Potsdam Declaration signed by Allied leaders called for immediate Japanese surrender – failing which the country would face 'prompt and utter destruction'. But in ignoring the ultimatum, the stubborn Hirohito regime can have had little idea of just how devastating that destruction could – and would – be.

A bench reserved for white people.

Apartheid

An Afrikaans word meaning 'separateness', apartheid was the formal policy of racial segregation which prevailed in South Africa for most of the second half of the 20th century, making it a pariah state among the nations of the world. Introduced by the National Party when it assumed power following the 1948 whites-only election, the policy classified the population in four racial groups: White, Black, Indian and Coloured (mixed race). Increasingly fearful of the urban migration of blacks seeking work, the white minority sought to defend itself by enacting laws separating the different groups and banning racially mixed marriages.

Apartheid ideologues, many of whom were Afrikaners of Dutch descent and devout Calvinist backgrounds, believed that it was God's will, no less, that different races should live apart. But there was also a hard commercial reality to the system, based on economic self-interest; why should non-whites reap the fruits, so the argument ran, of predominantly white labours? The majority black population was subjected to humiliating measures such as the hated 'pass laws' and their forced resettlement into homelands, known as *bantustans*. The international community turned its back on the regime, imposing wide-ranging economic sanctions and banning South Africa from major sporting events. While this external pressure was an undoubted contributory factor, the decisive blows that undermined the foundations of apartheid came with the collapse of Soviet communism in 1990 and the civil unrest which had been growing steadily inside the country in spite of the government's brutal attempts to stifle it.

Apartheid was finally abolished following protracted negotiations in the early 1990s between the government of F W De Klerk and the principal black party, the ANC (African National Congress). In 1994 South Africa held its first free, non-racial elections, and Nelson Mandela was chosen as president and head of a government of national unity.

WHEN:
1948–1994
WHERE:
South Africa
DEATH TOLL:
Estimates vary, but one authoritative source puts the number of deaths in political violence during the apartheid era as high as 21,000. Almost exclusively black deaths, these include the notorious Sharpeville Massacre of 1960 and the Soweto Uprising of 1976–1977.
YOU SHOULD KNOW:
The vile nature of the apartheid regime is often best captured in its more bizarre details, such as the 'comb test' used in the racial classification process. If a comb drawn through someone's hair got stuck, that person was identified as African.

The Great Leap Forward

WHEN:
1958–1961
WHERE:
China
DEATH TOLL:
The famine that was a direct consequence of the Great Leap Forward fiasco caused the death of at least 20 million people, with some sources putting the figure at twice this. It is the worst famine in recorded history.

Ten years after the Communist victory in China and the establishment of the People's Republic the new state was growing rapidly. For its leader Mao Zedong, however, the pace of development was not fast enough and in 1958 he announced the Great Leap Forward, a radical and hugely ambitious programme to propel China into the ranks of advanced industrial nations. Conceived as a five-year plan, its central element was the complete overhaul of Chinese agriculture. Private property and land ownership were abolished and the traditional peasant farmers were corralled into large communes, over 26,000 of them. Farming was collectivized and farming methods reorganized along industrial lines. On top of this, much of the rural labour force was diverted to manning over half a million 'backyard furnaces' erected in the countryside; these were supposed to implement Mao's bizarre vision of a cottage industry replicating the output and quality of heavy industry in steel manufacture.

Incredibly, one of Mao's goals in the Great Leap Forward was for China to surpass Britain in steel production in five years. Things indeed began well but the whole programme started to fall apart within a year. The redeployment of labour meant that crop cultivation was neglected at critical times, nor had the peasant workers been trained in the new farming methods. When they did return to the fields they often lacked the equipment and tools they needed as these had been melted down in the furnaces to produce low-grade steel. Poor weather combined with incompetence to produce terrible harvests in both 1959 and 1960. The resulting starvation and malnutrition were on an almost unimaginable scale. Mao had to concede that the plan had failed; it was finally abandoned in 1961.

Chinese propaganda poster of Mao Zedong

The Cultural Revolution

The failure of China's Great Leap Forward strengthened the hands of moderates in the ruling Communist Party who favoured a more centrally planned style of development. Seeing his position within the party threatened, Mao Zedong re-asserted his authority in 1966 by launching the Great Proletarian Cultural Revolution. An unrelenting barrage of propaganda presented this as nothing less than a move to reclaim the heart and soul of the nation, which Mao claimed had been contaminated by 'revisionist' elements and 'bourgeois' influences. History, however, enables us to see Mao's initiative for what it truly was: a brazenly successful ploy to hold on to power which masqueraded as an exercise in revolutionary fervour.

Mao's principal shock troops in this programme of ideological cleansing were the Red Guards, radical young activists recruited from secondary schools and universities who were blindly obedient to the Chairman's every whim. Unleashed on the long-suffering Chinese population, which was still recovering from the Great Famine, these youthful zealots rampaged around the country, brandishing Mao's *Little Red Book* of doctrinal exhortations while railing against the 'Four Olds' of thoughts, culture, customs and habits. Anyone in a position of authority was deemed suspect and liable to harassment, torture or even arbitrary execution. The more educated you were, the greater the danger; members of the intellectual and urban elite were despatched to the countryside and forced to work in the fields and on construction projects.

The behaviour of Red Guard units soon led to chaos and civil unrest. After two years Mao had to call in the army to restore order, and thousands of Red Guards were sent to remote areas of the country to be 're-educated' among the peasantry.

Nigeria-Biafra war

WHEN:
1967–1970
WHERE:
Eastern Nigeria
DEATH TOLL:
During the conflict more than one million people died in battle, through ethnic cleansing or (the vast majority) from starvation.
YOU SHOULD KNOW:
The thriller writer Frederick Forsyth was a war reporter for the BBC during the conflict before leaving to become a freelance after showing alleged bias towards the Biafrans – one of many Europeans sympathetic to their cause. His first book was not the world-famous bestseller *The Day of the Jackal* but *The Biafra Story*, published in 1969 to try and tell the world how grievously Biafran people were suffering.

An undernourished Biafran child at a refugee camp in Gabon.

The boundaries of African colonies seized by European countries in the 19th century were arbitrary, representing lines drawn on a map rather than reflecting territories occupied by subjugated peoples. This had the potential for almost limitless tribal conflict as former colonies were granted their freedom after World War II, for emergent nations often contained ethnic groups with traditional rivalries and the ensuing struggle for supremacy could be savage.

This was clearly illustrated by Nigeria's experience after independence in 1960. The new nation sought to combine groups divided by ethnicity and religion – a process leading to serious tensions that culminated in two military coups from which Northerners emerged triumphant. When the Northern coup resulted in the murder of military and civilian members of the Igbo (or Ibo) people in 1967, they declared their homeland independent as the Republic of Biafra under the leadership of Lt Col Emeka Ojukwu. Despite recognition by some African states and tacit support from countries like France and Israel, the Nigerian FMG (Federal Military Government) wouldn't allow the oil-rich eastern region to secede.

In the increasingly vicious Nigeria-Biafra war that followed, Igbos fought gallantly but the FMG had infinitely superior forces and ruthlessly drove back the defenders. Appalling hardship ensued for the civilian population, with massacres reported as FMG forces advanced and famine took hold after the Nigerian government blockaded Biafra and banned Red Cross aid. As the world sat on its hands and ignored the developing humanitarian disaster, hundreds of thousands died of malnutrition before Biafran resistance was crushed in 1970. This dreadful tragedy did have one positive legacy. French doctor Bernard Kouchner was so moved by the fate of starving Biafrans – especially the legion of children – that he founded Médecins sans Frontières. This developed into one of the world's most effective aid agencies.

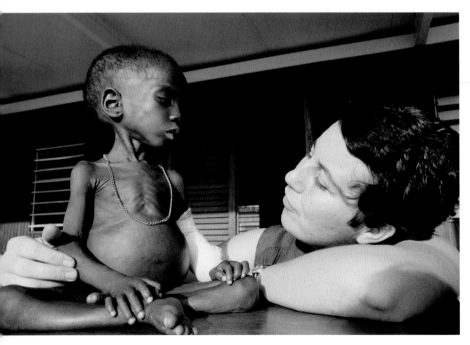

Famine and Khmer Rouge genocide

Communism and Southeast Asia endured a stormy relationship after World War II, as China exported its political philosophy throughout the region. Both Americans and French discovered in Korea and Vietnam respectively how hard it was to roll back this seemingly inexorable tide, and Cambodia became independent in 1953 when French Indochina collapsed under the assault of Ho Chi Minh's Viet Minh communist army.

This constitutional monarchy under Prince Sihanouk remained neutral during the Vietnam War, until Sihanouk was ousted in 1970 by an American-backed coup. Forced to seek refuge in Beijing, he became the figurehead for communist Khmer Rouge insurgents, whose cause was greatly aided when America bombed Cambodia in an attempt to suppress guerrilla activity. Cambodia's civil war ended in 1975 when capital city Phnom Penh fell to Pol Pot's Khmer Rouge.

The new regime started destroying evidence of Western influence, emptying cities and force-marching the urban population into the countryside to engage in hopelessly inadequate agricultural projects. As starvation and disease set in, this policy alone would have created a significant humanitarian disaster. But the Khmer Rouge didn't stop there.

Minorities were persecuted and killed in large numbers and the biters were bitten – high on the hit list were ethnic Chinese. Other targets included Cham Muslims and anyone who could remotely be described as 'intellectual', a term that included everyone wearing spectacles. The infamous Tuol Sleng Prison became a centre for mass murder and there were rural sites – chillingly nicknamed the Killing Fields – where countless others were executed. As hundreds of thousands of Cambodians fled into Thailand, the genocide intensified. By November 1978, when Vietnam invaded and put an end to Khmer Rouge excesses, at least 1.25 million Cambodians had died from starvation or genocide out of a population of 7.5 million. The total was probably much greater.

WHEN:
1976–1978
WHERE:
Cambodia
DEATH TOLL:
Unknown. Estimates vary from 1.25 million to three million deaths directly caused by Khmer Rouge activities.
YOU SHOULD KNOW:
In 1979, following the Khmer Rouge's defeat at the hands of Vietnamese forces, the movement's *de facto* leader Pol Pot fled into the jungles on Cambodia's border with Thailand where he maintained the pretence of leading a legitimate government. He died aged 69 in 1998 while under house arrest, having fallen out with a Khmer Rouge faction led by his rival Ta Mok. It is rumoured that Pol Pot was poisoned.

Horrifying evidence of genocide.

421

Refugees await treatment in the hospital tent of humanitarian organization Médecins sans Frontières.

Ethiopian 'Live Aid' famine

WHEN:
1984–1988
WHERE:
Ethiopia
DEATH TOLL:
Despite the best efforts of relief agencies and donor governments, the famine still resulted in an estimated one million deaths, the majority in 1984 before it came to international attention.
YOU SHOULD KNOW:
Live Aid concerts at Wembley Stadium in London and Philadelphia's JFK Stadium became one of the most widely watched live TV events ever staged, with an estimated audience of 400 million. The original intention was to raise £1 million through ticket sales, but when the final revenue total was calculated the figure was a staggering £150 million. Even so, Live Aid's real triumph was in inflaming public opinion to a degree that governments simply couldn't ignore, thus greatly enhancing the relief effort.

The world might have remained supremely indifferent to famine that took Ethiopia in its iron grip during 1984. But late that year a BBC crew documented the rapidly intensifying disaster with reporter Michael Buerk using evocative phrases like 'the closest thing to hell on earth' and 'a biblical famine in the 20th century'. Graphic reports and harrowing pictures of starving children galvanized British and, as the publicity bandwagon rolled, worldwide public opinion.

Rock stars Bob Geldof and Midge Ure wrote a charity song entitled *Do They Know It's Christmas?*, assembled a group named Band Aid and released the record to support Ethiopian famine relief. It went to Number One, selling 3.5 million copies in Britain alone. Mightily encouraged, Geldof organized Live Aid in July 1985, when simultaneous pop concerts in London and Philadelphia raised a vast sum for Ethiopian famine relief.

Had it not been for this magnificent effort – and equally significant official interventions such as food drops by governments spurred into action by newly aroused public awareness – the famine could have been every bit as serious as the great Ethiopian famine that killed 3.5 million people a century before. Even so, the country saw a serious humanitarian disaster unfold before the famine ended in 1988.

The Ethiopian government was interested only in fighting insurgencies in the north (by the Tigrayan People's Liberation Front) and south (Oromo Liberation Front), while continuing friction was caused by the troubled federation with Eritrea. Half of all national resources were devoted to military spending, even as low rainfall caused a succession of poor harvests. This imbalance ensured that no efforts were made to prepare for the impending famine, while medical provision was run right down. It was a recipe for prolonged suffering that would cost innumerable lives and see millions of Ethiopians become displaced and destitute.

Halabja attack

The disparate communities of Iraq – majority Shi'ites, Sunnis and Kurds – were ruled with an iron hand by President Saddam Hussein, who came to power after deposing his Arab Socialist Ba'ath Party leader and friend Ahmed Hasan Al-Bakr in 1979. Indicating his future *modus operandi* as a supreme human rights abuser, all potential rivals for the top job were arrested, murdered . . . or both. In classic dictatorship style Saddam Hussein then attempted to defuse internal tension by declaring a patriotic war on an external 'enemy' – the new Shi'ite-led Iranian regime. Hostilities lasted from 1980 to 1988, cost up to 1.5 million lives and ended in a bloody and indecisive stalemate.

Meanwhile, the troublesome Kurds of northern Iraq posed a problem for Saddam's regime. This proud and would-be-independent people favoured the Iranian cause as the lesser of two evils, so Kurds and Iranians had combined to resist government forces that unleashed Operation Anfal in 1986 to terrorize and subjugate a Kurdish rural population that harboured insurgents. The operation was led by Saddam's feared cousin Ali Hassan al-Majid. Chemical Ali was his nickname, earned after deadly chemical warfare became his game.

This was acquired after a ruthless poison gas attack on the town of Halabja, which had been liberated during the closing months of the Iraq-Iran conflict by Kurdish *peshmerga* guerrillas. Saddam Hussein couldn't afford to lose the Anfal campaign, and ordered al-Majid to use air-dropped mustard gas and the nerve agents sarin, tabun and VX on Halabja and surrounding villages, backed by a conventional offensive intended to crush the Kurdish revolt once and for all. Thousands died immediately, mostly civilians, and thousands more would suffer long-term health problems as a result of the chemical attack. Subsequently Halabja itself was virtually destroyed by bombing and a ground attack.

WHEN:
March 16–17 1988
WHERE:
Iraqi Kurdistan, Iraq
DEATH TOLL:
The world's largest chemical weapons attack on a civilian population is thought to have killed up to 5,000 people and certainly no fewer than 3,500, with over 7,000 more injured out of a population of 80,000.
YOU SHOULD KNOW:
Ali Hassan al-Majid, Saddam Hussein's cousin and the infamous instrument of the dictator's repressive regime, was captured when Coalition forces invaded Iraq in 2003 and in 2007 was sentenced to death for crimes against humanity, war crimes and genocide.

An Iraqi Kurd soldier stands in the cemetery at Halabja where victims of the chemical weapons attack are buried.

Rwandan genocide

WHEN:
April to July 1994
WHERE:
Rwanda
DEATH TOLL:
At least 500,000, probably 800,000,
perhaps one million
YOU SHOULD KNOW:
Following the RPF's victory a
government of national unity was
established in Rwanda, which
prohibited any discrimination on the
basis of ethnicity, race or religion and
now bans any emphasis on Hutu or
Tutsi identity in any part of the
political process. But the work of
reconstruction and reconciliation has
been slow.

The German colony of Rwanda fell under Belgian control after World War I and became independent in 1962. But this small country in Central Africa had the sort of tribal tensions that dogged many newly freed African nations. Two main tribal groupings lived in this verdant area, which also encompassed neighbouring Burundi. Hutus were in the majority, with Tutsis forming an elite minority.

After independence, Hutus took power in Rwanda and supported fellow Hutus in opposing Burundi's minority Tutsi government, whose army orchestrated genocidal retribution after a Hutu rebellion in 1972. When a Hutu president was elected in Burundi's first democratic elections in 1993 and assassinated by the Tutsi-dominated army, civil war erupted. Meanwhile, inter-tribal conflict was also raging in Rwanda, after the Tutsi-dominated Rwandan Patriotic Front (RPF) invaded from Uganda in 1990.

On April 6 1993 Burundi's replacement Hutu President, Cyprien Ntaryamira, was flying into Rwanda in company with Rwandan President Juvénal Habyarimana during yet another attempt to broker a peace deal between warring factions in both countries. But their plane was shot down on the approach to Rwanda's capital of Kigali, killing all aboard. Blaming Tutsis for the assassination, members of the Hutu Interahamwe ('Those who stand together') and Impuzamugambi ('Those with a single goal') paramilitary organizations began the indiscriminate murder of Tutsis and moderate Hutus. Mass genocide continued unabated for four months as neighbour fell upon neighbour with violent savagery. The world watched in horror – and ineffectually protested – as the ongoing genocide was directed by an influential Hutu group known as the Akazu made up of the dead President Habyarimana's inner circle. It continued alongside a renewed civil war until the Tutsi RPF emerged triumphant, thus ending the genocide and causing two million Hutus to flee from Rwanda to neighbouring countries in anticipation of Tutsi revenge.

*Rwandan refugees fleeing from
Rwanda to Kivu.*

Darfur conflict

Has it been a prolonged case of genocide or merely ongoing mass murder? The US government boldly announced it was the former, while the United Nations cautiously claimed that in the absence of 'provable genocidal intent' it was the latter. But semantics hardly matter to the devastated civilian population of Darfur, collectively the three Sudanese states of West, South and North Darfur, who have been subjected to a prolonged killing spree.

Displaced Sudanese women walk past an armoured personnel carrier of the United Nations-African Union Mission in southern Darfur.

The relentless Darfur conflict began in February 2003 when the SLA (Sudan Liberation Army) and JEM (Justice and Equality Movement) took up arms against the Sudanese government. Insurrection was caused by the Arab-dominated government's perceived discrimination against the mainly black inhabitants of Darfur. This uprising was viciously countered by the government-sponsored Janjaweed militia recruited from nomadic Afro-Arab Abbala tribes. As always in such conflicts, it is hard to ascertain the truth with any certainty. Each side has accused the other of unspeakable atrocities, while the international community periodically indulged in futile attempts to mediate (over 50 peacekeepers have been killed in Darfur) – or even exert any influence over the Sudanese government.

At least two million Darfurian civilians have been displaced, many fleeing to neighbouring Chad and the Central African Republic where they are sometimes pursued and attacked by Janjaweed fighters, exacerbating regional tensions. The combination of military engagements, malnutrition, disease and genocide/mass murder has taken a terrible toll. Just how terrible is a matter of conjecture. The Sudanese government claims a figure in the low tens of thousands, while other estimates go up to half a million. But all agree that a particularly unpleasant aspect of the conflict is the extensive use of rape by armed militias as a weapon of terror, underlining the Darfur conflict's status as one of the 21st century's most intractable humanitarian disasters.

WHEN:
2003 onwards
WHERE:
Western Sudan
DEATH TOLL:
Unknown, but estimated at anywhere up to 500,000 fatalities from all conflict-related causes.
YOU SHOULD KNOW:
The ICC (International Criminal Court) at The Hague filed genocide, crimes-against-humanity and murder charges against Sudanese President Omar al-Bashir in 2008. But like the UN the court, too, was uncertain about the use of the term 'genocide'. When an optimistic arrest warrant was issued, the genocide counts had been quietly dropped for 'lack of sufficient evidence'.

425

ENVIRONMENTAL & ECOLOGICAL DISASTERS

Easter Island

WHEN:
Not known exactly, but sometime
between the 14th and the 19th
centuries.
WHERE:
Rapa Nui (Easter Island),
Pacific Ocean
DEATH TOLL:
At its peak the Polynesian civilization
on Easter Island is thought to have
had a population in excess of
10,000. By 1877 a mere 111
islanders were left.
YOU SHOULD KNOW:
Rapa Nui now belongs to Chile,
3,600 km (2,250 mi) to the east.

Fittingly for one of the most remote inhabited places on earth, an air of mystery has always surrounded Easter Island. Lying in the southeastern Pacific Ocean over 1,600 km (1,000 mi) from its closest island neighbour, Easter Island is famous worldwide for the extraordinary stone sculptures which maintain a brooding presence over the island. Hewn out of the local volcanic rock these monumental figures, known as *moai*, have been puzzling archaeologists ever since they were first seen by Europeans in the 18th century and now stand as tantalizing markers of a vanished civilization.

First settled by Polynesian seafarers – the Rapanui – about AD 700, Easter Island quickly developed a complex, sophisticated culture which flourished in a lush environment where dense forests supported a rich flora and fauna and food was plentiful, both on land and in the surrounding seas. By the time Dutch explorer Jacob Roggeveen visited the island in April 1722, however, much of this culture had disappeared and the population had declined drastically to just 2,000, having outstripped the resources available to sustain it. Thus a society had effectively destroyed itself by overexploiting its environment.

The island's trees were the most serious loss since they had supported a varied plant and bird life and had limited the erosion of fertile top soils, especially the Easter Island palms which had grown as high as 24 m (80 ft) and had been used for the hulls of the islanders' great sea-going canoes. The notion that the Easter Island people committed ecological suicide is popular among today's harbingers of environmental doom, although other experts believe that the consequences of European contact – slave-trading, alien diseases and whaling – had a more decisive and damaging impact.

Increasing global population

WHEN:
From the 1750s onwards
WHERE:
Global
TOLL:
A large percentage of the world's
population already lives on or
below the poverty line, with famine
a regular occurrence, so the
consequences of an additional
three billion people arriving within
the next 40 years are potentially
catastrophic.

The evolution, survival and advance of any species are dependent on the available resources. Left to nature, the population of each species will settle at a sustainable level. This may fluctuate according to unusual events like abundant years or disease, but will essentially remain stable. When circumstances change permanently a species will either adapt and flourish or fade away and become extinct.

The one species that has managed to bend this rule to its own advantage is the most advanced animal of all – *Homo sapiens*. In the beginning, around 60,000 years ago, it is estimated that there were no more than a million humans on earth. This population remained stable for millennia, limited by the restricted food supply available to primitive hunter-gatherers. But once man learned how to farm the land, rapid population growth followed.

Human intelligence and drive harnessed agriculture and technology to exploit nature's bounty to such good effect that by the 14th century world population had reached 450 million. There were setbacks – plague pandemics and natural disasters – but these proved to be no more than blips on the soaring population graph. By 1750 the figure was 791 million. In 1850 it had leapt to 1.26 billion, and by 1950 it had reached 2.52 billion. In 2050 Planet Earth will be inhabited by an estimated 9.75 billion people!

But is this huge population sustainable? Can all those mouths be fed, even using modern techniques like genetically modified crops? Will the continuing plunder of dwindling natural resources lead to catastrophic consequences for the environment that all living creatures depend on? These are questions that will perforce remain speculative until it becomes apparent whether or not human ingenuity can continue to support limitless population expansion. Common sense suggests the answer must be 'no', but the doomwatch scenario indicates that this may not become apparent until Planet Earth has become irreparably damaged.

YOU SHOULD KNOW:
It is currently estimated that the world's population increases by around 225,000 people every day. Ironically, developed nations, such as Japan and many European countries, are expected to suffer negative population growth as birth rates decline and longevity increases, meaning that smaller and smaller working populations have to support more and more elderly folk.

View of overpopulated São Paulo, Brazil, with a population that is due to reach 20 million people by 2035

Extinction of species

WHEN:
From about 1800 onwards
WHERE:
Global
DEATH TOLL:
It is estimated that in addition to countless species that have become extinct over time – many in recent centuries as a result of human activity or predation – one half of all species of life on earth will become extinct within the next 100 years if the destruction of Earth's biosphere continues at its present rate.
YOU SHOULD KNOW:
One extinction that is almost guaranteed is that of the *Geochelone abigdoni* tortoise. There is just one left in the world – Lonesome George, the last remaining Galapagos giant tortoise of a species once found on the isolated island of Pinta. But many of 100-year-old George's genes may live on as attempts have been made to mate him with a similar but different subspecies of tortoise and scientists hope that DNA will help them identify other pure-bred specimens on the neighbouring island of Isabela. The quest to save his species has made George a potent conservation icon.

Evolution is as old as time itself: species adapt to cope with a changing environment, and new species emerge while the least adaptable ones die out. There were at least five great mass extinctions in prehistory. The most recent – a mere 65 million years ago – is the best known, for it wiped out all those impressive dinosaurs. In more recent times – for the past 50,000 years or so – the process of extinction has continued with more than a little active assistance from the burgeoning human race. In this context, it is estimated that 99.9 per cent of all species that ever lived have become extinct.

Extinction is defined as the moment when the last living specimen dies, though in practice a species is doomed when the breeding population is reduced below a sustainable level. This can happen for many reasons, including climate change and failure to compete as more effective species evolve over time. But the pace with which human activity has already contributed to the extinction of species since the start of the 19th century is truly horrifying and, even more worryingly, species extinction appears to be happening at an ever-increasing rate.

Much to the dismay of conservationists, wholesale habitat destruction and global warming threaten imminent mass extinctions. On a practical level, many endangered species are now subject to controlled captive breeding programmes in the hope of ensuring their survival. And experiments are being carried out to roll back the clock and reverse earlier extinctions by cloning. DNA from the remains of an extinct species is used to create a laboratory embryo that can be implanted into a similar host species; it was the stuff of fiction in *Jurassic Park*, but attempts to re-create the extinct Pyrenean ibex have already been made. Other target species are the Tasmanian tiger (*Thylacinus cynocephalus*), a relatively recent casualty, and the much more ancient woolly mammoth.

A collection of models of extinct animals at England's Tring Zoological Museum

Toxic waste in Love Canal

William T Love was a visionary who, in the 1890s, hoped to build a model community powered by hydroelectricity. His scheme required the construction of a short canal between the upper and lower Niagara River at Niagara Falls, New York State. But, in 1910, the money ran out; Love Canal was abandoned half-dug. In 1942 the site was acquired by the Hooker Chemical Company as a chemical waste dump. By the time it was sold for one dollar in 1953, Love Canal was filled with a toxic detritus of benzene, toluene, dioxins, heavy metals, hydrocarbons and worse. The site was 'sealed' with impermeable clay, and town planners allowed a school and some hundred houses to be built on it.

By the 1970s residents were reporting an exceptional incidence of miscarriages, birth defects and general health problems, and were linking them to the stinking puddles, bubbling chemical ooze and corroding oil drums popping up in their gardens and backyards. The worst affected homes were evacuated, but health problems multiplied even where state officials claimed there was no contamination. During 1979–1980 only four out of 22 births were normal. Defects included three ears, a double row of teeth and severe mental retardation. Children playing outdoors came home with burns on exposed skin.

Independent scientific studies were dismissed as 'useless housewife data' – until one of the housewives organized a mass street protest. By forcing the story of Love Canal onto the political agenda, Lois Gibbs exposed the catalogue of contempt shown by local and state authorities for residents' welfare. The Senate and even the President called for immediate action and proper investigation. But as soon as the fuss died down, Love Canal fell off the agenda again. The state continued to pursue its policy of playing for time and avoiding accountability. It's not over yet – that 'housewife' is slowly and surely winning her battle.

A child endangered by the toxic dump waves a protest banner.

WHEN:
1942 onwards
WHERE:
Love Canal, City of Niagara Falls, New York State, USA
TOLL:
Nobody can guess the true extent of the disaster. Tens of thousands of people are still ingesting toxic poisons from Love Canal (from the groundwater if nothing else), despite the Federal Emergency declared in 1978, the $356 million recovery costs paid by the Occidental Chemical Corporation (Hooker's successor), or the more than $100 million paid out by the authorities.
YOU SHOULD KNOW:
Around 59 kg (130 lb) of dioxin were buried there: 100 g (4 oz) can kill a million people. Some of the birth defects are permanent genetic mutations. No amount of money can change that. But Lois Gibbs, the campaigning housewife, has already changed the future by founding the Center for Health, Environment and Justice (CHEJ) which in 20 years has helped 10,000 American and international community-based groups discover how to organize and flex their grassroots power.

Paradise under threat:
the contamination of Mapua

WHEN:
Contamination 1945–1988;
botched clean-up in progress from
1999 onwards
WHERE:
Mapua, Tasman Bay, South Island,
New Zealand
TOLL:
The whole saga has been
educational. Mapua has caused
scientific, sociological, political and
economic text books to be rewritten
as the environmental implications
become more properly understood.
That's great, but it hasn't yet
restored faith in its non-hazardous
attractions for residents and visitors,
nor convinced its faraway
consumers of the safety of its
luscious produce. Mapua's disaster
is less what *has* happened, and
more what *could yet* happen.
YOU SHOULD KNOW:
After several years of buck-passing,
the ground-remediation contractors
have withdrawn, the government's
finite promise of 'help' for the
operation has lapsed, and the site
is now controlled again by the
local council – and since all the
legal consents necessary to
monitor a second clean-up (or
sealing) have also lapsed, Mapua is
pretty well back where it started,
but better informed. It's becoming
a modern parable.

The story of Mapua is a classic example of the long-term consequences of mankind's cavalier disregard for the natural environment. Mapua is one of the small, tranquil communities perched on the coastline of New Zealand's Tasman Bay – renowned for its wonderful beaches, benign Mediterranean climate and idyllic landscape of olive trees and vineyards, woods and orchards, with a backdrop of hazy blue hills in the distance. Mapua should be an earthly paradise but, some 20 years ago, woke up to the worm in its paradisaical apple.

In 1932, the Fruitgrowers Chemical Company built a plant to manufacture pesticides and from 1945 onwards the company began to produce a range of more than 80 different pesticide compounds involving 124 different chemicals. These included DDT, paraquat, organomercury and organochlorine pesticides. The risks associated with these hazardous compounds were not fully understood, and for years they were continually flushed through waterways, leaching into the ground and contaminating the foreshores of the estuary.

The plant, in the middle of a residential area and next to the estuary itself, was closed in 1988. It was only when houses were to be built that the full extent of the contamination became apparent. A 1999 project to clean up the 5.5 hectare (14 acre) site went horribly wrong. Mapua residents were appalled to discover that the clean-up operation had not been properly monitored, and not only was the ground still badly contaminated but potentially lethal dioxins had been released into the air, mercury had been spread to a wider area, and quantities of copper had leached into the groundwater and estuary.

The contamination of Mapua has been called New Zealand's greatest toxic disaster. It is a supreme irony that New Zealand, the world's greatest champion of 'greenness', should countenance such delay in making Mapua safe.

London's great smog

Throughout the 19th and early 20th centuries London was notorious for the thick fogs which often descended on the city in the late autumn. These 'London particulars' were not so much an atmospheric effect as the consequent pollution from a vast and dense urban population. Unchecked factory emissions mingled in the city air with smoke from half a million domestic coal fires to produce a phenomenon for which a new term was coined: smog. The image of the murky, mist-shrouded streets of Victorian London has been immortalized in the novels of

Charles Dickens and the adventures of Sherlock Holmes; indeed, fog has been dubbed 'the greatest character in 19th-century fiction'.

These 'pea-soupers' (a reference to the yellowish hue the fogs often had) may have been a part of London's unique appeal, but they also caused serious disruption and disease. Things came to a head in 1952. A new monarch was on the throne, giving promise of better times ahead, but the close of the year brought a stark reminder of bad old days. In early December a period of high humidity, freezing temperatures and an anticyclone causing very still air produced a heavy accumulation of domestic coal smoke. With smoke and sulphur dioxide levels in the foul-smelling air ten times higher than normal, the dense fog hung over London for four long days, bringing the city to a standstill. Cars were abandoned, conductors walked in front of their buses with flares, washing turned black on the line, theatres closed because no one could see the stage.

The smog exposed the failure of existing pollution controls and led directly to the Clean Air Act of 1956, which permitted local authorities to designate smoke control areas and to regulate what fuels could be burned in people's homes.

ABOVE: *A London double-decker bus makes its way along the fog-blanketed Embankment.*

LEFT: *Thick fog shrouds Trafalgar Square.*

WHEN:
December 5–9 1952
WHERE:
London, UK
DEATH TOLL:
During the winter of 1952 there were reckoned to have been at least 4,000 more deaths in London than normal for the time of year, mostly caused by respiratory conditions in infants and the elderly, such as bronchial asthma and pneumonia.
YOU SHOULD KNOW:
The Act took several years to come into full effect, during which time London continued to suffer periodic dense smogs; as late as December 1962, 750 people died as a direct result of one. This type of air pollution finally disappeared as urban overcrowding was tackled and people gradually switched to gas and electricity.

Soldiers watch the mushroom cloud that followed one of the detonations in 1958.

Marshall Islands atom bomb tests

WHEN:
July 1 1946 to August 18 1958
WHERE:
Bikini and Enewetak Atolls, Marshall Islands, South Pacific
TOLL:
More than 50 years later, Bikini is still uninhabitable. Among the Marshall islanders generally there has been an exceptionally high incidence of birth defects, growth retardation and thyroid cancer as a result of exposure to nuclear fallout. Many of the islanders believe they were used as guinea pigs to test the effects of excessive radiation. The USA paid $150 million in compensation but the Bikini islanders are still in exile.

America plunged the world headlong into the Atomic Age by unleashing its devastating new invention on Hiroshima and Nagasaki to bring World War II to an apocalyptic conclusion. The nuclear scientists who had worked on the Manhattan Project researching the atom bomb were appalled by what they had created and strongly advised against any further testing. But the US military wanted to play with their new weaponry; their excuse was that they needed to observe the after-effects of radioactive fallout, about which hardly anything was known.

The Marshall archipelago, a sparsely populated paradise in the Pacific Ocean, was selected as a suitably remote region. Bikini, an atoll of 23 islands, was forcibly cleared of inhabitants and, over the next 12 years, 67 nuclear tests were carried out at both Bikini and neighbouring Enewetak Atoll. In 1954 a 15-megaton hydrogen bomb (equivalent to about 1,000 Hiroshimas) was tested, to far more devastating effect than had been anticipated. It vaporized three of Bikini's islands. The H-bomb created a fireball nearly 5 km (3 mi) in

434

diameter and scattered radioactive debris over a vast area of more than 100,000 sq km (40,000 sq mi) leaving a 1.5 km-wide (mile-wide) crater in the bed of the lagoon. Radioactive ash rained down on the neighbouring atolls, causing the inhabitants to suffer severe burns and sickness.

Today, more than 50 years after the last test, Bikini and Enewetak are still contaminated with radioactive fallout. At first sight, the environment appears to be like the Garden of Eden but, although the lagoon is teeming with fish, they are unsafe to eat, as is the radioactive produce of the land. As comedian Bob Hope put it: 'As soon as the war ended, we located the one spot on earth that hadn't been touched by war and blew it to hell'.

YOU SHOULD KNOW:
Bikini swimwear, first introduced as a fashion item in 1946, was named after Bikini Atoll. The smallest one-piece contemporary swimsuit had been called the Atome, which enabled bikini designer Louis Réard to pun that he had 'split the Atome'. Advertisers had a field day with such slogans as: 'like the bomb, the bikini is small and devastating'.

Acid rain

Acid rain kills wildlife, erodes buildings and turns lakes into dark lifeless bodies of water. It is created in industrial heartlands and affects great swathes of the planet. Nowhere is it more destructive than in lakes and forests in Scandinavia. In winter the jet stream blows from east to west around northern Europe and at times it narrows to become a very efficient carrier of pollutants. While Europe's industrial core has done much to alleviate pollution in its locality by building ever taller chimneys, this has only served to spread toxic gases further. Coal-fired power stations are the biggest culprits. They release sulphur dioxide molecules into the atmosphere, which then mix with naturally occurring particles to produce acid rain.

Even small amounts of pollutants can upset delicate ecosystems. Very low concentrations can cause PH levels to fall below 5, when fish eggs will not hatch and insect larvae will not develop, removing a vital part of the food chain. This has the knock-on effect of depriving birds and mammals of much of their diet. Acid rain not only affects areas where it falls directly, but can also be carried through large river systems into bodies of water several miles away.

The effects can be seen most markedly when travelling through Finland, where lake after lake has an eerie mirror-like appearance, providing a perfect reflection of the surrounding forested hills. Gas desulphurization at the source of the pollution has done something to alleviate the problem, but it will take generations for the Scandinavian countryside to recover. It is a sad irony that Scandinavians are pioneers in green living – but they can do little to prevent the drift of rain across their borders.

WHEN:
1950s onwards
WHERE:
Scandinavia, North America, China and Russia
TOLL:
As well as the devastating effect on wildlife, the particles associated with acid rain have been linked to several forms of cancer and respiratory diseases.
YOU SHOULD KNOW:
International agreement is the only way forward. The European Union has vowed to reduce emissions that cause acid rain by 60 per cent within the next decade. While acid rain can be caused by naturally occurring phenomena such as volcanic eruptions, it is only by limiting our own emissions that the lakes of Scandinavia can be restored to their former vibrancy.

Desiccation of the Aral Sea

WHEN:
1960s onwards
WHERE:
Uzbekistan and Kazakhstan
TOLL:
By 2007, the Aral was only a tenth of its original size. As the sea has shrunk, it has retreated by up to 100 km (60 mi) from its original shoreline. As a result the entire regional ecosystem has been upset and the local climate has become far more extreme, seriously affecting the lives of five million people. The fishing industry, which used to supply the Soviet Union with a sixth of its catch, is moribund. Raging dust storms blow poisons through the atmosphere causing endemic respiratory and eye problems. Chemical pollution from a combination of industrial waste and pesticides and fertilizers is not only a permanent health hazard but has also caused genetic damage. Infant mortality is higher than anywhere else in the developing world.
YOU SHOULD KNOW:
In June 2004, researchers predicted that the Aral would have completely dried up in another 15 years, leaving only a vast toxic salt bowl. Recently the UN has stepped in and given backing to the Kazakh government to restore water to the Aral. This has met with more success than expected, giving a ray of hope; but Uzbekistan, still economically dependent on its cotton industry, has shown little interest in following suit.

The fate of the Aral Sea has been described as the greatest manmade ecological catastrophe. Once the world's fourth largest inland body of water, a giant oasis in the middle of the barren Central Asian wilderness, for millennia the Aral Sea sustained life and provided bounteous supplies of fish for the region's inhabitants. The sea was fringed by busy fishing villages and pristine beaches; people flocked to its healing saline waters and hunted wildlife along the shoreline.

Until the mid 20th century, the Aral was fed by two torrential rivers. The Amu Darya (Oxus) and Syr Darya (Jaxartes) pour down from the towering mountains on China's border, cutting two great swathes through the steppes of Uzbekistan and Kazakhstan. But when the USSR was at its height, Central Asia was turned over to agro-industry, specifically cotton monoculture. Innumerable canals were built to redirect river water into the endless miles of cotton fields. By 1960 more river water was being diverted than not; the Aral Sea started to shrink and the fertile Amu Darya delta to dry up. Throughout

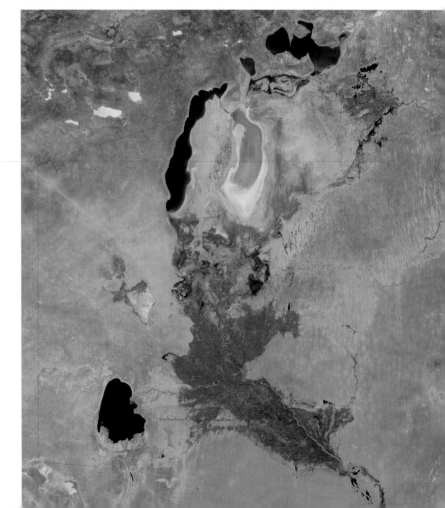

The shrunken waters of the Aral Sea appear to be emerald green and black in this dramatic satellite image.

the 1960s and 1970s the sea level continued to drop as more and more water was sidetracked to meet the insatiable demands of the cotton industry, without a thought for the consequences. In 35 years the Aral Sea's depth dropped by more than 19 m (62 ft).

The powers that be saw it happening, but nobody did anything and the imperative of instant profit took precedence over long-term wellbeing. By 2003, the Aral Sea had been reduced to four polluted puddles in a barren salt flat contaminated with pesticide and fertilizer residue. Today, the fishing villages of the Aral Sea are a tragic sight. Once thriving communities have become ghost towns, and abandoned boats lie half buried in the toxic mud. You might think you were in hell.

Yokkaichi air pollution

Located in Japan's Mie Prefecture, Yokkaichi is an important industrial town noted for the manufacture of such diverse products as porcelain, cars, textiles and chemicals. It owes its thriving economy to the port that was built in 1872 and in 1897 it was afforded 'modern city' status; its future was assured.

During the postwar push for progress, Yokkaichi became ever more reliant on chemical production and plants sprang up all over the city. Like many northern cities of England or those of the 'Rust Belt' in the USA, the production and processing of hazardous materials was carried out with scant regard for the local environment and, by the early 1960s, the burning of petroleum products in Yokkaichi had reached high enough levels to cause several episodes of severe smog. The first case of pulmonary disease linked to industrial pollution was reported as early as 1961 and it became normal practice for people to mask their faces with handkerchiefs while walking around the city on their daily business.

Levels of sulphur dioxide in the air became dangerously high and began to have a seriously detrimental effect on the respiratory systems of the local population. Initial efforts to alleviate the problem were woefully inadequate. The height of industrial chimneys was raised in an effort to spread the pollutants over a larger area, but this did little to help. The smogs continued and soon hundreds of people were presenting with chronic obstructive pulmonary disease (COPD), chronic bronchitis and bronchial asthma.

In 1970 a class-action lawsuit against the biggest polluter, Showa Yokkaichi Oil, finally led to effective action being taken. Through a process of gas desulphurization, the harmful chemicals were removed from the atmosphere and the last case of pulmonary disease linked to local heavy industry was reported in 1988.

WHEN:
1961–1988
WHERE:
Yokkaichi, Japan
DEATH TOLL:
Two deaths have been directly linked to asthma caused by the smog and research indicates that mortality rates from COPD were between ten and 20 times greater in Yokkaichi than in the rest of Mie Prefecture.
YOU SHOULD KNOW:
Although Yokkaichi has now cleaned up its act, it will forever be remembered for the pollution-induced asthma which carries its name. Today most cases of 'Yokkaichi asthma' are to be found in China, where a lack of environmental control is harming much of the urban population.

The *Torrey Canyon*

It seems inconceivable that a well-found ship could run aground in daylight and good weather. Famously, Admiral Sir Cloudesley Shovell managed it in 1707 when he wrecked his whole fleet on the rocks of the Scilly Isles after making a navigational mistake – but he had no way to determine his longitude. In the same waters 260 years later, the *Torrey Canyon* had no such excuse. *Torrey Canyon* was one of the first 'supertankers', a 300 m (930 ft) giant laden with 119,000 tons of Kuwaiti crude oil bound for Milford Haven. It had every navigational aid on board, except common sense.

Torrey Canyon's Captain changed course to pass between the Scilly Isles and the mainland in a fit of pique because his new Third Officer had presumed to take the more usual seaward route to Milford without consulting him. Newly awake, distracted, the Captain then initiated a series of farcically minor errors of command and interpretation. After he failed to disengage the automatic helm properly, he was left spinning the useless wheel at the vital moment. Correcting the mistake was impossible. The huge ship raced at over 16 knots onto Pollard's Rock, one of the Seven Stones reef. Six reinforced internal tanks ruptured, but the *Torrey Canyon* was held fast even after her back broke and the heavy swell pushed a vast oil slick towards both Cornwall and France. Nothing like it had ever happened before. The Prime Minister ordered RAF bombers to finish her off and burn the oil. The use of 42,450 kg (1,000 lb) bombs and 1,350 kg (3,000 lb) of napalm partially succeeded, but over three months huge tracts of coastline were ruined as thick, toxic sludge continued to drift ashore.

The secondary disaster was the damage caused by the remedial detergents. Infinitely more toxic than anything in use today, they were used in innocence but caused more serious and enduring damage than the oil itself.

The Torrey Canyon *blazes.*

WHEN:
March 18 1967
WHERE:
The Seven Stones, Scilly Isles, UK
DEATH TOLL:
One Dutch salvage worker was killed. Otherwise the damage was environmental, and on a colossal scale. Around 190 km (119 mi) of Cornwall's, and 80 km (50 mi) of Brittany's coastlines were drenched in red-brown sludge that killed at least 60,000 seabirds, and possibly three times as many. Regular forms of tourism suffered for years, even though eco-tourism got a kick-start (and a name) from volunteers who flocked to help on both sides of the Channel. More significantly, the disaster prompted international conventions on the use of the sea, pollution, and clean-up operations that have fundamentally changed maritime law.
YOU SHOULD KNOW:
The systems on ships' bridges have been modified to reduce the sort of mistakes made by the Captain of the *Torrey Canyon*. Royal Navy ships are now fitted with a device called a 'Torrey Canyon switch' that cancels the automatic helm mechanism when the wheel is rotated more than 15 degrees.

The *Atlantic Empress* and the *Aegean Captain*

When they embraced, the *Atlantic Empress* and the *Aegean Captain* were not sweethearts. They were VLCCs (Very Large Crude Carriers), each 350 m (1,000 ft) long and laden with over 200,000 tonnes of oil. The *Empress* was bound for Beaumont, Texas, from Saudi Arabia; the *Captain* was heading for Singapore from Aruba. They met in the evening in thick fog and heavy rain 29 km (18 mi) east of Tobago and 160 km (100 mi) northeast of the Orinoco Delta in Venezuela. At 19.15 the *Empress* smashed into the *Captain*'s bows, fracturing the forward tanks of both ships in a massive explosion of flames and dense smoke, and splattering both Greek crews with burning oil. The ships became funeral pyres and were abandoned.

Trinidad and Tobago's Coast Guard saved the *Aegean Captain* by containing the fire and enabling the crew to retake control. It limped to safety in Curacao. The *Empress* was a drifting inferno, but tugs risked immolation to get tow lines aboard and pull its dreadful cargo further from some of the world's loveliest (and most valuable) beaches. Two days later, it had left a slick of crude oil and naphthalene across 260 sq km (100 sq mi). Four aircraft and seven specialist boats bombarded it with dispersants. After a week, the heavily listing ship was still blazing when two explosions shattered the remaining tanks, doubling the rate of spillage to some 15,000 gallons an hour. As it poured from the stricken tanker, it ignited, fuelling a 2 km (0.6 mi) burning wake. There was one further explosion; then, two weeks after the original collision, the still-blazing *Empress* sank in deep water off Barbados. Its cargo of 276,000 tonnes was the largest amount of crude oil ever lost from a single ship.

WHEN:
July 19 1979
WHERE:
Off Tobago, Caribbean Sea
DEATH TOLL:
A total of 26 sailors from both ships were killed or disappeared, presumed dead and 50 crew members were seriously injured or burned. Because none of the oil reached the beaches, no impact studies were ever made of the damage to wildlife or the ocean floor from the 287,000 tonnes of heavy crude that was lost. The *Aegean Captain* was declared a 'CTL' (Constructive Total Loss) and broken up after her remaining oil was transferred. The collision became a major event in litigation because at the time oil prices were extremely high. It led to a 'significant change' in salvage law after the salvors claimed compensation for their efforts in trying to prevent both a major spill and major shore pollution.
YOU SHOULD KNOW:
Among shipping and oil companies, the tug that saved the *Aegean Captain* is as famous as the collision itself. The *Oceanic* salvage tug was a veteran of rescue operations. For the *Aegean Captain* it was like having Red Adair fly in to cap your oil well.

The Atlantic Empress *is aflame and spewing heavy smoke after the catastrophic collision.*

Castillo de Bellver oil spill

WHEN:
August 6 1983
WHERE:
Saldanha Bay, South Africa
TOLL:
There were no human casualties but
the spill left 1,500 gannets heavily
contaminated by oil. The colony had
gathered on a nearby offshore island
for the breeding season.
YOU SHOULD KNOW:
At the time damage was also
feared from a 'black rain' of oil
droplets which fell from the air after
the accident. However, no adverse
effects on local crops or grazing
lands were observed over the
long term.

The impact of human activity on the planet and the consequences of that activity going wrong are nowhere as dramatically demonstrated as in the case of marine oil spills. Images of traumatized seabirds, their plumage caked in thick, viscous oil, offer heart-breaking reminders of the fragile balance existing between the natural world and man's exploitation of its resources.

The *Castillo de Bellver* was a Spanish-registered supertanker which in August 1983 was *en route* from the Persian Gulf to Spain with a cargo of 252,000 tonnes of crude oil. As it crossed Saldanha Bay off the coast of South Africa, 110 km (70 mi) northwest of Cape Town, the massive vessel caught fire. The cause remains unclear but the effect was an instant inferno as the oil burned uncontrollably. Firefighters were quick to the scene; although they were unable to save the ship, they managed to rescue the crew before the blazing vessel broke in two and its stern section sank to the seabed. At this point the tanker was in deep water 40 km (25 mi) off the coast, and some 100,000 tonnes of oil, still in its tanks, may have accompanied the stern to the bottom.

A few days later the still floating bow section was towed further offshore and sunk with the aid of controlled explosives. Around 50,000–60,000 tonnes of oil are estimated to have spilled into the sea or burned, but – remarkably given the scale of the accident – there was relatively little environmental damage. This was thanks to factors such as wind direction and location. Judicious spraying with dispersants meant that local beaches were not significantly threatened by oil slicks and luckily there was little damage to local fish stocks.

Exxon Valdez oil spill

WHEN:
March 24 1989
WHERE:
Prince William Sound, Alaska, USA
TOLL:
There were no human casualties
but the environmental damage was
enormous. Over a quarter of a
million seabirds and 3,000 sea
otters are thought to have died as a
result of the oil pollution.
YOU SHOULD KNOW:
Years of litigation followed, and it
was not until 2004 that the Exxon
oil corporation was finally ordered
by the US courts to pay $4.5 billion
in damages for the oil spill. The
tanker itself was repaired,
renamed and put back into service,
although it is banned from ever
returning to Alaska.

Although it comes way down the list of the world's worst oil disasters in terms of the volume of oil spilled into the ocean, the *Exxon Valdez* accident in 1989 has gained particular notoriety for two reasons. First, it occurred in US waters (it remains the largest such spill in America's history) and was thus subject to unusually intense media scrutiny, and second, those waters were in Alaska, one of the planet's great pristine wildernesses, its ecosystem at that time still relatively unaffected by human intervention.

Alaska in the late 20th century found itself in the front line of a worldwide conflict between conservation and exploitation as big business sought to tap the huge oil deposits of the remote US state. An environmental disaster was probably on the cards sooner or later and it occurred as the 211,000-tonne supertanker *Exxon Valdez* was making its way from the terminal at Valdez down Prince William Sound to the open waters of the Gulf of Alaska. The ship was bound for California with a full cargo of crude oil. A slight change of course to avoid small icebergs in the narrow channel proved catastrophic when the mighty vessel struck a reef and ran aground in the darkness. The hull was punctured and oil began to spill into the sea. Eventually an estimated 42 million litres (11 million US gallons) of oil were lost, polluting an area of 1,300 sq km (500 sq mi) and devastating 2,100 km (1,300 mi) of Alaska's coastline.

Although a massive clean-up operation was mounted, involving over 10,000 workers, a combination of shallow water and the poor flush in the Sound magnified the impact of the spill on the environment's rich wildlife and fish stocks. It is an impact still being felt more than 20 years later.

Crude oil from the tanker
Exxon Valdez *contaminates*
Alaska's Prince William Sound.

Gulf War oil spill

WHEN:
January 21 1991
WHERE:
Persian Gulf
TOLL:
No loss of human life was directly
attributable to the oil spill, but
thousands upon thousands of fish,
birds, animals and plants were
destroyed.
YOU SHOULD KNOW:
After the Gulf War was over, a
massive clean-up was embarked on.
Some of the oil was recovered,
some was washed ashore, mainly in
Saudi Arabia, and some evaporated.
A long-term study monitored 22
separate locations in a Saudi
Marine Wildlife Sanctuary: by 2007
six locations had returned to their
previous state, two had not improved
at all, and the remainder were still
affected by various degrees of
pollution. So, 16 years after the war,
the area was far from fully recovered.

On August 2 1990 Iraqi president Saddam Hussein invaded Kuwait, provoking instant condemnation from the international community. The UN immediately imposed economic sanctions, while President George Bush Senior organized a 32-nation military coalition and dispatched US troops to Saudi Arabia.

The coalition's assault began with bombing raids on January 17 1991 and, just one week later, Iraq deliberately dumped millions of gallons of crude oil from Kuwait's Sea Island terminal into the Persian Gulf, apparently to prevent US Marines from landing. This wanton sabotage produced the worst oil spill in history, and it was exacerbated by other sources of leaking oil – several damaged tankers, a Kuwaiti oil refinery and an Iraqi oil terminal. Some 770 km (478 mi) of coastline, from southern Kuwait to Saudi Arabia's Abu Ali Island, was smothered in oil and tar, wiping out almost all plant and animal species living there and destroying an already fragile ecosystem.

Coalition forces successfully accomplished their mission of ejecting the Iraqis from Kuwait and the war was over by February 28. But during the fighting it had of course been impossible to deal with the disaster, which covered 1,550 sq km (600 sq mi) of the sea's surface, and was about 13 cm (5 in) thick.

The Persian Gulf contains superb coral colonies and beds of sea grass and algae that are home to dugongs and sea turtles as well as fish and birds, all of which were severely affected, as were the coastline's many beaches, mangrove swamps and salt marshes. There is uncertainty regarding the exact amount of oil that was spilled, but it was more than twice the size of the previous record-breaker, the Ixtoc 1 oil well blow-out in the Gulf of Mexico.

Red Adair Co. workers guide an oil well capping device into place over a spouting well head in Kuwait.

Marcopper mining disaster

In 1969 the Marcopper Mining Corporation began open-cut mining at Mount Tapian on Marinduque Island in the Philippines. Marinduque is a poor region and most inhabitants rely on agriculture and fishing for their livelihoods. Unhappily, the mining operation caused pollution of the waterways and deaths from poisoning in the population.

By 1990 Mount Tapian was worked out and a new site opened nearby. A tunnel leading from the old mine to the Boac River was sealed and the resulting pit took the waste from the new San Antonio copper mine. At the same time a dam was built in the Mogpog River in case the Tapian pit was not sufficiently large. People soon noticed that waste was seeping into the river and poisoning the fish. In 1993 the dam collapsed, polluting farmland and killing two children.

On March 24 1996 the seal of the pit tunnel broke, releasing millions of tons of waste into the Boac River. The effect was dramatic: flash floods inundated whole villages with polluted water up to 2 m (6 ft) deep, fields were drowned, drinking water was contaminated, and 20 villages had to be evacuated. The Boac River was declared dead.

Although there was severe contamination, Marcopper denied that its waste was toxic. A UN mission declared the river system to be an environmental disaster, and the communities near the mouth of the river to be significantly affected. Canadian mining company Placer Dome, who owned 40 per cent of Marinduque's mines, pledged to clean up the river. However, they too denied responsibility, selling out the following year after making a token contribution towards the rebuilding of houses and infrastructure repairs. They argued that all remaining problems were Marcopper's responsibility – but Marcopper went bankrupt.

The abandoned, rusting remains of a pipeline left over from the Marcopper Mining Corporation operation lie on Calancan Beach on Marinduque Island.

WHEN:
March 24 1996
WHERE:
Boac River region of Marinduque Island, The Philippines
DEATH TOLL:
No one died as a result of the flooding on the day of the disaster, but subsequently many villagers, especially children, presented with toxic-waste related illnesses, many of which proved fatal.
YOU SHOULD KNOW:
A special fund was set up to compensate thousands of villagers for the loss of their land, homes and livestock. Most have received nothing. The British Columbian Committee for Human Rights in the Philippines called Placer Dome's position 'obscene' after the company declared profits of Can$31 million for the first quarter of 2005. Local residents were given roughly Can$22 in compensation for the death of a child.

Martin County sludge spill

WHEN:
October 11 2000
WHERE:
Martin County, Kentucky, USA
TOLL:
No human lives were lost, but the
number of fish, birds, mammals,
amphibians and plants that were
killed amounted to millions.
YOU SHOULD KNOW:
Jack Spadaro headed an
investigation into the catastrophe,
but the newly formed Bush
administration decided to cut it
short, fearing that Massey Energy
would be charged with serious
violations. Eventually they were
charged with only two out of eight
possible violations, and got away
with a fine of $110,000. Jack Spadaro
was removed from his job on
specious grounds, but has since
been re-employed, though demoted,
and sent to work in West Virginia.

The Appalachian Mountains run from Newfoundland in Canada to central Alabama in the USA. Certain regions of this ancient and beautiful range, such as Tennessee, West Virginia, Pennsylvania and Kentucky, contain natural gas, minerals and vast coal deposits. Coal is the major source of fuel for energy production in the USA, with more than a billion tonnes mined annually. Inevitably there is a price to pay: coal slurry.

Mining is an important industry in Martin County, Kentucky, a small area with a population of fewer than 12,000, 37 per cent of whom live below the poverty line. During the night of October 11 2000, a terrible accident occurred when the bottom of a coal sludge reservoir broke open into an abandoned mine beneath, allowing 1.16 billion litres (306 million gallons) of sludge to seep out of the mineshaft and into two tributaries of the Tug Fork River.

Local residents woke to find Wolf Creek and Coldwater Fork smothered with black waste. Coldwater Fork, a 3 m (10 ft) wide stream, had become a 91 m (100 yd) wide river creeping inexorably forward, covering gardens and ground floors, and polluting wells; the water supply for over 27,000 people was contaminated. All the way down to the Ohio River, hundreds of kilometres of streams were polluted with toxins, killing all the aquatic life including an estimated 1.6 million fish, as well as small mammals such as muskrat and mink.

Jack Spadaro, Head of the National Mine Health and Safety Academy, discovered that the mine owners, the Massey Energy Company, had suffered a previous spill from the same reservoir in 1994. Although the company had announced that steps had been taken to solve the problem, one of their engineers admitted it wasn't true and that they knew another spill was inevitable sooner or later.

Prestige oil spill

WHEN:
November 13–19 2002
WHERE:
Bay of Biscay 250 km (155 mi) off the
Galician coast of Spain
TOLL:
No human lives were lost, but the
loss of marine and bird life is
incalculable.

On November 13 2002 the *Prestige*, a single-hulled oil tanker registered in the Bahamas and owned by a Liberian-registered corporation, ruptured one of its tanks during a storm in the Bay of Biscay. The ship was carrying heavy fuel oil and the Captain asked the Spanish authorities to help him into port, as he feared his ship might sink.

But first Spain, then France and finally Portugal denied him entry. The Captain soon reported that a section of his hull had sheared away and oil was spilling. On November 19, the *Prestige* broke in half and sank, releasing more than 20 million gallons of oil. The resulting oil slick polluted thousands of kilometres of beautiful coastline in Spain and France, and sank onto the seabed in an ecologically sensitive area of coral reefs, affecting all the marine and bird life. The Galicians, whose livelihood depends on the fishing industry, were dealt a terrible blow when all offshore fishing was banned for six months.

Thousands of volunteers organized a major clean-up operation. It was so successful that the following year Galician beaches were awarded more Blue Flags than in any of the preceding years.

The *Prestige* disaster is rated as even worse than that of the *Exxon Valdez*, not simply because the spill was larger but because the warmer waters caused higher toxicity. The Spanish government originally announced that only 17,000 tons of oil had been spilled, but by 2004 it transpired that the true figure was more than 80 per cent of the entire cargo. A study of the *Mytilus galloprovincialis* mussel revealed that by 2006 neither the mussels nor their environment had been restored to health. It is thought that it will take at least ten years for the ecosystem to get back to normal.

YOU SHOULD KNOW:
New oil slicks were found near the wreck of the *Prestige* in March 2006. It was estimated that between 16,000 and 23,000 tons of oil remained in the wreck, rather than the much lower figure given by the Spanish government, and that the microbiological agents that had been pumped into the hold to hasten the breakdown of the remaining oil had not worked, which could lead to yet another horrendous spill.

The Prestige *sinks after failing to find a safe haven.*

Three Gorges Dam

WHEN:
2006
WHERE:
Sandouping, Hubei Province, China
TOLL:
The loss of homes and land
experienced by around 1.25 million
people displaced by the Three
Gorges Reservoir, plus potentially
serious ecological consequences that
have not yet become fully manifest.
YOU SHOULD KNOW:
The numbers associated with the
dam are mind-numbing – it is
2,335 m (7,662 ft) long and 101 m
(331 ft) high. Construction
commenced in 1994 and the main
structure was completed in 2006,
creating a reservoir covering an area
of 1,045 sq km (403 sq mi) supplied
by a catchment area of one million
sq km (386,100 sq mi). The dam's 32
turbines are capable of generating
22,500 MW and a substantial
percentage of the $39 billion
construction cost was recouped
even before the dam's full generating
capacity came on line.

As the New World Order (NWO) transfers economic power from West to East, another sort of power underpins that inexorable process – electricity. That's the energy source supporting the relentless advance of the NWO's leading player, China. Despite the damaging global-warming effect of coal-fired power stations, insatiable appetite for energy means this method remains the principal source of China's electricity supply. However, any possibility of generating 'green' electricity is welcome, especially if it brings additional economic benefits, and one such project is the massive Three Gorges Dam.

Electricity generated by the Three Gorges Dam will be carbon neutral, but this and other gains must be balanced against the disastrous ecological cost in other areas, highlighting the compromises that must always be made when undertaking any major infrastructure project. And so it was for this huge engineering development on the Yangtze River, destined to become the world's largest electricity-generating plant.

On the up side is an unending supply of cheap hydroelectricity, improvement of the Yangtze River's navigation potential and ability to control downstream flooding. The price? Carbon dioxide emitted during the manufacture of millions of tonnes of concrete used to build the dam made a significant contribution to the acceleration of global warming. Perhaps more significantly, the dam had terrible consequences for the huge number of people displaced from land subsequently flooded as the Three Gorges Reservoir filled, plus the loss of important archaeological and cultural sites to the rising waters.

Added to that is a very real ecological downside – a sharp decrease in the river's ability to flush away vast quantities of pollutants discharged into its waters, downstream erosion, upstream sedimentation and a marked increase in the number of project-related landslides. The most deadly possibility is that a serious earthquake could breach the dam, with horrendous consequences.

*The vast Three Gorges
Dam project*

Rainforest destruction

Aerial view of a typical deforested area in Paraná, Brazil

Once upon a time, rainforests wrapped around the earth's equator like an unbroken green girdle – and that time was not long ago, though now rainforests are disappearing at an alarming rate. These very special biological treasure houses contain a huge diversity of plants and animals. They are also home to many different indigenous peoples who have resisted the destructive march of modern civilization. While many tribes remain, representing unique primitive cultures, others have simply been swept away along with their forest homelands.

Quite apart from the catastrophic reduction of rich biological ecosystems containing all sorts of undiscovered pharmaceutical resources, the destruction of rainforests has other major ecological implications. Yet wholesale clearances happened throughout the 20th century and the pace of destruction has continued to speed up in the 21st century, despite widespread awareness of the negative consequences for the future of all life on earth, including the future of the human race.

The world has an insatiable appetite for timber, and illegal logging with the tacit support of corrupt governments is a major cause of rainforest loss. So, too, is acute need for cash crops in poor countries blessed by huge expanses of rainforest. Coupled with rising demand for food and green fuel, this ensures that crude slash and burn is used to clear forest land where beef cattle can be raised or crops like palm oil or soya grown.

Rainforests are too valuable to lose, for they help regulate climate by absorbing one fifth of the harmful greenhouses gases emitted by human activity, thus slowing the potentially deadly process of global warming and climate change. However, forest burning that contributes significantly to global warming continues apace, while those capable of preventing this unfolding ecological disaster of epic proportions are often complicit in accelerating rainforest destruction.

WHEN:
20th and 21st centuries
WHERE:
Global
TOLL:
Continuing damage to an ecosystem vital to the future of every species on earth.
YOU SHOULD KNOW:
Rainforests once covered 14 per cent of the world's land surface, an area now more than halved, and if destruction continues at the same rate there will be no rainforest left inside 40 years. Over 100 distinct plant, animal and insect species are lost to deforestation every day – a huge negative when over 25 per cent of pharmaceuticals are derived from rainforest ingredients and less than one per cent of its trees and plants have been tested. The population of Amazonian Rainforest Indians has fallen from around ten million to 200,000, and 90 indigenous tribes were lost in the 20th century alone.

Climate change

WHEN:
20th and 21st centuries
WHERE:
Global
DEATH TOLL:
Incalculable. Countless natural
disasters that have claimed hundreds
of thousands of lives between them
are said by many to be caused (at least
in part) by global warming. While there
is almost certainly some truth in these
claims, it is impossible to prove that
any particular natural disaster has
been caused by, or even influenced by,
global warming.
YOU SHOULD KNOW:
The major climate-change summit that
took place in Denmark towards the
end of 2009 was billed as the last
serious opportunity to secure a binding
international agreement to limit the
emission of greenhouse gases before
global warming started to run out of
control. It ended in disarray with
complete failure to secure any sort of
meaningful deal.

A melting iceberg

Even the most sceptical of critics now admit that global warming is
a fact of life, so their line has switched from 'it isn't actually
happening' to 'it's actually happening but it's part of a natural cycle
rather than manmade'. But few scientists now doubt that the earth's
atmosphere is warming as millions of tonnes of greenhouse gases –
mainly carbon dioxide – are created annually by the relentless
burning of fossil fuels and destruction of forests that help to
neutralize harmful emissions.

While developed and developing nations alike acknowledge the
potentially disastrous consequences of global warming, they can't
agree on remedial action. The two super-polluters – the USA and
China – refuse to make any firm commitment to reduce emissions,
illustrating the key reason why global warming remains such an
intractable problem. Developed countries are unwilling to take the
economic pain and reduced living standards that would stem from
cutting back on existing levels of emission and restricting growth.
Developing countries won't slow economic growth and frustrate the
entirely reasonable ambition of their people to share living
standards enjoyed in the developed world. So nothing significant
gets done.

The best projections suggest that – in the absence of drastic
efforts to reduce the emission of greenhouse gases – the world's

Evidence of crippling drought

average temperature will rise by at least 1°C to 6.5°C in the 21st century, with the probable rise towards the top of the range – or even beyond – as the process becomes self-sustaining and feeds off itself. The consequences will be catastrophic, with rapidly rising sea levels engulfing low-lying land, erratic and violent weather patterns, desertification of large areas and mass species extinctions. The gloomiest sages ever foresee a very real threat to the continued existence of the species responsible for creating and failing to check global warming: *Homo sapiens*.

Detritus covers the banks of a river close to the sea, opposite the 400-year-old village of N'gor at the westernmost tip of Africa.

Threats to the world's oceans: pollution and over-fishing

During the 20th century, our oceans were fouled by pollution of all kinds and now contain increasing numbers of dead zones, where pollution-fed algae deprive existing marine life of oxygen. Oil spills from tankers are the most visible manifestation of pollution, but make up only a small percentage of the total. As holidaymakers avoid flying to limit their carbon footprints, more and more cruise liners take to the seas, and these floating towns discharge millions of gallons of detergent-laden 'grey water', oily bilge water and raw sewage. Even worse is the effect of runoff pollution: all over the world, a toxic cocktail of chemicals from factories and agriculture, along with the steady drip of oil from engines of all sorts, slowly but surely leaches into the water. We also toss waste of all kinds directly into the sea where floating plastic litter kills millions of seabirds, marine mammals and fish.

We also kill fish intentionally, and the 20th century population explosion greatly increased demands on fish stocks worldwide, resulting in the near extinction of several species. Quotas and controls may have saved some, such as cod and tuna, but marine biologists are concerned by the decrease in variety of species, as well as numbers, in the fishing grounds. Invasive and indiscriminate fishing methods endanger not just fish, but also ocean life – deep trawling, for example, destroys the fragile ecosystem of the seabed, where unknown species are still occasionally discovered.

The oceans cover 70 per cent of our planet and remain largely unexplored. We know more about outer space than we do about what goes on in the depths of the ocean, and we are only just beginning to appreciate both the importance and the vulnerability of our oceans and seas. As the warnings of environmentalists start to be heeded, we just have to hope it is not already too late.

WHEN:
20th and 21st centuries
WHERE:
Worldwide
TOLL:
Incalculable
YOU SHOULD KNOW:
In 1992 a cargo of thousands of brightly coloured bath toys fell into the Pacific; they spent nearly a year in the Subpolar Gyre, a counter-clockwise current, before circling the Pacific. For more than ten years, flotillas of yellow ducks were tracked as they journeyed around the world in different directions. They have been valuable to oceanographers studying currents and a delight to beachcombers who find them.

Honey bee colony collapse

Beekeepers expect to lose some bees, but in recent years a rapid increase in unexplained mass desertions by worker bees has prompted investigation, research and an official name: Colony Collapse Disorder (CCD). Also called Honey Bee Depopulation Syndrome, it is characterized by the complete disappearance of workers from the hive, leaving only the queen, immature brood and stores of honey and pollen. It is widespread in the USA and Canada as well as much of Europe; beekeepers have been reporting losses of a staggering 60 to 90 per cent of their hives.

Theories on the causes abound. Outside 'interference', such as climate change or microwaves from mobile phone masts, has been suggested; it may be that foraging bees are somehow disorientated and cannot find their way back to the hive. CCD could also be linked to pesticide or fungicide poisoning; possible culprits include pest-control characteristics in modified GM crops and new nicotine-based insecticides.

Or CCD could be due to disease. Sick bees are known to leave their hives to die and tests continue on various fungal infections, mites and viruses. The virulent Israel Acute Paralysis Virus has been identified in many CCD hives. It is commonly carried by the 'vampire mite', *Varroa destructor*, known to weaken the bees' immune system. In Spain, the parasite *Nosema ceranae* has recently been found as a constant in affected hives.

It is probable that CCD is the result of a combination of factors but, whatever the cause, the effect should not be underestimated. At risk is not only the honey on our toast, but also the ability of plants to cross-fertilize and reproduce, affecting the diet of the insects, birds and animals that feed on them and ultimately upsetting the ecological balance of the planet.

WHEN:
2006 onwards
WHERE:
North America and much of Europe, with cases increasingly reported worldwide.
TOLL:
Unknown. But bees serve the vital purpose of plant pollination. Without their aid, who knows what the consequences will be?
YOU SHOULD KNOW:
'Migratory beekeeping' has increased in the USA. Hives are transported around the country, from farm to farm, crop to crop, for pollination purposes. Many beekeepers earn more from bee rental than from honey production.

Bees make a vital contribution to the ecological balance of the planet.

Jiyeh power station oil spill

WHEN:
July 14–15 2006
WHERE:
Jiyeh, Lebanon
TOLL:
Incalculable effect on eastern
Mediterranean fish stocks and
bird life
YOU SHOULD KNOW:
After the spill, an overwhelming
majority in the UN General Assembly
passed a resolution that Israel should
contribute to the cost of the
clean-up. Israel refused, citing as a
defence its own 'ecological disasters'
from Hezbollah shelling.

In July 2006, during renewed conflict between Israel and the Lebanon, Israeli bombers hit a power plant at Jiyeh, south of Beirut, and vast quantities of heavy fuel oil escaped from damaged tanks into the sea. The Lebanon had no experience of this type of ecological disaster, which was a potential threat to the whole eastern Mediterranean, and called for international aid. Funding, expertise and specialized equipment came promptly from all over the world, but continued Israeli bombing and a naval blockade prevented immediate assessment or treatment of the damage. For nearly a month a 10 km (6 mi) wide oil slick drifted with the tides and not only continued to pollute the Lebanese coast but also threatened to spread to Turkey, Cyprus and beyond.

The spillage was estimated at around 30,000 tonnes. Beaches and harbours along a third of the Lebanese coast were smothered in thick black sludge and the sea was transmuted from limpid blue to an evil-smelling pitch-black brew. Underwater surveys revealed that oil sediment had sunk onto the seabed. The United Nations Environmental Programme expressed grave concern about the potential environmental and economic effects of the spill. Hundreds of thousands of fish, including spawning tuna, were contaminated, as were the endangered green turtles of the Mediterranean and hundreds of thousands of birds.

A coalition of environmental groups worked on clearing land and sea and on a waste-management project to remove and safely dispose of the contaminating sludge. In August 2009 a UN report recommended the establishment of a fund to provide assistance and support for eastern Mediterranean countries affected by similar events in the future.

A layer of sticky crude oil covers the Ramlet el-Beida public beach in Beirut.

Kingston Fossil Plant spill

Among the meandering waterways of the Tennessee Valley lies the Kingston Fossil Plant, sited at Watts Barr Lake reservoir, about 60 km (40 mi) west of Knocksville, a well-known spot for bird-watching. The plant converts five million tons of coal a year into electricity for the atomic reactor at nearby Oak Ridge and when it was built in the 1950s this was the largest plant of its kind in the world. In the main plant, pulverized coal is burnt to make steam; the process leaves a large residue of talc-fine ash, known as 'coal fly ash', which is mixed with water to stabilize it. Once the sediment has settled it is removed to a 'dredge cell' to dry out.

On December 22 2008, after days of heavy rain, a section of the massive clay walls of the dredge cell gave way, releasing millions of gallons of coal fly ash slurry and causing the biggest-ever environmental disaster of its kind in the USA. The slurry flowed along the river valley, damaging houses and power lines in its path, and covering an area of more than 1 sq km (0.5 sq mi) in a thick layer of grey sludge. Inevitably, the run-off flowed into the local waterways, killing thousands of fish and poisoning the bird life.

The plant's owners, the Tennessee Valley Authority, quickly reassured residents that water upstream still met drinking water standards and that the slurry was not toxic – independent tests suggested significant levels of toxic metals – and promised an immediate clean-up. They faced outcry, accusations and demonstrations from local people and environmental groups nationwide and were blamed not only for the spill – reportedly, the unlined tank had undergone repairs for leaks regularly for some years – but also for disposal methods generally.

This aerial view shows homes that were destroyed when a pond retention wall collapsed at the Tennessee Valley Authority's Kingston Fossil Plant.

WHEN:
December 22 2008
WHERE:
Kingston, Tennessee, USA
TOLL:
Fortunately, residents in the area were evacuated before the spill reached their homes, but the environmental damage has been enormous.
YOU SHOULD KNOW:
The TVA emphasized the importance of regaining the public's trust. Among the goals set out in their year-on report was the provision of 'health assessments' for local people.

DISASTERS CAUSED BY TERRORISM

Wall Street bombing

WHEN:
September 16 1920
WHERE:
Wall Street, New York, USA
DEATH TOLL:
The bomb left 38 dead and 400
injured, most of them messengers,
secretaries and junior clerks setting
out on their lunch-hour break. It
caused $2 million-worth of damage
($18 million in today's terms).
YOU SHOULD KNOW:
The perpetrators of the bombing
were never caught. A note,
discovered the following day in a
nearby mailbox, threatened: '. . . Free
the political prisoners or it will be
sure death for all of you. American
Anarchist Fighters', from which it
was deduced that an anarchist
group was behind the attack. But
investigations never led anywhere
and 20 years later the FBI finally
closed the file.

Terrorist attacks on America's financial institutions are not new.
Although the scale of the 1920 Wall Street bombing is dwarfed by 9/11,
at the time it was a tragedy of similarly momentous proportions. America
was shaken to its core: *The Washington Post* described the bombing as
an 'act of war', there was an immediate security crackdown, and initial
horror quickly turned to indignation and defiance.

Just before noon on September 16, an old horse-drawn wagon pulled
up in the street just outside 'The Corner', headquarters of the world's
leading financier J P Morgan. Across the road were the US Sub-Treasury
and the Assay Office and round the corner was the New York Stock
Exchange. As the church bells struck noon, the wagon's driver jumped
down and vanished. Seconds later there was a massive explosion.

The wagon had been loaded with 45 kg (100 lb) of dynamite and
packed with 230 kg (500 lb) of cast-iron weights (of the sort used in
sash-window frames) – a peculiarly deadly shrapnel. One of the sash
weights was rocketed to the 34th floor of a nearby building by the force
of the blast, and windows shattered 800 m (0.05 mi) away. When the air
cleared, the cobbled street was a fearful sight – a grotesque scene of
mutilated bodies and scattered limbs strewn in a sea of shattered glass.
The horse had been blown apart – a solitary leg lay poignantly draped
across a doorstep.

Within minutes, police, medics and troops were on the scene. By mid
afternoon Wall Street had been cleared up and the New York Stock
Exchange defiantly declared that tomorrow would be business as usual.
The next day, thousands of New Yorkers congregated at noon and one of
the largest crowds in the city's history sang *The Star-Spangled Banner*
in a spontaneous demonstration of patriotic fervour.

*Crowds gather on the steps of
the Stock Exchange and around
an upturned vehicle.*

King David Hotel bombing

The King David is the most famous hotel in Jerusalem. Opened not far from the Jaffa Gate in 1931, its pink sandstone has always been a conspicuous landmark of opulence; and with a clientele of political, military and wealthy international elites, it has been a *de facto* government building for whoever is in power. In 1946 the hotel was home to the British Secretariat. The south wing was the British Mandate's military, civil, judicial, police and communications headquarters.

It was a red rag to Irgun, the Stern Gang and Haganah, three underground Jewish groups with a track record of ruthless political violence. Whether you call them terrorists or freedom fighters depends on your point of view. Irgun's leader, the future Israeli Prime Minister Menachem Begin, paid lip service to avoiding 'individual terror' but was

The damaged King David Hotel

happy to kill indiscriminately to fight his 'war'. Briefly united as the 'Jewish Resistance Movement', the gangs feared British betrayal of the promise of an exclusive Jewish homeland. They were also unscrupulous about taking what they wanted at gunpoint. Their protest was to bomb the King David. Dressed as Arabs, they smuggled 225 kg (500 lb) of explosives in milk churns into the hotel basement. The blast brought down all seven stories of the south wing, crushing more staff and fellow Jews than British administrators.

The international response was universal disgust. The Jewish Agency, attempting to achieve some sort of parity at the negotiating table, called the gangs 'criminals', and Zionist leader David Ben-Gurion denounced Irgun as 'enemies of the people'. Ben-Gurion understood how the global confusion following World War II had delayed the peaceful resolution of legitimate Jewish aspirations. Bombing the King David Hotel was a cowardly demonstration of contempt for the broader Jewish consensus: *menschlichkeit* (humanity) and murder don't mix.

WHEN:
July 22 1946
WHERE:
King David Hotel, Jerusalem, Israel
DEATH TOLL:
91 dead (including 41 Arabs and 17 Jews) and 45 injured. Because the hotel was such a potent symbol, the bombing achieved a disproportionate significance. It increased British jitters and hastened the setting up of Israel. The bombing was not an Israeli disaster, but an Arab disaster, because it taught the fledgling Israeli leadership that by force of arms they could disenfranchise the Palestinians. The King David Hotel was bombed in the cause of *Eretz Israel* (greater Israel), a policy which was fundamental to Israeli aspirations.
YOU SHOULD KNOW:
The attainment of *menschlichkeit*, or humanity, is one of the ideals of the Jewish faith: to live the life of a well rounded, ethically grounded, 'good' man (*mensch*).

The Dublin and Monaghan bombings

The timing of the bombs was critical. The Ulster Workers' Council (UWC) had paralyzed Northern Ireland by striking in an attempt to de-rail the Sunningdale Agreement, which was a last-ditch effort to reconcile Ulster's warring factions. The bombings resulted in a cynical insurance that nobody could trust anyone else.

Dublin firemen and police walk through rubble caused by three powerful bombs detonated in cars that had been parked in the heart of the city.

WHEN:
May 17 1974
WHERE:
Dublin and Monaghan town, Republic of Ireland
DEATH TOLL:
33 dead and 258 injured, the majority of whom were young women.
YOU SHOULD KNOW:
The full truth is unlikely ever to emerge about the bombings. It doesn't help that the covert intelligence unit directly concerned with the actual Dublin and Monaghan bombers included a *bona fide* British Army hero – Captain Robert Nairac. Nairac's determinedly courageous undercover activities led to his torture and execution by the Provisional IRA, for which he was awarded a posthumous George Cross.

In Dublin, three car bombs exploded almost simultaneously across the city in the early evening rush hour of May 17 1974, killing 26 people. Ninety minutes later, seven died in another blast in Monaghan. Hundreds were maimed. Sammy Smyth, press officer to both the loyalist Ulster Defence Association (UDA) and the UWC declared 'I am very happy about the bombings in Dublin. There is a war with the Free State and now we are laughing at them'.

Nobody doubted loyalist involvement in the outrage, but nobody claimed responsibility either. Instead, official enquiries in the Republic were concluded with inexplicable speed and with no results, let alone arrests or charges. It was quiet – too quiet. The depth and efficiency of official silence bred a growing certainty among republicans that the loyalist bombers had had seriously powerful help on their mission.

It took 20 years for hard evidence to start to emerge, and a further 15 for probability to become fact. In 1993, a Yorkshire Television documentary included former British Army officers who confirmed specific links between an Armagh loyalist group and a British Intelligence undercover team. Over several years, evidence mushroomed to show that the team had supplied weapons, ammunition and expertise for a number of loyalist atrocities, of which the Dublin and Monaghan bombings were the worst. Trials, appeals, retrials and acquittals have come and gone leaving the victims unavenged. Despite the evidence, the proof remains locked up for fear of rocking Northern Ireland's precarious political boat.

Siege in Masjid al-Haram (Grand Mosque)

The *Hajj* is the pilgrimage all Muslims strive to make at least once in their lives to their holiest site, the Kaaba: a plain cuboid building in the great courtyard of the Masjid al-Haram in Mecca. The Grand Mosque's courtyard holds 300,000 people who, in the ritual *Tawaf*, all circulate in unison anti-clockwise round the sacred Kaaba seven times, creating a great swirl of humanity in motion.

In the Islamic calendar it was New Year's Eve of the year 1400, the last day of *Hajj*, and tens of thousands of pilgrims were milling around the Grand Mosque courtyard. Several hundred among them suddenly donned red headbands and produced automatic weapons. Proclaiming their leader was the new Mahdi (Messiah), they denounced the Saudi monarchy for 'betraying Islamic principles'. The sacrilege stunned Saudi guards into inaction: religious law prevents them committing acts of violence inside the Mosque without direct authorization. In a few seconds the terrorists shot or disarmed them and began herding hostages by the hundred into the hallowed Kaaba itself.

A two-week running battle involved tanks, artillery and rockets; an eye-witness suggested that 'probably well over a thousand' died. Thousands – soldiers, hostages and terrorists alike – shared a bloodbath in the secret labyrinth of hundreds of hermits' chambers, hidden beneath the shrine. Here the terrorists had prepared themselves for the long haul by amassing a hoard of weapons and supplies, ingeniously (and profanely) smuggled into the mosque in coffins.

By the time the carnage ended (after Saudi forces were given a blueprint of the labyrinth by none other than Osama bin Laden's billionaire father), the Islamic world was inflamed with fury. Ayatollah Khomeini of Iran blamed the US and Israel; US installations from Bangladesh to Turkey were stoned, and two US personnel were killed when rioters burned the embassy in Pakistan. But the unthinkable truth was actually that Muslim was battling Muslim for ultimate control of their religious creed.

WHEN:
November 20 1979
WHERE:
Masjid al-Haram (the Grand Mosque), Mecca, Saudi Arabia
DEATH TOLL:
Officially, Saudi security forces suffered 127 dead and 451 wounded. No figure was given for hostages, but it is thought to have been hundreds. Of the terrorists, 117 died in the siege and a further 63 were later publicly beheaded by the sword simultaneously in eight Saudi cities.
YOU SHOULD KNOW:
The siege was a disaster for Islam. It was the first time Wahhabi zealots from Saudi Arabia had found common cause with jihadi extremists from Egypt's Islam Brotherhood. Later, that same combination of fanatics would become known as al-Qaeda. Meanwhile, the attack and its suppression served to nurture growing aspirations among disaffected Islamic sects everywhere.

Iranian students praying outside the US Embassy.

Bologna's neo-fascist bombing

WHEN:
August 2 1980
WHERE:
Bologna Centrale Station,
Bologna, Italy
DEATH TOLL:
Until Madrid, it was Europe's worst
terrorist incident with 85 dead and
over 200 injured. Those convicted of
the bombings were members of the
neo-nazi NAR (Nuclei Armati
Rivoluzionari). They happily admitted
other murders, but not these. Freed
in 1990 after the revelations, they
were then retried, and sentenced to
life in 1995 . . . and released again
after the intervention of the deputy
head of one of Italy's secret services.
The Bologna bombing is a terrifying
reminder of how 'things we don't
know we don't know' can be deadly.
YOU SHOULD KNOW:
The main clock at Bologna station is
forever stopped at 10.25, and
August 2 has been designated the
annual Memorial Day in Italy for all
terrorist massacres. The day
culminates in a concert in Bologna's
Piazza Maggiore.

Bologna's beautiful, medieval arcades empty in high summer heat. On an August Saturday morning one of the few crowded places is the air-conditioned Centrale Station waiting room. The bombers chose well. In the confined space, the suitcase bomb packed with high-quality TNT collapsed the ceiling on everyone inside, destroyed most of the main station building, and wrecked the Ancona to Chiasso express train at platform one. Hundreds lay dead and injured and Italy was shaken to its core. Bologna represents the country's soul, and Italians were united in their distress.

From the start, official investigations were mired in disinformation. Only with hindsight can partial truth be disentangled from conspiracy theory, and the result is even more fantastic. Long afterwards, Licio Gelli and others were convicted of planting false leads, including a second bomb 'found' in Bologna station in 1981, to suggest an international group of terrorists. Then Gelli was found to be leader of Propaganda Due (P2), a secret Masonic lodge whose existence was unknown until late 1981. P2 was nothing less than a right-wing government in waiting, comprised of serving Cabinet ministers, Vatican bankers, Italian secret service commanders, and top movers and shakers.

In 1987, P2 'arranged' for four known neo-nazi terrorists to be convicted of the bombings; but by 1990 declassified documents began to emerge showing that both NATO and the CIA were intimately involved with a 'parallel' army, part of NATO's anti-communist European network. Known in Italy as Gladio (every country uses a local name), it engaged in electoral subversion and terrorist acts. In 2000, another investigation by the Italian Senate into the bombing concluded that the bombers were 'men inside Italian state institutions and . . . men linked to the structures of United States intelligence'. In the febrile political atmosphere of the 1970s and 1980s, morality apparently counted for nothing.

Rescue vehicles line the streets near the train station in Bologna.

Grand Hotel:
the Brighton bombing

The imposing Grand Hotel on Brighton's seafront has often been the first choice of British political parties for their annual party conferences. On October 12 1984 it was fully occupied by the Conservative Party. As usual, the best suites and rooms facing the sea were occupied by the most important people: Prime Minister Margaret Thatcher and her most senior Cabinet colleagues and friends.

The predictability of it all was a gift to the Provisional IRA. Three weeks earlier, long before security teams began to check the hotel, one of them had stayed as a guest and planted a huge bomb among the VIP rooms upstairs. The explosion at 02.54 in the morning tore the front wall off the Grand Hotel, collapsed eight floors vertically on top of one another, killed five and maimed 34 people. Mrs Thatcher wasn't among them.

Her incredible luck (and the sturdy Victorian construction of the building) left Mrs Thatcher on her feet to preside over the propaganda of the aftermath. The shattered debris of the Grand Hotel was intended by the IRA to showcase the destruction of the political elite and the futility of their democratic notions. The disaster for Britain is that in the end it did. Despite the personal courage of the Thatchers, Tebbits and dozens more, the hotel bombing led to the creation of a 'ring of steel' around senior members of the political establishment.

The bomb-damaged Grand Hotel

WHEN:
October 12 1984
WHERE:
Grand Hotel, Brighton, Sussex, UK
DEATH TOLL:
The bomb killed five and left 34 injured. Among the injured were Trade and Industry Secretary Norman Tebbit and his wife. Tebbit made a full recovery but his wife was permanently confined to a wheelchair. Some years later the couple's legendary courage came to be valued as transcending politics, and as the embodiment of a Churchillian spark which would be an asset to any political force.
YOU SHOULD KNOW:
In the middle of the rescue operation, and mindful that his boss intended to open the Conference that morning on time, Conservative Party Treasurer Alistair McAlpine arranged for Marks and Spencer to open early so that everyone who had lost their clothes in the attack could get new ones.

Air India Flight 182

A policeman guards the wreckage of Flight 182.

WHEN:
June 23 1985
WHERE:
Atlantic Ocean
DEATH TOLL:
329 passengers and crew (including 280 Canadians and 84 children)
YOU SHOULD KNOW:
An explosion took place at Tokyo's Narita International Airport an hour before Flight 182 was downed. Two baggage handlers were killed and four were injured as a bomb concealed in luggage exploded prematurely before it could be loaded onto Air India Flight 301 to Bangkok, thus saving the lives of 177 passengers and crew.

The mid-air destruction of Air India's Boeing 747 *Emperor Kanishka* ranks as Canada's largest mass murder. For Flight 182 in June 1985 originated from Montreal, flying via London and Delhi to Bombay with a majority of Canadian passengers. A terrorist bomb in the forward cargo hold detonated at an altitude of 9,400 m (31,000 ft), 190 km (120 mi) off Ireland's southwest coast – at the time the deadliest terrorist attack involving an airliner. While some passengers and crew survived the explosion and decompression, none lived through the subsequent break up and crash into the Atlantic. Over 130 bodies were recovered; nearly 200 were 'lost at sea'.

The attack's perpetrator was a mysterious 'Mr Singh' who made assorted flight bookings using different first names. He arranged for his baggage – a brown Samsonite suitcase containing the bomb – to be transferred from Canadian Pacific Flight 60 from Vancouver to Toronto onto Flight 182 for Bombay. He had a confirmed booking on Flight 60, checked in but didn't fly. His booking on Flight 182 was provisional but he still persuaded the Canadian Pacific Air Lines agent to mark his suitcase for transfer to the Bombay flight, thus sealing the 747's fate. This procedure seems incredibly lax in the light of modern security routines, but back in 1985 commercial airliners had yet to become prime terrorist targets.

As always in such cases, the official reaction was to promise that the culprits – thought to be members of a Sikh separatist group called the Babbar Khalsa – would be brought to book. But in the event, despite a prolonged investigation by Canadian authorities that took many years – and charges being brought against prime suspects – the only conviction secured was that of bomb-maker Inderjit Singh Reyat. He served five years after pleading guilty to manslaughter in 2003.

Remembrance Day bombing

Enniskillen is the largest town in County Fermanagh, one of six counties within the province of Ulster that remained part of the United Kingdom after the rest of Ireland began its journey to full independence when the Irish Free State was formed in 1921. But this division would leave a lasting legacy of bitterness among those nationalists who believed then and passionately continue to believe that their homeland should never have been partitioned. But the Protestant majority in Northern Ireland expressed equal conviction that remaining within the UK was essential, and set about moulding a province that sustained their pre-eminence at the expense of Ulster's substantial Catholic minority.

This was the backdrop for 'The Troubles' – sectarian violence that erupted from 1969 after Catholics began agitating for improved civil rights and an end to Protestant discrimination – and marked the start of a 30-year armed struggle waged by the Provos (Provisional Irish Republican Army or IRA) against the *status quo*, as represented by Protestants and the 'occupying' British Army that swiftly arrived to try and keep the peace.

Two decades on the Provos (or elements thereof) planted a bomb in Enniskillen's Reading Rooms, timed to go off on the morning of 1987's Remembrance Sunday – the day set aside to commemorate soldiers (many of them Irish) who gave their lives in World War I. The blast was symbolically scheduled to attack the security forces in general and the British Army in particular. The violent explosion killed ten civilians, all Protestants, and one member of the Royal Ulster Constabulary. Another 63 people were injured. But the attack proved counterproductive. The world was horrified by the atrocity and Sinn Fein, the IRA's political wing, lost electoral support among Fermanagh's Catholic population despite unconvincing denials that the IRA's Northern Command had sanctioned the bombing.

WHEN:
November 8 1987
WHERE:
Enniskillen, Northern Ireland, UK
DEATH TOLL:
12 (11 at the time and one victim who died after being in a coma for 13 years).
YOU SHOULD KNOW:
To emphasize the IRA's serious intention of creating mayhem on that Remembrance Sunday – and devalue its denial of 'official' involvement – a second and larger bomb was planted to devastate a wreath-laying ceremony at nearby Tullyhommon, attended by members of the Boys' and Girls' Brigades, spectators and a few uniformed representatives of the security forces. Mercifully, that one failed to explode.

The Cenotaph at Enniskillen with the devastated community centre in the background

Hipercor bombing

WHEN:
June 19 1987
WHERE:
Barcelona, Spain
DEATH TOLL:
21 died (15 immediately) and 45
were badly injured.
YOU SHOULD KNOW:
Two of the bombers were caught
after three months and each
sentenced to 794 years in prison. In
2003 Caride Simon – who led the
three-man ETA cell that carried out
the Hipercor bombing – received a
790-year prison sentence after being
extradited from France, while Santi
Potros was given a similar sentence
for ordering the bombing.

Along with Northern Ireland, Spain's Basque region was one of two European hotspots for terrorist activity – with militant operations in both places commencing towards the end of the 1960s. And just as the IRA exported its bombing campaign to mainland Britain, so ETA (Euskadi Ta Asskatasuna, translating as 'Basque Homeland and Freedom') mounted attacks outside the territory it sought to 'liberate'.

In June 1987 one such attack took place in Catalonia on Avinguda Meridiana, an important Barcelona street. A powerful incendiary bomb weighing 200 kg (440 lb) was placed in the boot of a stolen Ford Sierra car. This was parked on a Friday afternoon in an underground car park beneath the Hipercor shopping centre. It would be the worst of many ETA attacks, surpassing a Madrid car bomb the previous year that killed 12 and injured 50. At around 16.12 the device exploded, destroying surrounding vehicles and blowing a large hole in the floor of the hypermarket, from which an intense fireball erupted. A number of people were burned to death or asphyxiated, while others were injured – some so badly that they subsequently died in hospital.

The blame game soon began. Faced with public outrage, ETA claimed that telephone warnings had been given. Indeed they had, though that didn't lessen responsibility for the bombing and its consequences. A lax response by the police and store management was also inexcusable. The first of three telephone warnings came an hour before the blast and police did mount a half-hearted search. Meanwhile, management decided not to clear the busy hypermarket as there had been bomb warnings that proved to be hoaxes in the past. Hipercor claimed the police should have made the evacuation decision while the authorities (surprise!) said it was the store management's call.

US Embassy bombings

The man who would become the USA's terrorist nemesis first came to international public attention in August 1988, after Osama bin Laden funded an audacious double strike on US embassies in Kenya and Tanzania. The attackers were members of Egyptian Islamic Jihad, a militant group active in Africa since the 1970s. Its leader was Ayman al-Zawahiri, a cultured surgeon and close associate of bin Laden, who founded the Islamist al-Qaeda group around this time.

Two massive truck bombs were constructed and a date set to coincide with the seventh anniversary of US troops arriving in bin Laden's homeland of Saudi Arabia. In Kenya, the truck gained entry to the Nairobi US Embassy compound in mid morning and detonated almost immediately, damaging the main building and

causing fearful loss of life – over 200 died and thousands were injured. At about the same time a refrigerated truck packed with high explosive exploded at the US Embassy in Dar es Salaam. It was as powerful as the Nairobi bomb, but casualty figures were much lighter. President Bill Clinton ordered retaliatory cruise missile strikes in Afghanistan and Sudan and a number of bombers were brought to book and jailed. Others were subsequently killed or captured, though some named culprits remain at large.

At the time, there were many theories regarding the motivation behind the bombings, including revenge for the CIA's alleged torture of captured members of Egyptian Islamic Jihad. But it is now thought that the plan was hatched for two reasons – firstly to hurt and humiliate America for failing to protect its own, secondly to try and provoke the USA into invading Afghanistan. The latter was eventually achieved as bin Laden's ambitious hope of provoking a long guerrilla war in 'the graveyard of foreign armies' duly came to pass.

Rescue workers pull a survivor from the wreckage.

WHEN:
August 7 1988
WHERE:
Nairobi, Kenya and Dar es Salaam, Tanzania
DEATH TOLL:
An estimated 223 were killed in both bombings (212 in Nairobi and 11 in Dar es Salaam).
YOU SHOULD KNOW:
Although the USA and its citizens were the prime target of these atrocities, only 12 of the dead were Americans (all in Nairobi). Ten Americans were seriously injured in Nairobi and two in Dar es Salaam. So most of the unfortunate victims were local people who just happened to be in the wrong place at the wrong time.

Pan-Am Flight 103

Lockerbie disaster

The word 'Lockerbie' has chilling resonance in the context of international terrorism, for just before Christmas in 1988 it was at 9,400 m (31,000 ft) above the quiet town of Lockerbie in the Scottish Borders that a bomb exploded in the forward cargo hold of Pan-Am Flight 103, a Boeing 747 named *Clipper Maid of the Seas* bound from London to New York. The jumbo's control systems were destroyed and the aircraft disintegrated within seconds. In addition to passengers and crew who died instantly, 11 people on the ground were killed when the 747's wing section fell on Lockerbie's Sherwood Crescent, igniting in an intense fireball.

Horror and grief experienced by victims' families were compounded by failure to achieve closure, because the origins of this dreadful terrorist outrage were never fully explained. A massive investigation by Scottish police was aided by America's FBI, and eventually two Libyans were tried in a Scottish court convened in The Netherlands. One was convicted, the other acquitted. But hard evidence of Libyan culpability was flimsy, and the fact that Libya gave up the accused for trial and admitted responsibility in 2003, also paying compensation, may have been motivated only by desire to have damaging US and UN trade sanctions lifted.

Libya is the chief suspect – Libyan leader Muammar al-Gaddafi's adopted daughter had been killed in an US air strike launched as part of a confrontation between the two countries. But – among others – credible culprits were Iranian extremists (avenging Iran Air Flight 655 shot down by American missiles over the Persian Gulf in 1987) and activists from the Palestine Liberation Organisation seeking to sabotage PLO talks with the US government. Responsibility for the Lockerbie bombing remains a tantalizing mystery that is unlikely to be solved, despite repeated calls for a new enquiry.

Police and investigators inspect what remains of the flight deck of Pan Am Flight 103.

WHEN:
December 21 1988
WHERE:
Lockerbie, Scotland, UK
DEATH TOLL:
270 (259 were aboard Flight 103, including 190 American citizens).
YOU SHOULD KNOW:
In 2009 the Scottish government's decision to release the only person convicted of the Lockerbie bombing – Libyan Abdelbaset al-Megrahi – on the compassionate grounds that he was suffering from terminal cancer was met with outrage in the USA, especially when he was greeted as a returning hero in Libya and comfortably outlived the three-month prognosis. His trial was not told that this 'humble' Libyan who was head of security for Libyan Arab Airlines had $2 million in a Swiss bank account.

Tokyo sarin attack

Religion and nerve gas don't normally go hand in hand, but that's the combination that brought terror to Tokyo in the mid 1990s. A new Japanese religious group called Aum Shinrikyo (roughly translating as Supreme Truth) was founded by one Shoko Asahara in 1984, drawing on Buddhist and Christian influences to round out his interpretation of yoga. Though controversial, Aum Shinrikyo (also called Aleph) was known for its leader's doomsday prophecy that saw all sorts of sinister conspiracies ending in World War III rather than for overt criminal activity. But all that changed in 1995.

Ten members of the group (five perpetrators, each with a getaway driver) carried out a sarin attack on one of the world's busiest commuter systems, timed to coincide with the morning rush hour when Tokyo Metro trains would be packed. An impure form of sarin – a deadly nerve agent classified as a weapon of mass destruction – had been formulated. Bags of liquid sarin were dropped on trains at prearranged stations and punctured with sharpened umbrellas, leaking their deadly contents as the attacker escaped. Three different lines were targeted. On the Chiyoda Line one of two bags was punctured, resulting in two deaths and over 230 serious injuries. During the first Marunouchi Line attack one died and nearly 360 were seriously injured, while the second caused no loss of life but over 200 injuries. The combined death toll on two Hibiya Line trains was nine dead and over 800 injuries.

The attack caused chaos, with injured victims lying around inside the subway system or at its entrances. Emergency services were criticized for handling the attack badly, though 5,500 people eventually made it to hospital. By 2004 eight members of Aum Shinrikyo had received death sentences for their part in the attack, including cult leader Shoko Asahara.

WHEN:
March 20 1995
WHERE:
Tokyo, Japan
DEATH TOLL:
12 died, over 50 commuters or station staff were left with long-term disabilities and more than 1,000 suffered temporary vision problems.
YOU SHOULD KNOW:
Forewarned was not forearmed – in 1994, members of Aum Shinrikyo released sarin from a refrigerated truck with a view to killing judges who were about to rule against the cult in a lawsuit. The judges survived, but seven people died and 500 were injured. The following year the much more dramatic Tokyo Subway attack occurred, for reasons that have never been satisfactorily explained.

Emergency services personnel prepare to enter the Tokyo Metro.

Manchester IRA bomb

WHEN:
June 15 1996
WHERE:
Manchester, UK
TOLL:
Thanks to the prior warning and speedy evacuation, nobody was killed, though 212 were injured, including a pregnant woman who was thrown 4.5 m (15 ft) into the air by the blast. Property damage was extensive, requiring major reconstruction accompanied by much new building and general regeneration of the city. Insurers paid out £411 million in claims, but the total bill was estimated at £700 million.
YOU SHOULD KNOW:
A red pillarbox stood close to the centre of the massive explosion, but survived the blast and even protected the mail within. It now bears a modest brass plaque commemorating the event.

The scene of total devastation in Manchester city centre

The Provisional IRA loved nothing better than a 'spectacular', and few attacks fitted the bill more impressively than the massive car bomb planted in the centre of Manchester in June 1996. Thanks to a telephone warning to the local television station no Mancunians were killed, but property damage was truly awesome.

In February 1996 the IRA ended a two-year ceasefire during which its political wing Sinn Fein had negotiated with the British government. Six bombs rocked London, starting with a device that killed two people near Canary Wharf on the Isle of Dogs, before the bombers turned to Manchester. A 1,400 kg (3,000 lb) bomb in a Ford Cargo van was parked in Corporation Street near the Arndale shopping centre. The telephone warning was given at 09.43 and the huge task of evacuating 80,000 people from the area began. It was completed by 10.46 when the bomb squad moved in and tried to neutralize the bomb using a robot. The attempt failed when, at 11.17, the largest peacetime bomb ever detonated in Britain exploded, destroying or damaging a third of the city centre's retail space. Behind the barriers, over 200 people were hurt, mostly by flying glass, including seven who were seriously injured.

Nobody was ever charged with the Manchester bombing, much less convicted. Ironically – though six men thought to be responsible for the planning were jailed in connection with other offences – the only people to face charges in connection with the attack were a policeman and a newspaper reporter. The former was charged with leaking the information that Greater Manchester Police had a prime suspect the Crown Prosecution Service refused to prosecute. He was acquitted. The newspaper reporter who broke the story was found to be in contempt of court for refusing to name his source.

Omagh bombing

After the British Labour Party's election victory in May 1997, the new Prime Minister, Tony Blair, declared that one of his first priorities was to be the securing of a peace settlement for Northern Ireland. For over 30 years the so-called 'Troubles' had blighted the lives of the province's citizens as paramilitary forces belonging to the two main religious groups, Protestants and Catholics, had waged a vicious and bloody sectarian war against one another and against the British troops stationed there. New life was now breathed into the stalled peace talks, and they received strong support from the Clinton administration in the USA. In April 1998, less than a year after taking office, Blair was able to sign the historic Good Friday Agreement with Irish leaders, establishing a devolved power-sharing assembly and executive for Northern Ireland and defining a new relationship between the United Kingdom and the Irish Republic.

Just four months later the fragility of the new agreement was demonstrated starkly when a huge 225-kg (500-lb) car bomb exploded in the centre of Omagh, a small market town in the farming country of County Tyrone. It was a Saturday afternoon in late summer and the town was crowded with shoppers. A telephone warning was issued but its vagueness meant that police were in fact evacuating the wrong area when the bomb detonated. The carnage was indiscriminate; both Protestants and Catholics died, and the heart was ripped out of a previously tight-knit community.

A dissident republican group, the Real IRA, claimed responsibility for the bombing. This attempt to derail the fledgling peace agreement failed, however, and the outrage was roundly condemned by all parties. The subsequent police investigation was heavily criticized for its failure to identify the perpetrators and apparent reluctance to press criminal charges.

WHEN:
August 15 1998
WHERE:
Omagh, County Tyrone, Northern Ireland
DEATH TOLL:
29 people were killed in the blast and hundreds suffered appalling injuries.
YOU SHOULD KNOW:
To this day only two people have been tried in connection with the bombing. One was acquitted and the other's conviction was later quashed.
A number of victims' families pursued a civil action through the courts which in June 2009 resulted in a £1.6m award of damages against four named leaders of the Real IRA.

The centre of Omagh after a car bomb ripped through the market town.

Engineers in a speedboat examine the damaged USS Cole.

Suicide attack on USS *Cole*

In October 2000 the United States Navy warship USS *Cole* was on its way to the Gulf when it stopped for re-fuelling in the Yemeni port of Aden. The mission of the guided missile destroyer was to join the US-led maritime intercept operations in the Gulf in support of the United Nations sanctions then in force against Saddam Hussein's regime in Iraq. As the vessel was being re-fuelled from a floating platform in the harbour several hundred metres offshore, two suicide bombers managed to get a small inflatable raft packed with high explosives right up against the *Cole*. That they were able to do so without arousing suspicion was probably because it was assumed they were helping to moor the ship to the platform. When the bombers detonated their charge it blew a gaping hole in the destroyer's side. The force of the explosion was so strong that buildings around the harbour shook. The stricken vessel immediately started to list but did not sink; it was eventually towed out of Aden for repairs and then returned to service.

It was widely assumed in the aftermath of the bombing that al-Qaeda had been the perpetrators, although the terrorist organization did not claim responsibility and there has never been conclusive proof that Osama bin Laden, or any of his senior leaders, ordered the attack. The suicide bombers both came from Yemen. Six men were subsequently tried and convicted by a Yemeni court, including the alleged ringleader, a Saudi who was described as al-Qaeda's operations chief in the Gulf. The ringleader was tried *in absentia* as he had previously been handed over to the USA; he remains in custody at the Guantanamo Bay detention centre.

WHEN:
October 12 2000
WHERE:
Aden, Yemen
DEATH TOLL:
17 US sailors were killed and over 40 injured. The two suicide bombers also died.
YOU SHOULD KNOW:
There was a widely held view at the time that the government of Sudan had aided and abetted the terrorists. A civil lawsuit launched by relatives of the victims resulted in a March 2007 ruling by a US federal court that Sudan was liable for the bombing attack. Around $13.4m of Sudanese assets frozen in the USA were awarded to the victims' families in compensation.

9/11

There can be no question that the defining event of the third millennium thus far has been the terrorist atrocities committed on September 11 2001; atrocities so breathtaking in their conception, so unimaginable in their execution, that they continue to beggar belief a decade afterwards. The world would never be the same again, its consciousness seared forever by three simple digits and a stroke.

New Yorkers had woken on that fateful late summer's day to clear blue skies. On their way to their offices in downtown Manhattan, some would have looked up shortly before 09.00 and noticed a plume of thick smoke pouring from one tower of the World Trade Center. As they were starting to digest reports that a passenger aircraft had flown into the tower, thousands looked on in horror and disbelief as another airliner crashed into the second tower. The tops of both towers were now shrouded in smoke and flames, and office workers trapped on the upper storeys made desperate telephone calls to families and loved ones. Barely an hour later the south tower suddenly collapsed, propelling a huge cloud of dust and ash through the streets of Lower Manhattan. Within minutes the north tower followed suit, and what was once one of the world's tallest and proudest buildings had been reduced to a pile of rubble.

Both aircraft were on routine scheduled flights when they were hijacked by al-Qaeda suicide terrorists after taking off from Boston. Almost simultaneously, another hijacked airliner was flown into the Pentagon building, 320 km (200 mi) away in Washington DC. A fourth passenger jet failed to reach its target – thought to have been the White House itself – and crashed into a field near Pittsburgh after the passengers fought back against their captors.

WHEN:
September 11 2001
WHERE:
New York; Arlington, Virginia; near Shanksville, Pennsylvania, USA
DEATH TOLL:
2,973 people were killed in the attacks, including all the passengers on the four jets and 19 terrorist hijackers.
YOU SHOULD KNOW:
Not surprisingly, there has been endless debate over what, if anything, should occupy Ground Zero, as the World Trade Center site has become known. The site is slowly being re-developed, but at its heart there will be a National Memorial to the victims of 9/11, comprising two enormous pools set within the footprints of the Twin Towers, their edges inscribed with the victims' names.

The horrifying moment when Flight 175 flew into the World Trade Center's south tower.

Bali bombing

WHEN:
October 12 2002
WHERE:
Kuta, Bali, Indonesia
DEATH TOLL:
202 dead and 240 seriously injured.
YOU SHOULD KNOW:
Jemaah Islamiyah was back in 2005, with attacks by suicide bombers at the Jimbaran resort village and Kuta (again) in South Bali. That time they killed 20 people, including five foreigners, and injured 129.

The scourge of militant Islam lashed the Indonesian island of Bali in October 2002, when the violent Islamist group Jemaah Islamiyah detonated bombs aimed at causing maximum damage to the island's all-important tourist industry. A small device went off outside the US Embassy in Bali's capital city, Denpasar, to make it clear that 'The Great Satan' had not been overlooked. In case the point was missed this bomb was packed with human excrement.

The prime target was the tourist hotspot of Kuta, where two suicide bombers wreaked terrible havoc. One carried a backpack bomb into the crowded Paddy's Pub nightspot and detonated it at 23.05. A few seconds later the second attacker set off a powerful 1,250-kg (2,750-lb) car bomb in a Mitsubishi van outside the nearby Sari Club. The area was densely populated by locals and full of holidaymakers enjoying a night out. Damage to life and property was massive. The car bomb left a smoking crater 1 m (3 ft) deep and the combined efforts of the murderous pair killed over 200 people and seriously injured around 250 others.

The majority of the victims were – as Jemaah Islamiyah intended – from overseas, with 88 Australians among the 152 foreign nationals who died. The local hospital was ill equipped to deal with the disaster and eventually some of the injured – especially those with horrific burns – had to be airlifted to Australia for treatment. The radical cleric Abu Bakar Bashir, said to be Jemaah Islamiyah's spiritual leader, denied that the organization was responsible. Indonesian courts disagreed, subsequently convicting him of conspiracy in connection with the 2002 Bali bombs. Three men convicted of complicity in the attacks were executed by firing squad in 2008. A number of suspects remain at large, and Indonesia is under constant threat of further attacks.

Visitors offer prayers at the site of the car-bomb blast in Kuta.

Nord-Ost siege

Russia and Chechnya have a troubled history of more or less continual strife. From medieval times, Christian Russia has constantly sought to impose its authority on its Muslim neighbour in the Caucasus, while the fervently nationalistic Chechens have fought for independence at every opportunity. During World War II, Stalin brutally repressed any dissidence with one of his infamous purges. The indiscriminate mass killings and deportations to Siberia have not been forgotten by the Chechen people.

When the Soviet Union crumbled in 1991, Chechnya once again made a bid for freedom. After some initial success, the Chechen forces were soon pulverized by the overwhelming might of the Russian army. A change of tactics was called for and from 2000 the separatists sought to achieve their ends through terrorism. It was in this context that on the night of October 23 2002, 42 heavily armed Chechen rebels sneaked into a Moscow theatre during a performance of the popular Russian musical *Nord-Ost* and took the entire 850-strong audience hostage. Their demand was straightforward: complete withdrawal of Russian forces from their homeland.

At first, in a bid to appear reasonable, the terrorists released 150 women, children and foreigners, but on the second day of the siege conditions inside the theatre started to deteriorate and a number of people were shot. On the morning of the third day, Russian special forces, who had set up their headquarters in a gay nightclub in the basement of the theatre complex, prepared for an all-out assault. Noxious gas was sprayed into the theatre to incapacitate the terrorists. Inevitably the hostages were affected too and many innocent people were killed by the gas. The heavy-handed approach of the authorities was widely criticized as displaying a callous disregard for the lives of ordinary Russian citizens.

Special forces prepare to enter the Moscow theatre.

WHEN:
October 23–26 2002
WHERE:
Dubrovka Theatre, Moscow, Russia
DEATH TOLL:
Officially 129 hostages and 33 terrorists died during the raid or shortly afterwards, but there have been claims that more than 200 civilians were killed and the authorities have covered up the true figure. More than 700 people were injured.
YOU SHOULD KNOW:
The gas used by the special forces to subdue the terrorists was vaporized fentanyl, a pain-relieving drug 100 times more powerful than morphine. The security services refused to disclose what the gas was; doctors and paramedics were simply left to guess what first aid they should administer to counteract its effects. As a result, many of the injured were permanently harmed by inappropriate treatment of fentanyl overdose.

Manila *Superferry 14* fire

WHEN:
February 27 2004
WHERE:
Manila Bay, Philippines
DEATH TOLL:
The official death toll is 116.
YOU SHOULD KNOW:
Abu Sayyaf is an Islamist separatist group which has a long history of extortion in order to fund its part in an insurgency in the south of the country. It came to worldwide prominence when, in 2000, foreign hostages were taken in the diving resort of Sipadan. A ransom of $25 million dollars was paid by Libya's Colonel Gaddafi which secured their release. Gaddafi's motives were questionable and the money paid was seen as aid for a cause he supported.

Sandwiched between the South China Sea in the west and the Philippine Sea in the east, the Philippines is a sprawling mass of a country consisting of over 7,000 islands. Its 85 million inhabitants are spread over 2,000 of them and linking them by boat is essential to the economy of the country. Unfortunately, the Philippines is no stranger to maritime tragedy as rough seas, collisions and conflagrations have all taken a heavy toll.

As the name implies, *Superferry 14* was no ordinary ship. Trumpeted as a 'festival' ship, it came into service in 2000 and brought luxury to what is normally a prosaic journey to and from the capital. Features included a business centre, lavish dining rooms, a beauty salon and even a karaoke bar.

Late in the evening of February 26 2004, the ferry left the capital and set out across Manila Bay on its journey to Bacolod City. Two hours into its journey it sent out a distress signal. An explosion near the engine room had caused extensive damage and the vessel lurched to one side as flames ripped through it. Of the 900 or so on board, those nearest to the fire were in the greatest danger and many jumped, burning, into the sea. Fortunately the US marines were doing exercises nearby and were on hand to assist the overwhelmed local coastguards with the rescue. However, more than 100 people lost their lives, although only 63 bodies were recovered.

Some five months after the disaster, it was revealed that the explosion on board had been caused by a bomb. The terrorist group Abu Sayyaf had tried to extort money from the ferry's owner and, when they were rebuffed, sent one of their operatives on board with a bomb placed inside a television set.

Madrid commuter train bombs

WHEN:
March 11 2004
WHERE:
El Pozo del Tío Raimundo, Calle Téllez, Santa Eugenia and Atocha Stations, Madrid, Spain
DEATH TOLL:
191 dead; more than 2,000 injured.

During the early stages of the second Iraq war, Spain provided the sixth largest contingent of forces in what George Bush had dubbed the 'Alliance of the Willing'. On October 18 2003, a message purporting to be from Osama bin Laden threatened reprisals against Spain, Britain and Australia among other allies of America. It was a message of defiance – al-Qaeda wanted to show that not only could it open up a new front against the West in Iraq but that it could also bring the war back to the countries ranged against it.

At some time on or before March 14 2004, 13 bag bombs were loaded onto four commuter trains at Alcalá de Henares Station, some

32 km (20 mi) from Madrid. The mobile phones used as their timing devices were set to go off when the trains were standing at stations *en route*, with the aim of causing maximum loss of life during the morning rush hour. Within a few minutes of each other, ten of the bombs exploded. Three of the trains were at stations, the other was just outside. Scores of people were killed and many hundreds more injured. It was the biggest loss of life through terrorism in Europe since the Lockerbie disaster of 1988.

With a general election just days away, the ruling conservatives sought to blame the Basque Separatist group ETA for the attack and arrests were made. However, it soon became clear that this was the work of Islamic extremists who, although not working for al-Qaeda, had taken their cue from Osama bin Laden. Just one month later, seven of the main suspects were killed in an explosion in a Madrid apartment when surrounded by police.

Workers and police examine the debris of a destroyed train at Madrid's Atocha station.

YOU SHOULD KNOW:
Although the majority of the victims were Spanish, people from 17 different countries were among the dead, including South Americans, Eastern Europeans and North Africans. Twenty-one people were tried and convicted for their part in the bombings.

7/7: the bombing of London's transport

WHEN:
July 7 2005
WHERE:
On Tube trains at Liverpool Street Station and Edgware Road Station, and in the tunnel between King's Cross and Russell Square stations, and on a bus at Tavistock Square, London, UK
DEATH TOLL:
56 died, including four suicide bombers, and more than 700 were injured, many of them very severely. Basic freedoms have been eroded, and Britain has been forced to live within new legal parameters that for many feel like a straitjacket. The effect of the 7/7 bombings has proved disastrous to the ties that bind society together – suspicion reigns.
YOU SHOULD KNOW:
The 7/7 atrocities have become London's 'badge of terrorism'. Unfortunately, apart from the individual displays of extraordinary courage and human kindnesses on the part of ordinary members of the London public at the time, there have been no positive outcomes.

On July 7 2005 during the morning rush hour, three bombs exploded simultaneously on London Underground trains. A fourth exploded an hour later, wrecking a red double-decker bus. Only the previous day London had celebrated being awarded the 2012 Olympic Games. Now the city was in shock.

Mobile and landline phone systems crashed as millions of Londoners sought information or reassurance – sparking ever wilder rumours of civic or government meltdown, crazy conspiracies and official cover-ups. When, finally, the traffic began to move again, the truth was found to be altogether starker than anyone had imagined: four suicide bombers had succeeded in bringing bloody mayhem to the capital. A random 52 Londoners were dead and more than 700 were injured as a result of Islamist extremism.

With some justification, the bombings induced a kind of panic in UK security agencies. Not knowing whether the bombings were the start of a more widespread attack, specialist police units were instructed to 'shoot to kill' anyone who was 'suspicious'. Just two weeks later a copycat series of bombings only failed because the detonators didn't work properly. This time the failed suicide bombers were caught; but, in the heightened atmosphere of paranoia that followed, the very next day an innocent Brazilian student, Jean Charles de Menezes, was gunned down by armed police without any warning as he sat on a train at Stockwell Station.

The death of de Menezes sobered the entire country. Since 7/7 Britain has learned that the price its citizens must pay for protection is permanently armed police and a 'surveillance society' that effectively removes the civil rights British citizens consider their birthright.

The London bus devastated by one of the three bombs.

The Red Sea bombings

The three suicide bombs that blew the heart out of Dahab in April 2006 were the third set of triple bombings in 18 months; 34 victims had died at Taba in October 2004, and 88 were killed and more than 200 injured at Sharm-el-Sheik in July 2005. Each time visitors thought it was safe to go back into the warm water of the Red Sea, the Egyptian shore resorts of the Sinai Peninsula became the focus for attack by Egypt's home-grown Wahhabi Islamic extremists. They weren't the only targets. Attacks in Cairo in 2004 and 2009 killed fewer people, but were just as effective at frightening off tens of thousands of free-spending visitors. After 1997, when 58 foreign tourists and their four guides were shot by Islamic terrorists as they walked from their bus to the noble ruins at Luxor, even the wonders of the pyramids seemed somehow diminished.

After Luxor, Egypt's tourist trade almost collapsed. It recovered slowly while the forces of Islamic extremism concentrated their malign ascendancy elsewhere. Egypt depends on tourism as one of the cornerstones of its economic survival. Unfortunately, its benefits barely reach the impoverished rural communities where Egypt's version of fundamentalism flourishes – the very communities who don't forgive Egypt for signing a peace treaty with Israel, and for whom the nation's secular regime is a daily affront to their ideology. Dahab turned personal tragedies into national disaster. Tourists – Russian, American, British, French and even Egyptian – were by definition infidels who deserved their fate, and so they died. And now Dahab has forced Egypt to abandon its secularity in all but name and seek compromises with the religious zealotry that has sought the state's destruction.

WHEN:
April 24 2006
WHERE:
Dahab, Sinai Peninsula, Egypt
DEATH TOLL:
23 dead and 62 wounded, including many Egyptians and people from at least ten other countries. The bombers were believed to come from Bedouin communities of the Sinai with known extremist sympathies and loose connections to al-Qaeda.
YOU SHOULD KNOW:
Egypt's tourist trade suffered badly, though it has proved amazingly resilient despite further attacks. Dahab inspired an unprecedented level of security measures at resorts and tourist sites – in itself a demonstration of the bombings' worst outcome. It seriously weakened Egypt's role as a leader among Arab nations, by making it impossible for the country to pursue its relatively quiet, laisser faire accommodations with its neighbours in Palestine, Israel, and the Arab world.

Egyptian shop owners and a wrecked store that was destroyed by a bomb.

477

Mumbai terror

The burning Taj Hotel

The world gawped in horror as the media transmitted rolling news of a terrorist rampage through the streets of Mumbai. The commercial hub of South Asia is no stranger to terrorism and, as the state elections approached in November 2009, the security services were well aware that there was likely to be a display of violence from one or other of the fanatical Muslim organizations intent on 'liberating' Kashmir from India's governance. But nobody could ever have anticipated the sheer gall of the attack: ten suicide terrorists, armed to the teeth with high-explosives, grenades and AK-47 assault rifles, attacked Mumbai from the sea. Their mission was to blow up the tower of the Taj Mahal Palace & Tower, Mumbai's most prestigious luxury hotel, in an oriental version of 9/11.

The reign of terror lasted for three days, orchestrated from thousands of miles away in Karachi using satellite-phone technology to relay orders that kept the Mumbai police on the hop. After landing on the beach in inflatable boats at the southern tip of the city, the terrorists split up and, as instructed, headed for carefully chosen high-profile targets – the Taj Mahal Palace, the nearby luxury Oberoi Hotel and exclusive Leopold Restaurant, the main railway station, a hospital and a Jewish community centre – where they rained bullets on terrified members of the public, hurled grenades and held hostages.

The rampage ended with the deaths of all but one of the terrorists. He confessed that he had been recruited by Lashkar-e-Taiba, a militant Islamist organization whose avowed aim is simple, if crazed: to wipe out India and all Jews everywhere, and create an Islamic state out of the disputed territory of Kashmir. Pakistan at first vehemently denied any connection, but reluctantly had to admit that the terrorists had sprung from Pakistani soil.

WHEN:
November 26–29 2008
WHERE:
Mumbai, India
DEATH TOLL:
At least 173 killed and 308 injured; nine of the ten terrorists also died.
YOU SHOULD KNOW:
The single surviving terrorist – 21-year-old Mohammed Ajmal Amir – shocked his interrogators by his willingness to swap sides: 'if you give me regular meals and money I will do the same that I did for them'. A village boy and petty criminal whose parents couldn't afford to send him to school, he'd joined Lashkar-e-Taiba not for any religious convictions but because he thought it would be exciting to learn how to use a gun.

Peshawar bombing

Peshawar is a city on the front line, only a few miles from the Taliban-held barren mountain badlands, the ill-defined border region between Pakistan and Afghanistan. Like all border cities, Peshawar is a cultural melting-pot: a city of smugglers and spies, traders and refugees, tribal factions and political intrigue. Afghanistan's troubles have always spilled over the border, but recently northwestern Pakistan has become swept up in the turmoil of its neighbour – with a vengeance.

The bombing of October 28 2009 was an unconscionable act of wickedness even by terrorist standards. A car exploded in a preserve of women and children: the women-only Peepal Mandi shopping street in the Meena Bazaar. The bomb was massive – 150 kg (330 lb) of explosives – and the blast could be heard throughout the city. It ripped through the congested alleys of the bazaar, where Peshawari housewives pass the time of day haggling with stallholders over piles of cheap fabric, costume jewellery and shoddy household goods.

The explosion caused an inferno. Highly inflammable artificial materials in the garment stalls immediately caught light, melting into lethal fireballs; a two-storey building collapsed and a mosque and four other buildings were badly damaged. The dead and injured lay strewn in the rubble in a scene from the apocalypse: bloody-faced screaming infants, terror-stricken mothers, and everywhere the smell of burning flesh in the air.

The emergency services failed to respond. The injured were ferried to hospital in rickshaws and taxis as there wasn't an ambulance in sight; and when the police finally arrived, they started firing into the crowd to 'restore order'. The attack was blamed on the Taliban, but they countered with accusations that it was the handiwork of American or government undercover agencies, designed to foment disgust with Islamists; or it could even have been a personal vendetta that went tragically awry.

WHEN:
October 28 2009
WHERE:
Peshawar, North West Frontier Province, Pakistan
DEATH TOLL:
More than 100 died and over 200 were injured, mostly women and children, in the deadliest terrorist attack in Peshawar's history.
YOU SHOULD KNOW:
Since 2007 a wave of terror bombings has engulfed Pakistan; they have become so commonplace that news of them scarcely registers in the Western media. In 2007 there were 18, rising to 25 in 2008 and more than 40 in 2009. 2010 got off to a horrifying start: there were nine bombings in January alone.

The explosion's searing aftermath

MASSACRES

St Bartholomew's Day massacre

WHEN:
August 24 1572
WHERE:
Paris, France
DEATH TOLL:
Estimates vary considerably. It is on record that 1,100 bodies were recovered from the River Seine alone. Based on this figure, the overall death toll has been calculated at anywhere between 5,000 and 20,000.
YOU SHOULD KNOW:
When the Pope heard of the massacre (in true Christian spirit!) he assembled all the cardinals to chant a celebratory *Te Deum*, ordered a medal to be struck in honour of the occasion and had commemorative frescoes painted at the Vatican.

Catherine de Medici observes victims outside the Louvre on the morning after the St Bartholomew's Day massacre.

In the 16th century religious reform movements were sweeping through Europe like wildfire, challenging the over-arching authority of the Catholic church and plunging the entire continent into turmoil. In France, the power struggles between Huguenots (protestants) and Catholics became known as the 'Wars of Religion'. The youthful King Charles IX, under the thumb of his mother Catherine de Medici, sat on the fence placating first one side then the other. During a rare break in the religious wars, Catherine arranged the marriage of her daughter Marguerite de Valois to the influential Huguenot Prince Henry of Navarre – to the utter dismay of the Catholics.

As Henry's wealthy retinue swanned into staunchly Catholic Paris, unrest was in the air. The populace, suffering from rising taxes and food prices, were outraged by the conspicuous luxury surrounding the wedding celebrations of August 18. Four days later, Admiral de Coligny, an important Huguenot political leader, was shot and injured in an assassination attempt. It was never established who was behind the attack but Catherine and Charles couldn't have been entirely unaware of the plot.

The following night, St Bartholomew's Eve, the wounded de Coligny was dragged from his bed and impaled on a pike; the next morning Paris awoke to find his corpse hanging by the ankles from Montfaucon gallows. This was the signal for a free-for-all, the worst eruption of sectarian mob-violence in the history of Europe. The Paris mob stormed through the city on a bestial rampage, a bloodbath that left thousands dead: in three days of carnage Huguenots all over the city were mercilessly hunted down regardless of age or gender.

The slaughter quickly spread to the provinces, almost all the Huguenot leaders were killed and thousands of ordinary people were either forced to convert to catholicism or fled for their lives to Holland and England.

Jamestown massacre

Strictly speaking, the Jamestown massacre didn't actually happen in Jamestown, the first English settlement in North America's Virginia Colony. After arriving in 1607, colonists got on well with the locals, trading iron tools and weapons with the Powhatan Confederacy in return for food. But Chief Powhatan soon realized that the incomers hadn't come to trade, but to steal his lands.

War broke out, but when the chief's daughter Pocahontas was captured in 1613 he sued for peace. Her marriage to tobacco planter John Rolfe in 1614 cemented an uneasy standoff, but when the old chief died power passed to his youngest brother, the belligerent Opechancanough. Still smarting from defeats suffered in the earlier conflict, he decided it would be desirable to drive out the interlopers.

In March 1622 an Englishman murdered his close advisor, Nemattanew. Opechancanough immediately planned a surprise attack on Jamestown and outlying settlements, but even the best plans can be undone by the smallest miscalculation – in this case Opechancanough's decision to entrust the murder of colonist Richard Pace to Pace's Native American servant Chanco. Chanco warned his master and Pace promptly rowed across the James River to raise the alarm in Jamestown. Forewarned was forearmed, and the fortified main settlement was unscathed.

But there was no time to warn those in smaller communities, mainly along the James River. Native Americans appeared with provisions to sell, before seizing any weapons that came to hand and killing men, women and children. Among the places to suffer the greatest number of casualties were Henricus, Wolstenholme Town and the neighbouring plantation of Martin's Hundred. A number of settlements were abandoned in the aftermath of Opechancanough's deadly slaughter, though his hope that the upstart English settlers would pack up their tents and steal away in the aftermath of their bloody reverse proved wildly misplaced.

A Native American attack on a farm during the Jamestown massacre.

WHEN:
March 22 1622
WHERE:
Colony of Virginia, North America (now Virginia, USA)
DEATH TOLL:
347 settlers were killed in the co-ordinated attacks, around one quarter of their total number.
YOU SHOULD KNOW:
Revenge was sweet for the colonists and sour for the Powhatans. In 1623, after a successful campaign by the colonists that destroyed his people's crops, Chief Opechancanough requested a peace parley. Vengeful Jamestown leaders William Tucker and John Potts poisoned liquor given to the Native Americans for the ceremonial toast, killing around 200 of their number and leaving 50 survivors to be slaughtered by the less-than-hospitable hosts.

British prisoners held in the guardroom later described as the Black Hole of Calcutta.

The Black Hole of Calcutta

Siraj-ud Daulah became Nawab of Bengal in April 1756 at the age of 23, succeeding his grandfather. The young independent ruler had learned at the old man's knee to be suspicious of British colonial ambitions in Bengal, as represented by a British East India Company that had established Fort William beside Calcutta's River Hooghly to advance its acquisitive commercial ambitions. The new Nawab was not happy when its defences were strengthened in anticipation of a confrontation with his French allies. In addition, the company was giving sanctuary to disgraced members of his entourage and seriously abusing trade privileges at the Nawab's expense.

Siraj-ud Daulah attacked Calcutta and laid siege to Fort William. After taking casualties most of the garrison managed to escape, leaving a small force under John Zephaniah Holwell to continue the fort's defence. Holwell was a company man whose military knowledge was confined to former employment as an army surgeon. After some of his mercenary troops deserted, Fort William was taken on June 19 1756.

Following this defeat, Holwell asserted that 146 assorted prisoners consisting of soldiers and civilians were crammed into a tiny guardroom measuring 4.3 m by 5.5 m (14 ft by 18 ft), packed in so tightly that the door could barely be closed. There were two small barred windows and the atmosphere was full of smoke from fires that still burned with the fort. Attempts to bribe guards on the balcony failed and repeated pleas for water resulted only in small amounts being passed through the windows, much of which was spilt. As thirst intensified, hysteria spread through the captives as those furthest from the windows struggled to reach fresh air and many were suffocated in the deadly crush. Holwell survived, but stated that over 120 other unfortunate captives did not.

The *Boyd* massacre

By the first decade of the 19th century Australia was an established British colony, but New Zealand remained a distant land ruled by Maori chiefs. Nonetheless, the place had resources – notably *kauri* trees ideal for ships' masts and spars – and trade possibilities were inviting. But it was a risky business, as those aboard the brigantine *Boyd* discovered to their cost.

The *Boyd* had transported convicts to Australia in 1809 and left Sydney Cove in October on the return voyage to Britain, sailing to Whangaroa on New Zealand's northern peninsula to pick up *kauri* spars. Commanded by Captain John Thompson, she carried home one TeAara (known as George) who was the son of a Maori chief. George was supposed to work his passage, but refused menial tasks and was flogged. Accepting punishment meekly, George directed *Boyd* to safe anchorage at Whangaroa, where he lived. Inwardly, he was seething with resentment at the way alien *pakeha* (Europeans) had treated him and complained to his father, demanding *utu* (revenge).

It wasn't long in coming. Led by helpful Maoris in canoes, Captain Thompson, his first officer and three men set off in their longboat to find suitable *kauri* trees. As they came ashore the Maoris fell on them with clubs and axes. Bodies were stripped and carried back to the Maori village to be prepared for a great cannibal feast. Some warriors disguised themselves in stolen clothes and returned to *Boyd* as night fell. Supported by others in canoes, they swarmed aboard and engaged in prolonged and bloody slaughter.

Five crew members – later killed – climbed into the rigging for a temporary reprieve, watching in horror as bodies were dismembered below in preparation for the forthcoming feast. Four people survived – two babies and two adults, who lived to tell the terrible tale of the *Boyd* massacre.

WHEN:
Late 1809 (exact date unknown)
WHERE:
Whangaroa, Northland, New Zealand
DEATH TOLL:
Precise figure unrecorded, but around 70 of *Boyd*'s passengers and crew were killed.
YOU SHOULD KNOW:
After being beached near the Maori village, *Boyd* was destroyed by explosion and fire, killing one culpable Maori chief and nine of his men who inadvertently ignited gunpowder they were trying to loot. A rescue mission recovered the four lucky survivors, but in 1810 whalers attacked a Maori village in reprisal for the massacre, killing 60 inhabitants. Sadly, it was the wrong village.

Peterloo

WHEN:
August 16 1819
WHERE:
Manchester, UK
DEATH TOLL:
15 are said to have died and between 600 and 700 protesters were injured, many seriously (both sets of figures are estimates).

YOU SHOULD KNOW:
Despite outrage expressed in liberal circles, the Peterloo massacre made little difference to the pace of reform in Britain. Indeed, the process actually suffered a set back when a panic-stricken government passed the Six Acts to prevent future demonstrations, thus gagging radical newspapers and labelling any meeting held to promote reform as 'an overt act of treasonable conspiracy'.

A cavalry assault on Manchester citizens gathered to protest against the Corn Laws and to agitate for Parliamentary reform.

Not for the last time, Britons would discover that winning a prolonged war was no guarantee of good times. The end of the Napoleonic Wars in 1815 was soon followed by an economic slump. This encouraged the growth of political radicalism, particularly among Lancashire's suffering textile workers. They deeply resented the rotten borough system that deprived them of parliamentary representation – resentment that reached fever pitch in 1819 when the Manchester Patriotic Union organized a great protest meeting.

The government feared armed insurrection and immediately despatched the 15th Hussars to Manchester. The meeting took place on a sunlit Monday in mid August on St Peter's Field, a space cleared for the imminent extension of St Peter's Street. The well-turned-out crowd assembled with military precision, travelling in from surrounding towns to join native Mancunians in hearing impassioned speeches by the likes of leading radical orator Henry Hunt.

As 80,000 protesters assembled, Manchester's magistrates were watching from a nearby house, primed to deal with possible trouble. At their disposal they had special constables, cavalry, infantrymen, an artillery unit and yeomanry – the latter being an inexperienced militia consisting mainly of tradesmen and publicans. Although it was a peaceful gathering, the magistrates issued arrest warrants for

platform speakers, enlisting the help of both yeomanry and hussars to enforce their ill-judged action. The Manchester and Salford Yeoman Cavalry charged the crowd, hacking to right and left with their sabres, soon to be followed by the regulars of the 15th Hussars.

In ten minutes it was all over. The terrified crowd had fled in all directions, leaving only the dead, dying and wounded behind on St Peter's Field. The speakers were in custody and it would not be long before the day's events were christened the Peterloo massacre, in ironic reference to the bloody Battle of Waterloo.

Fall of Tripolista

The Ottoman Empire once spanned three continents, but by the 19th century this lumbering behemoth was getting ragged around the edges as subject peoples started agitating (and sometimes fighting) for their freedom from harsh Turkish rule. Revolutionaries began the Greek War of Independence in 1821, but the journey would be long and bloody. Revolts against Ottoman rule broke out in various parts of the country and the first big home successes came in southern Greece, the Peloponnese, where insurrectionists won a decisive victory at the Battle of Valtetsi and then laid siege to Tripolista, the largest city and an important Ottoman administrative centre.

In addition to many thousands of Turks, the city contained a large Jewish population and numerous Ottoman refugees from successful Greek attacks elsewhere in the Peloponnese. The somewhat inefficient siege lasted for months, punctuated by occasional sorties by Turkish cavalry and protracted negotiations between attackers and defenders. But on September 23 – shortly after cleverly giving a large Albanian contingent safe passage out of Tripolista and thus weakening the garrison – the attackers decided that Turkish defenders were deliberately prevaricating in the hope of delaying matters until Ottoman troops arrived to lift the siege. They found a weak spot in the walls and successfully stormed the town.

What followed the fall of Tripolista is almost too awful to contemplate. The Greeks looted with wild abandon and savagely slaughtered every non-Christian they could lay hands on – Turk and Jew alike – often inflicting terrible tortures on those suspected of concealing valuables. Limbs were amputated, screaming victims were slowly roasted over open fires and pregnant woman were slashed open. Heads were cut off, children were chased and killed like stray dogs and after two days the last remnants of Tripolista's terrified population were rounded up and brutally massacred.

WHEN:
From September 23 1821
WHERE:
Tripolista (now Tripoli), Peloponnese, Greece
DEATH TOLL:
The most authoritative estimates suggest that upwards of 30,000 Turks and Jews were killed by rampaging Greeks after the fall of Tripolista.
YOU SHOULD KNOW:
Many moderate Greek leaders were horrified by the massacre at Tripolista, and it would not be long before the independence movement split into warring political and military factions, though Greece finally did achieve nationhood in 1832 after Russia, Britain and France intervened on behalf of the embattled Greeks.

'Big Foot', the leader of the Sioux tribe, lies frozen on the battlefield of Wounded Knee, South Dakota.

Massacre of Wounded Knee

The beautiful Black Hills of South Dakota were, for the Lakota Sioux, a sacred spiritual and ancestral home. An 1868 treaty guaranteed lands where they could roam freely but, following the discovery of gold, the area was occupied by miners and settlers. The Sioux refused to be confined and after the humiliation of the battle of Little Big Horn the US government tightened control. Early in 1890 the authorities attempted to suppress native culture by dividing the Great Sioux Reservation into five smaller areas, separating the tribes and forcing them to farm the arid land. The Sioux found spiritual solace in the Ghost Dance.

A Nevada mystic called Wovoka had revived this ancient ritual; his teachings of an earthly paradise-in-waiting swept through the Native American nation. Though he preached harmony, the Sioux believed that, wearing sacred 'bullet proof' Ghost Shirts, they would be instrumental in the disappearance of their colonial masters. White officials were alarmed: interpreting spiritual fervour as a war dance, they banned its performance on the reservations.

Scattered tribes began to move south; Chief Sitting Bull was killed during his arrest and his tribe went to join his half brother Big Foot. But as the 120 men and 230 women and children trekked over the frozen plains, they were intercepted by the Seventh Cavalry and

WHEN:
December 29 1890
WHERE:
Wounded Knee creek,
South Dakota, USA
DEATH TOLL:
25 soldiers and about 200 unarmed
Sioux died.
YOU SHOULD KNOW:
Today South Dakota is one of the
USA's poorest states, and the
remaining Native American tribes are
dependent on the tourism industry.
The Wounded Knee Massacre Site is
a neglected cemetery in the
grindingly poor Pine Ridge Indian
Reservation.

'escorted' to a site near Wounded Knee creek. Commander Colonel James Forsyth positioned four Hotchkiss machine guns around the camp and early next morning ordered the Sioux to surrender arms. As they handed in their weapons one man accidentally loosed a shot, provoking fierce hand-to-hand fighting.

Then the artillery fired. Dead and wounded were left lying where they fell as a blizzard enveloped them. Many attempting escape died of cold. Forsyth was exonerated. A record ten Medals of Honour were awarded.

Badung *Puputan*

The beautiful island of Bali is renowned for its glorious landscapes and beaches, palaces and temples, and its unique culture. Terrorist bombs in 2002 and again in 2005 shocked the world; but violent death is nothing new to the Balinese. A *Puputan* is a Balinese ritual mass-suicide ceremony, an alternative to surrender. In a series of *Puputan* suicides between 1894 and 1908, thousands died in the face of colonial forces.

The Dutch came to Indonesia in the 17th century, though contact with Bali was limited to trade until military intervention was prompted by the Balinese custom of 'salvaging' wrecked ships. When a large frigate that had run aground was looted, the Dutch retaliated. It took their vastly superior forces three campaigns to shatter Balinese defences, but from the 1850s they gradually gained a foothold and by 1900 much of the island was under control.

Another plundered ship provided an excuse for action on the south coast: the Sixth Military Expedition arrived in September 1906. The Rajah of Badung rejected an ultimatum and the Dutch landed on Sanur Beach on September 14. The troops marched on Denpasar.

The town appeared deserted, the only sound an ominous drumming from the palace. As the soldiers approached, a silent procession emerged. At its head was the Rajah in his palanquin, followed by his court, guards, priests, wives and children all wearing white cremation robes and splendid jewels. Each carried a *kris* (ceremonial lance).

The procession halted, the Rajah stepped down and at his signal a priest plunged a *kris* into his heart. Now all turned daggers on themselves and each other. Unnerved by this horrifying display and startled by a stray gunshot, the Dutch opened fire as women mockingly hurled jewels and coins. The gunfire continued. The mound of corpses grew . . .

WHEN:
September 20 1906
WHERE:
Denpasar, Bali
DEATH TOLL:
Approximately 1,000
YOU SHOULD KNOW:
The Balinese honoured the sea deity *Batara Baruna*, and accepted as gifts from the gods ships wrecked on their reefs. Ships, passengers and cargoes were shared between the local Rajah and the 'salvagers'.

The Amritsar massacre

WHEN:
October 13 1919
WHERE:
Amritsar, Punjab, India
DEATH TOLL:
According to the official British record 379 were killed and 1,100 injured.
YOU SHOULD KNOW:
Brigadier Dyer admitted to a court of enquiry that he hadn't attempted to disperse the crowd because he didn't want to risk losing face. In 1940 Lieutenant Governor O'Dwyer was shot dead at Caxton Hall, London, by Udham Singh who, as a teenager, had witnessed the massacre and regarded O'Dwyer as the man crushing the spirit of India.

During World War I the Sikh battalions indentured into the British Army won universal respect for their incredible bravery. At the end of the war they returned home to the Punjab to find themselves no longer respected as equal 'comrades in arms' but treated as subservient 'natives' by the British military administration. Inevitably the nationalist unrest that had already been stewing boiled over. The government rushed through an anti-terrorist law in 1919 empowering it to imprison suspects without trial and when a huge crowd gathered in Amritsar to demand the release of two activists, troops opened fire. The subsequent rioting resulted in fatalities on both sides. Brigadier Reginald Dyer arrived to restore order and the Lieutenant Governor of the Punjab, Sir Michael O'Dwyer, announced stringent restrictions on freedom of assembly.

The thousands of Sikhs who travelled to Amritsar from all over India to celebrate the New Year festival of *Baisakhi* knew nothing of the new emergency laws in the Punjab. They had simply come to worship at their holiest shrine, the Golden Temple – as they did every year. They joined the throng in Jallianwala Bagh, a small high-walled park near the Golden Temple where a peaceful political protest was being held in defiance of the government crack-down.

Dyer (who afterwards claimed he had been 'confronted by a revolutionary army') positioned armoured cars and machine guns at the main gate, blocking the exit. Without warning he suddenly ordered his men to shoot at the closely confined, penned-in crowd. Machine guns blazed until the ammunition ran out – after ten minutes the park was piled with bodies. Some were shot in the back as they fled, some were trampled in the chaos, some jumped into a well to avoid the bullets.

This unprovoked act of carnage was condemned worldwide, ultimately furthering the cause of Indian nationalism.

British Brigadier General R E H Dyer was responsible for killing between 380 and 1,000 unarmed Indian Sikh adults and children.

Bath school disaster

Bath is an ordinary little town in rural Michigan, and May 18 1927 was an ordinary spring morning: men went off to work and mothers saw their children off to the new 'consolidated' school, the pride of the community. At 08.45 an explosion shattered the calm. By the time neighbours reached Andrew and Nellie Kehoe's farm, it was blazing. As the townspeople tried to quench the flames, they heard another violent blast, this time from the direction of the school. With terrible foreboding, they raced over there.

One wing had collapsed completely. Children's bodies were strewn among a tangled heap of wreckage. Desperate parents struggled to shift rubble and timbers, frantically searching for their children, weeping over the dead, and comforting the injured.

Andrew Kehoe arrived in his pickup and, as school superintendent Emery Huyck went to speak to him, Kehoe fired his rifle into the back of his truck, setting off a round of shrapnel-packed dynamite. The blast killed him, Huyck and several others. All day, people worked flat out rescuing survivors from the ruins, pausing only while 230 kg (500 lb) of unexploded dynamite found hidden in the school was de-activated.

Kehoe had planned the outrage carefully, accumulating the huge quantities of explosives from different shops without arousing suspicion (farmers commonly used dynamite in those days). As school handyman, he had ready access to the building to wire up the bombs.

It turned out he was in serious financial difficulties, which he blamed on taxes levied to build the new school. Recently, his wife's medical expenses had added to his problems. Kehoe had battered Nelly to death before blowing up the farm. Her charred body was found the next day, along with his last message on a board hung from a fence: 'Criminals are made, not born'.

Rescuers searching for victims among the ruins of Bath school.

WHEN:
May 18 1927
WHERE:
Bath, near Lansing, Michigan, USA
DEATH TOLL:
38 children and seven adults died; 61 people were injured.
YOU SHOULD KNOW:
The school was rebuilt but demolished in 1975 to make room for a park commemorating the victims. A bronze plaque fixed to a white boulder lists their names.

Japanese infantry and cavalry troops marched through the triple-arched Chungsun Gate that leads to Nanjing.

The rape of Nanjing

WHEN:
December 1937 to January 1938
WHERE:
Nanjing, China
DEATH TOLL:
Possibly as many as 300,000 – half the city's inhabitants. Between 20,000 and 80,000 women and girls were raped, brutalized, and often left for dead.
YOU SHOULD KNOW:
The rape of Nanjing was one of the worst atrocities in modern history. Only the heroism of German businessman John Rabe and the handful of other Westerners who had remained in the city prevented thousands more from being exterminated. Rabe used his Nazi Party membership as leverage to persuade the Japanese to leave the Safety Zone relatively unscathed.

When the Japanese invaded northeastern China in the 1930s, the Chinese were in the middle of a bloody civil war; but by 1937 they had established a sufficiently united front to offer fierce resistance to the Japanese at Shanghai. Nevertheless the city finally fell to the Japanese. Nationalist China's leader, Chiang Kai-shek, realizing that defeat at Nanjing (at that time China's capital city) was inevitable, moved his government and elite troops to Peking at the beginning of December. On December 13 Japanese troops smashed into Nanjing; their orders were to take no prisoners.

Though superior in numbers, the Chinese troops in Nanjing were completely untrained; they crumbled in the face of the Japanese onslaught. In Japanese eyes, their abject defeatism made them utterly contemptible, undeserving of life. They were rounded up and slaughtered – the executions provided 'training' for the young Japanese soldiers.

After the elimination of the military, the Japanese turned on the women. Thousands, of all ages, were savagely gang-raped and murdered. Later, any pretty girls were forced to become slave-prostitutes or 'comfort women' for the occupying army. Meanwhile, the officers turned murder of civilians into a grisly sport to entertain their men.

Half the population of Nanjing died in six weeks of carnage. The only survivors were those who made it to the International Safety Zone, an enclave (marked out by Red Cross flags) set up by 15 extraordinarily courageous Westerners who refused to decamp. Japan's High Command, mindful of international opinion, forbade shelling of the safety zone, but marauding troops would randomly enter and drag off civilians for execution.

In late January, the Japanese forced everyone who had fled into the safety zone to return to their homes, claiming that order had been restored. But Nanjing was quiet only because everyone was dead.

Tsuyama massacre

In an era when society has perforce become accustomed to the regular incidence of tragedies involving disturbed loners who run amok, indulging in apparently motiveless killing sprees, it is hard to imagine the unbelieving horror that the first such event recorded in modern times – the Tsuyama massacre – engendered in prewar Japan.

The perpetrator was 21-year-old Mutsuo Toi, a young man with a reputation for *Yobai* (night crawling) – creeping into the beds of women in the locality in the hope that they would allow sexual intercourse. The orphaned Mutsuo had been brought up by his grandmother and was an outgoing boy, but when his beloved sister married in 1934 he quickly became withdrawn. In 1937 he was diagnosed with tuberculosis – then an incurable disease that had carried off both his parents and imposed a powerful social stigma. When the girls in his village near the city of Tsuyama started giving him the cold shoulder, the over-sexed Mutsuo started planning a most terrible revenge.

He assembled a *katana* (traditional curved Japanese sword), axe and Browning shotgun. In the early hours of a night in May 1938, Mutsuo cut the power supply to his small community and embarked on a deadly mission. First, he beheaded his 71-year-old grandmother with an axe. Then he attached twin electric torches to his head and stalked through the village, entering homes and slaying unsuspecting occupants. In the course of the night he killed 27 and seriously injured five more, two of whom would later succumb to their wounds. This awful toll was roughly half the village's population. Before dawn, Mutsuo Toi shot himself fatally in the chest, leaving suicide notes that explained his sense of despair at contracting tuberculosis and anger at the behaviour of those neighbours – especially young women – who had shunned him.

WHEN:
May 21 1938
WHERE:
Kaio, near Tsuyama, Okayama Prefecture, Japan
DEATH TOLL:
31 (including the killer)
YOU SHOULD KNOW:
In one suicide note Mutsuo Toi claimed that it had been necessary to kill his own grandmother in order to spare her the shame of being branded as the woman who brought up a mass murderer.

Katyn massacre

In 1939 Poland was a rabbit torn apart by wolves as Nazi Germany invaded from the west and Soviet Russia from the east. Following inevitable victory, the Soviets set about dealing with a multitude of Polish prisoners including army officers, soldiers, pilots and prominent citizens such as intellectuals, policemen, landowners, lawyers, priests and bureaucrats. After releasing most ordinary soldiers, the NKVD secret police under the feared Lavrentiy Beira still held some 40,000 unfortunate Poles in various camps, principally Kozelsk, Starobielsk and Ostashkov.

These prisoners were subjected to an intense programme of interrogation, designed to determine if each could be persuaded to adopt a pro-Soviet attitude or would remain defiant. The reason for this process became apparent on March 5 1940 when the ruling Soviet Politburo responded positively to Beira's request that thousands of Polish 'nationalists and counter-revolutionaries' should be executed.

This gruesome policy was carried out from early April. Occupants of the Kozelsk camp were taken to three sites – NKVD headquarters in Smolensk, Smolensk slaughterhouse and an established NKVD killing field in Katyn Forest. The vast majority, mainly military personnel but including hundreds of civilians, were taken into the woods, never to reappear. After their invasion of Russia, a tip-off led the Germans to the Katyn site, where they exhumed 4,500 corpses, each with hands tied and a pistol shot to the neck. This discovery was a huge propaganda coup for the Nazis, though the Soviets vehemently denied their involvement and continued to do so long after the end of World War II.

In 1990, Russian authorities finally admitted that the Katyn massacre was carried out by the NKVD, but still refused to accept the heinous mass killing as either genocide or a war crime. This ensured that none of those responsible could ever be brought to trial.

*A partially emptied mass grave
in Katyn forest*

228 incident

Supporters of the pro-independence Taiwan Solidarity Union form the number 228 in a rehearsal for a massive rally.

The Republic of China (ROC) sounds impressive, but now consists only of Taiwan (formerly the island of Formosa) off the Chinese mainland's southeastern coast. Formosa was restored to China after World War II, having been seized by Japan in the 19th century. General Chiang Kai-shek's ROC took possession in 1945, imposing a Kuomintang (KMT) government – the KMT being the ROC's ruling political party.

The ROC's arrival was not altogether welcome. The populace – though ethnically Chinese – was accustomed to Japanese rule, spoke a distinct dialect and became less than impressed by the KMT regime. Economic conditions were chaotic in the aftermath of war and the Taiwanese soon observed that their inefficient but authoritarian new government was riddled with nepotism and corruption.

Tension built, the flashpoint coming in February 1947, when agents from the Tobacco Monopoly Bureau raided the premises of a woman selling illegal cigarettes. A crowd gathered as they confiscated her stock, stole her life savings and hit her over the head when she protested. Angry locals surged forward but the agents escaped after firing into the crowd, killing one man. This ignited the spontaneous outbreak of civil disorder and insurrection that erupted the next day, which would become known as the 228 incident.

When security forces fired on peaceful protesters, dissidents took control of the capital city, Taipei, and much of the island. But while ROC authorities pretended to negotiate on the angry population's demands for better governance, they were secretly gathering a large military force on the mainland. This arrived on March 8 and proceeded to crush the rebellion brutally. The prolonged massacre involved the execution of many thousands of Taiwanese people, guilty or not. The outcome was harsh martial law and repressive one-party rule, known as the 'White Terror', that would last for four decades.

WHEN:
From February 28 1947
WHERE:
Taiwan
DEATH TOLL:
Unknown, though estimates start at 10,000 and go up to 30,000 and beyond.
YOU SHOULD KNOW:
The '228' comes from the date (second month, 28th day) when the anti-government rising began, with such terrible consequences for so many Taiwanese citizens when the military subsequently arrived to punish them for their temerity in seeking self-determination.

South African protesters lie dead after police opened fire on a demonstration in Sharpeville.

The Sharpeville massacre

Apartheid in South Africa became institutionalized in the 1940s and by 1960, under the government of the ultra-right National Party with Hendrik Verwoerd at the helm, black South Africans were existing under an intolerably oppressive regime. The ANC (African National Congress) opposition party had proved ineffectual and some members, impatient with its passive stance, formed the breakaway movement of the PAC (Pan Africanist Congress) – their agenda being to mobilize the masses.

The PAC's charismatic leader Robert Sobukwe organized an anti-pass campaign. The loathed pass books effectively restricted freedom of movement for black Africans; they were the primary means by which the government implemented segregation, a constant reminder of discriminatory laws. PAC supporters were to gather without their pass books and give themselves up for arrest at the nearest police station. Sobukwe informed the police of the proposed action, stressing its non-violent nature.

On the morning of March 21 more than 5,000 protesters gathered in Sharpeville and headed for the police station, ignoring the low-flying jets (intended to intimidate the demonstrators). But the police refused to make any arrests; instead they lined up Saracen armoured vehicles. PAC leaders started to move people away. At 13.15 – by which time the crowd numbered only hundreds – the police started shooting at bemused protesters. As bodies started to fall, the demonstrators turned and ran. Many were shot in the back.

Despite worldwide condemnation, the South African government backed the police story – they had fired in self-defence. A state of emergency was declared and more than 18,000 arrests were made. Both the PAC and ANC were banned. Increasingly at odds with world opinion, South Africa withdrew from the Commonwealth in 1961. But Sharpeville marked a transition from passive resistance to armed activism – although it took another 30 troubled years before the apartheid laws were finally repealed.

WHEN:
March 21 1960
WHERE:
Sharpeville, Gauteng (then part of Transvaal), South Africa
DEATH TOLL:
According to official records there were 69 deaths, including eight women and ten children, and 180 injured of which 31 were women and 19 children.

YOU SHOULD KNOW:
Afterwards the police claimed the protesters had been carrying guns, spears and *knobkerries* (walking-stick clubs); poignant documentary photographs show only shoes, hats and a few bicycles scattered among the bodies.

My Lai massacre

America was bogged down in its anti-communist war against North Vietnam when in January 1968 Viet Cong guerrillas joined the regular North Vietnamese army to launch the Tet Offensive – a massive attack on US positions. Although the Americans stood their ground, they were badly shaken by the scale of the assault and the morale of the troops, already low, plummeted to their boots.

In March 1968, Charlie Company had only been in action for three months but they were already living on their edge of their nerves: five of them had been killed and others had been injured by mines or booby traps. They'd learned that absolutely anyone might be Viet Cong and that any patrol might be their last.

As part of a retaliatory search-and-destroy mission, Charlie Company was sent to My Lai, a village that was supposedly a Viet Cong hideout. Three platoons under Second Lieutenant William Calley were dropped by helicopter just after dawn on March 16. The jittery GIs found no Viet Cong; instead they loosed some bullets on civilians. These first few indiscriminate shootings stirred a bestial bloodlust: the soldiers ran amok, attacking anything that moved – old men, women, children, babies, even animals – with a savagery that defies description. They used any weapon that came to hand in an orgy of violence that included rape and mutilation. Groups of civilians were rounded up and Lieutenant Calley personally supervised their mass execution.

The massacre was recorded as a 'fierce firefight' in which 128 Viet Cong and 22 civilians had been killed. The true horror of the My Lai massacre was successfully covered up by the Pentagon for 18 months, eventually coming to light in November 1969. The sickening revelations provoked a storm of anti-war protests throughout the USA. America had had enough.

WHEN:
March 16 1968
WHERE:
My Lai, Vietnam
DEATH TOLL:
US reports suggest 347 dead; there are 504 names on the memorial.
YOU SHOULD KNOW:
It later became apparent that officers far more senior than Lieutenant Calley had been complicit in encouraging the massacre. Of the 26 GIs sent for trial only Lieutenant Calley was convicted. He received a life sentence of which he served three years under house arrest before being quietly released.

American military Bell UH-1D Iroquois ('Huey') helicopters in flight during the My Lai massacre.

Tlatelolco massacre

WHEN:
October 2 1968
WHERE:
Mexico City, Mexico
DEATH TOLL:
The official version was four dead
and 20 wounded, but it is thought to
be between 200 and 300 dead. More
than 1,000 were injured or arrested.
YOU SHOULD KNOW:
Recently declassified US documents
suggest American involvement. While
the CIA recognized the 'graft and
dishonesty' of the PRI, both
governments saw the prevention of
any disruption to the Olympic Games
as paramount, and at the time the
US stood by Diaz Ordas.

In Mexico the coalition PRI (*Partido Revolucionario Institucional*) government had begun to confront the problems of the poor but when Gustavo Diaz Ordas came to power in 1964 it was on a platform emphasizing business rather than social programmes. Students were the first to express outrage: demonstrations at the National University in Mexico City in 1966 were squashed by federal troops. The grassroots CNH student movement was formed to take up the fight for factory workers and rural peasants. Students distributed leaflets in streets and on buses, gradually gaining sympathy for their fight against government corruption and repression.

As Mexico City prepared for the 1968 Olympic Games, building hotels, athletics facilities and a subway system, discontent came to a head. The CNH saw the Olympic Games, with the world's attention on the city, as an opportunity to gain support. The orderliness of a huge demonstration on August 1 proved to the public that the students were not simply communist agitators, but Diaz Ordas was determined to stop further protests at all costs.

On October 2 about 10,000 students gathered in the Plaza de las Tres Culturas in the city's Tlatelolco district for a peaceful rally. The square was surrounded by 5,000 soldiers backed by tanks and armoured cars. A helicopter hovered, a flare blazed, and as demonstrators and bystanders gazed upwards the troops opened fire into the crowd. The bloodshed continued into the night. Bodies, dead or alive, were carted off in military trucks.

Newspapers reported a few casualties after security forces returned fire in the face of armed student provocateurs. Not until 2001, after the end of the PRI's 70-year repressive reign, did President Vicente Fox order the release of government documents relating to the tragic 'Night of Tlatelolco'.

Police captured a van full of students after sealing off and searching all buildings on Tlatelolco Plaza.

Kent State shooting

In May 1970, soldiers of the Ohio National Guard fired 67 live rounds at a group of unarmed students at Kent State University. Four were killed. The world was appalled.

When Richard Nixon was elected president in 1968 he promised to end the war in Vietnam, but his announcement on April 30 1970 of the US invasion of Cambodia, coming after the revelations about My Lai, provoked protests nationwide. At Kent State there was a mass demonstration the following day, and in town that night bottles were hurled at shop windows, cars and the police. Next day the mayor asked the Ohio National Guard to maintain order. They found their Reserve Officer Training Corps building ablaze, surrounded by a cheering crowd. The National Guard used tear gas, made arrests, and set up camp. By May 3 there were nearly 1,000 guardsmen on campus. Governor Rhodes described the protesters as a 'well-trained, militant revolutionary group'.

University officials tried to prevent a protest scheduled for May 4, but about 2,000 students gathered anyway. When the National Guard ordered the crowd to disperse and fired tear gas, the students returned a fusillade of stones and gas canisters, chanting 'pigs off campus'. Guardsmen advanced with fixed bayonets and the students backed off. Both sides hesitated, not knowing what to do next. Some guardsmen on top of a hill suddenly opened fire on the scattered students in the distance below. Two of the casualties weren't even demonstrators – they were just on their way to classes.

Some 4,000,000 students came out on protest strike all over America and a violent demonstration in Washington followed. Inquiries and legal actions dragged on, but none of the soldiers (who all claimed they had been in fear for their lives) was ever brought to trial.

Clasping her head in anguish, a woman reacts with horror upon seeing the body of a student who was shot and killed by National Guardsmen during a war protest rally at Kent State University.

WHEN:
May 4 1970
WHERE:
Kent State University, Ohio, USA
DEATH TOLL:
Four killed, nine wounded.
YOU SHOULD KNOW:
The photograph of a screaming girl kneeling over the body of a dead student became an enduring image of the anti-Vietnam War movement, winning a Pulitzer Prize for photography student John Filo.

Bloody Sunday

WHEN:
January 30 1972
WHERE:
Derry, Northern Ireland, UK
DEATH TOLL:
13 dead, 13 injured (one of whom died later).
YOU SHOULD KNOW:
Some of the most outstanding public art in the world was created as a result of Bloody Sunday. The Bogside Artists collective painted the 'People's Gallery' – 12 giant murals depicting the Troubles and Bloody Sunday on the walls of the houses along Rossville Street in the heart of Bogside. They are intended as an enduring memorial and an uplifting message of hope for the future.

In the late 1960s Northern Ireland was torn by factional violence between Catholic Nationalists and protestant Unionists. After two rioters were shot dead by soldiers in July 1971, the IRA stepped up its campaign. On August 9 internment was introduced and demonstrations banned. Disorder raged throughout the province and more than 30 soldiers had been killed in IRA attacks by the end of the year. Some of the worst fighting was in Derry (or Londonderry to the Unionists), a border city with a Catholic majority and a long history of anti-British sentiment. The IRA barricaded Derry, establishing no-go areas for the British Army and the RUC.

The Northern Ireland Civil Rights Association organized a protest in Derry against internment and on January 30 a cheerful crowd of some 15,000 left the Creggan area. The route was diverted from the city centre and the march continued down Creggan Hill to Free Derry Corner in the Bogside. A group of youths crossed the barricades, hurling abuse and stones at British troops who dispersed them with tear gas, water cannon and rubber bullets. Soldiers of the Parachute Regiment then moved in to make arrests but within minutes bullets were flying; the soldiers had opened fire on the demonstrators. Several were shot in the back as they fled.

Anglo-Irish relations hit rock bottom. An inquiry was conducted by Lord Justice Widgery, which promptly discounted all eye-witness statements and upheld the official version of events – that the paratroopers had reacted to gunfire and nail bombs. The Widgery Tribunal was never accepted by the people of Northern Ireland, who demanded further investigation. Eventually, in January 1998 the Saville Inquiry was set up by Prime Minister Tony Blair to re-examine Bloody Sunday. The inquiry still hasn't made its report. The latest estimate for publication is March 2010.

A man and his child walking past an Ulster Volunteer Force mural on the Shankill Road, Belfast.

Kingsmill mass murder

If ever the phrase 'cycle of sectarian violence' had deadly meaning it was during Northern Ireland's 'Troubles', especially in the Republican heartland of South Armagh during the mid 1970s. On December 31 1975 the Irish National Liberation Army (INLA) killed three protestants in a bomb attack on a pub in Gilford. On January 6 the Ulster Volunteer Force (UVF) murdered six Catholics from the Reavey and O'Dowd families. Retaliation took place the following day and represented one of the worst targeted killings of the entire Troubles.

A minibus carrying home 15 textile workers and a driver dropped four Catholics in Whitecross before proceeding along Kingsmill Road towards Bessbrook. It was stopped at what the occupants assumed to be a police or army checkpoint and they got out in anticipation of a search. They were immediately surrounded by 12 armed men, but when Catholics were ordered to step forward assumed it was a UVF ambush and tried to persuade the one remaining Catholic not to reveal himself. When he did, he was told to run and not look back. The gunmen were Republicans, later claiming to represent the South Armagh Republican Action Force. In the next minute 11 protestants were shot down in a hail of gunfire. Amazingly, one survived what was later described as 'a horrifying scene of carnage' despite having 18 gunshot wounds.

Notwithstanding much speculation and the naming of names by the Reverend Ian Paisley under the protection of British parliamentary privilege, neither members of the murder squad nor the Republican faction they represented were ever identified beyond doubt and no charges were brought in relation to the killings. Most thought the South Armagh Republican Action Force was a cover name for members of the South Armagh Brigade of the Provisional Irish Republican Army (PIRA).

WHEN:
January 5 1976
WHERE:
Near Bessbrook, South Armagh, Northern Ireland, UK
DEATH TOLL:
Ten died at the scene.
YOU SHOULD KNOW:
It has been calculated that Northern Ireland's Troubles between 1969 and 2001 cost nearly 3,300 lives in the province. Republican groups or individuals were responsible for over 2,000 of those deaths. But the Kingsmill atrocity was the last in the series of mass tit-for-tat murders that took place in South Armagh during the 1970s, supposedly because a deal to end such killings was agreed between the Irish Republican Army and Ulster Volunteer Force.

Bodies of the followers of cult leader Jim Jones are seen at the Jonestown commune in Guyana, where more than 900 members of the People's Temple Christian Church committed suicide.

The Jonestown massacre

On November 18 1978 the news from Guyana that 914 people had been found dead in an apparent suicide pact was both a terrible shock and unsurprising. And nowhere was this dual response felt more strongly than in California: most of the dead had been members of the People's Temple Christian Church in San Francisco, then famously a haven for 'free-thinking crazies' (the Temple's services included faith healing, visions, and seeking advice from extraterrestrials).

Led by the charismatic 'Reverend' Jim Jones, in 1977 the group hurriedly removed to a jungle encampment ('Jonestown') in Guyana after Californian and Federal authorities began ferreting too deeply into Jones's activities.

Jones had prepared his flock well – if 'persecution' got too bad, they would enter paradise together. Former cult members in the US had alleged human rights abuses. When US Congressman Leo Ryan and several news teams were despatched to Guyana to question him, Jones ordered them gunned down at the airstrip as they tried to leave with disillusioned devotees. Ryan and five others died.

This created the 'state of emergency' for which Jones had primed his flock with countless rehearsals. He doled out the cocktail of soft drink and cyanide. Photographs show a sort of nightmare family garden party of willing victims collapsed in sociable heaps. Did the 276 children thirstily want more, or have to be coaxed? If anyone was reluctant, they died anyway, either poisoned or shot until Jones, last man standing, shot himself through the right temple. Neat, rounded, plausibly cultish – case closed. Except that Jones's body was 12 m (40 ft) from his gun.

Conspiracy theorists love the Jonestown massacre. Jones had huge opportunities – legal and illegal – to make Swiss-bank-serious money in California. His brainwashed flock of bodyguards, thugs and slaves was always expendable. Official enquiries settled for the 'loony cult mass madness' option; and Pandora's box remains closed.

WHEN:
November 18 1978
WHERE:
'Jonestown', Guyana
DEATH TOLL:
There were 914 deaths.The bodies of 412 apparent suicides were not claimed by relatives; they are buried in a mass grave in Oakland, CA.
YOU SHOULD KNOW:
In the early 1970s, Jones became prominent in social welfare programmes in the San Francisco area, and his ability to turn out large numbers of people was valued by sympathetic politicians, including the mayor and the state governor.

Sabra and Shatila

The history of the Middle East's only democracy is soaked in the blood of Arabs who tried to destroy the new state of Israel from the day it was proclaimed and Israelis who died defending their homeland. Both sides have perpetrated atrocities that seem unbelievable to outside observers, who do not share or entirely understand traditional passions that drive the combatants. No atrocity was more awful than Israel's failure to stop (let alone give tacit encouragement for) the brutal massacre of Palestinians in Lebanon's long-established Shatila refugee camp and the surrounding Sabra area.

Lebanon was in the grip of civil war from 1975 to 1990. Although alliances constantly shifted, the conflict was essentially between the Christian Phalangists (backed and armed by Israel) and the Palestine Liberation Army (backed by Arab states). The PLO was attacking Israel from Southern Lebanon and Israel invaded Lebanon in June 1982 – a move condemned by the United Nations.

A deal was done between Israel and Lebanon's President Bachir Gemayel, a Phalangist, whereby Beirut would not be occupied by Israeli Defence Forces (IDF) if PLO fighters were evicted from the city. This was going smoothly when Gemayel was assassinated in a massive bomb blast set by a Syrian agent, further destabilizing an already volatile situation. In defiance of international agreements, Israeli Defence Minister Ariel Sharon ordered an invasion of Palestinian-dominated West Beirut to gain control of Sabra and Shatila camp – hotbeds of PLO activity.

By mid September the IDF had completely surrounded Sabra-Shatila and sent in Christian militia forces to 'clean out terrorist nests'. Bent on avenging their leader, Phalangists swept through the refugee communities indiscriminately slaughtering men, women and children. The IDF knew full well what was happening, but prevented any Palestinians or local Lebanese from escaping and lit the area by night with flares so the killing could continue around the clock. The United Nations later declared that this terrible massacre was an act of genocide.

WHEN:
September 16–18 1982
WHERE:
West Beirut, Lebanon
DEATH TOLL:
Unknown. Estimates vary wildly from 700 dead to over 3,500, but the probable figure is around 2,000.
YOU SHOULD KNOW:
In 1983 a government enquiry found that Israel was 'indirectly responsible' for the Sabra and Shatila killings. Ariel Sharon was found personally culpable for 'ignoring the danger of bloodshed and revenge' and forced to resign, which he did reluctantly. Such is the nature of Israeli politics that Sharon returned triumphantly to serve as prime minister from 2001 to 2006.

A Palestinian woman cries out as civil defence workers carry the body of one of her relatives away from the rubble of her home in the Palestinian refugee camp of Sabra, in West Beirut.

Hungerford

WHEN:
August 19 1987
WHERE:
Hungerford, Berkshire, UK
DEATH TOLL:
16 dead; 15 wounded
YOU SHOULD KNOW:
Though dozens of people tried to alert the police from the beginning, the local telephone system was so antiquated that it jammed. Nobody had mobiles then, at least not there. The two local policemen did their best – but one was among the first to be killed, in his car. More senior officers simply had no communications system, either to block minor roads into the area or to co-ordinate any kind of strategy (if they'd had one). The situation was truly beyond anyone's experience.

In America, it is called a 'spree killing'. In the UK, nothing like it had ever happened before, so it was known simply as 'the biggest mass murder in British history' – which was not technically true, but represented the magnitude of the nation's trauma. Nothing was the same afterwards.

A major factor in the shock felt as the story emerged was its location. Hungerford is a little market town in the county of Berkshire. It's a quiet, ancient place set in gentle green countryside on the edge of Savernake Forest, for centuries a hunting preserve of Royalty and a renowned beauty spot.

Late one summer's morning, a 27-year-old unemployed labourer called Michael Ryan went to Savernake, as he often did: he had boasted of 'creeping up on picnic parties without them knowing'. This time he took a 9mm Beretta pistol, a Chinese assault rifle and a Kalashnikov semi-automatic, and shot a nurse as she picnicked with her two small children. Then he returned to Hungerford, stalking the streets and firing arbitrarily into cars, at bystanders, and anyone who caught his eye. There are no explanations. Presumably Ryan was playing out some dark, internal fantasy. It cost 16 innocent people their lives, and 15 more suffered serious injuries. He even shot his own mother, at her hearth, before setting fire to the family house and that of their neighbour.

Hungerford resembled a war zone, with bodies lying unattended and dozens of folk hiding behind hedges and ducking down back lanes. Long before Ryan barricaded himself in his old school, the sky was full of media and police helicopters. Reporters were trying to make their reputations and getting in the way of the police response – part of the horror of Hungerford is that there wasn't one; Ryan shot himself at 18.52 at the school.

Blankets cover the windows of a taxi in Hungerford containing the body of one of the victims of gunman Michael Ryan.

Tiananmen Square

Truthfully, what the world remembers best about Tiananmen Square in 1989 is one of the 20th century's defining images: 'Tankman'. Alone, he faced down a column of army tanks for half an hour, standing resolute and unmoving, until he raised his arm to extend a gauntlet of peace, a flower, to the muzzle of the cannon pointed straight at him. The world held its breath at his courage, not yet quite understanding that his gesture derived all its power from the violent confrontation that had taken place on the previous two days, and the massacre which still continued in the nearby streets.

'Tankman' facing the army in Tiananmen Square.

Dissent had been rumbling in a China eager for liberal reform and by May 1989, regular demonstrations had grown into mass protests led by students but with tacit support from urban workers and citizens. Weeks of inconclusive marches brought up to a million protesters to Tiananmen Square, China's most symbolic rallying point; and around 1,000 students began a hunger strike there. Government elders dismissed them as lackeys of 'bourgeois liberalism' and ordered in the troops. By June 2 both sides had resorted to violence as the army sought to clear Tiananmen Square. Casualties mounted.

In fact most students left Tiananmen Square voluntarily, trying to avoid a bloodbath. The massacre took place in the surrounding streets. Tanks rolled over bodies and soldiers kept up withering semi-automatic fire on packed crowds who had no chance of escape. Students fought back where they could – but though the Chinese Army (PLA) is composed mainly of draftees, who might be expected to be sympathetic, unarmed protesters were brutally suppressed. Using the excuse of martial law, and the cover of night, troops literally crushed what had become a rebellion.

Thankfully, as 'Tankman' proved, though the soldiers won the 'battle', they simultaneously realized they could not win the moral war.

WHEN:
June 2–5 1989
WHERE:
Tiananmen Square, Beijing, China
DEATH TOLL:
Exact casualty figures remain a Chinese state secret. Student organizations can name 1,100 dead known to them.
YOU SHOULD KNOW:
Workers and other civilians supported the protesters constantly with food, water, money and goodwill. Many times, rickshaw drivers braved the firing in no-man's-land to pick up wounded citizens and students and get them to hospitals.

Batticaloa

WHEN:
August to September 1990
WHERE:
Kattankudy and Sathurukondan,
Batticaloa District, Sri Lanka
DEATH TOLL:
About 450 Muslim men and boys,
and about 350 Tamil men, women
and children.
YOU SHOULD KNOW:
Sri Lanka is one of the few places on
earth where massacres are endemic.
In 1990, in the Batticaloa district
alone, about 1,100 Tamils were killed
by known SLA officers: there have
been no prosecutions.

The uneasy relationship between Tamils and Sinhala has persisted for centuries, with cyclical exchanges of political power effected by means including war, economic dependence and turning-a-blind-eye coexistence. Periodically, the opposition explodes in frenzied violence – at which both sides have considerable practice – without any warning.

In 1990 there was just such an explosion at Batticaloa, on Sri Lanka's east coast – considered by the whole country to be a Tamil region not often involved with outright military confrontation. Episodes of violence there have generally consisted of ambushes, bombings and 'guerrilla actions'. Severe incidents (any of which would be international headlines in most countries) in which 20 or 30 people might be made to 'disappear' or be found dead and mutilated, increased in number until August 3 when armed Tamil Tiger personnel butchered 103 Muslims from the mosque at Kattankudy. The next day they killed over 300 men and boys from the Meera Jumma mosque on the Kandy-Batticaloa road, and about 40 more from the nearby Hussainya mosque.

Retaliation came in the shape of the SLA (Sri Lanka Army) and Muslim guards, who on September 9 (known as Black September Day) took 158 Tamil civilians sheltering in the East University (Refugee) Campus plus 184 Tamil villagers from Sathurukondan village and caused all 342 to 'disappear'.

The Tamil attacks of August had included single-shot executions of men with their hands bound and horrific, very public mutilations by machetes, grenades and machine guns. SLA/Muslim attacks left less bloody evidence but many mass graves. Neither side achieved anything except more dates to be remembered with further violence. In the 20 years since, peace declarations have been made and refuted and actual war has flared repeatedly. The Batticaloa massacres serve only as a terrible example of pointless tit-for-tat violence executed on the civilians who have least to gain from either side winning power.

National Bosses Day at Luby's

Luby's Cafeteria was a popular restaurant on US Highway 190 at Killeen, Texas, right next to America's biggest military base, Fort Hood. The lunchtime crowd was bigger than usual with folk from Killeen's small businesses affectionately celebrating 'National Bosses Day'. Around 80 people were at the tables when Luby's huge plate-glass window crashed inwards as 35-year-old George Hennard, from nearby Belton, rammed his Ford Ranger pickup truck straight through it. In the stunned silence, a local vet rushed to the driver's window to offer help. He was the first to die. Hennard shot him point blank. Then he clambered from the cab yelling 'This is what Belton did to me!', and opened fire.

Patrons and staff screamed and dived for cover. There was rising panic as they realized Hennard's truck blocked the obvious exit. They tried to shrink into invisibility under tables – but Hennard stalked the room, ramming pistols against heads and chests and blasting his victims away. One woman saw her father charge Hennard, only to be shot down. Another patron risked his life by hurling himself through a window to create an escape route for everyone else.

Hennard calmly reloaded and kept firing, a semi-automatic in either hand. He didn't stop his methodical slaughter even when four policemen screeched up and returned his fire. Finally, wounded and cornered by the police, he turned a gun on himself 14 long minutes after his shattering entrance, leaving 23 dead or dying, and another 20 groaning from their injuries.

Until Virginia Tech in 2007, Luby's was America's deadliest 'spree killing'. It defied explanation or even speculation. As Bishop John McCarthy, who led a service at Killeen, said of the murders: 'Today the lives of the citizens of Killeen are changed. We . . . faced death, but death in a meaningless context'. It wasn't even a tragedy – just an empty, pointless disaster.

WHEN:
October 16 1991
WHERE:
Luby's Cafeteria, Killeen, Texas, USA
DEATH TOLL:
24 dead (including the perpetrator) and 20 wounded.
YOU SHOULD KNOW:
The woman whose father died charging Hennard also saw her mother killed by him. Distraught that she had left her own (legal) handgun in her car as Texas law demanded, she lobbied the Texas legislature – and in 1995 Texan law was changed to allow residents with gun permits to 'carry *and conceal*' their weapons. Had the law existed before Luby's, Hennard could have been stopped almost immediately.

Officials removing bodies from Luby's Cafeteria

Waco

WHEN:
April 19 1993
WHERE:
Mount Carmel, Waco, Texas, USA
DEATH TOLL:
80 (including 23 children under 17 –
14 of whom were fathered by
Koresh). The FBI and ATF have always
claimed that the disaster was a
'mass suicide' because the Branch
Davidians started the fires. But the
ATF bulldozed the site making it
impossible to recover forensic
evidence of the fires' origins or
composition, so we'll never know.
YOU SHOULD KNOW:
If it's possible to say so, the Waco
siege had its lighter moments. One
man arrived from Florida claiming to
be 'Jesus's brother' and wanting a
chat. Another claimed he was Jesus
himself, and would the ATF please
let him pass so he could 'go in and
set Koresh straight on who Christ
really was'.

In 1990, when he took control of the Branch Davidians religious cult, David Koresh believed he was an angel with a direct channel to God. Disillusioned ex-members accused him retrospectively of offences that brought him under the intense scrutiny of the FBI, ATF (Alcohol, Tobacco and Firearms), and Texan authorities. The ATF planned to arrest him at Mount Carmel, the cult's compound outside Waco on February 28 1993, and made no secret of their intentions.

Koresh had long denounced his 'persecution' by the government as 'satanic' and been dismissed as paranoid. Now the ATF was proving him right. They moved in on the compound's wooden buildings with around 75 armed agents and three helicopters. Nobody knows who fired first, but four ATF agents died and another 16 were wounded in the hail of bullets between them and the 130 Branch Davidians inside. Several Branch Davidians were hit, including Koresh, whose prestige rose as it became public knowledge that he had always predicted that 'the Apocalypse would begin when the American army attacked Mount Carmel'.

The stand-off lasted 51 days. There were negotiations at presidential level, defections from Koresh's following, and 'hostage releases' (from the government's standpoint, though in fact Koresh just sent out the children who wanted to leave). The world learned just how badly US authorities had handled the situation; and though Koresh didn't look great either, he was clearly genuine, and genuinely provoked. Finally the FBI went in with tear gas (knowing it was flammable in a house that used oil lamps), tanks, armoured vehicles and automatic weapons. By noon, flames were rising in several places. Nine Branch Davidians ran for it as the wooden structures were engulfed in a white-hot, partly chemical blaze. Koresh died with 79 of his willing followers. For a long time he had prophesied the manner of his end and his 'immortality'. The FBI and associates fulfilled his prophesy.

Flames engulfing the Branch Davidian compound in Waco, Texas.

The Solar Temple killings

Later, when the authorities pieced it together, it became obvious that the three mass killings were planned as one. The five deaths in Morin Heights near Montreal, the 22 in Cheiry, and 25 in Granges, both in Switzerland, shared both a date and a *modus operandi*. Most of the victims wore some kind of exotic regalia that matched drapery and other ceremonial arcana decorating the rooms where they were found; and the bodies were arranged to form circles, extending outwards like the rays of the sun.

All the victims belonged to the secretive cult of the Order of the Solar Temple, known to authorities in France, Switzerland and Francophone Canada as a surprisingly *haut-bourgeois* affiliation of roughly 450 subscribers to a paternalistic hierarchy which promised to initiate them, by degrees, to its esoteric secrets borrowed randomly from Rosicrucian sects. At a time when unbridled capitalism felt threatened by social disintegration, it wasn't hard for the Temple's founders to find suggestible adherents with lots of money to donate ($93 million by 1993, when Canadian police began a general surveillance).

Those 'chosen' to evolve would have 'to leave in fire' – abandon their physical bodies in 'arks of safety' which would afterwards be burned to prevent earthly contamination – and make a 'death voyage' to a higher consciousness on the star Sirius. As Swiss Forensics discovered, waverers were shot or stabbed or suffocated, including the children.

The Solar Temple's founders were among the Swiss dead, but even that didn't prove they believed their own utopian fiction. Evidence clearly showed that one or more members with intimate knowledge of the Temple's affairs was both alive and on the loose. For anyone prepared to organize it, the Temple provided a perfect scenario for mass murder: people paid you money, and went, willy-nilly, to their salvation. There was always a genuine mass suicide to take the blame.

Charred ruins of the chalet where 25 sect members died.

WHEN:
October 4 1994
WHERE:
Cheiry and Granges-sur-Salvan, Switzerland, and Morin Heights, Montreal, Quebec, Canada. All the buildings were owned by the Solar Temple.
DEATH TOLL:
52 dead, around two-thirds of whom were suicides
YOU SHOULD KNOW:
The Solar Temple massacres continued. In 1995 16 died in France; in 1997 five died (after freeing three deeply unwilling teenagers) in Quebec; and in 1998 police prevented another mass suicide of 30 members in the Canary Islands. It is not known how many of the dead were 'awakened', and thus allowed to poison themselves after shooting the others. Anyone deemed a 'traitor' was executed without being 'transitioned' to safety on Sirius.

509

Genocide in Srebrenica

The euphoria of independence didn't last long in most Balkan countries. As the former Yugoslavia fragmented, age-old sectarian, ethnic and tribal rivalries were revived. In 1993 UN forces called in to buffer the antagonism between Bosnian Serbs and Bosnian Muslims had designated several 'Safe Areas' for civilians. One of these was Srebrenica. By July 1995, as Bosnian Serb forces laid siege to the enclave, Srebrenica was crammed with Muslims under the protection of 600 UN Dutch troops to whom they had surrendered their weapons.

On the afternoon of July 11 Serb commander Ratko Mladic, having humbugged the UN peacekeepers, entered Srebrenica like some beaming Goering, festooned with news crews. Fearing the worst, that night 15,000 Muslim men (civilians and unarmed ex-fighters) attempted a mass break out across the hills. They were heavily shelled and many were recaptured. Next day Mladic ordered that all men between the ages of 12 and 77 be held in trucks and warehouses for 'interrogation for suspected war crimes'; while convoys of buses deported 23,000 women and children to distant 'Muslim territory'.

The killings had already begun in the village of Kravica when the UN forces in nearby Potocari handed over 5,000 Muslims in their charge to the Serbs in return for 14 Dutch hostages taken earlier. The 2,000 elderly and infirm men were separated, driven away and killed. Under Mladic 'ethnic cleansing' quickly became methodical and organized. If they weren't hunted down in the forests, unarmed men were pushed into warehouses or just lined up and machine-gunned, with a bullet or bayonet in the neck for certainty. Bratunac, near Srebrenica, was one favoured killing ground – because Serbs had already used it in 1992 when they tortured 350 Muslims to death. This time the victims had to dig their own graves before being shot; 400 were simply buried alive, bulldozed into the earth. In total 8,000 men and boys died in the genocide. It was the worst atrocity in Europe since World War II.

Portraits of Bosnian Muslims who were victims of the 1995 Srebrenica massacre.

WHEN:
July 11–15 1995
WHERE:
Srebrenica district,
Bosnia-Herzegovina
DEATH TOLL:
8,000 men and boys. Almost as ugly as the genocide itself was the Serbs' attempt to cover up their crime. They moved the mass graves and tried to camouflage them. Srebrenica massacre sites are still being discovered – only 3,000 bodies have so far been found.
YOU SHOULD KNOW:
A video of Ratko Mladic shows him strutting through Srebrenica on July 11, saying to camera 'the time has come to take revenge on the Turks'. After it was shown at the trial of Radovan Karadzic (Mladic's commander-in-chief) in The Hague, Karadzic said his only regret was that 'some Muslim men got away'. For the rest of the world, bringing the murderers to justice is one thing – learning that membership of the UN carries a very real responsibility to keep its promises is more difficult. The Bosnian Muslims of Srebrenica had been 'guaranteed' a safe haven.

Dunblane

There were 29 small children in the gymnasium of Dunblane Primary School when Thomas Hamilton walked in and opened fire at point-blank range. Using several automatic firearms, he sprayed and re-sprayed the room. In just three minutes 16 children were dead or dying along with their teacher, and 12 were wounded. Just one of the five and six year olds escaped the carnage physically unscathed. Then, without pausing, Hamilton shot himself. It was the worst multiple murder Britain had ever known.

Hamilton's dogged focus on young children as his victims made the Dunblane massacre even more horrific than Hungerford, nine years earlier. Michael Ryan, the Hungerford killer, had been deemed a fantasist whose violence had been nourished by a lifetime of voluntary isolation from normal societal interchange. As police and psychologists desperately sought to identify Hamilton's motivation – if only to help grief-ravaged parents make some sense of the horror – it became clear that Hamilton had *been* isolated. Facts about him included being rejected as a suitable leader of all manner of boys' clubs, including the Boy Scouts, over a number of years; and he certainly had a clinical 'persecution complex', evidenced by his dozens of complaints to councils, parliament, the police, the Ombudsman and even the Queen about his mental stability being questioned. Yet his firearms licence was not revoked, and afterwards his keen membership of a gun club was interpreted as a 'behavioural tryout'.

Finally, he was rejected as a voluntary worker by the Dunblane Primary School. After a lifetime trying to belong to the community, his awful, bloody revenge was symbolic. Instead of the adult authorities who had systematically excluded him – *without ever, once, offering him any kind of counselling for his perceived and stated shortcomings* – Hamilton attacked those they held most dear, their children.

WHEN:
March 13 1996
WHERE:
Dunblane Primary School, Dunblane, Scotland, UK
DEATH TOLL:
17 (16 children and their teacher), plus 12 wounded
YOU SHOULD KNOW:
After talking to witnesses who saw Hamilton cross the school playground, push past two staff members in a corridor, and pass the dining room before entering the gym, a senior forensic psychiatrist stated that Hamilton's primary motive was suicide, and that 'it was not my impression that he particularly relished the killing spree or wanted to prolong it'. We don't need to forgive Hamilton, but we do need to understand that if we ostracize the 'weird' and 'suspicious', and ignore their complaints about it, we shouldn't be surprised if they eventually do terrible things.

A policewoman lays flowers at the gates of Dunblane Primary School the morning after a vigil at the town's cathedral for the victims of the shooting.

Heaven's Gate cult suicide

WHEN:
March 26 1997
WHERE:
Rancho Santa Fe, near San Diego,
California, USA
DEATH TOLL:
39 (plus two cult members who
killed themselves later)
YOU SHOULD KNOW:
When contacted early in March
about taking part in *Louis Theroux's
Weird Weekends* series, Heaven's
Gate refused the invitation, saying it
'would be an interference with what
we must focus on'.

In March 1997 in a house in California police found 39 bodies lying neatly in their bunk beds, their heads and torsos covered by purple cloths. All were wearing black shirts and trousers; in their pockets they each had a $5 note and three quarter coins; each had an armband patch reading 'Heaven's Gate Away Team'. They had all drunk a cocktail of vodka and phenobarbital and wrapped their heads in polythene bags.

Heaven's Gate was one of many millennial and UFO-based cults in the USA. It was originally set up in the early 1970s by Marshall Applewhite together with Bonnie Nettles, who died in 1985. They were known as 'Do' and 'Ti' and believed themselves to be 'The Two' (two 'witnesses' mentioned in the *Book of Revelation*). The cult combined various beliefs – Christian salvation and apocalypse, evolutionary advancement and travel to other worlds. Members renounced family and worldly goods to live a communal life of asceticism and celibacy in a rented mansion they described as a monastery. They called each other brothers and sisters and knew that the next level of existence would be free from gender and sexual activity – some, including Applewhite, underwent castration.

Central to their faith was the idea that the earth, controlled by evil powers, was about to be 'recycled' and that they must leave it immediately, to be ready for 'replanting' in another container (body) at a higher level. A video shot just before the suicides shows cult members thrilled by the prospect of joining a UFO hidden behind the Halle-Bopp comet, which they regarded as a celestial marker. They had timed their departure to coincide with the comet's closest approach to earth.

*One of 39 members of the
Heaven's Gate cult who
committed suicide.*

Columbine High School shooting

The Columbine massacre was one of the deadliest school shootings in US history, its circumstances and aftermath inflicting untold trauma on American culture.

Eric Harris, aged 18, and Dylan Klebold, 17, armed themselves with homemade bombs, sawn-off shotguns, semi-automatic rifles, pistols and knives. Their objective was an all-out assault on the Columbine High School in the suburban town of Littleton, outside Denver. They planned a diversionary explosion to draw off emergency services, then they would explode two more bombs inside the school and pick off survivors as they ran. Their intention was to kill hundreds of people, dwarfing the Oklahoma City carnage with an obscene disaster that would forever besmirch American history.

When the two interior bombs fizzled but failed, they swaggered through the school shooting at anything and anyone. It was fun, especially in the packed cafeteria where their terrified peers shrank under the tables hoping to escape notice and make a break for it.

It's taken a decade of deconstruction for the police, FBI, survivors, victims' families, public and Michael Moore (who made the seminal film *Bowling for Columbine*) to reach any kind of cogent explanation for the murders. Prolonged study of video and notebook diaries show that Harris and Klebold had spent a year planning this major atrocity in detail. Columbine School was merely convenient. They weren't even seeking fame, they just wanted to hurt as many people as possible. Harris was a clinical psychopath and Klebold a troubled adolescent with a suicidal tendency.

The true, almost unspeakable, horror of the Columbine massacre is that, had the boys been older with greater technical knowledge, they would have committed a far deadlier crime. On the front page of his journal, Harris had scrawled: 'I hate the f*****g world'.

In this image from television, a Columbine High School student is rescued by emergency personnel during the shooting.

WHEN:
April 20 1999
WHERE:
Columbine High School, Littleton, Jefferson County, Colorado, USA
DEATH TOLL:
13 (12 students and one teacher) dead; 23 injured
YOU SHOULD KNOW:
Repercussions of the massacre continue. America watched the siege unfold on live TV, and the subsequent national debates cover access to guns, school security systems, violence on TV and in video games, and police 'procedures' (the sensitive issues of why the police failed to enter the school and shoot the two boys; and why they left a teacher to bleed to death on TV; and whether the job of a policeman includes taking risks). 'Columbine' has entered American vocabulary in all kinds of contexts, and none of them are pleasant.

Massacre at Kanungu

WHEN:
March 16–17 2000
WHERE:
Kanungu, Uganda
DEATH TOLL:
330 at Kanungu (the police clearing the ashes believed it could be as many as 550), with a further 725 or so recovered from several locations. The dead included a number of children.
YOU SHOULD KNOW:
Indoctrinated cult members were given an extended 'home leave' in 1998. The dates coincided with the treatment for bipolar disorder and manic depression, in a Kampala mental hospital, of Joseph Kibwetere, the preacher who was Mwerinde's accomplice. There's a price on his head for murder.

As the millennium loomed, Christianity in Africa blossomed to equal or surpass the number of its European adherents. African Christians are especially attracted by charismatic offshoots of the Catholic and Anglican creeds, and Uganda's traditional culture of obedience, respect and loyalty makes it unusually fruitful for new sects. The more exciting, the better. Hoping to find what the executive secretary of the Uganda Joint Christian Council described as 'easy answers to the difficult questions', there were plenty of eager takers for the strong spiritual leadership offered by Credonia Mwerinde, founder of the apocalyptic sect called The Movement for the Restoration of the Ten Commandments of God.

Mwerinde presented herself as a redeemed Mary Magdalene who had turned away from sin after 'a vision of the Virgin Mary' and was therefore fit to dictate terms on other people's waywardness. With a talented preacher as partner, she built up a dedicated following in southwest Uganda. Rules were strict: separation of families, celibacy, absolute silence, obedience and commitment to a millennial 'rapture'. This last was conditional on donating all your worldly goods to Mwerinde.

Having prepared her followers for the millennium, Mwerinde had to explain why the world hadn't ended. She blamed it on their concealed 'sins' and quickly re-scheduled for March 16. On that night, she locked them in their prayer hall and set them on fire.

The fireball killed at least 330, but it was just the beginning. Across southwest Uganda, a series of mass graves revealed more than 700 bodies, stabbed, strangled and burned. Very probably there are more still. The cult's leaders were not among them – they were last seen driving north with suitcases full of valuables.

The heart-breaking credulity of their victims, up to the last minute of horrified disillusion, stripped the crime of any pretension to religious suicide. This was mass murder at its ugliest, and was without doubt planned 'with malice aforethought'.

Beslan school hostage massacre

Chechen militant with hostages in the gym of Beslan school.

September 1 was the first day of school in the sleepy North Ossetian town of Beslan, when parents, teachers and children celebrate 'The Day of Knowledge' by wearing their best clothes and school uniforms. Instead of a party with music and dancing, they stepped into a brutal nightmare. Clubbed and beaten into the school gym by Chechen militants, more than 1,200 civilians found themselves at the mercy of gun-toting fanatics prepared to abuse, torture, maim and kill them in pursuit of concessions from the Russian government, their 'oppressors'. In the convoluted morality that guided competing territorial claims in the Caucasus (Russia, Chechnya, Ingushetia and North Ossetia could not even agree a rationale for their bitter confrontations), the hostages were to be expendable human pawns.

The screams and chaos that accompanied the initial shooting quickly settled into the groans of the wounded and whimpering of children denied water, food and the lavatory. The toxic sweat of fear mingled with vomit and rotting corpses. The militants had moved swiftly to wire the school with explosives, and several were living grenades – suicide bombers anxious to make their mark with the world looking on and Russian Special Forces among the thousands of surrounding troops. Handfuls of hostages escaped, but catastrophe was inevitable.

After 51 hours, Russian assault troops rushed the school using tanks, rocket-propelled grenades, flame throwers, helicopter gunships and anti-personnel high explosives. As whole sections of wall collapsed on some of the hostages, bombs were triggered, and the school erupted. Explosions continued throughout a 12-hour gunfight, in which hostages were shot indiscriminately by their 'rescuers'. With no fire crews and few ambulances to help, bystanders braved the inferno to get some of the hundreds of injured hostages to safety in private cars; 334 of their friends, neighbours and children were already dead.

WHEN:
September 1–3 1994
WHERE:
Beslan, North Ossetia
DEATH TOLL:
At least 334 died, including 186 children. Most of the militants were also killed, and it's not clear if they or the many injured who died in hospital are included in that total (because the Russian government conducted at least one mass burial of more than 125 people). Many other hostages 'survived' but remain too traumatized to resume their former lives, and several have committed suicide.
YOU SHOULD KNOW:
The Beslan massacre was a manufactured crisis intended to aggravate the great powers rather than to achieve a local objective. Behind every sobbing Beslan mother is the cynical and underhand power politics of governments.

Virginia Tech

WHEN:
April 16 2007
WHERE:
The campus of Virginia Polytechnic Institute and State University, Blacksburg, Virginia, USA
DEATH TOLL:
33 dead (27 students, five faculty members, and Cho) and 23 wounded.
YOU SHOULD KNOW:
Cho's imaginary life included calling himself 'Question Mark'; a 'supermodel' girlfriend called 'Jelly' who 'travelled by spaceship'; and reporting to his room mate that he was 'vacationing with Russian Prime Minister Vladimir Putin' having 'grown up with him in Moscow'. But a Senior in Cho's class who read his one-act play told a friend: 'This is the kind of guy who is going to walk into a classroom and start shooting people'.

The massacre at the campus of Virginia Polytechnic Institute and State University (Virginia Tech) was the deadliest peacetime shooting by an individual in US history. What Seung-Hui Cho demanded was a blood sacrifice from the world. His choice of victims was almost random. The exception was the first one, the girl he shot as she slept; her boyfriend was a straight arrow whom Cho happened to see at the firing range where he practised. If he made Cho feel inferior, it was entirely in Cho's imagination.

Everything was in his imagination; it always had been. Since childhood he had remained uncommunicative, even with his family, and his self-isolation grew more extreme when he got to Virginia Tech. His English professor noticed the anger expressed in writing projects, and pleaded with college authorities to get Cho to seek help. But that would have infringed his civil rights – like the privacy laws which prevented Virginia Tech ever knowing that Cho's mental health had been the subject of much previous anxiety.

Cho paused after the first two shootings. He returned to his room and wrote a manifesto of his loathing for the world. In it he praised the Columbine High School killers as 'martyrs'. Then he mailed it to NBC News. Meanwhile the police chased the wrong man, not bothering to tell the college of the nightmare – currently arming himself with guns he'd collected in previous weeks – stalking the campus.

Cho waited two hours for classes to begin, chained the doors of one of the halls shut behind him, and worked his way through four full classrooms, blazing

Seung-Hui Cho went on a deadly rampage at Virginia Tech University.

away. In less than 15 minutes, he reduced them to blood and gore, only stopping when the police blasted open the hall doors. Then he reversed one of his pistols and shot himself. An enquiry later noted that if Cho's human rights hadn't prevented Virginia Tech from 'connecting the dots', 33 lives might have been saved.

Fort Hood

Despite the 9/11 catastrophe, the USA's much-hyped intelligence community yet again failed to head off a preventable disaster. Major Nisal Malik Hassan's attempts to contact al-Qaeda and radical Muslim clerics were closely monitored, but the decision was taken to watch rather than reel him in, hoping to land bigger fish.

So the 39-year-old US Army psychiatrist was free to attend his place of work early one afternoon in November 2009, carrying two handguns – a semi-automatic FN pistol and .357 Magnum revolver – plus lots of ammunition. The Soldier Readiness Center at Fort Hood was busy processing personnel returning from or leaving for overseas tours of duty when Hassan produced the FN pistol and started shooting, discharging over 100 rounds in quick succession.

Moments later 13 people – 12 soldiers and one civilian worker – lay dead or dying, while 30 others had been felled with gunshot injuries. As Hassan chased a wounded soldier out of the building, civilian base police officers arrived. Sergeant Kimberly Munley exchanged shots with Hassan before falling to the ground after being hit three times.

Sergeant Mark Todd then took up the fight. Hassan missed him twice before being shot himself. He fell unconscious to the ground with four bullet wounds and was handcuffed by Todd.

After regaining consciousness in hospital, Hassan was charged with 13 counts of premeditated murder, leaving investigators to puzzle over his motivation. He was a practising Muslim of Jordanian origin, who had expressed interest in suicide bombings and had close contact with Anwar al-Awlaki, his *imam* at the mosque in Falls Church, Virginia, which was also attended by two 9/11 hijackers. Various theories were advanced to explain the massacre, from Hassan's reluctance to accept an imminent Afghanistan posting to fury that his superiors refused to prosecute soldiers who had admitted committing atrocities against Muslims in the course of psychiatric sessions.

WHEN:
November 5 2009
WHERE:
Fort Hood, near Killeen, Texas, USA
DEATH TOLL:
Unlucky 13 (plus the unborn child of a casualty, Private First Class Francheska Velez, one of three women killed)
YOU SHOULD KNOW:
Shortly after the Fort Hood shootings Major Nisal Hassan's lawyer announced that his client had been paralyzed from the waist down and was unlikely to walk again.

Responders using a table as a stretcher to transport a wounded soldier to an awaiting ambulance.

DISASTROUS CONSEQUENCES

The Donner party

The lure of a better life on America's West Coast saw thousands of mid-19th-century pioneers pack their lives into covered wagons and attempt an arduous journey to a promised land. Among them, in 1846, were two families from Illinois: the Donners and the Reids. After travelling with a large wagon train for two months along the California Trail, the Donner party arrived at Little Sandy River in modern-day Wyoming. There, the disastrous decision to follow a new route was made.

George Donner duly led 87 people in 23 wagons to Fort Bridger and the supposedly quicker Hastings Cutoff, where the travellers endured great hardship crossing the Wasatch Mountains and Great Salt Lake Desert. Far worse, they took three weeks longer to reach Elko than those who had stayed on the proven California Trail – a delay that would ultimately prove fatal.

When the Donner party finally reached the forbidding Sierra Nevada Mountains in late October a snowstorm blocked their pass, preventing wagons from progressing. Low on supplies, the stranded emigrants divided into two groups and camped, slaughtering their oxen for food.

In mid December a group of 15 (later known as the Forlorn Hope) fashioned snowshoes and headed into the mountains. Close to death, seven survivors reached safety in January 1847. They survived only by resorting to cannibalism, eating fallen colleagues after they died. Of those who remained behind, 14 were dead when the first relief party arrived from California in February and saved 21 emigrants. Three further missions rescued the rest, though cannibalism again broke out before the last survivor was collected in April.

Had the Donner party stuck to the California Trail, they would have been through the mountains before the pass became snowbound. But they couldn't resist the shortcut that never was . . . and paid the price.

The Donner party on the way to the summit, 1846

Deaths of Burke and Wills

One riding accident and a minor oversight led to the demise of two pioneering Australian explorers – Robert O'Hara Burke and William John Wills. They led the first expedition to cross Australia from south to north, leaving Melbourne in 1860 to the cheers of vast crowds. Equipment failure, arguments and slow progress dogged the venture, but eventually the expedition reached Coopers Creek – at the outer limit of European exploration. There, Camp 65 was established. Leaving William Brahe in charge, Burke and Wills took two men and set out for the Gulf of Carpentaria.

They made it, but the demanding journey took two months with bad weather and dwindling supplies hindering their return. One died but the other three reached Camp 65 on April 21 1861. Brahe's depot party should have waited for 13 weeks, but actually stayed for 18. But on the morning of the very day that Burke, Wills and John King arrived, one of Brahe's men broke a leg, an accident precipitating hasty departure for Menindee to the south. If that was bad luck, what followed was an avoidable tragedy.

Beneath a 'Dig Tree' Brahe buried supplies and blazed the trunk. The returning explorers retrieved the food, but rather than following Brahe to Menindee, Burke headed towards the distant cattle station of Mount Hopeless, after burying an explanatory note. Disastrously, he neglected to re-mark the Dig Tree.

Meanwhile, Brahe met up with a relief party and returned to Coopers Creek. But in the absence of any sign that the Gulf Party had survived, he again departed – though Burke, Wills and King were still close by. They abandoned their attempt to reach Mount Hopeless and also returned to Coopers Creek. Some seven weeks later Burke and Wills died on the same day. John King survived.

Robert O'Hara Burke and William John Wills set out from the Royal Park in Melbourne to begin their exploration of Central Australia in 1862.

WHEN:
Around the end of June or early July 1861 (officially June 28 1861)
WHERE:
Coopers Creek, Queensland, Australia
DEATH TOLL:
Seven – apart from Burke and Wills, five other expedition members also died.
YOU SHOULD KNOW:
Wills returned to the Dig Tree at the end of May to bury his journals and notebook in the cache, along with bitter criticism of Brahe for not leaving animals or more supplies behind – little realizing that if he had thought to blaze the tree himself, all three surviving members of the Gulf party would already have been rescued by Brahe.

Chaos in the street outside the Victoria Music Hall, Sunderland, when, at a conjuring performance by Mr and Miss Fay, 183 children died in a stampede.

Victoria Hall crush

There's nothing that causes greater grief than the death of a child, which made events at Sunderland's Victoria Hall on a June afternoon in 1883 truly horrifying. The hall was hosting a children's variety show put on by Mr Fay, who billed the performance as 'The Greatest Treat For Children Ever Given' and promised that every child would have the chance of receiving a gift after the show.

Two thousand children paid their penny and packed in, half upstairs and half down. They were entranced by the entertainment, not least when the climax just after five o'clock saw Mr Fay magically producing pigeons that were allowed to fly free. But the best was yet to come. True to his word, Mr Fay and his assistants started throwing small presents, resulting in a frantic scrum in the stalls.

Those in the gallery watched the excitement below with increasing dismay. Treats should have been distributed upstairs, but this was badly organized and eager youngsters assumed the tempting action was downstairs. There was a stampede for the staircase, but the inward-opening door at the bottom had been bolted in a position that only allowed one child at a time to pass, a fact that would have disastrous consequences.

A crush occurred at the bottom of the staircase. In moments, a

WHEN:
June 16 1883
WHERE:
Sunderland, County Durham (now Tyne and Wear), UK
DEATH TOLL:
183 children (114 boys and 69 girls), with around 100 more injured, some seriously
YOU SHOULD KNOW:
Public outrage at the Victoria Hall tragedy led to a new law requiring public venues to be fitted with an adequate number of emergency exits that opened outwards, resulting in the development of the type of push-bar doors that are still in widespread use in Britain today.

tightly packed mass of children eight or ten deep piled up, compressed by the weight of those pressing from above. When order was eventually restored, the scale of the tragedy became apparent. Nearly 200 children between the ages of three and 14 had died from compressive asphyxia, most aged seven to ten. The scenes as frantic parents scanned long rows of small bodies, many mangled, were unbelievably harrowing. Some families lost all their young ones and the whole town went into mourning.

Khodynka tragedy

There was nothing grander than a Russian Imperial coronation, and great festivities had been planned to accompany the accession of Tsar Nicolas II on May 13 1896. To ensure that the population appeared suitably ecstatic, Muscovites would be encouraged to celebrate with the help of coronation gifts from their new absolute monarch. The appointed day was May 18. Bars and booths for distributing gifts were erected in a town square in northwest Moscow, at the beginning of present-day Leningrad Prospect. This had been chosen because it adjoined Khodynka Field, a large open space capable of accommodating the large number of people who were expected to attend.

The plan was an unqualified success, for a vast crowd (later estimated to have contained up to 500,000 people) gathered on Khodynka Field by dawn, in anticipation of receiving their gifts – a commemorative mug, bread roll, slice of sausage and piece of gingerbread. There would also be free beer.

A large force of police was present to maintain order, but the 1,800 officers proved entirely ineffectual in the face of unfolding events.

Suddenly, a rumour started that there was insufficient beer for everyone and not enough gifts to go round. The consequences were catastrophic. The crowd pressed forward, creating a disastrous crush. Panic swept through the assembled masses, and in the ensuing rush to escape more than 1,300 were trampled to death, with a similar number injured.

The triumph Tsar Nicholas had anticipated ended in tragedy. He was genuinely distressed and spent the day visiting hospitalized victims with his wife, Alexandra. But he allowed his own better judgement to be overruled by diplomatic advisers and attended a celebration ball at the French embassy that same evening, a decision that didn't go down well with the shocked Russian public.

WHEN:
May 18 1896
WHERE:
Moscow, Russia
DEATH TOLL:
1,389 people were killed and over 1,300 injured.
YOU SHOULD KNOW:
The event that sparked the Khodynka tragedy – the coronation of a Russian emperor – would never be repeated. Nicholas II was the last tsar to rule, abdicating in 1917 before being executed with his family by Bolsheviks at Yekaterinburg in 1918. Opponents nicknamed him 'Nicholas the Bloody' as a result of Khodynka, the massacre of peaceful protesters by the Imperial Guard in 1905, and anti-Semitic pogroms.

Barnsley Public Hall disaster

WHEN:
January 11 1908
WHERE:
Barnsley, South Yorkshire, UK
DEATH TOLL:
16 (all children)
YOU SHOULD KNOW:
The Barnsley Public Hall is now the town's Civic Hall. A commemorative plaque listing the names and ages of victims was recently unveiled by the mayor following a major refurbishment, serving as a reminder of how deeply a tragedy that has never been forgotten affected the people of Barnsley.

New-fangled cinematography was still a great novelty in 1908, so the youngsters who trooped towards Barnsley Public Hall one Saturday afternoon that January were in a state of high excitement. The boys and girls who hurried along the town's Eldon Street were looking forward to a cinematographic display and children's variety show mounted by the World's Animated Picture Company that would cost them a then-not-inconsiderable penny apiece. But despite the price there were plenty of takers.

As the hall started to fill, a voice was heard to shout 'Fire'. This may have been as a result of a genuine belief that there was a fire in the building – though in fact there wasn't – but a more likely explanation is that it was some over-excited individual's misplaced idea of a joke. Whatever the reason for this alarming cry, the immediate consequences proved to be tragic.

A disorderly stampede ensued, as panic-stricken children sought to escape from the imagined threat. Most of the assembling audience managed to reach the open air with no more harm done than assorted minor cuts and bruises. But that would not be the case for some of those already upstairs, and youngsters who were still trying to ascend the narrow staircase leading to the gallery.

Wrongly assuming they were in mortal danger, children from the gallery rushed downstairs and thereby actually put themselves in harm's way. They met those coming up who had no idea that anything was wrong and tumbled over them – a head-on collision that created a fatal crush in the confined space. When the panic subsided and order was restored, rescuers were horrified to discover that 16 children aged between four and nine had died from asphyxia, after the weight of pressing bodies compressed their lungs.

Captain Scott's polar assault

WHEN:
January to March 1912
WHERE:
Antarctica
DEATH TOLL:
Five
YOU SHOULD KNOW:
Though Amundsen beat Scott to the South Pole and the race ended disastrously for Scott's polar party, the *Terra Nova* Expedition did do much valuable scientific work – and Captain Scott's tragic death captured the public imagination and ensured that he became a national hero.

He was famous following the *Discovery* Expedition, but Robert Falcon Scott's burning ambition – to be first at the South Pole – remained unfulfilled when the ambitious naval officer launched his second Antarctic foray in 1910. The *Terra Nova* Expedition was intended to expand scientific knowledge, but Scott had the Pole as his coveted objective – spurred on by learning that Norwegian explorer Roald Amundsen had joined the race.

Ultimately, bad luck and misjudgements would have disastrous consequences for the British team. A delay when *Terra Nova* was trapped in pack ice for three weeks meant the main supply point for the polar assault – One-Ton Depot – was located further north than intended. Scott didn't fully exploit the potential of husky dogs. Finally, he impulsively added an extra man for the final push.

The polar party consisted of Scott, Edward Wilson, H R Bowers, Lawrence Oates and Edgar Evans. On January 17 1912 they reached their goal after much gruelling sledge-hauling, only to find a Norwegian flag – using dogs, Amundsen had beaten them by five weeks. The 1,300 km (800 mi) return journey across hostile terrain was a nightmare. Evans died on the fearsome Beardmore Glacier and the others were handicapped by shortage of provisions caused by taking the fifth man, plus snow blindness and physical exhaustion.

On March 16 Oates sacrificed himself to try and save the others, leaving their tent with the immortal words 'I'm going outside and may be some time.'. The survivors struggled on, but were caught in a blizzard that precluded further travel. They lived on for nine days, with Scott himself last to die on March 29. The final irony was that they were just 18 km (11 mi) short of salvation offered by One-Ton Depot – but 38 km (18 mi) beyond the point where it should have been located.

The members of Captain Scott's ill-fated expedition to the South Pole (left to right): Lawrence Oates, H R Bowers, Robert Falcon Scott, Edward Wilson and Edgar Evans.

The 1913 Massacre

WHEN:
December 24 1913
WHERE:
Calumet, Michigan, USA
DEATH TOLL:
73 died, mostly children
YOU SHOULD KNOW:
The depth of feeling in the mining community may be gauged by the fact that their name for this disastrous event – the 1913 Massacre – is still widely used rather than the less judgmental 'Italian Hall Disaster', squarely placing blame for the deadly shout of 'Fire' on the mining companies, who funded a shadowy group called the Citizens Alliance that made every effort to disrupt the strike. After the disaster, they kidnapped and shot a union leader who wouldn't accept a substantial donation in return for exonerating them. Instead, he accused the Alliance of being responsible and refused to be cowed when they put him on a train and told him to leave the state . . . or else.

Michigan's Copper Country was in turmoil from July 1913, as miners struck for union recognition, shorter hours, extra pay and a return to two-man drills. Unrest was sparked by the introduction of a new one-man drill. Miners rightly feared this innovation would lead to job losses and isolation as they were forced to work alone rather than in traditional groups – groups that were often drawn from single families.

The struggle became increasingly bitter as mining companies hired blackleg labour and the Michigan state militia was deployed to break up strikers' gatherings. But their resolve held firm and leaders like Big Annie Clemenc worked tirelessly to maintain morale as the strike dragged on into the hard winter. She hit on the idea of organizing a Christmas party sponsored by the union for which the strikers sought recognition, the Western Federation of Miners.

Calumet on Lake Superior's Keweenaw Peninsula was the chosen venue. Miners and their families gathered on Christmas Eve in the upstairs function room of the Italian Hall, which had shops on the ground floor. Spirits lifted at the thought of a few brief hours in which wretched circumstances could be forgotten, but someone had other ideas. A loud voice shouted 'Fire' and the yell led to instant panic in the crowded hall. People dashed for the narrow staircase *en masse* and a crush developed at the exit door.

The consequences were predictable, and tragic. Over 70 men, women and children died and in the aftermath the miners were quick to blame a company agitator for the fatal shout. Though highly credible, this accusation was never proved and an unsatisfactory inquest promptly cleared the mining companies of culpability. The Italian Hall has been demolished and the site of the tragedy is now a memorial garden.

Assassination of Franz Ferdinand

Life looked sweet for 49-year-old Archduke Franz Ferdinand of Austria-Este in 1914. He had married for love and the starchy Austrian court was finally accepting his wife. Franz Ferdinand was also fabulously wealthy and heir to the mighty Austro-Hungarian Empire.

It all came to a violent end on June 28. Franz Ferdinand was in the Austro-Hungarian province of Bosnia and Herzegovina, accompanied by his beloved wife Sophie. The visit was not popular with everyone. Balkan politics were turbulent, and the neighbouring

Kingdom of Serbia coveted Bosnia. The Royal couple were travelling through Sarajevo in an open-topped car when a grenade was thrown and though Franz Ferdinand was unhurt, members of his entourage were injured and bystanders were peppered with shrapnel.

Franz Ferdinand and Sophie later insisted on visiting the victims in hospital. Returning to the palace, their open car took a wrong turn. As the driver manoeuvred in a side street a young Austrian citizen named Gavrilo Princip seized his opportunity. Approaching the car, he shot both Franz Ferdinand and Sophie with a Browning pistol. Both died within moments.

Princip belonged to the Serb-supported Young Bosnia movement and the Black Hand. Both groups were dedicated to uniting territories seized by Austria-Hungary that contained South Slav peoples, by violent means if necessary. But Princip's act had disastrous consequences that went far beyond the Balkans, contributing significantly to the outbreak of World War 1.

Deeply insulted by the assassination, Austria-Hungary declared war on the country behind the outrage, Serbia. This set the Triple Alliance (Austria-Hungary, Germany and Italy) against Serbia's allies in the Triple Entente (Russia, France and Britain). Momentum became unstoppable and the deadliest conflict in history erupted. Two lives taken in Sarajevo thus led directly to the death of over 15 million combatants in the Great War.

After swallowing a cyanide pill which only made him sick, Gavrilo Princip was dragged from an angry crowd and arrested for shooting Archduke Franz Ferdinand and his wife.

WHEN:
June 28 1914
WHERE:
Sarajevo, Bosnia and Herzegovina
DEATH TOLL:
Two very important people
YOU SHOULD KNOW:
Gavrilo Princip tried to commit suicide after the attack. His cyanide capsule failed to work and the pistol was wrestled from his hand before he could use it on himself. He was too young to receive the death penalty, but was given a long prison sentence and kept in harsh conditions that contributed to his death from tuberculosis in 1918 – without seeing the creation of the united Yugoslavia of which he dreamed.

527

Introduction to Australia of the cane toad

WHEN:
1935 and 1936
WHERE:
Queensland, Australia
DEATH TOLL:
Many millions of native animals, notably cane toad predators like the Northern Native Cat, monitor lizards, land snakes and freshwater crocodiles whose populations have declined significantly as a result of eating the poisonous amphibians.
YOU SHOULD KNOW:
One of the chemicals produced by a cane toad in defensive mode is bufotoxin, which induces pleasantly mild hallucinations and is a banned Class 1 drug in Australia. Unfortunately, thrill seekers who lick cane toads in the hope of achieving a 'high' ingest a cocktail of powerful toxins that can prove fatal . . . and has been on several recorded occasions.

Graeme Sawyer, founder of the Northern Territory group known as Frog Watch, holds a cane toad, left, and a native frog at a billabong south of Darwin. Sawyer and his group have laid traps in an attempt to reduce the rapid spread of the cane toad.

It was Puerto Rico's fault. The Caribbean island introduced the Giant Neotropical Toad (officially *Bufo marinus*) from nearby Central America in the early years of the 20th century, in an attempt to control damaging beetle infestations in sugar cane plantations. The cunning plan worked, establishing this large terrestrial amphibian as the sugar planters' friend and earning it the popular name 'cane toad'.

But this is not a nice creature, growing as it does to a maximum length of around 38 cm (15 in), weighing in at up to 2.65 kg (5.8 lb) and protecting itself by excreting deadly toxins. The warty cane toad is a prolific breeder and its tadpoles, too, can prove fatal when ingested by predators. Undeterred by this alarming CV, and encouraged by results in Puerto Rico and Pacific islands like Hawaii, a few hundred cane toads were introduced to Australia in 1935.

A half-hearted study into the newcomers' feeding habits was conducted – which failed to detect the fact that they would prove ineffectual in controlling the very beetles they were expected to eradicate – before over 60,000 toadlets were released into the Queensland cane fields the following year. It ultimately proved to be a disastrous decision. Not only did the interlopers fail to control pests that were ravaging the sugar cane, but they also had a hugely negative impact on indigenous wildlife.

From relatively small beginnings the population expanded to the point where it is estimated in the hundreds of millions, with an increasing range that now encompasses the whole of Queensland plus large areas in New South Wales and Northern Territory.

Australia's isolation ensured that it developed a balanced ecological system, but the introduction of feral species like rabbits, domestic cats and foxes after colonization – and latterly the cane toad – has seriously disrupted the natural order of things.

Bethnal Green disaster

The eastern extension to London's Central Line was under construction in the 1930s, but was incomplete when World War II began in 1939. However, many of the new Underground line's deep tunnels had been finished and these proved useful when Hitler's bombers started to pound the city. Some housed factories, others were used as shelters – a safe if uncomfortable refuge for the population during air raids. One such was Bethnal Green station, which had seen almost constant use during the Blitz of 1940 and 1941.

But by 1943 the tide was turning against Goering's Luftwaffe. Raids on London were infrequent, usually occurring only as retaliation after the RAF bombed German cities. And so it was on March 3, following a heavy attack on Berlin. At 20.17 that evening Civil Defence sirens sounded in the East End and the people of Bethnal Green followed a well-established routine. They hurried to their station and filed into the dimly lit underground booking area, heading for narrow stairs that led to the platform where they could find refuge from the imminent raid.

What they didn't know was that a secret type of anti-aircraft rocket was about to be launched in nearby Victoria Park, with unexpected and horrifying consequences. At 22.27 a 60-rocket salvo was fired. The loud roar was a new and frightening sound, terrifying those at the station and causing the crowd to surge towards the first 19-step staircase that led to safety. Narrow stairs and hysterical people are a familiar ingredient of tragedy, and so it proved. A woman at the front tripped and fell, starting a chain reaction. Within seconds over 300 people were forced into the constricted stairwell by the pressure of those pushing from above. The result was devastating, as over 170 died of asphyxia and crush injuries.

WHEN:
1943
WHERE:
London, UK
DEATH TOLL:
173 (172 at the scene; one subsequently died in hospital), including 70 children
YOU SHOULD KNOW:
The Bethnal Green disaster was Britain's largest loss of civilian life in a single incident during World War II, eclipsing the 68 casualties inflicted by one bomb in Balham, South London.

Introduction of cats to Marion Island

Far from land in the sub-Antarctic region of the Indian Ocean lie the Prince Edward Islands. There are just two small islands in the group – Prince Edward Island and Marion Island – and the only human inhabitants are the South African National Antarctic Programme's staff at a research station.

After intermittent occupation by sealers, wreck hunters and those collecting *guano* for fertilizer, the islands were claimed by South Africa in 1947 and the research station was established on Marion Island, a rocky volcanic peak around 19 km (12 mi) long and 12 km (7 mi) wide, surrounded by towering cliffs.

When the new buildings suffered a mouse infestation, a simple solution was adopted. In 1949 five domestic cats were imported to see off the unwelcome rodents; but someone forgot to have them neutered. The consequences were disastrous. Within 30 years there were 3,500 feral cats on Marion Island, feasting not on mice but the very birds the scientists were there to study. The fearsome felines were particularly fond of petrels, burrowing birds that were easy meat in the breeding season. Some species became extinct on Marion Island and it was only a matter of time before they all went, with even penguin and albatross chicks suffering severe depredation.

It had to stop, and stop it did – not in the kindest of ways. In 1977 a specific feline virus was introduced, wiping out most of the cat population, and thereafter resistant animals were culled by trapping and night shooting. By the mid 1990s the cats were gone, though some suggest a few hardy moggies may still lurk in hidden corners. The unintended consequences of introducing non-native animals to a balanced natural habitat were plain to see, but in this case it was ultimately possible to limit the damage. It isn't always so.

Notting Hill race riots

Britain has long been a haven for immigrants. This enriches the nation, though not without difficulties along the way. Echoes of Sir Oswald Moseley's pre-war British Union of Fascists attacking the Jewish population of London's East End could still be heard in the 1950s, not least because the right-wing baronet had founded the Union Movement in 1948. It soon had a new target.

A wave of immigration from the Caribbean after World War II contributed to economic recovery but created social tension –

particularly in areas where newcomers settled in large numbers, causing the local working-class population to feel that its hegemony was threatened. Meanwhile, rebellious youngsters were breaking free from traditional constraints and roaming the streets in gangs. They disliked immigrants, parroting the slogan 'Keep Britain White', and by 1958 were becoming increasingly bold. A series of racially motivated incidents took place in Notting Hill, West London, but ironically the one that had disastrous consequences involved an attack by white youths on a white woman.

On August 29 she was with her Jamaican husband, rounding on the gang when they shouted racial taunts. Seeing her again the next evening, they pelted her with bottles and stones before hitting her with an iron bar. This sparked an explosion. White mobs attacked West Indian homes, occupants fought back and the infamous Notting Hill race riots began. The police proved unable to prevent violent disturbances and rioting, which continued for several nights until it petered out.

Over 100 people were charged with offences ranging from grievous bodily harm to affray (72 were white, 36 black), but the real significance of the Notting Hill riots was their role in bringing simmering racial tensions to national prominence, beginning a debate on the pros and cons of mass immigration that continues in Britain to this day.

Police arrest a white man and woman during a race riot in Notting Hill.

WHEN:
August 30 to September 5 1958
WHERE:
London, UK
TOLL:
With good reason, London's black population acquired lasting suspicion that the Metropolitan Police was biased against their community, a problem that still exists 50 years on despite strenuous efforts to eradicate institutionalized racism within the force and to build bridges with ethnic minorities.
YOU SHOULD KNOW:
The famous Notting Hill Carnival was started by Claudia Jones in 1959 in an attempt to ease the tensions caused by the previous year's riots and make a positive contribution to the state of race relations in Britain.

A man carries a Nile perch of 80 kg in Kasinyi, Entebbe, Uganda.

Introduction of Nile perch to Lake Victoria

Lake Victoria is Africa's largest lake – and home to one of the world's largest freshwater fish. The man-sized Nile perch can grow to around 2 m (over 6 ft) and slam the scales down to 200 kg (530 lb). But *Lates niloticus* is no native, and debate raged in the 1950s with one side promoting the introduction of Nile perch for commercial reasons and the other issuing dire warnings that such a move would decimate one of the world's most diverse fish environments.

The 'pro' lobby triumphed, but not by winning the argument. Nile perch were surreptitiously slipped into Lake Victoria from Uganda around 1954, so the genie was already out of the bottle when official introductions followed in 1962 and 1963. But did this prove disastrous, as naysayers predicted?

In fact, both sides were right. Once established, the Nile perch of Lake Victoria made a massive contribution to the economies of three countries, supporting not only 150,000 fishermen but also those working in related industries like processing and transport. On the other hand, the fierce new predator decimated original fish stocks with negative consequences for the area's traditional fishing communities. Whatever view is taken, everyone agrees that the introduction is a classic example of the negative impact aliens can have on an established ecosystem.

And the spectacular commercial success of the Lake Victoria fishery may not last. Over-fishing is dramatically reducing Nile perch stocks, and the good times could be coming to an end. Just as cow pasture ploughed to grow arable crops produces spectacular initial yields that drop away as the natural fertilizer is exhausted, so the boom years for fishermen on Lake Victoria may be coming to an end as the bill for meddling with Nature is presented.

WHEN:
Early 1950s and early 1960s
WHERE:
Lake Victoria,
Uganda/Kenya/Tanzania
DEATH TOLL:
Countless millions of native fish, with many of Lake Victoria's 500 species vanishing altogether.
YOU SHOULD KNOW:
Sometimes, painful eco-lessons *do* get learned. The Australian state of Queensland – having suffered mightily following the introduction of cane toads in the 1930s – has made it a serious offence to be found in possession of a live Nile perch. It is thought that – should the dominant predator become established in local waters – it would swiftly decimate the popular native barramundi, a similar but smaller fish.

Bangladesh tube wells

Bangladesh is a desperately poor country, with most of its 140 million citizens living in abject poverty. The former East Pakistan lies on the Bay of Bengal and is one of the world's most densely populated countries. This is a nation of low-lying land with extensive deltas where Himalayan rivers empty into the sea and the annual monsoon invariably causes severe flooding that displaces vast numbers of people.

Ironically for a country that practically floats, a major concern is sickness caused by poor sanitation and a shortage of uncontaminated drinking water. It is estimated that around a quarter of deaths in Bangladesh stem from water-related diseases; so when the fledgling democracy emerged from civil war with Pakistan in the early 1970s, foreign governments and NGOs (Non-Governmental Organizations) were quick to offer aid.

It was imperative to address the chronic problem of inadequate drinking water and there was a concentrated aid focus on the creation of tube wells. Even sophisticated versions are simple, consisting of a stainless steel pipe bored down to an underground water supply with an electric pump lifting water into a small reservoir that often does double duty as the village bathhouse. In Bangladesh, millions of shallow tube wells were created using hand pumps rather than unavailable electricity. This well-meaning policy seemed to make absolute sense, and nobody anticipated the disastrous consequences of this wholesale infrastructure investment.

Unfortunately, much of Bangladesh's groundwater turned out to be infused with arsenic. The problem was not identified until the 1990s, when it became apparent that many of the tube wells were seriously contaminated – to the point where the World Health Organisation described it as 'the largest mass poisoning in history'. In seeking to solve one acute health problem with the best of intentions, a ticking medical time bomb had been unleashed.

WHEN:
1970s to the present day
WHERE:
All over Bangladesh
DEATH TOLL:
Unknown, but a significant number of deaths caused by cumulative arsenicosis (poisoning) and assorted arsenic-related cancers have already been recorded . . . with many thousands more expected in the years ahead.
YOU SHOULD KNOW:
Once the problem was understood, a concerted programme (keenly supported by the very aid agencies that had inadvertently contributed to the problem in the first place) to eliminate contaminated wells was initiated, with a view to ensuring that all tube wells in Bangladesh would deliver arsenic-free water by 2013.

A Bangladeshi villager shows his palms, which have been affected by arsenic contamination.

Space shuttle *Challenger*

WHEN:
January 28 1986
WHERE:
Above the Atlantic off Cape
Canaveral, Florida
DEATH TOLL:
Seven
YOU SHOULD KNOW:
A stroke of bad luck contributed to
the *Challenger* disaster. One feasible
launch in warmer weather, on
January 26, was postponed because
Vice President George Bush wanted
to stop off at the Kennedy Space
Center and watch the launch on the
following day, *en route* to Honduras.
Ironically that launch, too, was
postponed.

Space shuttle Challenger
explodes shortly after take-off.

Spend billions of dollars, utilize the cutting-edge design and engineering
capabilities of the world's most technologically advanced nation and what
have you got? For NASA (the USA's National Aeronautics and Space
Administration) the answer was a snappy acronym – STS.

The Space Transportation System has at its heart the iconic space
shuttles – reusable craft used for orbital flight that became operational in
the early 1980s. Things had gone quiet for NASA after America won the
race to the moon back in 1969, and the STS programme revived public
interest and showed arch-rival Russia that old-fashioned rocketry wasn't
the only route to the stars.

The STS consists of three main elements. The shuttle is the reusable
orbiter vehicle (OV), propelled into space with the help of an external
fuel tank (ET) and two reusable solid rocket boosters (SRBs). This
incredibly sophisticated system has many thousands of components.
Among the least expensive are O-ring seals on the SRBs. Engineers had
warned that these might fail if the external temperature was too low, but
each launch was a major event that had to take place within a relatively
short time window.

There were several delays to the launch caused by problems like unsuitable weather conditions or minor equipment failures. It was unusually cold on the morning of January 28 and ice had formed on *Challenger*'s gantry, but NASA was desperate to get the mission away and decided to go ahead. It took just 73 seconds from launch to dramatically demonstrate how disastrous the decision to ignore chill conditions had been. The weakened O-ring on the right-hand rocket booster failed. A plume of flame scorched outwards, setting in motion a train of events that swiftly destroyed *Challenger* and took the lives of the seven crew, including 'people's astronaut' Christa McAuliffe.

Mecca tragedies

The Hajj is the world's largest pilgrimage, drawing a vast crowd to Mecca every year. It is the fifth pillar of Islam and demonstrates the solidarity of Muslims everywhere. Attending the Hajj at least once in a lifetime is an obligation for every able-bodied Muslim who can afford the trip – an edict that has seen attendance rising sharply as a result of global prosperity and easy air travel.

The month of Hajj now attracts up to four million visitors annually, posing huge logistical difficulties for the Saudi Arabian authorities. They have not always succeeded in dealing with the vast crowds and the sheer weight of numbers can have disastrous consequences. There have been many serious crowd incidents over recent years, cumulatively costing many lives. The worst accident occurred on July 2 1990, when 50,000 worshippers were allowed to converge simultaneously on the 500 m (1,640 ft) al-Mu'aysam tunnel connecting Mecca to the huge tented encampment of Mina, below Mount Arafat, during the Eid al-Adha (Feast of the Sacrifices) at the end of the Hajj. The tunnel collapsed and 1,426 died, mostly pilgrims from Turkey and Indonesia.

In May 1994 there was a stampede at Mina during a ceremony where pilgrims stone three pillars representing the devil. This time 270 died, mainly Africans. A catastrophic fire destroyed 70,000 tents on the Plain of Mina in 1997, probably started by an exploding gas cylinder. After the fire, 217 bodies were recovered and 1,300 were treated in hospital. The following year 118 died during another stampede after police opened a walkway on the Jamraat Bridge, causing a fatal surge.

Sadly, it won't be the last tragedy at Mecca. For as long as devout pilgrims gather in their millions each year, the Hajj will sometimes be a time of mourning as well as celebration.

WHEN:
1990, 1994, 1997 and 1998
WHERE:
At and around Mecca, Saudi Arabia
DEATH TOLL:
1,426 (1990); 270 (1994); 217 (1997); 118 (1998)
YOU SHOULD KNOW:
Although the casualty figures for disasters at Mecca seem bad enough, some commentators have suggested that the Saudi authorities deliberately understate the totals in order to mitigate criticism of their stewardship of the Hajj – which, in fairness, is the world's most demanding crowd-control challenge.

Kidnapping of Gorbachev

By the mid 1980s, the Soviet Union was creaking. The Communist Party's absolute control from Moscow had failed to deliver for assorted nations that had been forcibly combined to create the Russianized superstate. The economy was stagnant, poverty was endemic and the tightly controlled peoples of this disparate empire were getting restive.

Cometh the moment, cometh the man. In 1985, a visionary new leader rose to power. Mikhail Gorbachev set about implementing a two-track reform plan. On one hand, *glasnost* (freedom of speech) would provide a safety valve for the frustrated people. On the other, *perestroika* (rebuilding) would address economic woes. But the long-suppressed ability to speak freely led to a wave of unrest, both in Russia itself and in satellite countries, especially as *perestroika* failed to deliver improved living standards.

By 1991, hardliners who once enjoyed absolute power became restive as they saw communist control start to slip. In a desperate move to regain control, they kidnapped Mikhail Gorbachev and mounted a coup. On August 19 they announced that Gorbachev was 'indisposed' and unable to govern. But this dramatic move proved to be a serious miscalculation with disastrous consequences for their cause.

The plotters were horrified by the subsequent uproar, with protests erupting in major cities throughout the Soviet Union. In desperation, they turned to the traditional totalitarian solution and sent in the army to restore order. When soldiers refused to fire on their fellow countrymen – as dramatically symbolized by pictures of future leader Boris Yeltsin addressing a Moscow crowd from the top of a tank – the coup was over. This failure proved terminal for the nationalists. Instead of restoring the Soviet Union to its former centralized strength, the fiasco ensured that the entire Union finally fell apart, along with Russian control over Eastern Bloc states like East Germany.

Soviet President Mikhail Gorbachev speaking in a video message taped on the second day of his captivity. Gorbachev said there had been an unconstitutional coup and that he was completely well. Gorbachev returned to Moscow on August 22 1991, after the coup had failed.

WHEN:
August 19 to August 21 1991
WHERE:
Moscow, Russia, Soviet Union
TOLL:
The thwarted aspirations of the old guard to restore the Communist Party's totalitarian control of the Soviet Union
YOU SHOULD KNOW:
There is no evidence that Mikhail Gorbachev originally envisaged an end to the Soviet Union, but the failed coup was the last nail in the Union's coffin and it almost immediately disintegrated into 15 separate countries . . . while Gorbachev himself had already won a Nobel Peace Prize for creating the conditions that allowed it to happen.

Cavalese cable car collision

When an EA-6B Prowler aircraft left the Aviano Air Base in northeastern Italy on February 3 1998, it was a routine assignment for pilot Captain Richard Ashby, his navigator Captain Joseph Schweitzer and two crew members. The Prowler – call sign 'Easy 01' – was a twin-engine jet used for electronic warfare belonging to the US Marine Corps. It should have been a mission that passed without incident but constraints imposed by military regulations were ignored, either by accident or design, with disastrous consequences.

Easy 01 was flying considerably faster – at 805 kph (500 mph) – and much lower at 110 m (360 ft) than it should have been. As the Prowler scorched through the valley near Cavalese in the Italian Dolomites it hit and severed cables supporting a moving cable car, sending the gondola crashing to the ground and killing all 19 passengers plus the operator. The plane had wing and tail damage but returned safely to base.

Military personnel all too often escape the consequences of reckless or illegal actions, and so it proved. A US court martial accused Ashby and Schweizer of negligent homicide and involuntary manslaughter, but they claimed on-board maps did not show the cables, they were unaware of speed restrictions and the plane's altimeter wasn't working. Even though the pilot admitted to flying at 300 m (1,000 ft) when the official minimum was 610 m (2,000 ft), both were dubiously acquitted.

This outraged public opinion in Italy, where the disaster was christened *Strage de Cermis* (Massacre of Cermis), after the adjacent mountain. There was a surge of anti-American feeling, hardly appeased when the two men were subsequently convicted on lesser charges of obstructing justice and conduct unbecoming of a gentleman for destroying the in-flight videotape. They were dismissed from the service, with Ashby getting a six-month prison sentence.

WHEN:
February 3 1998
WHERE:
Near Cavalese, Trento, Italy
DEATH TOLL:
20 dead (all adults, from six different countries).
YOU SHOULD KNOW:
Cavalese wasn't the safest of places to ride a cable car. In a previous incident in 1976 a steel cable broke, sending a cabin plunging down the mountainside. The heavy overhead assembly then crashed down on top. One 14-year-old girl survived the world's worst cable-car accident, 42 died.

Ski equipment lies amid debris from the smashed car of the Mt Cermis cable car line.

The Columbia *space shuttle breaks apart upon re-entry. Viewed from the Owens Valley Radio Observatory at 05.54.*

Space shuttle *Columbia*

The National Aeronautics and Space Administration's rather dull designation of its first spaceworthy shuttle was OV-102 (for Orbiter Vehicle). But to the wider world it would always be *Columbia*, pioneer of an entirely new sort of space flight from the USA. NASA launched *Columbia* for the first time in 1981 and it would go on to fly 27 successful missions.

Tragically, the 28th proved to be its last. After spending 300 days in space, completing over 4,800 orbits of the earth and flying around 200 million kilometres (125 million miles) in a long and honourable career, *Columbia* would self-destruct. The cause seemed innocent enough – a piece of insulating foam that detached from the external fuel tank during launch and hit the left wing – but the consequences of this near-routine happening proved disastrous for NASA's unlucky 113th shuttle mission.

Engineers suspected damage to *Columbia*'s thermal tile cladding, but NASA vetoed a space walk to check on the basis that nothing could be done anyway. It is debatable whether a close inspection of the damage would have allowed the astronauts or NASA to somehow save the day, but at least it might have given the doomed crew a chance. As it was, re-entry proved to be catastrophic. The holed wing was incapable of withstanding intense temperature as superheated gases entered and destroyed the wing structure, causing the rest of the shuttle to break apart. Horrified observers on the ground saw a fiery smoke trail high in the sky, even as mission control realized that *Columbia* had been tragically lost.

The second fatal destruction of a shuttle effectively ended the orbiter programme. Though a number of further flights were planned and executed, NASA decided that the way forward would be Orion, developed from the successful multiple-stage Apollo spacecraft of an earlier era.

WHEN:
February 1 2003
WHERE:
Above Texas, USA
DEATH TOLL:
All seven crew members
YOU SHOULD KNOW:
There was already a peak in Colorado's Sangre de Cristo Mountains – Challenger Point – named in memory of the previous lost shuttle. It would soon be joined by its immediate neighbour, which became Columbia Point to commemorate the second disaster. The crew were also honoured by the naming of the Columbia Hills on Mars, which may one day be visited by their successors in space.

Stockwell shooting

On July 21 2005, there was an attempt to paralyze London's transport system and kill a large number of people. Mercifully, four bombs planted at three Tube stations and on a bus failed to explode, but the memory of the fatal London 7/7 bombings two weeks before was fresh and security forces were jumpy. With the help of CCTV pictures, the Metropolitan Police mounted a massive manhunt for the would-be bombers.

Intelligence had quickly linked a block of flats in South London with one of the suspects, and it was under surveillance the following morning when 27-year-old Jean Charles de Menezes emerged from the communal entrance and was identified as a possible suspect by the watching 'Frank'. The undercover soldier thought the Brazilian national resembled one of the suspects caught on CCTV. But Frank was relieving himself and couldn't video Jean Charles, so no picture was transmitted to Gold Command at police HQ.

The consequences of this ill-timed call of nature would soon prove fatal. Plainclothes policemen followed Jean Charles to Stockwell station, where the young electrician picked up a newspaper and boarded a waiting train. Meanwhile, Gold Command ordered that the presumed bomber should be prevented from entering the Underground system. Three surveillance officers followed him onto the train, swiftly followed by a specialist firearms team.

A volley of shots rang out, eight hitting Jean Charles de Menezes who was killed instantly. The tragedy revealed the existence of a 'shoot to kill' policy where an imminent terrorist threat existed, though the Metropolitan Police initially tried to justify the killing by falsely claiming that a warning had been shouted, then further muddied the waters before admitting their mistake the following day. They then issued an apology, but that was scant consolation to the innocent victim's distraught family.

WHEN:
July 22 2005
WHERE:
London, UK
DEATH TOLL:
One
YOU SHOULD KNOW:
Although the Stockwell shooting revealed serious organizational failings within the Metropolitan Police, no individual was ever punished for their part in the unjustifiable killing of Jean Charles de Menezes, though the Met itself was fined under Health and Safety legislation. Thoughtful commentators described Jean Charles as another victim of terrorism, because he died as a result of official over-reaction to the terrorist threat that at times bordered on hysteria.

Alex Pereira, cousin of Jean Charles de Menezes who was killed by police at Stockwell tube station, at Jean Charles' shrine outside Stockwell tube station in London.

PLACES

Corbis 10, 22, 24, 25, 69, 162-163, 205, 253, 309, 314, 327, 434, 174 top; /Akintunde Akinleye/Reuters 370; /Dominique Aubert/Sygma 402-403, 421; /Kapoor Baldev/Sygma 359; /Orlando Barria/epa 75; /Zohra Bensemra/Reuters 425; /Bettmann 6 centre, 23, 28, 29, 30, 32, 36, 37, 42, 44, 47, 48, 53, 54, 56, 94, 98, 100, 101, 102, 120, 122, 130, 164, 168, 169, 170, 173, 176, 180, 197, 199, 201, 225, 233, 235, 241, 245, 250-251, 259, 260, 263, 274, 275, 279, 304, 305, 313, 318, 322, 325, 329, 331, 334, 342, 343, 345, 346, 356, 375, 378, 379, 385, 405, 406, 407, 408, 410, 413, 416, 417 below, 417 above, 433 below, 433 above, 439, 456, 457, 461, 482, 486, 488, 490, 491, 492, 498, 499, 520, 521, 527; /Jonathan Blair 61, 430; /Gene Blevins/LA Daily News 518-519, 538; /Nic Bothma/epa 450; /Brazilian Air Force/Handout/XinHua/Xinhua Press 161; /Bojan Brecelj 7 centre, 404; /Carlos Cazalis 429; /Charles Caratini/Sygma 424; /China Newsphoto/Reuters 367; /Andy Clark/Reuters 462; /Lloyd Cluff 50; /Fridmar Damm 307; /Alain DeJean/Sygma 332; /Kieran Doherty/Reuters 159; /EFE 228; /epa 68, 445; /Yves Forestier 509; /David J. & Janice L. Frent Collection 227; /Paulo Fridman 447; /Robert Galbraith/Reuters 78; /Gianni Giansanti/Sygma 460; /J A Giordano 287; /Todd Gipstein 284; /David Gray/Reuters 528; /Klaus Heirler/dpa 95; /HO/Reuters 516; /Jeremy Horner 2-3 centre, 76; /Rob Howard 471; /Hulton-Deutsch Collection 91, 105, 177, 203, 226, 230, 319, 349, 352, 355, 415, 496, 525; /Hyogo Prefectural Government/epa 63; /Sergei Ilnitsky/epa 193; /Kamerareportage/Sygma 186; /Karen Kasmauski 213; /Alain Keler/Sygma 422; /Andras Kisgergely/Reuters 153; /Tony Korody/Sygma 272-273, 281; /Legnan Koula/epa 6 top, 219; /Kim Kulish 512; /Simon Kwong/Reuters 495; /Jacques Langevin/Sygma 59; /Lebrecht Music & Arts 254; /Guo Lei/XinHua/Xinhua Press 271; /Lisbon City Museum/Handout/Reuters 15; /Peter MacDiarmid/epa 476; /Peter MacDiarmid/Reuters 298; /Francis R. Malasig/epa 86; /Anatoly Maltsev/epa 72; /Michael Maslan Historic Photographs 257; /Paul McErlane/epa 500; /Richard Melloul/Sygma 139, 280; /Gideon Mendel 82; /Joao Abreu Miranda/epa 393; /Grzegorz Momot/epa 368; /Emilio Morenatti/epa 365; /Nasa 436; /Mike Nelson/epa 477; /Michael Nicholson 165, 376; /Namir Noor-Eldeen/Reuters 423; /NTV/Via Reuters TV/Reuters 515; /Thierry Orban 60; /Katie Orlinsky 3 right, 8-9, 87; /Louie Psihoyos/Science Faction 449; /Ed Quinn 189; /Andy Rain/epa 539; /Reuters 21, 154, 187, 194-195, 217, 248, 296, 338-339, 366, 467, 472, 473, 505, 533; /Reuters TV/Reuters 112; /Boris Roessler/dpa 6 bottom, 269; /Ron Sachs/CNP 247; /Damir Sagolj/Reuters 510; /Schenectady Museum/Hall of Electrical History Foundation 324; /Leonard de Selva 224; /Guo Jian She/Redlink 80; /Tokyo Shimbun 467; /Christian Simonpietri/Sygma 420; /Skyscan 438; /Stringer/Mexico/Reuters 192; /Swim Ink 2, LLC 419; /Peter Turnley 302-303, 335; /Harish Tyagi/epa 478; /Aaron Ufumeli/epa 221, 268; /Underwood & Underwood 172, 198; /Robert Wallis 143; /Ira Wyman/Sygma 212; /Gong Zhihong/Xinhua Press 220; /Hoch Zwei/NewSport 301.

Getty Images 229, 267, 270, 336; /AFP 265, 266, 299, 503, 532, 536; /Jaakko Avikainen/AFP 149; /Bloomberg via Getty Images 443; /Pablo Cuarterolo/AFP 190; /Hulton Archive 39, 119, 127, 256, 290, 317, 483, 484, 522; /George William Joy 316; /Luis Magan/Cover 211; /Leonard McCombe/Time & Life Pictures 208; /National Geographic 306; /Popperfoto 310, 320; /SSPL 374; /Tom Stoddart Archive 246; /Time & Life Pictures 286, 308, 497.

Press Association Images/Dita Alangkara/AP 85; /AP 2 left, 5 top, 34, 45, 46, 49, 77, 79, 110, 113, 117, 124, 125, 126, 140, 142, 145, 146, 157, 174 below, 182, 206, 207, 222-223, 231, 232, 234, 237, 239, 292, 326, 328, 333, 341, 347, 350, 380, 383, 386, 409, 459, 466, 480-481, 494, 502, 513, 531; /apply pictures 175; /Sayyid Azim/AP 156; /Paul Barker/PA Archive 468; /Stacy Bengs/AP 2 centre, 399; /Jaques Boissinot/The Canadian Press 64; /Peter Busomoke/AP 514; /Harry Cabluck/AP 353; /Felice Calabro/AP 537; /Dave Caulkin/AP 504; /David Cheskin/PA Archive 214; /ChinaFotoPress/Photocome 446; /Danie Coetzer/Africa Visuals/Press 7 bottom, 109; /CP Photo/Granma/Raul Corrales/AP 330; /Malcolm Croft/PA Archive 210; /Ben Curtis/AP 452; /Saurabh Das/AP 188; /Dave Dawson/AP 133; /Peter Dejong/AP 442; /Jerome Delay/AP 7 top, 337; /dpa 58, 323, 418; /DS/AP 431; /John Gaps III/AP 441; /Albert Gea/AP 73; /Haraz N. Ghanbari/AP 451; /Greg Gibson/AP 426-427; /Thomas Grimm/AP 282; /Libor Hajsky/AP 238; /Ron Heflin/AP 507; /Mohammad Iqbal/AP 479; /Yun Jai-Hyoung/AP 392; /James Jim James/PA Archive 289; /Kerstin Joensson/AP 395; /Peter Jordan/PA Archive 297; /Ken Karuga/AP 465; /Brian Kersey/AP 394; /Myung Jung Kim/PA Archive 71; /Ross Kinnaird/EMPICS Sport 88-89, 107; /Sgt. Jason R. Krawczyk/AP 517; /Landov 83; /Louis Lanzano/AP 5 bottom, 300; /Pete Leabo/AP 388; /Marty Lederhandler/AP 240, 261; /Charles Lindbergh/AP 33; /Dimitri Messinis/AP 470; /A3498 Marcel Mettelsiefen/DPA 249; /Mikami/AP 264; /Neil Munns/PA Archive 114-115, 152; /Amr Nabil/AP 155; /Na-Son Nguyen/AP 372-373, 397; /Anja Niedringhaus/AP 475; /Gurinder Osan/AP 401; /PA Archive 31, 132, 136, 144, 148, 181, 184, 236, 242, 243, 244, 277, 278, 283, 288, 312, 321, 354, 362, 384, 463; /PA Photos/PA Archive 138; /Joel Page/AP 66; /Wade Payne/AP 453; /Yvon Perchoc/AP 160; /David J Phillip/AP 67; /Suzanne Plunkett/AP 454-455; /Karel Prinsloo/AP 70; /Reuters 5 centre; /Robert Rider-Rider/AP 41; /Peter Robinson/EMPICS Sport 106; /Rossiiskaya Gazeta Newspaper 400; /Stefan Rousseau/PA Archive 511; /Hasan Sarbakhshian/AP 74; /Stefano Sarti/AP 150; /Reed Saxon/AP 285; /SMG 90; /Dale Sparks/AP 340; /Christof Stache/AP 293; /STR/AP 361; /Justin Sutcliffe/AP 62; /Bela Szandelszky 396; /Alessandra Tarantino/AP 84; /Topham Picturepoint 18, 93, 121; /Andrew Vaughan/The Canadian Press 111; /K Vindefallet/AP 387; /Bruce Weaver/AP 3 centre, 534; /Susan Weems/AP 508; /Peter Winterbach/AP 458; /Chris Young/PA Archive 191; /Matty Zimmerman/AP 97.

Superstock/Image Asset Management Ltd 315.

Cover Photography:

Corbis front main image, back image 1, back image 5; /Akintunde Akinleye front image 1; /Kieran Doherty front image 5; /Jeremy Horner front image 4; /Na-Son Nguyen/AP back image 3; /Romeo Ranoco, front image 3; /Boris Roessler/dpa, front image 6; /Paul Souders back main image; /Aaron Ufumeli/epa back image 4. **Getty Images**/Popperfoto back image 6. **Press Association Images**/AP front image 2; /PA Archive back image 2.